Opinions of the Press

"The volume may be commended as learned and valuable."—*Times*.

"No one has done more to advance the study of our early constitutional history than Mr. Round, since the Bishop of Oxford ceased to write. In the volume before us Mr. Round has collected a series of historical studies of the eleventh and twelfth centuries. Among them is the brilliant study on knight-service in England which appeared in the pages of the English Historical Review."—*Literary World*.

"Mr. Round has already made himself a name as a minute, cautious and indefatigable historical inquirer. This book will preserve and increase his reputation."—*Speaker*.

"No one in this generation has done more for the study of *Domesday* than Mr. Round, and we heartily welcome the republication of his teachings and able papers."—*Manchester Guardian*.

"The test of Mr. Round's merits is that the next generation will never want to know how much rubbish he has swept or helped to sweep away. He has done more than any one scholar to put us in the way of reading *Domesday Book* aright."—*English Historical Review*.

"The whole book leaves the stamp of deep research and of a singularly unbiassed mind."—*Spectator*.

FEUDAL ENGLAND

FEUDAL ENGLAND

HISTORICAL STUDIES ON THE XITH AND XIITH CENTURIES

BY

J. H. ROUND, M.A.

Author of "Geoffrey de Mandeville: a Study of the Anarchy"

"Patres nostri et nos hanc insulam . . . in brevi edomuimus, in brevi nostris subdidimus legibus, nostris obsequiis mancipavimus."—WALTER ESPEC (1138)

ARDVA·QVÆ·PVLCRA

London
SWAN SONNENSCHEIN & CO. LTD.
25 HIGH STREET, BLOOMSBURY
1909

First Edition, *June*, 1895.
Reissued *January*, 1909.
Reprinted, *May*, 1909.

PREFACE

THE present work is the outcome of a wish expressed to me from more than one quarter that I would re-print in a collected form, for the convenience of historical students, some more results of my researches in the history of the eleventh and twelfth centuries. But to these I have added, especially on Domesday, so much which has not yet seen the light, that the greater portion of the work is new, while the rest has been in part re-written. The object I have set before myself throughout is either to add to or correct our existing knowledge of facts. And for this I have gone in the main to records, whether in manuscript or in print. It is my hope that the papers in this volume may further illustrate the value of such evidence as supplementing and checking the chroniclers for what is still, in many respects, an obscure period of our history.

As a foreign scholar has felicitously observed :—

Je lis avec plaisir le chroniqueur qui nous raconte les événements de son époque. Les détails anecdotiques, les traits piquants dont son œuvre est parsémée font mes délices. Mais comment saurai-je s'il dit la vérité si les pages qu'il me présente ne sont pas un roman de pure imagination ? Dans les chartes, au contraire, tout est authentique, certain, précis, indubitable. Leur témoignage est contradictoire-ment établi, sous le contrôle de la partie adverse, avec l'approbation et la reconaissance de l'autorité souveraine, en présence d'une imposante assemblée de notables qui apposent leur signature. C'est la plus pure de toutes les sources où il soit possible de puiser un renseignement historique.[1]

[1] *Table chronologique des chartes et diplômes imprimés concernant l'histoire de la Belgique.* Par Alphonse Wauters, vol. i., p. xxxi.

vii

An instance in point will be found in the paper on
" Richard the First's change of seal."

A collective title for a series of studies covering the
period 1050-1200, is not by any means easy to find. But
dealing as they do so largely with the origins of " Feudal
England," I have ventured to give them this title, which
may serve, I hope, to emphasise my point that the feudal
element introduced at the Conquest had a greater influence
on our national institutions than recent historians admit.[2]
Even Domesday Book has its place in the study of feudalism,
re-arranging, as it does, the Hundred and the Vill under
Fiefs and " Manors."

To those in search of new light on our early mediæval
history, I commend the first portion of this work, as
setting forth, for their careful consideration, views as
evolutionary on the Domesday hide and the whole system
of land assessment as on the actual introduction of the
feudal system into England. Although I have here brought
into conjunction my discovery that the assessment of
knight-service was based on a five-knights unit, irrespective
of area or value, and my theory that the original assessment of land was based on a five-hides unit, not calculated
on area or value, yet the two, one need hardly add, are, of
course, unconnected. The one was an Anglo-Saxon system,
and, as I maintain, of early date ; the other was of Norman
introduction, and of independent origin. My theories were
formed at different times, as the result of wholly separate
investigations. That of the five-hides unit was arrived at
several years ago, but was kept back in the hope that I
might light on some really satisfactory explanation of the
phenomena presented. The solution I now propound can
only be deemed tentative. I would hope, however, that the
theories I advance may stimulate others to approach the
subject, and, above all, that they may indicate to local
students, in the future, the lines on which they should
work and the absolute need of their assistance.

[2] See pp. 247, 262, 536-8.

Perhaps the most important conclusion to which my researches point is that Domesday reveals the existence of two separate systems in England, co-extensive with two nationalities, the original *five hides* of the "Anglo-Saxon" in the south, and the later *six carucates* of the "Danish" invaders in the north.[3]

No one, I may add, is better qualified to carry further these enquiries than Prof. Maitland, whose brilliant pen has illumined for us the origins of English law. Himself engaged on the study of Domesday, he kindly offered to withhold his conclusions until my work should have appeared.[4]

Among the fresh points here discussed in connexion with Domesday Book will be found the composition of the juries by whom the returns were made, the origin and true character of the " Inquisitio Eliensis," and the marked difference of the two volumes compiled from the Domesday returns.

Of the six early surveys dealt with in conjunction with Domesday, I would call attention to that of Leicestershire as having, it would seem, till now remained absolutely unknown. It has long been a wish of mine to deal with these surveys,[5] not only as belonging to a period for which we have no records, but also as illustrating Domesday Book. In "The Knights of Peterborough" will be found some facts relating to Hereward "the Wake," which seem to have eluded Mr. Freeman's investigations, and even those of Mr. Tout.

In case it should suggest itself that these papers, and some in the other portion of the work dwell at undue length on unimportant points, I would observe that apart from the fact that even small points acquire a relative importance

---

[3] See p. 573.

[4] Prof. Maitland informs me that since the appearance of his *Select Pleas in Manorial Courts*, he has discovered the earlier occurrence of the word "leet" (see p. 101).

[5] See *Domesday Studies.*

from our scanty knowledge of the time, there are cases in which their careful investigation may lead to unforeseen results. At the last anniversary of the Royal Society, Lord Kelvin quoted these words from his own presidential address in 1871 :—

Accurate and minute measurement seems to the non-scientific imagination a less lofty and dignified work than looking for something new. But nearly all the grandest discoveries of science have been but the rewards of accurate measurement and patient, long continued labour in the minute sifting of numerical results.

The same principle applies to the study of institutional history. Whether we are dealing with military service, with the land, with finance, or with the king's court, "the minute sifting" of facts and figures is the only sure method by which we can extend knowledge.

To those who know how few are the original authorities for the period, and how diligently these have been explored and their information exhausted, the wonder will be not so much that there is little, as that there was anything at all yet left to discover.

In a work dealing with the history of the eleventh and twelfth centuries, a writer must inevitably find himself at times dealing with the same subjects as the late Professor Freeman. Without in any way disparaging the genius of that eminent man, one may deem it a duty to correct the errors into which he fell, and conscientiously to combat, as an obstinate and mischievous superstition, the conviction of his pre-eminent accuracy and authority on matters of fact. It would be far pleasanter to dwell only on his merits ; but when one finds that, in spite of the proofs I have been producing for years, Mr. Herbert Fisher, representing the Oxford school of history, can still declare Mr. Freeman to have reached "the highest standard of scholarly exactitude," [6] it is evident that the works of the Regius

[6] *Fortnightly Review*, December, 1894, pp. 804-5.

Professor are still surrounded by a false glamour, and that one must further expose his grave liability to error. I cannot suppose that any competent scholar who may carefully peruse this work will in future venture to deny that, in spite of his many and his splendid gifts, Mr. Freeman was as liable as any of us to error, or that however laudable his intentions, he was capable of precisely the same inaccuracy and occasionally of the same confusion as he denounced so bitterly in others.

It is, indeed, my contention, as I have already explained,[1] that to these denunciations of the errors of others is largely due the conviction of Mr. Freeman's supreme accuracy. The question raised may seem to affect the whole method of history, for if, as has been said, it is the argument of the scientific historian that we ought to prefer accuracy of fact to charm of presentment and to literary style, the proof that his method fails to save him from erring like any "literary" historian strikes at the root of his whole contention.

Yet it is not the scientific method, but its prophet himself that was at fault.

Although I am here only concerned with inaccuracy in matters of fact, I would guard myself against the retort that, at least, Mr. Freeman's errors are of little consequence as compared with that obliquity of vision which led Mr. Froude, at all hazards, to vindicate Henry the Eighth. Without insisting on an absolute parallel, I trace a resemblance even here. Just as his bias against the Roman church led Mr. Froude to vindicate Henry in order to justify the breach with Rome, so Mr. Freeman's passion for democracy made him an advocate on behalf of Harold, as "one whose claim was not drawn only from the winding-sheet of his fathers." I have elsewhere maintained, as to Harold's election "by the free choice of a free people," that Mr. Freeman's undoubted perversion of the case at this "the central point" of his history, gravely impairs his

[1] *Quarterly Review*, July, 1892.

narrative of the Conquest, because its success, and even its undertaking, can actually be traced to that election.[8]   Unless we realise its disastrous effect on the situation both at home and abroad, we cannot rightly understand the triumph of the Duke's enterprise.

It had been my hope, in the present work, to have avoided acute controversy, but the attitude adopted, unfortunately, by the late Professor's champions has rendered that course impossible.   One can but rejoice that his accuracy should find strenuous defenders, as it removes the reluctance one would otherwise feel in continuing to criticise it now.   A case is doubly proved when proved in the teeth of opposition. But one expects that opposition to be fair, and the line my opponents have taken throughout cannot, by any stretch of courtesy, be so described.   My difficulty, indeed, in dealing with their arguments on the Battle of Hastings, is that they do not affect or even touch my case.   In spite of their persistent efforts to obscure a plain issue, there is not, and there cannot be, any "controversy" as to Mr. Freeman and the "palisade."   For, while fully recognising that the *onus probandi* lay on those who assert its existence, he failed, on his own showing, to produce any proof of it whatever.[9]   Mr. Archer has ended,[10] as he began,[11] by deliberately ignoring Mr. Freeman's words,[12] on which my case avowedly rests, and without suppressing which he could not even enter the field.   This, indeed, I have explained so often, that I need not again have disposed of his arguments had not Mr. Gardiner, in the exercise of his editorial discretion, allowed him to make certain statements,[13] and refused me the right of exposing them.   A typical example will be found on p. 353.[14]

[8] See *Quarterly Review* as above.

[9] See pp. 340-347.

[10] *English Historical Review*, July, 1894.

[11] *Contemporary Review*, March, 1893, pp. 335-355

[12] *Norman Conquest* (2nd Ed.), iii. 763-4.

[13] *English Historical Review*, as above.

[14] I have, therefore, been obliged to refer in some detail to these

It is not only demonstrable error that justifies critical treatment ; no less dangerous, if not more so, is that subtle commixture of guess-work and fact, which leaves us in doubt as to what is proved and what is merely hypothesis. In his lecture on " The Nature of Historical Evidence," the late Professor himself well brought out the point :—

Many people seem to think that a position is proved if it can not be disproved. . . . Very few see with Sir George Lewis— though Sir George Lewis perhaps carried his own doctrine a little too far—that in a great many cases we ought to be satisfied with a negative result, that we must often put up with knowing that a thing did not happen in a particular way, or did not happen at all, without being furnished with any counter-statement to put in the place of that which we reject.[15]

The question is whether a statement can be proved, not whether it can be disproved. Cases in point will be found on pp. 379, 389, 433-5.

It may, in view of certain comments, be desirable, perhaps, to explain that the study on the origin of knight-service appeared in Mr. Freeman's lifetime,[16] and that my open criticism of his work began so far back as 1882. It will be seen, therefore, that I challenged its accuracy when he was himself able to reply.

To those who may hold that in these studies excessive attention is bestowed on Anglo-Norman genealogy, I commend the words, not of a genealogist, but of the historian Kemble :—

It is indispensable to a clear view of the constitutional law and governmental institutions of this country, that we should not lose sight of the distribution of landed estates among the great families, and that the rise and fall of these houses should be carefully traced and steadily borne in mind. . . .

Amidst all the tumult and confusions of civil and foreign wars ; statements, while for those I have already disposed of I have given the references to the *Q.R.* and *E.H.R.*

[15] *Methods of Historical Study*, p. 141.

[16] *English Historical Review*, July, 1891-January, 1892.

throughout religious and political revolutions; from the days of Arminius to those of Harald; from the days of Harald to our own; the successions of the landowners and the relations arising out of these successions, are the running comment upon the events in our national history: they are at once the causes and the criteria of facts, and upon them has depended the development and settlement of principles, in laws which still survive, in institutions which we cling to with reverence, in feelings which make up the complex of our national character.[17]

The paper on "Walter Tirel and his wife" may serve to show that in this department there is still needed much labour before we can hope for a perfect record of the great houses of the Conquest.

I have to thank Mr. Murray for his kind permission to make use of two of the articles I have contributed to the *Quarterly Review.* Some of the studies have previously appeared in the *English Historical Review,* and these are now republished with Messrs. Longmans' consent. Lastly, I would take the opportunity afforded by this preface of acknowledging the encouragement my researches have derived from the approval not only of our supreme authority —I mean the Bishop of Oxford—but also of that eminent scholar, Dr. Liebermann, whose name one is proud to associate with a work on mediæval history.

J. H. ROUND.

[17] *The Names, Surnames, and Nicknames of the Anglo-Saxons.* Read at Winchester, September 11th, 1845.

[NOTE.—I have not thought it needful to include in the index names of persons or places only introduced incidentally in illustration of arguments. The prefix "Fitz," as in *Geoffrey de Mandeville,* has been retained as a useful convention, whatever the actual name may have been.]

TABLE OF CONTENTS

PART I.—TERRITORIAL STUDIES.

PART II.—HISTORICAL STUDIES.

PAGE

PART I

TERRITORIAL STUDIES

PART I

TERRITORIAL STUDIES

DOMESDAY BOOK

THE true key to the Domesday Survey, and to the system of land assessment it records, is found in the *Inquisitio Comitatus Cantabrigiensis.* Although the document so styled is one of cardinal importance, it has, from accident, been known to few, and has consequently never succeeded in obtaining the attention and scientific treatment it deserved. The merit of its identification belongs to Mr. Philip Carteret Webb, who published in 1756 a paper originally read before the Society of Antiquaries, entitled, *A Short Account of Danegeld, with some further particulars relating to William the Conqueror's Survey.* It is difficult to speak too highly of this production, remembering the date at which it was composed. Many years were yet to elapse before the printing of Domesday was even begun, and historical evidences were largely inaccessible as compared with the condition of things to-day. Yet the ability shown by Mr. Webb in this careful and conscientious piece of work is well seen in his interesting discovery, which he announced in these words :—

In searching for the *Liber Eliensis,* I have had the good fortune to discover in the Cotton Library a MS. copy of the Inquisition of the jury, containing their survey for most of the hundreds in Cambridgeshire. This MS. is written on vellum in double columns and on both sides of the page. It is bound up with the *Liber Eliensis*, and begins at p. 76*a* and ends at p. 113. It is written in a very fair but ancient character, not coeval with the Survey, but of about the time of Henry II. It was given by Mr. Arthur Agard to Sir Robert Cotton, and is marked Tiberius A. VI. 4. Your lordship and the Society will be of opinion that this is a discovery of importance, and what had escaped the observation of Sir H. Spelman, Mr. Selden, and other antiquarians. A part of this valuable morsel of antiquity is already transcribed, and in a few weeks I hope to be able to communicate the whole of it to the Society (p. 26).

Mr. Webb's discovery was known to Kelham, and duly referred to by him in his *Domesday Book Illustrated* (1788). It was also known to Sir Francis Palgrave, strong in his acquaintance with manuscript authorities, who alluded (1832) to the fact that "fragments of the original inquisitions have been preserved,"[1] and described the MS. Tib. A. VI., of which "the first portion consists of the *Inquisitio Eliensis*, extending, as above mentioned, into five counties; it is followed by the inedited *Inquisitio*," etc.[2] It is, however, undoubtedly ignored in Ellis's *Introduction to Domesday Book* (1833), and "even the indefatigable Sir Thomas Duffus Hardy," writes Mr. Birch,[3] "has omitted all notice of this manuscript in his *Descriptive Catalogue of Manuscripts relating to the History of Great Britain and Ireland*, vol. ii. (1865)." This, however, is not strictly the case, for in his notice of the Domesday MSS. he observes in a footnote :—

The Cottonian MS. [Tib. A. VI.] has also a second and unique portion of this survey, which was not printed in the edition published by the Record Commission in 1816. It commences "in Grantebriggesira, in Staplehouhund," and ends imperfectly "et vicecomiti regis v. auras."

These words prove that Sir Thomas had inspected the MS., which duly begins and ends with the words here given.

It is certain, however, that Mr. Freeman, most ardent of

---

[1] *English Commonwealth*, II. ccccxliv.   [2] *Ibid.*
[3] *Domesday Book*, p. 42.

Domesday students, knew nothing of this precious evidence, and remained therefore virtually unacquainted with the *modus operandi* of the Great Survey. The pages, we shall find, of the *Inquisitio* afford information that no one would have welcomed more eagerly than himself. Perhaps, therefore, it is not surprising that Mr. N. E. S. A. Hamilton, when editing this document for the Royal Society of Literature (1876), should have supposed that it had been overlooked till then, or that he was "the first to bring its importance to light" (p. iv.) It is, however, much to be regretted that Mr. De Gray Birch should have strenuously insisted that Webb (whose paper he actually names) and Kelham "appear to have been strangely ignorant of the true and important nature of this manuscript,"[4] and should have repeated this assertion[5] after I had shown at the Domesday Commemoration (1886) that the honour of the discovery really belonged to Mr. P. C. Webb. One may claim that Webb should have his due, while gladly expressing gratitude to Mr. Hamilton for his noble edition of the *Inquisitio*, which has conferred on Domesday students an inestimable boon.[6]

The printing of the document in record type, the collation throughout with Domesday Book, and the appending of the *Inquisitio Eliensis*, edited from three different texts, represent an extraordinary amount of minute and wearisome labour. The result is a volume as helpful as it is indispensable to the scholar.

I propose in this paper to take up anew the subject, at the point where Mr. Hamilton has left it, to submit the text to scientific criticism, to assign it its weight in the scale of authority, and to explain its glossarial and its illustrative value for the construction and the contents of Domesday Book.

---

[4] *Athenæum*, 1885, I. 472, 566-7 ; *Domesday Book*, 1887, p. 44.

[5] *Domesday Studies* (1891), II. 488.

[6] *Inquisitio Comitatus Cantabrigiensis.* Cura N. E. S. A. Hamilton, 1876.

I. Nature of the "Inq. Com. Cant."

Exact definition is needful at the outset in dealing with this document. The *Inquisitio Comitatus Cantabrigiensis*, which is entered on fos. 76-113 of Tib. A. VI., must be carefully distinguished from the *Inquisitio Eliensis* on fos. 38-68. Mr. Hamilton doubted whether any one before him "had distinguished between" the two, but this, we have seen, was a mistake. The distinction however is all-important, the two documents differing altogether in character One would not think it necessary to distinguish them also from the so-called *Liber Eliensis* (which is not a survey at all) had not Mr. Eyton inadvertently stated that our document has been printed under the title of *Liber Eliensis*.[7]

The *Inquisitio Comitatus Cantabrigiensis* (hereafter styled "the I.C.C.") deals with the county of Cambridge alone, but, in that county, with the lands of all holders. The *Inquisitio Eliensis* (which I propose to style the I.E.") deals with several counties, but, in these counties, with the lands of the abbey alone. The latter was duly printed, with Domesday Book, by the Record Commission; the former remained in manuscript till printed by Mr. Hamilton.

Mr. Hamilton describes his record at the outset as "the Original Return made by the *Juratores* of the county of Cambridge in obedience to the Conqueror's mandate, from which the Exchequer Domesday for that county was afterwards compiled by the King's secretaries," and as "the original source from which the Exchequer Domesday for that county was derived." Mr. Birch here again repeats the words, insisting "that we have in this very precious Cottonian MS. *the original source* from which the Exchequer Domesday of Cambridgeshire was compiled."[8]

Such a description is most unfortunate, being not only inaccurate but misleading. All that we are entitled to pre-

---

[7] *Notes on Domesday* (1877), reprinted 1880, p. 15.

[8] The italics are his own, *Domesday Book*, p. 42. Cf. *Domesday Studies*, II. 486-7.

dicate of the document is that it is *apparently a copy* of the
original returns from which Domesday Book was compiled.
For "the original source" of both we must look to the now
missing returns of the jurors, the primary authority from
which Domesday Book and the *Inquisitio Com. Cant.* are
independently derived. This distinction is all-important,
reducing, as it does, the *Inquisitio* from the rank of an
"original" to that of a secondary authority on the same
level with Domesday Book.[9] Mr. Hamilton, like Mr. Webb
before him, assigned the handwriting of the *Inquisitio* to
about the close of the twelfth century. The copy of the
returns which it contains, therefore, was made about a
century later than the returns themselves.

The problem then that we have to solve is this : "Is the
I.C.C. an actual transcript of these original returns, and
if so, is it faithful?" I will not, like Mr. Hamilton, assume
an affirmative, but will attempt an impartial enquiry.

The two paths which we must follow in turn to arrive
at a just conclusion are (1) the construction of the I.C.C.,
(2) collation with the *Inq. Eliensis.* For I hope to show
that the latter record must have been derived from the
same source as the *Inq. Com. Cant.*

Following the first of these paths, we note at once that
while *Domesday Book* arranges the Manors according to
fiefs, the *Inq. Com. Cant.*, on the contrary, arranges them by
hundreds and townships. Its system is regular and simple.
For every hundred it first enumerates the principal jurors
who made the return, and then gives the return itself,
arranged according to townships (*villæ*). These townships
are thus the units of which the Manors they contain are
merely the component fractions. This is precisely what
we should expect to find in the original returns, but it only
creates a presumption ; it does not afford a proof. For instance, it might be reasonably urged that these copies may

---

[9] It is not even *proved* that the I.C.C. is copied from the original
returns themselves. There is the possibility of a MS. between the two.
See *Addenda*,

have omitted certain items in the returns, just as Domesday Book omitted others.

To reply to this objection, we must turn to the second path ; that is to say, we must collate the *Inquisitio Eliensis* with the *Inq. Com. Cant.* I shall prove below that the latter cannot have been taken from the former, which only covers a portion of its field, and that, on the other hand, the former cannot have been taken from the latter, because the *Inquisitio Eliensis* is accurate in places where the *Inq. Com. Cant.* is in error. Consequently they must both have been derived independently from some third document. This being so, if we should find that their versions agree closely, we may fairly infer that each is intended to be a faithful reproduction of the above "third document." In other words, if neither version omits items which are given in the other, we are entitled to assume that the copy is in each case exhaustive, for two scribes working independently are not likely to have systematically omitted the same items from the document before them.

What then was the "third document" from which they both copied? Obviously it was either the original returns of the Domesday jurors, or a copy (exhaustive or not) of these returns. Now we cannot suppose that two scribes, working, as I have said, independently, would both have worked, not from the original returns themselves, but from a copy, and that the same copy of these returns—a copy, moreover, of the existence of which we have no evidence whatever. Moreover, in this hypothetical copy, there would, we may safely assert, have been some clerical errors. These would have duly re-appeared in both the *Inquisitiones*, and collation with Domesday Book would enable us to detect them. Yet in no single instance, though each of them contains errors, have I found a clerical error common to both. We are thus driven to the conclusion that in both these *Inquisitiones* we have copies of the actual returns made by the Domesday jurors.

One of the postulates in the above argument is that the

Inq. Com. Cant. and the *Inq. Eliensis* "agree closely" in their versions. Here is an instance in illustration[10] :—

I.C.C.	I.E.
Meldeburna pro x. sol[idis] se defendebat T.R.E. et modo pro viii. Et de his x. hidis tenet predictus abbas ii. hidas et I[am.] virgam. v. carrucis est ibi terra. Una carruca et dimidia, et una hida et una virga in dominio, et dimidia carruca potest fieri. iii. carucæ villanis. vi. villani, ix. bordarii, iii. cotarii, dimidium molendinum de iii. solidis, et viii. denariis. Pratum v. carrucis. Pastura ad pecora villæ, ccc. oves iii. minus, xxxiiii. porci. Inter totum valet c. sol., et quando recepit totidem. T.R.E. vi. lib. Hæc terra jacet et jacuit in ecclesia sancte AEdel. de eli in dominio. Et de his x. hidis tenet Wido de Reb' curt de rege, &ca., &ca.	Meldeburne pro x. hidis se defendebat in tempore R.AED. et modo pro viii. Et de his x. hun[dredis] tenet abbas de eli ii. hidas et i. v[irgam]. v. carucis ibi est terra. I. caruca et dimidia, et i. hida et dimidia, in dominio, et dimidia caruca potest fieri. iii. carucæ hominibus. vi. villani, ix. bordarii, iii. cotarii. Pratum v. carucis. i. molendinum de ii. solidis et viii. denariis. Pastura ad pecora villæ. oves ccc., iii[es.] minus, et xxxiiii. porci. Inter totum valet v. lib. Quando recepit v. lib. T.R.E. vi. lib. Hæc terra jacet et jacuit in ecclesia sancte AEdel' ely in dominio. In eadem villa habet Guido de Raimbecurt de rege, &ca., &ca.

These extracts are typical and instructive. They leave, in the first place, no doubt upon the mind that both are versions of the same original. This, which proves my postulate, will be shown below to possess a further and important bearing. But while these versions closely agree, we notice (1) independent blunders, (2) slight variants in diction. As to blunders, we see that the I.C.C. has "sol[idis]" where the I.E. has the correct "hidis," while, conversely, the I.E. reads "hun[dredis]" where the I.C.C. has, rightly, "hidis." Again the I.C.C. allots to demesne an assessment of a hide and a virgate, but I.E. a hide and a half (*i.e.* two virgates). Collation with Domesday Book confirms the former version. Conversely, the I.C.C.

---

[10] These extracts are *extended* and *punctuated* to faciliate the comparison. Important extensions are placed within square brackets.

assigns to the mill the value of three shillings and eightpence, but the I.E. of two shillings and eightpence. Collation with Domesday Book confirms the latter. Turning
now to the variants, we may express them more clearly
thus:—

I.C.C.		I.E.
T.R.E.	=	in tempore R.ÆD.
predictus abbas	=	abbas de eli.
villanis	=	hominibus.
dimidium molendinum	=	i. molendinum.
c. sol.	=	v. lib.
totidem	=	v. lib.
de his x. hidis tenet	=	in eadem villa habet.

These prove that verbal accuracy was not aimed at by the
transcribers. The same freedom from its trammels is seen
in the transposition of the "mill" and "meadow" passages, and, indeed, in the highly abbreviated form of the
I.E. entries (in which a single letter, mostly, does duty for
a word), which shows that the original version must have
been either extended in the I.C.C., or (more probably) abbreviated in the I.E.

We are now in a position to advance to the criticism of
the text of the *Inq. Com. Cant.*, and to inquire how far it
can be trusted as a reproduction of the original returns.
In other words, are its contents more or less trustworthy
than those of Domesday Book?

It might, no doubt, be fairly presumed that a simple transcript of the original returns was less likely to contain
error than such a compilation as Domesday Book, in which
their contents were (1) re-arranged on a different system,
(2) epitomised and partly omitted, (3) altered in wording.
Mr. Hamilton, indeed, who was naturally tempted to make
the most of his MS., appears to have jumped at this conclusion; for he speaks in his preface (p. xii.) of its "superior
exactness," and gives us no hint of omissions or of blunders.
There are, however, plenty of both, as will be seen from the
lists below, which do not profess to be exhaustive.

But we will first examine the instances adduced by Mr. Hamilton. Out of ten examples in proof of its value, five are cases in which "the want of precision in Domesday" leaves the identity of the tenant-in-chief "undefined." It is difficult to comment on these statements, because in all five cases the name is as carefully recorded in Domesday as in the I.C.C. Mr. Hamilton's error can only, it will be found, have arisen from comparing the I.C.C. not with Domesday Book, but with the extracts therefrom printed in his work, which, being torn from their place, do not, of course, contain the tenant's full name, which in Domesday itself is given at the head of the list from which they are taken. Moreover, as it happens, this test demonstrates not the inferiority, but (in one instance at least) the superiority of Domesday, the I.C.C. (fo. 97, col. 2) reading "Hanc terram tenuit comes alanus" (*sic*), where Domesday has (rightly) "Hanc terram tenuit Algar comes." The former must have wrongly extended the abbreviated original entry.[11]

Another of Mr. Hamilton's examples is this :—

"Hæc terra fuit et est de dominio æcclesiæ" (Domesday) is abbreviated from a long account of the holdings of Harduuinus de Scalariis and Turcus homo abbatis de Rameseio in the Cotton MS.

But, on referring to the passage in question, we find that the Domesday passage : "Hæc terra fuit et est de dominio æcclesiæ" has nothing to do with that "long account," but corresponds to the simple formula in the I.C.C., "Hanc terram tenuerunt monache de cet'ero T.R.E. et modo tenent." The example which follows it is this :—

At pp. 38, 39 we see a curious alteration in the value of the land, which had risen from xv. lib. "quando recepit" and T.R.E. to xvii. lib. at the time the return was made, and dropped again to xvi. lib. in the Domesday Survey.

[11] Curiously enough, the cases in which the I.C.C. does really supplement the Domesday version, that is, in the names of the holders T.R.E. and of the under-tenants T.R.W., were left unnoticed by Mr. Hamilton.

This strange comment implies the supposition that the I.C.C. records an earlier survey than Domesday Book, whereas, of course, they are derived from the same returns, so that the discrepancy of xvi. and xvii. is merely a clerical error. One more instance, the "curious reading" *harlestone* in the I.C.C., is shown below to be merely an error in that MS. Such are eight of the examples adduced by Mr. Hamilton. The remaining two merely illustrate not the superior accuracy, but the greater elaboration of the I.C.C. It has been absolutely necessary to dispose of these examples, in order to show that a critical estimate of the value of the I.C.C. has yet to be made.

Taking the omissions in the MS. first, we find some really bad ones. On fo. 79A (2), collation with Domesday gives this result :—

I.C.C. (p. 12).[12]	D.B. (I. 196A).
II. hidas et dimidiam et x. acras tenuerunt. [................ ....]. Non potuerunt recedere sine licentia.	Tenuerunt ii. hidas et dimidiam et x. acras. Nec isti potuerunt recedere absque licentia abbatis. Et xix. sochemanni, homines regis E., tenuerunt ii. hidas. Non potuerunt recedere absque licentia.

A similar "run on" omission is found on ᵢ 109A (1) :—

I.C.C. (p. 79.)	D.B. (I. 200A, 193A).
Tenet Radulfus de bans de [Widone de] rembercurt terciam partem unius virge. I. bovi ibi est terra, et est bos [.............. ....] Valet et valuit semper xii. den.[13]	Tenet Radulfus de Widone iii^{ciam} partem i. virgatæ [Terra est i. bovi], et ibi est bos. Valet et valuit ii. sol., et vendere potuit, et iiii^{tam} partem unius Avere vicecomiti invinit. In Oreuuelle tenet eadem æcclesia iiii^{tam} partem unius virgatæ. Terra est dimidio bovi et valet xii. den.

[12] The references to pages are to those of Mr. Hamilton's edition. The portions within the square brackets are the passages omitted.

[13] In this instance the omission is so gross that it attracted Mr. Hamil-

Another instance of "running on" occurs on fol. 105A (1), where "xviii. cotarii" (p. 67) is proved by Domesday to stand for "xviii. [bordarii x.] cotarii." Again on fo. 79 (B) 2 we have this :—

I.C.C. (p. 14).	D.B. (I. 195 B 1).
Eadiua unam hidam habuit et unam virgam [.................. ....] Socham huius habuit ædiua T.R.E.[14]	Tenuit Eddeua i. hidam et i. virgatam et Wluui homo ejus i. hidam et i. virgatam. Socam ejus habuit Eddeua.

So, too, on fo. 100B (1) :—

I.C.C. (p. 52).	D.B. (I. 190A).
XI. carruce villanis xv. [villani, xv. bordarii, xi. servi. Unum mol' de xvi. denariis, et alii duo mol' de xxxii. denariis. Pratum] xvi. carrucis.	XV. villani et xv. bordarii cum xi. carucis. Ibi xi. servi, et i. molinus de xvi. denariis et alii duo molini de xxxii. denariis, Pratum xvi. carucis.

The importance of such an omission as this lies in the proof of unintelligent clerkship and want of revision which so unmeaning an entry as "xv. xvi. carrucis" supplies.

Omissions of another character are not infrequent. On fo. 95B (1) an entire holding of a virgate (held by a sokeman of Earl Alan) is omitted (p. 34). Another sokeman of Earl Alan (p. 32) has his holding ($\frac{1}{4}$ virgate) omitted on the same folio (95A, 1), so is an entire holding of Hardwin's (p. 36) on fo. 96A, (2). A demesne plough ("i. caruca") of

ton's notice. He admits in a footnote that his MS. "confounds two separate entries." It would, however, be more correct to say that the MS. here omits a portion of each. It is easy to see how the scribe erroneously "ran on" from the first portion of one entry to the second portion of another. This entry has a further value, for while D.B. convicts the I.C.C. of omitting the words "de Widone," it is itself convicted, by collation, of omitting the entry, "Terra est i. bovi."

[14] The I.C.C. here wholly omits one of the three holdings T.R.E. "The three hides and a virgate," at which the estate was assessed, were thus composed :—(1) three virgates held by Huscarl, (2) a hide and a virgate held by Eadgyth, (3) a hide and a virgate held by Wulfwine, her man. It is this last holding which is omitted. Note here that the Domesday "hide" is composed as ever (*pace* Mr. Pell) of four virgates.

Hugh de Port (p. 8) is omitted (78A, 1), and so are the ploughs ("et iiii. villanis") of Aubrey's villeins (p. 9) a few lines lower down. On fo. 90A (1) the words "ibi est terra" are wanting (p. 15),[15] and so are "non potuit" on fo. 100 (A) 1.[16] The word "recedere" is left out on fo. 103B (2),[17] and "soca" just before (103 (B) 1).[18] "Odo" is similarly wanting on fo. 90A (1).[19] The note also on the Abbot of Ely's sokeman at Lollesworth (p. 95), is wholly omitted (fo. 113, B, 2), though found both in Domesday Book and in the *Inquisito Eliensis.*[20]

Turning now to the clerical blunders, we find an abundant crop. We may express them conveniently in tabular form :—

Folio		Page
76 (*a*) 2.	"Auenam lvii. nummos," *for* "Aueram (ve)l viii. denarios" (D.B.)	2
76 (*b*) 1.	"Hominis" *for* "ho(mo)"	3
77 (*a*) 2.	"In dominio et iii. villani," *for* "una caruca in dominio et iii. villanis"	7
Ibid.	"Mille de anguillis dimidium de piscina," *for* "i. millen' et dimidium anguill'" (D.B.)	7
78 (*b*) 2.	"iiii. in dominio carucæ et iiii. hidæ in diminio," *for* "iiii. carucæ et iiii. hidæ in dominio". . . .	11
79 (*a*) 1.	"cuius honor erat," *for* "cuius ho(mo erat" . .	12
79 (*b*) 2.	"iiii*or.* bobus," *for* "iiii. bord(arii". . . .	14
91 (*b*) 2.	"valent iii.," *for* "valent iii. den.". . . .	21
92 (*b*) 2.	"xliii. car(ucis) ibi e(st) terra." *for* "xl. acras terræ".	25
95 (*a*) 2.	"has v. h(idas) tenet," *for* "de his v. h(idis) tenet"	33
95 (*b*) 1.	"et pro iiii. virgis," *for* "et pro iii. virgis" . .	34
95 (*b*) 2.	"unam virgam minus," *jor* "dimi' virg' minus" (D.B.)	35
96 (*b*) 1.	"dimidiam virgam," *for* "i. virg'" (D.B.) .	38
97 (*b*) 1.	"Clintona," *for* "Iclintona"	41

[15] "i. caruce [ibi terra] et est caruca."

[16] "Ita quod [non potuit] dare vel vendere" (p. 50).

[17] "Potuerunt [recedere] qua parte voluerunt"—p. 62 (Mr. Hamilton noticed this omission).

[18] "Sed [soca] eius remansit ædiue" (p. 61).

[19] "Tenet [Odo] de comite Alano" (p. 15).

[20] "Soca tantum hominis abbatis de Ely remansit æcclesiæ" (D.B.); "sine socha" (I.E.).

Folio				Page
97 (*b*)	2.	"unam hidam," *for* "dimidiam hidam" (D.B.)	.	42
100 (*a*)	1.	"Terra est vi. carucis," *for* "Terra est v. carucis"[21]		50
100 (*a*)	2.	"ii. h(idas) et dimidiam virgam," *for* "ii. hidas et i. virgam et dimidiam"[22] (D.B.)		50
100 (*b*)	2.	"vii. sochemanni," *for* "iii. soch[emanni]"[23].	.	52
101 (*a*)	2.	"homities," *for* "homines" . . .	.	54
101 (*b*)	2.	"tenet pic' vicecomes quendam ortum de rege ii. hide." *for* "tenet pic' vicecomes de rege ii. hidas"[24]	.	55
102 (*a*)	1.	"ii. boves," *for* "ii. bord(arii)" . . .	.	56
104 (*b*)	1.	"iiii. hidas et i. virgam," *for* "iii. hidas et i. virgam" (D.B.)		65
105 (*b*)	2.	*bis* "Rahamnes," *for* "Kahannes" . .	.	60
106 (*a*)	1.	"pro vi. hidis" (*bis*), *for* "pro vii. hidis"	.	70
109 (*b*)	2.	"Fulcuinus tenet de comite Alano iii. cottarios," *for* "Fulcuinus tenet de comite Alano. iii. cottarii".	.	82
110 (*b*)	1.	"viiii. h(idis)," *for* "viii. h(idis)" . .	.	84
111 (*a*)	2.	"liii. carrucis est ibi terra," *for* "iiii. car' est ibi terra"		87
110 (*a*)	1.	"ely tenuit ii. h(idas), *for* "ely tenuit i. h(idam)" (I.E.)		83

Besides these, Ralf "de bans" is often entered as Ralf "de scannis." Again, we find such blunders as this :—

I.C.C.	D.B.
Hugo de portu tenet sneileuuelle. Pro v. hidis se defendebat T.R.E. et modo facit *de feudo episcopi baiocensis* (p. 3).	Ipse Hugo tenet *de feudo episcopi baiocensis* snellewelle. Pro v. hidis se defend[ebat] semper.
Tenuit Turbertus i. hidam sub abbate de eli. *Et in morte* ita quod non potuit dare neque separare ab ecclesia extra dominicam firmam monachorum T.R.E. (p. 63).	Tenuit Turbern i. hidam de abbate. Non poterat separare ab æcclesia extra firmam monachorum T.R.E. *nec in die mortis ejus.*

[21] The latter is the reading of D.B., and is the right one because confirmed by I.E.

[22] This, like the similar cases where D.B. is given as the authority for the second reading, is proved arithmetically (*vide infra*).

[23] The I.C.C. enumerates only *three*, which is the number given in D. B.

[24] The words "quendam ortum" had occurred just before, and are here wrongly repeated.

Abuerunt de soca S. Ædel' ii. hidas et dimidiam virgam *de ely* T.R.E. (p. 65).

Habuerunt ii. hidas et dimidiam vir[gatam] de soca S. Ædeldride *de Ely*.

In all these three cases the italicised words are misplaced, and in all three the explanation is the same, the scribe having first omitted them, and then inserted them later out of place. Having now criticised the text of the I.C.C., and shown that it presents no small traces of unintelligent clerkship, if not of actual ignorance of the terms and *formulæ* of Domesday, I turn to the text of Domesday Book, to test it by comparison with that of the I.C.C.

II. Criticism of the Domesday Text

Among the omissions are, on i. 195 (*b*) 1, "Item et reddebat viii. den. vel aueram si rex in vicecomitatu venit" (p. 5). At Kirtling (p. 11), "et v^{ta.} caruca potest fieri [in dominio]" is omitted (i. 202 *a*). So is (p. 25) a potential demesne plough of John fitz Waleran (i. 201 *b*). The Countess Judith's sokemen at Carlton (pp. 20, 21) have their values omitted[25] (i. 202, *a*, 2). "Habuerunt dimidiam hidam, et," is omitted (p. 28) in the entry of two sokemen of Godwine (201, *b*, 2). On i. 196 (*a*) 1, "Terra est i. bovi" is wanting (p. 79). More important, however, are the omissions of whole entries. These are by no means difficult to account for, the process of extracting from the original returns, the various entries relating to each particular fief being one which was almost certain to result in such omissions.[26]

[25] "Inter totum valent et valuerunt xii. den." This was *exclusive* of the value of the Manor, which by the way the I.C.C. gives as sixteen pounds and D.B. at six pounds, one of those cases of discrepancy which have to be left in doubt, though D.B. is probably right.

[26] Mr. Eyton, in his *Notes on Domesday* (p. 16), called attention to this. "The result," he wrote (of the Lincolnshire Domesday), "as to arrangement, is in certain instances just what might have been expected from some haste of process. . . . The hurried clerks were perpetually overlooking entries which they ought to have seen."

Moreover, two entries were occasionally thrown into one, a dangerous plan for the clerks themselves, and one which may sometimes lead us to think that an entry is omitted when it is duly to be found under another head. Lastly, the compilers of Domesday Book had no such invaluable check for their work as was afforded in the original by entering first the assessment of the whole township, and then that of each of its component Manors separately. But of this more below.[27] The only wonder is that the omissions are, after all, so few. Perhaps even of these some may be only apparent. Hardwin's half-hide in *Burwell* (p. 6) is wanting; so is Aubrey's half-virgate in *Badburgham*, according to Mr. Hamilton (p. 36), but the oversight is his. A virgate held in Trumpington by a burgess of Cambridge (p. 51) would seem to be not forthcoming, but its position was somewhat anomalous.[28] Guy de Rembercurt held a hide and a virgate in *Haslingefield* (p. 73), though we cannot find it in Domesday; and in *Witewelle* (Outwell) two hides which were held by Robert, a tenant of Hardwin (p. 81), are similarly omitted, according to Mr. Hamilton but will be found under " Wateuuelle" (198 *b*, 2).

There are cases in which the I.C.C. corrects D.B., cases in which D.B. corrects the I.C.C., and cases in which the I.C.C. corrects itself. There are also several cases of discrepancy between the two, in which we cannot posi-

---

[27] Mr. Eyton (*ibid.*, pp. 17, 18), while ignoring this valuable and most mportant feature, notes the employment of a similar device in Domesday Book itself in the case of Yorkshire. "Against such errors and redundancies a very simple but effective precaution seems to have been adopted by some clerk or clerks employed on the Yorkshire notes. Before transcription was commenced an index was made of the loose notes of that county. This index gave the contents of each Wapentac or Liberty in abstract under the appropriate title ; then the measure in carucates and bovates of each item of estate ; and lastly (interlined) some hint or indication to whose Honour or fief each item belonged. This most clerkly device will have saved the subsequent transcribers much trouble of roll-searching and a world of confusion in their actual work."

[28] " Warra jacet in trompintona, et terra in grantebrigga."

tively pronounce which, if either, is right. A singular
instance of both being wrong is found in the case of Soham.
The assessment of this township was actually eleven hides,
its four component holdings being severally assessed at
nine and a half hides less six acres, half a hide, one hide,
and six acres. The I.C.C. at first gives the total assessment as eleven hides and a half, while D.B. erroneously
assesses the first of the four holdings at six hides and forty
acres in one place, and nine hides and a half in the other,
both figures being wrong. A most remarkable case of yet
another kind is found in *Scelford* (Shelford). Here the entry
in I.C.C. agrees exactly with the duplicate entries found in
D.B. Yet they both make nonsense.[29] But on turning to
the *Inquisitio Eliensis* we obtain the correct version. As
this is a very important and probably unique instance, the
entries are here given in parallel columns :—

Inq. Eliensis.	*Inq. Com. Cant.*	*D.B.*	*D.B.* i. 198 (*a*) 2.
i. hidam et dim. et vi. acras quas tenuerunt vi. sochemanni de socha abbatis ley, de quibus non potuerunt dare nec recedere nisi iiiᵉˢ· virgas absque ejus licentia. Et si alias vendidissent tres virgas, predictus abbas semper socham habuit T.R.E.	Tenuerunt vii. (*sic*) sochemanni i. hidam et dim. et vi. acras de soca abbatis de ely. Non potuerunt recedere sed soca remanebat abbati.	i. 198 (*a*) 2. Tenuerunt vii. (*sic*) socheman ni i. hidam et dim. et vi. acras de soca abbatis. Non [30] potuerunt recedere cum terra, sed soca remanebat æcclesia de ely.	Tenuerunt vii. (*sic*) socheman ni i. hidam et dim. et vi. acras de soca abbatis de ely. Non potuerunt recedere cum terra, sed soca remanebat æcclesiæ Ely.

[29] To say that the sokeman "non potuerunt recedere *sed* soca remanebat abbati," is nonsense, because if they were not able "recedere," the
question of "soca" could not arise. The formula "sed soca," etc., is
only used in cases where there *was* a right "recedere."

[30] In this case the "n[on]" has been added by interlineation.

Here the *Inquisitio Eliensis* version shows us that the estate had two divisions held by different tenures. Three virgates the sokemen were not free to sell; the other three they might sell, but if they did, "predictus abbas semper socham habuit."[31] The two divisions of the estate are confused in the other versions. But all three of these correspond so exactly that we are driven to assign the error to the original returns themselves. In that case the compiler (or compilers) of the I.E. will have corrected the original return from his own knowledge of the facts, which knowledge, I shall show, he certainly possessed.

This brings us to the *errors* of Domesday. For comparison's sake, I here tabulate them like those of the I.C.C. :—

Folio   Page

i. 189 (*b*) 2. "mancipium," *for* "inuuardum" (I.C.C.) . . 4

i. 195 (*b*) 1. "Terra est ii. carucis et ibi est," *for* "Terra est i. carucæ et ibi est" 15

i. 199 (*b*) 1. "xxx. acras," *for* "xx. acras" I.C.C.) . . 15

i. 196 (*a*) 2. "iiii. villani . . . habent iii. carucas," *for* "iiii. villani . . . habent iiii. carucas" . . . 21

i. 199 (*b*) 1. "De hac terra tenet," *for* "adhuc in eadem villa tenet" (?)[32] 29

i. 198 (*a*) 1. "tenet Harduuinus i. virgatam" *for* "tenet Hardeuuinus dim. virgatam" (I.C..C) . , . . 38

i. 194 (*b*) 1. "ii. hidas et i. virg. terræ," *for* "ii. hidas et una virg. et dimidiam" (I.C.C.) 64

i. 199 (*b*) 2. "xvi. sochemanni," *for* "xv. sochemanni" . . 65

i. 198 (*b*) 1. "tenet Durand . . . i. hidam et i. virg.," *for* "tenet Durand i. hidam et dim. virg." 67

[31] The meaning, I think, is clear, though badly expressed, "alias" being, seemingly, put for "illas."

[32] This error arose thus : The original return (*see* I.C.C.) ran : " De his v. hidis " (*i.e.* in "Campes") tenet Normannus de Alberico dimidiam hidam." The Domesday scribe read this hurriedly as implying tha Norman's half hide was part of Aubrey's estate here (two and a half hides), whereas it was reckoned and entered as a *separate* estate.

Comparing the omissions and errors, as a whole, in these two versions of the original returns, it may be said that the comparison is in favour of the Domesday Book text, although, from the process of its compilation, it was far the most exposed to error. No one who has not analysed and collated such texts for himself can realise the extreme difficulty of avoiding occasional error. The abbreviations and the *formulæ* employed in these surveys are so many pitfalls for the transcriber, and the use of Roman numerals is almost fatal to accuracy. The insertion or omission of an " x " or an "i" was probably the cause of half the errors of which the Domesday scribes were guilty. Remembering that they had, in Mr. Eyton's words,[34] to perform "a task, not of mere manual labour and imitative occuracy, but a task requiring intellect—intellect, clear, well-balanced, apprehensive, comprehensive, and trained withal," we can really only wonder that they performed it so well as they did.

Still, the fact remains that on a few pages of Domesday we have been able to detect a considerable number of inaccuracies and omissions. The sacrosanct status of the Great Survey is thus gravely modified. I desire to lay stress on this fact, which is worthy of the labour it has cost to establish. For two important conclusions follow. Firstly, it is neither safe nor legitimate to make general

[32] Proved by collation with I.C.C. and I. E., which agree with each other.

[34] *Notes on Domesday*, p. 16.

inferences from a single entry in Domesday. All conclusions as to the interpretation of its *formulæ* should be
based on *data* sufficiently numerous to exclude the influence
of error. Secondly, if we find that a rule of interpretation
can be established in an overwhelming majority of the
cases examined, we are justified, conversely, in claiming
that the apparent exceptions may be due to errors in the
text.

The first of these conclusions has a special bearing on
the theories propounded by Mr. Pell with so much ingenuity
and learning.[35] I have shown, in an essay criticising these
theories,[36] that the case of Clifton, to which Mr. Pell attached
so much importance,[37] is nothing, in all probability, but one
of Domesday's blunders, of which I gave, in that essay,
other instances. So, too, in the case of his own Manor of
Wilburton, Mr. Pell accepted without question the reading,
" *six* ploughlands," as representing the " primary return,"[38]
althongh that reading is only found in the most corrupt,
of the three versions of the *Inquisito Eliensis*, while the
two better versions (B and C texts) agree with Domesday
Book, and with the abbreviated return at the end of the
A text itself (Tib A. VI. fo. 67, *b*, 1), in giving the ploughlands as *seven*. Really it is nothing but waste of time to
argue from a reading which is only found in one out of
five MSS., and that one the most corrupt.

This brings me to the existence and the value of duplicate
entries in Domesday. Mr. Hamilton describes as "a
curious reading" the words in the I.C.C., "sed soca remanebat *Harlestone*." Now it so happens that in this case
we have five separate versions of the original entry: one
in the I.C.C., one in the I.E., and three in Domesday Book.
Here they are side by side :—

[35] *Domesday Studies*, pp. 227-363, 561-619.
[36] " Domesday Measures of Land " (*Archæological Review*, Sept.,
1889 ; iv. 130).
[37] *Domesday Studies*, 188, 354.
[38] " vi. earucis ibi est terra." See *Addenda*.

I.C.C. (p. 46.)	I.E. (p. 106.)	D.B. (I. 200, *a*, 2.)	D.B. (*ib.* in margin.)	D.B. (I. 191, *a*, 2.)
Et potuit recedere quo voluit sed soca remanebat Harlestone.	Potuit recedere cum terra sua absque ejus licentia, sed semper remansit socha ejus in ecclesia sancte Ædel' ut hund testantur.	Recedere cum terra sua potuit, sed soca remansit æcclesiæ.	Vendere potuit, sed soca Abbati remansit.	Potuit recedere sine licentia ejus, sed soca remansit Abbati.

The value of such collation as this ought to be self-evident. It is not only that we thus find four out of five MSS. to be against the reading " Harlestone " (which, indeed, to any one familiar with the survey is obviously a clerical error), but that here and elsewhere we are thus afforded what might almost be termed a bilingual inscription. We learn, for instance, that the Domesday scribe deemed it quite immaterial whether he wrote " recedere cum terra ejus," or " vendere " or " recedere sine licentia." Consequently, these phrases were all identical in meaning.[39]

Considerable light is thrown by the I.C.C. on the origin of these little known duplicate entries in Domesday. In every instance of their occurrence within the limits of its province they are due to a conflict of title recorded in the original return. They appear further to be confined to the estates of two landowners, Picot, the sherriff, and Hardwin d'Eschalers, the titles of both being frequently contested by the injured Abbot of Ely. Why the third local offender, Guy de Raimbercurt, does not similarly appear, it is difficult to say. He was the smallest offender of the three, and Picot the worst; but it is Hardwin's name which occurs

---

[39] Compare the equivalent tenure recognised in William of Poitier's charter to Bayonne :—" Le *voisin* qui voulait abandonner la cité sans esprit de retour avait le droit de vendre librement tout ce qu'il possédait maisons, prairies, vergers, moulins."

most frequently in these duplicate entries.[40] The principle which guided the Domesday scribes cannot be certainly decided, for they duplicated entries in the original return which (according to the I.C.C.) varied greatly in their statements of tenure. Thus, to take the first three :—

I.C.C.	D.B.
fo. 79 (*b*) 1, " Tenet Harduuinus descalariis." [41]	I. 190 (*b*) 2, "Tenet Harduinu *sub abbate.*"
	I. 199 (*a*) 2, " Tenet Harduinus."
fo. 90 (*b*) 2, " Tenet Harduuinus *de abbate.*"	I. 190 (*b*) 1, "Tenet Harduinus de Escalers *de abbate.*"
	I. 199 (*a*) 2. " Tenet Harduinus."
fo. 92 (*a*) 2, " Tenet Harduuinus *de rege*	I. 199 (*b*) 2, "Tenet Harduinus *de abbate.*"
	I. 199 (*a*) 2, "Tenet Harduinus.'

Here, whether the original return states Hardwin to hold (1) of the abbot, (2) of the king, or (3) of neither, the scribes, in each of the three cases, enter the estates (*A*) under the Abbot's land, as held of the Abbot, (*B*) under Hardwin's land, as held *in capite*. And it is singular that in all these three cases the entry of the estate under the Abbot's land is the fuller of the two.[42]

[40] We have three separate statements (of which more anon) of the aggressions of these three men on the Abbey's lands. Taking the one printed on pp. 175-177 of Mr. Hamilton's book, we find that of the twelve estates grasped by Hardwin, all but one or two can be identified as the subject of duplicate entries in Domesday. (A disputed hide and a half in " Melrede," though not mentioned in this list, is also entered in duplicate.) But neither of the estates seized by Guy de Raimbercurt is so entered in Domesday. The first two of those which Picot is accused of abstracting are entered in duplicate, but not the following ones. There is one instance of a duplicate entry of another character, relating to half a virgate (D.B., i. 199, *b*, 2, gives it erroneously as half a hide, but D.B., i. 190, *a*, 1, rightly as half a virgate), which Picot, as sheriff had regained for the king against the " invading " Aubrey.

[41] The I.E. adds " sub abbate ely " in each case, but is, from its nature, here open to suspicion.

[42] This is not always the case. At Whaddon, for instance, the entry

On the whole it would appear that the domesday scribes did not consistently carry out a system of duplicate entry, though, on the other hand, these entries were by no means due to mere clerical inadvertence, but were prompted by a doubt as to the title, which led to the precaution of entering them under the names of both the claimants.

But the chief point of interest in these same entries is that they give us, when we add the versions of the I.C.C. and the I.E., four parallel texts. At some of the results of their collation we will now glance.

I.C.C.	I.E	D.B.	D.B.
(fo. 92, *b*, 2.)	(p. 107)	(I. 190, *b*, 2.)	(I. 199, *a*, 2.)
Hanc terram tenuerunt iii. sochemanni homines ab-batis de ely. Non potuerunt *recedere absque licentia ejus.*	Hanc terram tenuerunt iii. sochemanni sub predicto abbate ely. Non potu-erunt *vendere terram suam sine eius licentia.*	Hanc terram tenuerunt iii. sochemanni homines ab-batis de ely. Non potuerunt *dare nec ven-dere absque ejus licentia terram suam.*	Hanc terram tenuerunt iii sochemanni. *Vendere* non potuerunt.
(fo. 79, *b*, 1.)	(p. 102.)	(I. 190, *b*, 2.)	(I. 199, *a*, 2.)
iiii. soche-manni tenuer-unt hanc terram T.R.E. Et non potuerunt *rece-dere sine licen-tia abbatis de ely.*	Hanc terram tenuerunt iiii. sochemanni. T.R.E. de ab-bate ely. Non potuerunt *rece-dere vel vendere sine licentia abbatis ely.*	Hanc terram tenuerunt iiii. sochemanni, nec, potuerunt *recedere sine licentia abbatis.*	Hanc terram tenuerunt iiii. sochemanni abbatis de ely. Non potuerunt *vendere.*

These extracts illustrate the use of the terms *dare, ven-dere, recedere,* etc. They are supplemented by those given below :—

under Hardwin's land is the fuller. It is noteworthy also that in this case the *later* entry (i. 198, *b*, 1) is referred to (" Hæc terra appreciata est cum terra Hardwini ") in the *earlier* one (i. 191, *a*, 2).

I.C.C.	D.B.	I.E.
76 (*a*) 1.	I. 196 (*b*) 1.	
Potuit dare sine licentia domini sui terram suam	Terram suam tamen dare et vendere potuit.	

76 (*b*) 2,	I. 199. (*a*) 2.	p. 101.
Absque eius licentia dare terram suam potuerunt, sed socham eorum habuit archiepiscopus.	Sine ejus licentiat poterant recedere et terram suam dare vel vendere, sed soca remansit Archiepiscopo.	Potuerunt dare vel vendere terram suam. Saca remansit abbati.

76 (*b*) 2.	I. 196 (*b*) 1.
Potuit dare cui voluit.	Potuit absque[48] ejus licentia recedere.

77 (*b*) 2.	I. 195 (*b*) 1.
Potuerunt recedere cum terra ad quem dominum voluerunt.	Potuerunt receder sine licentia eorum.

I.C.C.	D.B.
78 (*a*) 1.	I. 190 (*b*) 1.
Potuerunt recedere cum terra sua absque licentia domini sui.	Dare et vendere potuerunt.

90 (*a*) 2.	I. 190 (*b*) 2.	p. 102.
Non potuerunt recedere sine licentia abbatis.	Non Potuerunt recedere sine ejus licentia.	Non potuerunt recedere vel vendere absque eius licentia.
	I. 200 (*a*) 2.	
	Non potuerunt vendere sine ejus licentia.	

---

[48] This same change of phrase is repeated four times on two pages (pp. 4, 5).

105 (*a*) 2	I. 200 (*a*) 1.	p. 109.
Potuerunt dare et vendere sine soca.	Terras suas vendere potuerunt. Soca de viii. sochemannis remansit in abbatia de ely.	Potuerunt dare vel vendere cui voluerunt, sed saca eorum remansit eidem abbati.
113 (*b*) 1.	201 (*a*) 1.	p. 112.
Potuerunt recedere sine soca.	Terram suam vendere potuerunt. Soca vero remansit abbati.	Potuerunt dare preter licentiam abbatis et sine soca.

No one can glance at these passages without perceiving that *dere*, *vendere*, and *recedere* are all interchangeably used, and that even any two of them (whether they have the conjunction "et" or the disjunction "vel" between them) are identical with any one. It would be possible to collect almost any number of instances in point. Further, the insertion or omission of the phrase "sine" (or "absque") "ejus licentia" is immaterial, it being understood where not expressed. So too with the words "cui voluit." In short, like the translators to whom we owe the Authorized Version, the Domesday scribes appear to have revelled in the use of synonym and paraphrase.[44] Our own conceptions of the sacredness of a text and of the need for verbal accuracy were evidently foreign to their minds.

Glancing for a moment at another county, we have in the Survey of Leicestershire a remarkable instance of a whole fief being entered twice over. It is that of Robert Hostiarius :—

Robertus hostiarius tenet de rege ii. car. teræ in Howes. Terra est iii. carucis. In dominio	Robertus filus W. hostiari. tenet de rege in Howes ii. cari terræ. Ibi habet i. car. in

[44] So, for instance :—

"de appulatione navis " (I.C.C.) = " de theloneo retis " (D.B.).
"ferarum siluaticarum " (I.C.C.) = " bestiarum siluaticarum " (D.B.).
"silua ad sepes refici." (I.C.C.) = " ne musad claud. sepes " (D.B.)

est i. **caruca** et iii. servi, et viii. villani cum i. bordario habent ii. car. . . .

dominio et iii. serv[os] et viii. villani cum i. bordario habentes ii. car. . . .

Idem [Turstinus] tenet de R. iiij. car. terræ in Clachestóne. Terra est ii. **caruca**. Has habent ibi iii. sochemanni cum ii. villanis et ii. bordariis. Ibi viii. acræ prati. Valuit et valet x. solidos.

Idem Turstinus tenet de Roberto in Clachestone iiii. car. terræ et Tetbald[us] ii. car. terræ. Ibi est in dominio i. caruca et iii. sochemanni et v. villani et iiii. (*sic*) bordarii cum iii. carucis et i. servo. Ibi xiii. acræ prati. Valuit et valet totum xx. solidos. Has terras tenuerunt T.R.E Outi et Arnui cum saca et soca.

Tetbald[us] tenet de Roberto ii. car. terræ in Clachestone. In dominio est i. caruca cum i. servo et iii. villani cum i. bordario habent i. car. Ibi vi. acræ prati. Valuit et valet x. solidos.

Here the last two entries (both relating to Claxton) have been boldly thrown into one in the second version, which also (though omitting the number of ploughlands) gives additional information in the name of Robert's father, and in those of his predecessors T.R.E. This is thus an excellent illustration of the liberty allowed themselves by the compilers of Domesday.

An instance on a smaller scale is found in the Survey of Cambridgeshire, where we read on opposite pages :—

In Witelesfeld hund'. In histetone jacet Wara de i. hida et dimidia de M. Cestreforde et est in Exsesse appreciata, hanc terram tenuit Algarus comes (i. 189 *b*).

In Witelesf' h'd. In histetune jac' Wara de hida et dimidia de Cestres' man. et est appreciata in Exexe. Algar comes tenuit (i. 190).

The second entry has been deleted as a duplicate, but it serves to show us that the scribes, even when free from error, were no mere copyists.[45]

[45] Compare the I.C.C. version on p. 116, *infra*.

III. "Soca" and "Theinland."

The extracts I have given above establish beyond a doubt the existence among the "sochemanni" of two kinds of tenure. We have (1) those who were free to part with (*vendere*) and leave *(recedere)* their land, (2) those who were not, *i.e.* who could not do so without the abbot's licence. This distinction is reproduced in two terms which I will now examine.

In the *Inquisitio Eliensis* and the documents connected with it there is much mention of the "thegnlands" of the Abbey. These lands are specially distinguished from "sokeland" (*terra de soca*). Both, of course, are distinct from the "dominium." Thus in one of the Conqueror's writs we read :—

Restituantur ecclesiæ terræ que in *dominio* suo erant die obitus Æduardi. . . . Qui autem tenent *theinlandes* que procul dubio debent teneri de ecclesia faciant concordiam cum abbate quam meliorem poterint, . . . Hoc quoque de tenentibus *socam* et *sacam* fiat.[46]

Now this distinction between "thegnland" and "sokeland" will be found to fit in exactly with the difference in tenure we have examined above. Here is an instance from the "breve abbatis" in the record of Guy de Raimbecurt's aggressions :—

In melreda ii. hidas et dim. virg.

In meldeburne ii. hidas et dim.[47] et dim. virg.

Hoc est iiii. hidas et iii. virg. Ex his sunt i. virg. et dim. *thainlande* et iiii. hidas et dim. [48] *de soca*.

On reference to the two Manors in question, there is, at first sight, nothing in the I.C.C., the I.E., or Domesday to distinguish the "thegnland " from the "sokeland." Of the

---

[46] *Inq. Com. Cant.*, pp. xviii., xix.

[47] "Et dimidiam" [hidam] is omitted in B, and (oddly enough) in Domesday itself.

[48] All three MSS. err here, as the reading should clearly be " dim. *virg.*"

first holding we read that it had been held T.R.E. by 10 *sochemanni* "de soca S. Edelride"; of the second, that it was held by "viii. *sochemanni*. . . homines abbatis de Ely." But closer examination of the I.C.C. reveals, in the former case, this distinction :—

De his ii. hidis et dimidia virga tenuit i. istorum *unam virgam et dimidiam.* Non potuit dare nec vendere absque licentia abbats. Sed alii novem potuerunt recedere et vendere cui voluerunt. [49]

Here then we identify the virgate and a half of "thein-land"—though held by a *sochemannus*—and this same distinction of tenure proves to be the key throughout. Thus, for instance, in the same document " Herchenger pistor" is recorded to have seized "in Hardwic i. hidam *thainlande* et dim. hidam et vi. acras *de soca*" (p. 177). Reference to the I.C.C., D.B., and the I.E reveals that the former holding had belonged to "v. sochemanni homines abbatis de ely," and that "isti non potuerunt dare neque vendere alicui extra ecclesiam S. Edeldride ely."[50] But the latter holding had belonged to a *sochemannus*, of whom it is said—" homo abbatis de ely fuit: potuit recedere, sed socam ejus abbas habuit." [51]

This enables us to understand the distinctions found in the summaries appended to the Cambridgeshire portion of the I.E., and recorded in the *Breve Abbatis.* Indeed they confirm the above distinction, for the formula they apply to holders "de soca abbatie ely" is: "illi qui hanc

---

[49] b. 65, This distinction between the one and the nine, but not the size of the holding, is preserved in D.B. ; while the I.E., though pre-serving it, gives the numbers as two and eight.

[50] This is the I.E. and D.B. version. For "extra ecclesiam," the I.C.C. substitutes "sine ejus [abbatis] licentia."

"Soca *remansit abbati*" is the D.B. and I.E. version. It should be noted that the I.E. and *Breve Abbatis* give "herchenger pistor" as the despoiler, while the I.C.C. and D.B. record him only as a " miles " of Picot the sheriff. This is a case which certainly suggests special local knowledge in the compiler of the former documents, who also gives the sokeman's name—Siward.

terram tenuerunt de soca T.R.E. vendere potuerunt, sed saca et soca et commendatio et servitium semper remanebat ecclesia de ely."

These terms are valuable for their definition of rights. Over the holder of land "de soco" the lord had (1) "saca et soca," (2) " commendatio et (3) servitium." If the land was thegnland then the Abbot received "omnem consuetudinem" as well.[52] We will first deal with the latter class, those from whom the Abbot received " consuetudo," and then those who held "de soca.'

For contemporary (indeed, slightly earlier) evidence, we must turn to the Ely *placitum* of 1072—1075.[53] The special value which this *placitum* possesses is found in its record of the services dne from *sochemanni*, and even from freemen. It thus helps to interpret the bald figures of Domesday, to which it is actually anterior. The first two instances it affords are these:—

In breuessan tenet isdem W. terram Elfrici supradicte consuetudinis. In brucge tenet ipse W. terram etfled ejusdem modi.

The *consuetudo* referred to was this :—

Ita proprie sunt abbati ut quotienscunque preceperit prepositus monasterii ire et omnem rei emendationem persolvere. Et si quid de suo voluerint venundare, a preposito prius licentiam debent accipere.

The corresponding entries in the I.E. run thus :—

"In Brugge una libera femina commend' S. Ædel. de lxxx. ac. pro manerio.

In Beuresham ten[uit] Ælfricus i. liber homo commed' S. Ædel.[54] lx. acras pro manerio " (p. 165).

---

[52] Thus " In Branmmeswelle . . . lxx. liberi homines unde abbas habuit sacam et socam et commendatio *et omnes consuetudines* . . . In eadem villa iiii. liberi homines* unde abbas habuit sacam et socam et commendationem" (p. 161).

[53] *Inq. Com. Cant.*, 192-5. See paper on it, *infra.*

[54] " In soca et commdantione abbatis de eli " (D.B., ii. 441).

* " Commend' abbati" (D.B., ii 387*b*).

Thus we obtain direct evidence of the services due from commended freemen owing "consuetudines." Turning now to those of *sochemanni*, we have this important passage :—

Willelmus de Warena tenet quadraginta quinque socamans in predicta felteuuella qui quotiens abbas preceperit in anno arabunt suam terram, colligent et purgabunt segetes, adducent et mittent in horrea, portabunt victum monachorum ad monasterium, et quotiens eorum equos voluerit, et ubicunque sibi placuerit, totiens habebit, et ubicunque forsfecerint abbas forsfacturam habebit, et de illis similiter qui in eorum terram forsfecerint.

Item Willelmus de uuarenna tenet triginta tres socamans, istius consuetudinis in Nortuuolda.

Item W. tenet quinque socamans istius modi in Muddaforda.

Supradictus Walterus et cum eo Durandus, homines hugonis de monte forti, tenent xxvi. socamans supradicte consuetudinis in Maraham.

Collating as before from the I.E. the relative entries, we find them run this :—

Felteuuelle . . . Huic manerio adjacebant T.R.E xxxiiii. homines cum omni consuetudine, et alii vii. erant liberi homines,[55] qui poterant vendere terras, sed soca et commendatio remansit S. Ædel. (p. 132).

In felteuuella tenet W. de uuarenna xli. sochemannos . . . Super hos omnes habebat S. Ædel. socam et commendationem et omnem consuetudinem. Illorum vii. liberi erant cum terris suis, sed soca et commendatio remanebat S. Ædel. (p. 139).

IIII. sochemanni adjacent (*sic*) huic manerio [felteuuella] T.R.E. Et modo habet eos W. de Warenna (p. 138).

Nortuualde . . . Huic manerio adjacebant T.R.E. xxx. sochemanni cum omni consuetudine. Et alii iiii. liberi homines qui poterant vendere terras, sed saca et commendatio remanebat S. Ædel. (p. 132).

In Nortuualde S. Ædel. xxxiiii. sochem [annos] . . . S. Ædel. [habuit] socam et commendationem et omnem consuetudinem de illis xxx. tantum; et iiii. erant liberi homines, socam et sacam et commendationem [super hos] S. Ædel. habebat [56] (p. 139).

[55] " Soca et commendatione tantum " (D.B.)
[56] "iiii. liberi homines soca et commendatione tantum" (D.B.).

Mundeforde . . . Huic manerio adjacebant T.R.E. septem sochemanni cum omni consuetudine (p. 132).

In Mundeforde S. Ædel. vii. sochemannos cum omni consuetudine (p. 139).

Huic manerio [Mareham] T.R.E. adjacebant viginti vii. sochemanni cum omni consuetudine, sed postquam Rex W. advenit, habuit eos hugo de Munfort preter unum (p. 130).

[Terre hugo de Munford.] In mareham xxvi. sochemanni quos tenet [*sic*] S. Ædel. T.R.E.[57] . . . hanc terram receperunt[58] pro escangio, et mensurata est in brevi S. Ædel. (p. 137).

Here then we identify these four cases: Feltwell, with its 41 *sochemanni* (more accurately described as 34 s. and 7 *liberi homines*) attached to one Manor and four to another —45 in all; Northwold, with its 33 or 34;[59] Muddiford with 5 or 7;[60] and Marham with its 26.

The three former Manors lay in the Hundred of Grimeshoe, the fourth northwards, towards the Wash. Just to the south of the three Manors, over the borders of Suffolk, lay Brandon, where Lisois de Moustiers had usurped the rights of Ely over six *sochemanni.*

In Lakincgeheda et in Brandona vi. sochemanni S. Ædel. ita quod non potuerunt vendere terras liberati liseie antecessori eudo[nis] dapif[eri] . . . Post eum tenuit eos eudo et tenet cum saca et soca (p. 142).

The record of the *placitum*, drawn up during the tenure of Lisois, shows us their limited services: " Isti solummodo arabant et c'terent (*sic*) messes ejusdem loci quotienscunque abbas præceperit." The difference between these services and the others we have seen recorded is considerable.

Yet another group of sokemen on Suffolk Manors rendered these services :—

Ita proprie sunt abbati ut quotienscunque ipse præceperit in anno arabunt suam terram, purgabunt et colligent segetes, portabunt victum monachorum ad monasterium, equos eorum in suis necessitatibus

---

[57] " T.R.E. ad socham" (D.B.).   [58] " Recep'" (D.B., ii. 238).
[59] The *Breve Abbatis* records 34.   [60] *Ibid.*, 7.

habebit [abbas], et ubicunque deliquerint emendationem habebit semper et de omnibus illis qui in terris eorum deliquerint.

This is practically the same definition as we had for the other group, and suggests that it was of wide prevalence A notable contrast is afforded by the entry: "In villa que vocatur Blot tenet ipse R. iiii. homines qui tantum debent servire abbati cum propriis equis in omnibus necessitatibus suis."

We have now examined the *consuetudines* due from those "qui vendere non potuerunt," and may turn to the rights exercised over the other class. Excluding "ser-vitium" (which is usually omitted as subordinate or com-prised in the others), these are: (1) "commendatio" (2) "saca et soca." The distinction between the two meets us throughout the survey of the eastern counties. A man might be "commended" to one lord while another held his *soca*. Thus we read of Eadwine, a "man" of the Abbot of Ely :—"Potuit dare absque eius licentia, sed socam comes Algarus habuit." [61] That is to say, he was "commended to the Abbot of Ely," but Earl Ælfgar had the right of "sac and soc" over him. [62]

So too in the case of three "liberi homines," commended to the Abbot in Norfolk. He had no right over them, but such as commendation conferred "non habebat nisi com-mendationem," while their "soca" belonged to the King's Manor of Keninghall. [63] Conversely, the Abbot of Ely had the "soca" of a "man" of Earl Waltheof, [64] and a "man"

---

[61] I.C.C., fo. 110 (*b*) 1. Cf. D.B., I. 199 (*a*) 2, and I.E., p. 110.

[62] "Socam comes Algarus habuit "=" soca remansit comiti Algaro." See, for instance, the similar case in which a "man" of Earl Waltheof "terram suam dare vel vendere potuit, sed abbas de Rameseia socam habuit" (I.C.C., fo. 112, *b*, 2), where D.B. has :—"dare potuit, sed soca remansit abbati de Ramesy" (i. 202, *b*, 1).

[63] "Et in eadem villa iii. liberi homines . . . de quibus abbas non habebat nisi commendationem : soca in kanincghala regis."

[64] "Hanc terram tenuit godmundus homo comitis Waltevi ; soca vero remansit abbati ely" (p. 115).

of John, Waleran's nephew.[65] "Commendatio," of course, took precedence as a right. Thus we read of the above three "liberi homines,"—"Hos liberos homines tenet [tenuit] Ratfridus, postea W. de Scodies, et abbas saisivit eos propter commendationem suam " (p. 133).

In the above extracts we saw "liberi homines qui vendere poterant" distinguished from "Sochemanni," who could not sell. But we also saw that the two classes were not always carefully distinguished. We find, moreover, that the "liberi homines" were themselves, sometimes, "not free to sell." Thus "tenuit anant unus liber homo sub S. Ædel. T.R.E. pro manerio ii. carucatas terræ sed non potuit vendere" (p. 142). Some light may be thrown on this by the case of the estate held by Godmund, an abbot's brother :—

Totam terram quam tenebat Gudmundus in dominio, id est Nectuna, sic tenebat T.R.E. de S. Ædel. quod nullo modo poterat vendere, nec dare ; sed post mortem suam debebat manerium redire in dominio ecclesiæ ; quia tali pacto tenuit Gudmundus de Abbate (p. 144).

With this we may compare these entries :—

In Cloptuna . . . Ædmundus commendatus S. Ædel. unam carucatam . . . quam non potuit vendere nec dare (p. 150).

In Brandestuna Ædmundus presbyter terram quam accepit cum femina sua dedit S. Ædel. concedente femina T.R.E. ea conventione quod non posset eam dare nec vendere. Similiter de Clopetona" (p. 152).

In these cases the holder had only a life interest. Exactly parallel with the second is the case of " Eadward," citizen of London, who gave lands to St. Paul's, reserving a life interest for himself and his wife,—" et mortua illa Sanctus Paulus hereditare debuit." [66]

The above commendation of Edmund the priest ought to be compared with that of "unus liber homo S. Ædel.

[65] "Unum liberum hominem unde abbas habet sacam et socam tantum " (p. 140).

[66] *Domesday Studies*, p. 556.

commendatus *ita quod* non poterat vendere terram suam sine licentia abbatis," and of "i. liber homo S. Ædel. commendatus *ita quod* non poterat vendere terram suam extra ecclesiam (sed sacam et socam habuit stigandus in hersham ").[67] Thus both those who were free to sell and those who were not, might belong to the class of "liberi homines." The essential distinction was one, not of status, but of tenure.

IV. THE DOMESDAY CARUCA.

Yet more definite and striking, however, is the information on the Domesday *caruca* afforded by collating D.B. with the I.C.C. I referred at the Domesday Commemoration (1886) to the problem raised by the *caruca*,[68] and recorded my belief that *in Domesday* the word must always mean a plough team of *eight* oxen. The eight oxen, as Mr Seebohm has shown, are the key to the whole system of the carucate and the bovate. In Domesday, as I argued, the *formula* employed involves of necessity the conclusion that the *caruca* was a fixed quantity. Such entries, moreover, as "terra i. bovi," "terra ad iii. boves," etc., can only be explained on the hypothesis that the relation of the *bos* to the *caruca* was constant. But as the question is one of undoubted perplexity, and as some, like Mr. Pell, have strenuously denied that the number of oxen in the Domesday *caruca* was fixed,[69] the evidence given below is as welcome as it is conclusive :—

I.C.C.	D.B.
fo. 96 (*a*) 2 : " Dimidiæ caruce est ibi terra."	I. 202 (*a*) 2 : "Terra est. iiii. bobus."
fo. 103 (*a*) 2 : " iiii. bobus est terra ibi."	I. 190 (*a*) 1 : "Terra est dimidiæ carucæ."
fo. 103 (*b*) 2 : "Dimidiæ caruce est ibi [terra]."	I. 196 (*b*) 2 : "Terra est iiii. bobus."
fo. 112 (*b*) 1 : "iiii. bobus est ibi terra."	I. 201 (*a*) 1 : "Terra est dimidiæ caruce."

[7] *cf. El. pp*, 140, 141.
[69] *Domesday Studies*, p. 187.

[68] *Domesday Studies*, p. 209.

fo. 112 (*b*) 2 : " iiii. bobus est   I. 202 (*b*) 1 : " Terra est iiii.
            ibi terra. Et ibi   bobus, et ibi
            sunt.   Pratum   sunt, et pratum
            dimidiæ caruce."   ipsis bobus."

It is absolutely certain from these entries that the scribes
must have deemed it quite immaterial whether they wrote
"dimidia caruca" or "iiii. boves"; as immaterial as it
would be to us whether we wrote "half a sovereign" or
"ten shillings." It is, consequently, as absolutely certain
that the Domesday *caruca* was composed of eight oxen as
that our own sovereign is composed of twenty shillings.
And from this conclusion there is no escape.[70]

Another point in connection with the *caruca* on which
the I.C.C. gives us the light we need is this :—

            I.C.C.   D.B.

fo. 102 (*a*) 2. " ii. carrucis ibi   I. 200 (*b*) 1. " Terra est iii.
est terra. Non sunt carruce nisi   carucis. Sed non sunt ibi nisi
sex boves."   boves."

Here the Domesday text is utterly misleading as it stands.
But the I.C.C., by supplying the omitted " sex," gives us at
once the right sense.

V. THE DOMESDAY HIDE.

Similar to its evidence on the Domesday "plough" is
that which the I.C.C. affords as to the hide and virgate. In
my criticism of Mr. Pell's learned paper, I strenuously
opposed his view that the *hida* of Domesday was composed
of a variable number of virgates, and I insisted on the fact
that the Domesday "virgate" was essentially and always
the *quarter* of the geldable "hide." [71] The following parallel
passages will amply prove the fact :—

[70] It is essential to bear in mind that the Domesday scribes had nothing
to guide them but the bare words of the return, so that if they thus
equated these expressions, they can only have done so because the rule
was of universal application.

[72] *Archæological Review*, vol. i., p. 286.

..C.   D.B.

fo. 102 (*a*) 1 : i. hidam et dimidiam et unam virgam.

i. hidam et iii. virgatas terræ.—i. 194 (*a*) 2.

fc. 102 (*a*) 1 : dimidiam hid m et dimidiam virg'.

ii. virg' et dimidiam—i. 194 (*a*) 2.

fo. 103 (*a*) 1 : dimidiam hid..m et dimidiam virg'.

ii.[as] virg' et dimidiam—i. 198 (*a*) 2.

fo. 103 (*b*) 1 : i. hida et dimidia et dimidia virg'.

i. hida et ii. virg' et dimidia—i. 190. (?) 2.

fo. 103 (*b*) 2 : i. hida et dimidia et i. virg'.

i. hida et iii. virg'—i. 198 (*b*) 1.

fo. 106 (*b*) 2 : iiii. hidæ et dimidia et una virg'.

iv. hidæ et iii. virg'—i. 200 (*b*) 1.

fo. 112 (*a*) 2 : xi. hidæ i. virg' minus.

x. hidæ et iii. virg—i. 192 (*b*) 1.

These are only some of the passages of *direct* glossarial value.[72] Indirectly, that is to say by analysis of the township assessments, we obtain the same result throughout the survey *passim*.[73] Here, again, we are able to assert that two virgates must have been to the scribes as obviously equivalent to half a hide as ten shillings with us are equivalent to half a sovereign. For here, again, the point is that these scribes had no knowledge of the varying circumstances of each locality. They had nothing to guide them but the return itself, so that the rule, in Domesday, of "four virgates to a hide" must have been of universal application.

But not only were there thus, in Domesday, four virgates to a hide; there were also in the Domesday virgate thirty Domesday acres. Mr. Eyton, though perhaps unrivalled in the study he has bestowed on the subject, believed that there were only twelve such acres, of which, therefore, forty-eight composed the Domesday hide.[74] It is, perhaps, the most important information to be derived from the

---

[72] Compare also the Exon. Domesday, where "Stoches," which is entered "pro. ii. virgatis et dim." appears in D.B. as dim. hida et dim. virga."

[73] See below, and *ante*, p. 17, note.   [74] *Key to Domesday*, p. 14.

I.C.C. that *a hundred and twenty* Domesday acres composed the domesday hide.[75]

We have the following direct statements :—

I.C.C.	D.B.
fo. 105 (*b*) 2 : "una virg' et x. acre in dominio."	i. 202 (*b*) 1 : "In dominio dimidia hida xx. acras minus."
fo. iii. (*a*) 1 : "tenet Rogerus comes xx. acras."	i. 193 (*b*) 1 : "tenet comes ii. partes unius virg'."

If 20 acres were identical with two-thirds of a virgate, there must, in a whole virgate, have been thirty acres; and if a virgate, *plus* 10 acres, was equivalent to half a hide *minus* 20 acres, we have again a virgate of thirty, and a hide of 120 acres. But the conclusion I uphold will be found to rest on no isolated facts. It is based on a careful analysis of the *Inquisitio* throughout. Here are some striking examples :—

fo. 92 (*b*) i. "Belesham pro x. hidis se defendit."

	H.	V.	A.
Abbot of Ely . .	9	0	0
Hardwin . . .			80
"Almar" . . .			40
	10	0	0

fo. 99 (*b*) 1 : "tenet hardeuuinus de scal' vi. hidas et i. virgam et vii. acras de rege."

	H.	V.	A.	
Ely Abbey. .	$2\frac{1}{2}$	0	9	
7 Sokemen .	$1\frac{1}{2}$	0	6	
3 Sokemen .	$\frac{1}{2}$	0	0	
"Alsi" . .	$\frac{1}{2}$	0	0	T. R. E.
2 Sokemen .		1	7	
5 Sokemen .		$3\frac{1}{2}$	0	
	6	1	7	

[75] It is to this evidence that I made allusion in *Domesday Studies* (p. 225). Similar evidence as to the Domesday carucate is found in the *Inq. El.* (Ed. Hamilton, pp. 156, 178) where "lx. acre" equate "dim. c[arucata]."

fo. 79 (*a*) **2** : "Suafham pro x. hidis se defendit."

	H.	V.	A.
Hugh de Bolebec . .	7½	0	10
Geoffrey . . .	1	3	0
Aubrey de Ver . .	½	0	20
	10	0	0

fo. 90 (*a*) "choeie et stoua pro x. hidis se defenderunt."

	H.	V.	A.
Odo . . .	1	0	0
Reginald . .	½	0	20 [76]
Picot (1) . .	3	3	0
Picot (2) . .	4½	0	10
	10	0	0

fo. 96 (*a*) **2** : "Pampeswrda pro v. hidis et xxii. acris se defenda

	H.	V.	A.
Abbot of Ely . .	2	3½	0
Two Knights . .	1	0	22
Ralf "de scannis" .		3	0
Hardwin . .			10
Picot . . .			5
Hardwin . .		½ [77]	0
A priest . .		½	0
	5	0	22

[76] D.B. erroneously reads "xxx." (30) by the insertion of an "x" too many. The I.C.C. correctly reads "xx." (20), its accuracy here being proved by the above arithmetic. Thus the I.C.C. corrects a reading which (1) would, but for it, appear fatal to the belief that 30 acres = a virgate ; (2) would upset the above arithmetic. This ought to be clearly grasped, because it well illustrates the element of clerical error, and shows how apparent discrepancies in our rule may be due to a faulty text alone.

[77] Here, as in the preceding instance, Domesday is in error, reading "one virgate" (" 1 virgata") where the I.C.C. correctly gives us half a virgate ("dimidiam virgam"). The remarks in the preceding note apply equally here.

fo. 107 (*a*) 2 : " Barentona pro x. hidis se defendit."

	H.	V.	A.
Robert Gernon	7	$1\frac{1}{2}$[78]	0
Chatteris Abbey	2	0	0
Ralf			20
Walter fitz Aubrey			40
Picot		$\frac{1}{2}$	0
	10	0	0

fo. 108 (*a*) 2 : " Oreuuella pro. iiii. hidis se defendit."

	H.	V.	A.
Earl Roger	1	$1\frac{1}{3}$	0
Durand		$3\frac{1}{3}$	0
" Sigar "		$1\frac{1}{3}$	0
Picot		$3\frac{1}{4}$	5
Walter fitz Aubrey		1	0
Robert		1	0
Ralf " de bans "		$\frac{1}{3}$	0[79]
Chatteris Abbey		$\frac{1}{4}$	0[79]
	4	0	0

This last example is, perhaps, the most remarkable of all in the accuracy with which the virgates and their fractions, by the help of the five acres, combine to give us the required total.

But, it may be asked, how far does the *Inquisitio*, as a whole, confirm this conclusion ? In order to reply to this enquiry, I have analysed every one of the Manors it contains. The result of that analysis has been that of the ninety-four townships which the fragment includes (not counting " Matingeleia," of which the account is imperfect) there are only fifteen cases in which my calculation

[78] Here, again, Domesday is in error, reading *two* and a half virgates, where the I.C.C. has *one* and a half.

[79] These two entries are by a blunder in the I.C.C. (see above, p. 12) erroneously rolled into one (of ⅛ virgate). In this case it is Domesday Book which corrects the I.C.C., and preserves for us the right version.

does not hold good, that is to say, in which the constituents as given do not equal the total assessment when we add them up on the above hypothesis of thirty acres to the virgate, and four virgates to the hide. This number, however, would be considerably larger if we had to work only from D.B., or only from the I.C.C. But as each of these, in several cases, corrects the errors of the other, the total of apparent exceptions is thus reduced. Hence I contend that if we could only get a really perfect return, the remaining apparent exceptions would largely disappear.

In some of these exceptions the discrepancy is trifling. Thus, at Triplow, we have two acres in excess of the 8 hide assessment—a discrepancy of $\frac{1}{480}$. At "Burch and Weslai" we have a deficit of 5 acres on 10 hides, that is $\frac{1}{240}$. At "Scelforda" the figures of D.B. gives us an excess of 7 acres on the 20 hide assessment, that is $\frac{7}{2400}$. The I.C.C. figures make the excess to be 12 acres.

Another class of exceptions is accounted for by the tendency of both texts, as we have seen, to enter a virgate too much or too little, and to confuse virgates with their fractions. Thus at "Litlingetona" our figures give us a virgate in excess of the assessment, while at "Bercheham"[80] and again at "Witlesforde" we have a virgate short of the amount. At "Herlestona" we have, similarly, half a virgate too much, and "Kingestona" half a virgate (15 acres) too little. Lastly, at "Wicheham," the aggregate of the figures is a quarter of a virgate short of the amount.

A third class of these exceptions is due to the frequent omission in the I.C.C. of estates belonging to the king. Thus at Wilbraham it records an assessment of ten hides represented only by two estates of four hides apiece. But on turning to Domesday (i. 189*b*) we read:—"Wilborham dominica villa regis est. Ibi ii. hidæ." The missing factor is thus supplied, and the apparent discrepancy disposed of.

---

[80] The I.C.C., which is very corrupt in its account of this township, gives us a deficiency of 1 hide o½ virgates.

So, too, at "Haslingefelda" (Haslingfield), where the I.C.C. accounts only for twelve hides and three virgates out of an assessment of twenty hides. Domesday here, again, supplies the missing factor in a royal Manor of seven hides and a virgate. We thus obtain, instead of an exception, a fresh illustration of our rule.

Haslingfield.

	H.	V.	A.
Rex	7	1	
Picot	4	3	
Count Alan	1	$\frac{1}{2}$	
The same	$\frac{1}{2}$		
Geoffrey de Mandeville . .	5		
Guy de Remberdcurt . .	1	1	3
Count Alan			12
	20	0	0

Domesday omits altogether, so far as I can find, the holding of Guy, an omission which would upset the whole calculation. But, in the case of Isleham, the apparent exception is due to the I.C.C., not to Domesday Book. Its assessment, in that document, is given as four hides. But the aggregate of its Manors, as there recorded, give us an assessment of three hides *plus* eighty acres. Here any one who was rash enough to argue from a single instance (as Mr. Eyton and Mr. Pell were too apt to do) might jump at the conclusion that the hide must here have been of eighty acres. Yet Domesday enables us to collect all the constituents of the "Vill," among them the king's estate, here again omitted. The real figures, therefore, were these :—

	H.	V.	A.	D.B.
The King	6	0	40	i. 189 *b*.
Bishop of Rochester . .	$1\frac{1}{2}$	0	20	i. 190 *b*.
Hugh de Port . . .	$1\frac{1}{2}$	0	20	i. 199 *a*.
Earl Alan . . .			40	i. 195 *b*.
	10	0	0	

Isleham, then, was a normal ten-hide township, and confirms, instead of rebutting, the rule that the geldable hide contained 120 acres.[81]

The remaining exceptions are "Somm[er]tona" partly explained by the omission of *terra Regis*, "Bathburgeham" (Babraham) with 21 acres short on an assessment of seven hides, and Carlton, which fitly closes the list of these exceptions. For here, on an assessment of ten hides, we have, according to the I.C.C., 27 acres short, but, according to D.B., $53\frac{1}{2}$ ($27+20+6\frac{1}{2}$). A demonstrable blunder in Domesday Book and a discrepancy between it and the I.C.C. are responsible, together, for the difference.[82] Thus we see how wide a margin should be allowed, in these calculations, for textual error.

It is necessary to remember that there were three processes, in each one of which error might arise :—

I. In the actual survey and its returns, "by reason of the insignificance of some estates, or by reason of forgetfulness, or inaccuracy, or confusion, or doubt on the part of local jurors and witnesses, or of the clerks who indited their statements."[83]

II. In the collection and transmission of the returns, by the loss of "a leaflet or rotulet of the commissioners' work."[84]

III. In the transcription of the returns into D.B., or into the I.C.C., *plus*, in the case of the former, the rearrangement and abridgment of the materials.

[81] The apparent exception was caused by the *Inq. Com. Cant.* reading "pro iiii. hidis," and omitting the words "xl. acras minus," the true assessment of the Manor, when the king's estate was excluded, being "three hides *less forty acres.*"

[82] The *blunder* consists in treating $6\frac{1}{2}$ (geld) acres as part of the Countess Judith's estate, whereas they had been reckoned separately ; the *discrepancy* is due to D.B. reading "ii. acras," where the I.C.C. has 'xxii. acras."

[83] Eyton's *Notes on Domesday*, p. 12.

[84] *Ibid.*, p. 13.

We may now quit this part of our subject, claiming to
have settled, by the aid of the I.C.C., a problem which has
puzzled generations of antiquaries, namely : "What was the
Domesday hide?"[85]   We have shown that it denoted a
measure of assessment composed of four (geld) virgates or
a hundred and twenty (geld) acres.   What relation, if any,
it bore to *area* and to *value* is a question wholly distinct, on
which the next portion of this essay may throw quite a new
light.

VI. THE FIVE-HIDE UNIT.

It is one of the distinctive and valuable features of tne
Inq. Com. Cant. that it gives us the total assessment for each
Vill of which it treats before recording the several Manors
of which that Vill is composed, the aggregate assesments of
which Manors make up the total assessment for the Vill.
In this feature we have something which Domesday does
not contain, and which (independently of its checking
value),[86] gives us at once those Vill assessments which we
could only extract from the Domesday entries by great
labour and with much uncertainty.   Let us see then if these
Vill assessments lead us to any new conclusions on the
whole assessment system.

The first point that we notice is this.   The *five-hide unit*
is brought into startling prominence.   No careful student,
one would suppose, of Domesday, can have failed to be
struck by the singular number of Manors in the hidated
portion of the realm, which are assessed in terms of the five-
hide unit, that is to say, which are entered as of five hides

---

[85] Dr. Stubbs' remarks "on the vexed question of the extent of the
hide" will be found in a note to his *Const. Hist.*, vol. i. (1874), p. 74.
Mr. Eyton (*Key to Domesday*, p. 14) asserted that the *Domesda* hide
contained 48 geld-acres.   Prof. Earle in his *Land Charters and Saxonic
Documents* (1888) reviews the question of the hide, but leaves it undetermined (pp. lii.--liii., 457--461).

[86] See above, p. 17.

or some multiple of five hides.   This is specially the case with towns, and some years ago, in one of my earliest essays, I called attention to the fact, and explained its bearing in connexion with the unit of military service.[87]   Yet no one, it would seem, has been struck by the fact, or has seen that there must be some significance in this singular preponderance of five-hide Manors.   Now what the *Inquisitio* here does for us is to show us that this preponderance is infinitely greater than we should gather from the pages of Domesday, and that when the scattered manors are pieced together in their Vills, the agregate of their assessments generally amounts either to five hides or to a multiple of the five-hide unit.   Thus the rural townships are brought into line with towns, and we learn that in both the assessment was based on the *five-hide unit.*

Let us now take a typical hundred and test this theory in practice :—

HUNDRED OF STAINES.

(*In. Com. Cant.*, pp. 11-17.)

Vill.			Hides.	Ploughlands.	Valets. (T. R. E.)		
Bottisham	.	.	10	20	£16	0	0
Swaffham (1)	.	.	10	16	11	10	0
Swaffham (2)	.	.	10	$13\frac{1}{4}$	12	10	0
Wilbraham	.	.	10	17	20	0	0
Stow-cum-Quy	.	.	10	11	14	10	0
			50	$77\frac{1}{4}$	£74	10	0

Here we have five Vills varying in area from 11 ploughlands to 20, and in value T.R.E., from £11 10s. to £20, all assessed alike at ten hides each.   What is the meaning of it?   Simply that ASSESSMENT BORE NO RATIO TO AREA OR TO VALUE in a Vill, and still less in a Manor.

Assessment was not objective, but subjective; it was not

---

[87] *Antiquary*, June, 1882, p. 242.   See also *Domesday Studies*, vol. i., p. 119.

fixed relatively to area or to value, but to the five-hide unit. The aim of the assessors was clearly to arrange the assessment in sums of five hides, ten hides, etc.

Take now the next hundred in the *Inq. Com. Cant.*:—

HUNDRED OF RADFIELD.

(Inq. Com. Cant., pp. 17-25).

	Hides.	Ploughlands.	Valets. (T.R.E.)		
Dullingham . . .	10	16	£19	5	0
Stetchworth . . .	10	$13\frac{1}{4}$	12	15	0
Borough Green and Westley	10	17	17	1	4
Carlton	10	$19\frac{1}{2}$	18	10	0
Weston	10	$19\frac{1}{4}$	13	15	0
Wratting	10	$15\frac{3}{4}$	8	8	0
Balsham	10	20	12	13	4
	70	$120\frac{3}{4}$	£102	7	8

Here again we have seven Vills varying in area from $13\frac{1}{4}$ ploughlands to 20, and in value from £8 8s. to £19 5s., all uniformly assessed at ten hides each. The thing speaks for itself. Had the hidation in these two hundreds been dependent on area or value, the assessments would have varied infinitely. As it is, there is for each Vill but one and the same assessment.

Note further that the I.C.C. enables us to localise holdings the locality of which is unnamed in Domesday : also, that it shows us how certain Vills were combined for the purpose of assessment. Thus Borough Green and Westley are treated in Domesday as distinct, but here we find that they were assessed together as a ten-hide block. By this means we are enabled to see how the five-hide system could be traced further still if we had in other districts the same means of learning how two or three Vills were thus grouped together.

We may now take a step in advance, and pass to the hundred of Whittlesford.

HUNDRED OF WHITTLESFORD.
(*Inq. Com. Cant.*, pp. 38-43.)

	Hides.	Ploughlands.			Valets. £ s. d.		
Whittlesford .	12 ⎫	11 ⎫		15 2 0 ⎫			
Sawston . .	8 ⎭ 20	9 ⎭ 20		19 0 0 ⎭ 34 2 0			
Hinxton . .	20	16		20 10 0			
Icklington .	20	24½		24 5 0			
Duxford . .	20	20¼		27 5 0			
	80	80¾		£106 2 0			

Here we are left to discover for ourselves that Whittlesford and Sawston were grouped together to form a twenty-hide block. And on turning from the above figures to the map we find the discovery verified, these two Vills jointly occupying the northern portion of the hundred. Thus, this hundred, instead of being divided like its two predecessors into ten-hide blocks, was assessed in four blocks of twenty hides each, each of them representing one of those quarters so dear to the Anglo-Saxon mind (*virgata*, etc.), and lying respectively in the north, south, east and west of the district. Proceeding on the lines of this discovery, we come to the Hundred of Wetherley, which carries us a step further.

HUNDRED OF WETHERLEY.
(*Inq. Com. Cant.*, pp. 68-83.)

	Hides.	Ploughlands.
Comberton . . .	6 ⎫	7 ⎫
Barton . . .	7 ⎬ 20	12 ⎬ 32
Grantchester . .	7 ⎭	13 ⎭
Haslingfield . .	20	22 [88]
Harlton . . .	5 ⎫	7 ⎫
Barrington . .	10 ⎬ 20	15⅜ ⎬ 27⅞
Shepreth . .	5 ⎭	5½ ⎭
Ordwell . . .	4 ⎫	5 5/16 ⎫
Wratworth . . .	4 ⎪	5⅝ ⎪
Whitwell . . .	4 ⎬ 20	5 ⎬ 29 5/16
Wimpole . . .	4 ⎪	5 ⎪
Arrington . . .	4 ⎭	8½ ⎭
	80	111 1/16

[88] The I.C.C. *omits* the king's Manor (7¼ hides, 8 ploughlands).

It is important to observe that, though the grouping is my own, the *order* of the Vills is exactly that which is given in the *Inq. Com. Cant.*, and by that order the grouping is confirmed. Note also how, without such grouping, we should have but a chaos of Vills, whereas, by its aid, from this chaos is evolved perfect symmetry. Lastly, glance at the four "quarters" and see how variously they are subdivided.

Advancing still on the same lines, we approach the very remarkable case of the adjoining Hundred of Long Stow.

HUNDRED OF LONGSTOW.

(*Inq. Com. Cant.*, pp. 83-89.)

	Hides.		Ploughlands.	
Eversden . . .	$8\frac{1}{3}$ ⎫		$13\frac{3}{8}$ ⎫	
Kingston . . .	$8\frac{1}{3}$ ⎬	25	$8\frac{9}{16}$ ⎬	$38\frac{9}{16}$
Toft and Hardwick .	$8\frac{1}{3}$ ⎭		$16\frac{1}{8}$ ⎭	
Gransden . .	5 ⎫		9 ⎫	
Bourne . . .	20 ⎬	25	$[23\frac{1}{2}]$ ⎬	$32\frac{1}{2}$
Gamlingay . .	20 ⎫			
Hatley . . .	$4\frac{1}{4}$ ⎫ 5 ⎬	25		
[Unnamed] . .	$\frac{3}{4}$ ⎭			
Croxton . . .	7 ⎫ 10			
Eltisley . . .	3 ⎭			
Caxton . . .	10 ⎬	25		
Caldecot . . .	$1\frac{3}{4}$ ⎫ 5			
Long Stow . .	$3\frac{1}{4}$ ⎭			

100

Now it is necessary to explain at the outset that, the *Inq. Com. Cant.* being here imperfect, it only gives us the first two of the above "quarters," its evidence ending with Bourne. But, by good fortune, it is possible to reconstruct from Domesday alone the remaining half of the Hundred, and thus to obtain the most valuable example of the system we are engaged in tracing that we have yet met with. The grouping I have adopted is based on the figures, but in some cases it is obvious from the map: Eltisley and Croxton, for instance, which form a ten-hide block, occupy a projecting portion of the county all to themselves, while Caxton adjoins them.

Several points are here noticeable. Observe, in the first place, how the twenty-five hide "quarter" which heads the list is divided into three *equal* blocks of 8⅓ hides each, just as we found in Wetherley Hundred that one of the twenty-hide "quarters" was divided into five *equal* blocks of four hides each. In these cases the same principle of simple equal division was applied to the quarter hundred as we saw applied to the whole hundred in the first two cases we studied—the Hundreds of Staines and of Radfield. Notice next how the two Vills of Toft and Hardwick, which are separately surveyed in Domesday under their respective names, are found from the *Inq. Com. Cant.* to have combined (under the name of "Toft") in a block of 8⅓ hides. Lastly, it should not be overlooked that the ¾ hide not localised in Domesday fits in exactly with Hatley to complete its five hides.

The chase now becomes exciting: it can no longer be doubted that we are well on the track of a vast system of artificial hidation, of which the very existence has been hitherto unsuspected. Let us see what further light can be thrown by research on its nature.

On looking back at the evidence I have collected, one is struck, surely, by the thought that the system of assessment seems to work, not as is supposed, *up from*, but *down to* the Manor. Can it be possible that what was really assessed was not the Manor, nor even the Vill, but the Hundred as a whole? This view is so revolutionary, so subversive of all that has ever been written on the subject, that it cannot be answered off-hand. We will therefore begin by examining the case of the Hundred of Erningford, which introduces us to a further phenomenon, the *reduction* of assessment.

B. H.

E

Domesday Book

Hundred of Erningford.

(Inq. Com. Cant., pp. 51 68.)

	Hides.		
	T.R.E.	T.R.W.	Ploughlands.
Morden (1) . . .	10 .	. 8 .	. 20
Tadlow . . .	. 5 .	. 4 .	. $10\frac{1}{2}$
Morden (2) . .	. 5 .	. 4 .	. $10\frac{3}{4}$
Clopton . . .	. 5 .	. 4 .	. 7
Hatley . . .	. 5 .	. 4 .	. 7
Croydon . . .	. 10 .	. 8 .	. $11\frac{1}{2}$
Wendy . . .	. 5 .	. 4 .	. $6\frac{3}{4}$
Shingay . . .	. 5 .	. 4 .	. 6
Litlington . .	. 5 .	. 4 .	. 11
Abington . .	. 5 .	. 4 .	. $3\frac{3}{4}$
Bassingburne . .	. 10 .	. 8 .	. 22
Whaddon . .	. 10 .	. 8 .	. $14\frac{3}{4}$
Meldreth . .	. 10 .	. 8 .	. $20\frac{1}{2}$
Melbourne . .	. 10 .	. 8 .	. $19\frac{1}{2}$
	100	80	171

Here we have, as in the last instance, a Hundred of exactly a hundred hides (assessment). But we are confronted with a new problem, that of reduction. Before we form any conclusions, it is important to explain that this problem can only be studied by the aid of the *Inq. Com. Cant.*, for the evidence both of Domesday and of the *Inq. El.* is distinctly misleading. Reduction of assessment is only recorded in these two documents when the Manor is identical with the Vill. In cases where the Vill contains two or more Manors, the Vill is not entered as a whole, and consequently the reduction on the assessment of that Vill as a whole is not entered at all.

After this explanation I pass to the case of the above Hundred, in which the evidence on the reduction is fortunately perfect. The first point to be noticed is that in four out of the five Hundreds that we have as yet examined, there is not a single instance of reduction, whereas here, on the contrary, the assessment is reduced in every Vill throughout the Hundred. That is to say, the reduction is *conterminous with the Hundred.* Cross its border into the Hundred of Wetherley, or of Triplow, and in neither district will you find a trace of reduction. Observe next that the reduction is *uniform* throughout the whole, being twenty per cent. in every instance. Now what is the inevitable conclusion from the *data* thus afforded? Obviously that the reduction was made on the assessment of the Hundred *as a whole*, and that this reduction was distributed among its several Vills *pro rata*.[89] Further research confirms the conclusion that these reductions were systematically made on *Hundreds*, not on Vills. There is a well-defined belt, or rather crescent, of Hundreds, in all of which the assessment is reduced. They follow one another on the map in this order: Erningford, Long Stow, Papworth, North Stow, Staplehow, and Cheveley. Within this crescent there lies a compact block of Hundreds, in no one of which has a single assessment been reduced. They are Triplow, Wetherley (? Cambridge[90]), Flendish, Staines, Radfield, Chilford, and Whittlesford. Beyond the crescent there lie " the two Hundreds of Ely," in which, so far as our evidence goes, there would seem to have been similarly no reduction. As the two horns of the crescent, so to speak, are the Hundreds of Erningford and Cheveley, we will now glance at the latter, and compare the evidence of the two.

---

[89] I do not here discuss the cause of the reduction. Indeed, this would be hard to discover; for the original assessment was distinctly low, whether we compare it with the aggregate of ploughlands or of valuation. It is true that the total of *valets* which had been £235 0s. 4d. T.R.E., and was £203 8s. 4d. at the time of the survey, had fallen so low as £161 18s. 4d., when the grantees received their lands, but, even at the lowest figure, the assessment was still moderate.

[90] " Burgum de Grentebrige pro uno Hundredo se defendebat."—*D.B.*, i. 189.

HUNDRED OF CHEVELEY.

(*Inq. Com. Cant.*, pp. 9-11.)

	T.R.E.				T.R.W.				Ploughlands.	
Silverley	$6\frac{1}{2}$⎱10	.	.	.	4⎱6	.	.	.	8⎱12	
Ashley	$3\frac{1}{2}$⎰	.	.	.	2⎰	.	.	.	4⎰	
Saxon Street	5	.	.	.	3	.	.	.	7[93]	
Ditton.	. 5	.	.	.	3 [92] (or 4)	.	10			
Ditton	. 10	.	.	.	1	.	16			
Kirtling	. 10	.	.	.	6	.	. 21			
Cheveley.	. 10 [91]									

50

As a preliminary point, attention may be called to the fact that the grouping of Ashley and Silverley, although they are surveyed separately in the *Inq. Com. Cant.*, is justified by their forming, as "Ashley-cum-Silverley" a single parish. So too, Saxon Street may be safely combined with Ditton, in which it is actually situate. We thus have a Hundred of fifty hides divided into five blocks of ten hides each, and thus presenting a precise parallel to the Hundred of Staines, the first that we examined.

And now for the reductions. As the Vill of Cheveley, unluckily, is nowhere surveyed as a whole, we have in its case no evidence. But of the five remaining Vills above (counting Ashley-cum-Silverley as one), four we see had had their assessments reduced on a *uniform* scale, just as in the Hundred of Longstow. Now this is a singular circumstance, and it leads me to this conclusion. I believe that, precisely as in the latter case, the assessment of the Hundred *as a whole* was reduced by twenty hides. This was equivalent to forty per cent., which was accordingly knocked off from the assessment of each of its constituent Vills. One of the Dittons is clearly an exception, having

---

[91] This figure is arrived at by adding to the "hida et dimidia et xx. acræ" of Domesday, and the *Inq. Com. Cant.* the "viii. hidæ et xl. acræ," which the latter omits, but which Domesday records. The sum is exactly ten hides.   [92] Domesday reads "iii.," and *Inq Com. Cant.* "iiii."   [93] I.C.C. reads "x."

nine hides, not four, thus knocked off. I would suggest, as the reason for this exception, that Ditton having now become a "dominica villa regis" (*Inq. Com. Cant.*, p. 10), was specially favoured by having a five-hide unit further knocked off its assessment, just as in the case of Chippenham (*ibid.*, p. 2).[94]

It has been my object in the above argument to recall attention to the corporate character, the *solidarité* of the Hundred. This character, of which the traces are preserved in its collective responsibility, even now, for damages caused by riot, strongly favours the view which I am here bringing forward, that it was the Hundred itself which was assessed for geld, and which was held responsible for its payment. Although this view is absolutely novel, and indeed destructive of the accepted belief, it is in complete harmony with the general principle enunciated by Dr. Stubbs, and is a further proof of the confirmation which his views often obtain from research and discovery. Treating of "the Hundred as an area for rating," he writes thus:—

There can be no doubt that the organisation of the Hundred had a fiscal importance, not merely as furnishing the profits of fines and the produce of demesne or folkland, but as forming a rateable division of the county. [95]

Now there are several circumstances which undoubtedly point to my own conclusion. We know from the *Inq. Com. Cant.* that the Domesday Commissioners held their inquiry in the Court of each Hundred, and had for jurors the men of that Hundred. Now if the Hundred, as I suggest, was assessed for geld as a whole, its representatives would be clearly the parties most interested in seeing that each Vill or Manor was debited with its correct share of the general liability. Again we know from the *Inquisitio Gheldi* that the geld was collected and paid through the machinery of

---

[94] " Per concessionem ejusdem regis" (Domesday). Compare also the five hides knocked off the assessment of Alveston by Henry I., and another ten hides off that of Hampton (Domesday Studies, pp. 99, 103).

[95] *Const. Hist.*, i. 105.

the Hundred; and its collectors, in Devonshire, are "Hun-
dremanni." The Hundred, in fact, was the unit for the
purpose.[96] Further, we have testimony to the same effect
in the survey of East Anglia. But as that survey stands
by itself, it must have separate treatment.[97]

I need not further discuss the collective liability of the
Hundred, having already shown in my "Danegeld" paper
how many allusions to it are to be found in Domesday in
the case of urban "Hundreds."[98] It is only necessary here
to add, as a corollary of this conclusion, that the assessment of a single Manor could not be reduced by the Crown
without the amount of that reduction falling upon the rest
of the Hundred. Either, therefore, that amount must have
been allowed ("computatum") to the local collector as
were *terræ datæ* to the sheriff, or (which came to the same
thing) the assessment on the Hundred must have been
reduced *pro tanto*.

I now proceed to apply my theory that the Hundreds
themselves were first assessed, and that such assessments
were multiples of the five-hide unit.

We are enabled from the *Inq. Com. Cant.* to determine the
assessments of eleven Hundreds.[99] Nine out of these eleven
Hundreds prove to have been assessed as follows :—

Erningford	100	hides.
Long Stow	100	,,
Triplow	90	,,
Staplehow	90 [100]	,,
Whittlesford	80	,,
Wetherley	80	,,
Radfield	70	,,
Cheveley	50	,,
Staines	50	,,

This list speaks for itself, but it may be as well to point

---

[97] See also *Domesday Studies*, i. 117.　　See below, p. 98.

[98] *Domesday Studies*, i. 122-130.

[99] The fragments of the Hundred of Papworth and North Stow, which
it contains, are too small to enable us to speak with certainty.

[100] Correcting the *Inq. Com. Cant.* by adding from Domesday the royal
Manors in Isleham and Fordham.

out how convenient for the Treasury was this system. At the normal Danegeld rate of two shillings on the hide, an assessment of fifty hides would represent £5, one hundred hides £10, and so on.

Can we discover in other counties traces of this same system? Let us first take the adjacent county of Bedfordshire.

I am anxious to explain that for the means of utilising the Bedfordshire evidence I am entirely indebted to the *Digest of the Domesday of Bedfordshire* by the late Rev. William Airy (edited by his son, the Rev. B. R. Airy[101]). It was, most happily, pointed out to the author by the Rev. Joseph Hunter "that what we want is not translations but analyses of the surveys of the several counties" (p. viii.). To this most true remark we owe it that Mr. Airy resolved to give us a "digest" instead of that usual "extension and translation," which is perfectly useless to the Domesday student. It is easy to take from the record itself such an instance as these Beauchamp Manors entered in succession (213): Willington 10 hides, Stotford 15; "Houstone" 5, Hawnes 5, "Salchou" 5, Aspley 10, Salford 5; but it is only Mr. Airy's work that enables us to reconstruct the townships, and to show how fractions—apparently meaningless—fit in, exactly as in Cambridgeshire, with one another. His work is all the more valuable from the fact that he had no theory to prove, and did not even add together the factors he had ascertained. His figures therefore are absolutely free from the suspicion that always attaches to those adduced to prove a case.

Risely.		Tempsford.		Wymington.	
H.	V.	H.	V.	H.	V.
7	0	1	$1\frac{3}{4}$	0	3
1	0	1	1	3	0
$\frac{1}{2}$	0	4	1	4	0
$\frac{1}{2}$	0	2	0	$\frac{1}{2}$	0
1	0	1	$0\frac{1}{4}$	0	3
				1	0
10	0	10	0	10	0

101 Bedford, 1881.

Cople.			Eversholt.			Clophill.	
H.	V.		H.	V.		H.	V.
4	0		2	0		5	0
5	3		$7\frac{1}{2}$	0		4	0
0	1		$0\frac{1}{2}$	0		1	0
10	0		10	0		10	0

Northill.			Portsgrove.			Chicksand.	
H.	V.		H.	V.		H.	V.
$1\frac{1}{2}$	0		1	0		$\frac{1}{2}$	0
$1\frac{1}{2}$	0		$7\frac{1}{2}$	0		$3\frac{1}{2}$	0
$\frac{1}{2}$	0		1	0		2	0
$6\frac{1}{2}$	0		$\frac{1}{2}$	0		3	0
						1	0
10	0		10	0		10	0

Eyeworth.			Holwell.			Odell.	
H.	V.		H.	V.		H.	V.
9	0		$3\frac{1}{2}$	0		$4\frac{1}{2}$	$0\frac{1}{3}$
1	0		$6\frac{1}{2}$	0		5	$1\frac{2}{3}$
10	0		10	0		10	0

Pavenham.			Houghton Conquest.			Dean.	
H.	V.		H.	V.		H.	V.
$2\frac{1}{2}$	0		5	0		4	0
5	0		$\frac{1}{2}$	0		2	$\frac{1}{2}$
$2\frac{1}{2}$	0		$4\frac{1}{2}$	0		2	$7\frac{1}{4}$
						0	$\frac{1}{2}$
10	0		10	0		10	$0\frac{1}{4}$

Of these fifteen ten-hide townships, the last is selected as
an instance of those slight discrepancies which creep in so
easily and which account for many apparent exceptions to
the rule. Passing to other multiples of the five-hide unit
we have:—

Oakley.			Thurleigh.			Blunham.	
H.	V.		H.	V.		H.	V.
4	0		0	1		4	1
1	0		$\frac{1}{2}$	0		0	1
			$\frac{1}{2}$	0		$\frac{1}{2}$	0
5	0		0	1		10	0
			3	0		15	0
			$\frac{1}{2}$	0			
			5	0			

Marston.			Roxton.		Dunton.		
10	{	2 less ½ virg.)	R.	V.	H.	V.	
		8 *plus* ½ virg.)	1	1	8	1 }	
			0	4	1	3 }	10
5	{	1	1	1	5	0)	
		½	7½	1	4½	0 }	10
		3	8	3	½	0)	
		½					
15	0		20	0	20	0	

I now give three illustrations of slight discrepancies:—

Streatley.		Sutton.			Eaton Socon.	
H.	V.	H.	V.		H.	V.
1	0	0	3		20	0
4	1	1	0		6	3
4⅓	0	1½	0		0	1½
0	⅔	1½	0	} 5	0	1½
0	⅔	0	3½		9	1
		0	1½		0	5½
9	3⅔	2	0		2	0½
		0	3		0	1
		½	0			
		0	1½		40	1
		1	0			
		9	0½			

In the first case there is a deficiency of $\frac{1}{120}$, and in the
second of $\frac{7}{80}$, while in the third we find an excess of $\frac{1}{180}$.
No one can doubt that these were really ten-hide, ten-hide,
and forty-hide townships. We have to allow, in the first
place, for trivial slips, and in the second for possible errors
in the baffling work of identification at the present day.
One can hardly doubt that if a student with the requisite
local knowledge set himself to reconstruct, according to
Hundreds, the Bedfordshire Domesday, he would find, as
in Cambridgeshire, that even where a township was not
assessed in terms of the five-hide unit, it was combined in
an adjacent one in such an assessment.

We will now cross the border into Huntingdonshire, and

enter the great Hundred of Hurstingston. This, which may be described as a *double* Hundred, was assessed, Domesday implies, at 200 hides. Quartering this total, on the Cambridgeshire system, we obtain 50 hides, and this quarter was the assessment allotted to the borough of Huntingdon.[102] The total assessment of the Hundred was thus accounted for :—

Huntingdon	50	hides.
St. Ives (Slepe)	20	,,
Hartford	15	,,
Spaldwick	15	,,
Stukeley	10	,,
Abbots Ripton	10	,,
Upwood	10	,,
Warboys	10	,,
Calne 6 Bluntisham $6\frac{1}{2}$ Somersham 8	$20\frac{1}{2}$ [103]	,,
Wistow [104]	9	,,
Holywell	9	,,
Houghton	7	,,
Wyton	7	,,
Broughton	4	,,
Catworth	4 [105]	,,
	$200\frac{1}{2}$	

Passing on into Northamptonshire, we come to that most curious document, which I shall discuss below (*see* p. 147),

(*see* p. 147)

[102] "Huntedun Burg defendebat se ad geldum regis pro quarta parte de Hyrstingestan hundred pro L. hidis."—*Domesday*, i. 203.

[103] Adjoining Manors held by the Abbot of Ely.

[104] I have not attempted to group these six Manors, as we have not sufficient information to warrant it. They would, however, form two groups of twenty hides each, or one of twenty-five and another of fifteen.

[105] There are five entries relating to Catworth (fos. 205*b*, 206, 206*b*, 217*b*), which, by the addition of 11 hides (1+1+3+2+3+1), would bring up its assessment to 15; but as they are all credited in Domesday to other Hundreds, and as there are *two* Catworths surveyed, I have adhered to the above figure.

and which was printed by Ellis (*Introduction to Domesday*, i. *187 et sq.*). Ellis, however, can scarcely have read his own document, for he speaks of it as a list " in which every Hundred is made to consist of *a hundred hides*." [106] This extraordinary assertion has completely misled Dr. Stubbs, who writes :—

The document given by Ellis as showing that the Hundreds of Northampton each contained a hundred hides seems to be a mere attempt of an early scribe to force them into symmetry. [107]

It is greatly to be wished that some one with the requisite local knowledge should take this list in hand and work out its details thoroughly. In capable hands it should prove a record of the highest interest. For the present I will only point out that its contents are in complete harmony with the results that I obtained on the Hundred in Cambridgeshire; for it gives us Hundreds assessed at 150 (four), 100 (nine), 90 (two), 80 (four), 60 (one), and 40 (one) hides, with a small minority of odd numbers. This list throws further light on the institution of the Hundred by its recognition of " double " and " half " Hundreds. Note also in this connexion the preference for 100-hide and 50-hide assessments, which here amount to thirteen out of the twenty instances above, and in Cambridgeshire to four out of nine. These signs of an endeavour to force such assessments into terms of a 50-hide unit will be dealt with below. [108]

In Hertfordshire, as indeed in other counties, there is great need for that local research which alone can identify and group the Domesday holdings. So far as single Vills are concerned, Bengeo affords a good illustration of the way in which scattered fractions work out in combination.

[106] *Introduction to Domesday*, i. 134. The italics are his own.
[107] *Const. Hist.*, i. 99.
[108] This point brings further into line the towns and the rural Hundreds, through the 100-hide and the 50-hide assessments of the former. (*See* my " Danegeld " Essay in *Domesday Studies*.)

	H.	V.
Count Alan	0	1
Hugh de Beauchamp	6	0
Geoffrey de Mandeville	3	1
Geoffrey de Bech	5	1
	6½	0
	1	1½
	0	5½
	0	3½
Peter de Valognes	0	0½
	25	0

If we now push on to Worcestershire, we find a striking case in the Hundred (or rather the triple Hundred [109]) of Oswaldslow. Its assessment was 300 hides; [110] and I am able to assert that of these we can account for 299, and that it contained Manors of 50, 40, 35, 25 (two), and 15 hides. [111] We have also, in this county, the case of the Hundred of Fishborough, made up to 100 hides, and remarkable for including in this total the 15 hides at which Worcester itself was assessed. The special value of this and of the Huntingdon instances lies in its placing the assessments of a borough on all fours with the assessment of a rural Manor, as a mere factor in the assessment of a rural Hundred. By thus combining town and country it shows us that the assessments of both was part of the same general system. This is a point of great importance.

This case of the Hundred of Fishborough is, however, peculiar. The entry, which was prominently quoted by Ellis (who failed to see its true significance), is this :—

[109] Edgar spoke of it as three Hundreds.

[110] "Unum hundret quod vocatur Oswaldeslaw in quo jacent ccc. hidæ."—*D. B.*, i. 172*b*.

[111] It also contained one 23-hide and two 24-hide Manors, which were once perhaps, of 25 hides. The church of Worcester also possessed, outside this Hundred, Manors (*inter alia*) of 20, 15, 10, and 5 hides. (*See* below, p. 173.)

In Fisseberge hundred habet æcclesia de Euesham lxv. hidæ. Ex his xii. hidæ sunt liberæ. In illo Hundredo jacent xx. hidæ de dodentreu. et xv. hidæ de Wircecestre perficiunt hundred." [112]

Now this entry is purely incidental, and its real meaning is this. In the true Hundred of Fishborough (adjoining Evesham on the east), Evesham Abbey held 65 hides (assessed value), of which 12 were exempted from payment of geld, a statement which can be absolutely verified from the details given. To this aggregate was added the 15 hides of Worcester (though in another part of the county), together with 20 hides of the distant *Hundred* of Dodden-tree. A total of 100 hides was that arrived at. Now the Hundred of Doddentree had itself made up to about 120 hides, [113] by the addition of 18 hides, which belonged to Hertford as to "firma." [114] A reduction, therefore, of 20 hides suggests a complicated process of levelling the local Hundreds, which may remind us how large a margin must be allowed for these arrangements.

Before leaving Worcestershire, attention should be called to the great Manor of Pershore, which Westminister Abbey held for 200 hides, and to the 100 hides connected therewith under the heading " Terra sanctæ Mariæ de Persore."

In Somerset we find some good instances, with the help of Mr. Eyton's analyses.

HUNDRED OF CREWKERNE.

Merriott (5+7) 12	} 15
Seaborough ($1\frac{1}{2}+1\frac{1}{2}$) 3	
Hinton St. George 13	} 25
In Crewkerne 12	

$$40$$

---

[112] D.B., i. 175*b*.

[113] I make the aggregate 118½ hides.

[114] " Quæ hic [Dodintret hundred] placitant et geldant et ad Hereford reddunt firmam suam." It would have been said in Cambridgeshire that their " wara " was in Doddintree Hundred.

HUNDRED OF WHITSTONE.

East Pennard ($19 + 1$)	20
Baltonsborough	5
Doulting ($14 + 3\frac{1}{4} + 2\frac{3}{4}$)	20
Batcombe ($10\frac{1}{4} + 2 + 7\frac{3}{4}$)	20
Ditcheat ($5 \times 5\frac{1}{2} \times 6\frac{1}{2} + 5\frac{1}{2} + 1 + 7$) . .	$30\frac{1}{2}$
Pilton ($6\frac{1}{2} + 3 + 5 + 5 + 2$)	$21\frac{1}{2}$
Stoke St. Michael	3
	120

There are also abundant cases of *Manors* which work out similarly such as Walton and its group ($4\frac{1}{2} + 5 + 3 + 2 + 3 + 2\frac{1}{2} = 30$), Butleigh ($7\frac{1}{2} + 8 + 2 + \frac{1}{2} + 2 = 20$). Again, in the Hundred of Frome we find eight Manors (Camerton, Englishcombe, Charterhouse Hinton, Norton St. Philip, Corston, Beckington, Cloford, and Laverton), assessed at 10 hides each, in addition to divided Manors, such as Road ($9 + 1$), and Tiverton ($7\frac{1}{2} + 2\frac{1}{2}$).[115]

We will now pass to Devon and examine the assessments of its Hundreds. Of these thirty-one are entered in the *Inquisitio Geldi*. Now, as four virgates went to the hide, such assessments as $25\frac{3}{4}$, $9\frac{1}{4}$ hides, show us that the simple doctrine of probability is in favour of only one Hundred in every twenty proving to be assessed in multiples of the five-hide unit. Yet we find that those so assessed form an absolute majority of the whole. When classified, they run thus—50 (four), 40 (one), 30 (two), 25 (four), 20 (five): total, 16 Hundreds.

It will at once be observed that these assessments are, as nearly as possible, on one half the scale of those we met with in Cambridgeshire and Northamptonshire. But this must be taken in conjunction with the fact that the Devon and Cornwall assessments are altogether peculiar. "In Devon and Cornwall, where the scope of the gheld-hide was enormous, it was necessary to introduce another quantity, intermediate between the virgate and the acre. This was the

---

[115] Eyton's *Somerset Survey*, ii. 25.

Ferndel or Ferdingdel, to wit, the fourth part of the next
superior denomination, the fourth part of the virgate." [116]
One might at first sight be tempted to suggest that the hide
was in these two counties a term of higher denomination
when we find Manor after Manor assessed at a fraction of
a hide, while in Cornwall the "acra terræ" was clearly a
peculiar measure.[117]   Yet in some Manors adjacent to Exeter
or to the neighbouring coast the assessment is much less
abnormally low, though even there moderate. There is
much scope, here also, for intelligent local research, although we may conclude, from the evidence of the Pipe
Rolls, that the hide represented the same unit here as elsewhere, as it would seem did the Devonshire Hundred, in
spite of its singularly low average assessment. Indeed, it
represented a larger, not a smaller, area than usual.   I
shall deal with this phenomenon below, and endeavour to
explain its significance. For the present it is only necessary to insist on the evidence that the Hundreds afford of
assessment on the five-hide system.

Indeed, though I definitely advance the suggestion that the
assessment was, in the first instance, laid upon the Hundred itself, and that the subsequent assessment of its Vills
and Manors was arrived at by division and subdivision,
the truth or falsehood of this theory in no way affects the
indisputable phenomenon of the five-hide unit. On the
prominence of that unit I take my stand as absolute proof
that the hide assessment was fixed *independently of area
or value*, and that, consequently, all the attempts that have
been made by ingenious men to discover and establish the
relation which that assessment bore to area, whether in
Vill or Manor, have proved not only contradictory among
themselves, but, as was inevitable, vain.

The late Mr. Eyton did much to destroy the old belief held

---

[116] Eyton's *Dorset Domesday*, p. 14.

[117] I drew attention in the *Archæological Review* (vol. 1.) to a Cornish
survey of 21 Ed. I. (*Testa de Nevill*, p. 204), in which every Cornish acre
contains a Cornish carucate.

by Kemble and other well-known writers that the Domesday hide was an areal measure and to substitute the sounder view that it was used as a term of assessment, and Mr. Chester Waters, in his *Survey of Lindsey* (1883), claimed tha the " key to the puzzle " had been thus finally discovered. Canon Taylor, on the other hand, at the Domesday Commemoration (1886), claimed that if his own most ingenious theory of the relation of the geld-carucate to area could be more generally extended, " many volumes of Domesday exposition, including, among others, Mr. Eyton's *Key to Domesday*, may be finally consigned *al limbo dei bambini*." [118] Mr. Pell's theories—the inclusion of which at enormous length in *Domesday Studies*[119] cannot be too deeply regretted—require a passing notice. According to him, the Domesday hide was virtually an areal term ; but the interests of truth and of historical research require, as to his confident calculations, very plain speaking. Although I devoted to the investigation of Mr. Pell's theories a deplorable amount of time and labour,[120] I would rather state the inevitable conclusion in the words of that sound scholar, Mr. W. H. Stevenson :—

All the fanciful calculations that Mr. Pell has based upon this assumption, including his delicious " Ready Reckoner," may be safely left to slumber in oblivion by the Domesday student who does not wish to waste his time.

The only abiding principle underlying Mr. Pell's calculations is that the figures in Domesday, or wherever found, have to produce a certain total that Mr. Pell has already fixed upon. To do this, virgates may mean hides, carucates may mean virgates, and, in short, anything may mean anything else.[121]

Although Mr. Eyton also indulged in " fanciful calculations," and committed the fatal error of combining facts and

[118] *Domesday Studies*, p. 172.

[119] " A New View of the Geldable Unit of Assessment of Domesday,' *Ibid.*, pp. 227-363, 561-619.

[120] *Archæological Review*, i. 285-295 ; iv. 130-140, 391.

[121] *Ibid.*, iv. 325.

fancies, he was at least on the right track in discarding the notion that the Domesday hide denoted a fixed area, and in treating it as a term of assessment. At the same time, the acceptance of my theory that this assessment was not determined by the real value of the Manor or Vill, but was unconnected with it, would be, of course, destructive of all his calculations.

The five-hide unit which lies at the root of my theory is found ever to the front, turn where we will. In Oxon.[122] we find entered in succession the Bishop of Lincoln's Manors 90, 60, 40, 50, 50 hides, while if we work through the southern extremity of the county (lying south of Ewelme), following the bend of the Thames, we find the assessments are as follows :—Preston Crowmarsh, 5 ; Crowmarsh Gifford, 10 ; Newnham Murren, 10 ; Mongewell, 10 ; Ipsden, 5 ; North and South Stoke, 20¼ ; Checkenden, 5 ; Goring, 20 ; Gethampton, 6½ ; Whitchurch, 10 ; Mapledurham, 10 ; Caversham, 20 ; Dunsden, 20 ; Bolney (8) and Lashbrook (12) 20 ; Harpsden, 5 ; Rotherfield, 10 ; Badgemoor, 5 ; Bix 5. So too on the western border we have in succession Churchill, 20 ; Kingham, 10 ; Foxcote (1) and Tilbury (14), 15 ; Lyneham, 10 ; Fyfield, 5 ; Tainton, 10 ; Upton, 5 ; Burford (8) and Widford (2), 10 ; Westwell, 5.[123]

Berkshire undoubtedly offers a fruitful sphere of study On the one hand, we have so large a proportion of Manors assessed at five, ten, fifteen, twenty hides, and so forth as to strike the reader at once without special research ; on the other, we find these archaic assessments reduced under the Conqueror in the most sweeping manner, and the old system thus effaced. Fortunately for us in this case its existence is recorded in the Domesday entries of the previous

---

[122] A curious hint of the grouping of Vills is afforded in Oxfordshire by Adderbury and Bloxham. Domesday first gives us an assessment of 34½ hides in the two, and then 15½ hides in Adderbury, making in all, for the two, 50 hides, the same as Banbury.

[123] This evidence is rendered available by the useful *Notes on the Oxfordshire Domesday*, published by the Clarendon Press in 1892.

assessments. What is here, as elsewhere, wanted is a thorough local analysis of the hidage, Hundred by Hundred. For no county is such an analysis more urgently needed.

In Bucks the Primate's three Manors are of 40, 5, 30 hides, while nine Manors of Walter Giffard follow one another with these assessments : 20, 10, 10, 20, $3\frac{1}{2}$, 10, 5, 5, 10; and in Gloucestershire we are met on every side by Manors of 5, 10, 15, 20 hides, and so on. In Surrey, the Primate's six Manors are assessed at 30, 20, 80, 5, 20, 14 hides. As a proof that this feature is in no way of my own creation, I will take the Wiltshire Manors selected by Mr. Pell for his tables. Seven out of the eleven selected by him are five-hide assessments, being 5, 10, 20, 40, 20, 5, 10. The marvel is that any one can have failed to observe the general occurrence of the fact.

In Middlesex the five-hide unit is peculiarly prominent. We have only to glance at the pages of Domesday to be struck by such assessments as Harrow (100 hides), Fulham (50 hides[124]), Isleworth (70 hides), Harmondsworth (30 hides), while on folios 129B-130, we have seven Manors in succession of which the assessments are 15, 35, 30, 30, $7\frac{1}{2}$, 15, 10, representing 3, 7, 6, 6, $1\frac{1}{2}$, 3, 2, multiples of the five-hide unit. But, here again, conspicuous as is this unit even in the case of Manors, its prevalence would be still more apparent if we could reconstruct the Vills. Thus, for instance, in the Hundred of Spelthorne we find these assessments :—

	Hides.				Fo.
Staines	19	.	.	.	128
" In Speletorne Hundred "	1	.	.	.	128*b*
" Hatone " . . .	$1\frac{1}{2}$	.	.	.	129
Haneworde . . .	5	.	.	.	129
" Leleham " . . .	2	.	.	.	129
" Exeforde " . . .	1	.	.	.	129
" Bedefunt " . . .	2	.	.	.	129
Felteham . . .	12	.	.	.	129
Stanwelle . . .	15	.	.	.	130

[124] 40 + 5 + 5.

	Hides				Fo.
" Bedefunde ".	10				130
" West Bedefunde ".	8				130
" Haitone "	$1\frac{5}{6}$ [125]				130
" Leleham "	8				130b
" In Hundredo de Spelethorne "	$\frac{2}{3}$ [126]				130b
" Cerdentone "	5				130b

" Exeforde " is Ashford, which " appears from a very early period till after the dissolution of the monasteries to have been an appendage of Stains."[127]   Thus we obtain an assessment of 20 hides for Staines *cum* Ashford. So too we have at once for Laleham an assessment of 10 hides, while that of East and West Bedfont was, we see, 20 hides. The most striking case, however, is that of Hatton ; for, if we add to its two named Manors the nameless estates in the above list, the four fit in like a puzzle, giving us an aggregate assessment of exactly five hides.

The hundred, therefore was assessed thus :—

	Hides
Stains with Ashford	20
Stanwell	15
West Bedfont	10
East Bedfont	10
Laleham	10
Feltham	12
Hanworth	5
Charlton	5
Hatton, etc	5

Let us now connect the territorial with the institutional unit. Dealing in my " Danegeld " essay with the evident assessment of towns in terms of the five-hide unit, I traced it to the fact that " five hides were the unit of assessment for the purpose of military service." [128]   The evidence I

---

[125] " Unam hidam et iii[es.] virgatas et iii[ciam.] partem de i. virgata."

[126] " Dimidiam hidam et iii[ciam.] partem dimidiæ hidæ."

[127] Lysons. So also Domesday : " *soco vero jacebat in Stains.*"

[128] *Domesday Studies*, i. 120. See also *supra*, p. 45, and the case of Northampton, *infra*.

have adduced in the present paper carries further its
significance ; but we must not allow its financial to obscure
its military importance.   I appealed, at that time, to the
Exeter instance :—

> Quando expeditio ibat per terram aut per mare serviebat hæc
> civitas quantum v. hidæ terræ ;

and to the service of Malmesbury :—

> Quando rex ibat in expeditione vel terra vel mari habebat de hoc
> burgo aut xx. solidos ad pascendos suos buzecarlos aut unum
> hominem ducebat secum pro honore v. hidarum.[129]

Of course this brings us to the notoriously difficult question of the thegn and his qualification.   With this I am
only concerned here so far as it illustrates the prevalence
of a five-hide unit.   Mr. Little, who holds that Maurer,
followed by Dr. Stubbs, has gone too far, and that " there
is no proof of any general law or widely prevalent custom
which conferred on the owner of five hides pure and simple
the title, duties, and rights of a thegn,"[130] sets forth his
view thus :—

> What then is the meaning of the frequent recurrence in the laws
> of possession of five hides of land as the distinctive mark of a
> particular rank ?   An explanation may be hazarded : at the end of
> the seventh century it was the normal and traditional holding of a
> royal *thegn*. . . .   It is not too much to infer from the parallelism
> of the two wergelds, that five hides formed also the regular endow-
> ment of a Saxon king's thegn.[131]

Dr. Stubbs' views will be found in his *Constitutional
History* (1874), i. 155-6, 190-92, and those of Gneist in his
Constitutional History (1886), i. 13, 90, 94.   The latter
writer follows Schmidt rather than Maurer, but sums up
his position in the words ; " Since under Ælfred and his
successors every estate of five hides is reckoned in the

---

[129] *Domesday*, i. 64*b*.
[130] *English Historical Review*, 1889, iv. 729.
[131] *Ibid.*, 728-9.

militia system as one heavy-armed man, the rank of a thane becomes the right (as such) of a possessor of five hides."

Lastly, it is an interesting and curious fact that we owe to the five-hide unit such place-names as Fivehead, Somerset; Fifehead, Dorset; Fifield, Oxon; Fifield and Fyfield, Wilts; Fyfield, Hants; and Fyfield, Essex—all of them in Domesday "Fifhide" or "Fifehide"—as well as Fyfield, Berks, which occurs in Domesday as "Fivehide." Philologists will note the corruption and its bearing on the original pronunciation.

To the probable antiquity and origin of the five-hide system I must recur, after glancing at the evidence for the northern and eastern districts of England.

VII. The Six-Carucate Unit.

The subject that I now approach is one of the highest interest. I propose to adduce for my theory convincing corroborative evidence by showing that the part which is played in the hidated district of England by the five-hide unit is played in the Danish districts by a unit of six carucates. In other words, where we look in the former for "v. hidæ," we must learn to look in the latter for "vi. carucatæ terræ."

One must dissociate at the outset this six-carucate unit from the "long hundred," or *Angelicus numerus*, with which Mr. Pell confused it. In Mr. Stevenson's instructive article on "The Long Hundred and its use in England,"[132] he has clearly explained that this reckoning only applied to a whole hundred, which if, a "long" hundred, was really 120. Any lesser number was reckoned in our usual manner. This is seen at once in the test passage at Lincoln (D.B., i. 336*a*), where, 1,150 houses are reckoned as "novies centum et lxx.," because "hic numerus Anglice computatur, id est centum pro cxx." [133] The persistence, in Lincoln-shire, of the long hundred is well shown in the *Inquisitiones post mortem* on Robert de Ros, 1311, among those printed by Mr. Vincent.[134] We there read of " c. acre terra arra-bilis per majorem centenam que valent per annum lx. s. prec' acre vj. den.," at Wyville and Hungerton (on the border of Leicestershire) ; while at Claxby and Normanby (in the north of the county) we have "cc. acras per min-orem centenam et valent c.s. prec' acre vj. d." Again, at Gedney (in the south-east), we have "cc. acre terre arra-bilis per majus centum et valent per annum xxiiij. li." prec' acre ij. s. et iiij[xx.] acre prati et valet per annum viij. li., prec' acre ij. s. Et cxiij. acre pasture per majus centum et valent per annum ix. li. xix. s. vi. d. prec' acre xviij. d." On the same property there were due " ccciiij[xx.] opera aut-umpnalia cum falcis, et valent xxxvj. s. viij. d., prec' operis j. den.," so that these also were reckoned by the long hundred.

Mr. Stevenson was not aware of this evidence, but admitted that as the Domesday passage refers to " such a Danish stronghold as Lincolnshire, it is not free from the suspicion of Danish influence." His own evidence from a 16th century rental[135] is subject to a similar criticism. For the general use, therefore, of the " long hundred " in Eng-land he is compelled to rely on the *Dialogus de Scaccario* and Howden's description of the new survey of 1198, the hide or ploughland " being described in both cases as of a hundred acres, where the " hundred " must have meant 120. But I venture to think that the use of this reckoning for the ploughland, or archaic " hide," does not establish its general

---

[133] Mr. Stevenson, perhaps, is rather too severe on Canon Taylor's "Carucate" remarks in the *New English Dictionary*. Strictly, no doubt, the Canon was mistaken, with Mr. Pell, in reckoning 120 as 144 "by the English number"; but the evidence in his paper on "the plough and the ploughland" seems to establish a practice of counting by twelve instead of ten.

[134] *Genealogist*, N. S., vi. 160-1.　　　[135] *Arch. Rev.*, iv. 322.

employment. In Domesday, certainly, it is only at Lincoln that we find it actually recognised, houses being reckoned everywhere else on the usual system.

I think, therefore, that we fairly may hold the *Anglicus numerus,* or long hundred, to have specially prevailed in the "Danish" districts, which were also assessed, we shall find, in sums of six and twelve. But what was the boundary of this Danish district? It was not the border between Mercia and Wessex, for Mercia was itself divided between the "six" and the "five" systems.[136] Of the two adjacent Mercian shires, for instance, of Leicester and Warwick (afterwards united under one sheriff), we find the latter decimal and the former duodecimal. The military service of Warwick and Leicester was arranged on the same method, yet Leicester sent *twelve* "burgesses" to the fyrd where Warwick sent *ten.* But, it may be urged, the two shires were divided by the Watling Street, the boundary (under the peace of Wedmore) of Danelaw. Was then the Danelaw the district within which the systems prevailed? No, for the Danelaw, under this treaty, included all Cambridgeshire and other hidated districts. The answer, therefore, which I propound is this : The district in which men measured by carucates, and counted by twelves and sixes, was not the district which the Danes *conquered,* but the district which the Danes *settled,* the district of "the Five Boroughs."

[136] On this point one may compare with profit "the making of the Danelaw" (858-878, by the late Mr. Green (*Conquest of England,* pp. 114-129), who had devoted to this subject much attention. He discusses the limits of Eastern Mercia, the district of the Five Boroughs, in the light of local nomenclature (*ibid.,* pp. 121-2), and includes within it, on this ground, Northamptonshire, while observing that the country about Buckingham, which formed the southern border of the "Five Boroughs," has no "byes." My own evidence is wholly distinct from that of local nomenclature, and defines more sharply the district settled and reorganized by the Danes. The hidation of Northamptonshire is peculiar, a unit of four (reminding one of the Mercian shilling) coming into prominence. Still, it was not carucated, but retained its assessment in hides.

Dependent on these "Five Boroughs" were the four shires of Leicester, Derby, Nottingham, and Lincoln. For two of the Boroughs, Lincoln and Stamford, both belonged to this last shire, which was, indeed, the stronghold of the system.[187] Between Stamford and Cambridge we have the same contrast as between Warwick and Leicester, for while Cambridge was divided into *ten* wards ("custodiæ"), Stamford was divided into *six*. Lincolnshire, as I have said, was the stronghold of the system, and it is in Lincoln itself that we find Domesday alluding *eo nomine* to the *Anglicus numerus*, the practice of counting 120 as 100.

Now in the peculiar district of which I am treating there occurs an important formula which covers Lincolnshire, Yorkshire, Derbyshire, and Notts. Domesday has nothing like it for the other parts of England. Here are the three passages in which we find it recorded :—

LINCOLNSHIRE.

Pax manu regis vel sigillo ejus data, si fuerit infracta, emendatur per xviii. hundrez. Unumquidque hundret solvit viii. libras. Duodecim hundrez emendant regi et vi. comiti. —i. 336*b*.

YORKSHIRE.

Pax data manu regis vel sigillo ejus, si fuerit infracta, regi solummodo emendatur per xii. hundrez, unumquidque hundret viii. libras.

Pax a comite data et infracta a quolibet ipsi comiti per vi. hundrez emendatur, unumquidque viii. libras,—i. 298*b*.

DERBY AND NOTTS.

In Snotingehamscyre et in Derbin scyre pax regis manu vel sigillo data, si fuerit infracta, emendatur per xviii. hundrez, unumquidque hundret viii. libras. Hujus emenadtionis habet rex ii. partes, comes terciam. Id est xii. hundred emendant regi et vi. comiti—i. 280*b*.

For comparison with these three pasages we may turn to

[137] Stamford is assigned to Lincolnshire by Domesday, but is now in Rutland. The "Rutland" of Domesday (the northern portion of the ocunty as at present constituted) was included, we shall find, in the carucated disirict by which it was surrounded on the north.

the charter of immunities confirmed to York Cathedral by
Henry I., Stephen, and Henry II.   We there read :—

Si quis enim quemlibet cujuscumque facinoris aut flagitii reum et
convictum infra atrium ecclesiæ caperet et retineret, universali judicio vi. *hundreth* emendabit ; si vero infra ecclesiam xii. *hundreth*
infra chorum xviii. . . . *In hundreth* viii. *libræ continentur.*[188]

As there were *twelve* carucates in the " Hundred," so it
paid *twelve* marcs, which, if we can trust the above explanation, themselves came to be termed a " Hundred."   Moreover, the " Hundreds " themselves were grouped in mutiples
of *six*.   So too the Yorkshire thegn who held *six* Manors or
less paid three marcs to the sheriff ; if he held more than
six, *twelve* marcs to the king (*Domesday*, i. 289*b*).

It is a special feature of the " Danish " district that each
territorial " Hundred " contained twevle " carucatæ terræ."
This point is all-important.   Just as a " Hundred " to an
Anglo-Saxon suggested one hundred " hides," so to the
Danes of this district it suggested twelve " carucates."
Nay, to the men of Lincolnshire there could be no more
question that twelve carucates made a " Hundred " than
there could be now, among ourselves that twelve pence
make a shilling.   If we turn to the Lindsey Survey,[139] a
generation later than Domesday, we obtain proof to that
effect.   We find that Survey, in three instances, adding up
all the estates of a tenant within a Wapentake, and giving
us the result in " Hundreds " and " carucates."   Here are
the actual figures :—

[138] Reg. Mag. Alb. at York, pars. ii. 1.   Quoted by Canon Raine, in
his edition of John of Hexham (who applies these *formulæ* to Hexham
itself,) p.61.

[139] *Vide infra*, p. 181, *et sq.*

Car.	Bov.		Car.	Bov.		Car.	Bov.
2	4		12	0		12	0
2	0		10	0		11	4
2	4		10	6		3	0
11	0		8	0		1	0
5	0		6	0		2	0
11	0		1	4		3	0
8	6		0	4		3	4
						1	0
						0	6
						2	0
						1	6
H. 3	6	6 [140]	H. 4	0	6 [141]	H. 3	5	4 [142]

Now we must oberve that these "Hundreds" are not
districts with "a local habitation and a name"; they are
merely sums of twelve carucates produced by compound
addition. We further find, at the head of the survey of
each Wapentake, a note that it is reckoned to contain so
many "Hundreds," with the explanation, in some instances
that in each "Hundred" were "xii. carucatæ terræ."[143]
But even here the real unit is shown to be "six carcuates,"
for several Wapentakes contain an odd "half-hundred,"
while in that of Horncastle this is actually entered as "six
carucates."

Here are the nineteen Wapentakes, with the number of
Hundreds assigned to each, and the number of "carucatæ
terræ" that such Hundreds would imply :—

[140] "Suma iii. hundr' et vi. car. et vi. bov."
[141] "Suma iiii. hundr' et x. car." (a wrong total).
[142] "Summa iii. hundr' et v. car. et iiii. bov."
[143] See also on these Hundreds Mr. Stevenson's remarks in *Eng.
Hist. Rev.*, v. 96, which have appeared since I made these researches.

WEST TRITHING.

Wapentake.	Hundreds.	Car. terr.
Manley	[ ]$\frac{1}{2}$	
Aslacoe	7$\frac{1}{2}$	90
Lawress	12	144
Corringham	5	60
Axholme	4	48
Well	7	84

NORTH TRITHING.

	Hundreds.	Car. terr.
Walshcroft	8	96
Haverstoe	7$\frac{1}{2}$	90
Bradley	3$\frac{1}{2}$[144] [and 3 bov.]	42$\frac{3}{8}$
Ludborough	3	36
Yarborough	14	168
Bolingbroke	8	96
Gartree	6	72

South Trithing.

	Hundreds.	Car. terr.
Candleshoe	10	120
Calceworth	10	120
Wraghoe	9	108
Hill	6	72
Lothesk	10	120
Horncastle	6$\frac{1}{2}$	78

All the above, it will be seen, are multiples of the six
carucate unit. That the aggregate of recorded "carucatæ
terræ" appears to differ, though slightly, from the totals
here given only shows how vain is the argument that,
because the recorded aggregates of Hundreds may often be
uneven figures, there could therefore have been no system
at work such as I contend there was. Clerical error and
special alterations have both to be allowed for.

It has never, so far as I know, been pointed out that
these Lindsay Trithings were so arranged as to contain an
approximately equal number of "Hundreds." So far as
it is possible now to reckon them, the South Trithing con-

[144] This appears to be a clerical error. The actual figures represent
"Hundreds."

tained 51½, the North Trithing 51½, and the West Trithing 49½. Fifty "Hundreds" would represent 600 *carucatæ*; and it is, to say the least, a singular coincidence that, in the archaic territorial list that has hitherto baffled investigation, the North Gyrwa, South Gyrwa, and Spalda are reckoned each at 600 hides.[145]

I shall now give some instances of Lindsey townships assessed on the basis of the six-carucate unit:—

	Car.	Bov.		Car.	Bov.
Willoughton . . .	3	5½	Thorganby	1	7
„ . . .	2	2½	„	0	5
			„	1	6
	6	0	„	0	6
			„	1	0
Faldingworth . . .	2	4			
„ . . .	1	0		6	0
„ . . .	2	4			
			Beelsby	4	4
	6	0	„	1	0
			„	0	4
Reepham	0	4			
„	0	6		6	0
„	4	6			
			Riby	1	4
	6	0	„	4	4
Thoresway	0	2		6	0
„	5	6			
			Rigsby	3	6
	6	0	„	2	2
Benniworth	2	4		6	0
„	3	4			
			South Kelsey . . .	4	4
	6	0	Thornton le Moor . .	1	4
				6	0

[145] The Northern division by threes and sixes is responsible, of course, or the six "sheaddings" of the Isle of Man. On their connexion with the "scypfylleth" of three Hundreds see Vigfusson in *Eng. Hist. Rev.* ii. 500.

These instances will illustrate the value of the Lindsey Survey in enabling us to group the fractional assessments which appear in Domesday Book. Here are some other varieties :—

	Car.	Bov.		Car.	Bov.
Dunholm	5	3	Barrow-on-Humber .	11	0
,, ...	2	5	,, .	1	0
,, ...	2	0			
,, ...	2	0		12	0
	——		South Elkington . .	4	0
	12	0	,, . .	8	0
				——	
Glentham	3	0		12	0
,, ...	0	10	Winteringham . . .	11	0
Glentham and Caenby	7	6	,, . . .	1	0
	——			——	
	12	0		12	0
Scotton	0	4	Nun Ormsby . . .	2	2
"	0	4	,, . . .	4	4
,, ...	2	0	,, . . .	2	2
,, ...	6	0		——	
	——			9	0
	9	0			
			Croxby	0	3
Irby-on-Humber . .	1	4	,, ...	0	5
,, . .	1	0	,, ...	1	0
,, . .	0	4	,, ...	1	0
	——			——	
	3	0		3	0
Somerby	2	4	Worlaby	2	2
,, ...	0	6	,, ...	0	6
	——			——	
	3	0		3	0

Lastly, to complete the parallel with the Leicestershire Hundreds *infra*, we may take this case (*cf.* p. 65, note 122):—

Claxby and Well	14
Claxby	10
	——
	24

Precisely the same system prevailed in Holland as in Lindsey, for the "Testa de Nevill" preserves for us the constituents of a Holland Wapentake, that of "Elhou":—

Pinchbeck .	. . . . .	. 12
Spalding .	. . . . .	. 12
Weston .	. . . . .	. 6
Moulton .	. . . . .	. 6
Whaplode and Holbeach	. . .	. 18
Fleet .	. . . . .	. 6
Gedney . . 8 } Lutton . . 4 }	. . . .	. 12
Sutton . . $9\frac{3}{4}$ } Tydd . . $2\frac{1}{4}$ }	. . .	. 12

84

The Lindsey survey would describe such a Wapentake as containing "7 Hundreds."

Crossing the border from Lincolnshire into Rutland (*i.e.* the Rutland of Domesday), we find the same system at work that meets us in the Lindsey Survey. We read :—

In Alfnodestou Wapent' sunt ii. Hundrez. In unoquoque [sunt] xii. carucatæ ad geldum. . . . In Martinesleie Wap' est i. hundret, in quo xii. carucatæ ad geldum.—*D.B.*, i. 293*b*.

On analysing the contents of these Wapentakes, we find this statement fully borne out, the former containing twenty-four, and the latter twelve, "carucatæ terræ." These are carefully contrasted throughout with the "terra carucæ" or areal measure.[146]

In Yorkshire, Notts and Derby, we have less direct evidence. Sawley, in Derbyshire, has indeed been alleged to be entered in Domesday as a Hundred of twelve caru-cates, but Domesday does not justify this assertion being

---

[46] The aggregate of these *areal* measures does not bear out the statement of Domesday regarding them, the former Wapentake containing eighty-four ploughlands, where Domesday allows it only forty-eight.

made.[147] I would rather trust to the notable formula, which, as I explained at the outset, is common to these counties for proof that they also were arranged in "Hundreds" of twelve carucates.

The prevalence, however, of assessment by sixes, threes, and twelves, meets us on every side, as does, in hidated districts, the assessments by fives and tens. At the outset, for instance, of the survey of Yorkshire we have the district "gelding" with the city assessed at eighty-four (12×7) carucates (which would be described in Lincolnshire as seven "Hundreds"). We have two lists of the details, which are given here.[148]

	Car. terræ.		Car. terræ.
Archbishop . . .	6	Archbishop . . .	6
Osboldeuuic . . .	6	Osboldeuuic . . .	6
Stocthun	6	Stochetun	6
Sa'bura	3	Sa'bure	3
Heuuarde	6	Heuuorde	6
Ditto	3		
Fuleford	10	Fuleforde	10
Round the City . .	3	Round the City . .	3
Cliftune	18	Cliftune	18
Roudclif	3	Roudeclif . . .	3
Ouertun	5	Ouertune	5
Sceltun	9	Scheltune	9
Mortun	3	Mortune	3
Wichistun . . .	1	Wichintun . . .	3
	"84"		"84"

These lists have a value independent of their illustration of the arrangement in threes and sixes. They show how Domesday breaks down, when it supplies a check upon its own evidence, by failing to make its details agree with its

---

[147] The entry is far more suggestive of the "Hundreds" (*vide infra*) in Leicestershire, on the border of which Sawley stood. This remark applies also to the entry (i. 291*b*) that Leake (Notts) "jacet in Pluntree Hund."

[148] See D.B., i. fos. 298, 298*b*, and fo. 379.

total; and they further show by the discrepancy between them how easily error may arise, and how rash it must be to argue from a single case.[149]

Yorkshire presents other traces, in its Hundreds, of the same system. Thus the townships in the Hundred of "Toreshou" follow one another in this order: 18, 18, 20, 6, 18, 8, 12, 12 (8 + 4), 6, 18, 8, 18, etc. (*infra* p. 88).

But my strong evidence is found in an invaluable survey of Leicestershire, unknown till now to historians,[150] which does for the carucated districts just what the *Inq. Com. Cant.* does for the hidated ones. Here we find the townships grouped in small blocks of from six to twenty-four "carucatæ terræ," as a rule with almost monotonous regularity. And these blocks are further combined in small local Hundreds, of which the very existence is unknown to historians and antiquaries,[151] and which are usually multiples, like the Lincolnshire Wapentake, of the six-carucate unit.

It will be remembered that in the case of Cambridgeshire, I selected for my first two examples a Hundred of 50 hides, composed of 5 Vills assessed at 10 hides each, and a Hundred of 70 hides, composed of 7 Vills, assessed at 10 hides each. In Leicestershire, precisely in the same manner, I shall begin with the simplest forms and select Hundreds of 36 and 48 carucates, composed of Vills uniformly assessed at 12 carucates each.

HUNDRED of SCALFORD.

Scalford	. . .	12 $(11\frac{1}{2} + \frac{1}{2})$
Goadby	. . .	12 $(6 + 6)$
Knipton	. . .	12 $(8\frac{3}{4} + 3\frac{1}{4})$
		$\overline{36}$

---

[149] As Mr. Pell did in the case of Clifton.

[150] *Vide infra*, p. 196.

[151] "There is no trace of any," writes Canon Taylor (*Domesday Studies*, i. 74).

HUNDRED OF KIBWORTH.

Kibworth (Beauchamp)	12
Kibworth (Harcourt) .	12
"Bocton" . . .	12
Carlton . . .	12 $(10 + 1\frac{1}{4} + \frac{3}{4})$
	—
	48

From these we may advance to other combinations :—

HUNDRED OF HARBY.

Harby and Plungar. .	18
Stathern . . .	18
	—
	36

HUNDRED OF TONG.

Tong	12
Kegworth . . .	15 $\left.\right\}18$
Worthington . .	3
"Dominicum" . .	12
	—
	42

HUNDRED OF LANGTON.

Langton (1)		$14\frac{1}{2}$ $(11\frac{1}{4} + 3\frac{1}{4})$
Thorp (Langton)	24	$3\frac{3}{4}$
Langton (2)		$5\frac{3}{4}$
Tur Langton		12
Shangton	24	12 $(10 + 2)$
		—
		48

With these types as clues we are in a position to assert that where the total assessment of a Hundred varies but slightly from a multiple of six, there must have been some slight error in one of the figures. Thus Hundreds of $35\frac{1}{2}$, $34\frac{13}{16}$ carucates, etc., may be safely assumed to have been Hundreds of 36 carucates; those of 41, $43\frac{7}{8}$, etc., would be of 42 carucates; those of $48\frac{7}{8}$, 50, etc., would be of 48 carucates. These slight discrepancies, precisely as in Lincolnshire, are accounted for by Vills of 6 or 12 carucates, being entered as of $5\frac{7}{8}$, $5\frac{13}{16}$, $6\frac{3}{4}$, or $11\frac{7}{8}$, 13, etc. Thus:—

B.H.
G

HUNDRED OF EASTWELL.

Vills.				Carucates.
Eastwell	.	.	.	$12 \quad (2 + 6 + 4)$
Eaton	.	.	.	$12\frac{1}{4} \quad (3\frac{1}{4} + \frac{9}{16} + 8\frac{7}{16})$
Branston	.	.	.	$12 \quad (7\frac{1}{2} + 4\frac{1}{2})$

$$36\frac{1}{4}$$

The most usual Leicestershire Hundreds are those of 36, 42, and 48 carucates, which, be it observed, would be described in the language of the Lindsey Survey as " Wapenta' es of 3, $3\frac{1}{2}$, and 4 "Hundreds" respectively. The name may be different : the thing is the same.[152]

It will have been seen by this Survey that the "Vills," single or grouped, were assessed precisely as in Cambridge-shire, save that there the assessment was reckoned in fives and tens, while here it was in sixes and twelves.

VIII. THE LEICESTERSHIRE "HIDA."

The case of Leicestershire introduces us to a very curious point. Leicestershire is not one of those counties to which the singular formula that I discussed above refers. This suggests that it was not arranged in "Hundreds" of twelve carucates. The above Survey confirms this, for it shows us Hundreds resembling in character those found in the hidated districts. But although the twelve-carucate unit of the "Hundred" is not found in Leicestershire, we do find in it a group-unit, and that unit is the *hida*. Just as we have seen the Hundred used in two wholly different senses, so also was the "hida." The quite peculiar way in which "hida" occurs in Leicestershire (which was not a hidated ♣ but carucated district) completely baffled Mr. Eyton, and was misunderstood by Mr. Pell.[158] Both writers failed to observe not only that the use of "hida" is here of

---

[152] As with *maenols* and *trevs* in North and South Wales.

[158] Mr. Pell tried to explain it by assuming that the Leicestershire *carucates* were really small virgates of the *hida* in question !

a peculiar character, but also that the normal "hida" of Domesday (from which they could not emancipate themselves) would be quite out of place in this carucated district.

The first point to grasp is that this Leicestershire "hida" was a term which, locally I mean, explained itself. It is used at least a dozen times in the Survey of Leicestershire without any mention of its contents. Those contents must have been, therefore, familiar and fixed. But what were those contents? Three incidental notices enable us to determine them :—

231 (*a*), 2 : "Ibi est i. hida et iiii[ta.] pars i. hidæ. Ibi sunt xxii. car' terræ et dimidia."

236 (*a*), 1 : " II. partes unius hidæ, id est xii. car' terræ."

237 (*a*), 2 : " II. partes unius hidæ, id est xii. car' terræ."

Just as the " Hundred " of Lincolnshire was a sum of twelve carucates, so the "Hide" of Leicestershire was a sum of *eighteen carucates*.[154] Working in the light of this discovery (for as such I claim it), we find that the other "hides," thus interpreted, give us an aggregate of "carucates" obviously suitable to the recorded ploughlands.[155] It may, however, be fairly asked why Domesday should speak in one place of half a "hide," and in another of nine "carucates"; in one place of a hide and a third, and in another of twenty-four carucates. The answer is that the singular love of variety which distinguishes Domesday in Cambridgeshire (as we saw) is at work here also. For instance, two equal estates are thus described: —" Willelmus iiii. car' terræ et dimidiam et iii. bovatas, et Rogerus iiii. car' terræ et vii. bovatas " (fo. 234*a*). The same instinct which led the scribe to enter these seven bovates as half a carucate *plus* three bovates, led him also to enter ten and a half

---

[154] This at once shows the absurdity of taking these eighteen carucates to be eighteen "virgates " of a normal hide, and of all the reasoning based thereupon.

[155] See morebelow on this point.

carucates as half a hide *plus* a carucate and a half (fo. 237*a*).

But to the rule I have established there is a single exception. We read of " Medeltone " in this shire : " Ibi sunt vii. hidæ et una carucata terræ et una bovata. In una-quaque hida sunt xiiii. carucatæ terræ et dimidia " (fo. 235*b*). The actual formula employed is unique for the shire, and the figures are specially given as an exception. But, with singular perversity, Domesday students have always been inclined to pitch upon the exceptions as representing the rule, forgetting that it was precisely in exceptional cases that figures had to be given. In normal cases they would have been superfluous.

Several years have elapsed since I wrote the above explanation, but I have decided to publish it exactly as it originally stood. In the meanwhile, however, Mr. Stevenson has dealt with the subject in an article on " The Hundreds of Domesday : the Hundred of Land " (1890).[156] He has ad-vanced the ingenious theory that the Leicestershire " hida " was only a clerical error for H[undred], and that it was really that " Hundred " of *twelve* carucates which we meet with in the Lindsey Survey. To prove this, he reads an entry on 236*a*, 1, as " Ogerus Brito tenet in Cilebe de rege ii. partes unius hidæ, id est xii. car[ucatæ] terræ," and claims that this gloss defines the " hida " as a " hundred " of twelve carucates. I confess that to me such a rendering is in the highest degree non-natural. If we speak of " two-thirds of a yard, that is twenty-four inches," we should clearly imply that the yard itself was thirty-six inches, not twenty-four. Similarly, I claim to render the " gloss " as implying that the " hida " itself contained eighteen caru-catæ, not twelve.[157] If I am right, Mr. Stevenson's sugges-tion that this " hida " was really a " Hundred " also falls to the ground.

[156] *English Historical Review*, v. 95.

[157] Mr. Stevenson, moreover, should surely, to obtain the meaning he wants, have extended *car* as " car[ucatarum]."

After careful study of the Domesday Survey of Leicestershire, I definitely hold that in that county "carucata terræ"
was the geld-carucate and "terra x car[ucis]" the actual
ploughlands.[158] Now there are only three instances in
which the Survey records the assessment both in terms of
the "hida" and in "carucatæ terræ," and in all three the
figures support my own theory. The Abbot of Coventry's
Burbage estate (231a, 2), where a "hide" and a quarter
equates 22½ "carucatæ terræ," is a test-case, and Mr.
Stevenson there takes refuge in a suggested "beneficial
hidation." The exact formula, no doubt, is peculiar, but
reference to the text shows that "s[un]t" has been inter-
polated between "ibi" and "xxii." I suspect that the
scribe had written "ibi" (from the force of habit) when he
ought to have written "id est."

I close this portion of my essay by applying my own
theory to the case of "Erendesbi" (Arnesby). The relative
entries are :—

"Episcopus Constantiensis tenet in Erendesberi ii[as.] car[ucatas]
terræ et dim. et unam bovatam (231)."

"W[illelmus] Pevrel tenet dim. hidam et iii. bovatas terræ in
Erendesbi (235)."

Put into figures they work out :—

	Car.	Bov.
Bishop of Coutances	2½	1
William Peverel	9	3
	12	0

So that Arnesby was a typical Vill assessed at twelve
carucates.[159]

---

[158] I also hold the formula "T. R. E. erant ibi x car[ucæ]" to refer to
ploughs, not ploughlands.

[159] Note that the assessment of 2⅔ cars. represented 2½ ploughlands,
and that of 9⅔ cars. only 7 ploughlands. No relation, therefore, can be
traced here.

IX. THE LANCASHIRE "HIDA."

There is one other case of a peculiar " hide " in Domesday. This is that which is found in the land " between
Ribble and Mersey," that district of which the description
offers so many peculiarities. We find it divided into six
hundreds, and of the " hides " in the first, that of (West)
Derby, we read : " In unaquaque hida sunt vi. carucatæ
terræ " (i. 269*b*). Whether or not that explanation applies,
as is believed, to the whole district, we have here again
a " Danish " place-name brought into direct relation with
the six-carucate unit. On the opposite bank of the Mersey
lay the Wirral peninsula, in which this system of assessment cannot be traced.

Mr. Green alluded to the Danish " byes " as found, by
exception, " about Wirral in Cheshire, [160] and held that
Norsemen from the Isle of Man had founded " the little
group of northern villages which we find in the Cheshire
peninsula of the Wirral." [161] I cannot find them myself.
In his " Notes on the Domesday Survey, so far as it relates
to the Hundred of Wirral " [162] (1893), Mr. Fergusson Irvine,
in a paper which shows, though somewhat discursive, how
much can only be done by intelligent local research, has
collated all the Domesday entries. " Raby " is the one place
I can there find in the peninsula with the " bye " termination ; while out of fifty-one entries twenty refer to places
with the English termination " tone," and the Anglo-Saxon
test-words " ham " and " ford " are found in four others.
There were, doubtless, Norse elements in the peninsula, but
they were not strong enough to change the place-names or
divide the land on their own system. In the same way,
Chester had its " lawmen," though it was not one of the
Five Boroughs, nor is what I have termed the Scandinavian
formula applied to Cheshire in Domesday. So, too, there

---

[160] *Conquest of England*, p. 121 *note*.
[161] *Ibid.*, p. 276.
[162] *Chester Archæolo*; *c il Journal*, vol. v.

were lawmen at Cambridge, and their heriot included eight pounds,[163] which occur in the above formula as the twelve marcs of the Danish "Hundred." Yet the whole system of Cambridgeshire was non-Danish. It was only, in short, where the northern invaders had settled down as a people that they were strong enough to divide the land anew and organise the whole assessment on their own system.

X. The Yorkshire Unit.

We have seen that the unit of assessment for the carucated districts of England was "vi. carucatæ terræ," just as five hides was the old unit in the south. We have also seen that the former reckoning extended over those districts which the Danish immigrants had settled. There remains the question whether the Danes had merely substituted six for five in the pre-existing arrangement, or had made a wholly new one for themselves based on actual area.

It is *primâ facie* not probable that they can have adopted the latter course, for the uniformity of their assessment proves its artificial character. Yet, in his remarkable paper on "The Ploughland and the Plough,"[164] Canon Taylor has arrived at the conclusion that

The geldable carucate of Domesday does not signify what the carucate usually signifies in other early documents. The "carucata ad geldum" is not as commonly stated by Domesday commentators, the quantity of land ploughed in each year by one plough, but it is the quantity tilled in one year *in one arable field* by one plough.[165]

This "novel and important proposition," as its author truly described it, was probably the most notable contribution to our knowledge that the Domesday Commemoration

---

[163] "De harieta Lagemanorum habuit isdem picot viii. lib," etc. (i. 189).

[164] *Domesday Studies*, i. 143-186.

[165] *Ibid.*, 157.

produced. The Canon's theory, which (so far as his own East Riding is concerned) he certainly seems to have established, is, at first sight, fatal to mine. But, on the other hand, my own theory can be proved no less clearly for Leicestershire, where the " carucate terræ " and the ploughs are often connected in about the same ratio as in Yorkshire.[166] This leads us to inquire whether, even in the East Riding (where his theory works best), we may not find traces of that assessment by the six-carucate unit which I advocate myself. Such traces in Yorkshire we have already seen,[167] but there is other and stronger evidence.

If we take the modern Wapentake of Dickering (the first on Canon Taylor's list) and examine its three Domesday Hundreds of Turbar, Hunton, and Burton, we obtain these results :—[168]

TURBAR HUNDRED.

Hundemanebi	24
Ricstorp, Mustone, Scloftone, and Neuton	18
Flotemanebi	6
Muston and Neuton	6
Fordun and Ledemare	6
Burton, Fulcheton, and Chelc. . . .	30
Chelc (2), Ergone, Bringeham, Estolf, Fodstone, and Chemelinge. . . .	19
Nadfartone.	23¾
Pochetorp	6
Helmeswelle and Gartune	44

[166] According to Canon Taylor's ingenious theory, the ratio should be 1 to 1 (for two-field Manors), or 2 to 1 for three-field Manors. But in Leicestershire there is a remarkable prevalence of the 3 to 2 ratio, which his theory can, at best, only explain as exceptional.

[167] *Supra*, p. 80.

[168] The figures are taken from the " Index " to the Hundreds at the close of the first volume of Domesday Book, and the names are arranged in the same order as they are there found.

HUNTON HUNDRED

Flaneburg and Siwardbi	24½	Gerendele	12
Marton	9	Ricton, Benton, and	
Bredinton	18	Spetton	24
Hilgertorp	6	Bocheton	12
Wivlestorp and Basin-		Fleuston	14 ⎫
gebi	12	Stactone	6 ⎬ 27
Frestintorp	9 ⎫	Foxhole	7 ⎭
Eleburne	½ ⎬ 29½		
Eston	6 ⎭		
Bovintorp	14		

BURTON HUNDRED.

Burton	12	Rodestain (8+8+8) .	24
Grenzmore (4+2) . .	6	Twenc	17¼
Arpen (4+8) . . .	12	Suauetorp	9
Chillon (30+11+7) .	48	Fornetorp (4+14 . .	18
Roreston (9+3) . .	12	Butruid	12
Logetorp (1½+5½) . .	7 ⎫	Langetou (9+6) . . .	15 ⎫
Thirnon	7	Buitorp	5
Ascheltorp (4+2) . .	6 ⎬ 36	Bruneton	3 ⎬ 42
Torp	3	Galmeton	8
Cherendebi	13 ⎭	Binneton	6 ⎭
Caretorp (5+4+3) . .	12	Widlaueston	5

The evidence of this last Hundred is so overwhelming that it cannot be gainsaid.[169]

I claim, therefore, that my theory holds good even in Canon Taylor's stronghold, but I do so without venturing to dispute the accuracy of his own. How far they can be reconciled I leave to others to decide.

There are certain difficulties, however, which his brilliant suggestion must raise. It is the essence of his theory that in a two-field Manor the ploughland of 160 acres (half

---

[169] There is plenty of similar evidence elsewhere in the shire. Thus we find the Craven Manors assessed at 6, 6, 6, 3, 3, 4, 6, 10, 2, 2, 3, 3, 3, 3, 3, 3, 2, 3, 3, 3 carucates. These assessments would give us 24 (6 + 6 + 6 + 3 + 3 + 3) + 24 (4 + 6 + 10 + 2 + 2) + 18 (3 + 3 + 3 + 3 + 3 + 3) + 11 (2 + 3   3).

fallow) was assessed at *one* "carucata terræ," while in
the three-field Manor the plonghland of 180 acres (a third
fallow) was assessed at *two*. This would be an obvious
and gross injustice. Again, remembering that, according
to the Canon, the proportion of "carucatæ" to ploughlands should be either 2 to 1 or 1 to 1, what are we to
make of such figures as these, taken at a venture from a
page of the Leicestershire Survey (232*a*, 1):—

Carucatæ.	Ploughlands.	Carucata.	Ploughlands.
1	2	12	8
1	$\frac{1}{2}$	$11\frac{1}{3}$	7
2	1	9	4
$5\frac{5}{8}$	4	7	6
2	1	6	5
$2\frac{5}{8}$	4	2	4
1	1	10	7
6	4	9	6
$8\frac{7}{8}$	6	$\frac{5}{8}$	$\frac{1}{2}$
$\frac{1}{2}$	$\frac{1}{2}$	6	4 (thrice)
28	22	$4\frac{7}{8}$	3

It is certainly difficult to discover any regular or consistent assessment in a system where the ploughland was
represented by anything from $\frac{1}{2}$ *carucata* to 2¼ *carucatæ*.
There is, however, in so many cases an approximation to
an assessment of three *carucatæ* for two ploughlands, that
there seems to have been some underlying idea, if we could
only trace it out. But for this there is needed a special
investigation of all the carucated counties, a work of great
labour and requiring local co-operation. If we could have
tables for each county, arranged Hundred by Hundred and
Vill by Vill, showing in parallel columns the ploughland
and the *carucatæ ad geldum*, we could then, and only then,
venture to speak positively. Till that is accomplished we
are not in a position to explain how a system of assessment, based on actual area, could result in aggregate assessments uniformly expressed in terms of the six-carucate
unit.

XI. GENERAL CONCLUSIONS.

In seeking a clue to the origin of that artificial assessment, of which the traces, whether more or less apparent,
linger on the pages of Domesday, I propose to exclude the
carucated district, because we require, as I have said, more
complete evidence as to the system pursued within it, and
because, being associated with the settlement of the Danes
it represents a later introduction, while the very name
"carcucate," as I observed in *Domesday Studies*, has, unlike
the mysterious "hide," an obvious connexion with the
ploughland. Confining ourselves to the district assessed in
terms of the " hide," we seek to learn the origin of the
system by which, as I contend, it was divided for the purpose of taxation into blocks, each of which was expressed
in terms of the five-hide unit.

Now if we follow the clue afforded by the Cambridgeshire evidence, and hold that the assessment was originally
laid not on the Manor, nor even on the Vill, but on the
Hundred as a whole,[170] it might be suggested that the
Hundred itself subdivided the amount among its constituent elements. In practice, indeed, from the nature of
the case, this principle must have prevailed in every *town*
assessed at a Hundred or Half-Hundred, for where an urban
community was assessed in "hides" the burgesses must,
as in later days, have settled among themselves the proportion to be borne by individuals or individual properties.
If, then, they were able to do this, and if, as I hold, town
and country were assessed on the same principle, as part
of the same system, what was to prevent their neighbours,
in the court of the rural Hundred, similarly distributing
among its constituents their respective shares of the common burden ?

We might even be tempted to go far further than this,
and to carry our discoveries to a logical conclusion. If, as
is asserted, direct taxation ("geld") began in England

---

[170] *Supra*, pp. 49, 63.

with the need for raising money to buy off the Danes, let us ask ourselves how the Witan would proceed when confronted with a demand, let us say, for £10,000. As there had been hitherto, *ex hypothesi*, no direct taxation, there would be no statistical information at their disposal, enabling them to raise by a direct levy the sum required. Their only possible resource, we might hold, would be to apportionate it in round sums among the contributory shires. Proceeding on precisely the same lines, the county court, in its turn would distribute the *quota* of the shire among its constituent Hundreds, and the Hundred court would then assign to each Vill its share. As the Vills were represented in the Hundred court, and the Hundreds in the Shire court, the just apportionment of the Shire's *quota* would be thus practically secured. The arrangement would, moreover, be as satisfactory to the Witan as it was fair to the contributors *inter se*; for, by this gradation of responsibility, the payment of the whole was absolutely secured. This explanation is very tempting, and, indeed, such a system of apportioning liability is to be traced from time immemorial in the Indian village community.[171] Moreover, if the ratio of "hides" to ploughlands were found to vary to any marked extent, according to county, the hypothesis that the quota, in the first instance, was laid upon each county would duly explain the ratio assessment being higher or lower in one county than in another.

But such an hypothesis would imply that this assessment dated only from the days of Æthelred, or *circ.* 1000. Now the five-hide unit, on the contrary, was undoubtedly an old institution. Church lordships, the easiest to trace, appear to have retained their hidation unchanged from early times, and the "possessio decem familiarum" of Bede seems to carry the decimal system back to very early days. Mr. Seebohm, indeed—though, like others, he had failed to

---

[171] Compare the "Reparto de la contribucion," found in the Spanish village communities, the members of which apportioned the assessment among themselves.

discover the existence of the five-hide system—saw in this "possessio" of Bede a connecting link with the Roman *decuria*, just as he saw in the Roman *jugatio* the possible origin of English hidation. And we must, of course, trace its artificial arrangement (1) either to the Romans, (2) or to the Britons—assuming them to have had the same system as existed in Wales for the food-rents, (3) or to the English invaders.

Arrested at this point by the difficulty of assigning to the system I have described its real origin, I dropped these studies for some years in the hope that there might come from some quarter fresh light upon the problem. As I cannot, however, for lack of evidence, propound a solution capable of proof, I will content myself with indicating the line of research that offers, I venture to think, the most likelihood of success.

The proportionate sums contributed by the several counties to the Danegeld present a fruitful field of enquiry, but one, it would seem, as yet unworked. Mr. Eyton, it is rue, observed that "in Devon and Cornwall the scope of the gheld-hide was enormous," [172] that is, in other words, the assessment was strangely low, but it did not occur to him to seek the cause of the phenomenon he observed. If, as was the case, West Wales was assessed on quite a different scale to the counties adjoining it on the east, it may suggest a conclusion no less important than that, when the latter were originally assessed, West Wales was not yet a portion of the English realm. But, before concluding that the hide assessment is proved to be as ancient as this, we must see whether it is possible to detect any principle at work in the total assessments of the several counties, any relation between their area and the sums they contributed to the geld as entered in the Pipe Roll of 1130, our first evidence on the subject.

For such an enquiry it is especially needful to insist on breadth of treatment. In the first place, the modern area

---

[172] Key to Domesday: Dorset, p. 14.

of the counties may vary more or less from the original extent;[178] in the second we have no proof that the assessment had always been the same, through the tendency in early days, no doubt, was to stereotype such figures. We must not, therefore attempt close or detailed investigation but if, on a review of the whole evidence, we detect certain broad features, uneffaced by the hand of time, we may fairly claim that we have in these the traces of a principle at work, the witness to a state of things prevailing in the distant past.

On comparing the contributions to a "geld" at two shillings on the hide with the (modern) area of counties, we find that a rate of about a pound for every seven square miles prevailed widely enough to be almost described as normal.

The three eastern counties work out thus :—

		Square Miles.		(At $\frac{1}{7}$).		Actual Sum.		
				£		£	s	d.
Norfolk	..	2,119	.	$302\frac{5}{7}$	.	330	3	2
Suffolk	..	1,475	.	$210\frac{5}{7}$	.	235	0	8
Essex	...	1,542	.	$220\frac{2}{7}$	.	236	8	0

In all three cases the proportion to the square mile is between a sixth and a seventh of a pound. In Cambridgeshire it is just under, in Sussex just over, a seventh :—

		Square Miles.		(At $\frac{1}{7}$).		Actual Sum.		
				£		£	s.	d.
Cambridgeshire		820	.	$117\frac{1}{7}$	.	114	15	0
Sussex	...	1,458	.	$208\frac{2}{7}$	.	209	18	6

Most remarkable, however, is this Midland group:—

	Square Miles.		(At $\frac{1}{7}$).		Actual Sum.		
			£		£	s.	d.
Leicestershire	700	.	100	.	100	0	0
Warwickshire .	885	.	$126\frac{3}{7}$	.	128	12	6
Worcestershire .	738	.	$105\frac{3}{7}$	.	101	5	7
Gloucestershire	1,224	.	$174\frac{6}{7}$	.	179	11	8
Somerset ..	1,640	.	$234\frac{2}{7}$	.	227	10	4

[178] The anomalous position of Rutland also was, of course, a disturbing element.

It is remarkable, not only for this agreement *inter se*, but also for the sharp contrast it presents to the groups of counties, lying respectively to the south-east and the north-west of it. The former approximates a rate twice as high, namely, *two*-sevenths of a pound to the square mile :—

	Square Miles.	[At $\frac{2}{7}$]	Actual Sums.
		£	£ s. d.
Buckinghamshire	. 745	. $212\frac{3}{7}$	. 204 14 7
Oxfordshire .	. 756	. 216	. 239 9 3
Berkshire . .	. 722	. $206\frac{2}{7}$	. 200 1 3
Wiltshire . .	. 1,354	. $386\frac{6}{7}$	. 388 13 0

Taking this group as a whole, it paid £1,032 18s. 1d., a curiously close approximation to the £1,021¼ which my suggested rate of $\frac{2}{7}$ would give. Middlesex was so exceptional a county, that one hardly likes to include it, but there also the rate was a little over two-sevenths.

On the other hand, the counties to the north-west of what I have termed the Midland group are assessed at a rate singularly low. Nottingham and Derby, with a joint area of 1,855 miles, contributed only £108 8s. 6d., representing one-seventeenth ; [174] while Staffordshire, with its 1,169 miles, is found paying £44 0s. 11d., a rate scarcely more than one twenty-seventh. Passing to the opposite corner of the realm, we have Kent, always a wealthy county, assessed at the phenomenally low rate of about one-fifteenth (£105 2s. 10d., as against 1,555 miles), rather less than half that of Essex to its north, and Sussex to its west.

It would seem impossible to resist the conclusion that in these widely differing rates we have traces of a polity as yet divided, of those independent kingdoms from which had been formed the realm. Kent, for instance, which had so steadily maintained, first, its independent existence, and then its local institutions, had succeeded in preserving an assessment that its neighbours had cause to envy. In the

[174] This low assessment is equally obvious in that of the several Manors.

west, Cornwall similarly enjoyed a low, indeed a nominal
assessment, while that of Devon, though higher than this,
was so significantly lower than those of Somerset and
Dorset [175] as to remind us that here, in part at least, the
"Welsh" long held their own. If the incidence of geld
were shown by shading a map of England, on the plan so
successfully adopted in Mr. Seebohm's great work, it
would show that the heavily assessed counties were those
which formed the nucleus of the old West-Saxon realm. [176]
All round this nucleus the map would shade off sharply,
another sudden change marking the Danish counties on
the north, the Jutish kingdom on the east, and the British
district in the south-west. It is, perhaps, worthy of remark that Shropshire was assessed twice as heavily as
the adjoining county of Stafford, possibly because part of
it was added, at a very early period, to the kingdom of the
West Saxons. If Mr. Eyton was right in his reckoning
that Kesteven was assessed twice as heavily as Lindsey,
and Lindsey, in turn, twice as heavily as Holland, it would
illustrate the survival of local distinctions even within
the compass of a modern county, as well as the "shading
off" tendency of which I have already spoken.

The point I have here endeavoured to bring out is that
if the system of artificial assessment were of Roman or
British origin, we should expect to find it fairly uniform
over the whole country, whereas we find, on the contrary,
the very widest discrepancies. It might be urged, perhaps,
that these were due to the differing conditions of particular
counties, to their more or less partial reclamation, for
instance, of the date when they were assessed. But this
would not account for the grouping I have traced, and
would imply that each county ought to differ indefinitely.

[175] Probably $\frac{1}{37}$, as against about $\frac{1}{6}$ for Somerset and Dorset jointly.

[176] See Mr. Green's maps in his work, *The Making of England*, and
Mr. Freeman's map of "Britain in 597," in vol. i. of his *Norman Conquest*.
The figures for Hampshire, unfortunately, are wanting in the roll of 1156,
as in that of 1130.

Nor would it explain the case of Kent, where a county that must have been foremost in early development and prosperity enjoyed a phenomenally low assessment.

Another objection that may be raised to my hypothesis is that the Hundred, as an area for police and rating, was a comparatively late institution, and that if the artificial system of assessment were as ancient as I suggest, it could not have operated, as we saw, in Cambridgeshire, it did operate, through the " Hundred." It is, however, admitted that the *thing* represented by the " Hundred " was, whatever its original name, of immemorial antiquity, as the intermediate division between the Vill and the Shire or kingdom. Approaching the subject from the legal standpoint, Prof. Maitland has pointed out that the Hundred having a proper court, which the Vill had not, was the older institution of the two, and has skilfully seized on the differentiation of villages originally possessing one name in common as a hint that some such subdivision may have been going on more widely than is known. It seems to me to be at least possible that the district originally representing a Hundred, and named, as we are learning, in most cases from the primitive meeting-place of its settlers, was reckoned as so many multiples of five or ten hides, and that this aggregate was subsequently distributed by its community among themselves.[177]

If it be not presumption to touch on the controversies as to the Hundred,[178] I would suggest that while agreeing with Dr. Stubbs, that the name of " Hundred " may be traced to the ordinance of Edgar,[179]—which did not, however, create the district itself,—I cannot reconcile it with the view to which he leans in his *Constitutional History*, that " under the name of geographical hundreds we have the variously

---

[177] Even if such assessment were not required, at first, for financial reasons, it might be necessary for such obligations as eventually formed the "trinoda necessitas."

[178] See Stubbs, *Select Charters*, pp. 67-69, and *Const. Hist.*, i. 96-99.

[179] *Select Charters*, p. 67.

B.H.   H

sized *pagi* or districts in which the hundred warriors settled"; and that we should "recognise in the name the vestige of the primitive settlement, and in the district itself an earlier or a later subdivision of the kingdom to which it belonged."[180]　For my part, I have never been able to understand the anxiety to identify the district known, in later days, as a "Hundred" with an original hundred warriors, families, or hides.　The significant remark on the "centeni" by Tacitus, that "quod primo numerus fuit, jam nomen et honor est," would surely lead us to expect that by the time of the migration the "Hundred" had become, like the "hide" of Domesday, a term even more at variance with fact.　Indeed, in his masterly "Introductory sketch," Dr. Stubbs observed that the "superior divisions" made by the "new-comers" would "have that indefiniteness which even in the days of Tacitus belonged to the Hundreds, the *centeni* of the Germans," and that their "system" would be "transported whole, at the point of development which it has reached at home."[181]

The suggestion I have made as to the origin of the five-hide system is tentative only, and must remain so until we have at our disposal for the whole hidated region that complete and trustworthy analysis of assessment, on the need of which I again insist, at the risk of wearisome iteration.

XII.　The East Anglian "Leet."

In Norfolk and Suffolk we find Domesday recording assessed values not, as everywhere else, at the outset of an entry, but at its close; not in terms of hides and carucates,

---

[180] Vol. i., pp. 98, 99　Cf. *Select Charters*, p. 67 : "It is sometimes stated that the Hundred is a primitive subdivision consisting of a hundred hides of land, or apportioned to a hundred families, the great objection to which theory is the impossibility of reconciling the historical Hundreds with any such computation."

[11] *Select Charters*, p. 6.

but in terms of shillings and pence. Instead of saying that
a Manor paid on so many "hidæ" or "carucatæ terræ,"
Domesday, in the case of these counties, normally employs
the phrase: "*x* denarii de gelto." Its meaning is that to
every *pound* paid by the Hundred as geld the Manor contributed *x* pence.[182] Thus, in the case of a Hundred assessed
at a hundred hides, the formula for a five-hide Manor
would be here "xii. denarii de gelto," instead of the usual
"defendit se pro v. hidis," or some such phrase as that.
There is an exact parallel to this method of recording
assessed values in the case of fractions of knights' fees
where portions of land are entered as paying so much
"when the scutage is forty shillings," instead of being
assessed in terms of the knight's fee.[183] This system would
seem, however, to have been understood imperfectly if at
all. I may, therefore, point out that its nature is clear
from the case of the Suffolk Hundred of Thingoe.

The case of this Hundred is singularly instructive. We
find its twenty "Vills" grouped in *blocks*, precisely as in
the Cambridgeshire Hundreds, and these blocks are all
equal units of assessment, like the ten-hide groups of the
hidated districts. But in this case we can go further still.
For we are not dependent on Domesday alone. The portion
of a special Survey executed about a century later (*circ.*
1185) for Abbot Sampson of St. Edmund's, which relates
to its Hundred, is fortunately preserved, and gives us the
name of the twelve "leets" into which this Hundred was
divided.[184]

Here are the divisions recorded in it, with the Domesday

[182] Thus, the first entry for East Anglia (ii. 109 *b*) has "de xx. solidis
reddit xvi. d. in gelto."

[183] Compare also the very curious system of "purses" adopted by the
Cinque Ports. The "purse" was £4 7*s.*, and to every "purse" Sandwich, for instance, paid twenty shillings, while, whenever it paid such
twenty shillings, its four "members" were assessed to pay three and
fourpence apiece towards it.

[184] "In hundredo de Tinghowe sunt xx. villæ ex quibus constituuntui
ix. lete, quas sic distinguimus." Gage's *Suffolk*, p. xii.

assessment (in pence) of each Vill placed against its name.

			£	s.	d.
I. { Barrow	. .	7			
Flemington	. .	6			
Lackford	. .	6			
		—			
		19	.	0	1	7
II. Risby	. .	20	.	0	1	8
III. { Saxham (*A*)	.	7			
Saxham (*B*)	.	7			
Westley	.	$6\frac{1}{2}$			
		—			
		$20\frac{1}{2}$		0	1	$8\frac{1}{2}$
IV. { Hengrave	. .	10			
Fornham	. .	10			
		—			
		20	.	0	1	8
V. { Ickworth	. .	$7\frac{1}{2}$			
Chevington	.	$6\frac{1}{2}$			
Hargrave	. .	7			
		—			
		21	.	0	1	9
VI. { Brockley	. .	7			
Rede	. .	7			
Manston	. .	6			
		—			
		20	.	0	1	8
VII. Whepstead	. .	20	.	0	1	8
VIII. { Hawstead	. .	$13\frac{1}{2}$			
Newton	. .	$6\frac{1}{2}$			
		—			
		20	.	0	1	8
IX. Horningsheath	.	20	.	0	1	8
X., XI., XII. Sudbury	. .	60	.	0	5	0
			£1	0	$0\frac{1}{2}$

The two records—Domesday and the Inquest—thus confirm one another, and their concurrent testimony establishes the fact not only that the Suffolk Hundred was divided into blocks of equal assessment, but that these blocks were known by the name of "leets."

Now Professor Maitland, in his Dissertation on the "History of the Word Leet,"[185] pronounces this "the earliest occurrence of the word" that he has seen. But I can carry it back to Domesday itself. Though not entered in the *Index Rerum*, we find it in such instances as these:—

"H[undredum] de Grenehou de xiv. letis" (ii. 119*b*).

"Hund[redum] et eim[idium] de Clakelosa de x. leitis" (ii. 212*b*).

I think it probable that in these cases the entry happened to stand first on the original return for the Hundred, and so—as in the I.E., where it is derived from the original returns,—the general heading crept in. Though Professor Maitland has to leave the origin of the word unexplained, it seems to me impossible to overlook the analogy between the Danish *lægd*, described by Dr. Skeat as a division of the country (in Denmark) for military conscription,[186] and the East Anglian *leet*, a division of the country (as we have seen) for purposes of taxation.

Sudbury, it will be observed, was *a quarter* of the Hundred of Thingoe,[187] just as Huntingdon was a quarter of a Hundred,[188] and Wisbech a quarter of a Hundred.[189]

Having thus obtained from the Hundred of Thingoe the clue to this peculiar system, we can advance to more difficult types. The Hundred of Thedwastre, for instance,

---

[185] *Select Pleas in Manorial Courts* (Selden Society), I., lxiii.—lxxvi.

[186] *Ibid.*, p. lxxvi.

[187] "De gelto v. sol'" (D.B., ii. 286*b*). Sudbury was an outlying portion of the Hundred of Thingoe, in which is situated Bury St. Edmunds, of which we read (D.B., ii. 372): "quando in hundredo solvitur ad geldum, i. libra, tunc inde exeunt lx. d. *ad victum monachorum.*" This substitution, apparently, of Sudbury (as three leets) for Bury St. Edmunds (of which the monks received the geld) deserves investigation.

[188] See p. 58.

[189] "Wisbeche, quæ est quarta pars centuriatus insulæ" (*Liber Eliensis* p. 192).

was divided not into twelve blocks, each paying twenty pence in the pound, but into nine blocks, each paying twenty-seven. This assessment allowed a margin of 3*d.* for every pound (*i.e.* £1 0*s.* 3*d.*); but in the case of Thedwastre the total excess was only 1½*d.* on the pound (*i.e.* £1 0 1½*d.*). I group the Vills *tentatively*, thus :—

				d.
I.	Barton			27
II.	Fornham	6½		26½
	Rougham	20		
III.	Pakenham	13½		
	Bradfield	5		26½
	Fornham St. Genevieve	8		
IV.	Thurston	16		
	Woolpit	11		27
V.	Rushbrook	7		
	Ratlesden	20		27
VI.	Hessett	18		
	Felsham	5		28
	Bradfield	5		
VII.	Gedding	5		
	Whelnetham	10		26
	Drinkston	11		
VIII.	Ampton	7		
	Tostock	10½		27½
	Staningfield	10		
IX.	Tinworth	14		
	Livermere	12		26

241½ (£1 0*s.* 1½*d.*)

The same unit of 27 (×9)—or, which comes to the same thing, 13½ (×18)—was adopted in Risbridge Hundred. In this case no less than five Manors are assessed at the same unit—13½*d.* So, again, in the Hundred of Blackbourn the units are 34½*d.* and 17¼*d.*, one Manor being assessed at the former, and five at the latter sum. Such is the key to the peculiar system of East Anglian assessment.

It is to be noted that "twenty shillings"[190] represents ten hides at two shillings on the hide (the normal Danegeld rate), and thus suggests that in Norfolk, as in Cambridge-shire, the Hundreds were normally assessed in multiples of ten hides. The point, however, that I want to bring out is that the Hundred, not the Manor, nor even the Vill, is here treated as "the fiscal unit for the collection of Danegeld."[191]

XIII. THE WORDS SOLINUM AND SOLANDA. [192]

Several years ago I arrived at the conclusion that the identity of these two words was an unsupported conjecture. So long as it remained a conjecture only, its correction was not urgent; but since then, as is so often the case, the result of leaving it unassailed has been that arguments are based upon it. There appeared in the *English Historical Review* for July, 1892, a paper by Mr. Seebohm, in which that distinguished scholar took the identity for granted, as his no less distinguished opponent, Professor Vinogradoff has done in his masterly work on *Villainage in England.*

I believe the alleged identity was first asserted by Arch-deacon Hale, who wrote in his *Domesday of St. Paul's* (1858), p. xiv. :—

The word *solanda*, or, as it is written at p. 142, *scolanda*, is so evidently a Latinized form of the Anglo-Saxon *sulung*, or plough-land, and approaches so near to the Kentish *solinus*, that we need scarely hesitate to consider them identical.

Let us start from the facts. In the Domesday of Kent we find the form *solin*, or its Latin equivalent *solinum*, used for the unit of assessment, like the hide and the carucate in other countries. In the Kent monastic surveys it is

[190] " In Sparle et in Pagrave, xviii. d. quando hundret scotabat xx solidos et in Acra vi. d. et in pichensam xii. d. quicunque ibi teneat " (ii. 119*b*). See also note 182.

[192] See Domesday Studies, p. 117.

[192] Reprinted from the *English Historical Review*, October, 1892.

found as *sullung* or *suolinga*. But when we turn to the
Domesday of St. Paul's, we find—first, that instead of
being universal, as in Kent, it occurs only in three cases ;
secondly, that the form is *solande, solanda, scholanda, scolanda,* or even (we shall see) *Scotlande* ; thirdly, that it is
not employed as a unit of assessment at all.

The three places where the term occurs in the Domesday
of St. Paul's are Drayton and Sutton in Middlesex, and
Tillingham in Essex. Hale would seem to have arrived at
no clear idea of what the word meant. At p. xiv. he wrote
that " a *solanda* consisted of two hides, but probably in
this case the hide was not of the ordinary dimension." At
p. lxxviii. he inferred, from a reference to " la Scoland "
in a survey of Drayton, that " ' ploughed land ' would
seem to be opposed to ' Scoland.' " At p. cx. he was led
by the important passage—" De hydis hiis decem, due
fuerunt in dominio, una in scolanda, et vii. assisae"—to
suggest that it "appears to denote some difference in the
tenure." This last conjecture seems the most probable.
If we take the case of Sutton and Chiswick, we read in the
survey of 1222 :—

> Juratores dicunt quod manerium istud defendit se versus regem
> pro tribus hidis preter solandam de Chesewich que per se habet
> duas hidas, et sunt geldabiles cum hidis de Sutton.

Hale (p. 119) believed that this *Solande de Chesewich* was
no other than the *Scotlande thesaurarii* of 1181, namely the
prebend of Chiswick. The above passage should further
be compared with the survey of Caddington (1222) :—

> Dicunt juratores quod manerium istud defendit se versus regem
> pro x. hidis . . . preter duas prebendas quae sunt in eadem
> parochia.

The formula is the same in both cases, and a *solanda* was
clearly land held on some special terms, and was not a
measure or unit of assessment at all. Indeed Hale himself
admitted that it could not be identified with one or with
two hides.

Fortunately I have discovered an occurrence of the word *solanda* which conclusively proves that it meant an estate, such as a prebend, and was not a unit of measurement. We have, in 1183, a "grant by William de Belmes, canon of St. Paul's, to the chapter of that church, of the Church of St. Pancras, situate in his *solanda* near London" (*i.e.* his prebend of St. Pancras), etc. [193] This solves the mystery. The three *solandœ* at Tillingham were no other than the three prebends—Ealdland, Weldland, and Reculverland—which that parish actually contained. [194]

Hale, however, misled Mr. Seebohm, who in his great work on the *English Village Community* (p. 54), wrote of Tillingham :—

There was further in this Manor a *double hide*, called a *solanda*, presumably of 240 acres. This double hide, called a *solanda*, is also mentioned in a Manor in Middlesex [Sutton], and in another in Surrey [Drayton] [195] ; and the term *solanda* is probably the same as the well-known "*Sollung*" or "*solin*" of Kent, meaning a " plough land."

Proceeding further (p. 395), Mr. Seebohm wrote :—

Generally in Kent, and sometimes in Sussex, Berks, and Essex, we found, in addition to, or instead of, the hide or carucate, or "terra unius aratri," *solins*, *sullungs*, or *swullungs*, the land pertaining to a "*suhl*," the Anglo-Saxon word for plough.

Unfortunately no reference is given for the cases of Sussex and Berks, and I know of none myself.

Turning now to the learned work of Professor Vinogradoff, we find him equally misled :—

Of the *sulung* I have spoken already. It is a full ploughland, and 200 acres are commonly reckoned to belong to it. The name is sometimes found out of Kent, in Essex for instance. In Tillingham, a Manor of St. Paul's, of London, we come across six hides

---

[193] Ninth Report on Historical MSS., App. I., 38.

[194] *Domesday of St. Paul's*, p. iv.

[195] This is a slip. Drayton was in Middlesex, and the words (which Mr. Seebohm quotes) are "cum *una* hida de solande."

"trium solandarum." The most probable explanation seems to be that the hide or unit of assessment is contrasted with the *solanda* or *sulland* [196] (sulung,) that is with the actual ploughland, and two hides are reckoned as a single *solanda* (p. 255).

Lastly, we come to Mr. Seebohm's reply to Professor Vinogradoff (*ante*, pp. 444-465). Here the identity is again assumed :—

Along with parts of Essex, the Kentish records differ in phraseology from those of the rest of England. Their *sullungs* of 240 acres occur also in the Manors of Essex belonging to St. Paul's, and the custom of gavelkind and succession of the youngest child mark it off as exceptional. Mr. Vinogradoff . . . shows that in the Kentish district, and in Essex, where the *sullung solanda* takes the place of the hide, and where gavelkind prevailed, the unity of the hides and virgates was preserved only for the purposes of taxation and the services; whilst in reality the holdings clustered under the nominal unit were many and irregular.

I yield to no one in admiration for Mr. Seebohm's work, but the question raised is so important that accuracy as to the fact is here essential. (1) *Sullung* is nowhere found in Essex, but only *solanda!* (2) *Solanda* does not occur "in the Manors" referred to, but at Tillingham alone; (3) In Essex it nowhere "takes the places of the hide," as it does in Kent; (4) The Essex instance adduced by Professor Vinogradoff is taken from a Manor where *solanda* does not occur.

Two issues—quite distinct—are involved. In the first place, Mr. Seebohm contends that Professor Vinogradoff must not argue from "the custom of Kent" to the rest of England, because (*inter alia*) Kent, unlike the rest of England, was divided into *sulungs*, which points to some difference in its organization. [197] This contention is sound, and is actually strengthened if we reject the identity of *sulung* and *solanda*. But, in the second place, he endeavours to explain away the Essex case of subdivision at

---

[196] I know of no authority for this form.

[197] The "*Lathes*" of Kent of course point in the same direction.

Eadwulfsness, to which the Professor appeals, by connecting it with the Kentish system through the term *solanda*.
This, as I have shown above, is based on a misreading of
the evidence, and is contrary to the facts of the case.

Let us then look more closely at the Essex instance of
subdivision. It is taken from one Manor alone, the great
"soke" of Eadwulfsness, in the north-east corner of the
county. This "soke" comprised the townships of Thorpe
"le soken," Kirby "le soken," and Walton "le soken"
(better known as Walton-on-the-Naze). Such names pro-
claim the Danish origin of the community, and it is noteworthy that the "hidarii," on whom the argument turns,
are found only at Thorpe and Kirby, the very two townships which bear Danish names. This circumstance points
to quite another track. That the system in this little
corner of Essex was wholly peculiar had been pointed out
by Hale, and it might perhaps have originated in the
superimposition of hides on a previous system, instead of
in the breaking up of the hide and virgate system. But
this is only a conjecture. The two facts on which I would
lay stress are that at Thorpe, according to Hale, "the
holders of the nine hides (in 1279) possessed also among
them seventy-two messuages," which, by its proportion of
eight to the hide, favours Mr. Seebohm's views; and that
the holdings of the "hidarii" were rigidly formed on the
decimal system (such as 60, 30, 15, 7½ acres, or 40, 20, 10,
5 acres),[198] unlike the holdings of an odd number of acres
on the Kentish Manors of St. Augustine's. The reason for
the Essex system was clearly the necessity of keeping the
holdings in a fixed relation to the hide, that their proportion
of the hide's service might be easily determined. These
two points have, perhaps, I think, been overlooked by both
of the eminent scholars in their controversy.

Before leaving the subject of the *sulung*, one should mention perhaps that it was divided (as Mr. Seebohm has ex-

---

[198] Professor Vinogradoff states, on the contrary, that "all are irregular in their formation."

plained) into four quarters known as *juga*, just as the hide
was divided into four virgates. Mr. Seebohm bases this
statement on Anglo-Saxon evidence,[199] but it is abundantly
confirmed by Domesday, where we read of Eastwell (in
Kent): "pro uno solin se defendit. Tria juga sunt infra
divisionem Hugonis, et quartum jugum est extra" (i. 13).
So far all is clear ; but Prosessor Vinogradoff, on the contrary, asserts that "the yokes (*juga*) of Battle Abbey (in
Kent) are not virgates, but carucates, full ploughlands"
(p. 225). This assertion is based on a very natural misapprehension. In the Battle Manor of Wye (Kent) we find
that the *jugum* itself was divided into four quarters, called
"virgates" which were each, consequently, the sixteenth,
not, as in the hidated district, the fourth of a ploughland.
Professor Vinogradoff, naturally assuming that the
"virgate" meant the same here as elsewhere, inferred that
four "virgates" (that is, a *jugum*) must constitute a full
ploughland. But this change of denotation goes further
still. The Battle Cartulary records yet another "virgate,"
namely, the fourth (not of a ploughland, but) of an acre!
This led me, on its publication, to wonder whether we have
here the clue to the origin of the somewhat mysterious
term "virgate." Starting from the acre, we should have
in the *virgata* (rood) its quarter, with a name derived from
the *virga* (rod) which formed its base in mensuration. The
sense of "quarter" once established, it might be transferred to the quarter of a *jugum*, or the quarter of a hide.
This is a suggestion which, of course, I advance with all
diffidence, but which would solve an otherwise insoluble
problem. The relation of the bovate to the carucate, and
of the *jugum* to the *sulung*, are both so obviously based
upon the unit of the plough-team that they raise no difficulty. But the term "virgate" does not, like them, speak
for itself. If we might take it to denote merely a "quarter"
of the hide, it would become a term of relation only, leaving
the "hide" as the original unit. Should this suggestion

meet with acceptance, it might obviously lead to rather important results.

Mr. Elton, in his well-known *Tenures of Kent*, attaches considerable importance to a list, " De Suylingis Comitatus Kanciæ et qui eas tenent," in the Cottonian MS., Cland. A. IV., which he placed little subsequent to Domesday. Having transcribed it for collation with the Survey, I came to the conclusion that it was not sufficiently trustworthy for publication. For the names, in my opinion, involve some anachronism. The feature of the list is that it shows us, as tenants-in-chief, the leading tenants of Bishop Odo ; and the change of most interest to genealogists is the succession of Patrick " de Caurcio " to the holding of Ernulf de Hesdin.

XIV. The " Firma Unius Noctis."

The curious and evidently archaic institution of the *firma unius noctis* was clearly connected with the problem of hidation. In Somerset the formula for a Manor contributing to this *firma* was :—

Nunquam geldavit nec scitur quot hidæ sint ibi (i. 85).

In Dorset it ran :—

Nescitur quot hidæ sint ibi quia non geldabat T.R.E. (i. 75).

In Wiltshire we read :—

Nunquam geldavit nec hidata fuit, *or* nunquam geldavit : ideo nescitur quot hidæ sint ibi.[200]

In all these entries the " hide " is recognised as merely a measure of assessment quite independent of area.

Hampshire affords us, in a group of Manors, a peculiarly good instance in point. Of Basingstoke, Kingsclere, and " Esseborne," we read :—

[200] The phrase " quot hidæ *sint* ibi " is of importance, because such *formulæ* as " T.R.E. geldabat pro ii. hidis, sed tamen *sunt* ibi xii. hidæ," have sometimes been understood to imply two geldable, but twelve arable hides, whereas both figures refer to assessment only.

Rex tenet indominio *Basingestoches.*　Regale manerium fuit semper.　Numquam geldum dedit, nec hida ibi distributa fuit . . .

Clere tenet rex in dominio.　De firma Regis Edwardi fuit, et pertinet ad firmam diei de Basingestoches.　Numerum hidarum nescierunt. . . .

Esseborne tenet rex in dominio.　De firma Regis Edwardi fuit. Numerum hidarum non habent . . .

Hæc tria maneria, Basingestoches, Clere, Esseborne, reddunt firmam unius diei (39).

Other Manors are found about the county displaying the same peculiarity.

Ipse rex tenet *Bertune.*　De firmâ Regis E. fuit, et dimidiam diem firmæ reddidit in omnibus rebus. . . . Nunquam in hid(is) numeratum fuit. . . . Numerum hidarum non dixerunt.

Ipse rex tenet *Edlinges* in dominio.　Hoc manerium reddidit dimidiam diem firmæ tempore Regis E.　Numerum hidarum nesciunt (38).

Manors, such as Andover, not hidated, clearly belonged to the same system, though neither their value nor their render is given.

Thus, then, within the limits of Wessex, in the four adjacent counties of Dorset, Somerset, Wiltshire, and Hants, we find surviving, at the time of the Conquest, an archaic but uniform system of provision for the needs of the Crown by the assignment of certain estates or groups of estates, the render of which was expressed in terms of the "firma noctis" or "firma diei," and which, unlike the country around them, had never been assessed in "hides."

Mr. Seebohm hints slightly at this *firma* system,[201] but only speaks of it as existing in Dorset.　Nor does he allude to the significant fact of such Manors having never been hidated.　It would lead us far afield to speculate on the origin of this system, or to trace its possible connection with the Welsh *gwestva.*[202]　Nor can we here concern ourselves with

[201] *English Village Community,* 212 note.

[202] We might also compare the *droit de gîte* on the other side of the Channel.

the few scattered traces of it that we meet with elsewhere in Domesday. Its existence in four adjacent counties, with non-hidation as a common feature, is the point I wish to emphasize.

The system of grouping townships in the west for the payment of a food-rent (*firma unius noctis*) was exactly parallel to the grouping in the east for the payment, not of rent but of "geld." We can best trace this parallel in Somerset, because the *firma unius noctis* of the days before the Conquest had been there commuted for a money payment at the time of Domesday. Turning to the Cambridgeshire hundred of Long Stow, we find one of its "blocks" (of twenty-five hides) divided into three equal parts, while another is divided into three parts, of which one is half the size of the two others. And so in Somerset we have Frome and Bedminster combined in one group for the payment of this *firma*, and the two Perrotts similarly combined with Curry. Frome and Bedminster are each assigned the same payment, but in the other group the contribution of one is half that of the two others.

Here are the Somerset groups of demesne, each charged with the render of a *firma unius noctis*.

	Commutation.			£	s.	d.
Somerton (with Borough of Langport) .	79	10	7			
Chedder (with borough of Axbridge). .	21	0	2½	100	10	9½
North Petherton	42	8	4			
South Petherton	42	8	4	106	0	10
Curry Rivell.	21	4	2			
Williton						
Carhampton				105	17	4½
Cannington.						
Frome.	53	0	5			
Bruton	53	0	5	106	0	10
Milborne Port (with Ilchester)				79	10	7
[Bedminster[203]				21	0	2½]

[203] I am indebted for these identifications to Mr. Eyton's work.

Of these two last, Milborne Port is entered as having paid three-quarters of a *firma noctis* under the Confessor, while Bedminster—though in the midst of this group of *firma* Manors—is alone in having no render T.R.E. assigned to it. One is tempted to look on the two as originally combined in one *firma* (like Somerton and Chedder), save that the whole width of the country divides them, while in the other cases the constituents are grouped geographically.

The Wiltshire Manors, each of which rendered a *firma unius noctis*, were—

	Ploughlands.	Valets.
Calne	29	
Bedwin	79	
Amesbury . . .	40	
Warminster . . .	40	
Chippenham . . .	100	£110
"Theodulveshide". .	40	£100

From the figures given for Somerset and Wilts, it may fairly be concluded that, in this district the value of the "firma" was about £105. In Somerset, however, there was clearly a special sum, £106 0s. 10d., on which calculations were based.

An examination of Mr. Eyton's statements on the *firma unius noctis* in Somerset and Dorset would prove a peculiarly conclusive test of his whole system.

In the case of Somerset one need not dwell on his giving its amount for the Williton group as £105 16s. 6½d., when the sum named is £105 17s. 4½d., although absolute accuracy is, in these matters, essential. We will pass at once to the bottom of the page (ii. 2), and collate his rendering of Domesday with the original :—

"T.R.E. reddebat dimidiam firmam noctis et quadrantem" (Domesday).

"Reddebat T.R.E. dimidiam noctis firmam et unum quadrantem" (Eyton).

Domesday gives the payment (in a characteristic phrase), as *three-quarters* [a half and a quarter] of a *firma noctis.*

Mr. Eyton first interpolates a " unum," and then overlooks the " quadrantem," with the result that he represents the due T.R.E. as a *firma dimidiæ noctis* (i. 77). So far, this is only a matter of error *per se*. But Domesday records the commutation of the due T.R.W. at £79 10s. 7d. This proves to be *three-quarters* of the commutation, in two other cases, for a whole *firma noctis* (£106 0s. 10d.) Mr. Eyton, however, imagining the due to have been only *half a firma* set himself to account for its commutation at so high a figure (i. 77-8). This he found no difficulty in doing. He explained that " this was not a mere commutation," but " was doubtless a change which took into consideration the extra means and enhanced value of Meleborne."

The probability is, then, that what we have called the *enhanced ferm*, was enhanced by something less than the gross profits we have instanced ; that is, that a part of those profits, say the Burgage rents, or some of them, had contributed to the *dimidia firma noctis* before the commutation.

All these ready assumptions, we must remember, are introduced to account for a discrepancy which does not exist. Great masses of Mr. Eyton's work consist of similar guesses and assumptions. Now, if these were kept scrupulously apart from the facts, they would not much matter ; but they are so inextricably confused with the real facts of Domesday that, virtually, one can never be sure if one is dealing with facts or fancies.

And far more startling than the case of Somerset is that of Dorset, the " Key to Domesday." Mr. Eyton here held that Dorchester, Bridport, and Wareham paid a full *firma unius noctis* each, the total amount being reckoned by him at the astounding figure of £312 (p. 70)! Exeter, which affords a good comparison, paid only £18 (as render), though the king had 285 houses there : the three Dorset towns in which, says Mr. Eyton, the Crown had 323 houses, paid in all, according to him, £312. The mere comparison of these figures is sufficient. But further, Mr. Eyton observes

(p. 93), that in 1156 "Fordington, Dorchester, and Bridport" were granted by Henry II. to his uncle, "as representing Royal Demesne to the annual value of £60." This is an instructive commentary on his view that Dorchester and Bridport alone rendered £208 per annum. Our doubts being thus aroused, we turn to Domesday and find that it does not speak of any of these towns as paying that preposterous *firma*. The right formula for that would be "reddit firmam unius noctis" (p. 84). Instead of that, we only have "exceptis consuetudinibus quæ pertinent ad firmam unius noctis" (p. 70). The explanation is quite simple. Just as in Somerset, Mr. Eyton admits, Langport and Ilchester, although boroughs, were "interned" in groups of Royal demesne, paying the *firma unius noctis*, so in Dorset the boroughs were "interned" in groups of Royal demesne. Indeed one of these groups was headed by Dorchester, and is styled by Mr. Eyton the "Dorchester group." But he boldly assumed that "Dorchester" must have two different meanings :—

[A] We assume about 100 acres to have belonged to the Domesday Burgh, and perhaps 882 acres to represent land, subinfeuded at Domesday, and annexed to Dorchester Hundred. [B] It follows that we assume about 429 acres, [to be that] . . . which here figures [fo. 75] under the name Dorchester.

It is not too much to say that any one, who refers to pp. 70-73, 78-101 of the *Key to Domesday*, will find that the singular misconception as to the Dorset Boroughs makes havoc of the whole calculation. But here again the point to be insisted on is not the mere mistake *per se*, but the elaborate assumptions based upon it and permeating the whole work.[204]

Apart from the Manors grouped for a *firma unius noctis*, if we take the comital Manors (*mansiones de comi-*

[204] It is a further and fundamental error that Mr. Eyton speaks of the *firma unius noctis* as "borough taxation," whereas it was essentially of the nature of rent, not taxes.

tatu) of Somerset, which were in the King's hands in 1086, we find their rentals given on quite a different principle to those of the Manors in private hands.

(1) They are entered as renders ("reddit"), not as values ("valet").

(2) The sums rendered are "de albo argento."

(3) In at least ten out of the fifteen cases, they are multiples of the strange unit £1 3*s*.

As this fact seems to have escaped Mr. Eyton's notice, I append a list of these Manors, showing the multiples of this unit that their renders represent :—

	£	s.	d.	
Crewkerne	46	0	0	. 40
Congresbury . . .	28	15	0	. 25
Old Cleeve . . .	23	0	0	. 20
North Curry . . .	23	0	0	. 20
Henstridge . . .	23	0	0	. 20
Camel . . .	23	0	0	. 20
Dulverton . . .	11	10	0	. 10
Creech St. Michael .	9	4	0	. 8
Langford	4	12	0	. 4
Capton[205] . . .	2	6	0	. 2

Whatever this strange unit represented, it formed the basis in these Manors of a reckoning wholly independent of the "hides" or ploughlands of the Manor, and as clearly artificial as the system of hidation I have made it my business to explain.

XV. "WARA."

The meaning of "Wara" is made indisputable by the I.C.C. When land was an appurtenance, *quoad* ownership, of a Manor in one township, but was assessed in another in which it actually lay, the land was said to be in the former, but its "wara" in the latter. As this "wara" was an integral part of the total assessment of the township,

---

[205] I am indebted for these identifications to Mr. Eyton's work.

it had to be recorded, under its township, in the I.C.C.
Here are the three examples in point:—

[HISTON.]   De his xx. hidis jacet Warra de una hida et dimidia
in hestitone de manerio cestreford.   Hanc terram tenuit comes
alanus (*sic*) et est appretiata in essexia (p. 40).

[SHELFORD.]   De his xx. hidis tenet petrus valonensis iii. hidas
de firma regis in neueport. . . .   Hæc terra est berewica in
neueport, sed Wara jacet in grantebrigge syra (p. 49).

[TRUMPINGTON.]   De his vii. hidis [tenet] unus burgensis de
grenteburga i. virgam.   Et Warra jacet in trompintona, et terra in
grantebrigga (p. 51).

To these I may add a fourth instance, although in this case
the name *wara* does not occur :—

[BATHBURGAM.]   De his vii. hidis tenet Picotus in manu regis
dimidiam hidam et dimidiam virgam.   Hæc terra jacet in cestre-
forda et ibi est appretiata xxx. sol. in essexia (p. 36).

The lands at Histon and "Bathburgam" were mere outlying
portions of the royal Manor of Chesterford in Essex, and
those at Shelford were a "berewick" of the royal Manor
of Newport, also in Essex.   But they were all *assessed* in
Cambridgeshire, where they actually lay.

So also we read under Berkshire (61*b*): "Hæc terra
jacet et appreciata est in Gratentun quod est in Oxene-
fordscire, et tamen dat scotum in Berchesire."   Again (203
b) we read under Pertenhall : "Hec terra sita est in Bede-
fordsire, set geldum et servitium reddit in Hontedunscyre."
A good instance of the same arrangement in another part
of England is found in those Worcestershire Manors which
were annexed as estates to Hereford, but which were
assessed in those Worcestershire hundreds where they
actually lay (see p. 61).

A similar expression is applied to the possession of
"soca."   Thus under Shelford we read :—

De hac terra adhuc tenuerunt iii. sochemanni dimidiam hidam sub
gurdo comite.   Non potuerunt recedere sine licentia comitis gurdi.
Et soca jacebat in Witlesforda (p. 48).

Here the land was in Shelford, but the jurisdiction (soca) was attached to Earl Gyrth's Manor of Whittlesford.

Prof. Vinogradoff has dealt with "the word *wara*" in his *Villainage in England* (i. 241-244), and asserts that the "origin and use of the term is of considerable importance." But he does not allude to the above evidence, and I cannot follow him in his argument. While rightly disregarding Mr. Pell's fanciful derivation from "warectum," he asserts that :—

We often find the expression "ad inwaram" in Domesday, and it corresponds to the plain "ad gildam [*sic*] regis." If a Manor is said to contain seven hides *ad inwaram*, it is meant that it pays to the king for seven hides. . . . The Burton cartulary, the earliest survey after Domesday, employed the word "wara" in the same sense.

One cannot disprove the first proposition without reading through all Domesday for this purpose. I can only say that I do not remember ever meeting in Domesday Book with such an expression. The solitary instance of its use known to me is in the *Liber Niger* of Peterborough (p. 159), where we read : "in Estona sunt iii. hidæ ad in Waram"; and there the relevant entry in Domesday has no such expression. Of the statement as to the Burton cartulary, one can positively say it is an error. Its "waræ" have quite another meaning and are spoken of as virgates would elsewhere be.

Collation with what I have termed the Northamptonshire geld-roll renders it clear that "wara," in Domesday, represents the old English word for "defence," in the sense of assessment, the "defendit se" formula of the great Survey leading even to the phrase of "Defensio x. acrarum," for assessment to Danegeld, which is found in the first volume of Fines published by the Pipe-Roll Society.

XVI. THE DOMESDAY "JURATORES."

I now approach the subject of the Domesday *juratores*.
The lists of these in the I.E. and in the I.C.C. afford priceless information. The latter gives us the names for all but
three of the Cambridgeshire hundreds, the former for all
Cambridgeshire (one Hundred excepted) and for three
Hertfordshire Hundreds as well. The opening paragraph
of the I.E. tells us "quomodo barones regis inquisierunt,
videlicet per sacramentum vicecomitis scire et omnium
baronum et eorum francigenarum et tocius centuriatus
presbyteri prepositi vi. villani [*sic*] uniuscuiusque ville."[206]
Careful reading of this phrase will show that the "barones
regis" must have been the Domesday Commissioners.
The difficulty is caused by the statement as to the oaths of
the sheriff, the tenants-in-chief *(barones)*, and their foreign
(? military) under-tenants *(francigenæ)*. The lists of *juratores* contain the names of many *francigenæ* in their respective hundreds, but, so far as I can find, of no tenants-in-
chief. The sheriff, of course, stands apart. His name
indeed in the I.C.C. is appended to the list of jurors for
the first Hundred on the list, but is not found in the I.E.
Moreover, it should be noted that the above formula speaks
of all the tenants-in-chief, but only of a single hundred
court. Two hypotheses suggest themselves. The one, that
the sheriff and *barones* of the county made a circuit of the
Hundreds, and then handed in, on their oaths, to the commissioners a return for the whole county ; the other, that
the circuit was made by the commissioners themselves,
attended by the sheriff and *barones*. In the former case it
is obvious that the commissioners would fail to obtain at
first hand that direct local information which it was their
object to elicit : and further, when we find the sheriff and
barones charged with wrongdoing in these very returns,
it is, to say the least, improbable that they were their own

[206] We should perhaps read this as explaining the composition of the
centuriatus, viz. : "the priests, the reeves, and six villeins from each Vill."

accusers, especially in the case of such a sheriff as Picot at once dreaded and unscrupulous.

It seems, therefore, the best conclusion that the Domesday commissioners themselves attended every Hundred-court, and heard the evidence, sometimes conflicting, of " French " and " English."[207]

The *order* in which the Hundreds occur must not be passed over, because their sequence distinctly suggests a regular circuit of the country. Here is the sequence given in our three authorities :—the I.C.C., the I.E., and the lists of jurors prefixed to the latter :—

Staplehow.	Staplehow.	Staplehow.
Cheveley.	Cheveley.	Cheveley.
Staines.	Staines.	Staines.
Radfield.	Flammenditch.	Erningford.
Flammenditch.	Childeford.	Triplow.
Childerford.	Radfield.	Radfield.
Whittlesford.	([208])	Flammenditch.
Triplow.	Triplow.	Whittlesford.
Erningford.	Erningford.	Weatherley.
Weatherley.	Weatherley.	Stow.
Stow.	Stow.	Papworth.
Papworth.	Papworth.	Northstow.
Northstow.	Northstow.	Chesterton.
	Chesterton.	Ely.
	Ely.	

On comparing the first two of these lists it will be found that (except in the case of three contiguous Hundreds, which does not effect the argument) the Hundreds are taken in a certain sequence, which is seen, on reference to the valuable map prefixed to Mr. Hamilton's book, to repre-

[207] Of this conflict there is a good instance, almost at the outset of the Cambridgeshire survey (p. 3) :—"Hanc terram posuit Orgarus in vadimonio . . . ut homines Goisfridi dicunt. Sed homines de hundredo neque breve aliquid neque legat' R.E. inde viderunt, neque testimonium perhibent."

[208] Whittlesford omitted, because in this Hundred no lands were held or claimed by the Abbey.

sent a circuit of the southern portion of the county from
north-east to north-west, followed by an inquest on the
district to its north, the " two Hundreds " of Ely.

The third list, on the other hand, misplaces the Hundreds
of Triplow and Erningford altogether, and wholly omits
that of Childeford.   The transposition and omission are both
notable evidence that the B and C texts, as I shall urge,
were derived from some common original which contained
these defects.

The essential point, however, is that a circuit was made
of the county whether merely by the sheriff, or, as seems
most probable, by the Domesday Commissioners themselves
—the " barones regis " of the record—who must have
attended the several Hundred-courts in succession.

But when we speak of the Hundred-court it is necessary
to explain at once that the body which gave evidence for
the Domesday Inquest was of a special and most interesting character.   It combined the old *centuriatus*—deputations of the priest, reeve, and six villeins from each
township *(villa)*—with the new settlers in the hundred,
the *francigenæ*.   A careful investigation of the lists will
prove that half the *juratores* were selected from the former
and half from the latter.   This fact, which would seem to
have been hitherto overlooked, throws a flood of light on
the compilation of the Survey, and admirably illustrates
the King's policy of combining the old with the new, and
fusing his subjects, their rights and institutions, into one
harmonious whole.   Conquerors and conquered were alike
bound by their common sworn verdicts.[209]

We have the lists, in all, for eighteen Hundreds, fifteen in
Cambridgeshire and three in Herts, of which two were

[209] Compare Wilkins, 125 (quoted by Palgrave, *English Commonwealth*, i. 464) on English and "Welsh" in Devon :—"Disputes arising
between the plaintiffs and defendants of the two nations were to be
decided by a court of twelve 'lawmen'—six English and six Welsh—
the representatives of the respective communities.   And it may be observed that the principle which suggested this dimidiated tribunal was
generally adopted in our border law."

"double." There were, practically, for each Hundred exactly eight *juratores*, half of them "French" and half "English." But the two "double" Hundreds had sixteen each, half of them "French" and half "English." Although it is recorded that "alii omnes franci et angli de hoc hundredo juraverunt," it is obvious that the eight men always specially mentioned were, in a special degree, responsible for the verdict. Their position is illustrated, I think, by the record of a Cambridgeshire *placitum* found in the Rochester chronicles. This is the famous suit of Bishop Gundulf against Picot the sheriff in the County Court of Cambridgeshire,[210] which affords a valuable instance of a jury being elected to confirm by their oaths the (unsworn) verdict of the whole court :—

Cum illis (*i.e.* omnes illius comitatus homines) Baiocensis episcopus, qui placito præerat, non bene crederet; præcepit ut, si verum esse quod dicebant scirent, ex seipsis duodecim eligerent, qui quod omnes dixerant jure jurando confirmarent.

Now we read of this jury :—

Hi autem fuerunt Edwardus de Cipenham, Heiuldus et Leofwine saca de Exninge, Eadric de Giselham, Wlfwine de Landwade, Ordmer de Berlincham, et alii sex de melioribus comitatus.

Investigation shows that the names mentioned are local. The land in dispute was a holding in Isleham in the Hundred of Staplehoe. One juror, Eadric, came from Isleham itself, two from Exning, one from Chippenham, one from Landwade, while the sixth, Ordmer, was an undertenant of Count Alan, in the Manor from which he took his name (Badlingham), and was a Domesday juror for the Hundred. These six, then, were clearly natives chosen for their local knowledge. The other six, chosen "de melioribus comitatus," were probably, as at the Domesday inquest, Normans (*Franci*). Thus the double character of the jury would be here too preserved, and the principle of testimony from personal knowledge upheld

[210] Wharton's *Anglia Sacra*, i. 339.

So again in the Dorset suit of St. Stephen's, Caen (1122),[211] the men of seven Hundreds are convened, but the suit is to be decided " in affirmatione virorum de quatuor partibus vicinitatis illius villæ." [212] Accordingly, " sexdecim homines, tres videlicet de Brideport, et tres de Bridetona, et decem de vicinis, juraverunt se veram affirmationem facturos de inquisitione terræ illius." The names of the jurors are carefully given : " Nomina vero illorum qui juraverunt, hæc sunt." Again in the same Abbey's suit for lands in London, " per commune consilium de Hustingo, secundum præceptum regis, elegerunt quatuordecim viros de civibus civitatis Londoniæ qui juraverunt." And in this case also we read : " Hæc sunt nomina illorum qui juraverunt. . . . Et hæc sunt nomina eorum in quorum præsentia juraverunt." [213]

This corresponds, it will be seen, exactly with the writ to which the *Inquisitio Eliensis* was, I hold, the return : " Inquire . . . qui eas (terras) juraverunt et qui jurationem audierunt " (*infra*, p. 133).

Enough has now been said to show that the names of the Domesday jurors recorded for each Hundred represent a jury of eight, elected to swear on behalf of the whole Hundred, and composed of four foreigners and four Englishmen, in accordance with the principle that the conflicting interests ought to be equally represented.[214]

We may take, as a typical set of *juratores*, those for the Hundred of Erningford, the survey of which, in Mr.

---

[211] Palgrave's *Commonwealth*, ii. 183.

[212] This seems of great importance as a very early instance of the *quatuor villatæ* system, on which see Gross's "The Early History and Influence of the Office of Coroner" (*Political Science Quarterly*, vol. vii., No. 4), where the researches of Prof. Maitland and others are summarised.

[213] Only four, however, of the fourteen actually swore : "reliquos vero decem quietavit Willelmus abbas, qui parati erant jurare."

[214] The number eight perhaps, is unusual for the jury of a hundred, but we have an instance in 1222, of a "jurata per octo legales cives Lincolniæ et præterea per octo legales homines de visneto Lincolniæ" (*Bracton's Note-book*, ii. 121) ; and see Addenda.

Hamilton's book, occupies pp. 51-68. I give them in their order:—

[Francigenæ.]	[Angli.]
Walterus Monachus.	Colsuenus.
Hunfridus de anseuilla.	Ailmarus eius filius.
Hugo petuuolt.	Turolfus.
Ricardus de Morduna.	Alfuuinus odesune.

All four *francigenæ* can be identified in the Hundred. Walter held a hide and a quarter in "Hatelai" from the wife of Ralf Tailbois; Humfrey, a hide and a quarter in "Hatelai," from Eudo dapifer;[215] Hugh, a hide and a half in "Melrede," from Hardwin de Scalers; and Richard, three virgates in "Mordune," from Geoffrey de Mandeville. Of the *Angli*, Colsuenus was clearly Count Alan's under-tenant at three townships within the Hundred, holding in all two hides; "Ailmarus," his son, was, just possibly, the "Almarus de Bronna," who was a tenant of Count Alan in two adjacent townships, holding two hides and three-eighths; "Turolfus" and "Alfuuinus" cannot be identified, and were probably lower in the social scale.

It will be observed that Colsweyn belongs to a special class, the English under-tenants. He is thus distinct at once from the *Francigenæ*, and from the villeins of the township. He and his peers, however, are classed with the latter as jurors, because they are both of English nationality. In the great majority of cases the English *juratores* cannot be identified as under-tenants, and may therefore be presumed to have belonged to the township deputations.

XVII. THE "INQUISITIO ELIENSIS."

The record known by this name has long been familiar to Domesday students, but no one, so far as I know, has ever approached the questions: Why was it compiled? When was it compiled? From what sources was it com-

---

[215] His surname is there omitted, but his identity is proved by Humphrey "de Anslevilla" occurring elsewhere as an under-tenant of Eudo.

piled? These three questions I shall now endeavour to answer.

First printed by the Record Commission in their "Additamenta" volume of Domesday (1816), its editor, Sir Henry Ellis, selected for his text the most familiar, but, as I shall show, the worst of its three transcripts (Cott. MS., Tib. A. VI.), though he knew of what I believe to be the best, the Trin. Coll. MS., O. 2, 1, which seems to be the one styled by him 68 B 2.[216]   In his introduction he thus described it :—

> The *Inquisitio Eliensis* is a document of the same kind with the Exeter Domesday; relating to the property of the Monastery of Ely recorded afterwards in the two volumes of the Domesday Survey (p. xiv.)

From this it would seem that Ellis believed the *Inquisitio,* at any rate, to be previous to Domesday Book, but he practically left its origin altogether in doubt.

Sixty years later (1876) the *Inquisitio* was published anew, but without any further solution of the points in question being offered.[217]   For this edition three MSS. were collated, with praiseworthy and infinite pains, by Mr. N. E. S. A. Hamilton. Taking for his text, like Ellis, the Cottonian MS. Tib. A. VI., which he distinguished as A, he gave in footnotes the variants found in the MSS. at Trinity College, Cambridge, viz. : O. 2, 41 (which he termed B), and O. 2, 1 (which he distinguished as C). In Mr. Hamilton's opinion (p. xiv.) the "C" text "appears to have been derived from the 'B' MS. rather than the Cottonian" ("A"). From this opinion, it will be seen, I differ wholly.

A careful analysis of the three texts has satisfied me beyond question that while C is the most accurate in detail, it is marred by a peculiar tendency to omission on the part of its scribe. This indeed, is its distinctive feature. Now B cannot be derived from C, because it supplies the latter's omissions. On the other hand, C can-

---

[216] So I conclude from his *Introduction to Domesday*, i. 22, note 2.
[217] *Inquisitio Comitatus Cantabrigiensis*, pp. 97 *et seq.*

not be derived from B, because it corrects, throughout, B's inaccuracies. Consequently they are independent. More difficult to determine is the genesis of A, the worst of the three texts; but as it virtually reproduces all the inaccuracies found in B (besides containing many fresh ones), without correcting any, it can only be inferred that B was its source. Thus we have on the one hand C, and, on the other B (with its offspring A), derived independently from some common source. And this conclusion agrees well with the fact that a long catalogue of lands abstracted from the House of Ely is found in C, but not in A or B,[218] and with the circumstance that the famous rubric ("Hic subscribitur inquisitio"), which heads the inquisition in A and B, is placed by C at the end of the lists of jurors.

Starting from this conclusion, let us now proceed to ask, What was the document from which B and C copied independently? Clearly, it was not Domesday Book, for outside the eastern counties they record the returns in full, like the *Inquisitio Com. Cant.* itself. Were they then taken from the original returns, or at least from the copy of those returns in the *Inq. Com. Cant.?* This point can only be determined by close analysis of the variants; if we find B and C containing occasionally the same errors and peculiarities, although copied independently, it follows that the document from which they both copied must have contained those same errors and peculiarities. Let us take the case of Papworth. The right reading, as given both in Domesday and the *Inq. Com. Cant.*, I have placed on the left, and the wrong reading, in B and C, on the right :—

[tenet abbas] ii. hidas et iii. virgas et dim. [virgam].	[tenet abbas] ii. hidas et dim. virgam et [220] iii. virgas.
I. hida et i. virga et dimidia [virga] in dominio.	I. hida et dimidia virga et una virga [221] in dominio.

[218] Ed. Hamilton, pp. 184-189.

[219] *Ibid.*, pp. 97, 101.   [220] C omits "et."

[221] Here the scribe of C, puzzled by the evident corruption of the text from which he copied, read "inv[enit]."

Here are some further illustrations of errors in the I.E. :—

D.B. and I.C.C.	I.E.
VIII. hidas et dimidiam et dimidiam virgam . . . In dominio iii. hidæ et dimidia (p. 18).	VIII. hidis et dimidia et dimidia virga . . . iii. hidæ et dimidia *et dimidia virga* in dominio (p. 104).
II. carruce in dominio. Et tercia potest fieri (p. 21).	IIII[or.] carruce . . . in dominio.
I. hida *et dimidia* et xii. acræ in dominio (p. 87).	I. hida et xii. acræ in dominio (p. 110."
tenet Radulfus de Picot (p. 85).	Rod[bertus] tenet de vice-comite (p. 110).
Johannes filius *Waleranni* (p. 27).	Johannem filium *Walteri* (p. 103).

Again, the clause "Tost[222] pro viii. hidis et xl. acris," which ought to head the Hardwick entries, is wrongly appended in the I.E. (p. 110) to a Kingston entry with which it had nothing to do. So too, "hoc manerium pro x. hidis se defendit (*sic*) T.R.E. et modo pro viii. hidis," which belongs to Whaddon, is erroneously thrown back by the I.E. (p. 107), into Trumpington, a Manor in another Hundred. It is singular also that all the MSS. of the I.E. read "iii. cotarii" (p. 101), where D.B. and the I.C.C. have iii. bordarii (p. 3), and "x. cotarii" (p. 101), where they have "x. bordarii" (p. 6): conversely, the former, in one place, read "xv. bordarii" (p. 107), where the latter have "xv. cotarii" (p. 63).

In comparing the text of the I.E. with that of the I.C.C., we shall find most striking and instructive variants in the lists of *juratores* for the several Hundreds. Take, for instance, the lists for the Hundreds of Cheveley and Staines, which follow one another in both MSS.

I.C.C.	I.E.
CAUELEIE.	CAUELAI.[223]
Ric[ardus]	Ric[ardus] *prefectus huius hundreti.*

---

[222] "Toft" (rightly) in C.

[223] Chauelæi, C.

Euerard[us] filius Brientii	Æduuard[us] *homo Alb[er]ici de uer*
Radulfus de hotot	Radulfus de hotot
Will[elmu]s de mara	Will[elmu]s de mara
Stanhardus de seuerlei	Standard [224] de seuerlaio
Frauuin[us] de Curtelinga	Frawinus [225] de quetelinge [226]
Carolus de cauelei *Brunesune*	Carlo de cauelaio [227]
Vlmar[us] homo Wigoni *et o[mne]s alii franci et angli juraverunt*	Wlmar' homo Wighen [228]

The second name on these lists can be conclusively tested.
For the relative entry in the I.C.C. is "Esselei tenet euerard[us] [229] filius brientii de Alberico." This proves that the
I.C.C. is right in reading "Euerard[us]," while the I.E. is
right in adding "homo Alb[er]ici de uer."

These are the lists for Staines Hundred.

I.C.C.	I.E.
STANE	STANAS
Harold[us]	Alerann[us]
Roger[us]	Rogger[us] *homo Walt[er]i giffardi*[230]
Aleranus *francigena*	
Ric[ardus] fareman	Ric[ardus] *þ[ræ] fectus hui [us] hundreti*
	Farmannus
Huscarl de suafham [281]	Huscarlo de suafham[281]
Leofuuin[us] *de bodischesham*	Leofuuin[us]
	Harald *homo Hard[uuini] de scalaviis*
Alric[us] de Wilburgeham *et omnes franci et angli.*	Aluric[us] de Wiburgeham *et alii omnes franci et angli de hoc hundreto.*

---

[224] Stanhard[us], B, C.   [225] Frauuis, C.
[226] Chertelinge, C.   [227] Cheleia, C.
[228] Wigeni, C. This was "Wigonus de mara" (I.C.C.) or "Wighen"
(D.B.) Count Alan's under-tenant at Ditton.
[229] Eurard[us] in D.B.
[230] "Juraverunt homines scilicet Alerann[us], Rogger[us] homo
Walteri Giffardi" omitted in C.
[231] A sokeman of the Abbot of Ely at Suafham.

In these two lists the points to strike us are that Harold is placed first on one list and seventh on another; Aleran third on one list and first on another; and "Fareman" distinguished more clearly in the I.E. than in the I.C.C. as a separate individual.

If we now collect from the other Hundreds some instances of instructive variants, we shall obtain important evidence.

I.C.C.	I.E.
Rob[ertus] de Fordham	Rob[er]tus *angli[cus]* de Fordham
Picotus vicecomes	[Omitted] [232]
Walterus Monac[us]	Walt[erus] [233]
Gerardus Lotaringus *de salsintona*	Girardus lotherensis *Herveus de salsitona*
Pagan[us] homo hardeuuini	Paganus *dapifer* Hard'
Rad[ulfus] de *scannis*	Radulfus de *bans* [234]
Fulco *Waruhel*	Fulcheus *homo vicecomitis*
Rumold[us] *de cotis*	Rumold *homo comitis Eustachio*
Will[elmu]s	Will[elmus] *homo picoti vice comitis*
Wlwi *de doesse*	Wlwi de *etelaie*
Godlid de *stantona*	Godliue

I.C.C.	I.E.
FLAMENCDIC	FLAMMINGEDICH
Robert[us] de Hintona	Rodb[er]t[us] de Histona
Fulcard[us] *de Dittona*	Osmundus parvus
Osmund[us] parvulus	Fulcold *homo abbatis de Ely*
Baldeuuinus *cum barba*	Baldeuuinus *cocus*
Æduuin[us] presbyter	Æduuinus presbyter
Ulfric[us] de teuersham	Wlfuric de teuersham
Silac[us] *eiusdem villæ*	Syla
Godwun[us] *nabesone*	Goduuine *de fulburne*

It is impossible to examine the italicised variations in these

[232] Staplehoe Hundred.
[233] This is a noticeable case because "mo" has been interlined in B text of I.E., and because this man can be identified in I.C.C. and D.B. as an under-tenant in the Hundred.
[234] The I.E. version ("bans") is the right one.

parallel texts without coming to the conclusion that they must have been independently derived from some common original, an original containing more detail than either of them. On the other hand, the comparatively close agreement between the texts of the actual returns in the I.C.C. and the I.E. leads one to infer that these were copied with far more exactitude than the comparatively unimportant surnames of the jurors. For us the value of these variations in the jurors' lists lies in the evidence afforded on the origin of the existing MSS.

The object of this careful scrutiny has been to prove that as certain errors and peculiarities are found in two independent MSS., they must have existed in the original document from which both were copied, and which was neither the I.C.C. transcripts nor the original Domesday returns. What then was this document? It was, and can only have been, the true *Inquisitio Eliensis*, the date and origin of which I shall discuss below. Further, I should imagine this document to have probably been a roll or rolls, which—on its contents being subsequently transcribed into a book for convenience—was allowed, precisely as happened to the Domesday rolls themselves, to disappear. In perfect accordance with this view we find the whole contents of the *Inquisitio* arranged for a special purpose, and no mere transcript of the Domesday returns. Thus, after abstracting all the entries relating to the Cambridgeshire estates, and subjoining a list of houses held in Cambridge itself, it proceeds to add up all the items independently, and record their total values to the Abbey. This analysis is carried out for several counties (pp. 121-124), and is, of course, peculiar to the *Inquisitio*, although inserted between the abstracts of the Domesday returns for Cambridgeshire and Herts. So too the breviate or short abstract of the estates (pp. 168-173), which was part of the original document—for it is found in all the derived MSS.—must have been specially compiled for it, and so also was the *Nomina Villarum* (pp. 174-183).

B.H.

K

Another peculiarity of the *Inquisitio* is the care with which it records the names of sokemen on the Abbey estates when omitted in the I.C.C. and D.B. This may lead us to ask whether its compilers supplied these names from their personal knowledge. We might think not, for in some cases they are recorded by the D.B. and the I.C.C., while in one (p. 106) the I.E. actually omits the name, reading only " quidam sochemanus," where the other two documents (p. 46) supply his name (" Fridebertus "). From this we might infer that the names were probably recorded in the original returns, but deemed of too slight importance to be always copied by the transcriber. Yet the balance of evidence leads me to believe that the I.E. did supply names from independent knowledge. With the values, however, the case is clearer. The I.E. contains special and exclusive information on the value of socman-holdings, and must, I think, have derived it from some other source than the original Domesday returns. Here are some instances in point.

I.C.C.

III. sochemanni fuerunt . . . secundus homo abbatis de Ely tenuit ii.[235] hidas . . . Potuerunt recedere (p. 83).

X. sochemanni . . . et i. istorum homo abbatis de Ely fuit. Dimidiam hidam habuit. Non potuit dare neque vendere, et ii. istorum, homines predicti abbatis, iii. virgas habuerunt, vendere potuerunt ; soca remansit abbati (p. 91).

I.E.

In Erningetone fuit quidam sochemannus, *Ædwardus*, et habuit i. hidam. Homo abbatis Eli fuit in obitu regis Ædwardi, sed terram suam vendere potuit ; sed soca semper S. Ædeldrede remansit (p. 110).

In Ouro fuit quidam sochemannus *nomine Standardus*, qui dimidiam hidam habuit sub abbate ely. Non potuit ire ab eo nec separare ab ecclesia *et valet viginti solidos*. Et modo habet Hardwinus. Et alii ii. sochemanni iii. virgatas habuerunt. Potuerunt dare vel vendere sine soca cui voluerunt et modo tenet Hardwinus. *Et valet* xv. *solidos* (p. 112).

---

[235] Rectius " I. hidam."

Et x[us] [sochemannus] homo abbatis de ely fuit. i. hidam et dim. habuit. Et omnes isti recedere potuerunt; et vendere terram suam cui voluerunt (p. 95).

Quidam sochemannus sub abbate eli i. hidam et dim. tenuit T.R.E. potuit dare sine licentiam (*sic*) eius, sine socha. Et modo Picot vicecomes tenet eam sub abbate ely. *Valet* x. *sol.* (p. 113).

This last passage, of itself, is full of instruction. Firstly, the I.E. alone gives the value of the holding. Secondly, the I.E. preserves the "sine socha" which qualifies the holder's right. Now D.B. gives the last clause as :—

Hi omnes terras suas vendere potuerunt. Soca tantum hominis abbatis de Ely remansit æcclesiæ.

This qualification corresponds with the "sine socha" of the I.E., and is, we should observe, wholly omitted in the I.C.C. Thirdly, the three versions of the original return employ three different words to express the same one— "recedere," "vendere," "dare." Fourthly, the superiority of the C text of the I.E. over B (which makes two blunders in this passage) and of B over its offspring A (which adds a third) is here well illustrated. Fifthly, the phrase "Picot vicecomes tenet eam sub abbate ely" differs notably from Domesday, which assigns the estate to Picot unre-servedly, and still more from the I.C.C. which reads "tenet Robertus de Picoto vicecomite in feudo regis."

The next example is taken from the township immedi-ately preceding.

I.C.C.

V. istorum (sochemannorum) homines abbatis de Ely fuerunt. Et unus istorum i. virg. et dim. habuit. Non potuit recedere. Et alii iiii. habuerunt v. hidas et i. virg. Potuerunt recedere sine soca (p. 95).

I.E.

fuerunt quinque sochemani T.R.E. unus istorum *sugga nomine* habuit una virg. et dim. sub abbate ely. Non potuit rece-dere. *Et valet* x. *sol.* Et alii iiiior sochemani v. hidas et i. virg. tenuerunt de abbate eli. Potuer-unt dare preter licentiam abbatis et sine socha et modo tenet eam Picot vicecomes de abbate ely *et valet* iii. *lib.* (p. 112).

I have said that in all these cases it might perhaps be held that the additional details found in the I.E. were not due to special information possessed by its compilers, but were derived from the original returns, though omitted by their other transcribers. It is possible, however, to put the matter to the test. If, anticipating for a moment, we find that we have, for the eastern counties, in Domesday the actual materials from which the compilers of the I.E. worked, we can assert that any additional details must have been supplied from their own knowledge. An excellent instance in point is afforded by Tuddenham, in Suffolk :—

D.B.

In Tudenham Geroldus i. lib' hominem . . . comend' Saxæ de abbate T.R.E. xii. ac' pro man', iii. bord' Semp' i. car. ii. ac' prati . . . val. iii. sol. ; et in eadem ii. liberi homines comend' i. sancte Æ. et alter comend' heroldi x. ac', et dim. car. et val. ii. sol. Hoc tenet Geroldus de R. [de Raimes] (ii. 423*b*).

I.E.

In Tudenham i. li. homo Ælfric' commend' S. Ædel' xii. ac' et iii. b. et i. c. et iii. ac' prati et val. viginti iii. s.

In eadem i. l. ho' hedric'[236] commend' S. Ædel' viii. ac' et val' xx. den. Hoc tenet R. de Raimes (p. 151).

One knows not, truly, which blunder is the worst, that of the Domesday scribe, who has converted a probable "S. æ," [237] *i.e.*, Ely Abbey, into "Saxæ," or that of the compiler of the I.E., who, by interpolating the word "viginti," has converted three shillings into three-and-twenty. But the point is that the latter could name the Abbot's sokeman (nameless in Domesday) and could supply his acreage and the value of his holding. The actual details seem to have been :—

	Acres.	Pence.
Abllot's sokeman	8	20
Harold's sokeman	2	4
	10	24

Domesday records the totals only.

[236] C text.   [237] Commend' "S. æ." is found on 386*b*, *ad pedem*.

Enough has now been said of the twelfth century transcripts in which alone are preserved to us the contents of
the *Inquisitio*. We have seen that they point to the
existence of some common original, which, while closely
parallel with Domesday, as a record of the Abbey's possessions, contained certain special features and additional information. Why, when, and from what sources that original
was compiled, I shall now endeavour to explain.

XVIII. THE ELY RETURN.

The theory I propound for the origin of the so-called
Inquisitio Eliensis is that it was the actual return ordered
by that writ of the Conqueror,[238] of which a copy is given
in all three MSS. (A, B, C) and which is printed in Mr.
Hamilton's book, on p. xxi. (No. VIII.). I give the wording
of the writ, followed by the heading to the *Inquisitio* with
which it should be closely compared.

Willelmus Rex Anglorum Lanfranco archiepiscopo salutem.
. . Inquire per episcopum Constantiensem et per episcopum
Walchelinum et per ceteros qui terras sanctæ Ædeldrede scribi et
jurari fecerunt, quomodo jurate fuerunt et qui eas juraverunt, et qui
jurationem audierunt, et qui sunt terre, et quante, et quot, et
quomodo vocate [et] qui eas tenent. His distincte notatis et scriptis
fac ut cite inde rei veritatem per tuum breve sciam. Et cum
eo veniat legatus abbatis.

RETURN.

Hic subscribitur inquisicio terrarum, quomodo barones regis inquisierunt,[239] videlicet per sacramentum vicecomitis scire et omnium
baronum et eorum francigenarum, et tocius centuriatus, presbiteri,
prepositi, vi. villani [*sic*] uniuscujusque ville; deinde quomodo
vocatur mansio, quis tenuit eam tempore R.E., quis modo tenet.

---

[238] From internal evidence I hold this writ to have been sent from over
sea. It cannot have been issued by William Rufus, for the Bishop of
Coutances rebelled against him in 1088, and William Rufus did not go
abroad till later in his reign.

[239] This is usually quoted "inquirunt," which is the wrong reading.

quot hide, quot carruce[240] in dominio, quot hominum, quot villani, quot cotarii, quot servi, quot liberi homines, quot sochemanni, quantum silve, quantum prati, quot[241] pascuorum, quot molendina, quot piscine, quantum est additum vel ablatum, quantum valebat totum simul,[242] et quantum modo, quantum quisque liber homo vel sochemannus habuit vel habet. Hoc totum tripliciter, scilicet tempore regis Æduardi, et quando Rex Willelmus dedit et qualiter modo sit, et si potest plus haberi quam habeatur.

Isti homines juraverunt, etc., etc.

Especially important is the fact that the return contains the jurors' names, in accordance with the express injunction to that effect in the Conqueror's writ.

Now if this theory meet with acceptance, and the writ be taken to refer, as I suggest, to the Domesday Inquest itself, it follows that the Bishop of Coutances and Bishop Walchelin were the heads of the Domesday Commission for this district. This, of course, has been hitherto unknown; but it adds to the presumption in favour of the facts that Bishop Walchelin is not mentioned in any of the Ely writs as taking part in the *placita* concerning the Abbey's lands, and that, therefore, the only Inquest in which he could have been concerned was the Domesday Inquest itself. It should be added, however, that these two Bishops may have been, respectively, the heads of two distinct commissions for adjoining groups of counties.

The heading to the *Inquisitio Eliensis* is so well known, and has been so often quoted by historians, that it is a gain to fix its *status*, the more so as it has been loosely described as the "official" instructions for the Survey itself. We may also determine the date of the writ as the very close of the Conqueror's reign. For it must have been

---

[240] The right reading.

[241] Quantum in C text.

[242] The text here seems to be corrupt, C reading "tunc" for "simul." As the "tunc" and "modo" formula is represented in the next clause, it seems more probable that "simul" is the right reading, and refers to the totals entered in the *Inquisitio*. In that case the words "et quantum modo" are an interpolation.

to think, it is there meaningless. The point is worth
labouring. We see that the phrase cannot have occurred
in the original returns, where all the entries relating to
Marham would have come together. But if it was only
applicable to Domesday Book itself—where the fiefs were
separated—then must the I.E. have copied from Domesday
Book.

This, indeed, is the point to which I am working. For
Essex, Norfolk, and Suffolk, I believe, the compilers of the
Inquisitio (1086-7) must have worked from the second
volume of Domesday as we have it now. We see it *firstly*,
in the order of the counties; *secondly*, in the absence of the
jurors' names; *thirdly*, in the system of entering the lands.
With a fourth and minute test I have dealt just above.

But to make this clearer, we must briefly analyse the
return. The Cambridgeshire portion extends from p. 101 to
p. 120. It extracts from the original returns, hundred by
hundred, all that relates to the Abbey of Ely. Following
this is a note of its possessions in the Borough of Cambridge [247] (pp. 120-1), and then summaries of the Abbey's
estates, in *dominium* and *thainland* and *socha*, in all six
counties, and of the lands held by Picot the Sherriff,
Hardwin d'Eschalers and Guy de Rainbudcurt, to which
it laid claim as its own (pp. 121-124). Then we resume
with Hertfordshire, the extracts from the original returns
(pp. 124, 125). Both the Cambridgeshire and Hertfordshire
portions close with the words, "De toto quod habemus,"
etc., referring to the totals worked out by the Abbey from
the entries in the original returns.

With Essex, we enter at once on a different system.
This portion, which extends from p. 125 to p. 130 (line 8),
is arranged not by Hundreds but by fiefs. It first gives the
lands actually held by the Abbey (as coming first in Domesday), and then those of which laymen were in possession.
To the latter section are prefixed the words: "Has terras

[247] This also seems to have been taken from the detailed original
returns.

calumpniatur abbas de ely secundum breve regis." From
Essex we pass to Norfolk, the entries for which, commencing on p. 130 with the words " In Teodforda," end on
p. 141 at " Rogerus filius Rainardi." These again are
divided into two portions, namely, the lands credited to the
Abbey in Domesday (pp. 130-136), and those which it
claimed but which Domesday enters under other owners
(pp. 137-141). Between the two comes the total value of
the former portion and a list of the Norfolk churches held
by the Abbey. Last of the Eastern counties is Suffolk,
which begins on p. 141 at " In Tedeuuartstreu hund.," and
ends on p. 166. This also is in two portions, but the
order seems to be reversed, the alleged aggressions on the
Abbey's lands coming first and its uncontested possessions
last. The latter portion begins on p. 153, where the B text
inserts the word " Sudfulc."

The following parallel passages are of interest as showing how closely the I.E. followed D.B. even when recording
a judicial decision.

<table>
<tr><td>D.B.</td><td>I.E.</td></tr>
<tr><td>In dermodesduna tenuerunt xxv. liberi homines 1 car. terræ ex quibus habuit sca. Al. com-mend. et socam T.R.E. Tunc vi. car. modo ii., et iii. acre prati, et val. xx. sol. Rogerus bigot[us] tenet de abbate, quia abbas eam derationavit super eum coram episcopo de sancto Laudo, sed prius tamen tenebat de rege (ii. 383).</td><td>In dermodesdun a tenuerunt xxv. lib. homines 1 car. terre ex quibus habuit S. Ædel. sacam et socam et commend. T.R.E. Tunc vi. car. modo ii., et iii· acre prati, et val. xx. sol. R. bigot tenet de Abbate quia Abbas eam dirationavit super eum coram episcopo constan-tiensi. Sed prius tamen tenuit de rege (p. 157.)</td></tr>
</table>

The one variation, the Bishop's style, has a curious parallel
in Domesday Book (i. 165), where under the rubric " Terra
Episcopi Constantiensis " we read " Episcopus de Sancto
Laudo tenet," etc.

We may take it then that the compilers of the *Inquisitio
Eliensis* worked for Cambridge and Herts from the original

returns, but, for the eastern counties, from the second volume of Domesday. What are the corollaries of this conclusion? They used, for some reason or other, the second volume of Domesday, but not the first—if, indeed, it then existed. Speaking for myself, I have always felt not a little uneasy as to the accepted date for the completion of Domesday Book.[248] Mr. Eyton went so far as to write :—

Imperial orders have gone forth that the coming Codex, the Domesday that is to outlive centuries, is to be completed before Easter (April 5th, in that year [1086]), when King William himself expects to receive it in his Court and Palace of Winchester (*Notes on Domesday*, 15).

And he explicitly stated that—

On any hypothesis as to the time taken by the different processes which resulted in Domesday Book, the whole, that is the survey, the transcription, and the codification, were completed in less than eight months, and three of the eight were winter months. No such miracle of clerkly and executive capacity has been worked in England since." [249]

But was it worked then? All that the chronicle says of the King is that the "*gewrita* wæran gebroht to him," a phrase which does not imply more than the original returns themselves.

Of course, the chief authority quoted is the colophon to the second volume :—

Anno millesimo octogesimo sexto ab incarnatione Domini vicesimo vero regni Willelmi facta est ipsa descriptio non solum per hos tres comitatus sed etiam per alios.

It seems to have been somewhat hastily concluded that because the Survey (" Descriptio Angliæ ") took place in

[248] So far back as 1887 I raised this question, writing : " Indeed, heretical though the view may be, I see no *proof* whatever that Domesday Book was itself compiled in 1086 " (*Antiquary*, xvi. 8).

[249] *Domesday Studies*, pp. 625, 626.

1086, Domesday Book (which styles itself *Liber de Wintonia*), was completed in that year. The phrase "per hos tres comitatus" proves, surely, that "descriptio" refers to the Survey, not to the book. [250]

I have never seen any attempt at a real explanation of the great difference both in scope and in excellence between the two volumes, or indeed any reason given why the Eastern counties should have had a volume to themselves. For a full appreciation of the contrast presented by the two volumes, the originals ought to be examined. Such differences as that the leaves of one are half as large again as those of other, and that the former is drawn up in double, but the latter in single column, dwarf the comparatively minor contrasts of material and of handwriting. So, too, the fulness of the details in the second volume may obscure the fact of its workmanship being greatly inferior to that of the first. Of its blunders I need only give one startling instance. The opening words of the Suffolk Survey, written in bold lettering, are "Terra Regis de Regione" (281*b*). I have no hesitation in saying that the last words should be "de *Regno*." Indeed, the second formula is found on 289*b*, as "Terra Regis de Regno," while on 119*b* under "Terra Regis," we read "hoc manerium fuit de regno." So also in the Exon Domesday "Terra Regis" figures as "Dominicatus regis ad regnum

---

[250] The most erroneous date that has been suggested for Domesday is the year 1080. Ellis wrote, referring to Webb's "short account," that "the Red Book of the Exchequer seems to have been erroneously quoted as fixing the time of entrance upon it as 1080" (i. 3). Mr. Ewald,* following in his footsteps, has repeated his statement (under "Domesday Book"), in the *Encyclopedia Britannica* ; and, lastly, Mr. de Gray Birch asserts on his authority that "this valuable manuscript" is not responsible for that date (*Domesday Book*, p. 71). All these writers are mistaken. The *Diologus de Scaccario*, indeed, does not mention a year, but Swereford's famous Introduction, in the Red Book of the Exchequer, does give us, by an astounding blunder, the fourteenth year of the Conqueror 1079-1080) as the date of Domesday (see below, p. 264).

* Author of *Our Public Records.*

pertinens." [251] The muddled order of the tenants-in-chief for Norfolk and for Suffolk—where laymen precede the church [252]—is another proof of inferiority, but only minute investigation could show the hurry or ignorance of the scribes.

Now, all this might, I think, be explained if we took the so-called second volume to be really a first attempt at the codification of the returns. Its unsatisfactory character must have demonstrated the need for a better system, which, indeed, its unwieldy proportions must have rendered imperative. So drastic and so successful, on this hypothesis, was the reform, that while these three counties had needed a volume of 450 folios, the rest of England that was surveyed—some thirty counties—was compressed into a single volume of 382 folios, and on a system which rendered consultation easier and more rapid. In every respect the first volume is a wonderful improvement on the second, but the authorities may have shrunk from ordering the latter to have been compiled *de novo*, when the work, though unsatisfactory, had once been done.

This, it must of course be remembered, is all hypothesis, an hypothesis suggested by the facts. If it were proved that at the time when the Ely return was made, the "second" volume had been compiled, and the "first" had not, I should have established my case. But it might be urged that the "first" volume did exist at the time, and that the Ely scribes used the returns instead, because they contained fuller information. To this I reply, so far as the details of the estates are concerned, that neither the terms of the writ nor the heading of the *Inquisitio* involved the inclusion of such details as Domesday Book omitted. If the scribes inserted them, it must have been merely because they inserted everything they found in the records

---

[251] I am not sure that even "the pertin(ent) ad rege(m)" of the "first" volume (100*b*) is not a mistake for "regnum."

[252] On fo. 17 is a curious deleted list of church fiefs in Essex, which has no business there.

from which they copied. It might still be urged that they
went to the returns for the names of the *juratores* ; but why,
if so, did they not do so for the three eastern counties? It
certainly seems to me to be the most satisfactory explanation that the materials supplied for compiling this return,
as being the recognised official records, were the so-called
"second" volume of Domesday, and (for the rest) the
original returns.

XIX. FIRST MENTION OF DOMESDAY BOOK.

No one now-a-days should require to be told that the
pseudo-Ingulf's dealings with Domesday are devoid of all
authority. Some, however, may still believe in the tale
found in that "Continuatio" of his chronicle which is
fathered on Peter of Blois. It is there that Ellis found
(putting Ingulf aside) the only case of an appeal to its
witness before the reign of John.[253]

With the "Continuatio" I shall deal below,[254] but I
would observe, while on the subject, that the "pseudo-
Ingulf" (charters and all) was, I believe, largely concocted
by the help of hints gathered from Domesday Book.

The absence of any authoritative mention, in its early
days, of our great record gives a special importance to an
entry in the *Chronicle of Abingdon* (ii. 115-6), where we
read that Abbot Faritius was impleaded by certain men :—

Sed is abbas in castello Wincestre coram episcopis Rogero
Saresberiensi, et Roberto Lincolniensi, et Ricardo Londoniensi, et
multis regis baronibus, ratiocinando ostendit declamationem eorum
injustam esse. Quare, justiciarorum regis judicio obtinuit ut illud
manerium, etc. . . . sed quia rex tunc in Normanniâ erat,
regina, quæ tunc præsens erat, taliter hoc sigillo suo confirmavit.

Then follows the Queen's writ, announcing the decision
of the plea held in the royal "Curia," together with the
names of the "barons" present. These names enable us to

---

[253] *Introduction to Domesday*, i. 354.
[254] *Vide infra*, p. 188.

determine a certain limit for the date of the plea. "Thurstinus Capellamus," for instance implies that it was previous to his obtaining the See of York in 1114, while the presence of Richard, Bishop of London, places it subsequent to 26th July, 1108. It must, therefore, have been held during the King's absence between July, 1108, and the end of May, 1109; or in his later absence from August, 1111, to the summer of 1113.

The action of the Queen in presiding over this *placitum* illustrates a recognised practice, of which we have an instance in Domesday itself (i. 238*b*), where it is stated that Bishop Wulfstan, "terram deplacitasse coram regina Mathilde in presentia iiii^{or.} vicecomitatuum." The Queen's description of the *Curia Regis* as "curia domini mei et mea" should be compared with the phrase employed by the Queen of Henry II., who, similarly acting in her husband's absence, speaks of the Great Justiciar as "Justicia Regis et mea."

But the essential portion of the passage before us is this :—

> Sciatis quod Faritius abbas de Abendona in curia domini mei et mea, apud Wintoniam in thesauro . . . *per Librum de Thesauro*, diratiocinavit quod, etc.

The court was held "in castello Wincestre," says the narrative, "apud Wintoniam in thesauro," says the record. Both are right, for the Royal Treasury was in Winchester Castle.[255]

But what was the "Liber de Thesauro?" I contend that it was Domesday Book, and can have been nothing else, For, passing now to the *Dialogus de Scaccario (circ* 1177), we there read in reply to an enquiry as to the nature of Domesday Book (which "in thesauro servatur et inde non recedit"): "*liber ille* de quo quæris sigilli regii comes est individuus *in thesauro*" (I. XV.). The connexion of the

---

[255] Henry, says Orderic, in 1100, "concito cursu ad *arcem Guentoniæ, ubi regalis thesaurus continebatur*, festinavit."

Book with the Treasury is brought out strongly in the *Dialogus*, and leads to the presumption, as Mr. Hall perceived, that the Treasury being originally at Winchester, the Book was there also—as indeed we see it was under Henry I.[256] On the date of its removal to Westminster, there has been much discussion between my friend Mr. Hall and myself.[257] Mr. Hall relies mainly on the *Dialogus de Scaccario*, and on the inferences he draws from it, for the early removal of Domesday to Westminister, and the establishment there of the royal Treasury. For myself, I claim for the Winchester Treasury greater importance and continuity than he is willing to admit. The leading records, of course, were stored there as well as treasure. We find William Rufus speaking of "meis brevibus . . . qui sunt in thesauro mea Wyntoniæ";[258] and we read that, on his father's death, "pergens apud Wincestre thesaurum patris sui . . . divisit: erant autem in thesauro illo lx. m[ille] libræ argenti excepto auro et gemmis et vasis et palliis."[259] Heming's Cartulary describes the Domesday returns as stored "in thesauro regali," and Henry of Huntington states that "inter thesauros reposita usque hodie servantur."[260] Now, as the Treasury was in Winchester Castle at the time of the above suit, and as it had been in 1100[261] and 1087, so it was still at the accession of Stephen in 1135, and at the triumph of Matilda in 1141. This is absolutely certain from the Chronicles, nor do they ever mention any other Treasury. Moreover, the contents of this Treasury in 1135—"erant et vasa tam aurea quam argentea"—correspond with those described by the *Dialogus* forty

---

[256] This account of the Winchester placitum is taken from my second article on "The Custody of Domesday Book" (*Antiquary*, xvi. 9-10).

[257] *Academy*, 13 Nov., 1886; *Domesday Studies*, p. 537 note; and Mr. Hall's *Antiquities of the Exchequer*, chap i.

[258] *Mon. Ang.*, iii. 86.

[259] *Hen. Hunt.*, 211; Richard of Hexham says of Henry I's charter of liberties that "in ærari suo apud Wintoniam [eam] conservari præcepit" (p. 142).

[260] *Domesday Studies*, 546-7.

[261] *Supra*, note 255.

years later:—"vasa diversi generis aurea et argentea." Lastly, there is a piece of evidence which has not yet been adduced, namely, that in his *Expugnatio Hibernica* (1188), Giraldus, speaking of that ring and letters which John of Salisbury declared had been brought by him from the Pope, and were "still stored in the Royal Treasury," writes of

Annulum aureum in investituræ signum . . . qui statim simul cum privilegio *in archivis Wintoniæ* repositus fuerat.

Giraldus certainly must have looked on the Royal Treasury at Winchester as the only recognised repository for all such objects as these.

Mr. Hall, indeed, has gradually modified his original position that "Ingulphus saw the Domesday register, as it now exists, at Westminster," and that it was sent there for good from Winchester "early in the reign of Henry I.,"[262] but he still places the establishment of "the" Treasury at Westminster, in my opinion, too early. It is the gradual decay of Winchester as the capital and seat of adminstration that makes it difficult to say positively when or how the national records, Domesday Books among them, were transferred to Westminster. We have seen at least that, in its early days, the "Liber de Wintonia," as it styles itself, had its home within the walls of the Royal castle of Winchester; and I cannot but think, now as at first, that it began by visiting Westminster for Exchequer sessions only.[263]

In any case, we have seen its witness appealed to on a far earlier occasion than had hitherto been known. In my paper on "An Early Reference to Domesday,"[264] I quoted an even earlier mention of the "Descriptio Angliæ," but here again the reference seems to make rather to the Domesday Survey itself than to Domesday Book, the "Liber de Thesauro."

[262] *Athenæum*, 27th Nov., 1886.
[263] See also *Domesday Studies*, 547 note.[2]
[264] *Domesday Studies*, 539 et sq.

B.H.   L

As an appendix to this paper, I give the pedigree of the Domesday MSS. according to the views I have expressed.[652]

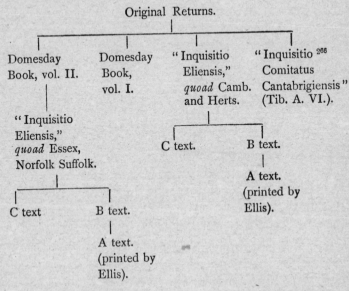

Original Returns.

Domesday Book, vol. II.

Domesday Book, vol. I.

"Inquisitio Eliensis," *quoad* Camb. and Herts.

"Inquisitio [266] Comitatus Cantabrigiensis" (Tib. A. VI.).

"Inquisitio Eliensis," *quoad* Essex, Norfolk Suffolk.

C text.

B text.

A text. (printed by Ellis).

C text

B text.

A text. (printed by Ellis).

[265] It will be observed that I do not touch the *Liber Exoniensis.*
[266] Possibly at second-hand, see p. 7 note, and Addenda.

THE NORTHAMPTONSHIRE GELD-ROLL.

THIS remarkable document was printed by Sir Henry Ellis (1833) in his *General Introduction to Domesday* (i. 184-187) from the fine Peterborough Cartulary belonging to the Society of Antiquaries (MS. 60). I shall not, therefore, reprint it here, but will give the opening entry as a specimen of its style :—

This is unto Suttunes (Sutton) hundred, that is an hundred hides. So it was in King Edward's day. And thereof is "gewered" one and twenty hides and two-thirds of a hide, and [there are] forty hides inland and ten hides [of] the King's ferm land, and eight and twenty hides and the third of a hide waste.

We have seen (*supra*, p. 59) that Ellis not only erred, but even led Dr. Stubbs into error, as to the character of the "hundreds" enumerated in this document. Except for that, I cannot find any real notice taken of it, although it has been in print over sixty years. It appears to be not even mentioned in Mr. Stuart Moore's volume on *Northamptonshire in Domesday*; and no one, it seems, has cared to enquire to what date it belongs, or what it really is.[1]

Now, although written in old English, it is well subsequent to the Conquest, for it mentions *inter alios* "Rodbertes wif heorles," who, we shall find, was Maud, wife of

---

[1] I have found, since this was written, that it was printed by Mr. T. O. Cockayne in his little-known *Shrine* (pp. 205-208), and pronounced by him (in error) to be "evidently" of the date 1109-1118.

the Count of Mortain. It also mentions William and Richard Engaine, Northamptonshire tenants in Domesday. On the other hand, it cannot be later than 1075, for it speaks of lands held by "the lady, the king's wife"; and this was Edith, Edward's widow, whose Northamptonshire lands passed to King William at her death in 1075. Of the very few names mentioned, one may surprise and the other puzzle us. The former is that of "the Scot King," holding land even then in a shire where his successors were to hold it so largely : the other is "Osmund, the King's writer," in whom one is grievously tempted to detect the future Chancellor, Saint and Bishop. But, apart from his identity, his peculiar style, exactly equating, as it does, the Latin "clericus regis," emboldens me to make the hazardous suggestion that we possibly have in this document an English rendering of a Latin original, executed in the Peterborough *scriptorium*.

For what was the purpose of the document? It may be pronounced without hesitation to be no other than a geld-roll, recording, it would seem, a levy of Danegeld hitherto unknown.[2] There are three features which it has in common with the rolls of 1084 : it is drawn up hundred by hundred ; it records the exemption of demesne ; and it specifies those lands that had failed to pay their quota.[3]

Its salient feature is one that, at first sight, might seem to impugn its authenticity. This is the almost incredible amount of land lying "waste." If we confine our attention to the land liable to geld represented by the first and fourth columns in my analysis below, we see that by far the

---

[2] I opposed in 1886 (*Domesday Studies* p.p. 86, 87) the accepted view that no Danegeld was levied by the Conqueror till the winter of 1083-4 and discussed (*ibid.*, 88-92) the *Inqisuitio Geldi*, which, as Mr. Eyton showed (*Key to Domesday*), belongs to that date. It has been persistently confused with the Exon Domesday (being bound up with it), as by Mr. Jones, in his Wiltshire Domesday (pp. xxxvii., 153 et sq.), and Professor Freeman (*Quart Review*, July, 1892, p. 22).

[3] It was connected, I find, by Mr. Cockayne with military service, not with Danegeld.

larger proportion of it is entered as "waste": yet this
witness to a terrible devastation is the best proof of its
authenticity; for it sets before us the fruits of those
ravages in the autumn of 1065, which are thus described
by Mr. Freeman, paraphrasing the English chronicle :—

Morkere's Northern followers dealt with the country about
Northampton as if it had been the country of an enemy. They
slew men, burned corn and houses, carried off cattle, and at last led
captive several hundred prisoners, seemingly as slaves. The blow
was so severe that it was remembered even when one would have
thought that that and all other lesser wrongs would have been forgotten in the general overthrow of England. Northamptonshire and
the shires near to it were for many winters the worse.

Mr. Freeman, had he read it, would have eagerly welcomed our record's striking testimony to the truth of the
Chronicle's words.

The devastation that our roll records had been well
repaired at the time of Domesday ; but we obtain a glimpse
of it in the Rockingham entry :—"Wasta erat quando rex
W. jussit ibi castellum fieri. Modo valet xxvi. sol."
(i. 220)

But it is not only that the entries of "waste" on our
roll are thus explained : they further prove it to be, as I
have urged, a "Danegeld" roll. For when we compare it
with the Pipe roll of 2 Hen. II. (1156), we find the latter
similarly allowing for the non-receipt of geld from land
"in waste"; and it is specially noteworthy that the portion thus "waste" is in every case, as on our roll, entered
after the others. The fact that the geld was remitted on
land that had been made "waste" is now established by
collation of these two records.

Incidentally, it may be pointed out that as our document
bears witness to the devastation of Northamptonshire in
1065, so the first surviving roll of Henry II. illustrates the
local range of devastation under Stephen. In Kent, which
had been throughout under the royal rule, the waste was

infinitesimal; in Yorkshire it was slight; but in the Midlands, which had long been the battle-ground of rival feudal magnates, it was so extensive that, as here in North-amptonshire after the Conquest, there was more land ex-empted as "waste" than there was capable of paying.

Before leaving this subject I briefly compare the cases of Northamptonshire and of East Sussex. In the former, we have seen, it is only our document that preserves for us evidence of the ravages in 1065; Domesday does not record them, because they had then (1086) been repaired. But in East Sussex, the entries are fuller; and as was observed by Mr. Hayley, an intelligent local antiquary :—

It is the method of Domesday Book, after reciting the par-ticulars relating to each Manor, to set down the valuation thereof, at three several periods, to wit, the time of King Edward the Confessor, afterwards *when the new tenant entered upon it*, and again at the time when the survey was made. Now it is to be observed in perusing the account of the Rape of Hastings in that book, that in several of the Manors therein *at the second of these periods*, it is recorded of them that they were waste, and from this circumstance it may upon good ground be concluded what parts of that Rape were marched over by, and suffered from the ravages of the two armies of the Conqueror and King Harold ; and indeed, the situations of those Manors is such as evidently shows their *then* devastated state to be owing to that cause.[4]

Mr. Freeman's treatment of this theory was highly characteristic. In the Appendix he devoted to the subject[5] he first contemptuously observed of the allusion to Harold's army :—

This notion would hardly have needed any answer except from the sort of sanction given to it by the two writers who quote Mr. Hayley. I do not believe that any army of any age ever passed through a district without doing some damage, but to suppose that Harold systematically harried his own kingdom does seem to me the height of absurdity.

[4] Quoted in Ellis's *Introduccion to Domesday*, i. 315-6.
[5] *Norm. Conq.*, iii 741-2.

And he, further, indignantly denied that such a King as Harold was "likely to mark his course by systematic harrying." Now, Mr. Hayley had never charged him with "systematic harrying;" he had merely traced with much ingenuity, the approach of his army to Senlac by the damage, Mr. Freeman admits, its passage, when assembled, must have caused.

The fact is that Mr. Hayley had, and Mr. Freeman had not, read his Domesday "with common care."[6] The latter started from the hasty assertion that

the lasting nature of the destruction wrought at this time is shown by the large number of places round about Hastings which *are returned in Domesday as* "waste."

Hence he argued, Harold, even had he been "Swegen himself"—

could not have done the sort of lasting damage which is implied in the lands being returned as "waste" *twenty years after.* The ravaging must have been something thorough and systematic, like the ravaging of Northumberland a few years later.

The whole argument rests on a careless reading of Domesday. It was on passages such as these that Mr. Hayley had relied :

Totum manerium T.R.E. valebat xx. lib. Et *post vasta fuit.* Modo xviii. lib. et x. sol.

Totum manerium T.R.E. valebat xiiii. lib. *Postea vastatum fuit.* Modo xxii lib.

Totum manerium T.R.E. valebat cxiiii sol. Modo vii. lib. *Vastatum fuit.*[7]

Thus, so far from being returned in 1086 as "waste," these Manors, we see, had already recovered from their devastation at the Conquest, and had even, in some cases, increased their value. And so Mr. Freeman's argument falls to the ground.

---

[6] The phrase employed by Mr. Freeman in criticising Prof. Pearson
[7] See Ellis, *ut supra.*

But as he was eager to vindicate Harold from a quite imaginary charge, I will try to clear William from Mr. Freeman's very real one. Having wrongly concluded that the ravages were "lasting," and must therefore have been "systematic," Mr. Freeman wrote:

There can be little doubt but that William's ravages were not only done systematically, but were done with a fixed and politic purpose (p. 413) . . . there can be little doubt that they were systematic ravages done with the settled object of bringing Harold to a battle. (p. 741).

Possibly the writer had in his mind the harrying of the lands of the Athenians, as described in the pages of Thucydides: but how can it have been politic for William, not only to provoke Harold, but to outrage the English people? It was Harold with whom his quarrel lay; and as to those he hoped to make his future subjects, to ravage their lands wilfully and wantonly was scarcely the way to commend himself to their favour: it would rather impel them, in dread of his ways, to resist his dominion to the death.

But if William's policy be matter of question, Domesday at least is matter of fact; and Mr. Freeman's followers cannot be surprised at the opposition he provoked, when we find him thus ridiculing a student for a charge he never made, and proved to have himself erred from his careless reading of Domesday.

I now append an analysis of the roll, showing the proportion of land "gewered,"[8] of "inland," of *terra regis*, of land which had not paid (in square brackets), and of "waste." The totals in square brackets are those given in the document; the others are those actually accounted for.

---

[8] "Wered," like "Wara" (*supra*, p. 115), refers to assessment, and corresponds with the "defendit se" phrase in Domesday. It seems here to represent the land which had actually paid.

	Inland.	Terra Regis.	Waste.	Total.	
Sutton	21⅔	40	10	28⅓	100 [100]
Warden	17¾	40		41¼	99 [100]
Cleyley	18	40		42	100 [100]
Gravesend . . .	18½	35	5	41½	100 [100]
"Eadbolds Stow"	23½	45	5	26½	100 [100]
"Ailwardsley" .	16½	40	[6½]	37	100 [100]
Foxley	16	30	21	33	100 [100]
Wyceste . . .	19[9]	40	20	21	100 [100]
Huxlow	8	15		39	62 [62]
Willybrook . . .	7	11	31	13	62 [62]
Upton Green . .	50	27	[3½]	29½[10]	110 [109]
Neuesland . . .	[80½][11]	59	[8]	12½	[160]
Navisford . . .	15	14		33	62 [62]
Polebrook . . .	10	20		32	62 [62]
Newbottlegrove .	44⅞	72		33⅛	150 [150]
Gilsborough . .	16	68		66	150 [150]
Spelho	20½	[Borough 25] [16]		28½	90 [90]
Wiceslea W. . .	10	40		30	80 [80]
Wiceslea E. . ,	15	34		31	80 [80]
"Stotfald" . . .	9⅛	40		50⅛	99¼ [100]
Stoke	18	[10]		12	[40]
Higham	49½	44		56	149½ [150]
"Malesley" . .	12	30	8	30	80 [80]
Corby	8½	12¼	12¼ [?4]	10¾	47¾ [47]
Rothwell . . .	10	20	7½ [7½]		45[12] [60]
"Andwertheshoe"	[?26][13]	25		39	[90]
Ordlingbury . .	29½	24½		21	80 [80]
"Wimersley" . .	41	60		49	150 [150]

The persons mentioned as not having paid can in most cases be identified. Thus "Robert the Earl's wife" is one

---

[9] Wrongly given by Ellis and Cockayne as "xviii."

[10] Wrongly given by Ellis as "viii. and xx."

[11] The MS. reads, "thus micel is gewered . . . viiii. and xx. hida and i. hida and viiii. and fifti hida inland." The text is clearly corrupt.

[12] There is no entry for "waste" in this hundred, so that possibly the words, "xv. hida westa" are omitted.

[13] There are clearly some words omitted here in the Peterborough transcript. We must read: "and thereof is 'gewered' [? 26 hide and] five and twenty hides inland.

of those in Rothwell Hundred, whose land was "unwered."
This was clearly Maud, wife of Count Robert of Mortain,
who had been given lands by her father, Roger of Mont-
gomery, at Harrington in this Hundred. Domesday, it is
true, where it figures as "Arintone," knows it only as
"Terra æcclesiæ de Grestain" (222 *b*); but a charter of
Richard I. (*per Inspeximus*) confirms to the Abbey "ex dono
Matildis Comitisse Moreton . . . xxxii. hidas terre quas
dederat ei pater suus Rogerus de Montegomerico, scilicet
apud Haxintonam (*sic*) viii. hidas, etc."[14] As the lands had
first been given to Roger, then by him to his daughter, and,
finally, by her to the Abbey, I cannot think our document
earlier, at any rate, than 1068. Edith, whose name proves
it not to be later than 1075, is entered as "the lady, the
King's wife," holding eight hides in Neuesland Hundred,
and again as a holder in Rothwell Hundred, under the
name of "the King's wife." Both entries, doubtless, refer
to her wide-spreading Manor of "Tingdene" (I. 222), parts
of which lay in both the above Hundreds. Of the other
holders we may notice "Urs" (? Urse d'Abetot), and
"Witeget the priest"; but these are quite eclipsed by
Richard and William Engaine, of whom the former occurs
twice and the latter thrice on the roll. In Spelho Hundred
"Richard" seems to be credited with ten hides at "Habin-
tune" on which "nan peni" had been paid. In Domesday
his holding at Abintone is given as *four* hides (i. 229). In
the same Hundred, William's land at "Multune" is in
default. Moulton is not entered under his fief in Domesday,
but under that of Robert de Buci we find a "William"
holding of him a hide and a virgate and a half in Moulton.
This was William Engaine, as was the "William" of our
roll; and in the Hen. I.-Hen. II. survey,[15] we find land in
Maulton entered as of Engaine's fee. Still more interesting is it to note that so late as 25 Ed. I. more than two
centuries after Domesday, John Engayne is found holding
half a fee in Moulton of Ralf Basset, and Basset of the

---

[14] *Monasticon*, vi. 1090.   [15] *Infra*, p. 215.

King *in capite*. For, as our Leicestershire survey shows,[16] the Domesday fief of Robert de Buci had passed to Basset, of whose heir, therefore, Engayne held, as his ancestor had held of Robert de Buci, in the days of William the Conqueror.

It is particularly instructive to follow out the Northamptonshire fief of William Engaine. In Domesday (i. 229) he is entered only as "Willelmus" holding 3½ hides in Pytchley (*Piteslea*), and Laxton (*Lastone*), worth at that time, £3 10s. "Vitalis" Engaine was his heir in 1130, for the Pipe Roll of 31 Hen. I. (p. 82) records his discharge of a debt to the crown "ut rehabeat terram suam de Laxetona." And this is confirmed by the survey of 1125 in the *Liber Niger* of Peterborough, where we read under "Pihtesle" (p. 162): "Et Vitalis reddit iii. solidos pro i. virga," this being the "i. virga" assigned to him in the list of Peterborough knights (*ib.*, p. 169). The "Rotulus de Dominabus" (1185) shows us the "Piteslea" estate in the hands of Margaret Engaine, makes it worth £6, and mentions that her heir was Richard Engaine (p. 14). The "Testa de Nevill" (p. 37) enters Richard "de Angayne" as holding five carucates of land in "Pettesle" and "Laxeton" worth £6 a year. It tells us, further, that he held them by serjeanty—" et est venator leporum, et facit servitium." From the nature of this return I assign it to the inquest of 1198, in which case it is of some value, as identifying five carucates under the new assessment with the 3½ hides recorded in Domesday.[17] Fulc de Lisures, on the other hand—the heir of the Richard Engaine of Domesday, returned himself in 1166, as the King's forester in fee, and attending the King's person, with his horn hanging from his neck.[18]

[16] Infra, p. 212.

[17] See my paper on "The great carucage of 1198" (*Eng. Hist. Rev.*, iii, 501 et sq.).

[18] "Et ego ipse custodio forestagium Regis de feodo meo ; et debeo ire cum corpore Regis in servitio suo paratus equis et armis, cornu meo in collo meo pendente."—*Lib. Rub.*, i 333.

The association of Pytchley with hunting is carried back even further still. For Richard and William Engaine had for their predecessor in title, Ælfwine the huntsman ("venator"), who owned their lands when King Edward sat upon the throne.

Among the lands deducted we observe in Spelho Hundred "fif and xx. hida byrigland." This represents the assessment in hides of the Borough of Northampton, and, so far as I know, is the only mention of that assessment to be found. In my paper on "Danegeld and the Finance of Domesday," I pointed out that Bridport and Malmesbury were assessed at five hides each, Dorchester, Wareham, and Hertford at ten hides, Worcester at fifteen, Bath and Shaftesbury at twenty, etc.[19] Northampton (we now see) was assessed in the same manner, and Chester and Huntingdon at no less than fifty hides each. Thus they admirably illustrate assessment in terms of the five-hide unit. We find this primitive system obsolete in 1130, when a borough gave an "auxilium" where its county paid Danegeld. But our roll implies that, here at least, it was already obsolete in the early days of the Conquest; for the twenty-five hides of "byrigland" are, for the payment of "geld," deducted from the Hundred.

From the date I have assigned to this document (*ante-*1075), it may fairly claim to represent our earliest financial record. Its illustrative value for Danegeld and the Hundred, and consequently for Domesday Book, will be obvious to every student.

[19] *Domesday Studies*, pp. 117-119.

THE KNIGHTS OF PETERBOROUGH

(*Temp.* HENRY I.)

THE interesting "Descriptio militum de Abbatia de Burgo" is found in the same MS. as the North-amptonshire Geld-roll.[1] It was printed by Stapleton in the appendix to his *Chronicon Petroburgense* (pp. 168-175)[2], but no attempt was made to date it. The name of Eudo Dapifer proves that it cannot have been compiled later than 1120. On the other hand, it cannot well be earlier than 1100, for some of the Domesday tenants had been succeeded by their sons—Robert (?) Marmion, for instance, by Roger, and Coleswegen by Picot—while the mention of "Gislebertus filius Ricardi," possibly the son of Richard of "Wodeford" (i. 224*b*), points in the same direction. As the majority of names, however, seem to be those of Domes-day tenants, it is probable that the list is not later than the Lindsey survey itself, if, indeed, it is not earlier. The first entry it contains is a good specimen of its value :—

Asketillus de Sancto Medardo tenet de abbatia de Burch in Hamtonascira x. hidas et iii. partes i. virgæ, et in Lincolnescira iii. carrucatas et inde servit se vi. milite. Et de feudo hujus militis dedit rex Willelmus senior Eudoni Dapifero in Estona hidam et dimidiam et mandavit de Normannia in Angliam Episciopo Con-stantiarum et R. de Oilli per breves suos ut inde darent ei excam-bium ad valens in quocomque vellet de iii. vicinis comitatibus; sed abbas noluit.

[1] Society of Antiquaries' MS. 60.
[2] Ed. Camden Society.

We duly find "Anschitillus" in Domesday, holding "Witheringham," Northants and "Osgodeby," Linc., of the Abbot (i. 221*b*, 345*b*). In the same way we are enabled to identify the "Rogerius Infans" of our list with "Rogerius" who held "Pilchetone," according to Domesday (i. 221*b*), of the Abbot, "Ascelinus de Waltervilla" with the "Azelinus" of Domesday (*ib.*), "Gosfridus nepos Abbatis," with "Goisfridus" who held in 'Sudtorp' (*ib.*), and "Rogerius Malfed" with that "Rogerius" who held of the Abbot at Woodford (i. 222). "Rogerus," on the other hand, who held in Domesday two hides at Milton, Northants (i. 221*b*), and seven bovates at Cleatham, Linc. (i. 346), is represented in our list by the entry :—

Turoldus de Meletona ii. hidas in Hamtonascira, et in Lindeseia vi. bovatas, et inde servit se altero milite (p. 171).

The chief lesson taught us here is the rashness of assuming the identity of tenants happening to bear the same name. For even among the few who are named as holding of the Abbot of Peterborough, we have found three Rogers quite distinct from one another.

The entries which follow are of value as absolute proofs of succession :—

DOMDESDAY.	DESCRIPTIO MILITUM.
In Dailintone tenet Ricardus de abbate iiii.ᵒʳ· hidas (i. 222).	Rodbertus filius Ricardi iiii. hidas in Hamtonascira, et inde servit se altero milite (p. 175).
In Risun habuit Elnod iiii. bovatas terre ad geldum . . . Nunc habet Colsuan de abbate Turoldo (i. 345*b*	Picotus filius Colsuaini habet dimidiam carrucatam in Rison, quam abbas dedit patri suo tali servicio quod esset ad placita abbatis et manuteneret res suas et homines suos in scira et in aliis locis (p. 175).

This second entry not only records a peculiarly interesting enfeoffment, but identifies 'Colsuan,' the Abbot's under-tenant at Riseholme, with no less a person than the conqueror's "English favourite Coleswegen, . . . an Englishman who, by whatever means, contrived to hold up his head among the conquerors of England."[3]

As sons, in such cases as these, have succeeded their fathers, it need not surprise us that our list comprises some names that are found in the *Liber Niger* survey of 1125.[4] Vivian, whom, it tells us, Abbot Turold had enfeoffed at Oundle (p. 175) occurs there in that survey (p. 158), as does Robert d'Oilli at Cottingham (pp. 159-173).[5] Vitalis ("Viel") Engaine had succeeded William (Engaine) at Pytchley both in our list and in the survey of 1125 (cf, *ante*, p. 155).

One of the most interesting and important points in this list of knights is the gleam of new light it throws on Hereward "the Wake." In it we read :—

Hugo de Euremou iii. hidas in dominio et vii. bovatas in Lincolne-shira, et servit pro ii. militibus.

Ansford iii. carucatas et servit pro dimidia hida (*sic*).

Now Hugh de Euremou is the name of the man who, according to the pseudo-Ingulf, married Hereward's daughter. Here we have proof of his real existence, and are enabled moreover to detect him, I claim, in that Hugh who, as a "miles" of the Abbot, held three hides at "Edintone" [Etton, Northants] in Domesday (i. 222). Mr. Freeman speaking of the vacancy at Bayeux in 1908, wrote :—

William at once bestowed the staff on Turold, the brother of

[3] *Norman Conquest*, iv. 219. We know *aliunde* that "Picot filius Colsuani" was the son of Colswegen of Lincoln. It would seem to be of this estate that we read in the "Clamores" :—"Abbas de Burg clamat iiii. bov. terræ in Risun terra Colsuani, et Wap' testatur quod T.R.E. jacuerunt in æcclesia Omnium Sanctorum in Lincolia."

[4] Society of Antiquaries' MS. 60. Printed by Stapleton *ut supra*.

[5] But possibly the Robert d'Oilli of our list may be the *first* Robert (who, as "Robertus" in Domesday, held Cranford of the Abbot), while the tenant of that name in 1125 may be the *second* Robert, entered in the Pipe Roll of 1130, and living *temp* Stephen.

Hugh of Evermont [*sic*], seemingly the same Hugh who figures in the legend of Hereward as his son-in-law and successor.[6]

But the French editors of Ordericus, in a note to the passage from which this statement was taken (iv. 18), speak of our man as "Hugue d'Envermeu, donateur du prieuré de St. Laurent d'Envermeu à l'Abbaye de Bec."[7]

Turning for a moment from Hugh to Ansford, we read in the Lincolnshire "Clamores":—

Terram Asford in Bercham hund' dicit Wapentac non habuisse Herewardum die quo aufugiit (D.B., i. 376*b*).

About this entry, as Mr. Freeman observed, "there can be no doubt." But as the result of his careful inquiry,[8] he limited "our positive knowledge," from Domesday, to this entry and to two in the text of the Lincolnshire survey (364*b*-377). It is strange that he did not follow up the clue the "Clamores" gave him. The relevant entry in the text of the Survey is duly found under the Peterborough fief:—

In Witham et Mannetorp et Toftlund habuit *Hereward* xii. bovatas terræ ad geldum. . . . Ibi Asuert [*sic*] homo abbatis Turoldi habet, etc. . . .
Berew[ita] hujus M. in Bercaham et Estou i. carucata terræ ad geldum. . . . Ibi Asford habet, etc. . . .
In Estov Soca in Witham iiii. bovatæ terræ et dimidia ad geldum. . . . Ibi Asfort de abbate habet, etc. . . . (i. 346).

This is the "terra Asford" referred to in the "Clamores," and, as amounting to $3\frac{1}{16}$ carucates, it is clearly the "iii. carucatas" assigned in our list to "Ansford." Thus, through his successor Ansford, we have at last run down our man; Hereward was, exactly as is stated by Hugh "Candidus," a "man" of the Abbot of Peterborough; and

---

[6] *William Rufus* i. 571. He makes it "Evermouth" in the *Norman Conquest.*
[7] Envermeu lay on the coast some 10 miles to the east of Dieppe.
[8] "The legend of Hereward" (*Norm. Conq.*, iv. [1st Ed.], 805).

his holding was situated at Witham on the Hill,[9] not far from Bourne, and, at Barholme-with-Stow a few miles off, all in the extreme south-west of the county. This is the fact for which Mr. Freeman sought in vain, and which has eluded Professor Tout, in his careful life of the outlaw for the *Dictionary of National Biography.*

We are now in a position to examine the gloss of Hugh " Candidus," showing how " Baldwin Wake " possessed the holdings both of Hugh and of Ansford : [10]—

Primus Hugo de Euremu. Baldwinus Wake tenet in Depinge, Plumtre, et Stove feoda duorum militum. . . . Et præterea dictus Baldewinus tenet feodum unius militis in Wytham et Bergham de terra Affordi. Et prædictus Baldewinus de predictis feodis abbati de Burgo debet plenarie respondere de omni forensi [servitio].

Here we see how the legendary name and legendary position of Hereward were evolved. The Wakes, Lords of Bourne, held among their lands some, not far from Bourne, which had once been held by Hereward. Thus arose the story that Hereward had been Lord of Bourne ; and it was but a step further to connect him directly with the Wakes, by giving him a daughter and heir married to Hugh de Evermou, whose hands had similarly passed to the Lords of Bourne. The pedigree-maker's crowning stroke was to make Hereward himself a Wake,[11] just as Baldwin fitz Gilbert (de Clare) is in one place transformed into a Wake.[12] The climax was reached when the modern Wakes revived the name of Hereward, just as " Sir Brian Newcome of Newcome " set the seal to his family legend by giving his children " names out of the Saxon calendar."

[9] With its hamlets of Manthorpe and Toft with Lound.

[10] Ed. Sparke *Historiæ Anglicanæ Scriptores* [1723].

[11] Professor Tout throws out the unlucky suggestion : "the *Wake, i.e.,* apparently the watchful one."

[12] See the new *Monasticon* on Deeping Priory, and the rubric to Baldwin's charter. The true parentage of Baldwin fitz Gilbert will be shown *infra* in the paper on " Walter Tirel and his wife."

Returning to Hereward himself, we find Mr. Freeman writing (of the spring of 1070) :—

At this moment we hear for the first time of one whose mythical fame outshines all the names of his generation, and of whom the few historical notices make us wish that details could be filled in from some other source than legend. . . . Both the voice of legend and the witness of the great Survey agree in connecting Hereward with Lincolnshire, but they differ as to the particular spot in the shire in which he is to be quartered. Legend also has forgotten a fact which the document has preserved, namely, that the hero of the fenland did not belong wholly to Lincolnshire, but that he was also a landholder in the distant shire of Warwick. But the Survey has preserved another fact with which the legendary versions of his life have been specially busy. Hereward, at some time it would seem, before the period of his exploits, had fled from his country.

Let us first dismiss from our minds the alleged fact as to Warwickshire. There is absolutely nothing to connect the Count of Meulan's tenant there with the Lincolnshire hero ; indeed Mr. Freeman admits in his appendix " that the Hereward of these entries may be some other person " (p. 805). Legend had an excellent reason for ignoring this alleged " fact " as had " romances " for having " perversely forgotten " to mention the deeds or the fate of William Malet in the Isle (Ib., p. 473). We must also dismiss the " fact "—" undoubted history " though it be (Ib., p. 805)—of Hereward's " banishment " at some time between 1062 and 1070. For the Survey gives no date ; it merely speaks of " die quâ aufugiit " (i. 376*b*), which phrase, in the absence of evidence to the contrary, must be referred to his escape from the " Isle," [14] when (1071) in the words of Florence, " cum paucis evasit." This at once explains the Domesday entry (*ante*, p. 160), for he would, of course, have forfeited his holding before that date.

[13] *Norm. Conq.* (1st. Ed.), iv. 455-6.
[14] *Norm. Conq.* (1st Ed.), iv. 484. Professor Tout, however, follows Mr. Freeman, and accepts an earlier " flight from England " as a fact. One must therefore insist that " the whole story has no historical basis."

"But leaving fables and guesses aside," in Mr. Freeman's words, "we know enough of Hereward to make us earnestly long to know more" (p. 456). My proof that the English hero was a "man" of the Abbot of Peterborough explains why "Hereward and his gang," as they are termed in the Peterborough Chronicle, "seem," Mr. Freeman is forced to admit, "to be specially the rebellious tenants of the Abbey," as distinct from the Danes and the outlaws (p. 459). And the vindication, on this point, of Hugh Candidus' accuracy makes one regret that Mr. Freeman, though eager for information as to Hereward, ignored so completely that writer's narrative. It is in absolute agreement with the Peterborough Chronicle, Mr. Freeman's own authority, but records some interesting details which the Chronicle omits.[15] These place Hereward's conduct in a somewhat different light, and suggest that he may really have been loyal to the Abbey whose "man" he was. His plea for bringing the Danes to Peterborough was that he honestly believed that they would overthrow the Normans, and that the treasures of the church would, therefore, be safer in their hands. He may perfectly well have been hostile to the Normans, and yet faithful to the Abbey so long as Brand held it; but the news that Turold and his knights were coming to make the Abbey a centre of Norman rule against him[16] would drive him to extreme courses. Professor Tout has made some use of Hugh, but says, strangely, that "the stern rule of the new Abbot Turold drove into revolt the tenants," when his rule had not yet begun.

Again, there is now no doubt where Hereward ought "to be quartered." Two other places with which the Domesday

---

[15] I am tempted, indeed, to suggest that Hugh may have had before him that lost local "account of Hereward's doings," which was inserted (but, according to my own view, in an abbreviated form) into the earlier chronicle, according to Professor Earle (see *Norm. Conq.*, iv. 461, note 3). This solution would explain everything, and would, if accepted, greatly increase the importance of Hugh's chronicle.

[16] Cf. William of Malmesbury *in loco*.

survey connects him are Rippingale and, possibly, Laughton to the north of Bourne. Living thus on the edge of the fenland, he may well have been a leader among "that English folk of the fenlands" who rose, says the Peterborough Chronicle, in the spring of 1070, to join the Danish fleet and throw off the Norman yoke. And the prospect of being ousted from his Peterborough lands by a follower of the new French abbot would have added a personal zest to his patriotic zeal.

Mr. Freeman, followed by Professor Tout,[17] holds that the story in the false Ingulf is not to be wholly cast aside, as it may contain some genuine Crowland tradition;[18] but he has not accurately given that story. It might hastily be gathered, as it was by him, that it was Hereward's mother-in-law who "very considerately takes the veil at the hands of Abbot Ulfcytel," whereas it was, according to the *Gesta*, his wife who did this. The *Gesta* version, he writes, "of Turfrida going into a monastery to make way for Ælfthryth is plainly another form of the story in Ingulf, which makes not herself but her mother do so." But if the *Historia Ingulphi* (pp. 67-8) be read with care, it will be seen that "mater Turfridæ," should clearly be "mater Turfrida," the reading that the sense requires. So there is here no opposition, and Ingulf merely follows the *Gesta* version.

As for the honour of Bourne, it can be shown from the *carta* of Hugh Wac in 1166, from our list of knights, and from the Pipe-Roll of 1130, to have been formed from separate holdings and to have descended as follows:—

[17] *Dictionary of National Biography.*
[18] Appendix on "the Legend of Hereward," *ut supra.*

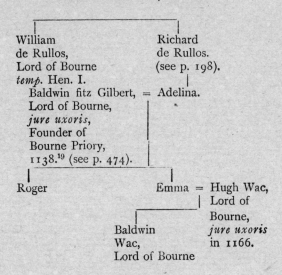

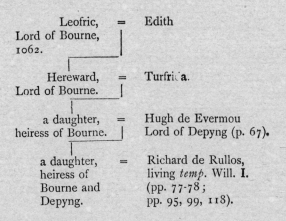

The Psuedo-Ingulf's version runs :—

It will be seen how skilfully the author of this famous forgery brings in the names of real people while confusing their connexion and their dates. Richard de Rullos, for in-

---

[19] The names of the churches he bestowed on the Priory illustrate the constituents of the Honour of Bourne.

stance, was living shortly before 1130, yet is here described as living under the Conqueror, though represented as marrying the great granddaughter of a man who was himself in the prime of life in 1062. The whole account of him as an ardent agriculturist, devoted to the improvement of live stock and the reclamation of waste, is quaintly anachronistic ; but the fact of his being a friend and benefactor to Crowland is one for which the writer had probably some ground. For my part, I attach most importance to his incidental statement that the daring deeds of Hereward the outlaw, " adhuc in triviis canuntur," an allusion, perhaps unnoticed, to a ballad history surviving, it may be, so late as the days when the forgery was compiled.

But, leaving Hereward, no entries in this list are more deserving of notice than those which bring before us the famous name of Nevile :—

Gislebertus de Nevila [tenet] ii. carrucatas in Lincolnescira, et servit Abbatiæ pro ii. hidis et inde inventi i. militem (p. 171).

Radulfus de Nevila [tenet] x. carrucatas in Lincolnescira et i. hidam et dimidiam in Hamtonascira et servit se tercio milite (p. 175).

Hugh Candidus wrote of the former :—

Heres Galfridi de Nevile tenet in Lincolnescire, scilicet in Waletone *(sic)* justa Folkingham, et Yoltorpe duas carrucatas terre et inde facit plenum servitium unius militis (p. 59).

With this clue we are enabled to detect Gilbert de Nevile in that " Gislebertus homo Abbatis," who held of the Abbot (D.B., i. 345*b*) at " Walecote " (Walcot near Folkingham), So also Hugh " Candidus " writes of the other Nevile fee :—

Heres Radulfi de Nevile tenet decem carrucatas terræ in Lincolnshire, scilicet in Scottone Malmetone ; et in Norhamtonscire unam hidam et dimidiam, scilicet in Holme, Rayniltorp, et inde facit plenum servitium trium militum (p. 55).

It is, then, Ralf de Nevile that we have in that " Radulfus homo Abbatis," who held of him at " Mameltune," and

" Rageneltorp " with " Holm " in Domesday (i. 345*b*, 346)— Manton, with Raventhorpe and Holme (near Bottesford, co. Linc.)—for Hugh, of course, has blundered in placing the two latter places in Northamptonshire.[20]   The *Testa*, more exact, enables us to add Ashby to Holme and Raventhorp as part of one estate, held as a single knight's fee. Scotton, in the same neighbourhood, was held by " Ricardus " in Domesday, but, in the hands of Nevile's heirs, represented a fee and a third.

Between Ralf and Gilbert de Nevile on fo. 346 we find " Gislebertus homo Abbatis " holding ten bovates at Hibaldstow. This was the " Gislebertus Falvel " of our return, not Gilbert de Nevile.

The last Domesday name I shall identify is that of the Abbot's under-tenant " Eustacius," who held of him at Polebrook, Clapton (Northants), and Catworth (Hunts). He was, I believe, the same as that Eustace who held land, as a tenant-in-chief, at Polebrook, Northants, and with that Eustace the sheriff (" Vice-comes ") who held (at Catworth, Hunts) also *in capite*.   Indeed the abbot's tenant is identified with the latter in the story of the foundation of Huntingdon Priory (*Mon. Ang.*, vi. 78), where, as in our list, we find that his two knights' fees soon passed to Lovetot.[21]

We may learn from this identification that two different tenants-in-chief and at least one under-tenant may prove to be all one man, just as, on the other hand, we found three

---

[20] The name of Ralf de Nevilla occurs in full in the Lincolnshire " Clamores " (i. 376*b*), annihilating the old assertion that this famous surname is nowhere found in Domesday. (See my letter in *Academy*, xxxvii. 373.)

[21] It is specially interesting to trace his holding at Winwick, Hunts, which then lay partly in Northants. As " Eustachius " he held *in capite* at " Winewincle " (i. 228), as " Eustachius Vicecomes " at " Winewiche " (i. 206), and as " Eustacius," a tenant of the Abbot, at " Winewiche " (i. 221). In the first two cases his under-tenants are given as " Widelard[us] " and " Oilard[us]," doubtless the same man. For " Winewincle " we should probably read " Winewicke." See also p. 222, *infra*

distinct Rogers among the Domesday under-tenants of the Abbot. An additional conclusion is suggested by the name " Eustachius de Huntendune," given to this sheriff in the *Inquisitio Eliensis*.[22] For we find Picot, the Sheriff of Cambridgeshire, similarly styled in Domesday (i. 200), " Picot de Grentebrige," " Ilbert de Hertford," I think, was the Sheriff of Hertfordshire,[23] and Hamo, a contemporary sheriff of Kent, attests a charter as " Hamo de Cantuaria." Turold, sheriff of Lincolnshire, is found as Turold " of Lincoln" (see p. 329), and Hugh, sheriff of Dorset, as Hugh of " Wareham," while Walter and Miles " of Gloucester," Edward and Walter " of Salisbury," are also cases in point. Hugh " of Leicester" was sheriff of Leicestershire *temp*. Henry I., while Turchil " de Warwic " (D.B., i. 240*b*) may possibly have owed that appellation to the fact that his father Ælfwine was sheriff of Warwickshire. Enough, in any case, has been said to show that it was a regular practice for sheriffs to derive, as often did earls, their styles from the capital town of their shire.

[22] *Inq. Com. Cant.*, Ed. Hamilton, p. 111.
[23] *Ib.*, 56, 192.

THE WORCESTERSHIRE SURVEY

(*Temp.* HENRY I).

WE have, in the case of the see of Worcester, the means of testing some of the changes which took place among its tenants within a generation of Domesday. This is a survey of that portion of its lands which lay within the county of Worcester. Although printed by Hearne in his edition of Heming's Cartulary (fos. 141, 141*d*, it escaped notice, I believe, till I identified it myself in *Domesday Studies* (p. 546). As it follows immediately on the transcript of the Domesday Survey of the fief, the fact that it represents a later and distinct record might, at first sight, be overlooked.

In spite of the importance of Heming's Cartulary in its bearing on the Domesday Survey, the documents of which it contains the transcripts have been hopelessly confused and misunderstood. Professor Freeman, dealing with them, came to utter grief,[1] and as for Mr. De Gray Birch, he not only took this Survey *temp.* Henry I. to be a portion of Domesday itself, which "should be collated with the orginal MS. at the Record Office,"[2] but even repeated Ellis's blunder,[3] that the names in a document *temp.* Bishop John [1151-7][4] represent "the list of jurors for the Hundred of Oswaldeslaw" at the Domesday Survey.[5]

---

[1] See my paper "An early reference to Domesday" (*Domesday Studies,* pp. 542-4).

[2] *Domesday Studies,* p. 513 ; *Domesday Book* (S.P.C.K.), p. 305

[3] *Introduction to Domesday,* i. 19.

[4] *Domesday Studies,* p. 547.

[5] *Domesday Book* (S.P.C.K,), pp, 78, 305.

From a writ entered on fo. 136 we may infer that there had been some dispute between the Sheriff and the Church of Worcester as to the number of hides in the county for which the latter should be rated.[6]   This Inquest or Survey was the consequence of that dispute, and resulted in the issue of the writ.   Its date is roughly determined by the facts that Urse d'Abetot was dead when it was made, while the Count of Meulan is entered as a tenant, so that we may probably date it as later (at the earliest) than 1108, and previous to the death of the Count of Meulan in July, 1118.[7]

Let us now compare, Manor by Manor, the earlier with the later Survey :—

DOMESDAY.	SURVEY *temp.* HENRY I.
Chemesege.	*Kemesige.*

Bishop	[13]	Bishop	13
Urso.	7	Walter de Beauchamp	9
Roger de Laci	2		
Walter Ponther	2	Hugh Puiher.	2
	24		24

Wiche.		*Wike.*	
Bishop	$3\frac{3}{4}$	Bishop	3
Urso.	$9\frac{3}{4}$	Walter de Beauchamp	$10\frac{1}{2}$
Robert Despenser	$\frac{1}{2}$	Nicholas (de Beauchamp?)	$\frac{1}{2}$
Osbern fitz Richard	1	Hugh fitz Osbern	1
	15		15

[6] There was a similar dispute about the same time in the case of Abingdon Abbey and its possessions in Berkshire (*Abingdon Cart.*, ii. 1600.

[7] This, however, as I have elsewhere shown must remain a presumption, as it is possible that, owing to the youth of his heir, he may have been entered as nominal tenant for some time after his death (see p. 190).

Fledebivie.

Bishop	7
Bishop of Hereford . . .	5
Urso	12
Robert Despenser . . .	5
Alricus archid[iaconus] . .	1
Roger de Laci.	10
	40

Fledebyri.

Bishop	3
Bishop of Hereford . . .	5
Walter de Beauchamp . .	22
Hugh de Laci	10
	40

Breodun.

Bishop	10
Monks	4
Ælricus Archd.	2
Urso	16
Durand	2
Brictric fil' Algar (in king's hands)	1
	35

Bredune.

Bishop	13
Monks	4
Walter de Beauchamp . .	16
Gile (? bertus)	1
King	1
	35

Rippel et Uptun.

Bishop	13
Ordric	1
Siward	5
Roger de Laci.	3
Urso	1
Ralph de Bernai (in king's hands)	1
Brictric fil' Algar (in king's hands)	1
	25

Rippel et Uptun.

Bishop	14
Hugh de Laci	3
Walter de Beauchamp . .	6
King	2
	25

Blochelei.

Bishop	$25\frac{1}{2}$
Richard	2
Ansgot	$1\frac{1}{2}$
Stephen fil' Fulcred . . .	3
Hereward	5
Monks	1
	38

Bloccelea.

Bishop	22
Bishop	2
Walter de Beauchamp . .	5
" Dæilesford "	3
" Eunilade "	5
Monks	1
	38

Tredingtun.

[Bishop	17]
Monks	2
Gilbert fil' Thorold . . .	4
	—
	23

Tredintun.

Bishop	17
Monks	2
"Langedun"	4
	—
	23

Norwiche.

Bishop	$3\frac{1}{2}$
Urso	$7\frac{3}{4}$
Ordric	$4\frac{1}{4}$
Alric Arch'	1
Walter Ponther . . .	$7\frac{1}{2}$
Herlebaldus	1
	—
	25

Northewike.

Bishop	$6\frac{1}{2}$
Walter de Beauchamp . .	10
Hugh Puiher	$7\frac{1}{2}$
King	1
	—
	25

Ovreberie cum Penedoc.

The Church of Worcester .	6

Werebyri et Penedoc.

. . . .	6

Seggesbarne.

The Church of Worcester .	3

Segesberewe.

. . . .	3

Scepwestun.

The Church of Worcester .	2

Scepwestune.

. . . .	2

Herferthun cum Wiburgestoke.

The Church of Worcester .	3

Herfortune cum Wiburga Stoke.

. . . .	3

Grimanleh.

The Church of Worcester .	2
Robert Despencer . . .	1
	—
	3

Grimeleage.

. . . .	2
Walter de Beauchamp . .	1
	—
	3

Halhegan cum Bradewesham.

The Church of Worcester .	1
Duo Radmanni	2
Roger de Laci	$3\frac{1}{2}$
Walter de Burh	$\frac{1}{2}$
Hugh de Grentmesnil . .	$\frac{1}{2}$
	—
	$7\frac{1}{2}$

Hallhagan cum Bradewasse.

(The Church of Worcester	1)
Walter de Beauchamp . .	$1\frac{1}{2}$
Roger de Laci	$3\frac{1}{2}$
Count of Meulan . . .	1
	—
	7

Cropetorn cum Neothetune.

Church of Worcester	. . 14
Robert Despencer	. . . 11
Urso . . ,	. . . 6
Abbot of Evesham	. . . 9
[*Ibid.*	. . 10]

50

Croppethorne.

Monks	 15
Walter de Beauchamp	. . 9
Robert Marmion	. . . 7
Abbot of Evesham	. . . 9
Ibid. "quiete a geldo"	. 10

50

Total for Oswaldslaw Hundred.

HIDES.	TENANTS.		HEMING'S TOTAL.
(*ut supra*).	(*ut supra*).		"He sunt ccc. hide ad
24	Bishop	93½	Osuualdes lauues hundret."
15			
40	Monks	39	
35	Walter de Beauchamp	90	" Episcopus habet in
25	King	4	dominio " . . xciiii.
38	Hugh Puher .	9½	" Monachi " . . . . xl.
23	Hugh de Laci .	13	"Walterus de Bealcamp " xx.[8]
25	Roger de Laci .	3½	
24	Robert Marmion	7	" Alii barones " . . lxiii.
50	Bishop of Hereford	5	" Rex " . . . . . iii.
—	Abbot of Evesham	19	
299	Hugh fitz Osbern	1	
	Count of Meulan	1	
	Gile (?bertus) .	1	
	Alii	12	
	Nicholas (? de		" Quiete apud Ham-
	Beauchamp) .	½	tun a geldo " . . x.

299   230

Huertelere.

Church of Worcester . . 20

Heortlabyri.

Bishop	15
Walter de Beauchamp . .	5

20

[8] MS. now destroyed here.

Vlwardelei.		*Wlfwardile.*	
Church of Worcester . .	5	Monks	5

Stoche.		*Stoka.*	
Church of Worcester . .	10	Monks	10

Alvievecherche.		*Ælfithe cyrce.*	
Church of Worcester . .	13	Bishop	13

Clive cum Lenc.		*Clive cum Leng.*	
Church of Worcester . .	$10\frac{1}{2}$	Monks	10

Fepsetenatun.		*Fepsintune.*	
Church of Worcester . .	5	Monks	1
Walter Ponther	1[9]	Hugh Puiher	1[9]
Roger de Laci	5	Hugh de Laci	5
	11		7

Hambyrie.		*Heanbyri.*	
Church of Worcester . .	14	Bishop	$13\frac{1}{2}$
		Walter de Beauchamp . .	$\frac{1}{2}$
			14

Ardolvestone et Cnistetone.		*Eardulfestun et Cnihtetun.*	
Church of Worcester (" de victu monachorum"). .	15	Monks	15

Total.		*" Summa in Kinefolka."*	
Bishop	$41\frac{1}{2}$	" Episcopus in dominio .	xli."
Monks	41	" Monachi	xli."
Walter de Beauchamp . .	$5\frac{1}{2}$	" Walterus de Bealcamp .	vi."
Hugh de Laci	5	" Hugo de Laci	v."
Hugh Puiher	1	" Hugo Puiher	i."
	94		94

In Oswaldeslaw .	. . . . .	299
Outside ditto .	. . . . .	94
		393

[9] " Non geldat."

Summa hidarum, quas episcopus habet in toto vicecomitatu est ccc. et quater xx. et xvii. cum his quas Abbas de Evesham tenet de OSWALDES LAUUE.[10]

It will be seen that of these 397 hides only 393 are accounted for above. The explanation is this. Of the five hides held in "Fepsintune" by the Church of Worcester in Domesday, only one is entered in the above list, the other four being wholly omitted, both in the list itself and in the total. These four omitted hides bring up the 393 to 397, the exact sum that we have to account for.

If the Manors in the above Survey are examined with care *seriatim*, it will be found that they bear manifest witness to the aggressions of Urse d'Abetot, who, we may gather from this Cartulary, was the *bête noire* of the Church of Worcester. The various extensions of his Domesday holdings, as at "Fledebyrie," where twelve hides had been increased to twenty-two, were partly due to the accession of the lands he inherited from his brother, but partly also to his absorption of the lands of other tenants and of portions of the episcopal demesne. All the benefit of these accessions passed to his son-in-law and successor, Walter de Beauchamp.

But perhaps the most important information that this Survey gives us is to be found in the light it throws on the succession to Robert "Dispensator." That he was brother to Urse d'Abetot is, of course, generally known. His relationship to the Marmions is the *crux*. I deal with it under the Lindsey Survey,[11] which shows us his Lincolnshire fief in the hands of Roger Marmion. In the present Survey we find that of the seventeen hides and a half which Robert Dispensator had held, at the time of Domesday, from the Bishop, only seven were held by Robert (not Roger) Marmion when this document was compiled, the rest being held by Walter de Beauchamp. We thus learn

[10] p. 116.
[11] *Infra*, pp. 181 *et sq*

that here, as in Leicestershire, the fief had been divided between the two.[12]

But this Survey further tells us—if we may trust the text—that, in this succession, Roger Marmion had been preceded by Robert. One may throw it out as a possible suggestion that, in addition to the wife of Walter de Beauchamp, Urse d'Abetot may have had a daughter who married Robert Marmion.[13] On the forfeiture of his son Roger, such a daughter would have pressed her claim, and, though the inheritance of Urse himself may, by special favour, have been regranted to Walter, she may have obtained a share of the fief of her uncle, Robert " Dispensator." But this can only be conjecture.

Of the other points of family history on which this Survey throws light, one may mention that Hugh " Puher " had succeeded Walter " Ponther," that Osbern fitz Richard (of Richard's Castle) had been succeeded by his son, Hugh fitz Osbern ; and that though, as in 1095,[14] the name of Hugh de Laci supplants that of his brother Roger, yet that, if we can trust the text, Roger had in one Manor been allowed to retain his holding, in accordance with a policy

---

[12] We are enabled by this Survey, and by the division it records, to carry up the history of Elmley, the original seat of the Beauchamps, to Domesday itself. The great Manor of Cropthorne, by Evesham, was held by the Church of Worcester. In Bengeworth, one of its "members," Urse d'Abetot, had seized an estate of five hides (*Heming's Cartulary* fo. 125b). His brother, Robert Despencer, had seized two other "members," Charlton ("Ceorlatuna") and Elmley (*ibid.*). In Domesday we are merely told that Robert held eleven hides in Cropthorne. But the present Survey fortunately mentions that the portion which fell to Marmion's share was seven hides in "Charlton." This leaves four hides for Elmley, which, added to the five hides of Urse d'Abetot in Bengeworth, makes exactly the nine hides here entered to Walter de Beauchamp. We thus learn how the Beauchamps became possessed of Elmley. And this calculation is confirmed by the entry in the *Testa* (p. 41): "Willelmus de Bello Campo . . . in Elmeleg in dominico iiij. hidas."

[13] It is worth noting that we find, in Domesday, both a Robert and a Walter holding of Urse in Worcestershire.

[14] See p. 312 *infra*.

which is believed to have been practised, namely, that of keeping a hold, however small, on the forfeited. The name of the Count of Meulan also, the supplanter of Grentmesnil, will be noticed, and that of a "Nicholas," whom, as the successor in a small holding of Robert Despencer, one might perhaps be tempted to identify with the mysterious Sheriff of Staffordshire, Nicolas de Beauchamp.

There are fragments of two other early surveys relating to Worcestershire, which, as they contain the names of Walter and of William de Beauchamp respectively, may be roughly assigned to the reigns of Henry I. and of Stephen. The first, which is found in an Evesham Cartulary,[15] is mainly an abstract of Domesday, but contains a later and valuable analysis of Droitwich, with an important reference to the Exchequer. The other [16] begins in the middle of a survey of what seems to be the Church of Worcester's fief, records the lands held, as under-tenant, by William de Beauchamp, and shows us the Domesday fief of Ralf de "Todeni" in the hands of his heir, Roger de "Toeni."

DROITWICH.

Hee sunt x. hidæ in Wich'. De Witton' petri corbezun ii. hidas. De feodo sancti Dionysii Ricardus corvus et Willelmus filiuv Oueclini tenent i. hidam. De sancto Guthlaco Willelmus filiuss Ricardi tenet i. hidam. De Johanne de Suthlega Ricardus filius Roberti tenet i. hidam. De Pagano filio Johannis Godwi tenet dimidiam hidam. De Waltero de bello campo Theobaldus et petrus tenent dimidiam hidam. De la Berton' de Gloucestra [see Glouc. Cartul.]. Randulf filius Ringulfi tenet dimidiam hidam. De monachis Gloucestrie Baldwinus et Lithulfus dimidiam hidam. De Comite Warewice Randulfus et Essulf filii Ringulf tenent iii. virgatas. De Waltero del Burc Randulf et Essulf dimidiam hidam. De West-monasterio Theobaldus et Walterus fil' Thorald i. hidam. De Almega fil' Aiulfi et mater ejus i. hidam. De Battona Aiulfus presbyter i. virgatam. De Wichebold Rogerus de Bolles i. virgatam. De monachis fil' Grim tenet i. virgatam. De Kinefare et Douerdale i. virgatam. Alewi caure et socii ejus dimidiam virgatam.[15]

---

[15] *Harl. MS.*, 3,763, fo. 80.
[16] *Cott. MS. Vesp.*, B. xxiv. fo. 8.

H[oc] debet computari ad Scacarium Regis vicecomiti Wirecestrie Habes x. hidas ad Danegeld et Wasto forestæ ii. hidas.

Et in Ederesfeld vi hid[æ]. Et in happeworda i. hid[a]. Et in Biselega i. hid[a]. Et in Burlega i. hyda.

FRAGMENT OF A SURVEY SUBSEQUENT TO 1130 AND PERHAPS

circ. 1150.

(*Cott. MS. Vesp.*, B. xxiv. fo. 8.)

. . . manerio de hambyry. Estona Ric' dimidiam hidam. In hundredo de Camele. In Waresleia v. hidæ de manerio de hertlebery. Summa quater xx. et xiii. hidæ.

In hundredo de persora habet ecclesia de Westmustier has terras quas tenet Willelmus de bello campo. Hekintona iii. hidæ et iii. virgatæ. Chaddesleia ii. hidæ. Langeduna Osmundi i. hida et dimidia. Colleduma iii. hidæ et iii. virgatæ. Graftona Ebrandi i. hida et iii. virgatæ. Flavel et pidelet v. hidæ. Newentona x. hidæ. Broctona Inardi iii. hidæ. Pidelet radulfi iii. hidæ. Berford v. hidæ Branefford i. hida. Wicha Inardi iii hidæ. Burlingeham ii. hidæ et i. virgata. Cumbrintona ii. hidæ. Poiwica Willelmi de bello campo i. hida. Newebolt i. hida. Medeleffeld i. hida de poiwica. An bergam i. hida. Olendene i. hida. Arleia i. virgata. Poiwica Inardi i. hida. Summa lx. hidæet dimidia.

In predicto hundredo de persora feudum Abbatis persore. Belega xxi. hidæ. Branefford i. hida. Wadberga iii. hidæ et dimidia. Cumbrintona i. hida et dimidia. Lega Ricardi dimidia hida. Walecote et torendune i. hida et dimidia.

In hundredo de Leisse tenet idem Willelmus Chirchlench iiii. hidas de abbatia de Evesham. Croulega v. hidas de feudo Osberti filii hugonis.

In hundredo de Clent. Belua viii. hidæ de feudo folwi paganelli. Salawarpa v. hidæ de feudo Rogeri Comitis. Item Salawarpa i. hida de feudo episcopi Cestrie. Chaluestona i. hida de feudo Roberti filii Archembaldi. Apud Wich dimidiam hidam Gunfrei. Item apud Wich i. hidam de terra Sancti Guthlaci quam Rodbertus filius Willelmi tenet. Item ibidem dimidiam hidam de Cormell' quam Gilebertus tenet. Cokehulla ii. hidæ et dimidiam de feudo regis. Hactona iii. hidæ de feudo episcopi baiocensis. Escreueleia i. hida. Summa tocius cclxiiii. hidæ et dimidia et dimidia virgata.

Terra rogeri de toeney. Esla iii. hidæ. Bertona iii. hidæ et iii. virgatæe. Alcrintona ii. hidæ. Linda ii. hidæ et ad halac i. hida. Mora hugonis i. hida et dimidia. Werueslega ii. hidæ et dimidia.

Alboldeslega ii. hidæ et dimidia. Rudmerlega i. hida et dimidia. Estlega i. hida Geldans et una hida quieta. Sceldeslega i. hida. Almelega Ricardi de portes xi. hidæ.

In the former of these two fragments we recognise in John of Sudeley the younger son of Harold, son of Earl Ralf. It would be of interest if we might identify his tenant, Richard fitz Robert, with the younger son of his brother Robert. The succession in the tenancy of the Crowland hide (St. Guthlac's) needs explanation. In Domesday (176) Urse held Dunclent of Nigel the physician, who held both here and at Droitwich under Crowland Abbey. It must have been through him at Droitwich also that William fitz Richard became tenant, for Robert fitz William (who was clearly the latter's son) held here of Walter de Beauchamp in the second fragment.

It is in tracing William de Beauchamp's succession, as under-tenant to his grandfather Urse, that we find the chief interest of the second fragment. He has succeeded him, for instance, as tenant to the Abbeys of Westminster, Pershore, and Coventry (the fief of the last having now become that of "the Bishop of Chester"). At Wadborough, however, it was Robert "Dispensator" whom he had succeeded as tenant of Pershore. In one case we find him holding of Robert fitz Erchembald, whose Domesday predecessor we thus learn was William Goizenboded (177b). We may also note his tenure of Madresfield (now Lord Beauchamp's seat),—the earliest mention, I think, of the place,—as a limb of Powick. Fulk Paynell, of whom William held at Beoley, had now succeeded to the Domesday fief of William fitz Ansculf, whose tenant "Robert" may have been Robert "Dispensator." Osbern fitz Hugh had similarly succeeded to the Richard's Castle fief held, in Domesday, by his grandfather.

I append a partial comparison of Domesday with the Henry I. survey so far as concerns Droitwich, where property, owing to its value, was divided among many owners.

DROITWICH.

DOMESDAY.	H.	*Temp.* Henry I.	H.
Willelmus filius Corbucion (Witone)	2	Petrus Corbezun (de Witton)	2
Church of St. Denis . . .	1	"De feodo sancti Dionysii Ricardus corvus et Willelmus filius Oueclini" . .	1
De Sancto Guthlaco Nigellus Medicus	1	De Sancto Guthlaco Willelmus filius Ricardi . . .	1
Heraldus filius Radulfi Comitis	1	De Johanne de Suthlega Ricardus filius Roberti .	1
		De Pagano filio Johannis Godwi	½
Urso tenet Witune in Wich et Gunfrid de eo . . .	½	De Waltero de Bello Campo Theobaldus et Petrus . .	½
Æcclesia sancti Petri de Glou.	½	De la Berton de Gloucestra Randulf filius Ringulfi . .	½
In Wich est dimidia hida quæ pertinet ad aulam de Glou.	½	De monachis Gloucestrie Baldwinus et Lithulfus .	½
		De Comite Warewice Randulfus et Essulfus filii Ringulf	¾
		De Waltero del Burc Randulf et Essulf	½
Ibi duo presbyteri [de Westmonasterio] tenet i. hidam que nunquam geldavit	1	De Westmonasterio Theobaldus et Walterus fil' Thorald	1
Isdem [Radulfus] tenent in Wich i. hidam de x. hidis [geldantibus].	1	De Almelega fil' Aiulfi et mater ejus	1

THE LINDSEY SURVEY

(1115-1118)

THIS "invaluable Survey," as Mr. Stevenson has termed it,[1] might be described as a miniature Domesday for each of the Wapentakes in the three trithings into which Lindsey was divided. For although drawn up, Wapentake by Wapentake, as is the Leicestershire Survey, Hundred by Hundred, the lands within each Wapentake described are grouped under the names of the holders of fiefs, instead of being entered Vill by Vill. It was doubtless compiled, like other surveys, in connexion with the assessment of the "geld."[2]

Remarkable from a palæographic standpoint, as well as from the nature of its contents, the record, which is found in a Cottonian MS. (Claud. C. 5), has been singularly unfortunate in its editors. As Mr. Greenstreet truly observed :—

The indefatigable Hearne, seeing that the manuscript related to a very ancient period of our history, and recognising its great importance, printed it in the Appendix to his " Liber Niger," but he does not appear to have properly examined either the question of the date of the writing, or the internal evidence . . . As a natural consequence of his superficial examination, he associates it wrongly with the reign of Henry II.

Stapleton, of course, knew better than this, and assigned

---

[1] *English Historical Review*, v. 96.
[2] I have discussed above (pp. 73-77) the bearing of its evidence on the problem of Domesday assessment, so need not recur to the subject here.

the survey at one time to *circ.* 1108,[3] but in his *Rotuli Scaccarii Normanniæ*[4] to 1106-1120. It was subsequently investigated and analysed with great care by Mr. Eyton, whose note-books, now in the British Museum, show that he adopted the sound method of comparing it in detail with Domesday Book. After his death Mr. Chester Waters issued (1883) an annotated translation of the text, with an introduction, analysis, etc., in which the place-names were carefully identified, and the same system of comparison with Domesday adopted.[5]

It is, unfortunately, necessary to explain that Mr. Waters in the table of contents described his translation as "from the Cotton MS., Claudius C. 5," and wrote on the opposite page :—

This MS. engaged the attention of Thomas Hearne, the antiquary, who has printed it amongst the additaments to his edition of the *Liber Niger Scaccarii*; but Hearne was one of those industrious but uncritical antiquaries who had no conception of the duties of an editor of the importance of accuracy.

Knowing the high opinion entertained of Mr. Waters's works,[6] I accepted his translation in all good faith as "from the Cotton MS." and was, I confess, not a little startled to discover from Mr. Greenstreet's facsimiles that it was made not from the Cotton MS., but from that inaccurate edition by Hearne, which Mr. Waters had mentioned only to denounce. On fo. 4*b* a whole line, containing three entries, was accidentally omitted by Hearne, and is, consequently, absent also from Mr. Waters' version. On collating the two, however, I found, to my great surprise, that matters were even worse than this, and that Hearne's text was far less inaccurate than Mr. Waters' own, the erroneous figures found in the latter being almost

---

[3] See note 31 below.   [4] Vol. II. p. xcvi.
[5] *A Roll of the Owners of Land in the parts of Lindsey.* ("Reprinted from the Associated Architectural Societies Reports and Papers").
[6] In consideration of which he received a pension on the Civil List

always correctly given by the "uncritical" Hearne. As for the version given by Mr. Waters, even in the very first Wapentake, there are three serious errors, five carucates being given as three, nine as seven, and eleven as two! And for Bradley Wapentake (p. 27), his figures are so erroneous that, according to him, "Radulf Meschin alone had 42 cars. 6 bovs. in this Wapentake," though his real holding was only 15 cars. 3 bovs. With another class of resultant errors I shall have to deal below.

To the enterprise of Mr. Greenstreet scholars were indebted for an *édition de luxe* of the record in facsimile, which made its appearance shortly after the treatise of Mr Waters. Unfortunately no attempt was made in the appended literal translation to identify the names of places or persons, while such a word as "[ap]pendiciis," which occasionally appears in the survey, is mistaken for a place-name "Pendicus." The book enjoys, however, the great advantage of an index.

The identification of places and of persons in Mr. Water's treatise shows extraordinary knowledge; but both Mr Eyton and Mr. Waters had the provoking habit of making important assertions without giving their authority. I expressed a wish in the *Academy*, at the time, that Mr. Waters would give us some clue as to his sources of information, but as he did not think fit to do so, we have to test his statements as best we can for ourselves. Now we learn from him on p. 36 that "Walter fitz William," a tenant at South Willingham, was "brother of Simon mentioned above," namely of "Simon fitz William (ancestor to the Lords Kyme)." This is impressive until we discover that the actual words in the survey (as indeed in Hearne's text) are "Walt[erius] fil[ius] Walt[eri]i" (fo. 11 *b*.)[7] To an expert such a test as this will prove significant enough. But to turn from an actual misreading of the text to cases in which are incorporated interlineations, not part of the

---

[7] There is a similar error on fo. 13, where the "William fitz Aubrey" of Mr. Waters proves to be "filius *Albrede*" (not Alb*erici*).

original text, but written in later times, we find Mr.
Waters—like other antiquaries who had followed Hearne's
text—stating that "Ranulf [Meschin] is twice styled in the
Roll Earl of Lincoln, but there is no record of his creation,
and no other authority for possession of the earldom"
(p. 8). The difficulty vanishes when we discover that this
supposed style was a mere interlineation made by a much
later hand.[8] So again we read on p. 30:—

Richard, Earl [of Chester], has 6 cars. in Barnetby-le-Wold,
where [William], the constable of Chester, is his tenant [as his father
was Earl Hugh's in Domesday].

But on turning to Mr. Greenstreet's facsimiles, we find
that the survey had nothing about "the constable of
Chester," the words "constabularia [*sic*] Cestrie" being
only a faint interlineation by a later hand.

And even where a reference to the true text does not at
once dispose of the matter, these statements of Mr. Waters
are, on other grounds, open at times to question. He
assumes, for instance, that Hugh fitz Ranulf, who occurs
as a landowner in the survey, was a younger son of
Ranulf Meschin, afterwards Earl of Chester (p. 12). No
such son would seem to be known; and this assumption,
moreover, does violence to chronology. For the pedigree
it involves is this:—

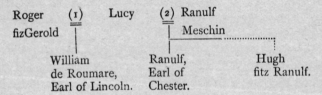

Roger (1) Lucy (2) Ranulf
fizGerold | Meschin
|
William Ranulf, Hugh
de Roumare, Earl of fitz Ranulf.
Earl of Lincoln. Chester.

Now William de Roumare was not old enough to claim
his inheritance from the Kiug till 1122, and his half
brother, Ranulf, was some years younger than he was, as
the words of Orderic imply in 1140. Consequently Hugh,
the youngest brother, can have been only a boy in 1212.

---

[8] Hearne duly prints it as an interlineation.

How then could he, as Mr. Waters alleges, have held a fief in right of his wife so early as 1115 or thereabouts?

In this assumption, however, he only follows Stapleton, to whom he here refers, and who relied on an abstract in the cartulary of Spalding (fol. 416 *a*, *b*.). This abstract which cannot, from its form, preserve the wording of the original charter, runs :—

Sciant tam presents quam futuri quod Hugo frater Rannulfi comitis Cestrie et Matild' uxor, ejus, fil' filia [*sic*] Lucie comitisse concesserunt, etc., etc.

Stapleton boldly rendered the obviously corrupt words as "son and daughter-in-law of the countess Lucia,"[9] and hence pronounced this Hugh to be "a married brother of the whole blood" to the *second* Randulf, Earl of Chester.[10] As he only knew their gift to Spalding to be "prior to 1141," no chronological difficulty was caused by this view; but the occurrence of Hugh's name in the Lindsey Survey, as already in possession of his small fief, at once raises the difficulty I have explained. The solution that occurs to me is that the Hugh fiz Ranulf of our survey, and the "Hugo frater Ranulfi Comitis Cestrie" of the Spalding charter, was a brother, not of the second but of the *first* Earl Ranulf, and that the words "fil' filia Comitisse Lucie" were introduced in error by the compiler, whose head was full of the Countess Lucy, and who had here confused the two Earls Randulf.

Stapleton, Mr. Waters has justly observed, was "*facile princeps* of Anglo-Norman genealogists."[11] Yet I venture to think that, as he here mistook a brother of the first Earl Ranulf for a son, so he confused William Meschin, another and better known brother, with William de Roumare, the Earl's stepson, afterwards Earl of Lincoln. William Meschin was not merely a considerable landowner in Lindsey,

[9] *Rolls of the Norman Exchequer*, II. clvi.
[10] He further hazarded the erroneous conjecture that Roheis, Countess of Lincoln, was his daughter.
[11] *Gundrada de Warrenne*, p. 9.

but had also estates in Northamptonshire and Leicestershire, as our survey of those counties show.[12] Stephen, according to Stapleton, created him Earl of Cambridge.

Remembering the *dictum* of Dr. Stubbs that " Stephen's earldoms are a matter of great constitutional importance," it is worth while to examine this earldom of Cambridge.

In one of Stapleton's greatest essays, that on Holy Trinity Priory, York,[13] he writes of this William Meschin, that—

By King Stephen he was made Earl of Cambridge, as we learn from the following extract from a charter of Alexander, Bishop of Lincoln, in 1139, founding the nunnery of Haverholm, in the parish of Ruskington, of the order of St. Gilbert of Sempringham. " But this donation . . . we have confirmed . . . by the testimony of Rannulph, Earl of Chester, and of William, Earl of Cambridge, his brother " (p. 34).

The words in the original are :—

Testimonio Rannulfi comitis Cestriæ et Willelmi comitis Cantebrigiæ fratris ejus (*Mon. Ang.*, vi. 949).

Now, though Stapleton is positive on the point, speaking again of " William Meschin, Earl of Cambridge " (p. 35), and though this learned paper well sustains his reputation, yet he has here beyond question gone astray. Earl Randulf, first of his name, appears as deceased in the Pipe Roll of 1130. He could not therefore have been the Earl Randulf of 1139, who was his son and namesake. Therefore the latter's "brother," the Earl of Cambridge, could not have been William Meschin, who was his father's brother.[14] A short chart pedigree will make the matter clear :—

---

[12] See pp. 210, 221, *infra*.

[13] pp. 1-237. Bound up in the York volume of the Royal Archæological Institute.

[14] Stapleton indeed exposed himself unconsciously by stating on the very same page that William Meschin's lands had passed to his heirs "prior to 1138," so that he could not be the Ear of 1139.

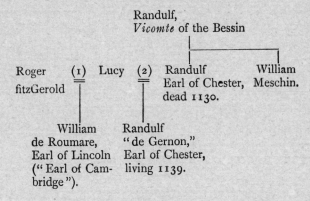

Randulf,
Vicomte of the Bessin

| Roger (1) | Lucy (2) | Randulf | William |
fitzGerold | | Earl of Chester, | Meschin. |
| | | dead 1130. | |

William
de Roumare,
Earl of Lincoln
("Earl of Cambridge").

Randulf
"de Gernon,"
Earl of Chester,
living 1139.

The pedigree shows my solution of the mystery. The two brother-earls of 1139 are those who are found so constantly together, and who were jointly concerned, next year, in the surprise of Lincoln, but who were really only *half*-brothers, though they spoke of one another as "frater."

The identity of the "Earl of Cambridge" is thus clearly established; but there of course remains the question why he is not here styled "Earl of Lincoln." Every mention of him as Earl of Lincoln is later, if this charter be rightly dated, so that he may possibly have changed his style. It is really strange that precisely as William, Earl of Lincoln, is here once styled Earl of Cambridge, so William, Earl of Arundel, is twice styled Earl of Lincoln, as I have shown in my *Geoffrey de Mandeville* (p. 324), though in that case also the fact had never been suspected. It is most tempting, if rash, to suggest that the reason why the Earl of Lincoln was at first Earl of Cambridge is that the Earl of Arundel (Sussex) was at first Earl of Lincoln, and thus kept him out of that title.

In any case an error has now been corrected, and one of Stephen's alleged earls disposed of.

The question of the date of this interesting survey is no less puzzling than important. Mr. Greenstreet held that "there is hardly any room for doubting" that it was previous to 1109. This conclusion was based on a misapprehension, and Mr. Waters claimed to have "established" the date as "between March 1114 and April 1116" (pp. 2-4). In this conclusion he would seem to have been anticipated by Mr. Eyton, as is shown by that writer's note-books,[15] but I cannot accept the identical and somewhat far-fetched argument on which they relied. They obtained their limit on the one hand from a passage in "Peter of Blois," and on the other from the fact that Robert, the King's son, is entered in the roll as "filius Regis," and "was therefore not yet Earl of Gloucester," whereas he was certainly Earl, they say, "before Easter, 1116," when he witnessed as Earl, a charter they both assign to that date.

Of the latter date I disposed in my paper "The Creation of the Earldom of Gloucester,"[16] in which I showed that Robert did not become Earl till several years later. The other evidence, if it cannot be disproved, cannot at least, be relied on. For, without asserting that the chronicle assigned to "Peter of Blois" is so daring a forgery as the "Historia Ingulphi," of which it is a "continuatio," it must be plainly described as absolutely untrustworthy. Apart from the passage on Cambridge University,[17] we have a description "Inclyti Comitis Leycestriæ Roberti tunc validissimi adolescentis, burgensiumque suæ dictæ civitatis" in 1113, and of his presence, with his knights, at the laying of the Abbey foundation stones next year.[18] Now the future Earl of Leicester was some nine years old at the time, and his father, the Count of Meulan, lived till 1118. So also, about the year 1114 we meet with "Milonis Comitis Herfordensis," who did not become Earl of Hereford till 1141, and whose father, Walter of Gloucester, was living long

---

[15] See on this point the important letters of Mr. Greenstreet and Mr. J. A. C. Vincent to the *Athenæum*, May 9 and June 27, 1885.

[16] *Geoffrey de Mandeville*, pp. 420 et sq.

[17] Ed. Gale, pp. 114, 115.

[18] *Ib.*, pp. 118, 119.

after 1114; while on the next page we find the notoriously false Countess Lucy legend, with the additional blunder of converting her son, the Earl of Lincoln, into her husband's brother![19]   It is in the midst of all this that we have the vital passage on which Mr. Waters relies :—

> We know from the *Continuator* [sic] *of Peter of Blois* (p. 121) that Stephen and his elder brother Theobald were on a visit to Henry I., at Oxford, at some period between 7th March and 1st August, 1114, when Theobald is described as Count of Blois, and Stephen as "pulcherrimus adolescens dominus postea rex Anglorum." It is manifest that at this date Stephen was not yet Count of Moreton, so the Roll must be later than 7th March, 1114 (p. 3).

The fact that this alleged visit is connected by " Peter " with intervention in favour of the Abbot of Crowland, will not lessen the suspicion under which the evidence must lie. Crowland was guilty of "hiring," Dr. Stubbs has severely observed, "Peter of Blois, or some pretended Peter who borrows an illustrious name, to fabricate for her an apocryphal chronicle."[20]

The actual proof of the survey's date is minute, no doubt, but conclusive. In the Lindsey Survey "the sons of Ragemer" (himself the Domesday under-tenant) are found holding of Walter de Gant; therefore their father, at the time of the survey, had been succeeded by them in this holding. But, as "Rachmar, son of Gilbert," he is found attesting a charter of Maud, Walter de Gant's wife, to Bridlington Priory, which is addressed to Thurstan, Archbishop of York, and which therefore must be later at the very least than his electiou, 15th August, 1114. Therefore Ragemer was alive after that date, and the survey, at the time of which he was dead, can consequently scarcely be earlier than 1115. On the other hand, we can scarcely place it later than the death of the great Count of Meulan in the summer of 1118,[21] though, as I have urged in the

---

[19] pp. 124, 125.
[20] *Lectures on Mediæval and Modern History*, p. 148.
[21] *Survey of Lindsey*, p. 2.

Genealogist, the lands he had held might still be assigned to "the Count of Meulan," till his fiefs were divided among his sons, who were boys at the time of his death. On the whole we may safely assign the survey to 1115-1118, and in any case it cannot possibly be later than the close of 1120.

As, according to Stapleton, the best authority, it is in this survey that the name of Marmion first appears in England, it may not be inopportune to examine here the accepted pedigree of that house. In the Roger Marmion of our survey we have its undoubted ancestor, but of Robert Marmion, who appears on its opening folio as a tenant of Walter de Gant at Winteringham, one cannot speak so positively. In Domesday Winteringham, as 12 carucates, was held of Gilbert de Gant by "Robertus homo Gilberti" (354b): in our Survey eleven [22] of these carucates were held of Gilbert's son Walter by Robert Marmion, and the twelfth *in capite* by Roger Marmion. Mr. Waters (p. 17) identifies the former with the Domesday under-tenant, which is a tempting solution, were not the Domesday Robert also under-tenant at Risby (which was held in our survey not by Marmion, but by Walter de St. Paul). It seems to me more probable that Robert, the under-tenant in our survey, was, as Mr. Waters, contradicting himself, elsewhere observes (p. 14), the son and heir of Roger. Yet of Roger Marmion's estate at Fulstow, Mr. Waters writes (p. 27): "Roger's father, Robert Marmion, was tenant there in Domesday of Robert Dispenser." This would give us an interesting clue. But on turning to Domesday (363b), we find that it is only one more mistake of Mr. Waters, its "Robertus" being no other than Robert Dispenser himself. [23]

[22] Mr. Waters, in error, states *two*.

[23] It is an illustration of the ignorance prevalent on early genealogy that even Mr. Freeman could write of "Mr. Chester Waters, than whom no man better deserves to be listened to on any point of genealogy,

Stapleton, who worked out the descent, held that Roger's son Robert, who had succeeded by 1130, and who was slain in 1143, was father of the Robert who died in 1218. I would rather interpolate another Robert between the two :—

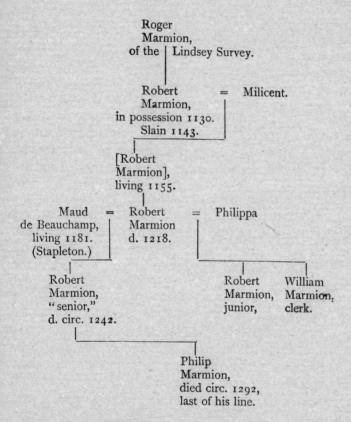

Roger Marmion, of the Lindsey Survey.

Robert Marmion, in possession 1130. Slain 1143. = Milicent.

[Robert Marmion], living 1155.

Maud de Beauchamp, living 1181. (Stapleton.) = Robert Marmion d. 1218. = Philippa

Robert Marmion, "senior," d. circ. 1242.

Robert Marmion, junior,

William Marmion, clerk.

Philip Marmion, died circ. 1292, last of his line.

The pedigree really turns on the charter of Henry III. in 1249, to Philip Marmion, confirming the royal charters to his ancestor. Mr. Stapleton declares that Henry inspected and confirmed—

especially of the Norman genealogy of the eleventh and twelfth centuries " (*Eng. Hist. Review*, iii. 690).

The charter which King Henry, his great-great-grandfather, had made to Robert Marmyon, great-grandfather of Philip Marmyon, of having warren in all his land in the county of Warwick, and especially at Tamworth; and likewise of the charter of King Henry, his uncle ["Avunculus noster" is the reading transcribed on the rolls, obviously in error for "atavus noster"], which he had made to the said Robert of having warren in all his land of Lindesay (*Rot. Scacc. Norm.*, II. cvi.).

This abstract is strangely inaccurate, considering that Stapleton had, clearly, examined the Inspeximus [24] for himself. Henry VI. inspected and confirmed—

(1) The charter of Henry I., granting Robert Marmion freewarren in Warwickshire (specially at Tamworth) as his father had.

(2) The charter of Henry II. (confirming the above charter), "T. Tom. Canc. apud Brugiam," and therefore granted in 1155.

(3) The charter of Henry III., who had inspected—

    (*a*) "Cartam quam Henr' rex avus [*sic*] noster [*i.e.* Henry II.] fecit Roberto Marmyon proavo Philippi Marmyun";

    (*b*) "Cartam Henrici regis avunculi nostri quam fecit Roberto";

and confirmed them as the charters, "H. Regis avi nostri et H. regis avunculi nostri," to Philip Marmion.

It is clear then that Henry III. inspected the charter of his grandfather ("avus") Henry II. (not as Mr. Stapleton wrote, his "great-great-grandfather"), in 1155, to Robert Marmion, "*pro*avus" of Philip. This, it will be seen, could only be the Robert whom I have inserted in the pedigree. Nor can Mr. Stapleton's "atavus" assumption be accepted in view of the facts. The "avunculus" and namesake of Henry III. would duly have been the "young king" Henry (crowned 1170). If "avunculus" is a clerical error, the word to substitute is "avus"; but the careful way in which the charter distinguishes the King's two predecessors is quite opposed to the idea that they were in both cases his grandfather.

As against the evidence afforded us by the charter of Henry III., we have the statements and documents relating to Barbery Abbey, a daughter of Savigny. It is alleged that the house was first founded in 1140[25] by that Robert Marmion who was slain at Coventry in 1143.[26] Stapleton accepted this without question. Yet, so far as documents are concerned, we have only the charter of Robert Marmion (1181), in which he speaks of his father Robert as beginning the foundation.[27] If that father were indeed the Robert who was slain in 1143, Stapleton's pedigree is duly proved as against that which I derive from Henry the Third's charter. But for this identification we have only, it would seem, the *obiter dictum* of the "Gallia Christiana" editors, while the fact that the first Abbot was appointed about 1177,[28] combined with the fact that Robert Marmion, in 1181, was avowedly completing that foundation which his father's death had arrested, certainly seems to point to his father's benefaction being then recent, and little previous to the said appointment of the first Abbot. In that case his father would be not the Robert who died in 1143, but a Robert who, as I suggest, came between the two.[29]

Leaving now this question of pedigree, there is a theory as to the name of Marmion which one cannot pass over in silence, because it has received the sanction even of Stapleton. Writing on the date of the Lindsey Survey, that eminent authority observes :—

---

[25] *Neustria Pia*, 68?.

[26] *Gallia Christiana* (1874), xi. 452.

[27] *Neustria Pia*, 881 ; *Gall. Christ.*, xi., Instr. 86.

[28] *Gall. Christ.*, xi. 452.

[29] Since this was written I have found that Mr. C. F. R. Palmer, in his admirable little treatise on the Marmion family (1875), duly inserts this intermediate Robert. Mr. Palmer has shown himself by far the best authority on the subject, and has printed a valuable charter of Stephen to Robert Marmion.

B.H.

O

Robert Le Despenser [*Dispensator*] was brother of Urso de Abbetot, whose other surname, Marmion, is equivalent in Norman French to the Latin word Dispensator; and as Robert Marmion died in 1107, it was probably in the following year that this catalogue was written.[30]

His meaning, though clumsily expressed, as was sometimes the case, is that the Latin "Dispensator" represented the name "Marmion." This theory would seem to be derived from the word "Marmiton" (not "Marmion") which means not a "Dispensator," but a scullion, the most despised of the menials employed in the kitchen. There was indeed in old French a rare word "Marmion," but according to Godefroy, it was equivalent to "Marmot," the name of the Marmoset. In any case, therefore, this illustrious surname, immortalized by Scott—

> They hailed him Lord of Fontenaye,
> Of Lutterworth and Scrivelbaye,
>   Of Tamworth tower and town—

had nothing to do with "Dispensator," but meant either a scullion or a monkey, and was one of those nicknames that the Normans loved to inexorably bestow on one another.

What was the actual relation of the Marmions to Robert "Dispensator" is a problem as yet unsolved. Mr. Waters wrote :—

It is generally believed that Scrivelsby and the rest of the Honour of Dispenser came to the Marmions through the marriage of Roger Marmion's grandson,[31] Robert Marmion, who was the husband of Matilda de Beauchamp, the grand-daughter of Urso de Abitot, and grand-niece of Robert Dispenser. But the Roll proves that Roger Marmion was the immediate heir of Robert Dispenser (p. 14).

I know of no such general belief. Stapleton, to whom one would naturally turn, had pointed out long before, in his

---

[30] Paper on "Holy Trinity Priory, York," p. 208 *note*. This identification is accepted by no less an authority than Mr. A. S. Ellis (*Domesday Tenants of Gloucestershire*, p. 69).

[31] *i.e.* according to Stapleton's pedigree.

"Rolls of the Norman Exchequer," that this survey proves Roger Marmion to have held the Lincolnshire fief of Robert "Dispensator,"[32] while those who have identified the latter magnate with Robert "Marmion" have traced the descent of Scrivelsby in the Marmions even from the Conquest.[33]

In any case, as I wrote in my *Ancient Charters* (1888) of a document there published :—

The succession of Urse [de Abetot] to this [Lincolnshire] fief is a genealogical discovery which throws a wholly new light on the very difficult problem of the relation of Marmion to Despenser, and is fatal to the assertion of Mr. Chester Waters that "Roger Marmion was the immediate heir of Robert Dispenser."

Moreover, in the Leicestershire Survey,[34] and still more in that of Worcestershire,[35] we have evidence that Robert's inheritance was shared between Beauchamp and Marmion which points there also to descent through Urse de Abetot. In my *Geoffrey de Mandeville* (pp. 313-315) I have suggested that in their rivalry for Tamworth,[36] the Marmions embraced the cause of Stephen, and the Beauchamps that of Maud, their variance being terminated under Henry II. by a matrimonial alliance. Such a compromise was common enough. It was agreed on in the case of Grantmesnil ; it was carried out at this very period in that of Fitzharding and Berkeley ; it was again resorted to at a later stage in the history of the house of Berkeley ; it was arranged in the case of Hastings ; and it was repeated in that of Boleyn, where the Butler inheritance was at stake.[37]

---

[32] And Mr. Palmer independently had done the same in his History of the Marmions (1875).

[33] Lodge's *Scrivelsby : the Home of the Champions.*

[34] See p. 214.   [35] See p. 175.

[36] It is certain that Tamworth originally belonged to Robert "Dispensator," and equally certain that it was held successively by Roger and Robert Marmion under Henry I.

[37] See my *Early Life of Anne Boleyn*, pp. 25-7.

THE LEICESTERSHIRE SURVEY

(1124-1129)

ASSERTING the importance of the Lindsey Survey, Mr. Chester Waters observed that "this is the sole record of its kind which deals with the interval between the completion of Domesday in 1086, and the compilation of the Pipe-Roll of 1129-1130, and that no similar return of the landowners of any other county is known to exist" (p. 2). And, indeed, it would seem that the survey to which I now address myself has hitherto remained unknown. It is found in the form of a late transcript on an unidentified roll in the Public Record Office.[1]

Comprising the whole of Gosecote Wapentake, and in part those of Framland and Gartree, it retains for these divisions the Domesday name of Wapentake—they are now "Hundreds"—while subdividing them into small "Hundreds," of which the existence seems to have been hitherto unsuspected. Proceeding, like the I.C.C., "Hundred" by "Hundred," and Vill by Vill, it enables us, like that document, to reconstitute the aggregate assessments, and thus affords priceless evidence on "the six-carucate unit."[2] But apart from this, it is invested with no small importance from that "great want of documentary evidence" for the reign of Henry I. which Mr. Hunter rightly lamented in his elaborate introduction to the first great roll of the Pipe (p. ii.). It affords us new and trustworthy evidence on the many vicissitudes of the great fiefs, and enables us, while

---

[1] Q.R., Misc. Bdle. 558, I.P.R., 8113; Knights' Fees, Com. Leic.
[2] See pp. 80-82.

tracing the fortunes of their owners, to see how the first Henry provided for his *novi homines*, showering escheats and royal demesne on the trusty officials he had raised "from the dust," as well as on his favourite nephew, Stephen, Count of Mortain.

The date of this survey is thus determined. The frequent mention of "Rex D[avid]" places it subsequent to his accession to the throne in April, 1124. On the other hand, the name of Ralf Basset (the justiciar) shows it to be anterior to his death; and he was dead before Mich., 1130 (*Rot. Pip.*, 31 Hen. I.). Moreover, it speaks more than once of Hugh de Leicester as "Vicecomes," and Hugh's shrievalty seems from the Pipe-Roll to have terminated at Mich., 1129. We may therefore place this survey between the spring of 1124 and the autumn of 1129, with a likelihood of its having been compiled nearer the latter date.

Text of the Survey.

. . . "Comes Lerc[estri]æ vj. car.

H[undredum] de [3] *Langeton'*.—In eadem villa Comes Lerc[estriæ] xj. car. et j. virg. Ibidem Ric[ardus] Basset iii. car. et. j. virg. In thorp Eustaci[us] iij. car. et. iij. virg. In alia Langeton' Abbas de Burg' iiij. car. et iii. virg. Ibidem Henricus de pport j. car. In thurlington idem Henricus xij. car. In sscanketon' Comes Lerc[estriæ] x. car. Ansch' ij. car.[4]

H[undredum] de Chiburd'.—In eadem villa xii. car. de feodo Ansch'. In alia chiburd' Walt[erus] de Bell' campo xj. car., Ricardus Basset j. car. In bocton Comes Leicestriæ xij. car. In carleton' idem Comes x. car. Et Monachi Sancti Arnulphi v. virg. Et de ssoch' Regis iij. virg.[5]

H[undredum] de Knossinton.—In eadem villa ij. car. de Honore. de Blida. Et Henricus de ferr' iij. car. et. iij. virg. In Osolinstona Rex D[avid] vij. car. In Picwell et in Lucerthorp de feudo Rogeri ed Moubray xv. car. In Neubotel Robertus de ferr' j. car. et dim.

---

[3] MS. "in."

[4] Langton, Thorpe Langton, Tur Langton, Shangton. Kibworth, Burton Overy, Carlton Curlieu.

In Burg' Marm' iij. car.   In Balbegrav: vj. car. iij. bov. minus de Soch[a] Regis.   In Mardefeud iij. car. de eadem Soch[a].   In alia Mardefeud iij. car.[6]

GOSECOTE WAP'.

H[undredum] de Lodinton[e], in Sceftinton[e] Norm[annus] de Verdun viij. car. et dim.   Ricardus Bass[et] iij. car. et dim.   In Gokebia Normannus de Verdun vj. car.   In Adelacston[e] v. car. et j. virg. de feodo Regis David.   Et de Soch[a] Regis iij. virg.   In Ludinton[e] Ricardus Basset xii. car.   In Thorp et in Twyford Ricardus de Roll[os] ix. car. j. bov. minus.   Ibidem Henricus de ferr[ariis] ix. car. j. bov. minus.   Et de Soch[a] Regis v. car.   Ex hiis Grimbaldus tenet dim. car. et Rex D[avid] j. car.   In Norton[e] x. bov.   Walter de Bello campo vj. car.   Et Roger de Moubray iiij. car. et iij. virg.[7]

H[undredum] de[8] Tilton.—In eadem villa ij. car. j. bov. minus de Soch[a] Regis.   Ibidem Walt[erus] de Bello campo iij. car.   Archiepiscopus[9] j. car.   In Neuton[e] Walter de Bello campo iiij. car.   Roger de Moubray viii. car.   In Lousebia Rex David xij. car.   In Watebergia Dominicum Regis iiij. car.   In Hallested Normannus de Verdun iij. car. j. virg. minus.[10]

H[undredum] de bebia.—In eadem villa Abbas de Croyland xij. car.   In Cahiham iiij. car. de Soch[a] Regis.   Comes Lercestrie ij. car.   In Hung'ton ix. car.   In Siglebia ix. car. et. vj. bov. et dim. de[11] Comite Lercestriæ.   Ibidem Comes Cestrie iij. car.   Ibidem Ricardus Basset ij. car.   Robertus de ferrer[iis] v. bov.[12]

H[undredum] de Barkbia.—In eadem villa v. car. de feodo de Belvar[o].   In Hamelton' et in thorp vi. car. de eodem feudo, et de feodo Comitis Lercestriæ j. car. et dim.   In Thormedeston Canonici iij. car.   In Crocheston[e] ij. car. et j. bov. et dim. de Soch[a] Regis.   In Neubold[e] Robertus de ferer[iis] j. car. et dim.   In Barnesby Rex iij. car. et dim. bov.   Ibidem Comes Lercestriæ xiij. bov.   In Gadesby [t]erra[13] Reg[is] viij. car. et dim. et dim. et dim. (*sic*) bov.

---

[6] Knossington, Owston, Picwell and Leesthorpe, Newbold, Burrow, Baggrave, Marefield.
[7] Skeffington, Allexton, Thorpe and Twyford, East Norton.
[8] MS. "in."   [9] MS. "Archid."
[10] Tilton, Loseby, Whadborough, Halstead.
[11] Interlined.   [12] Beeby, Keyham, Hungerton, [? Sileby].
[13] MS. injured here.

Ibidem Episcopus Lincolniensis viij. bov. Comes Lercestriæ j. car. et dim. bov. Ricardus Basset dim. car. Rex D[avid] ij. car.[14]

H[undredum] de Essebia.—In eadem villa Rex David v. car. Ibidem Hugo de Lerc[estria] j. car. In Humberstay Roger de Ram[is] viij. car. Ibidem Walter de Mustere j. car. Rad[ulfus] de Martinwast iij. car. In Mardegrave Comes Lercestriæ xij. car. In thurmedeston idem Comes car. (*sic*). Idem in Burstall ix. car. Idem in Anlepia vij. car. Idem in Anesting[e] vj. car.[15]

H[undredum] de Resebia.—In eadem villa Ricardus Basset v. car. Ibidem Comes Cestrie ij. car. et dim. Rex David iiij car. et dim. In Quenburg[o] xij. car. de feodo de Belvar[o]. In Siefton[e] Comes Lercestriæ xij. car. In Brokesbya Comes (*sic*) Cestrie v. car. Rex David j. car. quam Pip[er]d tenet. In Quenebia vj. car. de feodo de Belvar[o]. In thurketleston[e] de feodo Comitis viij. car. In Cropeston[e] iiij. car. In Rodeleia terra Regis v. car.[16]

H[undrednm] de Magna Dalbia.—In eadem villa Episcopus Lincolniensis ix. car. et dim. Radulfus Basset j. car. et iij. bov. Ibidem Wil[elmus] Gam[erarius] j. car. In frisebia Comes Cestrie iij. car., et de Soch[a] Regis viij. car. In Rederbia Comes cestrie vi. car. In Asfordebia Comes Lercestriæ xiij. car. In Wartnadeby de Soch[a] Regis vi. car.[17]

Hundredum de Dalbia super Wald'.—In eadem villa ix. car. de feodo Edwardi de sar[esbiria], Comes Lercestrie iij. car. In Grimestona de Soch[a] Regis iij. car. j. bov. et dim. minus. Ricardus Basset iij. car. In Saxebia Comes Lercestrie v. car. et de Soch[a] Regis j. car. In Siwaldebia Comes Lercestrie vj. car. In Cosinton[e] Comes Cestrie vj. car. In Horton[e] Robertus de Jor' ij. car.[18]

H[undredum] de Turstanestona.—In eadem villa Thomas x. car. et iij. virg. Ibidem Roger de Moubray xiiij. bov. In Wileges ij. car. de eodem feudo. In Rachedal[e] vj. car. de eodem feudo. In Houbia

[14] Barkby, Hambleton, Thorpe, Thurmaston, South Croxton, Barsby Gaddesby.
[15] Ashby, Humberstone, Belgrave, Thurmaston, Birstall, Wanlip, Ansty.
[16] Rearsby, Queensborough, Syston, Brooksby, Rothley, Thurcaston, Cropston.
[17] Great Dalby, Frisby, Rotherby, Asfordby, Wartnaby.
[18] Dalby on the Wolds, Grimston, Saxelby, Sileby, Cossington, Hoton.

vij. car. et j. virg. de feodo Thome.   Ibidem de feodo Albemarl' iiij. car. et iij. virg.[19]

H[undredum] de tunga.—In eadem villa cum appendiciis xij. car. de feodo Roberti de ferr[ariis].   In Caggworth Comes Cestrie xv. car.   In Wrdintona iij. car. secundum cartam Regis et s[uper] dictum[20] hominum hundredi xij. car.[21]

H[undredum] de[22] *Luaeb'.*—In eadem villa j. H[ida] et xiij. car. cum appendiciis.   In cherlega vj. car. et dim.   In Dixeleia et in Geroldon et in Thorp ix. car.   In Hantirna est dim. H[ida].[28]

H[undredum] de Beltona.—In eadem villa Normannus de Verdon vj. car.   In Overton[e] Ricardus Basset iiij. car.   In Wrdinton[e] j. car.   In alia Overton[e] Robertus de ferr[ariis] ij. car., ibidem Comes Cestrie j. car.   In Stanton Robertus de ferr[ariis] ij. car.   Ibidem Normannus de Verdon iij. car.   In Dailescroft Philippus de Bello Campo Maresc[allus] j. car.   In Doninton Comes Cestrie cum appendiciis xxij. car. et dim.   In Witewic Comes Lercestrie j. car. et dim.   Ibidem Robertus de ferr[ariis] j. car. et dim.[24]

H[undredum] de Dichesword.—In eadem villa Robertus de ferr[ariis] vj. car. et j. virg. Comes cestrie vj. car.   Ibidem Comes iij. car. et dim.   Normannus de Verdon j. car. et ij. bov.   In Hanthirn[e] ix. car.   In Widesers iij. car. Willelmi de Gresel[e].   Idem in Lintona j. car.   In blakefordeb[ia] Comes Lercestriæ iij. car.   In Culverteb[ia] ij. car. et Robertus de ferr[ariis] j. car.   In Wodete Robertus de ferr[ariis] j. car. et dim.   In Alton[e] Comes Lercestriæ j. car. et dim.   Idem in Raveneston[e] j. virg. et dim.   Ibidem Comes Cestrie iij. virg. et dim.   Et Comes War' ij. car.   In Suipestona Hugo vic[ecomes] ij. car.[25]

H[undredum] de Seyla.—In eadem villa Robertus de ferr[ariis] vij. car.   In alia Seyla idem vj. car.   Idem in Bocthorp j. car.   Idem in appelbia j. car. et j. bov.   Idem in Strecton j. car. et dim.   Idem in Durantestorp ij. car. quas Walkelinus tenet.   Idem in Swepeston[e]

[19] Thrussington, Ragdale, Hoby.
[20] MS. illegible.   [21] Tong, Kegworth, Worthington.
[22] MS. "in."
[23] Loughborough, Charley, Dishley, Garendon, Thorpe, Hathern.
[24] Belton, [?Coleorton], Worthington, Staunton Harold, Castle Donington, Whitwick.
[25] Diseworth, Hathern, Linton (Derby), Blackfordby, Ravenstone, Snibston.

vj. car. In Neuton ij. car. In Actorp dim. car. In Chilteston
Comes cestrie j. car. Idem in Alpelbia dim. car. In Assebia Comes
Lercestriæ iij. car. In Pakinton Hugo Vicecomes v. car. Idem in
Osgodesthorp dim. car. In scegla Henricus de Alben[eio] ij. car.
que pertinent ad defencionem de Swepeston[e].[26]

H[undredum] de Shepesheved.—In eadem villa Comes [   ][27] et
in wacthon[e] et in Lokinton et in Aminton ij. h[idas] et dim. et
iiij. car. In Wacton[e] Normannus de Verdon ij. car. et ij. bov.[28]

FRAMELAUND WAP'.

H[undredum] de caleverton[e].—In eadem villa xij. car. de feodo
Willelmi de Alben[eio]. In Someredebia Robertus de ferr[ariis] v.
car. Ibidem Roger de Moubray vj. car. Ibidem Robertus Marm-
[ion] iij. car. et in Burg[o] iij car. In Dalbia Robertus de ferr[ariis]
v. car. et j. bov. de feodo tessun. Ibidem Roger de Moubray xv.
bov. In Wittok Walt[erus] de bello campo j. car. et dim. In Gille-
thorp Roger de Moubray iij. car. Idem in Burg[o] j. car. In
Neubold Robertus de ferr[ariis] j. car. et dim.[29]

H[undredum] de Estwell.—In eadem villa Robertus de ferr[ariis]
ij. car. Ibidem Roger de Moubray vj. car. Robertus de insula iiij.
car. In aitona idem Robertus iij. car. et ij. bov. Et de Belvero dim
car. et dim. bov. Ibidem Robertus de insula viij. car. et ij. bov. et
dim. In Branteston[e] Episcopus Lincolniensis vij. car. et dim.
Robertus de Insula iiij. car. et dim.[30]

H[undredum] de Melton[e].—In eadem villa Roger de Moubray xv.
car. Idem in Burton[e] xj. car. et vij. bov. Et de Honore blide iij.
car. Robertus de ferr[ariis] ix. bov. In Fredebia ix. car. et ij. bov.
et dim.[31]

H[undredum] de Chirchebia.—In eadem villa Roger de Moubray
xxiiij. car. Idem in chetlebia viiij. car. In Sixtenebia iiij. car. et
dim. de eodem feudo. Ibidem Rex D[avid] iiij. car. et dim. In
alebia ix. car. de feudo Rogeri. Ibidem Rex David iij. car.[32]

[26] Seal (Nether and Over), Bogthorpe, Appleby, Stretton on le Field,
Donisthorpe, Swepston, Oakthorpe, Ashby, Pakington, Osgathorpe.
[27] Blank in MS.   [28] Sheepshed, Whatton, Lockington.
[29] Cold Overton, Somerby, Burrow, Dalby, Withcote, Newbold.
[30] Eastwell, Eaton, Branston.
[31] Melton Mowbray, Burton Lazars, Freeby.
[32] Kirby Bellars, Abkettleby, Sysonby.

H[undredum] de Droctona.—In eadem villa Comes de Moretonio
xij. car. In thorp Comes Lercestriæ xij. car. In brantingbia vj. car.
de eodem feodo. In Ringolfestorp ij. car. et ij. bov. de eodem feodo.
Robertus de ferrer[iis] j. car. et vj. bov. In Wyfordebia iiij. car. et
dim. de blide. Roger de Moubray j. car. et dim. In chetelby et
Holewell[e] ix. car. de feodo Basset. Episcopus Lincolniensis j.
car.[88]

H[undredum] de Scaldeford.—In eadem villa Rex David xj. car. et
dim. Ricardus Basset dim. car. In Goutebia Roger de Moubray
vj. car. In Knipton Comes de Moriton[io] viij. car. et vi. bov., et
Willelmus de Alben[eio] iij. car. et ij. bov.[84]

H[undredum] de[85] Waltham.—In eadem villa Comes Lercestriæ
xvj. car. et dim. Alanus de creon ij. car. et dim. In Stonesbia
idem Alanus viij. car. In Caston Robertus de ferr[ariis] ix. car.[86]

H[undredum] de Barcheston.—In eadem villa Willelmus de Alben-
[eio] xxiij. car. G. Camerarius j. car. In Saltebia et berthaldebia xx.
car. de feodo Peuerelli. In Garthorp Willelmus Mesch[in] vij. car.[87]

H[undredum] de Sproxcheston[e].—In eadem villa Rex David viij.
car. Alanus de Creon ij. car. Ibidem filius Gilberti ij. car. In
Bucheminest[re] et in Seustern[e] ix. car. et dim. de feodo Episcopi
Lincolniensis. Ibidem Robertus de ferer[iis] dim. car. Willelmus
Mesch[in] v. car. In Sessebia Rex David iij. car. Robertus de
ferrer[iis] iiij. car.[88]

H[undredum] de Claxton[e].—In eadem villa xvi. car. et dim. et dim.
bov. Ibidem Henricus Tuchet xj. car. j. bov. minus. In Houwes
de feodo de Beluer vij. car. et dim.[89]

H[undredum] de Stapelford.—In eadem villa x. car. de feodo Roberti
de ferrer[iis]. In Wymundeham et in thorp xxvij. car. et dim. de
eodem feodo. Ricardus Basset iij. car. et dim.[40]

H[undredum] de Herdebia.—In eadem villa et in plungar xvij. car.

---

[88] Nether Broughton, Thorpe, Brentingby, Wyfordby, Abkettleby,
Holwell.
[84] Scalford, Goadby, Knipton.
[85] MS. "in."   [86] Waltham, Stonesby, Coston.
[87] Barkstone, Saltby [?Bescoby], Garthorpe.
[88] Sproxton, Seustern, Buckminster, Saxby.
[89] Clawson, Hose.
[40] Stapleford, Wymondham, Edmondthorpe.

de feodo Willelmi de Alben[eio]. Ibidem Ricardus Basset j. car. In Stacthirn Willelmus de Alben[eio] viij. car. et dim. Ibidem Roger de Moubray viij. car. Robertus de Insula j. car. et dim.[41]

H[undredum] de Botlesford.—In eadem villa et Moston et Normanton[e] Willelmus de Alben[eio] xxxij. car. Ibidem Agnes de Gaunt ij. car. In Moston[e] Robertus de Insula j. car. et dim.[42]

[H]undredum de crocstona.—In eadem villa Comes Maur[itonii] xxiiij. car. In Harestan idem Comes xij. car."[43] . . -
[FINIS].

The work of identifying the places named in this survey is difficult, not only from the corruption of the text, but also from the fact that many of them are only obscure names, needing, for their perfect ascertainment, local knowledge. A careful study of the map will show that these Leicestershire "Hundreds," unlike those to which we are accustomed in the hidated districts, were strangely intermingled among themselves. Another of their peculiarities is that just as we find the reconquered "shires" named each after its capital town, so these "Hundreds" were each named after one of their Vills instead of after some natural object—probably the meeting-place of the primitive moot [44]—as so often in the south of England.

It is important to observe that, except for this survey, we should not even have known of the existence of these "Hundreds" in Leicestershire. And when we compare the entry on our roll—"Framelaund Wap'. Hundredum de Calevertone. In eadem villa xii. car."—with that in the Derbyshire Domesday: "Morelestan Wepentac. Salle Hundred. In Salle et Draicot et Opewelle . . . xii. car." (i. 273), it is scarcely possible to resist the conclusion that, in this passage relating to Sawley, divided only by a river

---

[41] Harby, Plungar, Stathern.

[42] Bottesford, Muston, Normanton.

[43] Croxton, Harston.

[44] See the valuable list, for Dorset, in Mr. Eyton's *Key to Domesday*, p. 143.

from Leicestershire, we have a glimpse of the same system
existing in Derbyshire also. That is to say, that Sawley
was not a "Hundred" of twelve carucates,[45] as has been
suggested,[46] but was the *caput* of a "Hundred" similar to
those of Leicestershire. I believe, indeed, that in our
survey we see the system on which these counties were
surveyed in 1086. The original returns will have been
drawn up Wapentake by Wapentake, and "Hundred" by
"Hundred." But when transcribed into Domesday Book
the entries were arranged under Wapentakes alone, and
the headings of the "Hundreds" omitted. In the case of
Sawley alone the heading slipped in, immediately preceding
the entry of the Manor, as it must have done on the original return. It is thus that I account for the mention of
"leets" slipping into the Norfolk Domesday, in two cases,
from the original return; [47] just as, in Cambridgeshire, the
total assessments of Impington and Chatteris have slipped,
from the original returns, into the *Inq. Eliensis*,[48] though
duly omitted in Domesday Book.

One more point should be noticed. The somewhat
mysterious entry of land belonging "ad defensionem de
Swepestone" is at once made clear when we compare it
with that "Defensio x. acrarum," to which I have appealed [49] in discussing "Wara," and which, like the
"wered" of the Northamptonshire geld-roll,[50] refers to
assessment for Danegeld.

We will now collate some of our "Hundreds" with the
relative entries in Domesday.

---

[45] The Lincolnshire "Hundred."
[46] Waters' *Survey of Lindsey*, p. 5; *Eng. Hist. Rev.*, v. 100; *supra*, p. 78.
[47] *Supra*, p. 101.
[48] Ed. Hamilton, pp. 113, 116.
[49] *Supra*, p. 117.
[50] *Snpra* p. 152.

LODINGTON HUNDRED.

(1086.)   (1124-9)

Skeffington.

Rex	12	Norman de Verdon	$8\frac{1}{2}$
		Richard Basset	$3\frac{1}{2}$

Tugby.

Rex	6	Norman de Verdon	6

Allexton.

Countess Judith	6	King David's fee	$5\frac{1}{4}$
		Rex	$\frac{3}{4}$

Lodington.

Robert de Buci	12	Richard Basset	12

Twyford.

Rex	$4\frac{1}{2}$	Richard de Rullos	$8\frac{3}{4}$
Thorpe Sackville.		Henry de Ferrers	$8\frac{3}{4}$

East Norton.

[? Rex	3]	[Richard Basset]	$1\frac{1}{4}$
Robert dispensator	$4\frac{1}{2}$	Walter de Beauchamp	6
Geoffrey de la Guerche	$4\frac{1}{2}$	Roger de Mowbray	$4\frac{3}{4}$
	12		12

TILTON HUNDRED.

Tilton.

Rex	2	Rex	$1\frac{3}{4}$
Robert Despencer	3	Walter de Beauchamp	3
Archbishop of York	1	Archbishop	1
	6		$5\frac{3}{4}$

Newton Burdet.

Geoffrey de la Guerche	6	Walter de Beauchump	4
Hubert *serviens*	$\frac{1}{2}$	Roger de Mowbray	8

Loseby.

Countess Judith	9	King David	12

Whadborough.

Rex	3	Rex	4

Halsted.

Rex	$2\frac{3}{4}$	Norman de Verdon	$2\frac{3}{4}$

BEBY HUNDRED.

Beby.

Crowland Abbey . . . . $10\frac{1}{2}$ Crowland Abbey 12

Keyham.

Rex . . . . 4 Rex 4

Hungerton.   9

Sileby.

Hugh de Grantmesnil . . $8\frac{1}{2}$ Earl of Leicester . . . $9\frac{13}{16}$

                          Earl of Chester 3

Rex . . . . $3\frac{1}{4}$ Richard Basset 2

                          Robert de Ferrers . . . $1\frac{1}{4}$

BARKBY HUNDRED.

Barkby.[51]

Robert de Todeni . . . 18   "Belvoir" 5

Hambleton. . . . .   "   6

Barkby Thorpe.

Adeliza de Grentmesnil . . $1\frac{1}{2}$ Earl of Leicester . . . . $1\frac{1}{2}$

Thurmaston.

Hugh de Grentmesnil . . 10

     "   "   . . $3\frac{1}{2}$ { Canons [of St. Mary de

                                 Castro, Leicester][52] . . 3

Croxton.

                          Rex . . . . $2\frac{3}{16}$

Newbold Folvile

Henry de Ferrers 1   Robert de Ferrers . . . . $1\frac{1}{2}$

Barnesby.

Rex . . . . $4\frac{5}{8}$ Rex . . . . $3\frac{1}{16}$

                          Earl of Leicester . . . $1\frac{5}{8}$

Gaddesby.

Rex . . . . $8\frac{3}{8}$ Rex . . . . $8\frac{9}{16}$

   "   1   Bishop of Lincoln . . . 1

Countess Judith . . . 2   Earl of Leicester . . . $1\frac{1}{16}$

                          Richard Basset . . . . $\frac{1}{2}$

                          King David 2

---

[51] Including Hambleton and Hungerton (6) in Domesday.
[52] By grant of Robert, Count of Meulan.

HUNDRED OF ASHBY.

Ashby Folvile.

Countess Judith	4[53]	King David	5
„ „	1½	Hugh of Leicester	1
Humfrey *camerarius*	1[54]		

Humberston.

Hugh de Grentmesnil?	Roger de Ramis	8
	Walter de Mustere	1
	Ralf de Martinwast	3

Belgrave.

Hugh de Grentmesnil	7	Earl of Leicester	12
Adeliza de Grentmesnil	1		

Thurmaston.

	Earl of Leicester . . . [10]

Burstall.

Hugh de Grentmesnil	6	Earl of Leicester	9

Wanlip.

"In manu Regis"	4	Earl of Leicester	7
Hugh de Grentmesnil	2	„ „	6[55]

REARSBY HUNDRED.

Reresby.

Robert de Buci	1¾	Richard Basset	5
Rex	1⅞	Earl of Chester	2½
Countess Judith	2½	King David	4½

Queneborough.

Geoffrey de la Guerche	9	"Belvoir"	12

Syston.

Hugh de Grentmesnil	9	Earl of Leicester	12

Brooksby.

Earl of Chester	2	Earl of Chester	5
Countess Judith	¾	King David	1

Quenby.

Robert de Todeni	2	"Belvoir"	6
„ „ (in South Croxton)	4		

[53] In Newbold. [54] In Barnsby
[55] Given (as 24 virgates) to Leicester Abbey.

Thurcaston.

Hugh de Grentmesnil . . 9   Earls ⌐of Leicester] . . . 8

Cropston.

Rothley.

Rex 5   Rex 5

DALBY HUNDRED.

Great Dalby.

Bishop of Lincoln . . . 8   Bishop of Lincoln . . . $9\frac{1}{2}$
Robert de Buci 1   Ralf Basset . . . . . . $1\frac{3}{8}$
Humfrey Cam. 1   William "Gam" 1

Frisby.

Rex (Barrow) 1   Earl of Chester 4
Rex 8   Rex 8

Retherby.

Rex (Barrow) . . . . . $2\frac{3}{4}$ Earl of Chester 6

Ashfordby.

Rex (Rothley) 12   Earl of Leicester . . . 13
Radulfus Framen . . . . $3\frac{1}{2}$

Wartnaby.

Rex 6   Rex 6

HUNDRED OF DALBY ON THE WOLDS.

Dalby on the Wolds.

Ralf fitz Hubert 9   Edward of Salisbury . . . 9
                            Earl of Leicester 3

Grimston.

Rex . . . . $2\frac{13}{16}$ Rex . . . . $2\frac{13}{16}$
Robert de Buci 3   Richard Basset 3

Saxelby.

Rex 1   Rex 1
                            Earl of Leicester 5

Sileby.

Hugh de Grentmesnil . . $8\frac{1}{2}$ Earl of Leicester 6

Cossington.

Earl of Chester 6   Earl of Chester 6

Hoton.

Robert de Lorz 4	Robert de Jor' 2

Thrussington.

Guy de Reinbudcurt . . . 12	Thomas . . . . . . 10¼?
[18]	Roger de Mowbray . . . 1¾

" Wilges."

Robert de Buci 2	Roger de Mowbray . . . 2

Ragdale.

Robert de Buci 6	Roger de Mowbray . . . 6

Hoby.

	Thomas 7¼
Dru de Bevrere 4¼	"Albemarle" 4¾

HUNDRED OF TONG.

Tong.

Henry de Ferrers 21½	Robert de Ferrers . . . 12

Kegworth.

Earl of Chester 15	Earl of Chester 15

Worthington.

Henry de Ferrers 4	
	3 or 12

In the case of this last Hundred our survey records a conflict of testimony and, in so doing, mentions incidentally (as would Domesday) the witness of the Hundred-court. Henry de Ferrers in the Domesday Survey, is credited with 21½ car. in " Tunge cum omnibus appendiciis," and with 4 in "Werditone" (i. 233). But here Tong, "cum appendiciis," is reckoned at 12 car. only. There remained, therefore, to be accounted for a large balance of car., and these the men of the Hundred assigned to his Manor of Worthington.

It is desirable to analyse some of the fiefs in our survey, and, by comparison with Domesday, to trace their descent or origin.

B.H.

P

Roger de Mowbray's fief.

<table>
<tr><td colspan="2">(1124-9.)</td><td colspan="2">(1086.)</td></tr>
<tr><td></td><td>car.</td><td colspan="2">[Geoffrey de la Guerche.</td></tr>
<tr><td>Picwell and Lucerthorp . .</td><td>15</td><td>Pichewelle and Luvestorp</td><td>14</td></tr>
<tr><td>East Norton . . . .</td><td>$4\frac{3}{4}$</td><td>East Norton . . . .</td><td>$4\frac{1}{2}$</td></tr>
<tr><td>Newton Burdet . . . .</td><td>8</td><td>Newton Burdet . . . .</td><td>6</td></tr>
<tr><td>Thrussington . . . .</td><td>$1\frac{3}{4}$</td><td></td><td></td></tr>
<tr><td></td><td></td><td colspan="2">[Robert de Buci.]</td></tr>
<tr><td>Wileges . . . . . .</td><td>2</td><td>Wilges . . . . . .</td><td>2</td></tr>
<tr><td>Rachedale . . . . .</td><td>6</td><td>Ragendele . . . . .</td><td>6</td></tr>
<tr><td></td><td></td><td colspan="2">[Geoffrey de la Guerche.]</td></tr>
<tr><td>Somerby . . . . . .</td><td>6</td><td>Dalby . . . . . .</td><td>4</td></tr>
<tr><td>Dalby . . . . . .</td><td>$1\frac{7}{8}$</td><td>,, ...</td><td>$2\frac{1}{2}$</td></tr>
<tr><td>Gillethorp . . . . .</td><td>3</td><td>Godtorp . . . . . .</td><td>$3\frac{1}{2}$</td></tr>
<tr><td>Burg . . . . . .</td><td>1</td><td>Burg . . . . . .</td><td>1</td></tr>
<tr><td>Eastwell . . . . .</td><td>6</td><td>Eastwell . . . . .</td><td>6</td></tr>
<tr><td>Melton . . . . . .</td><td>15</td><td>Melton . . . . . .</td><td></td></tr>
<tr><td>Burton . . . . . .</td><td>$11\frac{7}{8}$</td><td>Burton . . . . . .</td><td>$11\frac{7}{8}$</td></tr>
<tr><td>[Fredebie . . . . .</td><td>$9\frac{5}{16}$</td><td>Fredebie . . . . .</td><td>10]</td></tr>
<tr><td>Chirchebia . . . . .</td><td>24</td><td>Cherchebi (17 + 7) . . .</td><td>24</td></tr>
<tr><td>Kettleby . . . .</td><td>9 (?)</td><td>Chettlebi . . . . .</td><td>8</td></tr>
<tr><td>Sixtenebia . . . .</td><td>$4\frac{1}{2}$</td><td>Sistenebi ($2\frac{1}{2}$ + 2). . . .</td><td>$4\frac{1}{2}$</td></tr>
<tr><td>Alebia . . . . .</td><td>9</td><td>Alebia . . . . . .</td><td>$7\frac{3}{4}$</td></tr>
<tr><td>Wyfordebia . . . .</td><td>$1\frac{1}{2}$</td><td>Wordebia . . . . .</td><td>$1\frac{1}{2}$</td></tr>
<tr><td>Goutebi . . . . .</td><td>6</td><td>Goutebi . . . . .</td><td>6</td></tr>
<tr><td>Stacthirn . . . . .</td><td>8</td><td>Stachetone . . . . .</td><td>$8\frac{1}{4}$</td></tr>
</table>

Anschitel's fief.

<table>
<tr><td></td><td>car.</td><td></td><td>car.</td><td></td></tr>
<tr><td>Scanketon'</td><td>2</td><td>Scantone</td><td>2</td><td>Robert de Veci.</td></tr>
<tr><td>Chiburd</td><td>12</td><td>Chiborne</td><td>12</td><td>Robert de Veci.</td></tr>
</table>

Edward of Salisbury's fief.

<table>
<tr><td>Dalby on the Wolds . . }</td><td>9</td><td>Dalbi . . . .</td><td>9</td><td>Ralf fitz Hubert.</td></tr>
</table>

William Meschin's fief.

<table>
<tr><td>Seustern . .</td><td>5</td><td>Seustern . . .</td><td>5</td><td>William Lovet.</td></tr>
</table>

Henry de Albini's fief.

<table>
<tr><td>Scegla . . . .</td><td>2</td><td>Sela . . . .</td><td>2</td><td>Nigel de Albini.</td></tr>
</table>

Gilbert's son's fief.

Sproxcheston . . 2 Sprotone . . . 2 Godfrey de Cambrai.

William Chamberlain's fief.

Great Dalby . . 1 Dalby . . . . 1 { Hunfridus Camerarius.

Thomas's fief.

Thrussington $10\frac{3}{4}$ }
Hoby . . $7\frac{1}{4}$ } 18   Thrussington . 18 Guy de Rembodcurt.

Count of Mortain's fief.

Broctone . .	12	Broctone . .	12	Rex.
Knipton . . .	$8\frac{3}{4}$	Cnipeton . .	$8\frac{3}{4}$	Rex.
Croxton . .	24	Croxton . .	24	Rex.
Harestan . .	12	Horstan . .	12	Rex.

Alan de Craon's fief.

Stoneby . . . 8 Stoneby . . . 8 Guy de Craon.
Waltham . . . $2\frac{1}{2}$ Waltham . . $2\frac{1}{2}$ Guy de Craon.
Sproxton . . . 3 Sproxton . . 2 Guy de Craon.

William de Albini's fief.

Cold Overton . 12 Cold Overton . 12 Dru de Bevrere.
Knipton . . . $3\frac{1}{4}$ Knipton . . . $3\frac{1}{4}$ Robert de Todeni.
Herdebi and
  Plungar . . 17 Herdeby . . . 17 Robert de Todeni.
Stacthirn . . . $8\frac{1}{2}$ Stacthirn . . $9\frac{3}{4}$ Robert de Todeni.
Bottlesford . . 32 Bottlesford . 24 (?) Robert de Todeni.

Henry Tuchet's fief.

Claxton . . . $10\frac{7}{8}$ Claxton . .6 }
Howes . .$4\frac{1}{2}$ } $10\frac{1}{2}$ Robert Hostiarius.
Robert Hostiarius.

Richard Basset's fief.

car.
Langton . . . $3\frac{1}{4}$
Chiburd . . . 1
Skeffington . . $3\frac{1}{2}$ Skeffington . . $3\frac{1}{2}$ Rex.
Lodington . . 12 Lodington . . 12 Robert de Buci.
Sileby . . . . 2 Sileby . . . $2\frac{1}{4}$ Rex.
Gaddesby . . $\frac{1}{2}$
Reresby . . . 5 Reresby . . . $1\frac{3}{4}$ Robert de Buci.
Grimstone . . 3 Grimstone . . 3 Robert de Buci.

Overton . . .	4	Overton . . .	4	Robert de Buci.
Kettleby and Holwell	9	Holwell . . .	5	Robert de Buci.
		Kettleby . . .	6	
Goatby . . .	6	Goatby . . .	6	Robert de Buci.
Scaldeford . .		Scaldeford . .	½	Robert de Buci.
Wymondham and Thorpe	3½	Wymondham .	3½	Robert de Buci.
Hardebi . . .	1	Hertebi . . .	1	Robert de Buci.

The fief of Richard Basset is that of a typical man, of one of those trusted officials who flourished under Henry the First. We know not the fate of Robert de Buci, a Domesday baron in Leicestershire and Northants; but as two, at least, of his Leicestershire estates passed, we have seen, to Mowbray, it was, we may infer, forfeiture or escheat that brought his fief into the king's hands, and enabled him to divide it among his own favourites. We learn from the evidence to which I am coming that the eight carucates in Swinford and Walcote, and the two in Little Ashby which Robert de Buci had held in 1086, were in the hands of Geoffrey Ridel ninety years later. We may then infer, though they are not included in the sphere of our survey, that they had been obtained, like the rest, by Basset *temp*. Hen. I.[56]

The elaborate fine made at Leicester, 31st June, 1176,[5] has an important bearing on the Bassets' Leicestershire possessions. Not only does it specify the lands they held at Swinford (with Walcote), Ashby, and Fleckney, but it mentions their fee of Madeley, Staffordshire. Now the descent of this Staffordshire fee can be traced by charters on the same roll.[58] One of these (No. 12) is a confirmation, by Robert de Stafford, of Madeley to Geoffrey Ridel, to be held as his "antecessores" had held it. This was Geoffrey, son of Richard Basset, by Maud Ridel, as is shown by the fact that the first witness to the charter is Hervey de Stret-

---

[56] See also *supra*, p. 155.
[57] *Infra*, p. 514.
[58] *Sloane Cart.*, xxxi. 4.

ton, who held two knights' fees of Stafford in 1166,[59] and that another is Robert Bagot, who held a quarter of a fee,[60] while Geoffrey Ridel himself then held one, namely, Madeley.[61] But the enrolling scribe confused him with his (maternal) grandfather and namesake (d. 1120), and thus wrongly assigned this charter to the reign of Henry I., and threw the whole descent into utter confusion. The right clue is found in a charter of Robert "de Toni" (*i.e.* de Stafford), "conceding" Madeley to Robert "de Busa" (*alias* "de Busci"), "per servitium unius militis." [62] This fee, therefore, must have come to the Bassets with the rest of the Buci estates; and we thus learn that this must have been late in the reign of Henry I., for the names of the witnesses to this charter prove that it must be subsequent to 1122.[63]

As Robert de Buci was then in possession, it cannot have been, here at least, till later that Basset succeeded him.

Among the points to be observed in the descent of the above fiefs are Edward of Salisbury's succession to that of Ralf fitz Hubert,[64] the appearance of Henry de Albini, founder of the Cainho line, as successor to Nigel, and the portions of the great Belvoir fief, held in Domesday by Robert de Todeni, now owned by Robert de L'Isle and William de Albini "Brito." In the midst of great but vanished names, it is pleasant to meet with one, at least, still surviving in the male line: William de Gresley, holder of Linton (a Derbyshire hamlet close to Gresley), had succeeded, there and at "Widesers," Nigel, a tenant of Henry de Ferrers

---

[59] *Liber Rubeus*, Ed. Hall, p. 266.

[60] *Ib.*, p. 268.

[61] *Ibid.*

[62] *Sloane*, xxxi. 4, No. 10.

[63] They are "Nigellus de Aubeni, Ran[ulfus] Comes Cestrie, Galfridus Cancellarius, Simon decanus Lincolnie, Willelmus fil' Reg', Thomas de Sancto Johanne, Willelmus de Aubeny Brito, Unfridus de Bohun et alii." The Dean's occurrence so late is worth noting.

[64] Compare "The Barons of Criche" (*Academy*, June, 1885).

in 1086 (D. B., i. 233 *b*).[65]   In this "Nigel," therefore, it would seem, we have Nigel de Stafford, Lord of Drakelow (D. B., i. 278).

I will close with the names of those who had succeeded the Domesday tenants-in-chief.

HEIRS.

Count of Meulan.	Earl of Leicester.
Earl Aubrey.	(Escheat.)
"Countess" Godgifu.	
"Countess" Ælfgifu.	Earl of Chester (Donnington).
Earl of Chester.	Earl of Chester.
Hugh de Grentmesnil	Earl of Leicester.
Henry de Ferrers.	Robert de Ferrers.
Robert de Todeni.	William de Albini.
Robert de Veci.	[Anschitil.]
Roger de Busli.	[Honour of Blyth.]
	⎰ Walter de Beauchamp.
	⎱ Robert Marmion.
Robert Dispensator.	Henry Tuchet ($10\frac{7}{8}$).
Robertus Hostiarius, ($10\frac{1}{2}$).	
Ralf Mortimer.	
Ralf fitz Hubert.	Edward of Salisbury.
Guy de Rembudcurt.	[Thomas.]
Guy de Craon.	Alan de Craon.
William Peverel.	Honour of Peverel.
William Buenvaslet.	Comes War'?
William Loveth.	Will. Meschin.
Geoffrey Alselin.	
Geoffrey de "Wirce."	[Escheat.]
Godfrey de Cambrai.	the son of Gilbert.
Gunfrid de Cioches.	
Humfrey Camerarius.	Willelmus Camerarius.
Drogo de Bevrere.	Albemarle.
Nigel de Albini.	Henry de Albini.
"Countess" Judith.	King David.

[65] That William was his son is proved by the Ferrers *Carta* (1166), which enters "Willelmus filius Nigelli" as the tenant of four fees under Henry I., and as succeeded, in 1166, by his son Robert.

THE NORTHAMPTONSHIRE SURVEY

(HEN. I.-HEN. II.)

THIS "Hydarium" of Northamptonshire is found in a Peterborough Cartulary (Cott. MS. Vesp. E. 22, fo. 94 et sq.). It is drawn up hundred by hundred, like the surveys of Leicestershire and of Lindsey, and is, therefore, probably connected with the assessment of Danegeld. Although it is of special value for reconstituting the Domesday Vills, the assessment it records so often varies from that which is found in Domesday that we cannot institute a close comparison. The introduction of a "parva virgata" further complicates the reckoning. That the original document was written on a roll is shown by the use of the pharse "per alium rotulum." The statement on fo. 97*b* that there ought, at one place, to be half a hide more "per rotulos Wyncestr[ie]," would seem to refer to Domesday ; but on the next page we read :—

In Pytesle Abbas de Burgo v. hid. [et] dim. set tamen in Rotulis Wyncestr[ie] vi. hid. et iii. parvas virgatas.

Since Domesday records this holding as "v. hid. et una virgata terræ," the reference (if the text of the survey is right) must clearly be to some other record preserved in the national treasury.

I append about a fifth of the Survey as a specimen of the whole.

HOKESLAWE.

Twywell. Albr[icus] camerar[ius] ii. hidas de feudo Abbatis de Thorneya. Ibidem de feudo Comitis David. Ibidem de feudo Abbatis Burgi i. magnam virgatam.

In Slipton i. hidam et unam virgatam de feudo Will'i de Corcy. Ibidem Ricardus filius Hugonis ii. partes unius hidæ de feudo Burgi. Ibidem Rogerus nepos Abbatis tertiam partem unius hidæ de eodem feudo.

In Suburc [Sudboro'] ii. hidas [et] dim. de feudo Westmonaster'. In Lofwyc [Luffwick] Th——[1] i. hidam et unam virgatam de feudo de Deneford. Ibidem Radulfus Fleming i. virgatam et dim. de feudo Comitis David. Ibidem Wydo frater ejus i. magnam virgatam de feudo de Thorneya.

In Drayton Albr[icus] camerar[ius] dimidiam hidam de feudo R[egis].

In Yslep [Islip] idem Albri[cus] de feudo Regis. Ibidem iiii^or. sokemanni Regis i. hidam de feudo Westmonaster'.

In Audewyncle [Aldwinkle] Abbas de Burgo iiii. hidas [et] dimidiam quas Ascelinus de Waterville tenet. Ibidem Galfridus de Glynton i. magnam virgatam de feudo Glovernie pertinens ad Barton. Ibidem Ricardus filius Wydonis iii. hidas dim. virg. minus de feudo Regine (*sic*).

Item in Benifeld [Benefield] Willelmus de Lisurs iii. magnas virg. de feudo Regis.

In Bernewelle [Barnwell] Robertus de ferariis vi. hidas et i. magnam virg. de feudo Regis. Ibidem Reginaldus le Moyne vi. hidas de feudo de Rammeseye.

In Lilleford Willelmus Olyfart v. hidas de feudo Regis Scotie.

NAUEFORD

In Tytheni [? Tichmarsh] Robertus de Ferr[ers] x. hid. Ibidem Ascelinus de Waterville iii. hid. et i. virg. et tres partes dim. hid. de Burgo.

In Thrapston Radulfus fil. Oger ii. hid. et i. virg. de feudo de Brunne. Ibidem Robertus filius Edelinæ i. hid. et i. virg. de feudo de Clare.

In Torpe et Achirche Ascelinus de Waterville vi. hid. [et] dim. de feudo Burgi.

In Clopton Walterus i. hid. et i. virg. de feudo Regis. Ibidem iii. hid. [et] dim. de feudo Burgi. Ibidem Ascelinus dim. hid. de feudo Burgi.

Wadenhowe [Wadenhoe]. Albricus de Ver ii. hid. et i. virg. de feudo Regis David. Ibidem Wymunt de Stok[e] i. virg. de feudo

---

[1] Or Sh——.

Burgi. Ibidem Rogerus Infans ii. parvas virg. de eodem feudo.
Ibidem Wivienus de Chirchefelde dim. hid. de eodem feudo.
Ibidem Galfridus de Gonthorp ii. hid. de eodem feudo. In Catteworthe i. hid. [et] dim. de feudo Burgi.

POKEBROC.

In Pokebroc Robertus de Cauz i. hid. et. i. virg. de feudo Regis.
Ibidem Walterus de Clopton ii. hid. et dim. de feudo Burgi. Ibidem
Rogerus Marmium i. hid. et i. virg. de eodem feudo.

In Armeston [Armston] de Burgelay ii. hid. [et] dim. de eodem
feudo. Ibidem Turkil i. hid. de eodem feudo. Ibidem Wydo
Maufee i. hid. de eodem feudo. Ibidem Galfridus de Gunthorp
ii. partes dim. hid. de eodem feudo. Ibidem Tedrik' iii. partes de
dim. hid. de eodem feudo.

In Pappele [Papley] i. hid.

In Lillington [Lutton] i. hid.

In Hennington Berengerus le Moyne ii. hid. [et] dim. de feudo
de Rammes[eye]. Ibidem Ricardus filius Gilberti i. hid. et i. virg. et
dim. de feodo Burgi. Ibidem Wydo Maufe dim. hid. et dim. virg.
de eodem feodo. Ibidem Reginaldus le Moyne dim. hid. et dim.
virg. de eodem feodo.

In Kynesthorp [Kingsthorp] Walterus de Lodington i. hid. et i.
virg. de feodo Burgi. Ibidem Willelmus de Chirchetot dim. hid. de
feodo Regis.

In Therninge [Thurning] Rogerus Marmioun iii. parvas virg. de
feodo Burgi.

In Ayston [Ashton] Abbas de Burgo iiii. hid. in dominico.
Ibidem Papilun dim. hid. de eodem feodo. Ibidem Leuenoth dim.
hid. de eodem feodo.

In Undele [Oundle] Abbas in dominico vi. hid. Ibidem Vivien
i. parvam virg.[2]

DUO HUNDRED DE NASSO.

In Stinton Willelmus de Lisurs ii. hid.

In Bernak Fulco paynel iii. hid.[3]

In Wirthorpe Abbas Croylaund ii. hid. Ibidem de feodo Eudonis
Dapiferi i. virg.

In Eston [Easton] Simon i. hid. [et] dim.

---

[2] See *Chronicon Petroburgense*, p. 158.
[3] See Bridges' *Northamptonshire*, ii. 491.

In Peychirche [Peakirk]. In Etton. In Northburgo dim. virg. In dominico Abbatis de Burgo sancti Petri lxx. hid. et iii. virg. et dim.

HUNDRED DE SUTTON.

In eadem villa [King's Sutton] Dominus Rex habit in dominico iiii. hid.

In eadem villa Willelmus de Quency i. hid. [et] dim. et parvam virg. terre de Comitat[u] Leycestr[ie]. Ibidem Alfredus viii. parvas virg. de Gilberto de Pinkeny. Ibidem Paganus i. hid. et dim. et i. parvam virg. de feodo Comit[is] Leycestr[ie], Robertus filius Osberti tenuit.

In Evenle i. hid. et i. parvam virg. de feodo Comitis[is] Leyc[estrie].

In Preston dim. hid. de feodo Comit[is] Leyc[estrie].

In Croulton [Croughton] iiiiᵒʳ. parvas virg. de feodo Comit[is] Leyc[estrie]. Ibidem Sewar' i. hid. et ii. parvas virg. de feodo Leyc[estrie]. Ibidem Brien filius Comitis i. hid. [et] dim. et ii. parvas virg. de feodo de Walinford.

In Neubottle Regis [*sic*] de Reynes vi. hid. et i. parvam virg. de feodo Comitis Leyc[estrie], Willelmus de Lepyn tenuit.

In furningho [Farningho] iiii. hid. de feodo Comitis Leyc[estrie].

In Cherlington [Charlton] Maynardus i. hid. [et] dim. et i. parvam virg. Ibidem Simon Chendut i. hid. [et] dim. de feodo de Berkamstede et i. parvam virg. Ibidem Odo dapifer viii. parvas virg. de feodo de Colescestra.

In Gremesbir' [Grimsbury] Aunsel' de Chokes ii. hid. et iiii. parvas virg. scil. quarta pars ii. hid.

In Middleton Willelmus Me[s]chin i. hid. et dim. et i. parvam virg. de feodo Willelmi de Curcy.

In alia Middleton [Middleton Chenduit] Simon Chendut ii. hid. de feodo de Berkamstede.

In Thayniford [Thenford] Mainfenn de Walrentone i. hid. Ibidem Robertus Basset i. hid de feodo de Walingford.

In Ayno [Aynho] Willelmus de Mandeville iii. hid.

In Middelton monachi de sancto Eu'ald [4] ii. hid.

In Walton i. hid. cum ii. virg. in Sutton quas Suouild tenuit.

In Gildeby i. hid. et vii. parvas virg. de feodo de Mortal' (*sic*).

---

[4] St. Evroul, Grantmesnil's in Domesday.

HUNDRED DE ALBODESTOWE.

In Chacombe iiii. hid. de feodo Episc. Lincoln.

In Evenle ii. hid. et (*sic*) i. parvam virg. minus quas Alouf de Merke tenuit.

In Thorpe [Thorpe-Mandeville] ii. hid.

In Stanes [Stene] Gilbertus de Pinkeny ii. hid.

In Colewyth [Culworth] Willelmus ii. hid. et iiii. parvas virg. Ibidem Otuer i. hid.

In Stotebyr[e] [Stotesbery] ii. hid. quas monachi Norht'[5] tenent.

In Rodestone [Radston] ii. hid. de feodo Comitis Cestr[ie].

In Wytefeld [Whitfield] Gilbertus de Monte ii. hid. et ii. virg. in dominico.

In Merston [Merston St. Lawrence] Radulfus Murdac iiii. hid. de feodo Comitis Leyc[estrie].

In Siresham Thomas Sorel i. hid. [et] dim. Ibidem Comes Leyc[estrie] i. parvam virg. Ibidem Gilo dim. hid. Ibidem Willelmus filius Alui' [? Alan] iiii. parvas virg.

In Helmendene [Helmedon] Willelmus de Torewelle iiii. hid. de feodo Comitis Leyc[estrie].

In Chelverdescote dim. hid. Idem. Comes Leyc[estrie].

In Brackle et Hausho [Hawes] idem Comes vii. hid. [et] dim.

HUNDRED DE WARDON.

In Wardon Ricardus foliot[6] ii. hid. [et] dim. et i. magnam virg., scilicet quarta pars i. militis de feodo Regis in capite.

In Estone [Aston] et Apeltreya [Apeltre] Willelmus de Bolonia vii. hid. de feodo Comitis de Mandeville.

In Bottolendon [Boddington] Fulco Paynel[7] ii. hid. una ex illis de feodo Cestr[ie]. Ibidem Willelmus Meschin i. hid. Ibidem i. hid. de feodo Episcopi Lincoln.

The only writer, it would seem, who has used this important survey is Bridges, who refers to it throughout in his *Northamptonshire* as of the time of "Henry II." A good instance of the confusion caused by this assumption is seen in the remarks of Bridges as to Barnack (ii. 491), where he

---

[5] St. Andrew's Priory, Northampton.
[6] The heir of Guy de Renbodcurt.
[7] Clearly Fulk Paynel the first, Founder of Tykford Priory.

is puzzled by our record, giving as its lord, not Gervase Paynell, but Fulc Paynell (who was really his grandfather). To refute his conclusion, it is sufficient to refer to the first name entered—that of "Albricus Camerarius." This was no other than Aubrey de Vere, a trusted minister of Henry I., who was made by him Great Chamberlain in 1133, and who was slain in May, 1141.[8] His Northamptonshire estate descended to his younger son, Robert, who, as " Robertus filius Albrici Camerarii," made his return as a Northamptonshire " baron " in 1166.[9] There can, therefore, be no confusion between Aubrey the Chamberlain (d. 1141) and his eldest son and namesake. Yet if, from the occurrence of his name, we pronounced the date of this survey to be 1133-1141, we should be in error. There are names belonging to an earlier, as to a later, date than his.

Among the earliest are " Ricardus filius Wydonis," the son and successor of Guy de Renbodcurt, a great Domesday tenant-in-chief ; Walter fitz Winemar, whose father was both a tenant *in capite* and under-tenant in Domesday ; and Ralf fitz Oger, whose name illustrates the value of these early surveys ; for the entry proves that Oger, the Northamptonshire tenant-in-chief (D.B., i. 228), was identical with Oger " Brito," the Lord of Bourne, Linc. (i. 364*b*), and that the son and successor of this Oger was Ralf. We also recognise Roger Marmion, who was succeeded, under Henry I., by Robert ; Nigel de Albini, the founder of the house of Mowbray ; Michael de Hanslape, who died under

---

[8] *Geoffrey de Mandeville*, p. 81.

[9] See also as to Twywell itself. *Mon. Ang.*, ii 603 :—

"Ego Albericus, regis camerarius terram de Twiwell quamdiu vixero de domino abbate Guntero et monachis de Thorneya per talem conventionem teneo ad firmam."

"Ego Robertus filius Albrici camerarii regis terram de Twiwelle quamdiu vixero de domino abbate Roberto et monachis de Thorneia per eandem conventionem in feodi firmam teneo per quam conventionem pater meus ante me tenuit."

The Great Chamberlain occurs again on fo. 97*b*, where we read :—

"In alia Adington Albric[us] Camerar[ius], ii. hid. de feodo Regis."

Henry I.; and "Robertus filius Regis," who became Earl of Gloucester *circ.* 1122. Other tenants, living *temp.* Hen. I., are William de Mandeville,[10] William Meschin, Richard Basset, Viel (Vitalis) Engaine, Baldwin fitz Gilbert, and Brian fitz Count. As for Ascelin de Waterville. and Alouf de Merke, they are found as under-tenants in Domesday itself. On the other hand, such a name as "Comes Warenn de Morteyn" points to the latter years of Stephen's reign, or to the early days of that of Henry II.; while the mention of the earldoms of Arundel, Ferrers (Derby) and Essex preclude, of course, an earlier date than 1140.

After careful examination, I propound the solution that this survey was originally made under Henry I., and was subsequently corrected here and there, to bring the entries up to date, down to the days of Henry II. The late transcriber, to whom we owe the survey in its present form, has incorporated these additions and corrections in a single text with the most bewildering result. We trace exactly the same process in the Red Book of the Exchequer. In the Black Book the later additions that were made to the barons' *cartæ* of 1166 are distinguished by the difference in handwriting. But in the Red Book these interpolations are found transcribed in the same hand as the genuine original returns. To the uninitiated this has been the cause of no small confusion. So, too, in the above list of Peterborough knights (p. 157), the very first entry, made *temp.* Hen. I., has been carried on by a later hand to the time of Henry III. But there Stapleton, who transcribed the list, carefully discriminated between the two.[11] It is probable that the lists of Abingdon knights, published in the Abingdon cartularly, are rendered untrustworthy in places from the same cause of error.

The transcriber's ignorance is clearly shown by such a name as "Comes Mauricius," which is evidently his erro-

---

[10] If, as probable, the son of the Domesday Baron.
[11] *Chronicon Petroburgense*, pp. 168-9.

neous extension of an original "Comes Maur'," *i.e.*, Count of Mortain! So also we are enabled to detect proof of the theory I advance in such an entry as "Willelmus Meschin de feodo Wellelmi de Curcy"; for William de Curcy held, *temp.* Henry II., the barony held by William Meschin (his maternal grandfather, according to Stapleton[12]) *temp.* Henry I. Thus, the original entry will have run "William Meschin," while a later hand, in his grandson's days, will have added, by way of substitution, "De feodo William de Curcy."[13] Our transcriber, combining the two, has, of course, made nonsense of the whole. The same explanation applies to the entry, "Robertus filius Regis de feodo Glovernie," where the first three words represent the original entry, while the others were added, probably under Hen. II., to connect the holding with the fief of [the Earl of] Gloucester. "Brien filius Comitis de feodo de Wallin[g]ford" is another instance in point, and so, I suspect, is "Odo (*sic*) dapifer de feodo de Colcestra"; for I take it that the entry was originally made in the lifetime of Eudo Dapifer (d. 1120) and that, as his "honour" passed into the King's hands, the "de feodo de Colcestra" was added at a later time.[14]

I have given sufficient of the survey to prove that, in spite of confusion and corruption, it possesses a real value If we take, for instance, Polebrook ("Pochebroc"), a township of five hides, we find that in Domesday (221*b*, 228) Eustace ("the Sheriff") held a hide and a quarter *in capite* and three hides and three quarters as a tenant of Peterborough Abbey (see p. 167). Now our survey shows us the former holding in the hands of Robert de Cauz, while

[12] *Holy Trinity Priory, York*, p. 35.

[13] Since this was written I have come across a curious confirmation of the hypothesis advanced. In the Lindsey Survey (Ed. Greenstreet), an entry on fo. 20, in the original ran: "Comes Odo [tenet] in Aldobi," above which a later hand has interlined, "De feodo Comitis Albemerle." It is curious that in the same survey another later interlineation— "Comes Lincoln"—was, though distinguished by Hearne, incorporated with the text by Mr. Waters (see p. 184).

[14] Eudo was identified with Colchester.

the other has been broken up, two-thirds of it passing to Walter "de Clopton" and one-third to Roger Marmion.

Just below, in the case of Hemington, also a Vill of five hides, which was equally divided between the Abbeys of Peterborough and Ramsey, we read in Domesday that "iii. milites" held the Peterborough half (221*b*). Our survey enables us to distinguish their tenancies—Richard fitz Gilbert holding a hide and three-eighths; Guy Maufe, five-eights of a hide, and Reginald le Moyne the same.[15] But we can go further and identify the first, from his holding, as the son of Gilbert Fauvel, the Domesday tenant (see p. 167); while the second was the heir, and probably the son of Roger Malfed (see p. 158).

One more instance may be given. Our survey reckons Clapton ("Cloptone") as five and a quarter hides, of which "Walter" held one and a quarter *in capite*. Here again he had succeeded Eustace, whose Domesday estate at "Dotone" (228) ought, as Bridges conjectured, to have been entered "Clotone."[16] On the other hand, his tenancy of the Abbot at "Clotone" had been broken up, half a hide of it passing to Ascelin de Waterville. All this goes to show that the fief of Eustace the Sheriff did not, as has been alleged, descend to his heirs.

Such an entry as "In Lilleford, Willelmus Olyfart v. hidas de feudo Regis Scotiæ" is peculiarly suggestive. It reminds us that David Holyfard, godson of King David of Scotland, and his protector in 1141, was the founder of the house of Oliphant; and in the family's possession of Lilford (which was held of the Countess Judith in 1086) we see the origin of their Scottish connexion. William "Olifard" was of Northamptonshire, and Hugh "Olifard" of Huntingdonshire in 1130;[17] while Hugh "Olifart" (of

---

[15] Giving a total of 2⅝, instead of 2½—a trivial discrepancy.

[16] It is singular that in Sussex the "Cloninctune" of Domesday is, conversely, an error for "Doninctune." The source of the error in both cases must have been the likeness of "cl" to "d" in the original returns, on which these names cannot have begun with a capital letter.

[17] *Rot. Pip.*, 31 Hen. I.

Stoke) was a knight of the Abbot of Peterborough in rather earlier days. The earliest member of the house, however, it would seem, on record is Roger Olifard, who witnessed (doubtless as his tenant) Earl Simon's charter to St. Andrew's, Northampton, granted, probably, not later than 1108. This, of course, is but one of the cases in which the son of a Norman house settled in Scotland through its Kings' connexion with the earldoms of Huntingdon and Northampton.

At the close of the survey I have here discussed there is a list of the knights of Peterborough (fos. 99*b*, 100) holding in Northamptonshire. It ought to be carefully compared with the one I have examined above (p. 157), being, it seems probable, about a generation later. Such entries as these, at least, are conclusive for the holding to which they refer :—

Paganus de Helpestun terciam partem unius militis (*Chronicon Petroburgenes*, p. 171).

Roger fil[ius] Pagan[i] in Helpestun terciam partem i. militis (Vesp. E. xxii., fo. 100).

In the same way, Roger Marmion had been succeeded by Robert. This second list is of special value from the fact that the Peterborough *carta* of 1166 gives no particulars of the knights or of their fees.

THE INTRODUCTION OF KNIGHT SERVICE INTO ENGLAND.[1]

The growth of knighthood is a subject on which the greatest obscurity prevails; and the most probable explanation of its existence in England, the theory that it is a translation into Norman forms of the thegnage of the Anglo-Saxon law, can only be stated as probable."—STUBBS, *Const. Hist.* i. 260.

IN approaching the consideration of the institutional changes and modifications of polity resulting from the Norman Conquest, the most conspicuous phenomenon to attract attention is undoubtedly the introduction of what it is convenient to term the feudal system. In the present paper I propose to discuss one branch only of that process, namely, the introduction of that military tenure which Dr. Stubbs has termed "the most prominent feature of historical feudalism."

In accordance with the anticataclysmic tendencies of modern thought, the most recent students of this obscure problem have agreed to adopt the theory of gradual development and growth. The old views on the subject are discredited as crude and unhistorical:[2] they are replaced by confident enunciation of the theory to which I have referred.[3] But when we examine the matter closely, when

[1] Reprinted, with additions, from the *English Historical Review*.

[2] "The belief which has come down to us from Selden, and the antiquarian school, a belief which was hitherto universally received, that William I. divided the English landed property into military fees, is erroneous, and results from the dating back of an earlier [? later] condition of things."—GNEIST *Const. Hist.*, i. 129.

[3] "There can be no doubt that the military tenure, the most prominent

B.H.   Q

we ask for details of the process by which the Anglo-Saxon thegn developed into the Norman knight, we are met at once by the frank confession that "between the picture drawn in Domesday and the state of affairs which the charter of Henry I. was designed to remedy, there is a difference which the short interval of time will not account for."[4] To meet this difficulty, to account for this flaw in the unbroken continuity of the series, a *Deus ex machinâ* has been found in the person of Ranulf Flambard.

Now this solution of the difficulty will scarcely, I venture to think, bear the test of investigation. It appears to have originated in Dr. Stubbs' suggestion that there must have been, between the days of Henry I. and of William I., "some skilful organising hand working with neither justice nor mercy"[5]—a suggestion subsequently amplified into the statement that it is to Ranulf Flambard "without doubt that the systematic organisation of the exactions" under William Rufus "is to be attributed,"[6] and that by him "the royal claims were unrelentingly pressed," his policy being "to tighten as much as possible the hold which the feudal law gave to the king on all feudatories temporal and spiritual."[7] There is nothing here that can be called in question, but there is also nothing, be it observed, to prove that either "feudal law" or "military tenure" was introduced by Ranulf Flambard. Indeed, with his usual caution and unfailing sound judgment, our great historian is careful to admit that "it is not quite so clear" in the case of the lay as of the church fiefs "that all the evil customs owed their origin to the reign of William Rufus."[8] And, even if they did, they were, it must be remembered, distinctly abuses—"evil customs," as Henry I. himself terms them in his charter—namely (in

feature of historical feudalism, was itself introduced by the same gradual process which we have assumed in the case of the feudal usages in general."—STUBBS, *Const. Hist.*, i. 261.

[4] Stubbs, *C. H.*, i. 260-1 So too Freeman.   [5] i. 261.

[6] i. 298.   [7] pp. 298, 301.   [8] i. 300.

the matter we are considering), "*excessive* exactions in the way of reliefs, marriages and wardships, debts to the crown, and forfeiture. In the place," we are told, "of *unlimited* demands on these heads, the charter promises, not indeed fixed amercements, but a return to ancient equitable custom."[9] All this refers, it will be seen, to the abuse of an existing institution, not to the introduction of a new one. The fact is that Ranulf's proceedings have been assigned a quite exceptional and undue importance. Broadly speaking, his actions fall under a law too often lost sight of, namely, that when the crown was strong it pressed, through the official bureaucracy, its claims to the uttermost; and when it found itself weak, it renounced them so far as it was compelled. Take, for instance, this very charter issued by Henry I., when he was "playing to the gallery," and seeking general support: what was the value of its promises? They were broken, says Mr. Freeman, to the Church;[10] they were probably broken, says Dr. Stubbs, to the knights;[11] and they were certainly broken, I may add, to the unfortunate tenants-in-chief, whom the Pipe-Roll of 1130 shows us suffering from those same excessive exactions, of which the monopoly is assigned to Ranulf Flambard, and which "the Lion of Justice" had so virtuously renounced. I might similarly adduce the exactions from the Church by that excellent king, Henry II. (1159), "contra antiquum morem et debitam libertatem"; but it is needless to multiply examples of the struggle between the interests of the crown and those of its tenants-in-chief, which was as fierce as ever when, in later days, it led to the provisions of the Great Charter. What the barons, lay and spiritual, complained of from first to last, was not the feudal system that accompanied their military tenure, but the abuse of that system in the excessive demands of the crown.

Mr. Freeman, however, who had an equal horror of

---

[9] *Select Charters*, p. 96.   [10] *Norm. Conq.*, v. 380.   [11] *C. H.*, i. 581

Ranulf Flambard and of the "feudal system," did not hesitate to connect the two more closely even than Dr. Stubbs, though invoking the authority of the latter in support of his extreme views. The passages to which I would invite attention, as expressing most concisely Mr. Freeman's conclusions, are these :—

The system of military tenures, and the oppressive consequences which were held to flow from them, were a work of the days of William Rufus.

If then there was any time when "the Feudal System" could be said to be introduced into England, it was assuredly not in the days of William the Conqueror, but in the days of William the Red. It would be more accurate to say that all that we are really concerned with, that is, not an imaginary "Feudal System," but a system of feudal land-tenures, was not introduced into England at all, but was devised on English ground by the malignant genius of the minister of Rufus.[12]

As the writer's line of argument is avowedly that of Dr. Stubbs, it is only necessary to consider the point of difference between them. Where his predecessor saw in Henry's charter the proof that Ranulf Flambard had abused the existing feudal system by "excessive" and "unlimited" demands, Mr. Freeman held, and endeavoured to convince us, that he had introduced not merely abuses of the system, but the actual system itself.[13] The question virtually turns on the first clause of the charter;[14] and it will not, I think, be doubted that Dr. Stubbs is right in adopting its natural meaning, namely, that the novelty introduced by Ranulf was not the *relevatio* itself, but its abuse in "excessive exactions." Indeed, even Mr. Free-

---

[12] *N. C.*, v. 377 ; cf. *History of William II.*, pp. 335, 337, "The whole system, a system which logically hangs together in the most perfect way, was the device of the same subtle and malignant brain."

[13] *Ibid.*, p. 374.

[14] " Si quis baronum meorum, comitum sive aliorum qui de me tenent, mortuus fuerit, heres suus non *redimet* terram suam sicut faciebat tempore fratris mei, sed justa et legitima relevatione *relevabit* eam."

man had virtually to admit the point.[15] If, then, the argument breaks down, if Ranulf cannot be shown to have "devised" military tenure, how are we to bridge over the alleged chasm between the date of Domesday (1086) and that of Henry's charter (1100)? The answer is simply that the difficulty is created by the very theory I am discussing : it is based on the assumption that William I. did not introduce military tenure,[16] combined with the fact that "within thirteen years after the Conqueror's death, not only the military tenures, but the worst abuses of the military tenures, were in full force in England."[17] But, here again, when we examine the evidence, we find that this assumption is based on the silence, or alleged silence, of Domesday Book.[18] Now no one was better aware than Mr. Freeman, as an ardent student of "the great Record," that to argue from the silence of Domesday is an error as dangerous as it is common. Speaking from a rather wide acquaintance with topographical works, I know of no pitfall into which the local antiquary is more liable to fall. Wonderful are the things that people look for in the pages of the great survey ; I am always reminded of Mr. Secretary Pepys' writing for information as to what it contained

[15] "In that charter the military tenures are taken for granted. What is provided against is their being perverted, as they had been in the days of Rufus, into engines of oppression,"—*N. C.*, v. 373.

[16] *N. C.*, v. 372 ; *C. H.*, i. 261.

[17] *N. C.*, v. 373.

[18] Palgrave, as Mr. Freeman observes, "strongly and clearly brought out the absence of any distinct mention of military tenures in Domesday." Dr. Stubbs more cautiously wrote : "The wording of the Domesday Survey does not imply that in this respect the new military service differed from the old." (*C. H.*, i. 262.) Mr. Freeman confidently asserts : " Nothing is more certain than that from one end of Domesday to the other, there is not a trace of military tenures as they were afterwards understood. . . . We hear of nothing in Domesday which can be called knight service or military tenure in the later sense." (*N. C.*, v. 370, 371). Mr. Hunt (*Norman Britain*) follows the same line, and Gneist, vouching Palgrave, Stubbs, and Freeman, repeats the argument. (*C. H.*, i. 130).

"concerning the sea and the dominion thereof." [19] Like other inquests, the Domesday Survey—"the great inquest of all," as Dr. Stubbs terms it—was intended for a special purpose; special questions were asked, and these questions were answered in the returns. So with the "Inquest of Sheriffs" in 1170; so also with the Inquest of Knights, if I may so term it, in 1166. In each case the questions asked are, practically, known to us, and in each they are entirely different. Therefore, when Mr. Freeman writes—

> The survey nowhere employs the feudal language which became familiar in the twelfth century. Compare, for instance, the records in the first volume of Hearn's *Liber Niger Scaccarii*. In this last we find something about knights' fees in every page. In Domesday there is not a word— [20]

it is in no spirit of captious criticism, but from the necessity of demolishing the argument, that I liken it to basing conclusions on the fact that in the census returns we find something about population in every page, while in the returns of owners of land there is not a word. As the inquest of 1166 sought solely for information on knights and their fees, the returns to it naturally contain "something about knights' fees in every page"; on the other hand, "the payment or non-payment of the *geld* is a matter which appears in every page of the survey" [of 1086] because "the formal immediate cause of taking the survey was to secure its full and fair assessment." [21] Nor is this all. When the writer asserts that "in Domesday there is not a word" about knights' fees, he greatly overstates his case, as indeed is shown by the passages he proceeds to quote. I shall be able to prove, further on, that knights' fees existed in cases where Domesday does not mention them, but even the incidental notices found in the Great

---

[19] "I spoke to Mr. Falconberge to look whether he could out of Domesday Book give me anything concerning the sea and the dominion thereof" (1661).

[20] *N. C.*, v. 465.　　　　[21] *Ibid.*, v. 4.

Survey are quite sufficient to disprove its alleged silence on
the subject.   As Mr. Freeman has well observed :—

Its most incidental notices are sometimes the most precious.   We
have seen that it is to an incidental, an almost accidental notice in
the Survey that we owe our knowledge of the great fact of the
general redemption of lands.[22]

Here then the writer does not hesitate to base on a single
accidental notice the existence of an event quite as widespread and important as the introduction of knight
service.[23]

I have now endeavoured to make plain one of the chief
flaws in the view at present accepted, namely, that it is
mainly grounded on the negative evidence of Domesday,
which evidence will not bear the construction that has
been placed upon it,—and further that, even if it did, we
should be landed in a fresh difficulty, the gulf between
Domesday and Henry's charter being only to be bridged
by the assumption that Ranulf Flambard "devised" and
introduced military tenure, with its results—an assumption,
we have seen, which the facts of the case not only fail to
support, but even discountenance wholly.

Let us pass to a second difficulty.   When we ask the
advocates of the view I am discussing what determined
the number of knights due to the crown from a tenant-in-
chief, we obtain, I venture to assert, no definite answer.
At times we are told that it was the number of his hides ;
at times that it was the value of his estate.   Gneist, who
has discussed the matter in detail, and on several occa-

---

[22] *N.C.,* p. 42.

[23] As so much stress has been laid on the argument from Domesday
it is desirable further to demonstrate its worthlessness by referring to
the Lindsey Survey (*vide supra, p.* 181).   This survey can only be a few
years previous to 1120, and was therefore made at a time when, *ex
hypothesi,* feudal tenures had been established for some time.   Yet here,
also, page after page may be searched in vain for any mention of
"knights" or "fees."

sions, has held throughout, broadly speaking, the same view : he maintains that "since Alfred's time the general rule had been observed that a fully equipped man should be furnished for every five *hidæ*, but it had never been established as a rule of law as in the Carlovingian legislation" :[24] consequently, he urges, "a fixed standard for the apportionment of the soldiery was wanting" at the time of the Conquest, and this want was a serious flaw in the Anglo-Saxon polity. William resolved to make the system uniform, and

the object that the royal administration now pursued for a century was to impose upon the whole mass of old and new possessors an equal obligation to do service for reward. The standard adopted in carrying out this system was approximately that of the five hides possession of the Anglo-Saxon period; yet with a stricter rating according to the value of the produce.[25]

The difficulty encountered in ascertaining this value was a main cause of the Domesday Survey being undertaken. This is Gneist's special point on which he invariably insists : "Domesday book laid the basis of a roll of the crown vassals";[26] upon it, "in later times, the fee-rolls were framed."[27] By its evidence, "according to the extent and the nature of the productive property, could be computed how many shields were to be furnished by each estate, according to the gradually fixed proportion of a £20 ground rent."[28] For "the *feuda militum* thus computed are no knights' fees of a limited area,"[29] but "units of possession," the unit being £20 in annual value.

Dr. Stubbs, on the other hand, while rejecting the view that military service, since the days of Alfred, had been practically fixed at one warrior for every five hides,[30] leans

---

[24] Gneist, *C.H.*, i. 132.   [25] i. 118.   [26] i. 156, 133, 124.
[27] i. 130.   [28] i. 156.   [29] i. 133.
[30] Stubbs, *C.H.*, i. 192. I do not quite understand the passage that "it is probable that the complete following out of the Frank idea [exact proportion of service to hides] was reserved for Henry II., unless his

nevertheless to the belief that the knight's fee was developed out of the five-hide unit, and that the military "service" of a tenant-in-chief was determined by the number of such units which he possessed. But, as he also recognises the £20 unit, there will be less danger of misrepresenting his views if I append *verbatim* the relevant passages :—

The customary service of one fully armed man for each five hides was probably the rate at which the newly endowed follower of the king would be expected to discharge his duty . . . and the number of knights to be furnished by a particular feudatory would be ascertained by inquiring the number of hides that he held.[31]	The value of the knight's fee must already have been fixed— twenty pounds a year.[32]
The number of hides which the knight's fee contained being known, the number of knights' fees in any particular holding could be easily discovered.[33]	It cannot even be granted that a definite area of land was necessary to constitute a knight's fee ; . . . It is impossible to avoid the conclusion that the extent of a knight's fee was determined by rent and valuation rather than acreage, and that the common quantity was really expressed in the twenty librates, etc.[35]
All the imposts of the . . . Norman reigns were, so far as we know, raised on the land, and according to computation by the hide: . . . the feudal exactions by way of aid . . . were levied on the hide.[34]	The variation in the number of hides contained in the knight's fee.[36]

military reforms are to be understood, as so many of his other measures are, as the revival and strengthening of anti-feudal and pre-feudal custom." *(Ibid.)* The allusion is, clearly, to the assize of arms ; but was that assize based on fixed quantities of land? Mr. Little has discussed the five-hide question in the *English Historical Review*, No. xvi. pp. 726-9 (*vide supra*, p. 68).

[31] i. 262.   [32] i. 262.
[33] *C. H.*, i. 386.   [34] 581.   [35] i. 264-5.   [36] i. 432.

Mr. Freeman's views need not detain us, for he unhesitatingly accepts Dr. Stubbs' arguments as proving that the Norman military tenure was based on "the old service of a man from each five hides of land." [87]

We find then, I submit, that the recognised leaders of existing opinion on the subject cannot agree among themselves in giving us a clear answer, when we ask them what determined the amount of "service" due from a Norman tenant-in-chief, or, in other words, how that "service" was developed in unbroken continuity from Anglo-Saxon obligations.

The third point that I would raise is this. Even assuming that the amount of "service" bore a fixed proportion—whether in pecuniary or territorial units—to the extent of possession, we are, surely, at once confronted by the difficulty that the owner of x units of possession would be compelled, for the discharge of his military obligations, to enfeoff x knights, assigning a "unit" to each. A tenant-in-chief, to take a concrete instance, whose fief was worth £100 a year, would have to provide *ex hypothesi* five knights; if, as was quite usual, he enfeoffed the full number, he would have to assign to each knight twenty librates of land (which I may at once, though anticipating, admit was the normal value of a knight's fee), that is to say, the crown would have forestalled Henry George, and the luckless *baro* would see the entire value of his estate swallowed up in the discharge of its obligations.[38] What his position would be in cases where, as often, he enfeoffed more knights than he required, arithmetic is unable to determine. I cannot understand how this obvious difficulty has been so strangely overlooked.

---

[87] "The growth of the system of knight's fees out of the older system of hides is traced by Stubbs. The old service of a man from each five hides of land would go on, only it would take a new name and a new spirit" (*N.C.*, v. 866).

[38] This argument, of course, applies, *mutatis mutandis*, to a five-hide unit as well.

The fourth and last criticism which I propose to offer on the subject is this. If we find that under Henry II.—when we meet with definite information—a fief contained, as we might expect, more " units of possession " than it was bound to furnish knights (thus leaving a balance over for the *baro* after subinfeudation), we must draw one of two conclusions : either this excess had existed from the first ; or, if the fief (as we are asked to believe) was originally assessed up to the hilt for military service, that assessment must, in the interval, have been reduced. In other words, Henry I.—if, as Dr. Stubbs in one place suggests,[39] he was the first to take a "regular account of the knights' fees"—must have found the land with a settled liability of providing one knight for every five hides, and must, yet, have reduced that liability of his own accord, on the most sweeping scale, thus, contrary to all his principles, ultroneously deprived himself of the " service" he was entitled to claim.

Having completed my criticisms of the accepted view, and set forth its chief difficulties, I shall now propound the theory to which my own researches have led me, following the same method of proof as that adopted by Mr. Seebohm in his *English Village Community*, namely working back from the known to the relatively unknown, till the light thrown upwards by the records of the twelfth century illumines the language of Domesday and renders the allusions of monks and chroniclers pregnant with meaning.

[39] *C. H.*, i 265.

I. THE "CARTAE" OF 1166.

In the formal returns (*cartae*) made to the exchequer in 1166 by the tenants-in-chief (*barones*) of England, of which the official transcripts are preserved in the *Liber Niger* and the *Liber Rubeus*, we have our earliest glimpse of the organisation of that purely feudal host among whom our lands had been parcelled out to be held, as I shall show, by military service. We have therefore, in them our best starting-point for an inquiry into the origin and growth of military tenure in England.

It may be well perhaps, at the very outset, to contrast these *cartae* of 1166 with those of the Domesday Inquest eighty years before. [40] For the essentially feudal character of the former is at once, by the comparison, thrown into relief. The original returns of the Domesday Inquest were made hundred by hundred; those of 1166 were made fief by fief. The former were made by the jurors of the hundred court; the latter by the lord of the fief. Thus, while the one took for its unit the oldest and most familiar of native organizations, the other, ignoring not only the hundred, but even the shire itself, took for its unit the alien organisation of the fief. [41] The one inquest strictly continued, the other wholly repudiated, the Anglo-Saxon system.

It is consequently worse than lost labour to examine these two inquests, based as they are on opposite systems, and giving us as they do a cross-division as if they were but successive editions of the national register or rate-book.

The first point to be considered is this: What was the information which the tenants-in-chief were called upon to

[40] Henry of Huntingdon (p. 207) speaks of the Domesday returns by the same name (*cartae*).

[41] Domesday *Book* occupies a medial position, being arranged under counties, but within each county, under fiefs.

supply in these returns? It was *not*, as Dr. Stubbs and
others have supposed, the amount of "service" due from
each fief to the crown.[42] The information asked for was
the number of "milites" actually enfeoffed by each "baron"
and his predecessors in title, with the number of "servitia"
due from each such "miles" to the "baron." In this distinction, missed by Dr. Stubbs, we find the key to the
problem. The crown, we shall see, must previously have
known the total amount of "service" due from each fief;
but what it did not know, and what it wished to know, was
the number of knights' fees which, up to 1166, had been
created on each fief.

Although there is great diversity in the form of return
adopted—a diversity which imparts to the *cartae* a pleasant
flavour of character—it may fairly be assumed that, as in
similar cases, they were called for throughout the realm
by one uniform writ. If we may deduce the purport of
that writ from the collation of those returns which refer to
it most explicitly, we must infer that the information asked
for was to be given under four heads :—

(1) How many knights had been enfeoffed before the
death of Henry I.?

(2) How many have been enfeoffed since?

(3) How many (if any) remain to be enfeoffed to complete the "service" due from the fief. Or, in other words,
what is the balance of your "service" remaining charge-
able to your "demesne"?

(4) What are the names of your knights?

In support of these statements I append the whole of the
relevant returns.

---

[42] Compare the *carta* of the bishop of Exeter, *Praecepistis mihi quod
mandarem vobis* non *quod servitia militum vobis debeam*, etc. Dr.
Stubbs writes : "The king issued a writ to all the tenants-in-chief of the
crown, lay and clerical, directing each of them to send in a cartel or report of the number of knights' fees for the service of which he was legally
liable."—*Const. Hist.*, i. 584.

BISHOP OF EXETER.

Praecepistis mihi quod mandarem vobis per breve meum sigillatum et apertum, non quot servitia militum vobis debeam, sed (1) quot habeam milites feffatos de tempore Regis Henrici avi vestri, et (2) quot post mortem ipsius, et (3) quot sint super dominium meum. [48]

ARCHBISHOP OF YORK.

Praecipit dignitas vestra omnibus fidelibus vestris clericis et laicis, qui de vobis tenent de capite in Eboracsira, ut mandent vobis per literas suas, extra sigillum pendentes, (1) quot milites quisquis habeat de veteri feffamento de tempore Regis Henrici avi vestri, scilicet de die et anno quo ipse fuit vivus et mortuus, et (2) quot habeat de novo feodamento feffatos post mortem bonae memoriae avi vestri ejusdem, et (3) quot feoda militum sint super dominium uniuscujusque, et (4) omnium illorum nomina, tam de novo feffamento quam de veteri feffatorum quae sint in illo brevi scripta, quia vultis quod si aliqui ibi sunt qui vobis nondum fecerunt ligantiam, et quorum nomina non sunt scripta in rotulo vestro, quod infra dominicam primam xl^ae ligantiam vobis faciant (p. 412).

BISHOP OF DURHAM.

Praecepit nobis, domine, vestra sublimitas, quod literis nostris sigillatis, extra sigillum pendentibus, vobis mandaremus (1) quot milites feffatos haberemus de veteri feffamento et (2) de novo, scilicet, anno et die quo Rex Henricus fuit vivus et mortuus et de [*sic*] post mortem ejus . . . (3) super dominium vero nostrum, de quo similiter mandare præcepistis, etc. (pp. 416, 418).

---

[48] The bishop of " Coventry " expresses it :—" numerum . . eorum si quos in dominio tenemus, et eorum nomina " (p. 263).

HERBERT DE CAS-
TELLO.

Michi et compari-
bus meis mandastis
ut vobis per breve
nostrum pendens ex-
tra sigillum, mandare-
mus (1) quot milites
antiquitus feodatos
de tempore Regis
Henrici avi vestri ha-
beamus et (2) quot
de novo feodamento.
. . . Et hii omnes
ligantiam et homa-
gium vobis fecerunt
(pp. 275–6).

ENGELARD DE
STRATTONE.

Michi et ceteris
comparibus meis qui
de vobis tenemus in
capite per litteras
vestras mandastis ut
vobis per breve nos-
trum pendens extra
sigillum mandaremus
(1) quot milites habe-
amus de veteri feoda-
mento de tempore
Henrici Regis avi
vestri, et (2) quot
habeamus de novo
feodamento (p. 276).

ROBERT DE BRIN-
TONE.

Michi et aliis com-
paribus meis per lit-
teras vestras innotu-
istis ut per fidem et
ligantiam quam vobis
debemus per breve
nostrum pendens ex-
tra sigillum mandare-
mus (1) quot milites
haberemus de veteri
feodamento de tem-
pore Henrici Regis
avi vestri, et (2) quot
milites haberemus de
novo feodamento
post tempus Regis
Henrici avi vestri, et
(3) quot milites ha-
beamus super domi-
nium nostrum. . . .
Et vobis quidem et
filio vestro ligantiam
et homagium fece-
runt (p. 277).[44]

Let me here break off for a moment to consider one of
the most important points suggested by this great inquest,
namely, the issue of the writs under which it was held. It
has been generally assumed that each tenant received his
writ direct from the crown; and a casual reading of the
cartae might, perhaps, favour such a view. I have, however, been led to the conclusion that a general writ was
issued to the sheriff of each county, and that its terms

[44] These references are to the pages of the forthcoming edition of the
Liber Rubeus. It will be observed that the second three returns are too
closely alike for accidental coincidence; the three Shropshire " barons "
who made them must have been in some communication. Note here
the remarkable use of the term " compares."

were communicated by him to the several tenants-in-chief, whose *capita baroniæ* lay within his jurisdiction.

Baderun of Monmouth has heard the writ read out in the county court;[45] Earl Patrick also has heard the writ read out.[46] William fitz Siward derives from the sheriff, he tells us, his knowledge of the writ:[47] even the bishop of Chester has received his instructions from the sheriff.[48] But more especially do I rely upon the return of the Archbishop of York because he recites the tenor of the writ in terms which can leave no doubt that it was addressed, through the sheriff, to the whole shire collectively.[49] If the Archbishop of York did not receive a special writ, we may fairly infer that no other tenant can have done so.

Further, I believe that as the "barons" received their instructions from the sheriffs, so they also sent in their returns through those officers. The memorandum, for instance, on the missing *carta* of Osbert fitz Hugh informs us that it was brought to the exchequer by William de Beauchamp. Now, William de Beauchamp was sheriff of the shire. This would account for the grouping of the returns " per singulos comitatus," as Swereford expresses it, and indeed this arrangement would but follow the existing practice of collecting the scutage shire by shire.

Returning now to the terms of the inquiry, it is obvious that the tenant (*baro*) to whom such queries were addressed must of necessity have belonged to one of these three classes—

(*a*) Those who had created *the exact number* of knights' fees sufficient to discharge their " service."

---

[45] Audivi praeceptum vestrum in consulatu Herefordiae.

[46] Audito praecepto vestro.

[47] Praeceptum vestrum, per totam Angliam divulgatum, per vicecomitem vestrum Norhumberlande ad me, sicut ad alios, pervenit.

[48] Mandavit nobis . . . Vicecomes Stephanus, ex parte vestra quatinus, etc.

[49] Praecepit dignitas vestra omnibus fidelibus vestris, clericis et laicis, qui de vobis tenent in capite in Eboracsira ut mandent, etc. . . . . Quorum ego unus, etc.

(*b*) Those who had created *more* than sufficient.

(*c*) Those who had created *less* than sufficient.

This last class requires some explanation. When the number of knights' fees created was not sufficient to discharge the baron's "service," the balance of that service remained charged on the noninfeudated portion of his fief, that is, on the "demesne," and was technically said to be "super dominium." It is all-important that this should be grasped, for it might otherwise be supposed that such a phrase as "quot milites super dominium" implied the existence of actual knights enfeoffed on the demesne, which, to those who realise the working of the system of knight-service, is an absolute contradiction in terms. This, it will be found, beautifully explains the first article of the Assize of Arms (1181)—that every tenant is to keep in stock harness for as many knights "quot habuerit feoda militum in dominio suo." [50] That is to say, that if, after deducting the knights actually enfeoffed, there remained due from his fief a balance of knight-service, he must keep in readiness harness sufficient for those knights whom he would have to provide himself to discharge that balance. [51]

Having made this point clear, I now pass to the immediate object of the inquest of 1166. What that object was, no one has as yet discovered. Dr. Stubbs, for instance, in his preface to the Pipe-Roll of 1166, writes : "On the immediate purpose for which the inquiry was made—and it can scarcely be doubted that it was for the collection of a scutage—we shall look for further information in the rolls of the succeeding years." My own researches enable me to assert that this inquest formed part of a financial

---

[50] It should be scarcely necessary to warn the reader against confusing the *dominium*, or non-infeudated portion of the entire fief, with the *dominium*, or demesne portion, of each Manor upon that fief

[51] An instance in point is afforded by the Bardolf barony (*i.e.* fief) *temp.* John :—" Heres Dodon' Bardulf tenet feoda xxv. militum per totum. Inde xv. milites sunt feoffati et x. feoda sunt super dominium" (*Testa de Nevill*, p. 19).

revolution hitherto ignored, which deserves to be compared with those other innovations in administration and finance that characterised the latter half of the twelfth century in England.

When we come to place side by side the returns of 1166 and the payments made upon those returns in 1168, we find (at least, on the lay fiefs) the same distinction in both between "the old feoffment" and "the new." But while the *returns*, as we saw, were made under three heads,[52] the *payments* were made under two, namely, under the two feoffments. The reason of this difference can be established beyond dispute : the exchequer clerks had, in every instance, added the returns under the *third* head to those under the *first*, and classed them together as "old feoffment." This is one of the points which, I think, have never been hitherto explained.

Plenty of examples might be given, but these two will suffice. Walter de Aincurt returns 24 fees *de veteri*, 5 *de novo*, and 11 *super dominium*. The exchequer, in 1168 records him as paying on 35 fees *de veteri*, and on 5 *de novo*.[53] Richard de Haie returns 11 fees *de veteri*, 4 *de novo*, and 5 *super dominium*. The exchequer records him as paying on 16 *de veteri*, and 4 *de novo*.

The main point, however, on which I propose to insist, is that these returns were intended to provide, and, as a matter of fact, did provide a new feudal assessment, wholly superseding the old one, in no case to the advantage of the tenant, but in many to the advantage of the crown. The *modus operandi* was as follows. Instead of either adhering to the old assessment (*servitium debitum*), or uniformly substituting a new one based on the fees actually created, the crown selected in every case whichever of these two systems told in its own favour and against the tenant of the fief. If he had enfeoffed fewer knights than his *servitium*

---

[52] (1) Old feoffment, (2) new feoffment, (3) demesne.

[53] He and his successors are consequently found paying, time after time, on thirty-five fees.

debitum required, the crown retained that *servitium* as the irreducible minimum of his assessment; but if he had created an excess of fees, the crown added that excess to his pre-existing assessment and increased the "service" due from him *pro tanto*. This discovery is no conjecture, but is capable of arithmetical demonstration.

It should be noticed how skilfully the queries were framed, in the inquest of 1166, to entrap the unwary tenant, and make him commit himself to the facts. If his enfeoffed knights were short of the required number, he was caught under the third query; if, on the other hand, he had an excess, he was caught under the others. Now, did the "barons," when they made their returns, anticipate this sweeping and unwelcome reform? Presumably not. They appear to have drawn up their *cartae* carefully and willingly, few of those who had an excess of knights taking even the precaution of mentioning their *servitium debitum*.[54] The church, moreover, from the terms in which her payments are thenceforth entered (*vide infra*), must have uniformly and systematically adopted an attitude of protest. Yet there is no trace of such protest in her returns. May we then infer that the crown sought to deliberately entrap its tenants? Two circumstances might favour that view. In the first place the tenants had to make their returns *extra sigillum pendentes*, thereby solemnly committing themselves;[55] in the second, the tenants would, of course,

---

[54] William de Beauchamp, of Worcestershire, is virtually a solitary exception. He inserts, *cavendi causa*, this significant clause:—"De hiis praenominatis non debeo Regi nisi servitium vii. militum, nec antecessores mei unquam plus fecerunt, sed quia dominus Rex praecepit michi mandare quot milites habeo et eorum nomina, ideo mando quod istos (*i.e.* 16) habeo fefatos de veteri feffamento; sed non debeo Regi nisi servitium vii. militum." But William was a sheriff at the time, and may have had special information which put him on his guard.

[55] Compare the case of the Irish bishops six years later (1172), who sent the king "litteras suas in modum cartae extra sigillum pendentes" (Howden). Note also that the addition of the seal made the return essentially a *carta*. In Normandy, the tenants by knight service were only required (1172) to seal the return (*breve*) of their *servitium debitum*.

have been tempted to conceal or understate their excess of knights, had they foreseen the use that the crown would make of their returns.

The question may very fairly be asked, "What check had the crown upon a tenant in the event of the latter omitting some of his 'excess' fees?" The answer is supplied, I think, by a clause in the invaluable return of the northern primate. He there requests that his return may be accepted "without prejudice," as a lawyer would say, in case of his omitting some small fees. That is to say, these formal returns might be brought up as evidence against tenants-in-chief who had omitted some of their fees, proving that they had thereby themselves disowned their right to the fees in question.[56]

Two points strike one strongly in the preparation of these returns. The first of these is the difficulty experienced in compiling a correct list of under-tenants and their holdings; the second is the employment of the "Inquest" as a means of ascertaining the particulars.

Taking the former of these, we find Hugh Wac writing, "si amplius inquirere possim, notificabo vobis"; and Guarine "de Aula," "si plus possim inquirere, faciam vobis scire"; so too the Bishop of Ely, "de hiis vero certi sumus, et si amplius inquirere poterimus libenter vobis significabimus"; and the Bishop of Bath, "si certiorem inquirere poterimus veritatem, nos illam vobis significabimus"; and Alfred of Lincoln, "si plus inquiri potest, inquirere faciemus." The bishop of Exeter makes his return, "sicut eam diligentius inquirere potui"; the Abbot of Tavistock, "quantum inde sollicitius inquirendo scire potuit." Hugh de Lacy, in a postcript to his return, adds a fee "quod oblitus sum"; while the Earl of Clare has to send in a

---

[56] The point is of some importance in its bearing on the right of the individual to assess himself, which is held in this case to have been exercised. "The assessment," writes Dr. Stubbs, "of the individual depended very much on his own report, which the exchequer had little means o checking."—*C.H.*, i. 585.

subsequent rider, containing an entry, "quod ego postquam misi cartam . . . recordatus sum."

From this difficulty it is a short step to the inquests which it seems in some cases to have necessitated. The Abbot of Ramsey heads his return, "Haec est inquisitio"; the Earl of Warwick similarly commences, "Hoc est quod inquisivi per homines." Earl Patrick makes his return, "secundum quod de probis et antiquis hominibus meis inquirere potui." "Fecimus inquirere," writes the Bishop of Bath, "per legales homines meos. . . . Haec autem per eos inquisivimus."

This brings us directly to the very important inquest referred to in the *carta* of the earl of Arundel:—

Dominus noster Rex Henricus quadam contentione quae surrexit inter milites de honore de Arundel de exercitu quodam de Walliis, elegit iiij. milites de honore, de melioribus et legalioribus, et antiquioribus . . . et fecit eos recognoscere servitia militum de honore, et super legalitatem et sacramenta eorum inde neminem audire voluit.

Mr. Eyton argued elaborately on genealogical grounds that this inquest must have taken place under Henry I., but indeed it is quite obvious from the language of the *carta* itself that this was so. It is, consequently, worthy of notice for its bearing on "the sworn inquest." While on this subject, attention may be called to the unique entry in the Pipe-Roll of 12 Henry II. (1166): "Alanus de Munbi debet xl. s. quia non interfuit Jurat' feodorum militum" (p. 8). Investigation proves (through what is known as the Lindsey Survey) that Alan was an under-tenant of the honour of Brittany, the successor of that Eudo who held in Mumby *temp.* Domesday. This fact throws light on the entry, by suggesting that the inquest referred to concerned the honour of Brittany, the number of fees in which was then and subsequently doubtful.

But to return. It is infinitely easier to trace the change brought about by the inquest of 1166 in the case of the church fiefs than of the lay ones. For on the former it was uniform and glaring. Previously to 1166 the church tenants had paid on their *servitium debitum* alone; after 1166 they paid, as a rule, on all the fees actually created upon the fief. Thus the assessment of the Bishop of Durham was raised at a blow from ten fees to more than seventy.[57] There were several equally striking cases among the prelates. Now, whether or not the church tenants feared something of the kind, they had generally been careful in their returns to set forth their *servitium debitum*, and when, in 1168, they were uniformly assessed on their total of fees, their uniform protest is expressed in the formula "quos non recognoscit" applied to the payment on their excess knights. Such is the meaning of this puzzling formula which is peculiar to the church fiefs.[58] In these cases it wholly replaces the *de veteri* and *de novo* assessment which, from 1166, was applied to the lay fiefs.

II. THE SERVITIUM DEBITUM.

The essential feature we have to keep in view when examining the growth of knight-service is the *servitium debitum*, or quota of knight-service due to the crown from each fief.

This has, I venture to think, been obscured and lost sight of in the generalizations and vague writing about the

---

[57] By one of those slips so marvellously rare in his writings Dr. Stubbs writes that "the Bishop of Durham's service for his demesne land was that of ten knights, but it was not cut up into fees" (i. 263). What the bishop said was that he owed no service for his demesne, because there were already over seventy fees created on his fief, though he only owed ten.

[58] This is one of the points on which Madox is completely at sea. He quotes the case of the Bishop of Durham (1168) as an instance of "Doubts about the number of knights' fees" (*Baronia Anglica*, p. 122); and he writes, of the above uniform formula: "This uncertainty about the number of the fees frequently happened in the case of ecclesiastical persons, Bishops, and Abbots."—*Exchequer*, i. 647.

"gradual process" of development. It is difficult for me to traverse the arguments of Gneist, Stubbs and Freeman, because we consider the subject from such wholly different standpoints. For them the introduction of knight-service means the process of subinfeudation on the several fiefs ; for me it means the grant of fiefs to be held from the crown by knight service. Thus the process which absorbs the attention of the school whose views I am opposing is for me a matter of mere secondary importance. The whole question turns upon the point whether or not the tenants-in-chief received their fiefs to hold of the crown by a quota of military service, or not. If they did, it would depend simply on their individual inclinations, whether, or how far, they had recourse to subinfeudation. It was not a matter of principle at all ; it was, as Dr. Stubbs, himself puts it, "a matter of convenience," [59] a mere detail. What we have to consider is not the relation between the tenant-in-chief and his under-tenants, but that between the king and his tenants-in-chief : for this was the primary relation that determined all below it.

The assumption that the Conqueror cannot have introduced any new principle in the tenure of land lies at the root of the matter. Assuming this, one must of course seek elsewhere for the introduction of knight service. Have not the difficulties of the accepted view arisen from its exponents approaching the problem from the wrong point of view ? The tendency to exalt the English and depreciate the Norman element in our constitutional development has led them I think, and especially Mr. Freeman, to seek in Anglo-Saxon institutions an explanation of feudal phenomena. This tendency is manifest in their conclusions on the great council : [60] it colours no less strongly their views on knight-service. In neither case can they bring themselves to adopt the feudal standpoint or to enter into the

[59] *C. H.*, i. 264.
[60] See my papers on "The House of Lords ; the Transition from Tenure to Writ" (*Antiquary*, Oct. and Dec., 1884, April, 1885).

feudal spirit.   It is to this that I attribute their disposition
to bring the crown face to face with the under-tenant—or
"landowner" as they would prefer to term him—and so to
ignore, or at least to minimise the importance of the tenant-
in-chief, the "middleman" of the feudal system.   Making
every allowance for the policy of the Conqueror in insisting
on the direct allegiance of the under-tenant to the crown,
and thereby checking the disintegrating influence of a
perfect feudal system, the fact remains what we may term
the "military service" bargain was a bargain between the
crown and the tenant-in-chief, not between the crown and
his under-tenants.   It follows from this that so long as the
"baron" (or "tenant-in-chief") discharged his *servitium
debitum* to the crown, the king had no right to look beyond
the "baron," who was himself and alone responsible for the
discharge of this service.   It is, indeed, in this responsibility
that lies the key to the situation.   If the under-tenant of a
knight's fee failed to discharge his service, it was not to
him, but to his lord, that the crown betook itself.   "I know
nothing of your tenant," was in effect the king's position ;
"you owe me, for the tenure of your fief, the service of so
many knights, and that service must be performed, whether
your under-tenants repudiate their obligations to yourself
or not."   In other words the "baron" discharged his service to the king, whereas the baron's under-tenants discharged theirs to their lord. [61]   So the *Dialogus* speaks of the
under-tenant's "numerum militum quos domino debuerat."

Let us then apply ourselves directly to the quotas of
military service due from the "barons" to the crown, and
see if, when ascertained, they throw any fresh light on the
real problem.

---

[61] See, for instance, the language used in the *carta* of Ralf de Worcester
(p. 441) : "Teneo de vobis in capite de veteri fefamento feodum i. militis,
unde debeo vobis facere servitium i. militis.   Et de eodem feodo Jordanus
Hairum debet mihi facere iiii[am] partem servitii," etc.   In Normandy
(1172), the phrase ran : "quot milites unusquisque baronum deberet
ad servicium regis, et quot haberet ad suum proprium servicium."

No attempt, so far as I know, has ever been made to determine these quotas, and indeed it was the utter want of trustworthy information on the subject that led Swereford to undertake his researches in the thirteenth century. Those researches, unfortunately, leave us no wiser, partly from his defective method and want of the requisite accuracy; partly from the fact that what he sought was not abstract historical truth, but practical information bearing on the existing rights of the crown. We must turn therefore to the original authorities: (1) the *cartae baronum*, (2) the annual rolls. These were the two main sources of Swereford's information, as they must also be of ours. In the next part of this paper I shall deal with the evidence of the rolls, as checking and supplementing the *cartae baronum*.

I shall analyse the church fiefs first, because we can ascertain, virtually with exactitude, the *servitium debitum* of every prelate and of every head of a religious house who held by knight-service. The importance of these figures, together with the fact that they have never, so far as I know, been set forth till now, has induced me to append them here in full detail.

SEE	SERVICE DUE. knights	SEE.	SERVICE DUE. knights
Canterbury	60	Bath	20
Winchester	60	London	20
Lincoln	60	Exeter	$17\frac{1}{2}$[62]
Worcester	50 [60]	"Chester"	15
Norwich	40	Hereford	15
Ely	40	Durham	10
Salisbury	32	Chichester	4 [2]
York	20 [7]		

[62] Sometimes Exeter pays on $15\frac{1}{2}$ (14, 33 Hen. II.), but $17\frac{1}{2}$ (2, 5, 7, 18 Hen. II.) is the normal amount. The explanation of this odd number is found in the *Testa de Nevill* (p. 226) where ("Veredictum militum de Rapo de Arundel") we read:—"Episcopus Exoniensis tenet de Domino Rege de Capellaria de Boseham vii. feoda militum et dimidium." The Bosham estate (as belonging to Osbern) had formed part of the episcopal

Every English see then in existence is thus accounted for with the solitary and significant exceptions of Carlisle and Rochester. The latter see, we know, had enfeoffed knights for their names (*temp.* Hen. I., I think, from internal evidence) are recorded in the *Textus Roffensis* (p. 223);[63] the former had been created after the date when, as I shall argue, the Conqueror fixed the knight-service due from the fees.

In the above list the figures in brackets refer to the assessments previous to 1166. Three changes were made at, or about, that date. The Bishop of Worcester, in accordance with the protest he had made from the beginning of the reign, obtained a reduction of his quota from sixty knights to fifty; while the Archbishop of York's *servitium* was raised from seven knights to twenty, and that of the

---

fief in Domesday, but (the bishops having founded a church there) we find it assessed and paying separately as 7½ fees.

[63] I have found a case bearing upon this point and reported at great length (Thorpe's *Registrum Roffense*, pp. 70 et sq.). It arose from an attempt of the Archbishop of Canterbury, in 1253, to distrain the Bishop of Rochester for the "auxilium ad filium regis primogenitum militem faciendum." The bishop "posuit se super recordum rotulorum de Scaccario, per quos rotulos poterit et illa quam rex contra episcopum et etiam illa quam archiepiscopus contra episcopum movit questio diffiniri. Didicerat enim episcopus per unum fidelem amicum quem in scaccario tunc habebat quod nunquam tempore alicujus regis pro aliquo feodo episcopatus aliquod fuit regi factum servicium vel datum scutagium. . . . Unde consulebat quod audaciter poneret se episcopus super recordum rotulorum de Scaccario, nichil enim tenet episcopus per baroniam de rege, sed per puram elemosinam, quod non est dicendum de aliquo episcopatu Anglie, nec de Archiepiscopatu, nisi dumtaxat de Karleolen. Cumque cum audacia institisset episcopus, quod decideretur per rotulos de Scaccario quibus creditur in omnibus illis sicut sancto evangelio," etc., etc. The barons of the exchequer examined the rolls, "a tempore primi conquestus" (?) and reported:—"nusquam invenerunt episcopum Roffensem solvisse aut dedisse aliquod servicium regibus temporale." But the dispute was not finally decided till 1259. The clue to the matter is found in the Canterbury "Domesday Monachorum" (8th Report Hist. MSS. i. 316), where a list of the archbishop's knights, perhaps coeval with Domesday (*vide infra*, p. 300), is headed by "Episcopus Roffensis" with a *servitium* of ten knights to the Primate.

Bishop of Chichester from two knights to four. These changes are known to us only from the details of the prelates' scutages; there is nothing to account for them in the relevant *cartae*, and we can only infer from the formula *quos recognoscit* that the two bishops whose *servitia* were increased acquiesced in the justice of the crown's claim.

Proceeding to the "service" of the religious houses :—

HOUSE.	SERVICE DUE. knights	HOUSE.	SERVICE DUE. knights
Peterborough . . .	60	Wilton	5
Glastonbury . . .	40 [60]	Ramsey	4
St. Edmundsbury .	40	Chertsey	3
Abingdon	30	St. Bene't of Hulme .	3
Hyde	20	Cerne [64]	2[3]
St. Augustine's . .	15	Pershore	2[3]
Westminster . . .	15 (?)	Malmesbury . . .	3
Tavistock	15 (?)	Winchcombe	2
Coventry . , . .	10	Middleton	2
Shaftesbury . . .	7 [10]	Sherburne	2
St. Alban's	6	Michelney	1
Evesham	5	Abbotsbury	1

The changes of assessment on religious houses were few, and are thus accounted for. Glastonbury, which paid on sixty knights in the first two scutages of the reign, paid on forty in the third and in those which followed. Pershore paid on three in the first scutage, protesting that it was only liable to two, and from 1168 it was only rated at two. Shaftesbury, which had paid on ten knights in the first scutage, was assessed at only seven in the third scutage and those which followed. Cerne also succeeded in getting its assessment reduced from three knights to two. With these changes should be compared the letter of Bishop Nigel of Ely to Ramsey Abbey certifying that it was only liable to an assessment of four knights. Two

[64] Cerne had to provide "ten" knights *ad wardam* at Corfe Castle, or "two" *ad exercitum* (*vide* cartam).

cases remain which require special treatment—Tavistock and Westminster.

Although Tavistock, in the first scutage, appears to have paid on the anomalous assessment of ten and a half knights its payment on fifteen in the two succeeding ones may fairly be taken as evidence that this was its *servitium debitum.*[65] Its abbot, however, made no reference to that *servitium* in his return, and—by an exception to the regular practice in the case of church fiefs—we find him charged, not on the fees, (1) "quos recognoscit," (2) "quos non recognoscit," but on those which were enfeoffed "de veteri," and "de novo" just as if he were a lay tenant. As his fees "de veteri" were sixteen, this figure recurs in successive scutages, until in 3 John we find him contesting as to one knight ("unde est contentio") who, doubtless, represented the difference between fifteen and sixteen.

The case of Westminster presents considerable difficulty, the entries relating to its payments of scutage being very puzzling. The abbey's fees lay chiefly in Worcestershire and Gloucestershire—especially Worcestershire—and it is under this county that we find it ultimately (*i.e.* from 1168 onwards) assessed at fifteen fees, an assessment which the abbot himself seems to have claimed, in the first scutage, as the right one.

Taking then the *servitium debitum* of all the church fiefs, at their earliest ascertainable assessment, we obtain this result :—

Bishops	$458\frac{1}{2}$
Heads of religious houses . . .	318
Capellaria de Bosham	$7\frac{1}{2}$
Grand total . . .	784 [66]

---

[65] This indeed is proved by an extract quoted by Madox (*Exchequer*) from the Roll of 22 Hen. II. (rot. 10*a*).

[66] The effect of all the changes of assessment we have traced under Henry II. would only be the reduction of this total to 774.

Far more difficult is the calculation of the *servitium debitum* from the lay fiefs. The list which follows is constructed from the evidence of the *cartae* and the rolls, and, though substantially correct, is liable to emendation in details. It only comprises those fiefs the *servitium* of which I have been able to ascertain with certainty or probability.

Robert "filius Regis"	100 [67]
Earl Ferrers	80 (? 60) [68]
Honour of Totness	75
Honour of Tickhill	60 (?) [69]
Robert de Stafford	60
Count of Eu	60 (?) [70]
Earl Warrenne	60 (?) [71]
Lacy of Pontefract	60
Roger de Mowbray	60 [72]
Earl of Essex	60
Walter fitz Robert (of Essex) . . .	50
Honour of Richmond	50 [73]
Gervase Paynell	50
Reginald de St. Valery	50 (?) [74]
Patrick, earl of Salisbury	40
Walter de Aincurt	40
William de Montfichet	40
Payn de Montdoubleau	40 [75]
William de Roumare	40 (?) [76]

[67] Roll of 11 Hen. II. (This was, of course, the son of Henry I. by Edith).

[68] The *custos* of his fief paid scutage for eighty knights in 1159, but he speaks "de meis lx. militibus" in his *carta*.

[69] The undoubted assessment in 1162. Afterwards it is found paying on sixty and a fraction.

[70] "Lx. milites . . . habere solebat pater meus" (*Carta*).

[71] This figure is given in the *Liber Niger*, but is really derived from his recorded payments.

[72] Tot habuit milites feodatos . . . scilicet lx. de antiquo feodo (*Carta*).

[73] In Yorkshire alone. In all England, many more.

[74] This figure is taken from the payments in 1161 and 1172

[75] Roll of 11 Hen. II.

[76] *Ibid.* It is impossible, within the compass of a note, to discuss the

Hubert de Rye	.	.	.	.	.	35
Hubert fitz Ralf (Derbyshire)	.	.	.	.	30
Walter de Wahulle	.	.	.	.	.	30
William fitz Robert (Devon)	.	.	.	.	30
William de Traci	.	.	.	.	.	30 [77]
Robert de Valoines	.	.	.	.	.	30 [77]
Maurice de Craon	.	.	.	.	.	30 [77]
William de Albini (of Belvoir)	.	.	.	30 [77]
Bernard Balliol	.	.	.	.	.	30 [78]
Roger de Arundel	.	.	.	.	.	30 [79]
Walter de Mayenne	.	.	.	.	.	30 (?) [80]

two consecutive and most important entries on the Roll (pp. 37-8), which represent a payment by the Earl of Chester on 20 fees, "pro feodo Turoldi vicecomitis," and by Richard de Camville on 40 fees, "pro feodo Willelmi de Romara." I called attention to the former entry in the *Academy* (21st April, 1888), but did not at that time explain it. Mr. R. E. G. Kirk undertook to explain "its real meaning" (*Genealogist*, v. 141), which, however, he completely mistook (*ib.*, July, 1891). The two entries, I think, should be read together as relating to the estates of the famous Lucy, the common ancestress of the earl and of William. If so, they may refer to a fief with an original *servitium* of 60 knights, of which one-third was in the hands of the Earl of Chester, and two-thirds in that of his cousin. Independently of the light they throw on the obscure history of this divided and contested fief, they are of value for the unique reference (in this Roll) to "noviter feffati" (*vide infra*). The total (including these) for the two fiefs is 66⅜. There is no return for the earl's Lindsey fief in 1166, but William de Roumare's return acknowledges 57 fees. If to these we add the 9½ fees which, it says, had formerly existed in addition, we obtain 66½. This suggests that the one fief of 1166 represents the two of 1165. It should be added that the Hampshire fief of William de Roumare is paid for as 20 fees in 1159 and 1162, and was similarly accounted for by Richard de Camville in both these years.

[77] Roll of 11 Hen. II.

[78] He omitted to send in a *carta* in 1166 ; but, both before and after, he paid on 30 fees.

[79] He twice pays on 30 fees before 1166, in which year his fief was held by Gerbert de Percy. Subsequently, as the honour of Poerstoke (Poorstock), it always pays on 30.

[80] This is a very difficult case. Walter's *carta* might easily be read as implying a *servitium debitum* of 20 fees, and his fief paid on 29 *de veteri* and 1½ *de novo*. But careful scrutiny reveals that the words "hos iiijor. milites qui has predictas terras tenent" are preceded by *six* names. If they refer, either to the four names immediately preceding, or (which is

Robert de Albini (Bucks)	.	.	.	.	25
Robert fitz Hugh	.	.	.	.	25
Alfred of Lincoln	.	.	.	.	25
Ralf Hanselin	.	.	.	.	25
William de Braose	.	.	.	.	25 [81]
Oliver de Traci	.	.	.	.	25 [81]
Gerard de Limesi	.	.	.	.	25 (?) [82]
Walter Waleran	.	.	.	.	20
Richard de Hay	.	.	.	.	20
Honour of Holderness	.	.	.	.	20
William de Windsor	.	.	.	.	20
Hugh de Bayeux	.	.	.	.	20
William de Vesci	.	.	.	.	20 (?) [83]
Daniel de Crevecœur	.	.	.	.	20 (?) [84]
Thomas de Arcy	.	.	.	.	20 (?) [85]
Hugh de Dover	.	.	.	.	15
Walter Bret	.	.	.	.	15
Baderon de Monmouth	.	.	.	.	15
Earl Richard de Redvers	.	.	.	.	15 [86]
Adam de Brus	.	.	.	.	15
Hamo fitz Meinfelin	.	.	.	.	15
Osbert fitz Hugh	.	.	.	.	15 (?) [87]
? Hugh de Scalers	.	.	.	.	15 [88]
? Stephen de Scalers	.	.	.	.	15
Gilbert de Pinkeni	.	.	.	.	15
Geoffrey Ridel	.	.	.	.	15

more probable) to the four knights who held his lands but rendered him no service, the total of his *servitium debitum* would, in either case, be 30.

[81] Roll of 11 Hen. II.   [82] He paid on 25 fees in 1162.

[83] "Feodum xx. militum de rege de veteri feffamento quod pater suus tenuit" (*Carta*).

[84] He paid on 20 fees in 1161, but the subsequent assessment of the fief varies considerably.

[85] He paid on 20 fees in 1162 and 1165, and returned his fees in 1166 as 20 *de veteri* and ¾ *de novo*.

[86] The scutages record him as paying always on 15 knights *quos recognoscit*—the formula for *servitium debitum*.

[87] His payment on 15 fees in 1161 probably represents his *servitium debitum*. His total enfeoffments were 23.

[88] Hugh and Stephen de Scalers are the names given in the *cartae*, but Henry and William de Scalers held the fiefs at the time.

Robert Foliot	. . . . . .	15
Robert de Choques	. . . . .	15
Robert de Caux	. . . . . .	15
William Paynell	. . . . . .	15 (?)
Richard de Reimes	. . . . .	10
Roger de Buron	. . . . . .	10
Richard fitz William	. . . . .	10
William fitz Alan	. . . . . .	10
Richard de Cormeilles	. . . .	10
Roger de Kentswell	. . . . .	10
William Trussebut	. . . . .	10
Nigel de Lovetot	. . . . . .	10
Manasser Arsic	. . . . . .	10
Richard de Montacute	. . . .	10
Wandrille de Courcelles	. . . .	10
Walter de Bolebec (Bucks)	. . . .	10
Robert de Hastings	. . . . .	10
Lambert de Scotenni	. . . . .	10
Drogo de Montacute	. . . . .	10 (?) [89]
William de Reimes	. . . . ,	10 (?) [90]
William de Helion	. . . . .	10 (?) [91]

Graeland de Thani of Essex owed seven and a half knights (the half of fifteen), and Roger de Berkeley probably the same. Those who owed a *servitium* of five knights were Robert fitz Harding, Baldwin Buelot, Simon de Cancy, Nigel de Lovetot (of the honour of Tickhill), Amfry de Cancy, Hugh de Dover (of the honour of Brunne),[92] Walter de Bolebec (Northumberland), Robert de Brus, Roger Bertram, and probably Stephen de Bulmer,[93] and Herbert "de Castello."

The cases in which the *servitium* can be shown not to

---

[89] He paid 10 marcs in 1168, though his *carta* only records $9\frac{5}{8}$ fees.

[90] A difficult fief to deal with, but almost certainly the half of an original Reimes fief owing 20 knights (*vide supra*).

[91] Apparently 15 at first, and 10 later.

[92] *i.e.* the Peverel Honour of Bourne, Cambridgeshire (held in Domesday by Picot, the Sheriff), not Bourne, Lincolnshire, held by the Wakes.

[93] He only pays on 5 fees in 1162, and the excess *de novo* in his *carta* is accounted for, he says, by the necessities of his position.

have been a multiple of five are comparatively few. That of Simon de Beauchamp of Bedford was 54, of William Fossard 33½, of Humphrey de Bohun 30½, of William Malet 20⅛, of Robert de Beauchamp (of Somerset) 17, of William fitz John (of Harptree) 13¾, of William Blund 12, of Hugh Wac 10⅛, of William de Ros, William fitz John (of Weston) and William de Beauchamp (of Worcestershire) 7, of John de Bidun and Jocelin de Lovaine 5½.[94] But these, it will be seen, are quite insufficient to overthrow the accumulated array of evidence on the other side, and some of them are, doubtless, capable of explanation. The Bohun fief, for instance, in 1162 paid on exactly 30 fees.

It is impossible to resist the inference, from such evidence as we have, that the amount of the *servitium debitum* was a matter of custom and tradition, and could not usually be determined by reference to written grants or charters. On this point the returns of three Essex tenants are most instructive, while their similarity is so striking, that, as in the case of the Shropshire *formulæ*, it can scarcely be due to accident. The Earl of Essex closes with the words : " et homines mei dicunt mihi quod debeo Domino Regi lx. milites." Walter fitz Robert, who follows him, writes : " et hoc mihi homines mei intelligere faciunt, quod debeo inde Regi servitium de l. militibus." William de Montfichet ends thus : " et hoc faciunt homines mei mihi intelligere—quod pater meus deserviebat per xl. milites." With these expressions we may compare those of William fitz Alan's tenants, who assert that his Norfolk fief "non debet domino Regi nisi i. militem . . . ut antiqui testantur"; that his Shropshire fief " non debet Regi nisi x. milites in exercitu . . . sicut antiqui testantur"; and that, as to his Wiltshire fief, " non sumus certi quod servitium debeat Regi de hoc tenemento." The Abbot of Chertsey, also, states his *servitium debitum* with the proviso "secundum quod scire possumus."[2] These expressions explain the uncertainty as to the *servitium*

---

[94] This is not proved for the latter fief.

debitum in such cases as the see of Worcester and Ramsey Abbey.[95]

The same principle applies to the relation between the tenant-in-chief and his under-tenant. Thus the very first entry in the *cartae* runs as follows :—

> Willelmus de Wokindone iiij. milites et dimidium ; et praeter hoc, ex testimonio curiae meae, dimidium exigo, quem ipse se non debere defendit.

Of another tenant on the same fief we read : " praeter hoc, *ex testimonio curiae meae*, adhuc j. militem exigo." Here, we see, appeal is made not to record evidence, but to oral testimony. So, too, the Bishop of Exeter adds this clause to his return :—

> Et praeter hos omnes, sicut *a multis audivi*, comes Gloucestriæ, et comes Hugo, et comes de Clare debent tenere de Exoniensi Episcopo ; sed nullum ei servitium faciunt vel recognoscunt.

Surely in all such cases as these the obvious inference is that the tenant had been enfeoffed *sine carta,* or in the very words of the Provisions of the Barons (1259) " feofatus sine carta a tempore conquestus vel alio antiquo feofamento" (§ 1).

And now for my theory. No one can have even glanced at the lists I have compiled without being instantly struck

---

[95] Compare with these allusions to a traditional *servitium debitum* the significant words of Wace (*Roman de Rou*) :—

> " Ne ke jamez d'ore en avant,
> Co lor a miz en covenant,
> N'ierent de servise requis,
> Forz tel ke solt estre al paiz,
> E tel come lor ancessor
> Soleient fere a lor Seignor,"—

which are the reply to the fears of the barons (*Norm. Conq.,* iii. 298 :—

> " Li servise ki est doblez
> Creiment k'il seit en feu tornez,
> Et en costume seit tenu
> Et par costume seit rendu (lines 11272 *et seq.*)"

by the fact that the "service" is reckoned in round numbers, and is almost invariably *a multiple of* 5, *if not of* 10.[96]
This discovery, of course, is absolutely destructive of the
view that it always represented the number of five-hide
(or £20) units contained in the fief. Further, the number
of differing fiefs assessed at precisely the same figure proves
that the assessment was wholly arbitrary and cannot have
been even the round sum which approximated most nearly
the number of such units.[97] What then was the true de-
terminant, in the light of these conclusions? I reply—*the
unit of the feudal host.*

"On the continent," writes Gneist, "fifty *milites*, or at
least twenty-five, were reckoned to one banneret; in
England, in proportion to the smaller scale of enfeoffments,
a smaller number appears to have formed the unit of the
constabularia." [98] He is right: the English *constabularia*,
where I find it referred to, consists of *ten* knights.[99] It is
interesting to trace this unit and its multiples recurring in
the narratives of Irish warfare, under Henry II., and in
other struggles.[100] We meet with it also in the grant by
the Empress to Geoffrey de Mandeville, in 1141, of "feodum
et servicium xx. militum," and in Stephen's grant to him
of "lx milites feudatos." [101]

The next step is to show that the Normans were familiar

---

[96] It can be shown that the "service" in Normandy was based on precisely the same five-knight unit.

[97] "The estates of the twenty greatest feodaries in Domesday Book
contain, according to the ordinary computation, 793, 439, 442, 298, 280,
222, 171, 164, 132, 130, 123, 119, 118, 107, 81, 47, 46, and 33 knights'
fees."—GNEIST (C. *H.*, i. 334).

[98] *Const. Hist.*, i. 289.

[99] For instance, the Abbot of St. Edmund's "quinquaginta milites"
are spoken of as "milites de quatuor constabiliis" with "decem miles
de quinta constabilia" (*Memorials of St. Edmunds*, Ed. Arnold, i.
269, 271).

[100] Robert fitz Stephen lands with 30 knights, Maurice de Prendergast
with 10, Maurice fitz Gerald with 10, Strongbow with 200, Raymond the
Fat with 10, Henry himself with either 400 or 500, etc.

[101] See my *Geoffrey de Mandeville*, p. 103.

with *servitium debitum* in terms of the ten-knight unit when they landed in England. For this we have only to refer to Wace. For in the " Roman de Rou," as quoted by Mr. Freeman himself, we find William fitz Osbern assuring the duke as to his barons :—

> Vostre servise dobleront :
> Ki solt mener vint chevaliers
> Quarante en merra volontiers,
> E ki de trente servir deit
> De sesante servir vos velt,
> E cil ki solt servir de cent
> Dous cent en merra bonement.[102]

The *servitium debitum,* therefore, was a standing institution in Normandy, and "to the mass of his (William's) followers," as Mr. Freeman frankly admits, [103] a " feudal tenure, a military tenure, must have seemed the natural and universal way of holding land." When we find them and their descendants holding their fiefs in England, as they had been held in Normandy, by the service of a round number of knights, what is the simple and obvious inference but that, just as Henry II. granted out the provinces of Ireland to be held as fiefs by the familiar service of a round number of knights,[104] so Duke William granted out the fiefs he formed in England ?

If to escape from this conclusion the suggestion be made that these *servitia debita* were compositions effected by English *antecessores*, it need only be answered that the fiefs acquired were wholly new creations, constructed from the scattered fragments of Anglo-Saxon estates. And though in the case of the church fiefs this objection might not apply, yet we have evidence, as I shall show, to prove that their *servitia* also were determined by the conqueror's will,

---

[102] Lines 11253 *et seq.* The figures, however, are far too large, and savour of poetic license.

[103] *N. C.,* v. 368.

[104] Meath with a *servitium debitum* of 100, Limerick of 60, Cork with two *servitia* of 30 each.

as indeed might be inferred from their close correspondence with those of the lay barons.

But if the lands of the conquered realm were so granted to be held by a *servitium debitum* of knights, the key of the position is won, and the defenders of the existing view must retire along the whole line ; for, as Mr. Freeman himself observed, " Let it be once established that land is held as a fief from the crown on condition of yielding certain services to the crown, and the whole of the feudal incidents follow naturally." [105]

I am anxious to make absolutely clear the point that between the accepted view and the view which I advance, no compromise is possible. The two are radically opposed. As against the theory that the military obligation of the Anglo-Norman tenant-in-chief was determined by the assessment of his holding, whether in hidage or in value, I maintain that the extent of that obligation was not determined by his holding, but was fixed in relation to, and expressed in terms of, the *constabularia* of ten knights, the unit of the feudal host. And I, consequently, hold that his military service was in no way derived or developed from that of the Anglo-Saxons, but was arbitrarily fixed by the king, from whom he received his fief, irrespectively both of its size and of all pre-existent arrangements. Such propositions, of course, utterly and directly traverse the view which these passages best summarise :—

The belief that William I. divided the English landed property into military fees is erroneous. . . According to the extent and the nature of the productive property it could be computed how many shields were to be furnished by each estate, according to the gradually fixed proportion of a £20 ground-rent.[106]

There is no ground for thinking that William directly or systematically introduced any new kind of tenure into the holding of English lands. There is nothing to suggest any such belief, either in the chronicles of his reign, in the Survey, which is his greatest monument, in the genuine or even in the spurious remains of his legisla-

---

[105] *N.C.*, v. 378. [106] Gneist, *C.H.*, i. 129, 156.

tion. . . . As I have had to point out over and over again, the grantee of William, whether the old owner or a new one, held his land as it had been held in the days of King Edward.[107]

There can be no doubt that the military tenure . . . was itself introduced by the same gradual process which we have assumed in the case of the feudal usages in general. We have no light on the point from any original grant made by the Conqueror to a lay follower; but . . . we cannot suppose it probable that such gifts were made on any expressed condition, or accepted with a distinct pledge to provide a certain contingent of knights for the king's service.[108]

If my own conclusions be accepted, they will not only prove destructive of this view, but will restore, in its simplicity, a theory which removes all difficulties, and which paves the way to a reconsideration of other kindred problems, and to the study of that aspect of Anglo-Norman institutions in which they represent the feudal spirit developed on feudal lines.

III. Scutage, Aid, and "Donum."

Precious for our purpose as are the *cartae* of 1166, their evidence, as it stands, is incomplete. It needs to be supplemented by the early Pipe-Rolls of Henry II.'s reign. By collating these two authorities we obtain information which, singly, neither the one nor the other could afford. All those entries on the rolls which relate to *scutagia*, *auxilia* or *dona* require to be extracted and classified before we can form our conclusions. Hitherto historians have remained content with repeating Swereford's *obiter dicta*, as extracted from the *Liber Rubeus* by Madox, without checking these statements by the evidence of the rolls themselves.

The question of Swereford's authority is one which it is absolutely necessary to deal with, because his statements

---

[107] Freeman, *N. C.*, v. 372, 371.

[108] Stubbs, *C. H.*, i. 261.

have been freely accepted by successive historical writers, and have formed, indeed, the basis on which their conclusions rest. Now the presumption is naturally in favour of Swereford's knowledge of his subject. His introduction to the *Liber Rubeus* is dated 1230, and he tells us that he had been at work among the records in the days of King John, under William of Ely [109] himself: he wrote with the actual rolls before him; he had been intimate with the leading officials of the exchequer, and enjoyed full knowledge of its practice and its traditions. I cannot wonder that, this being so, his positive assertions should have been readily believed, or that Mr. Hall, when, for a short time, I was associated with him in preparing the Red Book for the press, should, with a kindly bias in favour of so venerable an authority, have shrunk from my drastic criticism of his famous introduction to that volume.

On the other hand we have Swereford's own admission that he worked from the rolls alone. [110] These rolls are, for all purposes, as accessible to us as they were to him, while we possess the advantage of having, in contemporary chronicles, sources of information which he did not use, and with which, indeed, he shows no sign of being even conversant. We must go, therefore, behind Swereford and examine for ourselves the materials from which he worked.

Passing, for the present, over minor points, I would fix on the "Great Scutage," or "Scutage of Toulouse," as the test by which Swereford's knowledge and accuracy must stand or fall. If he is in error on this matter, his error is so grievous and so far-reaching that it must throw the gravest doubt on all his similar assertions. The date of the expedition against Toulouse was June, 1159 (the host having been summoned at Mid-Lent): from the chroniclers we learn that, to provide the means for it, and especially to pay an army of mercenaries, a great levy was made in England and beyond sea. The roll of the following

[109] Mr. Hall informs me that is the name of the official referred to.
[110] " Prout rumor ex rotulis ad me devenit."

Michaelmas records precisely such a levy, and the payments so recorded must have been made for the expenses of this campaign. But we can go further still ; we can actually prove from internal evidence that sums accounted for on the roll of 1159 were levied expressly for the Toulouse campaign. [111] Yet we are confidently informed by Swereford that this levy was for a Welsh war, and that the scutage of Toulouse is represented by the levies which figure on the rolls of 1161 and 1162. He appears to have evolved out of his inner consciousness the rule that a scutage, though fixed and even paid in any given year, was never accounted for on the rolls till the year after. [112] But as even this rule will not apply to his calculation here, one can only suggest that he was absolutely ignorant of the date of the Toulouse campaign. [113] The value of Swereford's calculations is so seriously affected by this cardinal error, that one may reject with less hesitation his statement that the scutage of 1156 was taken for a Welsh war, and not, as there is evidence to imply, for a campaign against the king's brother. Swereford, again, may be pardoned for his ignorance of the fact that scutage existed under Henry I., [114] but when he unhesitatingly assigns the Domesday Survey to the fourteenth year of the Conqueror (1079-1080), he shows us that the precision of his statements is no proof of their accuracy. On both these points he has misled subsequent writers. [115]

The incredible ignorance and credulity even of officials

[111] See p. 279 *infra*.

[112] "Et nota quod quandocumque assidentur scutagia, licet eodem anno solvantur, annotantur tamen in annali anni sequentis" (*Red Book*, ed. Hall, p. 8).

[113] It is just possible that the source of his error is to be found in a solitary entry on the roll of 1163: "Advocatus de Betuna reddit compotum de vi. li. xiii. s. iiii. d. de auxilio exercitus de Tolusa" (p. 9)— which refers to the levy of 1161.

[114] "Temporibus enim regis Henrici primi . . . nec inspexi vel audivi fuisse scutagia assisa" (p. 5).

[115] *Vide supra*, p. 140 *note*.

at the time are illustrated by the fact that the Conqueroi was generally believed to have created 32,000 knights' fees in England, and that Swereford plumed himself on his independence in doubting so general a belief.[116]   His less sceptical contemporary, Segrave, continued to believe it, and even Madox hesitates to reject it.

The persistent assertion that the *Cartae Baronum* were connected with, and preliminary to, the *auxilium ad filiam maritandam* of 1168 is undoubtedly to be traced to Swereford's *ipse dixit* to that effect. He distinctly asserts that the aid was fixed (*assisum*) in the thirteenth year (1167), that the returns (*cartae*) were made in the same year (1167), and that the aid was paid and accounted for in the fourteenth year (1168).[117] Modern research, however, has shown that the returns were made quite early in 1166, while the youthful Matilda, we know, was not married till October, 1168. This throws an instructive light on Swereford's *modus operandi*. Finding from the rolls that the payments made in 1168 were based on the returns in the *cartae*, and not being acquainted with the date of the latter, he jumped to the conclusion that they must have been made in 1167, it being his (quite uusupported) thesis that all levies were fixed in the year preceding that in which they were accounted for on the rolls.

Proceeding further, we find him explaining (p. 9) that he omits the aid of 1165, "quoniam probata summa auxilii propter hoc non probatur numerus militum." And yet this aid, the last to be taken before the returns of 1166, is of special value and importance for the very purpose he speaks of. It is, indeed, an essential element in the evidence on which I build ; and this compels me to discuss the point in some detail.

Those who contributed towards this aid either (1) gave arbitrary sums for the payment of *servientes*—whose num-

[116] Illud commune verbum in ore singulorum tunc temporis divulgatum."

[117] See *Red Book of the Exchequer*, pp. 5, 8.

ber was almost invariably some multiple of five—or (2)
paid a marc on every fee of their *servitium debitum*. We
are only here concerned with those who adopted the latter
course. Now let us take the case of those who adopted this
alternative in the counties of Notts and Derby, and compare their payments with their *servitium debitum* as known
to us from other sources.

Payments (1165).				Service (1166).
Hubert fitz Ralf 30 *marcae*	.	.	.	30 knights
Ralf Halselin 25 ,,	.	.	.	25 ,,
Robert de "Calz" 15 ,,	.	.	.	15 ,,
Roger de Burun 10 ,,	.	.	.	10 ,,

In this case there is no doubt as to the *servitium debitum*,
for it is ascertained from the *cartae* themselves. Having
then proved, by this test, the exact correspondence of the
payments, I turn to the case of Devonshire.

Payments (1165).					Service (1166).
Robert "filius Regis" 100 *marcae*	.	.	.		unknown
William de Traci 30	,,	.	.	.	,,
William de Braose 25	,,	.	.	.	,,
Oliver de Traci 25	,,	.	.	.	,,
Abbot of Tavistock 15	,,	.	.	.	15 knights [118]
William fitz Reginald 1	,,	.	.	.	1 ,,
Ralf de Valtort 1	,,	.	.	.	1 ,,
Robert fitz Geoffrey 1	,,	.	.	.	1 ,,

Here we are supplied by this roll with four important
servitia which would otherwise be absolutely unknown to
us. And they happen to be of special interest. For while
the *carta* of William de Braose returns twenty-eight fees,
and that of Oliver de Traci twenty-three and a half
(though he pays on thirty and a half),[119] their payments in
1165, by revealing their *servitium debitum*, show us that
their fiefs represent the two halves of the Honour of Barnstaple (which, therefore, was assessed at 50 knights) then

[118] See list of church fiefs.
[119] His *carta* is corrupt.

in their respective hands. Again, William de Traci returns his fees in his *carta* as twenty-five and three-quarters, and says nothing about any balance on his *dominium*, as he should have done. Hence we should not have known his *servitium* but for the roll of 1165.

Swereford's extraordinary failure to understand this roll aright is possibly due to the fact that most of the relevant payments are entered without mention of their object. He seems to have been very dependent upon the rolls explaining themselves, and to have worked in the spirit of a copying clerk rather than of an intelligent student.

One more example of his errors will suffice. In his abstracts from the aid "ad maritandam primogenitam filiam regis" (1168), we read :—

Abbas Gloucestriæ de promissione, sed non numeratur quid ; sed in rotulo praecedenti dicitur :—Abbas Gloucestriæ debet xxxviij. l. ij. s. vj. d. de veteri scutagio Walliae.

Now (1) the amount of the abbot's contribution is duly entered on the roll ("xl. marcas de promissione de eodem auxilio"), and it is not paid in respect of fees, but is a voluntary proffer ; (2) the phrase in the preceding roll is not "de veteri *scutagio*," but "de veteri *exercitu*" ; (3) the payment there recorded represents a contribution of 50 *servientes*, and had nothing to do with scutage, for the abbot (as Swereford should have known) did not hold by military service, and ought not, therefore, to figure in his lists at all.[120]

Let us turn, therefore, to the rolls themselves. Now, although the language of the exchequer was not so precise as we could wish, it is possible, more or less, to distinguish and classify these levies. Thus, we have of course a typical "aid" in the levy for the marriage of the king's daughter (1168), while, on the other hand, we have an equally typical "scutage" in 1156, in the payments made by the church tenants in lieu of military service.

[120] "Abbas Gloucestrie tenet omnes terras in libera elemosina."— *Testa*, p. 77.

On the institution of "scutage" there has been much misconception. It is placed by our historians among the great innovations wrought by Henry II., who is supposed by them to have introduced it in 1156.[121] Here we see, once again, the danger of seeking our information on such points secondhand, instead of going straight to the fountainhead for ourselves.

John of Salisbury implies that scutage was no novelty in 1156 when he writes, not that the king imposed it, but that he "*could not remit* it." This inference is at once confirmed by the appearance of scutage *eo nomine* in the reign of Henry I.

The following charter is found in the (MS.) *Liber Eliensis* (Lib. III.), No. xxi., and in the Cottonian MS. Nero A. 15 :—

H. rex Anglorum Archiepiscopis, Episcopis, Abbatibus, Comitibus, etc. Salutem. Sciatis me condonasse Ecclesiæ S. Æetheldredæ de Ely pro Dei amore et anima Patris et Matris meae et pro redemptione peccatorum meorum, et petitione Hervei ejusdem Ecclesie Episcopi 40 libras de illis 100 libris quas predicta Ecclesia solebat dare de *Scutagio* quando *Scutagium* currebat[122] per terram meam Anglie : ita quod Ecclesia amodo inperpetuum non dabit inde nisi 60 libras quando *Scutagium* per terram evenerit, et ita inperpetuum sit de predictis libris Ecclesia predicta quieta. T. Rogero Episcopo Saresberiensi, Gaufrido Cancellario meo et Roberto de Sigillo et Willelmo de Tancarvilla et Willelmo de Albineio Pincerna et Radulfo Basset et Gaufrido de Clintona et Willelmo de Pondelarche. Apud Eilinges in transitu meo.

---

[121] "A new impost specially levied (1156) upon some of the ecclesiastical estates under the name of *scutage*" (Norgate's *Angevin Kings*, i. 433). "The famous scutage, the acceptance of a money composition for military service, alike for the old English service of the fyrd" [this, of course, is a misconception], "and for the newer military tenures, dates from this (1159) time" (Freeman's *Norman Conquest*, v. 674). "The term *scutage* now (1156) first employed. . . . As early as his second year (1156) we find him collecting a scutage, a new form of taxation" (Stubbs' *Const. Hist.*, i. 454, 458, 581, 590).

[122] The phrase "debet scutagium quando currit" is of course, a normal one.

This is followed by (No. xxii.) a grant of Charteris Abbey to the church of Ely; [123] and this again is followed, in a register of Charteris Abbey, [124] by a remission of 6s. 7d. Wardpenny hitherto paid by that abbey. The first and third charters receive singular confirmation, being thus accounted for in the Pipe-Roll of Henry I. :—

Et idem Episcopus debet ccxl. li. ut rex clamet eum quietum de superplus militum Episcopatus, et ut Abbatia de Cateriz sit quieta de Warpenna (p. 44).

This entry, moreover, connects the *scutagium* with the system of knight-service (*superplus militum*).

It is delicious to learn, on comparing the records, that the virtuous king who made these grants for the weal of his parents' souls and the remission of his own sins, extorted from the church, for making them, an equivalent in hard cash. [125]

Again, the (MS.) Cartulary of St. Evroul contains a confirmation by Randulf, Earl of Chester (1121-9) of his predecessor (d. 1120) Earl Richard's benefaction, "liberam et quietam ab *escuagio*," etc., etc. The list of the Abbot of Peterborough's knights (see p. 157) is a further illustration of knight-service *temp.* Henry I., while the entry as to Vivian, who was enfeoffed by Abbot Turold: "servit pro

---

[123] "Teste Gaufrido Cancellario et Willelmo de Albineio Pincerna et Gaufrido de Clintona et Pagano fil Johannis. Apud Sanctum Petrum desuper Divam."

[124] Cott. MS. Julius A. i. 6, fo. 74a.

[125] These charters have an independent value for the light they throw, in conjunction with the roll, on the movements of the king. The roll itself alludes to the occasion on which the king crossed from Eling— "ex q[uo] rex mare transivit de Eilling[es]"—and as it is assigned to Michaelmas, 1130, the entry cannot refer to his departure at that very date, especially as these charters are not paid for among the *nova* proceedings of the year. They must therefore have been granted at his previous departure (Aug., 1127), when he must have crossed from Eling and have gone to S. Pierre sur Dive (and Argentan) in Normandy. Pleas were heard before him at Eling on this occasion (*Rot. Pip.*, pp. 17, 38), and are referred to in a charter of Stephen to Shaftesbury Abbey.

milite *cum auxilio*" (*Chron. Petrob.*, p. 175), must refer to
the somewhat obscure "auxilium militum" of the period.
So also, it would seem, must the curious charter of Eustace,
Count of Boulogne,[126] in which he speaks of his knights
serving: "sive *in nummis*, sive in exercitu, sive in guarda,"
under Henry I. Most important of all, however, is a passage
on which I have lighted since this essay first appeared. In
reading through the letters of Herbert (Losinga), Bishop of
Norwich (d. 1119), I found this appeal to the Bishop of
Salisbury, in the king's absence from England :—

In terris meis exiguntur quinquaginta libræ pro placitis, cum
earundem terrarum mei homines nec in responsionem nec in facto
peccaverint.[127] Item *pro militibus sexaginta libræ* quos [? quas]
tanto difficilius cogor reddere, quanto annis præteritis mea substantia
gravius attenuata est (Ed. *Giles*, p. 51).

The sum is that to which the Ely contribution is reduced
by the above charter, and the death of the writer in 1119
proves the early date of the payment.

Indeed, a little consideration will show that payment in
lieu of military service, which was the essential principle
of scutage, could be no new thing. The two forms which
this payment might assume—payment to a substitute, or
payment to the crown—both appear in Domesday as
applicable to the fyrd ; the former is found in the
"Customs" of Berkshire, the latter in other passages.
From the very commencement of knight-service, the
principle must have prevailed ; for the "baron" who had
not enfeoffed knights enough to discharge his *servitium
debitum*, must always have hired substitutes to the amount
of the balance. Nor is this a matter of supposition : we
know as a fact, from the *Abingdon Chronicle* and the *Ely
History*, that under William I. knights were so hired.[128]
Here it should be noted, as a suggestive fact, that the

---

[126] Printed in *Athenæum*, 2nd Dec, 1893.
[127] Cf. *Geoffrey de Mandeville*, p. 105.
[128] "Abbas locum sibi commissum munita manu militum secure
protegebat ; et primo quidem stipendiariis in hoc utebatur" (*Cart.*

"forty days" of military service, though bearing no direct proportion either to the week or to the month, do so to the marc and to the pound. The former represents $4d.$, and the latter $6d.$, for each day of the military service.[129] It may fairly be assumed that this normal "scutage" would be based on the estimated cost of substitutes paid direct. Thus the only change involved would be that the tenant would make his payments not to substitutes, but to the crown instead.

There is a valuable entry bearing on this point in the roll of 8 Hen. II. (p. 53). We there read :—

Et in liberatione vii. militum soldariorum de toto anno quater xx. et iiii. li. et xviii. s. et viii. d. Et in liberatione xx. servientium de toto anno xxx. li. et vi. s. et viii. d. Et in liberatione viii. Arbalist' viii. li. et xvi. sol. Et in liberatione v. vigilum et i. Portarii vi. li. et xvi. d.

This represents $8d.$ a day to each of the seven knights for a year of 364 days, which, be it observed, corresponds precisely with the statements in the *Dialogus* : —"Duo milites bajuli clavium quisque in die viii. [den.] *ratione militiae* ; asserunt enim quod equis necessariis et armis instructi fore teneantur," etc. (i. 3). And so, we see, a scutage of two marks, such as that which was raised for the expedition of Toulouse (1159), would represent, with singular accuracy, $8d.$ a day for the forty days of feudal service, or exactly a knight's pay. Again the pay of the *serviens*, recorded in

Abingdon., ii. 3). "Unde abbas tristis recedens conduxit milites," etc. (*Historia Eliensis*, p. 275). So too Bishop Wulfstan is found "pompam millitum secum ducens qui stipendiis annuis," etc. (W. Malmesb.)

[129] It is singular that in his admirable work *The English Village Community*, pp. 38-9, Mr. Seebohm connects "the normal acreage of the hide of 120 a., and of the virgate of 30 a., with the scutage of $40s.$ per knight's fee," and argues that "in choosing the acreage of the standard hide and virgate, a number of acres was probably assumed corresponding with the monetary system, so that the number of pence in the *scutum* should correspond with the number of acres assessed to its payment." It need hardly be observed that the institution of scutage was, on the contrary, long posterior to that of a hide of 120 acres.

this passage, works out at a penny a day for a year of 364 days, which has an important bearing, we shall find, on the roll of three years later (11 Henry II.). A similar calculation shows that the porter received 2*d.* a day, and the *vigil* 1*d.*—the very pay assigned him in the *Dialogus* (i. 3). There is another similar passage in the roll of 14 Hen. II. (p. 124):—

Et in liberatione i. militis et ii. Portariorum, et ii. vigilum de Blancmost' xviii. li. et v. sol. Et in liberatione xl. servientum de Blancmust' de xxix. septimanis xxxiii. li. et xvi. s. et viii. d. Et xx. servientibus qui remanserunt xxiii. septimanas xiii. li. et viii. s. et iiii d.

Here again the knight's pay works out at 8*d.* a day, while the porters, the watchmen, and the *servientes* received 1*d.* Specially valuable, however, are the entries (to which no one, I think, has drawn attention) relating to the small standing guards kept up in the summer months at "Walton" and Dover.[180] Eventually the payments to these guards were made from the central treasury ("exitus de thesauro"), and are therefore appended, on the rolls, to the list of *combustiones* where no one would think of looking for them.

On the roll of 10 Hen. II. we find:—" Liberatio iiii. militum et ii. servientum de Waletone a festo Ap. Phil' et Jac' usque ad festum S. Luce xxiiii. li. et xx. d." This works out at exactly 8*d.* a day for the *miles*, and 1*d.* for the *serviens*. On the roll of the next year the five knights at Dover are paid £25 for 150 days' service, or exactly 8*d.* a day each. So too on the roll of the thirteenth year we read:—"Liberatio iiii. militum de Waletone xxiii. li. et ix. s. et iiii. d. de clxxvi. diebus. . . . Et ii. servientibus de clxxvi. diebus xxix sol. et iiii. d." Here again the *miles* gets 8*d.*, the *serviens* 1*d.* a day. It is needless to multiply

[180] Walton was at the mouth of the Orwell and the Stour, and was thus an exposed port towards Flanders as Dover was towards France. It is noteworthy that when the Earl of Leicester did invade England from Flanders a few years later, it was at " Walton" that he landed.

instances, but it may be added that similar calculcations show the sailors of Richard's crusading fleet to have received 2*d.* and their boatswains 4*d.* a day.

It is, perhaps, possible to trace a complete change of policy in this matter by the crown. The Conqueror, we may gather from divers hints, was anxious to push forward the process of subinfeudation, that as many knights as possible might be actually available for service. As the chief danger lay, at first, in the prospect of English revolt it was clearly his policy to strengthen to the utmost that " Norman garrison," as we may term it, which the feudal system enabled him to quarter on the conquered land.[181] But as the two races slowly coalesced, the nature of the danger changed : it was no longer a question of Norman *versus* Englishman, but of danger to the crown from war abroad and feudal revolt at home. Thenceforth its policy would be no longer to encourage personal service, but rather payment in lieu thereof, which would provide the means of hiring mercenaries, a more trustworthy and useful force. Clearly the accession of the Angevin house would, and did, give to this new policy a great impetus.

The first levy to which the rolls bear witness is that of 1156. As this was only raised from the *church* fiefs, Henry II. was, as yet, confining himself strictly to the precedent set him, as we know, in his grandfather's reign. This levy was at the rate of *one pound* on the fee, and was made on the old assessment (*servitium debitum*).

I have already shown that the levy in question was not, as alleged, an innovation. Dr. Stubbs writes : " The peculiar measure of the second year was the collection of scutage from the knights' fees holding of ecclesiastical superiors,[182] a measure which met with much opposition

---

[181] Compare Will. Pict. : "Custodes in castellis strenuos viros collocavit ex Gallis traductos, quorum fidei pariter ac virtuti credebat, cum multitudine peditum et equitum, ipsis opulenta beneficia distribuit," etc.

[182] Should not this rather be "from ecclesiastical tenants-in-chief hold-

B.H.   T

from Archbishop Theobald at the time;[133] and speaking of William of Newburgh, he suggests that "possibly in William's estimation the consent of St. Thomas took from the scutage on church fees its sacrilegious character."[134] But if the institution was fully recognised under Henry I., how was it "sacrilegious?" Theobald's "opposition" in 1156 can only be inferred from the king's reply explaining the necessity for the levy,[135] and was clearly directed, not against the principle, but by way of appeal against the necessity in that instance. Miss Norgate holds that "no resentment seems to have been provoked by the measure," although she sees in it "the origin of the great institution of scutage."[136] Then there is the question of the object for which the levy was made. Swereford says "pro exercitu Walliæ,"[137] and this misled, through Madox, Dr. Stubbs (who wrote "the scutage of 1156 was also for the war in Wales,"[138]) and Gneist.[139] The former writer, however, has elsewhere[140] pointed out that "its object was to enable Henry to make war on his brother"; and Miss Norgate gives the same explanation.[141] Swereford's error, I believe, can undoubtedly be traced to an entry on the Pipe-Roll of

ing by military service"? For it was neither collected from knights' fees, nor with reference to their existing number.

[133] Preface to *Gesta Henrici Regis*, II. xciv. So too *Const. Hist.*, i. 454: "The practice was, as we learn from John of Salisbury, opposed by Archbishop Theobald"; and (i. 577) "Archbishop Theobald had denounced the scutage of 1156"; and (*Early Plant.*, p. 54) "he made the bishops, notwithstanding strong objections from Archbishop Theobald, pay scutage."

[134] Preface to *Gesta Henrici Regis*, II. xcviii.

[135] "Honori et utilitati ecclesiae tota mentis intentione studiosius invigilabit. Verum interim," etc. John of Salisbury, Ep. cxxviii. Note that "ecclesiae" is the church at large, not the see of Canterbury.

[136] *Angevin Kings*, i. 443.

[137] *Red Book*, p. 6.

[138] Preface to *Gesta Henrici Regis*, II. xcv.

[139] *Const. Hist.*, i. 454.

[140] *Ibid.*, i. 164.

[141] *Angevin Kings*, i. 458. Both writers quote the passage from John of Salisbury (Ep. cxxviii.), on which this explanation is based.

the 3rd year (1157) recording the payment by the Abbot of Abbotsbury of two marcs "de exercitu Walie."[142] But this must refer to the Welsh campaign of that year, not to the foreign trouble of the year before.[143]

The next levy was "the scutage of Toulouse" in 1159. This, "the great scutage" of Miss Norgate, [144] is, strange as it may seem, on the Pipe-Roll itself almost uniformly styled not a scutage, but a *donum.* The explanation given by Swereford is wholly inadequate, and is this: "Intitula-turque illud scutagium *De Dono* ea quidem, ut credo, ratione quod non solum prelati qui tenentur ad servitia militaria sed etiam alii abbates, de Bello et de Salopesbiria et alii tunc temporis dederunt auxilium."[145]

Miss Norgate, adopting this explanation, writes :—

The reason doubtless is that they were assessed, as the historians tell us, and as the roll itself shows, not only upon those estates from which services of the shield were explicitly due, but also upon all lands held in chief of the crown, and all church lands without distinction of tenure; the basis of assessment in all cases being the knight's fee, in its secondary sense of a parcel of land worth twenty pounds a year. Whatever the laity might think of this arrangement, the indignation of the clergy was bitter and deep. The wrong inflicted on them by the scutage of 1156 was as nothing compared with this, which set at nought all ancient precedents of ecclesiastical immunity, and actually wrung from the church lands even more than from the lay fiefs.[146]

I am obliged to quote the passage *in extenso,* because, in

---

[142] His *servitium debitum* was one knight.

[143] The force for the Welsh campaign was raised, as we learn from Robert de Monte (*alias* de Torigni), "by demanding that every three knights should, instead of serving in person, equip one of their number," as Dr. Stubbs rightly puts it (*Const. Hist.*, i. 589), and not, as he elsewhere writes (preface to *Gesta Henrici Regis*, II. xciv.), by requiring every two to add to themselves a third, "by which means, if we are to understand it literally, 90,000 knights would appear from 60,000 knights' fees." The real number would probably be under 2,000.

[144] "This impost, which afterwards came to be known in English history as the 'Great Scutage'" (*Angevin Kings*, i. 459).

[145] *Liber Rubeus*, p. 6.   [146] *Angevin Kings*, i. 461.

this case, the accomplished writer betrays a singular confusion of ideas, and misrepresents not only the levy, but also the point at issue. The whole passage is conceived in error, error the more strange because Miss Norgate enjoyed over her predecessors the advantage of writing with the printed roll before her. The lay estates were not, as implied ("all lands held in chief of the crown"), in any way exceptionally assessed: in no case was the basis of assessment the unit alleged by the writer; and as to the "church lands," a reference to the roll will show that all over England there were only eight cases in which those not owing "services of the shield" contributed (and that in no way as an assessment on imaginary knights' fees) to this levy, while in six out of the eight their contributions were so insignificant that their collective amount barely exceeded £50.[147]

The true explanation is probably to be found in the fact that only a portion of the tax was raised by way of scutage. As this great levy has been wrongly supposed to have consisted of a scutage alone,[148] and as it played an important part in the development of direct taxation, I propose to set forth, for the first time, the various methods by which the money was raised. These were eight in number:—

I. (FIXED.) A *donum* of two marcs on the fee from the under-tenants of the church, raised *by fiefs* on the old assessment (*servitium debitum*).

II. (FIXED?) A *donum* of (it is said) two marcs on the fee from the under-tenants of the lay barons, raised partly *by counties* and partly b*y fiefs*.

III. (ARBITRARY.) A *donum* from the church tenants-in-chief themselves, irrespective of their fees.

IV. (ARBITRARY.) A *donum* from some of the non-

---

[147] The abbots of Shrewsbury, Thorney, and Croyland; the abbesses of Barking, Winchester, and Romsey. The total of their *dona* amounted to £51 13*s*. 4*d*.

[148] Not, however, by Dr. Stubbs (Preface to *Gesta Henrici Regi*s, II. xciv.-xcvi.).

feudal religious houses (tenants *in elemosina*, and not by military service).

> V. (ARBITRARY.) A *donum* from the towns.
> VI. (ARBITRARY.) A *donum* from the sheriffs.
> VII. (ARBITRARY.) A *donum* from the Jewries.
> VIII. (ARBITRARY.) A *donum* from the moneyers.

Of these, the *first* was strictly regular, being merely a repetition of the scutage of 1156, at the rate of two marcs instead of twenty shillings. The *second* presents some difficulty. Subject to correction, there are some fifteen cases in which the payment is made separately by fiefs, and in which the rate is clearly two marcs, while there are twenty-two in which the *milites* of the county pay as a group through the sheriff, and in which, therefore, we cannot actually test the rate of the levy or the manner of raising it. Swereford's *ipse dixit* as to the rate in these latter cases was probably based on analogy, here our only guide.

With the *third* and *fourth* divisions we return to sure ground. To them I invite particular attention, because it is to them (and especially to the third) that apply the complaints of the church chroniclers, and not (as has always, but erroneously, been supposed) to the perfectly legitimate levy of two marcs on the fee. It is necessary to emphasise the fact that the matter has been wholly misunderstood. The bitter complaint of John of Salisbury that Henry, on this occasion, "omnibus (contra antiquum morem et debitam libertatem) indixit ecclesiis ut *pro arbitrio* ejus satraparum suorum conferrunt in censum," would have been without meaning had it referred (as alleged) to the latter levy (or even to the insignificant sums contributed *ut supra* by eight foundations); but when we learn that, over and above this legitimate levy, a far larger sum was arbitrarily wrung from the church, the truth and justice of the protest are at once made evident. I here give two tables illustrative of this exaction. Each is divided into three columns. In the first column I give the number of the knights due from each bishopric and each religious house. In the second column I give the marcs due, and paid on this occasion, on the old assessment (*servitium debitum*). In the third will be found the exaction complained of, namely, the *dona* extorted from the spiritual "barons" themselves.

Sees.	Knights due.	*Donum* of Knights (in marcs).	*Donum* of Tenant (in marcs).
Winchester	60	120	500
Lincoln	60	120	500
Worcester	60	120	200
Norwich	40	80	200
Bath	20	40	500
London	20	40	200
Exeter	17½	35	150
Chester	15	30	100
Durham	10	20	500
York	7	14	500
Total	—	619	3,350

Religious Houses.	Knights due.	*Donum* of Knight (in marcs).	*Donum* of Tenant (in marcs).
Peterborough	60	120	100
St. Edmund's	40	80	200
Glastonbury	40	80	—
Abingdon	30	60	60
Hyde	20	40	150
St. Augustine's . . .	15	30	220
St. Alban's	6	12	100
Evesham	5	10	60
Wilton	5	10	20
Ramsey	4	8	60
St. Benet of Hulme . .	3	6	30
Pershore	3	—	7½
Chertsey	3	6	60
Cerne	3	6	—
Winchcombe	2	4	7½
Middleton	2	4	—
Sherburne	2		10
Abbotsbury	1	2	7½
Total	—	482	1,092½

We thus obtain a grand total of 1,101 marcs raised from the church by legitimate scutage, and 4,442½ (or, adding the *dona* from non-feudal houses, 4,700) marcs by special imposition.[149] This distinction at once explains the real extortion of which churchmen complained;[150] and shows that it had nothing to do with scutage, but was a special imposition on the church fees from which the lay ones were exempt.[151] The idea of the impost was not improbably the adjustment of inequalities in cases where the knight-service was a quite inadequate assessment; the precedent created was not forgotten, and it proved in later days a welcome source of revenue.

The discovery of this exaction identifies, it will be seen, in spite of Swereford's error, the levy accounted for on the roll with the famous "scutage of Toulouse." And if even further proof were needed, it is found in an incidental allusion which clinches the argument. Giraldus Cambrensis (iii. 357) refers to Bishop Henry of Winchester assembling all the priests of his diocese "tanquam ad auxilium postulandum (dederat enim paulo ante quingentas marcas regi Henrico *ad expeditionem Tholosanam*)." The sum here named is that which he paid in 1159, as my table shows. Its destination is thus established, as also, it may be noted, the means by which he was expected to recoup himself.

As to the scutage on the lay fiefs, the general impression, broadly speaking, is that Henry replaced his English feudal host by an army of mercenaries paid from the proceeds of

---

[149] Dr. Stubbs, independently, reckons the total payments of the church at £3,700 (*Gesta Henrici Regis*), which does not differ greatly from the above calculation (£3,167 6s. 8d.).

[150] " Ille quidem gladius quem in sancte matris ecclesiae viscera vestra paulo ante manus immerserat cum ad trajiciendum in Tolosam exercitum tot ipsam marcarum millibus aporiastis." Gilbert Foliot (Ep. cxciv.).

[151] "Nec permisit ut ecclesiae saltem proceribus coæquarentur in hac contributione vel magis exactione tam indebita quam injusta." John of Salisbury (Ep. cxlv.). Swereford, though confused in his account of the tax, points out that levy was made " non solum super praelatos, verum *tam super ipsos*, quam super milites suos" (*L.R.*, p. 6).

a scutage of two marks per fee on all lands held by military service.[152] But is that impression confirmed by the evidence of the rolls? Without setting forth the evidence in detail, I may sum it up as amounting to this: that the grouped payments found under twenty-two counties[153] present, I think, a total of 1,895 marcs, while those of the fiefs which paid separately amounted to 666. This gives us a grand total of 2,561 marcs, representing, of course, 1,280 knights. Now although the amount of knight-service due to the crown from its English realm has been, as we shall see, absurdly exaggerated, the above number, I need scarcely say, must represent a minority of the knights due from the lay fiefs. This sets the matter in quite another aspect. In spite of the passage in Robert de Monte, on which the accepted view is based,[154] the roll presents proof to the contrary, and indeed the words of Robert show that he knew so little of the levy in England as to believe that it was wholly arbitrary. There are, perhaps, indications that the fiefs which, on this occasion, paid scutage, were largely those in the king's hands,[155] and if we add to these the escheated honours, of which the scutage would be paid through the sheriffs, we must conclude that the great bulk of the tenants who had a choice in the matter served abroad with their contingents and did not pay scutage.

[152] Gneist, for instance, writes: "The first general imposition took place in 5 Henry II. for the campaign against Toulouse, with two marks per fee from all crown vassals" (*C.H.*, i. 212).

[153] Entered as "Dona militum comitatus," not to be confused with the "dona comitatus," a special levy of the following year (6 Hen. II.), raised, it will be found, from the western counties, from Stafford in the north to Devonshire in the south.

[154] "Rex . . . nolens vexare agrarios milites . . . sumptis lx. solidis Andegavensium in Normannia de feudo uniuscujusque loricae et de reliquis omnibus tam in Normannia quam in Anglia, sive etiam aliis terris suis, secundum hoc quod ei visum fuit, capitales barones suos cum paucis secum duxit, solidarios vero milites innumeros" (p. 202, ed. Howlett).

[155] This was certainly the case with the fiefs of Simon de Beauchamp and the Earl Ferrers, two of the most considerable.

Before taking leave of "the great scutage," another point demands notice. Gervase of Canterbury sets forth its proceeds in terms of great precision :—

Hoc anno rex Henricus scotagium sive scutagium *de Anglia* accepit, cujus summa fuit centum millia et quater viginti millia librarum argenti (i. 167).

Quite desperate attempts have been made to reconcile this statement with the actual sums raised. In his preface to the *Gesta Henrici Regis*, Dr. Stubbs suggests that Gervase included in his total the scutage of two years later (1161), but adds that, if so, the rolls are very incomplete. In his *Constitutional History* he speaks of "this [scutage] and a very large accumulation of treasure from other sources, amounting, according to the contemporary writers, to £180,000" (i. 457), but admits, in a footnote, that "the sum is impossible," and throws out as probable a different explanation. Miss Norgate writes that "the proceeds, with those of a similar tax levied upon Henry's other doiminions, amounted to some £180,000." [156] But Gervase distinctly states that this sum was raised *from England*. Now the actual sum raised, *by scutage*, in England (1159) was £2,440 in all, as I reckon it, while the special clerical impost produced some £3,130 in addition. Consequently, no ingenuity can save the credit of Gervase. He was not, after all, worse than his fellows. We shall find that when medieval chroniclers endeavour to foist on us these absurd sums they require much bolder handling than they have ever yet received.

Pass we now to the *third* levy, that of 1161. For this the rate was again *two marcs* on the fee according to Swereford (followed, of course, by subsequent writers), though the study of the roll (7 Henry II.) reveals that in many cases, on the lay fiefs at least, the rate was *one* marc. Both this and the levy of the following year are most

---

[156] *Angevin Kings*, i. 462.

difficult to deal with in every way. We have seen that an entry on the roll of 1163 led Swereford to believe that the levy of 1161 was made for the Toulouse campaign, and Dr. Stubbs has made the suggestion that it might have been raised to defray "debts" incurred on that occasion ; [157] but the difficulties in the way of accepting this view seem insuperable. [158]

The *fourth* levy, which is that of 1162 (8 Henry II.), was at the rate of *one* marc, and is recorded by Swereford, but not by Dr. Stubbs. [159] Though richer in names than that of 1161, it is even less useful for our purpose, as the sums entered are most irregular, perhaps owing to the adoption of a new method of collection. [160] Neither of these levies affords, in the absence of corroboration, trustworthy evidence on the *servitium* of any lay fief.

The *fifth* levy, on the other hand, in 1165 (11 Henry II.), affords most valuable evidence, although it is ignored by Swereford and by those who have followed him. It is, however, of a singular character. The money was raised, we gather from the roll, on two different systems :—

(I.) By a *fixed* payment at the rate of one mark on the fee (old assessment).

(II.) By an *arbitrary* payment of certain mysterious sums, which prove to be multiples of the unit 15s. 3d. But there is no fixed proportion to be traced between the

---

[157] "A second scutage was raised in the seventh year, probably for payment of debts incurred for the same war, the assessment being in this, as in the former case, two marks to the knight's fee." (Preface to *Gesta Henrici Regis*, p. xcv.)

[158] If it was raised for this purpose, it must have been levied either (1) from *all* tenants-in-chief, which it certainly was not ; or (2) from the *same* contributors as in 1159, which a comparison of the two rolls will at once show it was not ; or (3) from a *new* set of contributors, which was also not the case, for the prelates, the Ferrers fief, etc., are found contributing as before.

[159] *Const. Hist.*, i. 582.

[160] Instead of a fief paying *en bloc*, it seems to have paid through the sheriffs of the counties in which it was situate.

amount paid and the number of *servitia* due. Numerous instances are found of a single knight's fee being charged with a sum equivalent to five of these mysterious units. Magnates, again, are found paying apparently strange sums, which prove on dissection to represent 50, 100, 200, and even 300 of these units. The clue to the mystery is found in an entry on the Pipe-Roll of the following year (12 Henry II.), which proves that this unit was the pecuniary equivalent of a *serviens*, and that the various payers had "promised" the king so many *servientes* for the war in Wales.[161] Such "promises" were evidently offers, made independently of the actual service due from the "promising" party. Following up this clue, we see that the Abbot of Abingdon must, like the Bishop of Hereford, have promised 100 "serjeants,"[162] that the Abbot of St. Alban's must have done likewise,[163] while the Bishop of London must have promised 150, *in addition*, be it noted, to paying a scutage of a marc on each knight's fee (20) of his *servitium debitum*.[164] For the rolls of 1162 and 1163 prove that he had duly paid the scutage of the former year, and that this was a further payment. The varying form of these entries should be observed, for it was evidently quite immaterial to the clerks whether they wrote "5 serjeants" or their equivalent—76 shillings and 3 pence.[165] Taking the pay of the *serviens* at 1*d.* a day, the unit in question would represent six months' pay (for a year of 366 days).

---

[161] "Episcopus de Heref' reddit compotum de lxxvi. libris et v. solidis de promiss[ione] c. Servientium de Wal'" (p. 84).

[162] "Abbas de Abendona reddit compotum de lxxvi. libris et v. solidis de promissione servientium in Waliam" (rot. 11 Hen. II., p. 74).

[163] "Abbas de Sancto Albano reddit compotum de lxxvi. libris et v. solidis de Exercitu' (*ib.*, p. 19).

[164] "Episcopus Lond' reddit compotum de xiii. libris et vi. sol. et viii. den. de Servicio militum. . . . Idem reddit compotum de exiiii. marcis et v. sol. de promissione servientium Walie" (*ib.*, p. 19).

[165] "Willelmus de Siffrewast reddit compotum de lxxvi. sol. et iii. den. . . . Hugo de Bochelanda reddit compotum de. v. servientibus" (*ib.*, p. 75). Compare the love of variety in Domesday, *supra*, pp. 36, 37, 83.

But, for our present purpose, we must confine ourselves to the scutage proper. The passage on which I would specially dwell is the entry on the roll in which the *custos* of the archbishopric of Canterbury "reddit compotum de cxiii. li. de Militibus de Archiepiscopatu de ii. Exercitibus" p. (109).[166] In the first place, we have here, surely, witness to the *two* Welsh campaigns of this year, which Mr. Eyton adopts, following Mr. Bridgeman,[167] but which Miss Norgate rejects.[168] Secondly, this sum resolves itself, on analysis, into two constituents of $84\frac{3}{4}$ marcs each. Now the return for the archbishopric the following year is: "Archiepiscopus habet iiij$^{xx.}$ et iiij$^{or.}$ et dimidium et quartam partem feffatos."[169] Having set forth this exact corroboration, I will briefly trace the *servitium* of the see. In 1156 and 1159 it pays no scutage when the other church fiefs do, but within six months of Theobald's death it pays to the scutage of 1161 on a *servitium* of 60 knights, being then in the hands of the crown. Under Becket, in 1162, it is once more omitted; but in 1165 it again pays, as we have seen, and now not on 60 knights but on $84\frac{3}{4}$. In 1168 it contributes, on the same amount, to the *auxilium*, and in 1172, but the latter year is the first in which the *recognoscit* formula is employed, enabling us to determine that, as in 1161, the *servitium debitum* was 60 knights.

The typical difference between these 60 knights and the $84\frac{3}{4}$ actually enfeoffed will serve to illustrate the point on which I insist throughout. Had the fee been held by its tenant, he would have raised $84\frac{3}{4}$ marcs, paid 60 to the crown, and kept $24\frac{3}{4}$ for himself.[170] But when a *custos* held

---

[166] "Scutagium de ii. exercitibus in next roll" (rot. 12 Hen. II.).

[167] *Itinerary of Henry II.*, p. 79 et seq. Compare also the payment from the Giffard fief "de secundo exercitu" (p. 25).

[168] *Angevin Kings*, ii. 180, note.

[169] *Liber Rubeus*, p. 193.

[170] This was the point on which Abbot Sampson insisted, against his knights, at St. Edmond's. In the case of Canterbury, the inquest of 1163 would have ascertained the actual number of the archbishop's knights and their fees.

the fief, he could keep nothing back, and therefore paid over the whole. We have, I think, an illustration of the same kind in the payment (p. 254, note 76) by the *custos* of the Romare fief, "de noviter feffatis" (*noviter*, be it observed not yet *de novo*).

Having brought the levies down to 1165, I hope it has now been made clear that the officials of the exchequer were well aware of the amount of *servitium debitum* from every fief, the levies being always based on the said amount. Swereford, therefore, was quite mistaken in the inference he drew from the inquest of 1166:[171] indeed, his words prove that he completely misunderstood the problem.

This was the last levy raised previous to the making of the returns (*cartae*) in 1166. These returns were followed in 1168 by the first levy on the new assessment. I have already dealt with the changes which this new assessment involved, but I would here again insist upon the fact that the church and the lay fiefs were not dealt with alike, the latter being assessed wholly *de novo*, while the former retained their old assessments, while accounting separately, and under protest, for the fees in excess of their *servitium debitum*. So far as the lay fiefs were concerned, their *servitia*, congenital with Norman rule, were now swept away. Here, from the single county of Northumberland, are three cases in point :—

[171] Ignorasse quidem haec [debita] servitia militaria Regis . . . successores subsequentium argumento non immerito potuit dubitare : quia cum Rex Henricus . . . traderet, a quolibet sui regni milite marcam unam . . . exegit, publico praecipiens edicto quod quilibet praelatus et baro quot milites de eo tenerent in capite publicis suis instrumentis significarent" (*Liber Rubeus*, p. 4)

1162.	1168.
De scutagio Walteri de Bolebec. In thesauro v. marcae.[172]	Walterus de Bolebec redd. comp. de iiii. marcis et dim. de eodem auxilio. Idem debet xlviii. s. et v. d. pro tribus Militibus et ii[abus.] terciis partibus Mil. de Novo feffamento.
De scutagio Stephani de Bulemer. In thesauro v. marcae.	Stephanus de Bulemer redd. comp. de iiii. marcis de eodem auxilio. Idem debet xxiii. s. et iiii. d. de i. milite et dim. et quarta parte Mil. de Novo feffamento.
De scutagio Radulfi de Wircestria. In thesauro i. marca.[173]	Radulfus de Wigornio redd. comp. de i. marca de eodem auxilio pro i. milite. Idem debet xiii. s. de dim. Mil. et de i. tercia et de i. septima parte Mil. de Novo feffamento.

The change thus made by the restless king was permanent in its effect, and thenceforth the only assessment recognised was that based upon the fees, which, by 1166, had been created *de veteri* and *de novo*.[174]

Before leaving the subject of this levy, there is one point on which I would touch. When we find, as we often do, that the sum paid in 1168 in respect of a fief does not tally with the number of fees recorded in the *carta*, we must remember that in the *Liber Niger* and *Liber Rubeus* we have not the original *cartae*, but only transcripts liable to clerical eror. Checking the *cartae* by these payments, we constantly find cases in which the number of fees should

[173] "Teneo de vobis . . feodum i. militis, unde debeo vobis facer servitium i. militis" (*Carta*).

[172] "De hoc predicto feodo debet Regi v. milites" (*Carta*).

[174] It must always be remembered that, as explained above, in case where the requisite number of knights had not been enfeoffed by 1166, the balance *de dominio* was added to those actually created, as *de veteri* together.

be slightly greater than is recorded in the *carta*.[175]   I suspect
that the transcriber, in these cases, has omitted entries in
the original *carta*, and this suspicion is strongly confirmed
by the fact that where the original return enables us to
test the transcript, we find in the great *carta* for the honour
of Clare that the original transcriber has omitted half a
fee of William de Hastinges, has left out altogether the
entry "Reginaldus de Cruce, *dimidium militem*," and has
changed the quarter fee of Geoffrey fitz Piers into half a
fee ; while in that of the Bishop of Chichester, Robert de
Denton's half fee is converted into a whole one.   The later
(Red Book) transcriber has made a further omission.

Another source of discrepancy may be found in the
dangerous resemblance of formulæ.   Thus the *carta* of
Ranulf fitz Walter records three and three-quarter fees
duly accounted for.   Yet his payment in 1168 is not £2 10s.
but £2 4s 5d.   The explanation is that the holding was
really three and one-third fees,[176] but the transcriber read
"iij[ᵃ] pars " (one-third) as " iij. partes " (three-quarters).

How easily such errors arose may be seen in the elaborate
entries on Simon de Beauchamp's fief.   Here the formula
"decem denarios quando Rex accipit marcam de milite," correctly reproduced in the Black Book, becomes " x. denar-
ius," etc., in the Red Book.   The former expression means
"*tenpence* in the marc" (*i.e.* one-sixteenth of a fee);
whereas the latter is equivalent to "*the tenth penny* in the
marc" (*i.e.* one-tenth of a fee), and upsets the whole

---

[175] Thus Daniel de Crevequer pays on one fee (*de veteri*) more than his
carta records, William de Tracy on half a fee (*de veteri*), Adam de Port
on one, the Earl of Gloucester on two, the Earl of Warwick on two and
a half, Maurice de Craon on one, the Abbot of Hulme on a quarter of a
fee, William de Albini (Pincerna) on one, Henry de Lacy on one and a
half, William de Vescy on one, Bertram de Bulemer on a half, and
William Paynell on one (these figures are all subject to correction).
The case of William de Vescy is specially conspicuous, because the
nineteen fees enumerated are distinctly spoken of as twenty.

[176] This brings it into relation with the *Constabularia* of which it thus
formed just a third.

reckoning. The correct formula is a not uncommon one and should be compared with the "de xx. solidis viii denarios" (eightpence in the pound) which is given as the holding of two knights of the honour of Clare, and represents the thirtieth of a fee.[177]

Lastly, I think that, on further examination, there are three fiefs of which the *servitia debita*, though at first sight irregular,[178] may fairly be brought into line as multiples of the *constabularia*. That of Bohun, though implied by the *carta* to be thirty and a half knights, paid in the fifth and eighth years on exactly thirty; that of Malet, though similarly given as twenty and one-sixth in the *carta*, is returned in the *Testa de Nevill* as exactly twenty;[179] that of Beauchamp of Hacche, though distinctly given as seventeen in the *carta*, will be found, on careful collation of the rolls for 7 and 8 Hen. II., to be claimed by the exchequer as $17 + 3$, *i.e.* 20.

Here also, perhaps, it may be allowable to glance at the foreign parallels to fiefs of sixty fees and smaller multiples of five. There is a charter of Charles the Fair (1322-8) "qua Alphonsum de Hispania 'Baronem et Ricum Hominem' Navarrae creat; et, ut Baronis et Rici Hominis statum manu tenere possit, eidem de gratia speciali 60 militias [knight's fees] in regno sua Navarrae concedit modo consueto tenendos et possidendos,"[180] while an edict of earlier date proclaims:—"De Vasvassore [*i.e.* baron] qui *quinque milites* habet, per mortem [? pro morte] ejus, emendetur 60 unciae auri cocti, et per plagam [? pro plaga] 30, et si plures habuerit milites, crescat compositio sicut numerus militum."[181]

---

[177] The same formula is found in Domesday applied to hidation in East Anglia, where the assessment of Manors is expressed not in terms of the hide, but in fractions of the pound. (*Vide supra*, p. 99).

[178] *Vide supra*, p. 257.

[179] "Willelmus Malet tenet Cari de Domino Rege et alias terras suas per servicium viginti militum" (p. 163).

[180] Ducange (1887), ii. 581.

[181] *Ib.*, viii. 255. Ducange indeed asserts that five knights was the

IV. THE TOTAL NUMBER OF KNIGHTS DUE.

"Ad hoc solicitius animum direxi ut per regna Angliae debita Regi servitia militaria quatinus potui plenissime percunctarer." [182] So writes Swereford, who proceeds to explain that neither the famous Bishop Nigel himself, nor his successor, Bishop Richard, nor William of Ely (*ut supra*) had left any certain information on the subject; while he (Swereford) could not accept the common belief that the Conqueror had created *servitia* of knights to the amount of 32,000. [183] The cause of his failure is found in the fact that he confused two different things: (1) the *debita Regi servitia*, which formed the only assessment of fiefs down to 1166; (2) the assessment based on the *cartae* of 1166, which superseded the *debita servitia*, and is not evidence of their amount. [184] But then, as I have already explained above, the exchequer official was concerned only with the actual claims of the crown; for him the original "service due" had a merely academic interest.

There are two estimates for the total of which we are in search. One is 32,000 knights; the other 60,000.

"Stephen Segrave," Dr. Stubbs reminds us, "the minister of Henry III., reckoned 32,000 as the number" (which confirms Swereford's statement); but he himself wisely declines to hazard "a conjectural estimate," [185] adding that "the official computation, on which the scutage was levied, reckoned in the middle of the 13th century 32,000 knights' fees, but the amount of money actually raised by Henry II. on this account, in any single year, was very far from

qualification in Normandy for barony, but the statement is based on a mistaken rendering and is elsewhere disproved.

[182] *Liber Rubeus*, p. 4.

[183] "Illud commune verbum, in ore singulorum tunc temporis divulgatum, fatuum reputans et mirabile, quod in regni conquisitione Dux Normannorum, Rex Willelmus, servitia xxxii. militum infeodavit" (*ib.*).

[184] Swereford, it is clear, failed to grasp the great change of assessment in 1166.

[185] *Const Hist.*, i. 432

B.H.

U

commensurate." Gneist repeats this figure, but holds that "as far as we may conjecture by reference to later statements, the number of shields may be fixed at about 30,000." [186]

On the wondrous estimate of 60,000 I have more to say. Started by Ordericus,[187] this venerable fable has been handed down by Higden and others, till in the *Short History of the English People* it has attained a world-wide circulation.[188] Dr. Stubbs has rightly dismissed the statement "as one of the many numerical exaggerations of the early historians";[189] but neither he nor any other writer has detected, so far as I know, the peculiar interest of the sum. What that interest is will be seen at once when I say that Ordericus, who asserts that the Conqueror had so apportioned the knight-service "ut Angliae regnum lx. millia militum indesinenter haberet" (iv. 7), also alleges that the number present at the famous Salisbury assembly (1086) was 60,000. It is very instructive to compare this "body whose numbers were handed down by tradition as no less than sixty thousand,"[190] with the "sixty thousand horsemen"[191]—"ut ferunt sexaginta millia equitum"—of thirteen years earlier, and with the number of the Norman invaders, "commonly given at sixty thousand,"[192] of seven

[186] *Const. Hist.*, i. 157. Dr. Stubbs rightly rejects Mr. Pearson's conjecture that the number of 32,000 applied to the hides, and that the number of knights' fees, calculated at five hides each, would be 6,400."

[187] "His temporibus militiam Anglici regni Rex Willelmus conscribi fecit et lx. millia militum invenit, quos omnes, dum necesse esset, paratos esse praecepit."

[188] "A whole army was by this means encamped upon the soil, and the king's summons could at any moment gather sixty thousand knights to the royal standard."

[189] *Const. Hist.*, i. 264. Compare pp. 16, 17.

[190] Freeman (*Norm. Conq.*, iv. 694).

[191] *Ib.*, iv. 562.

[192] *Ib.*, iii. 387. In *Social England* (i. 373) we read that "William is believed to have landed in England with at least 60,000 men, 50,000 horse and 10,000 foot." But on turning to p. 306 of that great effort of co-operative genius, we learn that only "some of William's ships carried

years earlier still. It is Ordericus, too, who states that the
treasure in Normandy at the death of Henry I. was £60,000.
His father seems to have left behind him the same sum
at Winchester, for, though the chronicle left the amount in
doubt, "Henry of Huntingdon," Mr. Freeman observed,
with a touch of just sarcasm, "knew the exact amount of
the silver, sixty thousand pounds, one doubtless for each
knight's fee." [193]   He also reminds us, as to the crusade of
William of Aquitaine, that "Orderic allows only thirty
thousand. In William of Malmesbury they have grown
into sixty thousand. Figures of this kind, whether greater
or smaller, are always multiples of one another." [194]

Pursuing the subject, we learn from Giraldus that the
Conqueror's annual income was 60,000 marcs.[195]   Fantosme
speaks of marshalled knights as

Meins de seisante mile, *e plus de seisante treis,*

and the author of the Anglo-Norman poem on the conquest
of Ireland gives the strength of the Irish host, in 1171, as
60,000 men. Even "Sir Bevis," if I remember right, slew
in the streets of London 60,000 men; and Fitz Stephen
asserts that, in Stephen's reign, London was able to turn
out 60,000 foot.[196]   It may, also, not be without significance
that 60,000 Moors are said to have been slain at Navas de
Tolosa, and that William of Sicily was said to have be-
queathed to Henry II. three distinct sums of 60,000 each.[197]

The fact is that "sixty thousand " was a favourite phrase
for a great number, and that "sixty " was used in this

horses to the number of from three to eight—as well as men." So the
number of his ships (396, according to Wace) is as great a difficulty as
the proportions of Noah's Ark.

[193] *William Rufus,* i. 17.

[194] *Ib.,* i. 313.

[195] "Annui fiscales redditus . . . ad sexaginta millia marcarum sum-
mam implebant."

[196] "Sexaginta millia peditum " (p. 4).

[197] "Sexaginta millia silinas de frumento, sexaginta millia de hordeo,
sexaginta millia de vino " (*Richard of Devizes,* ed. Howlett, p. 396).

sense just as the Romans[198] had used it in classical times and just as Russian peasants (I think I have read) use it to this day. The "twice six hundred thousand men," who were burning to fight for England,[199] and the £180,000 (60,000 × 3) of Gervase (1159), are traceable, doubtless, to the same source.

How strangely different from these wild figures are the sober facts of the case! The whole of the church fiefs, as we have seen, were only liable to find 784 knights, a number which, small as it was, just exceeded the entire knight-service of Normandy as returned in 1171. As to the lay fiefs it is not possible to speak with equal confidence. I have ventured to fix the approximate *quota* of 104 (more or less), of which 92 are in favour of my theory: 48 fiefs, of five knights and upwards, remain undetermined.[200] If the average of knights to a fief were the same in the latter as in the former class, the total contingents of the lay barons would amount, apparently, to 3,534 knights; but, as the latter one includes such enormous fiefs as those of Gloucester and of Clare, with such important honours as those of Peverel and Eye, we must increase our estimate accordingly, and must also make allowance for fiefs omitted and for those owing less than five knights (which are comparatively unimportant).

Making, therefore, every allowance, we shall probably be safe in saying that the whole *servitium debitum*, clerical and lay, of England can scarcely have exceeded, if indeed it reached, 5,000 knights.

Indefinite though such a result may seem, it is worth obtaining for the startling contrast which it presents to

---

[198] "Sexaginta accipitur indefinite de magno numero. Sexcenti saepe usurpatur pro numero ingenti et indefinito" (Forcellini, *Totius Latinitatis Lexicon*).

[199] "Bis sex sibi millia centum" (*Carmen de bello Hastingensi*).

[200] It must be clearly understood that these figures cannot be absolutely accurate. Some honours are omitted, it seems, in the returns from which we have to work, and for these allowance must be made.

the 60,000 of Ordericus, to the 32,000 of Segrave,[201] and to the 30,000 of Gneist. The only writer, so far as I know, who has approximated, by investigating for himself, the true facts of the case, is Mr. Pearson ;[202] but his calculations, I fear, are vitiated by the unfortunate guess that the alleged 32,000 fees were really 6,400 of 5 hides each. It is a hopeless undertaking to reconcile the facts with the wild figures of medieval historians by resorting to the ingenious devices of apocalyptic interpretation.

V. THE NORMAL KNIGHT'S FEE

Much labour has been vainly spent on attempts to determine the true area of a knight's fee. The general impression appears to be that it contained five hides. Mr. Pearson, we have seen, based on that assumption his estimate of 6,400 fees, and other writers have treated the fee as the recognised equivalent of five hides. The point is of importance, because if we found that the recognised area of a knight's fee was five hides, it would give us a link between the under-tenant (*miles*) and the Anglo-Saxon thegn. But, as Dr. Stubbs has recognised, the assumption cannot be maintained ; no fixed number of hides constituted a knight's fee.

The circumstance of a fee, in many cases consisting of five hides, is merely, I think, due to the existence of five-hide estates, survivals from the previous *régime*. We have an excellent instance of such fees in a very remarkable document, which has hitherto, it would seem, remained unnoticed. This is a transcript, in Heming's Cartulary, of a hidated survey of the Gloucestershire Manors belong-

---

[201] "[1235] Sicut Stephanus Segrave . . . asserebat et affirmabat vetus scutagium ad xxxii. millia scuta assumabatur et irrotulabatur ; et ad tantundem plene et plane potuit novum scutagium de novis terris assumari" (*Ann. Monast.*, i. 364).

[202] "Nine thousand for all England would be a large estimate at any time in the twelfth century" (*Early and Middle Ages*, i. 375).

ing to the see of Worcester. I believe it to be earlier than Domesday itself, in which case, of course, it would possess a unique interest. Here are the entries, side by side, relating to the great episcopal Manor of Westbury (on Trym), Gloucestershire.

CARTULARY.	DOMESDAY.
Ad *uuestbiriam*[203] pertinent l. hide. xxxv. hidas in dominio habe*t*[203] episcopus, et milites sui habent xv. hidas. In icena*t*une v. hidas, In com*t*una v. hidas, In bi*s*copes *s*toke v. hidas.	Huesberie. Ibi fuerunt et sunt l. hidae. . . . De hac terra hujus Manerii tenet Turstinus filius Rolf v. hidas in Austrecliue et Gislebertus filius Turold iii. hidas et dimidiam jn Contone, et Constantinus v. hidas jn Icetune. . . . De eadem terra hujus Manerii tenet Osbernus Gifard v. hidas et nullum servitium facit. . . . Quod homines tenent (valet) ix. libras.

The three five-hide holdings, we find, figure in both alike, but Gilbert fitz Thorold's holding of three hides and a half appears in addition in Domesday. The inference, surely, would seem to be that Gilbert was enfeoffed between the date of the survey recorded in the Cartulary and the date of the Domesday Survey. If so, the former survey is, as I have suggested, the earlier; and in that survey we have the three tenants of five-hide holdings described *co nomine* as the bishop's *milites*.

In the *cartae* of 1166 we have fees of 5 hides,[204] of 4,[205] of 6,[206] of 10,[207] of 2½,[208] and even of 2;[209] also of 5 carucates,[210] of 11,[211] and of 14.[212] Cartularies, however, are richer in evidence of this discrepancy. Thus the six fees of St. Albans contained 40 hides (an average of 6⅔

---

[203] The italics represent Anglo-Saxon characters.

[204] *Lib. Rub.*, pp. 188, 214, 237, 238, 292.

[205] pp. 211, 214. [206] pp. 214, 292. [207] p. 292. [208] pp. 200, 210.

[206] p. 210. [210] pp. 390, 444. [211] p. 429. [212] pp. 431-2.

hides each), the figures being $5\frac{1}{2}$, 7, $8\frac{1}{2}$, 6, $5\frac{1}{2}$, $7\frac{1}{2}$.[213]   So too in the Abingdon Cartulary (ii. 3) we find four fees containing 19 hides, three containing 14, a half-fee 4, a fee and a half 13, one fee, 10, 5, 9. On the other hand, if we take 20 *librates* as the amount of the fee—which it was already, as Dr. Stubbs observes, in the days of the Conqueror—the *cartae* confirm that conclusion.[214] We must therefore conclude that the knight's fee, held by an under-tenant, consisted normally of an estate worth £20 a year, and was not based on the "five hides" of the Anglo-Saxon system.

VI. The Early Evidence.

We will now work upwards from the *cartae* to the Conquest.

Allusions to early enfeoffment are scattered through the *cartae* themselves. Henry fitz Gerold begins his return: "Isti sunt milites Eudonis Dapiferi," and Eudo, we know, "came in with the Conqueror." We learn from another return (*Lib. Rub.*, p. 397) that Henry I. had given William de Albini, "Pincerna, de feodo quod fuit Corbuchun xv. milites feffatos." Now this refers to "Robertus filius Corbution," a Domesday tenant in Norfolk. The *Testa*, again, comes to our help. Thus we learn from Domesday that Osbern the priest *alias* Osbern the sheriff (of Lincolnshire) was William de Perci's tenant at Wickenby, co. Lincoln, but the *Testa* entry (p. 338*a*) proves that William had enfeoffed him in that holding by the service of one knight.[215] So too Count Alan (of Brittany) had enfeoffed his tenant Landri at Welton in the same county for the service of half a knight (*ib.* 338*b*), and we find his son, Alan fitz

---

[213] M. Paris, *Additamenta*, p. 436. This list, which seems scarcely known, is very valuable for its early date, being, I think, about contemporaneous with the *cartae* of 1166.

[214] *L. R.*, pp. 229, 245, 356.

[215] " Et predictus Willelmus dedit predictas tres carucatas terre Osberto vicecomiti pro servicio unius militis."

Landri, tenant there to Count Stephen, a generation later than Domesday, in the Lindsey Survey. The barony of Bywell in Northumberland, we read in the *Testa* (p. 392*a*), had been held by the service of five knights [216] since the days of William Rufus, who had granted it on that tenure. [217] After this we are not surprised to learn that the barony of Morpeth had been held "from the Conquest" by the service of four knights, and that of Mitford as long by the service of five (*ib.*, p. 392*b*), or that those of Calverdon, Morewic, and Diveleston had all been similarly held by military service "from the Conquest." In Herefordshire, again, John de Monmouth is returned as holding " feoda xv. militum a conquestu Anglie. [218] So too Robert Foliot claims in his *carta* (1166) that his predecessors had been enfeoffed " since the conquest of England ; " [219] and William de Colecherche, that his little fief was " de antiquo tene-mento a Conquestu Angliae " (*L. R.*, p. 400) ; Humphrey de Bohun enumerates the fees " quibus avus suus feffatus fuit in primo feffamento quod in Anglia habuit " (*Ib.*, p. 242), and refers to his grandfather's subsequent enfeoffments in the days of William Rufus (p. 244), while Alexander de Alno similarly speaks of subinfeudation " tempore Willelmi Regis " (p. 230). To take one more instance from the *cartae*, an abbot sets forth his *servicium* due to Henry, " sicuti debuit antiquitus regibus predecessoribus ejus " (p. 224). This brings us to the instructive case of Ramsey Abbey.

Dr. Stubbs refers to a document of the reign of William Rufus as " proof that the lands of the house had not yet been divided into knights' fees." [220] But he does not men-tion the striking fact that the special knight-service for which the abbot was to be liable is distinctly stated to have

[216] Together with castle-guard of thirty knights at Newcastle.

[217] " Post tempus domini Regis Willelmi Ruffi, qui eos feoffavit."

[218] *Testa*, p. 69.

[219] " Post Conquestum Angliae " (*Liber Rubeus*, p. 332).

[220] *Const. Hist.*, i. 263.

been that for which his "predecessors" had been liable. [221]
As this charter is assigned to 1091-1100, the mention of
"predecessors" would seem to carry back this knight-
service very far indeed.   And we have happily another
connecting link which carries downwards the history of
this knight-service, as the above-named charter carries it
upwards.   This is the entry in the Pipe-Roll of 1129-30 :—

Abbas de Ramesia reddit compotum de xlviij. li. xj. s. et vj. d. pro
superplus militum qui requirebantur de Abbatia (p. 47). [222]

Further, we have a notable communication to the abbot
from Bishop Nigel of Ely, which must refer to the scutage
of 1156 or to that of 1159 (probably the former) :—

Sciatis quod ubi Ricardus clericus [223] reddidit compotum de
scutagio militum vestrorum ad Scaccarium ego testificatus sum vos
non debere regi plusquam quatuor milites, et per tantum quieti estis
et in rotulo scripti. [224]

Lastly, we have the return in the Black Book (1166) :—

Homines faciunt iiii. milites in communi in servitium domini regis,
ita quod tota terra abbatiae communicata est cum eis per hidas ad
prædictum servitium faciendum.

Prof. Maitland, writing on the Court of the Abbey of
Ramsey, in the thirteenth century, observes that,—

The Abbot is bound to provide four knights, and (contrary to
what is thought to have been the common practice) he has not split
up his land into knights' fees so that on every occasion the same
four tenants shall go to the war . . . the process by which the
country was carved out into knights' fees seems in this case to have
been arrested at an early stage. [225]

---

[221] " Et deinceps tres (milites) mihi habeat *sicut antecessores sui
faciebant* in septentrionali parte fluminis Tamesie" (1091-1100).—*Ramsey
Cartulary*, i. 234.

[222] Compare the Ely entry (*supra* p. 269) for " superplus."

[223] Could this have been Richard fitz Nigel himself?

[224] *Ramsey Catulary* i. 255.   Compare with this expression "in rotulo
scripti," the Conqueror's command (*infra*), that the number of knights
"in annalibus annotarentur."

[225] Select Pleas in Manorial Courts, p. 50.

The case of Ramsey was undoubtedly peculiar, but in the third volume of the Cartulary, now published, we have (pp. 48, 218) fuller versions of the Abbot's return in 1166. The second of these is specially noteworthy, and reads like a transcript of the original return.[226] Here we see separate knights' fees duly entered, with the customary formula "debet unum militem." But the service was certainly provided in 1166 and afterwards "per hidas." Further enquiry, therefore, is needed ; but we have in any case, for Ramsey, a chain of evidence which should prove of considerable value for the study of this difficult problem.

The phenomenon, however, for which we have to account is the appearance from the earliest period to which our information extends of certain quotas of knight-service, clearly arbitrary in amount, as due from those bishops and abbots who held by military service. When and how were these *quotas* fixed ? The answer is given by Matthew Paris—one of the last quarters in which one would think of looking—where we read that, in 1070, the Conqueror

episcopatus quoque et abbatias omnes quae baronias tenebant, et eatenus ab omni servitute seculari libertatem habuerant, sub servitute statuit militari, inrotulans episcopatus et abbatias *pro voluntate sua* quot milites sibi et successoribus suis hostilitatis tempore voluit a singulis exhiberi (*Historia Anglorum*, i. 13).

This passage (which perhaps represents the St. Albans tradition) is dismissed by Dr. Stubbs as being probably

---

[226] It enables us to correct such an entry in the Black Book as "Radulfus Maindeherst," by identifying him with Ralph Mowyn, the tenant at Hurst. It supplies an entry as to Henry de "Wichetone" (Whiston) which is omitted in L. R., and entered in L. N. with wrong name and wrong holding ; and, better still, it shows that Silvester of Holwell held only 2 hides, not 12, as given in error, both in L. N. and L. R. The existence of this error in both bears, of course, on their relation (cf. p. 287, *supra*).

" a mistaken account of the effects of the Domesday survey." [227]

But the Abingdon Chronicle, quite independently, gives the same explanation, and traces the *quota* of knights to the action taken by the Crown :—

Quum jam regis edicto in annalibus annotarentur quot de episcopiis quotve de abbatiis ad publicam rem tuendam milites (si forte hinc quid causae propellendae contingeret) exigerentur, etc. [228]

Moreover, the Ely Chronicle bears the same witness, telling us that William Rufus, at the commencement of his reign,—

debitum servitium quod pater suus imposuerat ab ecclesiis violenter exigit. [229]

It also tells us that, when undertaking his campaign against Malcolm (1072), the Conqueror

jusserat tam abbatibus quam episcopis totius Angliae *debita militiae obsequia* transmitti ; [230]

and it also describes how he fixed the *quota* of knights due by an arbitrary act of will. [231] The chronicler, like Matthew. Paris, lays stress upon the facts that (1) the burden was a wholly new one ; (2) its incidence was determined by the royal will alone. [232]

Here, perhaps, we have the clue to the (rare) clerical exemptions from the burden of military tenure, such as the abbeys of Gloucester and of Battle. [233]

[227] *Const. Hist.*, i. 357. Gneist writes that Matthew's statement "is for good reasons called in question by Stubbs" (*C. H.*, i. 255, note).

[228] *Cartulary of Abingdon*, ii. 3.

[229] *Historia Eliensis* (ed. 1848), p. 276.   [230] *Ib.*, p. 274.

[231] " Praecepit illi (*i.e.* abbati) ex nutu regis custodiam xl. militum habere in insulam." *Ib.*, p. 275. This is the very *servitium debitum* that appears under Henry II.

[232] Compare for the initiative of the crown, the Domesday phrase, " miles jussu regis," and the statement that Lanfranc replaced the drengs of his see by knights at the royal command (" Rex praecepit.")

[233] Madox writes (*Baronia Anglica*, p. 114) bitterly and unjustly : " In

The beginnings of subinfeudation consequent on the Conqueror's action are distinctly described in the cases of Abingdon and Ely, and alluded to in those of Peterborough[234] and Evesham. At the first of these, Athelelm

primo quidem stipendariis in hoc utebatur. At his sopitis incursibus . . . abbas mansiones possessionum ecclesiae pertinentibus inde delegavit, edicto cuique tenore parendi de suae portionis mansione.[235]

At Ely, the abbot

habuit ex consuetudine, secundum jussum regis, prætaxatum militiae numerum infra aulam ecclesiae, victum cotidie de manu celerarii capientem atque stipendia, quod intollerabiliter et supra modum potuit vexare locum. . . . Ex hoc compulsus quasdam terras sanctæ Ædeldredae invasoribus in feudum permisit tenere . . . ut in omni expeditione regi observarent, [et] ecclesia perpetim infatigata permaneret.[236]

For Canterbury we have remarkable evidence, not, it would seem, generally known. In Domesday, of course, Lanfranc's *milites* figure prominently ; but the absence of a detailed return in 1166 leaves their names and services obscure. Now in the Christ Church Domesday there is a list of the Archbishop's knights,[237] in which are names corresponding with those of his tenants in 1086. It can, therefore, be little, if at all, later than the Conqueror's reign. It is drawn up exactly like a *carta* of 1166, giving the names of the knights and the service due from each. Its editor, instead of printing this important document in full,

process of time, several of the religious found out another piece of art. They insisted that they held all their land and tenements in frankalmoigne, and not by knight-service." In the cases he quotes, "this allegation" was perfectly correct, and was recognised as such by the judges.

[234] Turoldus vero sexaginta et duo hidas terrae de terra ecclesiae Burgi dedit stipendiariis militibus" (*John of Peterborough*, ed, Giles).

[235] *Cart Abingdon.*, ii. 3.

[236] *Liber El.*, p. 275.

[237] "De militibus Archiepiscopis." 8th Report on Historical MSS., i. 316.

has, unfortunately, given us six names only, and—mistaking the familiar "d[imidium]" and "q[uarterium]" of the list for "d[enarios]" and "q[uadrans]"—asserts that the contributions of the knights are "evidently . . . expressed in terms of the shilling and its fractions,"[288] thus missing the essential point, namely, that they are expressed in terms of knight-service.

As Lanfranc had done at Canterbury, as Symeon at Ely, as Walter at Evesham, as Athelelm at Abingdon, so also did Geoffrey at Tavistock,[239] and so we cannot doubt, did Wulfstan at Worcester. The *carta* of his successor (1166) distinctly implies that before his death he had carved some thirty-seven fees out of the episcopal fief. Precisely as at Ely, he found this plan less intolerable than the standing entertainment of a roistering troop of knights.[240]

The influence of nepotism on subinfeudation, in the case of ecclesiastical fiefs, is too important to be passed over. On every side we find the efforts of prelates and abbots thus to provide for their relatives opposed and denounced by the bodies over which they ruled. The Archbishop of York in his *carta* explains the excessive number of his knights : "Antecessores enim nostri, non pro necessitate

---

[288] *Ibid.*

[239] A charter of Henry I. (*Mon. Ang.*, vi. 496) addressed "Willelmo Episcopo Exoniensi et Ricardo filio Baldwini vicecomiti" (see p. 330) contains the clause : "Prohibeo ne aliquis præter monachos ipsas terras amplius teneat vel alias aliquas quæ de dominio ecclesie fuerunt, exceptis illis quas Gaufridus abbas dedit *ad servicium militare.*" Abbot Geoffrey is said to have died in 1088. A curious difficulty has been raised about the words in italics. It is argued in Alford's *Abbots of Tavistock* (p. 68) that as, according to Mr. Freeman, military tenures did not exist in Abbot Geoffrey's day, there was perhaps a second Abbot of that name to whom that charter refers. But he is only introduced by Mr. Alford under protest ; and we see now that there is no need for him. Henry's charter being witnessed by Ralph, Archbishop of Canterbury, William, the King's son, and the Count of Meulan, at Odiham, belongs, I may observe, to 1114--1116.

[240] "Qui stipendiis annuis quotidianisque cibis immane quantum populabantur (Will. Malmesb., *Gesta Pontificum*).

servitii, quod debent, sed quia cognatis et servientibus suis providere volebant, plures quam debebant Regi feodaverunt." The Abbot of Ely, we are told by his panegyrist, enfeoffed knights by compulsion, "non ex industria aut favore divitum vel propinquorum affectu." [241] Abbot Athelelm of Abingdon, says his champion, enfeoffed knights of necessity; [242] but a less friendly chronicler asserts that, like Thorold of Peterborough, he brought over from Normandy his kinsmen, and quartered them on the abbey lands. [243] The Tavistock charter of Henry I. restored to that abbey the lands which Guimund, its simoniacal abbot (1088--1102), had bestowed on his brother William. Abbot Walter of Evesham and his successor persisted in enfeoffing knights "contradicente capitulo." [244]

So, during a vacancy at Abbotsbury under Henry I., "cum Rogerus Episcopus habuit custodiam Abbatiæ, duas hidas, ad maritandam quandam neptem suam, dedit N. de M., contradicente conventu Ecclesiæ." [245] Henry of Winchester has left us a similar record of the action of his predecessors at Glastonbury. [246] His narrative is specially

---

[241] *Liber Eliensis*, p. 275.

[242] *Cart. Abingdon.*, ii 3.

[243] *Ib.*, p. 233 : "misit . . . in Normanniam pro cognatis suis, quibus multas possessiones ecclesiae dedit et feoffavit, ita ut in anno lxx. de possessionibus ecclesiae eis conferret."

[244] Cott. MS. Vesp. B. xxiv. f. 8, "Randulfus frater abbatis Walterii habet in Withelega iii. hidas de dominio, etc. etc. . . . dono Walterii Abbatis contradicente capitulo." This was the "Rannulfum (sic) fratrem ejusdem Walteri abbatis . . . qui cum fratre suo tenebat illud placitum" *temp. Will. I.*), whom the Bishop of Worcester's knights challenged to trial by battle (Heming's *Chart. Wig.*, ed. Hearne, p. 82). His holding was represented in 1166 by the fees of Randulf de Kinwarton and Randulf de Coughton. Other cases of contested enfeoffment by Abbots Walter and Robert are those of Hugh Travers and Hugh de Bretfertun.

[245] See the *carta* of 1166, which explains how this holding became half a fee.

[246] "Miles quidam, Odo nomine, dono praedecessoris mei Sifridi abbatis, ob graciam cusjusdam consobrinae suae, quam idem Odo conjugem duxerat . . . tria maneria de dominio sibi astrinxerat . . .

valuable for the light it throws on the power of subsequent
revocation, perhaps in cases where the corporate body had
protested at the time against the grant. Of this we have a
striking instance in the grants of Abbot Æthelwig of Evesham, almost all of which, we read, were revoked by his
successor.[247] Parallel rather to the cases of Middleton and
Abbotsbury (*vide cartas*) would be the action of William
Rufus during the Canterbury vacancy.[248]

It was to guard against the nepotism of the heads of
monastic houses that such a clause as this was occasionally
inserted :—

Terras censuales non in feudum donet : nec faciat milites nisi in
sacra veste Christi.[249]

And by their conduct in this matter, abbots, in the Norman
period, were largely judged. But this has been a slight
digression.

Now that I have shown that in monastic chronicles we
have the complement and corroboration of the words of
Matthew Paris, I propose to quote as a climax to my argument the writ printed below. Startling as it may read,
for its early date, to the holders of the accepted view, the
vigour of its language convinced me, when I found it, that
in it King William speaks; nor was there anything to be

invitis fratribus. Alius quidam . . . dono abbatis . . . tamen
absque fratrum consensu manerium possidebat" (*Domerham*, p. 306).

[247] "De his terris quas, ut diximus, suo tempore acquisivit, quibusdam
bonis hominibus pro magna necessitate et honore ecclesiae dedit, et inde
Deo et sibi fideliter quamdiu vixit serviebant" (*Chronicon Evesh.*, p. 96).
His successor, Walter (1077-1086), incited by his own young relatives,
"noluit homagium a pluribus bonis hominibus quos praedecessor suus
habuerat suscipere eo quod terras omnium, si posset, decrevit auferre"
(*ib.*, p. 98). In the result, "dicitur quod fere omnes milites hujus abbatiae
haereditavit" (*ib.*, p. 91).

[248] He begged Anselm that "terras ecclesiae quas ipse rex, defuncto
Lanfranco, suis dederat pro statuto servicio, illis ipsis haereditario jure
tenendas, causa sui amoris, condonaret" (*Eadmer*).

[249] Foundation charter of Alcester Priory.

gained by forging a document which admits, by placing on record, the abbey's full liability.[250]

W. Rex. Anglor[um] Athew' abbati de Euesh[am] sal[u]ten. Precipio tibi quod submoneas omnes illos qui sub ballia et i[us]titia s[un]t quatin[us] omnes milties quo mihi debent p[ar]atos h[abe]ant ante me ad octavas pentecostes ap[ud] clarendun[am]. Tu etiam illo die ad me venias et illos quinque milites quos de abb[at]ia tua mihi debes tec[um] paratos adducas. Teste Eudone dapif[er]o Ap[ud] Wintoniam.[251]

Being addressed to Æthelwig, the writ, of course, must be previous to his death in 1077, but I think that we can date it, perhaps, with precision, and that it belongs to the year 1072. In that year, says the Ely chronicler, the Conqueror, projecting his invasion to Scotland, "jusserat tam abbatibus quam episcopis totius Angliae debita militiae obsequia transmitti," a phrase which applies exactly to the writ before us. In that year, moreover, the movements of William fit in fairly with the date for which the feudal levy was here summoned. We know that he visited Normandy in the spring, and invaded Scotland in the summer, and he might well summon his baronage to meet him on 3rd June, on his way from Normandy to Scotland, at so convenient a point as Clarendon. The writ, again, being witnessed at Winchester, may well have been issued by the king on his way out or back.

The direction to the abbot to summon similarly all those beneath his sway who owed military service is probably explained by the special position he occupied as "chief ruler of several counties at the time.[252] We find him again,

---

[250] Three other documents are found on the same folio. Of these the first is addressed to Lanfranc, Odo of Bayeux, Bishop Wulfstan, and Urse d'Abetot, and witnessed by Bishop Geoffrey (of Coutances) and (like our writ) by Eudo Dapifer, being also witnessed, like it, at Winchester. It is noteworthy that it grants Æthelwig the Hundred of Fishborough "in potestate et *justitia* sua."

[251] Cott. MS. Vesp. B. xxiv. f. 15[18].

[252] "Rex commisit ei curam istarum partium terrae . . . ita ut

two years later (1074), acting as a military commander.
On that occasion the line of the Severn was guarded
against the rebel advance by Bishop Wulfstan, "cum
magna militari manu, et Ægelwius Eoveshamnensis abbas
cum suis, ascitis sibi in adjutorium Ursone vicecomite
Wigorniae et Waltero de Laceio cum copiis suis, et cetera
multitudine plebis." [253]   The number of knights which constituted the *servitium debitum* of Evesham was five then as
it was afterwards, and this number, as we now know, had
been fixed *pro voluntate sua,* in 1070, by the Conqueror.

We find allusions to two occasions on which the feudal
host was summoned, as above, by the Conqueror, and by
his sons and successors.   William Rufus exacted the full
servitium debitum to repress the revolt at the commencement of his reign. [254]   Henry I. called out the host to meet
the invasion of his brother Robert. [255]   In both these instances reference is made to the questions of "service
due" that would naturally arise, [256] and that would keep
the *quotas* of knight-service well to the front.   That these
quotas, however, as I said (*supra,* p. 257), were matter of
memory rather than of record, is shown by a pair of early
disputes. [257]

omnium hujus patriae consilia atque judicia fere in eo penderent" (*Hist.
Evesham*).

[253] Florence of Worcester.

[254] "Cernens itaque rex grande sibi periculum imminere, debitum
servitium . . . exigit" (*Liber Eliensis,* p. 276).

[255] "Rex Henricus contra fratrem suum Robertum, Normanniae
comitem, super se in Anglia cum exercitu venientem, totius regni sui
expeditionem dirigit" (*Cart. Abingdon,* ii. 121).

[256] In the former case, between the crown and its tenant; in the latter,
between the tenant and his under-tenant.

[257] "Idem [Godcelinus de Riveria] dicebat se non debere facere servitium, nisi duorum militum, pro feudo quem tenebat de ecclesia, et abbas
et sui dicebant eum debere servitium trium militum" (*Cart. Abingdon,*
ii. 129). "Cum a quodam duos milites ad servicium regis exigerem (tantum
enim inde deberi ab olim a commilitonibus didiceram) ipse toto conatu
obstitit, unius dumtaxat se militis servicio obnoxium obtestans."—Henry
Abbot of Glastonbury (*Domerham,* p. 318).

B.H.   X

Let us pass, at this point, to the great survey. I urged
in the earlier portion of this paper that the argument from
the silence of Domesday is of no value. Even independently
of direct allusions, whether to the case of individual holders,
or to whole groups such as the *milites* of Lanfranc, it can
be shown conclusively that the normal *formulae* cover unquestionable military tenure, tenure by knight-service.[259]

An excellent instance is afforded in the case of Abingdon
Abbey (fol. 258*b*-259*b*), because the *formulae* are quite normal and make "no record of any new duties or services
of any kind."[259] Yet we are able to identify the tenants
named in Domesday, right and left, with the foreign knights
enfeoffed by Athelelm to hold by military tenure,[260] owing
service for their fees "to Lord as Lord." There are some
specially convincing cases, such as those of Hubert, who
held five hides in a hamlet of Cumnor,[261] and whose fee is
not only entered in the list of knights:[262] but is recorded to
have been given before Domesday for military service.[263]
Another case is that of William *camerarius*, who held Lea
by the service of one knight;[264] so too with the bishop
of Worcester's Manor of Westbury-on-Trym, where the
homines of Domesday appear as *milites* in a rather earlier
survey.[265]

[258] Thus undermining Mr. Freeman's argument : "We hear of nothing
in Domesday which can be called knight service or military tenure in
the later sense ; the old obligations would remain ; the primeval duty of
military service, due, not to a lord as lord, but to the state and to the
king as ts head, went on," etc. (*Norm. Conq.*, v. 371).

[259] *Norm. Conq.*, v. 865.

[260] *Cartulary of Abingdon*, ii. 3-7.

[261] " In Winteham tenet Hubertus de Abbate v. hidas de terra villanorum " (i. 58*b*).

[262] " Hubertus i. militem pro v. hidis in Witham " (p. 4).

[263] " In Wichtham de terra villanorum curiae Cumenore obsequi soli-
torum, illo ab abbate cuidam militi nomine Huberto v. hidarum portio
distributa est " (p. 7).

[264] See *Cart. Ab.*, ii. 138. Cf. *Domesday*, i. 58*b* : " Willelmus tenet de
abbate Leie."

[265] See p. 294.

Again, take the case of Peterborough. The Northampton-shire possessions of that house are divided by Domesday (fol. 221) into two sections, of which the latter is headed " Terra hominum. ejusdem ecclesiae," and represents the subinfeudated portion, just as the preceding section contains the *dominium* of the fief.[266] Here " Terra hominum ejusdem " corresponds with the heading " Terra militum ejus " prefixed to the knights of the Archbishop of Canterbury (fol. 4). The Peterborough *homines* are frequently spoken of as *milites* (fol. 221*b*, *passim*), and even where we only find such *formulae* as " Anschitillus tenet de abbate "., we are able to identify the tenant as Anschetil de St. Medard, one of the foreign knights enfeoffed by Abbot Turold.[267]

But it is not only on church fiefs that the Domesday under-tenant proves to be a feudal *miles*. At Swaffham (Cambr.) we read in Domesday (fol. 196) "tenet Hugo de Walterio [Gifard]."[268] Yet in the earlier record of a *placitum* on the rights of Ely, we find this tenant occurring as " *Hugo de bolebec* miles *Walteri Giffard*," while in 1166 his descendant and namesake is returned as the chief tenant on the Giffard fief. The same *placitum* supplies other illustrations of the fact.[269] The cases taken from the Percy fief and from the honour of Britanny afford further confirmation, if needed, of the conclusions I draw.[270]

It will startle the reader, doubtless, to learn that there is in existence so curious a document as a list of knights' fees drawn up in Old English. Headed " these beth thare Knystene londes," etc., and terming a knight's fee a " knystesmetehom," it has been placed by the Editors of

---

[266] This distinction, it will be found, is preserved in Henry's Charter of Liberties (1101): "nec . . . aliquid accipiam [1] de dominico ecclesiae vel [2] de hominibus ejus."

[267] See my paper on " The Knights of Peterborough," *supra*, p. 157.

[268] In the transcript of the original returns it is : "habet hugo de bolebech . . . de waltero giffard."

[269] *Inquisito Eliensis* (*O.* 2. 1), f. 210, *et seq.* (see below, page 459).

[270] See p. 205.

the new *Monasticon* (ii. 477) among documents of the
Anglo-Saxon era, but belongs, I think (from internal
evidence), to about the same period as the *cartæ* (1166).
The original is extant in a Cartulary now in the British
Museum.

VII. THE WORCESTER RELIEF (1095).

It was urged in the earlier part of this paper that Ranulf
Flambard had been assigned a quite unwarrantable share
in the development of feudalism in England. But so little
is actually known of what his measures were that they
have hitherto largely remained matter of inference and
conjecture. It may be well, therefore, to call attention to
a record which shows him actually at work, and which
illustrates the character of his exactions by a singularly
perfect example.

The remarkable document that I am about to discuss is
printed in Heming's "Cartulary" (i. 79-80).[271] It is therefore most singular that it should be unknown to Mr. Freeman—to whom it would have been invaluable for his
account of Ranulf's doings—as it occurs in the midst of a
group of documents which he had specially studied for
his *excursus* on "the condition of Worcestershire under
William."[272] It is a writ of William Rufus, addressed to
the tenants of the see of Worcester on the death of Bishop
Wulfstan, directing them to pay a "relief" in consequence
of that death, and specifying the quota due from each of the
tenants named. The date is fortunately beyond question ;
for the writ must have been issued very shortly after the
death of Wulfstan (18th Jan., 1095), and in any case before
the death of Bishop Robert of Hereford (26th June, 1095),
who is one of the tenants addressed in it. As the record is
not long, and practically, as we have seen, unknown, one
need not hesitate to reprint it.

[271] Hemingi *Chartularium* (ed. Hearne), 1723.
[272] *Norman Conquest*, vol. v.

W. Rex Anglorum omnibus Francis et Anglis qui francas terras tenent de episcopatu de Wireceastra, Salutem. Sciatis quia, mortuo episcopo, honor in manum meam rediit. Nunc volo, ut de terris vestris tale relevamen mihi detis, sicut per barones meos disposui. Hugo de Laci xx. libras. Walterus Punher xx. libras. Gislebertus filius turoldi c. solidos. Rodbertus episcopus x. libras. Abbas de euesham xxx. libras. Walterus de Gloecestra xx. libras. Roger filius durandi [quietus per breve regis][273] x libras. Winebald de balaon x. libras. Drogo filius Pontii x. libras. Rodbert filius sckilin c. solidos. Rodbert stirmannus lx. solidos. Willelmus de begebiri xl. solidos. Ricardus and Franca c. solidos. Angotus xx. solidos. Beraldus xx. solidos. Willelmus de Wic xx. solidos. Rodbertus filius nigelli c. solidos. Alricus archidiaconus c. solidos. Ordricus dapifer[274] xl. libras. Ordricus blaca[275] c. solidos. Colemannus[276] xl. solidos. Warinus xxx. solidos. Balduuinus xl. solidos. Suegen filius Azor xx. solidos. Aluredus xxx. solidos. Siuuardus xl. solidos Saulfus xv. libras. Algarus xl. solidos. Chippingus xx. solidos.

Testibus Ranulfo capellano & Eudone dapifero & Ursone de abetot. Et qui hoc facere noluerit, Urso & bernardus sasiant et terras et pecunias in manu mea.

The points on which this document throws fresh light are these. First, and above all, the exaction of reliefs by William Rufus and his minister, which formed so bitter a grievance at the time, and to which, consequently, Dr. Stubbs and Mr. Freeman had devoted special attention. On this we have here evidence which is at present unique. It must therefore be studied in some detail.

Broadly speaking, we now learn how " the analogy of lay fiefs was applied to the churches with as much minuteness as possible.[277] One of the respects in which the church fiefs

[273] Interlineation.
[274] *Dapifer* to Bishop Wulfstan.
[275] He witnessed, as "Ordric Niger," the *conventio* between Bishop Wulfstan and Abbot Walter of Evesham, and was perhaps Bishop Wulfstan's reeve (Heming, p. 420).
[276] Probably Bishop Wulfstan's chancellor.
[277] Although, from his ignorance of this document, Dr. Stubbs was not aware of Ranulf's *modus operandi*, its evidence affords a fresh illustration of his unfailing insight, and of his perfect grasp of the problem even

differed from those of the lay barons was, that on the one hand they escaped such claims as reliefs, wardships and " marriage," while, on the other, their tenants, of course, also escaped payment of such " aids " as those " ad filium militem faciendum " or " ad filiam maritandam." In this there was a fair " give and take." But Ranulf must have argued that bishops and abbots who took reliefs from their tenants ought, in like manner, to pay reliefs to the crown. This they obviously would not do ; and, indeed, even had they been willing, it would have savoured too strongly of simony. And so he adopted, as our record shows, the un-warrantable device of extorting the relief from the under-tenants direct. This was not an enforcement, but a breach, of feudal principles ; for an under-tenant was, obviously, only liable to relief on his succession to his own fee.[278]

It would be easy to assume that this was the abuse re-nounced by Henry I.[279] But *distinguo.* The above abuse was quite distinct from the practice of annexing to the revenues of the crown, during a vacancy, the temporalities. This, which was undoubtedly renounced by Henry, and as undoubtedly resorted to by himself and by his successors afterwards, was, however distasteful to the church,[280] a

in the absence of proof. " The analogy," he writes, " of lay fiefs was applied to the churches with as much minuteness as possible. . . . Ranulf Flambard saw no other difference between an ecclesiastical and a lay fief than the superior facilities which the first gave for extortion. . . . The church was open to these claims because she furnished no opportunity for reliefs, wardships, marriage, escheats, or forfeiture " (*Const. Hist.*, pp. 298-300).

[278] It has been urged to me that relief on *mutatio domini* was a recog-nised practice, but I cannot find proof of it in English feudalism.

[279] " Nec mortuo archiepiscopo, sive episcopo, sive abbate, aliquid accipiam de dominico ecclesiae vel de hominibus ejus donec successor in eam ingrediatur."

[280] There is a very important allusion to it, as introduced under Rufus, in the *Abingdon Cartulary*, ii. 42: " Eo tempore [1097] infanda usurpata est in Anglia consuetudo, ut si qua prelatorum persona ecclesiarum vita decederet mox honor ecclesiasticus fisco deputaretur regis."

logical deduction from feudal principles, and did not actually wrong any individual. It could thus be retained when the crown abandoned such unjust exactions as the Worcester relief, and it afforded an excellent substitute for wardship, though practically mischievous in the impulse it gave to the prolongation of vacancies.

There are many other points suggested by the record I am discussing, but they can only be touched on briefly. It gives us a singularly early use of the remarkable term "honour," here employed in its simplest and strictly accurate sense; the same term was similarly employed, we have seen, in the case of Abingdon (1097), where we also find the fief described as reverting to the crown *vacante sede*.[281] It further alludes to a special assessment by "barons" deputed for the purpose; it affords a noteworthy formula for distraint in case of non-payment; and it gives us, within barely nine years of the great survey itself, a list of the tenants of the fee, which should prove of peculiar value.

If the sums entered be added up, their total will amount to exactly £250. It is tempting to connect this figure with a *servitum debitum* (*teste episcopo*) of 50 fees at the "ancient relief" of £5 a fee; but we are only justified in treating it as one of those round sums that we find exacted for relief under Henry II., especially as its items cannot be connected with the actual knights' fees. The appended analysis will show the relation (where ascertainable) of sums paid to hides held.

[281] Compare the words of the chronicle on the king claiming to be heir of each man, lay or clerk, with the expression "honor in manum meam rediit."

DOMESDAY, 1086.			THE RELIEF, 1095.		
	h.	v.		£	s.
Roger de Laci	23	2	Hugh de Laci	20	0
Walter Ponther . . .	10	2	Walter Punther . . .	20	0
Gilbert fitz Thorold . .	7	2	Gilbert fitz Thorold . .	5	0
Bishop of Hereford . .	5	0	Bishop Robert [of Hereford]	10	0
Abbot of Evesham . .	9	0	Abbot of Evesham . .	30	0
Walter fitz Roger . . .	8	0	Walter de Gloucester .	20	0
Durand the sheriff . .	6	0	Roger fitz Durand . .	10	0
			Winebald de Balaon . .	10	0
Drogo	10	0	Drogo fitz Ponz . . .	10	0
Schelin	5	0	Robert fitz Schilin . .	5	0
			Robert Stirman . . .	3	0
Anschitil	2	0	Anschitil de Colesbourne	10	0
			Roger de Compton . .	1	0
Eudo	1	3	Eudo	3	0
			William de Begeberi . .	2	0
			Richard & Franca . . .	5	0
Ansgot	1	2	Angot	1	0
			Berald	1	0
			William de Wick . . .	1	0
			Robert fitz Nigel . . .	5	0
Ælfric the archdeacon .	4	0	Ælfric the archdeacon .	5	0
Orderic } . . . . . Orderic	6	1	Orderic the *Dapifer* . .	40	0
			Orderic Black	5	0
			Coleman	2	0
			Warine	1	10
			Baldwin	2	0
			Swegen fitz Azor . . .	1	0
			Alfred	1	10
			Siward	2	0
Siward	5	0	Sawulf	15	0
			Ælfar	2	0
			Cheping	1	0
				£250	0

The comparison of these two lists suggests some interesting conclusions. Roger de Laci, forfeited early in the reign for treason, had been succeeded by his brother Hugh.

"Punher" supplies us with the transitional form from the
"Ponther" of Domesday to the "Puher" of the reign of
Henry I. The identity of the names is thus established.
Walter fitz Roger has already assumed his family surname
as Walter de Gloucester, and his uncle Durand has now
been succeeded by a son Roger, whose existence was unknown to genealogists. The pedigree of the family in the
Norman period has been well traced by Mr. A. S. Ellis in
his paper on the Gloucestershire Domesday tenants, but he
was of opinion that Walter de Gloucester was the immediate
successor in the shrievalty of his uncle, Durand, who died
without issue. This list, on the contrary, suggests that the
immediate successor of Durand was his son Roger, and that
if, like his father, he held the shrievalty, this might account
for the interlineation remitting, in his case, the sum due.
In this Roger we, surely, have that "Roger de Gloucester"
who was slain in Normandy in 1106, and whom, without
the evidence afforded by this list, it was not possible to
identify.[282]

The chief difficulty that this list presents is its omission
of the principal tenant of the see, Urse d'Abetot. One can
only assign it to the fact of his official position as sheriff
enabling him to secure exemption for himself, and perhaps
even for his brother, Robert "Dispensator." Their exemption, however accounted for, involved an arbitrary assessment of all the remaining tenants, irrespective of the
character or of the extent of their tenure. With these
remarks I must leave a document, which is free from anachronism or inconsistency, and as trustworthy, I think, as
it is useful.

It is my hope that this paper may increase the interest in
the forthcoming edition of the *Liber Rubeus* under the care
of Mr. Hubert Hall, and that it may lead to a reconsideration of the problems presented by the feudal system as it

---

[282] " Rogerium de Glocestra, probatum militem, in obsessione Falesiae
arcubalistae jactu in capite percussum " (*William of Malmesbury*, ii. 475).

meets us in England. Nor can I close without reminding the reader that if my researches have compelled me to differ from an authority so supreme as Dr. Stubbs, this in no way impugns the soundness of his judgment on the *data* hitherto known. The original sources have remained so strangely neglected, that it was not in the power of any writer covering so wide a field to master the facts and figures which I have now endeavoured to set forth, and on which alone it is possible to form a conclusion beyond dispute.

PART II

HISTORICAL STUDIES

PART II

HISTORICAL STUDIES

NORMANS UNDER EDWARD THE CONFESSOR

IT is probable that in spite of all the efforts of that school which found in Mr. Freeman its ablest and most ardent leader, the "fatal habit," as he termed it at the outset of his *magnum opus* "of beginning the study of English history with the Norman Conquest itself," will continue, in practice, to prevail among those who have a choice in the matter. It was characteristic of the late Professor to assign the tendency he deplored to "a confused and unhappy nomenclature," for to him names, as I have elsewhere shown,[1] were always of more importance than they are to the world at large. More to the point is the explanation given by Mr. Grant Allen, who attributes to the unfamiliar look of Anglo-Saxon appellatives the lack of interest shown in those who bore them. And yet there must be, surely, a deeper cause than this, an instinctive feeling that in England our consecutive political history does, in a sense, begin with the Norman Conquest. On the one hand it gave us, suddenly, a strong, purposeful monarchy; on the other it brought us men ready to record history, and to give us— treason though it be to say so—something better than the

---

[1] *Quarterly Review*, June, 1892, pp. 9, 10.

arid entries in our jejune native chronicle. We thus exchange aimless struggles, told in an uninviting fashion,
for a great issue and a definite policy, on which we have
at our disposal materials deserving of study. From the
moment of the Conqueror's landing we trace a continuous
history, and one that we can really work at in the light of
chronicles and records. I begin these studies, therefore,
with the Conquest, or rather with the coming of the
Normans. For, as Mr. Freeman rightly insisted, it is with
the reign of Edward the Confessor that "the Norman Conquest really begins":[2] it was "his accession" that marked,
in its results, "the first stage of the Conquest itself."[3]

As he, elsewhere, justly observed of Edward :—

Normandy was ever the land of his affection. . . . His
heart was French. His delight was to surround himself with com-
panions who came from the beloved land, and who spoke the beloved
tongue, to enrich them with English estates, to invest them with the
highest offices of the English kingdom . . . His real affections
were lavished on the Norman priests and gentlemen who flocked to
his court as to the land of promise. These strangers were placed in
important offices about the royal person, and before long they were
set to rule as Earls and Bishops over the already half conquered soil
of England. . . . These were again only the first instalment of
the larger gang who were to win for themselves a more lasting settlement four and twenty years later. In all this the seeds of the Conquest were sowing, or rather, . . . it is now that the Conquest
actually begins. The reign of Edward is a period of struggle between natives and foreigners for dominion in England.[4]

One has, it is true, always to remember that if Edward,
on his mother's side, was a Norman, so was Harold, as his
name reminds us, on his mother's side, a Dane. Nor is it
without significance that, on the exile of his house (1051),
he fled to the Scandinavian settlers on the Irish coast, and
found, no doubt, among them those who shared his almost
piratical return in 1052.[5] The late Professor's bias against·

[2] *N. C.*, i. 525, 526.   [3] *Ibid.*   [4] *Ibid.*, ii. 29, 30.
[5] Mr. Freeman admits that his crews "probably consisted mainly of

all that was "French," together with his love for the
"kindred" lands of Germany and Scandinavia, led him,
perhaps, to obscure the fact that England was a prey
which the Dane was as eager to grasp as the Norman.
But this in no way impugns the truth of his view that
"the Norman tendencies of Edward" paved the way for
the coming of William. Nor can we hesitate to begin the
study of the Norman Conquest with the coming of those,
its true forerunners,—

> " Ke Ewart i aveit menéz
> Et granz chastels è fieux dunez,"

and with whom may be said to have begun the story of
Feudal England.

Professor Burrows is entitled to the credit of setting
forth the theory, in his little book upon the Cinque Ports,[6]
that Edward the Confessor "had evidently intended to
make the little group of Sussex towns, the ' New Burgh '
[? afterwards Hastings], Winchelsea, and Rye a strong
link of communication between England and Normandy,"
by placing them under the control of Fécamp Abbey.
He holds, indeed, that Godwine and Harold had contrived
to thwart this intention in the case of the latter; but this,
as I shall show in my paper on the Cinque Ports, arises
from a misapprehension. This theory I propose to develop
by adding the case of Steyning, Edward's grant of which
to Fécamp is well known, and has been discussed by Mr.
Freeman. It might not, possibly, occur to any one that
Steyning, like Arundel, was at that time a port. But in a
very curious record of 1103, narrating the agreement made
between the Abbot and De Braose, the Lord of Bramber,
it is mentioned that ships, in the days of the Confessor,
used to come up to the "portus S. Cuthmanni" [the patron

adventurers from the Danish Saxons of Ireland, ready for any enterprise
which promised excitement and plunder" (*N. C.*, ii. 313).

[6] *Historic Towns; Cinque Ports*, pp. 26-9.

saint of Steyning], but had been lately impeded by a bridge that had been erected at Bramber. Here then was another Sussex port placed in Norman hands. Yet this does not exhaust the list. Mr. Freeman seems to have strangely overlooked the fact that the great benefice of Bosham, valued under the Confessor at £300 a year, had been conferred by Edward on his Norman chaplain, Osbern, afterwards (1073) Bishop of Exeter, whose brother, in the words of the Regius Professor, was the "Duke's earliest and dearest friend," and who, of course, was of kin both to William and to Edward. Now this Bosham, with Thorney Island, commanded a third Sussex harbour, Chichester haven.[7]

But at London itself also we find the Normans favoured. The very interesting charter of Henry the Second, granted by him, as Duke of the Normans, in 1150 or 1151, to the citizens of Rouen, confirms them in possession of their port at Dowgate, as they had held it from the days of Edward the Confessor.[8] Here then we have evidence—which seems to have eluded the research of our historians, both general and local—that, even before the Conquest, the citizens of Rouen had a haven of their own at the mouth of the Walbrook, for which they were probably indebted to the Norman proclivities of the Confessor.

The building of "Richard's Castle" plays a most important part in Mr. Freeman's narrative of the doings of the Normans under Edward the Confessor. We hear of its building, according to him, in September, 1051:—

Just at this moment another instance of the insolence and violence of the foreigners in another part of the kingdom served to stir up men's minds to the highest pitch. Among the Frenchmen who had flocked to the land of promise was one named Richard the son of Scrob, who had received a grant of lands in Herefordshire. He and

---

[7] See for Osbern, Mr. A. S. Ellis's *Domesday Tenants in Gloucestershire*, p. 18. May not Peter, William's chaplain, Bishop of Lichfield, 1075, have similarly been the Peter who was a chaplain of Edward?

[8] Chéruel's *Histoire de Rouen pendant l'époque communale*, i. 245.

his son Osbern had there built a castle on a spot which, by a singularly lasting tradition, preserves to this day the memory of himself and his building. The fortress itself has vanished, but its site is still to be marked, and the name of Richard's castle, still borne by the parish in which it stood, is an abiding witness of the deep impression which its erection made on the minds of the men of those times. . . . Here then was another wrong, a wrong perhaps hardly second to the wrong which had been done at Dover. Alike in Kent and Herefordshire, men had felt the sort of treatment which they were to expect if the King's foreign favourites were to be any longer tolerated.[9]

Accordingly, Godwine, Mr. Freeman wrote, demanded (8th September, 1051) "the surrender of Eustace and his men and of the Frenchmen of Richard's Castle." In a footnote to this statement, he explained that "'The castle' [of the Chronicle] undoubtedly means Richard's Castle, as it must mean in the entry of the next year in the same Chronicle."[10] Of the entry in question (1052) he wrote "'The castle' is doubtless Richard's Castle . . . Here again the expressions witness to the deep feeling awakened by the building of this castle."[11] So, too, in a special appendix we read :

A speaking witness to the impression which had been made on men's minds by the building of this particular Richard's Castle, probably the first of its class in England, is given by its being spoken of distinctively as "the castle" even by the Worcester chronicler (1052 ; see p. 309), who had not spoken of its building in his earlier narrative.[12]

We have, thus far, a consistent narrative. There was in Herefordshire one castle, built by Richard and named after him. It had been the cause of oppression and ravage, and its surrender, as such, had been demanded by Godwine in 1051. A year later (September, 1052) Godwine triumphs; "It was needful to punish the authors of all the evils that had happened" (p. 333); and "all the French-

[9] *N.C.*, ii. 136-8   [10] *Ibid.*, p. 140.
[11] *Ibid.*, p. 309.   [12] *Ibid.*, p. 607.

men" who had caused them were at last outlawed. But now comes the difficulty, as Mr. Freeman pointed out :—

The sentence did not extend to all the men of Norman birth or of French speech who were settled in the country. It was meant to strike none but actual offenders. By an exception capable of indefinite and dangerous extension, those were excepted 'whom the King liked, and who were true to him and all his folk' (ii. 334). . . . We have a list of those who were thus excepted, which contains some names which we are surprised to find there. The exception was to apply to those only who had been true to the king and his people. Yet among the Normans who remained we find Richard, the son of Scrob, and among those who returned we find his son Osbern. These two men were among the chief authors of all evil (ii. 344).

That is to say, the Lord of Richard's castle, on whose surrender and punishment Godwine had specially insisted, was specially exempted, as guiltless, when Godwine returned to power.[18]

In me, at least, this discrepancy aroused grave suspicion, and I turned to see what foundation there was for identifying the offending garrison of 1051 with that of Richard's castle. I at once discovered there was none whatever.

We have here, in short, one of those cases, characteristic, as I think, of the late Professor's work, in which he first formed an idea, and then, under its spell, fitted the facts to it without question. The view, for instance, of the unique position of Richard's castle as "*the* castle" at the time is at once rendered untenable by the fact that, on the return of Godwine, Normans fled "some west to Pentecostes castle, some north to Robert's castle," in the words of the Chronicle.[14] Moreover, the former belonged to Osbern, "whose surname was Pentecost" (*cognomento Pentecost*), who, as we learn from Florence, was forced to surrender

---

[18] "Norman Richard still held his castle in Herefordshire" (Hunt's *Norman Britain*, p. 69).

[14] Mr. Clark refers to this passage, adding :—" So that these places, probably like Richard's castle, were in Norman hands" (*M.M.A.*, i. 37).

it and leave the country, as was also the fate of another castellan, his comrade Hugh.[15]

It is important to observe the clear distinction between Richard, son of Scrob, of Richard's castle, and Osbern Pentecost, of Pentecost's castle, of whom the former was allowed to remain, while the latter was exiled. But it is another peculiarity of Mr. Freeman's work that he was apt to confuse different individuals bearing the same name.[16] In this instance, he boldly assumed that "Pentecost, as we gather from Florence [?] . . . is the same as Osbern, the son of Richard of Richard's castle, of whom we have already heard so much" (ii. 329), although the latter, a well-known man, is always distinguished as the son of his father, and never as Pentecost. And he further assumes that "Pentecost's castle" was identical with Richard's castle, "the first cause of so much evil" (*ibid.*). These identifications led him into further difficulty, because Osbern, the son of Richard, is found afterwards holding "both lands and offices in Herefordshire" (ii. 345). To account for this, he further assumes as "certain that Osbern afterwards returned" (*ibid.*). This assumption led him on to suggest that others also returned from exile, and that "their restoration was owing to special entreaties of the King after the death of Godwine" (ii. 346). The whole of this history is sheer assumption, based on confusion alone.

Now let us clear our minds of this confusion, and keep the two castellans and their respective castles apart. On the one hand, we have Richard, the son of Scrob, who was left undisturbed at his castle, and was succeeded there by

[15] "Osbernus vero, cognomento Pentecost, et socius ejus Hugo sua reddiderunt castella."

[16] I have noted several cases in point, that of Walter Giffard being the most striking. But we also read in *William Rufus* (ii. 551) that "Henry, son of Swegen, who comes so often under Henry the Second, is the unlucky descendant of Robert, son of Wymarc," that is to say, Henry "of Essex," who was a son of Robert, not of Swegen, and who belonged to a wholly different family and district.

his son Osbern; [17] on the other hand, we have Osbern, "whose surname was Pentecost," and who had to surrender his castle, to which the guilty Normans had fled, and to go into exile. Can we identify that castle? I would venture to suggest that it was no other than that of Ewyas Harold in the south-west corner of Herefordshire, of which Domesday tells us that Earl William had *re*-fortified it ("hoc castellum refirmaverat"), implying that it had existed, and been dismantled before the Conquest. It heads, in the great survey, the possessions of Alfred of Marlborough, and although its holder T.R.E. is not mentioned, we read of the two Manors which follow it: "Hæc duo maneria tenuit Osbernus avunculus Alveredi T.R.E. quando Goduinus et Heraldus erant exulati" (i. 186). Mr. Freeman, of course, assumed that this Osbern was identical with Osbern, the son of Richard, the Domesday tenant-in-chief. This assumption is not only baseless, but also most improbable: for Alfred was old enough to be father-in-law to Thurstan (Mortimer), a Domesday tenant, and would scarcely therefore be young enough to be nephew to another Domesday tenant-in-chief. I would suggest that his uncle was that Osbern "Pentecost" who had to surrender his castle and flee on the return of Godwine and Harold. This would exactly fit in with the Domesday statement, as also with the dismantling of Ewyas Castle.[18]

Ewyas Harold fits in also with the chronicle's mention of the Normans fleeing "west" to Pentecost's castle.

We have now seen that Richard's castle did not stand alone, and that there is nothing to identify it with that Herefordshire castle ("ænne castel") of which the garrison had committed outrages in 1051, and which is far more likely, so far as our evidence goes, to have been "Pentecost's

[17] "Worse than all, the original sinners of the Herefordshire border, Richard and his son Osbern, were still lords of English soil, and holders of English offices" (iv. 53).

[18] Named, as Mr. Freeman pointed out, after Harold, son of Earl Ralph, not after Harold, son of Godwine.

Castle." Mr. Freeman rightly called attention to "the firm root which the Normans had taken in Herefordshire before 1051, which looks very much as if they had been specially favoured in these parts" (ii. 562); and he argued from this that Earl Ralf had probably ruled the shire between 1046 and 1050. The Earl would naturally have introduced the foreign system of castles, as he did the foreign fashion of fighting on horseback. Indeed, speaking of the capture of Hereford in 1055, Mr. Freeman wrote :—

It is an obvious conjecture that the fortress destroyed by Gruffyd was a Norman castle raised by Ralph. A chief who was so anxious to make his people conform to Norman ways of fighting would hardly lag behind his neighbour at Richard's castle. He would be among the first at once to provide himself with a dwelling-place and his capital with a defence according to the latest continental patterns (ii. 391).

But if this is so, he would have built it while he ruled the shire (as Mr. Freeman believed he probably did) from 1046 to 1050, and would, in any case, have done so on taking up its government in 1051.[19] Consequently he would have had a castle and garrison at Hereford in 1052. But Mr. Freeman, describing Gruffyd's raid in that year into Herefordshire, and finding a castle mentioned, assumed that it could only be Richard's castle,[20] although, a few lines before, he had admitted the existence of other castles in the shire.[21] Even in 1067 he would have liked to hold that Richard's castle was the only one in Herefordshire, but the words of the chronicle were too clear for him.[22]

[19] "That Ralph succeeded Swegen on his final banishment in 1051, I have no doubt at all" (ii. 562).

[20] "'The castle' is doubtless Richard's castle. . . . Here again the expressions witness to the deep feeling awakened by the building of this castle" (ii. 309).

[21] "The Norman lords whom Eadward had settled in Herefordshire proved but poor defenders of their adopted country. The last continental improvements in the art of fortification proved vain to secure the land" (*ibid.*).

[22] Florence (1067) speaks of the 'Herefordenses castellani et Richardus

I have endeavoured to make clear my meaning, namely, that Mr. Freeman's view that "Richard's castle" stood alone as "*the* castle," and that Richard and his garrison were the special offenders under Edward the Confessor, is not only destitute of all foundation, but at variance with the facts of the case. When we read of Herefordshire (1067) that—

The Norman colony, planted in that region by Eadward and so strangely tolerated by Harold, was still doing its work. Osbern had been sheriff under Edward, even when Harold was Earl of the shire, and his father Richard, the old offender, still lived (iv. 64)—

we must remember that the conduct of Harold was only strange if Richard, as Mr. Freeman maintained, was "the old offender." If, as Florence distinctly tells us, he was, on the contrary, void of offence, Harold's conduct was in no way strange.[23]

Let us now turn from the Herefordshire colony, planted, I think, not so much by King Edward as by his Earl Ralph, just as Earl William (Fitz Osbern) planted a fresh one after the Conquest.

filius Scrob' as the opponents of Eadric. I could almost have fancied that the words 'Herefordenses castellani' referred to 'the castle' in Herefordshire (see vol. ii. p. 139); but the words of the Worcester chronicler 'þa castelmenn on Hereforda' seem to fix the meaning to the city itself" (iv. 64).

[23] I have no hesitation in offering these criticisms, because Mr. Freeman's views have been embraced throughout by Mr. Hunt, who has followed closely in his footsteps. For instance :—

"A private fortress . . . would seem even stranger to us now than it seemed to our forefathers when Richard the son of Scrob raised the first castle on English ground" (*Norm. Conq.*, v. 640).

"It was the first fortress which was raised in England for the indulgence of private insolence and greed, and not for the protection of Englishmen; it was to be the first of many, and the evil deeds which Richard's men wrought were a foretaste of the evil times when fortresses such as his were common in the land" (*Norman Britain*, p. 64).

Mr. Hunt, therefore, survives to defend the position.

Among the Normans allowed to remain, on the triumph of Godwine's party in 1052, Florence mentions " Ælfredum regis stratorem." On him Mr. Freeman thus comments :—

Several Ælfreds occur in Domesday as great landowners, Ælfred of Marlborough (Osbern's nephew) and Ælfred of Spain, but it is not easy to identify their possessions with any holder of the name in Edward's time. The name Ælfred and Edward and the female name Eadgyth seem to have been the only English names adopted by the Normans. The two former would naturally be given to godsons or dependants of the two Althelings while in Normandy [*i.e.* after 1013].[24]

An appendix, in the first volume, devoted to Ælfred the giant—who appears in Normandy, *circiter* 1030—claims that Ælfred is a name so purely English that the presumption in favour of the English birth of any one bearing it in this generation is extremely strong," [25] and that it was only adopted by "a later generation of Normans." Mr. Freeman seems to have been unaware that in Britanny the name of Alfred enjoyed peculiar favour. I find it there as early as the 9th century,[26] while I have noted in a single cartulary seventeen examples between 1000 and 1150. Among these are "Alfridus frater Jutheli" (*ante* 1008) and Juthel, son of Alfred (1037). Now, at the Conquest, "Judhael, who from his chief seat took the name of Judhael of Totnes, became the owner," in Mr. Freeman's words, "of a vast estate in Devonshire, and extended his possessions into the proper Cornwall also." But we know from charters that this Judhael was the son of an Alfred, and was succeeded by another Alfred, who joined Baldwin of Redvers at Exeter in 1136.[27] In the same county, as Mr. Freeman reminds us, we have another Breton tenant-

[24] Vol ii. p. 345.
[25] Vol. i. p. 747.
[26] About 849 ; Alfret Machtiern, 868 ; Alfritus tyrannus, 871 ; Alfrit presbyter, 872 ; filius Alurit, 879.
[27] Gesta Stephani.

in-chief, "Alvredus Britio." In all this I am working up
to the suggestion that the well-known Alfred of Lincoln
was not, as Mr. Freeman holds, an Englishman,[28] but a
Breton. We have not only the overwhelming presumption
against any considerable tenant-in-chief being of English
origin, but the fact that his lands were new grants. When
we add to this fact that his heir (whether son or
brother) bore the distinctively Breton name of Alan,[29] we
may safely conclude that Alfred was not only a foreigner
but a Breton. But the strange thing is that we do not stop
there; we have a Jool (or Johol) of Lincoln, who died in
1051[30] after bestowing on Ramsey Abbey its Lincolnshire
fief.[31] Thus we have an Alfred and a Juhel "of Lincoln,"
as we have an Alfred and a Juhel "of Totnes"; and in
Juhel of Lincoln we must have a Breton settled in England under the Confessor.

The name of "Lincoln" leads me to another interesting discovery. "Both Alfred of Lincoln and the sheriff
Thorold," Mr. Freeman wrote, "were doubtless Englishmen."[32] And speaking of Abbot Turold's accession in
1070, he observed that Turold was "a form of the Danish
Thorold, a name still [1070] familiar in that part of England, one which had been borne by an English sheriff.[33]

Now this Thorold (*Turoldus*) has been the subject of much
speculation by Mr. Stapleton, Mr. Freeman,[34] etc., in con-

[28] iii. (2nd ed.) 780; iv. 214.
[29] See the Lindsey Survey.
[30] *Ramsey Cartulary*, iii. 167.
[31] *Ibid.*, i. 208; ii. 74.   *Domesday*, i. 346*b*.
[32] iii. (2nd Ed.) 780.
[33] iv. (1st Ed.) 457.
[34] *Ibid.*, 778-780. Mr. Freeman spoke of him as "a kind of centre"
for the inquiry, and stated that in Domesday 346*b* we have "Turoldus
vicecomes" as a benefactor of Spalding priory. This is an error, for the
words there are "dedit S. Gutlaco" (*i.e.* Crowland). He also urged that
"we must not forget the Crowland tradition" about him "preserved by
the false Ingulf." But the fact is that "Ingulf" made him into *two* (1)
"Thuroldus Vicecomes Lincoln," whose benefaction to Crowland (D.B.,

nection with William Malet and the mysterious Countess
Lucy, but the facts about him are of the scantiest, nor, I
believe, has any one succeeded in finding him actually
mentioned in the Conqueror's reign, though he is referred
to in Domesday. This, however, I have now done, lighting
upon him in a passage of considerable interest *per se*. In
the "De miraculis sancti Eadmundi" of Herman we read
that when Herfast, Bishop of Thetford, visited Baldwin,
Abbot of St. Edmund's, to be cured of an injury to his
eye, the Abbot induced him to renounce his claim to
jurisdiction over the Abbey :—

In sacri monasterii vestiario, præsentibus ejusdem loci majoris
ætatis fratribus, sed etiam accitis illuc ab abbate quibusdam regis
primoribus, qui dictante justitia in eadem villa regia tenebant placita·
Quorum nomina, quamvis auditoribus tædio, tamen sunt veræ rationis
testimonio; videlicet Hugo de Mundford, et Rogerius cognomento
Bigot, Richardus Gisleberti comitis filius, ac cum eis *Lincoliensis
Turoldus* et HispaniensisAl veredus, cum aliis compluribus.[85]

The date of this incident can be fixed with certainty as
1076-9 ; and it is of great interest for its mention both of
the eyre itself and of those "baron's" who took part in it ;
there can be no question that "Turoldus" was the mysterious Thorold, sheriff of Lincolnshire, taking his name
from Lincoln.[36] He was, therefore, not "an English sheriff"
of days before the Conquest, but a Norman—as were his
fellows—who died before Domesday.[87]

i. 346*b*) was confirmed in 806 (!) and subsequently (pp. 6, 9, 15, 19),
(2) "quidam vicecomes Lincolniæ, dictus Thoroldus. . . . de genere
et cognatione illius vicedomini Thoroldi qui quondam," etc. (p. 65). It
is the one living in "1051," to whom the Spalding foundation was
assigned.

[85] *Memorials of St. Edmund's Abbey*, i. 63-4. Herman wrote from
personal knowlege.

[36] There are plenty of instances of this practice, as at Exeter, Salisbury,
Gloucester, Leicester, etc.

[37] It may be well here to allude to a still more remarkable commission,
some twenty years later, namely in 1096, when William Rufus sent "in

The name of William Malet, connected with that of Thorold, reminds me of a suggestion I once made,[88] that he held Aulkborough, in Lincolnshire, T.R.E., "and was, to that extent, as M. le Prèvost held, 'established in England previously to the Conquest.'"

Stapleton, whose name in such matters rightly carries great weight, maintained that because the Manor was held in 1086 by Ivo Tailbois, and is stated in Domesday "to have previously belonged to William Malet," it must have been alienated by William by a gift in frank marriage with a daughter, who must, he held, have married Ivo. But I pointed out, firstly, that "it is not the practice of Domesday to enter Manors held *in maritagio* thus," and gave an instance (i. 197) "where we find Picot holding lands from Robert Gernon, which lands are entered in the Gernon fief with the note: 'Has terras tenet Picot Vicecomes de Roberto Gernon in maritagio feminæ suæ.'" I can now, by the kindness of Dr. Liebermann, add the instance of the Mandeville fief in Surrey, where we read of "Aultone":—
'De his hidis tenet Wesmam vi. hidas de Goisfrido filio comitis Eustachii; hanc terram dedit ei Goisfridus de

---

quadragesima optimates suos in Devenesiram et in Cornubiam et Exoniam, Walcalinum, videlicet, Wyntonensemep iscopum, Randulphum regalem capellanum, Willelmum Capram, Hardinum Belnothi filium (*i.e.* Elnoth or Eadnoth ; *see* Greenfield's *De Meriet pedigree*, p. 6) ad investiganda regalia placita.   Quibus in placitis calumpniati sunt cuidam (*sic*) mansioni abbacie Taviensis," etc.   (Tavistock cartularly in *Mon Ang.*, ii. 497).   This eyre cannot be generally known, for Mr. T. A. Archer, in his elaborate biography of Ranulf Flambard, does not mention it.   The association of Bishop Walkelin with Ranulf is specially interesting because they are stated to have been left by the king next year (1097) as joint regents of the realm.   The name, I may add, of "Willelmus filius Baldwini" among those to whom the consequent charter is addressed, *Mon. Angl.*, ii. 497, is of considerable importance, because it is clearly that of the sheriff of Devon, and is proof therefore that Baldwin the sheriff (Baldwin, son of Count Gilbert) had left a son William, who had succeeded to his shrievalty by 1096, and who was in turn succeeded by his brother, Richard Fitz Baldwin, sheriff under Henry I.

[88] *Genealogist*, viii. 4.

Mannevil cum filia sua " (i. 36).[89]   In addition to this argument I urged that "in default of any statement to the contrary, we must always infer that the two holders named
in the survey are (*A*) the holder T.R.E., (*B*) the holder in
1086." This would make William Malet the holder T.R.E.

Another "Norman" on whom I would touch is "Robert
fitz Wimarc," so often mentioned by Mr. Freeman.   I
claim him too as a Breton, on his mother's side at least, if
Wimarc, as seems to be the case, was his mother, for that
is a distinctively Breton name. Mr. Freeman queried the
Biographer's description of him as "regis consanguineus,"
when at Edward's death-bed ;[40] but he is clearly the
"Robertus regis consanguineus" of the Waltham charter.[41]
He was also of kin to William.[42]

The last on my list is Regenbald "the Norman chancellor of Edward," as Mr. Freeman termed him throughout.
He must have had, I presume, some authority for doing so :
but I cannot discover that authority ; and, in its absence,
the name, from its form, does not suggest a Norman origin.[43]
Of Regenbald, however, I shall have to speak in another
paper.

[89] Dr. Liebermann asks whether Geoffrey's daughter was not thus "the
first wife, else unknown, of the future King of Jerusalem."

[40] *N. C.*, iii. 576.   [41] *Ib.*, ii, 673.   [42] *Ib.*, iii. 416.

[43] Mr. A. S. Ellis has suggested that "Elward filius Reinbaldi " (D.B.,
i. 170*b*) King's thegn in Glo'stershire "was evidently a son " of the chancellor. This suggestion is highly probable, and in any case, the thegn
bearing this English name, it may fairly be presumed that his father
Reinbald was not of Norman birth.

MR. FREEMAN AND THE BATTLE OF HASTINGS.

ᵃ Ὅταν ὁ ἰσχυρὸς καθωπλισμένος φυλάσσῃ τὴν ἑαυτοῦ αὐλήν, ἐν εἰρήνῃ ἐστὶν τὰ ὑπάρχοντα αὐτοῦ. ἐπὰν δε ἰσχυρότερος αὐτοῦ ἐπελθὼν νικήσῃ αὐτόν, τὴν πανοπλίαν αὐτοῦ αἴρει ἐφ᾽ ᾗ ἐπεποίθει.

IT might well be thought the height of rashness to attempt criticism, even in detail, of Mr. Freeman's narrative of the Battle of Hastings. For its story, as his champion has well observed, is "the centre and the very heart of Mr. Freeman's work ; if he could blunder here in the most carefully elaborated passage of his whole history he could blunder anywhere ; his reputation for accuracy would be gone almost beyond hope of retrieving it." [1] And indeed, it may fairly be described as Mr. Freeman's greatest achievement, the point where he is strongest of all. He himself described the scene as the "battle which is the centre of my whole history," and reminded us that

on its historic importance I need not dwell ; it is the very subject of my history. . . . Looking also at the fight simply as a battle, it is one of the most memorable in all military history.

That is the first point. The second is, that in his battle pieces our author was always at his best. Essentially a concrete historian, objective as Macaulay in his treatment, he loved incident and action ; loved them, indeed, so well, that he could scarcely bring himself to omit the smallest details of a skirmish :—

[1] Mr. T. A. Archer (*Contemporary Review*, March, 1893, p. 336).

E ripenso le mobili
Tende, e i percossi valli,
E 'l campo dei manipoli,
E l'onda dei cavalli.

Precentor Venables has well described

that wonderful discourse, one of his greatest triumphs—in which, with flashing eye and thrilling voice, he made the great fight of Senlac—as he loved to call it, discarding the later name—which changed the fortunes of England and made her what she is, live and move before his hearers.

My third point is, that his knowledge of the subject was unrivalled. He had visited the battle-field, he tells us, no less than five times, accompanied by the best experts, civil and military, he could find ; he had studied every authority, and read all that had been written, till he was absolutely master of every source of information. He had further executed for him, by officers of the Royal Engineers, an elaborate plan of the battle based on his unwearied studies. Never was historian more splendidly equipped.

Thus was prepared that "very lucid and quite original. account of the battle," as Mr. G. T. Clark describes it, which we are about to examine ; that "detailed account of the battle" that Mr. Hunt, in his *Norman Britain*, describes as written "with a rare combination of critical exactness and epic grandeur."

THE NAME OF "SENLAC."

Before we approach the great battle, it is necessary to speak plainly of the name which Mr. Freeman gave it, the excruciating name of "Senlac." It is necessary, because we have here a perfect type of those changes in nomen-clature on which Mr. Freeman insisted, and which always remind one of Macaulay's words :—

Mr. Mitford piques himself on spelling better than any of his neighbours ; and this not only in ancient names, which he mangles in defiance both of custom and of reason. . . In such cases

established usage is considered as law by all writers except Mr.
Mitford . . . but he proceeds on no principle but that of being
unlike the rest of the world. Every child has heard of Linnæus;
therefore Mr. Mitford calls him Linné. Rousseau is known all over
Europe as Jean Jacques; therefore Mr. Mitford bestows on him the
strange appellation of John James.

None of Mr. Freeman's peculiar "notes" is more familiar
than this tendency, and none has given rise to bitterer
controversy or more popular amusement. "Pedantry"
was the charge brought against him, and to this charge
he was as keenly sensitive as was Browning to that of
"obscurity." Of both writers it may fairly be said that
they evaded rather than met the charge brought against
them. The Regius Professor invariably maintained that
accuracy, not "pedantry," was his true offence. Writing,
in the *Fortnightly Review*, on "The Study of History," he
set forth his standing defence in these words:—

I would say, as the first precept, Dare to be accurate. You
will be called a pedant for doing so, but dare to be accurate all the
same.
He who shall venture to distinguish between two English
boroughs, between two Hadriatic islands, when the authorized
caterer for the public information thinks good to confound them,
must be content to bear the terrible name of pedant, even if no worse
fate still is in store for him.

Was, then, our author a mere pedant, or was this the
name that ignorance bestowed on knowledge? For an
answer to this question, "Senlac" is a test-case. "Every
child," in Macaulay's words, had heard of the Battle of
Hastings; it was known by that name "all over Europe"
from time immemorial. Unless, therefore, that name was
wrong, it was wanton and mischievous to change it; and,
even if changed, it was indefensible to substitute the name
of Senlac, unless there is proof that the battle was so styled
when it was fought.
As to the first of these points, the old name was in no
sense wrong. Precisely as the battle of Poitiers was fought

some miles from Poitiers, so was it with that of Hastings. Yet we all speak of the Battle of Poitiers, although we might substitute the name of Maupertuis more legitimately than that of Senlac. The only plea that Mr. Freeman could advance was that people were led by the old name to imagine that the battle was fought at Hastings itself! Of those who argue in this spirit, it was finely said by the late Mr. Kerslake that,—

instead of lifting ignorance to competence by teaching what ought to be known, they cut down what ought to be known to the capacity of those who are deficient of that knowledge. Instead of making them understand the meaning of the ancient and established word "Anglo-Saxon," they disturb the whole world of learning with an almost violent attempt to turn out of use the established word, which has been thoroughly understood for ages.

The simple answer to Mr. Freeman's contention is, that it is needless to make the change in histories, because those who read them learn that the fight was at Battle ; while as to those who do not read histories, it is obvious that such a name as "Senlac" will in no way lighten their darkness.

The change, therefore, was uncalled for. But it was not merely uncalled for ; it was also absolutely wrong. "To the battle itself," Mr. Freeman wrote, "I restore its true ancient name of Senlac." In so doing the writer acted in the spirit of those who "restore" our churches, and who gave that word so evil a sound in the ears of all archæologists, Mr. Freeman himself included. I am reminded of the protest of the Society of Antiquaries on hearing "with much regret that a fifteenth-century pinnacle" at Rochester Cathedral "is in danger of destruction in order that a modern pinnacle, professing to represent that which stood in the place in the twelfth century, may be set up in its stead." Precisely such a "restoration" is Mr. Freeman's "Senlac." Professing to represent the ancient name of the battle, it is substituted for that name which the battle has borne from the days of the Conqueror to our own. In William of Malmesbury as in Domesday Book we read of "the Battle of Hastings" (*Bellum Hastingense*), and all Mr. Freeman's efforts failed admittedly to discover any record or any writer who spoke of the Battle of Senlac (*Bellum Senlacium*) save Orderic alone. Now Orderic wrote two generations after the battle was fought; the name he strove to give it fell from his pen stillborn; and the fact that this name was a fad of his own is shown by what Mr. Freeman suppressed, namely, that Orderic, in the same breath, tells us that Battle Abbey was founded as "cœnobium Sanctæ Trinitatis Senlac," whereas we learn from Mr. Freeman himself that

the usual title is "ecclesia Sancti Martini de Bello," "ecclesia de Bello," or, as we have seen, in English "pæt mysnter æt pære Bataille." The fuller form, "Abbas Sancti Martini de loco Belli," appears in Domesday, 11*b*: but it is commonly called in the Survey "ecclesia de Labatailge."

So much for Orderic's authority.

So violent an innovation as this of our author's could not pass unchallenged. Mr. Frederic Harrison threw down the gauntlet (*Contemporary Review*, January, 1886), attacking, in a brilliant and incisive article, Mr. Freeman's "pedantry" along the whole line. But he chiefly complained of

a far more serious change of name that the "Old English" school have introduced; which, if it were indefinitely extended, would wantonly confuse historical literature. I mean the attempt to alter names which are the accepted landmarks of history. It is now thought scholarly to write of "the Battle of *Senlac*" instead of "the Battle of *Hastings*." As every one knows, the fight took place on the site of Battle Abbey, seven miles from Hastings; as so many great battles, those of Tours, Blenheim, Cannæ, Chalons, and the like, have been named from places not the actual spot of the combat.

But since for 800 years the historians of Europe have spoken of "the Battle of Hastings," it does seem a little pedantic to rename it. . . . The sole authority for "Battle of Senlac" is Orderic, a monk who lived and wrote in Normandy in the next century. Yet, on the strength of this secondary authority, the "Old English" school choose to erase from English literature one of our most familiar names.

Mr. Freeman's rejoinder must be noticed, because singularly characteristic. Treating Mr. Harrison "de haut en bas," he expressed surprise that his friends should expect him to reply to an article which had merely amused him, and—unable, of course, to adduce any fresh authority for "Senlac"—denounced his critic for a "reckless raid into regions where he does not know the road." For this charge there was no foundation in the matter of which we treat. Mr. Freeman persisted that he had given the battle "the only name that I found for it anywhere" (which we have seen was not the case), and sarcastically observed that "so to do is certainly 'pedantic,' for it conduces to accuracy."

The truth is simply that the site of the battle had no name at all. As the professor himself wrote :—

The spot was then quite unoccupied and untilled; nothing in any of the narratives implies the existence of any village or settlement; our own Chronicle only describes the site as by "the hoar apple-tree" ("He com him togenes æt *þære* haran apuldran").

Consequently, when men wished to speak of the great conflict, they were driven, as in similar cases, to term it the Battle of Hastings, or, if they wished to be more exact, they had to describe it, by periphrasis, as fought on "the site which is now called Battle."

Henry of Huntingdon, our author tells us, is guilty, though otherwise well informed, of "a statement so grotesquely inaccurate as that Harold 'aciem suam construxit in *planis Hastinges.*'" Why "grotesque"? It would be strictly accurate to describe a battle, even seven miles from Salisbury, as fought on Salisbury Plain; while, as to the word "plain," his horror of field-sports may have caused Mr. Freeman's ignorance of the fact that another such stretch of Sussex Down is known as "Plumpton Plain."[2] But the fact is that the whole difficulty arose from that singular narrowness that cramped our author's mind, and

---

[2] Mr. Freeman saw nothing grotesque in Orderic's description of Exeter, as "in plano sita" (*Norm. Conq.*, iv. 153), though its site "sets Exeter distinctly among the hill cities" (Freeman's *Exeter*, p. 6).

that lies at the root, when rightly understood, of his most distinctive tenets. For he was a pedant, after all. And, observe, this "pedantry" did, in practice, conduce not to true accuracy, but to the very reverse. Paradoxical though this may sound, it is literally true. Let us take a striking instance. In his account of the attack on Dover in 1067, Mr. Freeman argued, "from the distinct mention of *oppidum* and *oppidani* in Orderic," that it was not the castle, as supposed, but the town that was attacked. And so convinced was he of this, that he forced his authorities into harmony with his view against their plain meaning. This was because he was not aware that Orderic—"my dear old friend Orderic," as in one place he terms him—was in the habit of using *oppidum* for castle. He must have afterwards discovered this; for his theory was tacitly and significantly dropped, and the old version substituted, in a subsequent edition. Again, an article on "City and Borough," which he contributed to *Macmillan's Magazine*, was based on the fundamental assumption that *civitas*, in the Norman period, must have had a specialized denotation. The fact that, on the contrary, the same town is spoken of as a *civitas* and as a *burgus*, cuts the ground from under this assumption, and, with it, destroys the whole of its elaborate superstructure. Our author's method, in short, placed him in standing conflict with every authority for his period. Never was "the sacredness of words" treated as of less account; never, indeed, were words more wantonly changed. What would Mr. Freeman have said had he known that the compilers of that sacrosanct record, Domesday Book itself, revelled in altering the wording of the sworn original returns? Such was the spirit of the men whose language he strove to limit by a terminology as precise as that of modern philosophy.

I may have wandered somewhat from "Senlac," but my object was to show that Mr. Freeman misunderstood twelfth-century writers by assigning to them his own peculiarities. It did not in any way follow from their speaking of a "Battle of Hastings" that they "grotesquely" supposed it to have been fought at the town itself : they allowed themselves an elasticity, both in word and phrase, which was so alien to himself that he could not realize its existence, and therefore accused them of ignorance because their language was different from his. In the same spirit he would never admit that the "Castellum Warham" of Domesday Book was no other than Corfe Castle, although, as Mr. Eyton and Mr. Bond have shown, the fact is certain.

But the *crux* is yet to come. To any one acquainted with "Old English" it must instantly occur that "Senlac" is not an English name. Mr. Freeman glided over this by simply ignoring the difficulty, but was he aware that the name in question, as "Senlecque" (or "Senlecques"), is actually found—in France? One is reminded of his own criticism on the name "Duncombe Park" :—

When the lands of Helmsley were made to take the name of Duncombe, a real wrong was done to geography. . . . How came a *combe* in Yorkshire? The thing is a fraud on nomenclature as great as any of the frauds which the first Duncombe, "born to carry parcels and to sweep down a counting-house," contrived to commit on the treasury of the nation.

How came a French "Senlac" in "Old English" Sussex? The name is as obviously foreign as "Senlis" itself, and the occurrence, in later days, of "Santlachæ" as a local field-name, cannot avail against this fact, or prove that this open down, in days before the Conquest, could have borne such a title. Therefore, when Mr. Freeman wrote that the English king "pitched his camp upon the ever memorable heights of Senlac," he was guilty, not only of anachronism, but of a "real wrong to geography," and, in the name of accuracy, he introduced error.[3]

[3] That I may not be accused of passing over any defence of Mr. Freeman, I give the reference to Mr. Archer's letter in *Academy* of 4th November, 1893, arguing, as against Mr. Harrison, that the story of a great "naval engagement" in 1066 may probably be traced "to the seaside associations of the name Hastings." Unfortunately for him, Mr. Freeman

I have gone thus carefully into this matter because the name has been meekly adopted by historians, and even by journalists, thereby proving the power of that tendency to fashion and imitation on which, in his *Physics and Politics,* Mr. Bagehot loved to insist. For my part I make an earnest appeal to all who may write or teach history to adhere to the "true ancient name" of the Battle of Hastings, and to reject henceforward an innovation which was uncalled for, misleading, and wrong.[4]

The Palisade.

The distinctive peculiarity of the English tactics, we learn from Mr. Freeman at the outset, is found in an entirely novel device introduced on this occasion by Harold. Instead of merely forming his troops in the immemorial array known as the shield-wall, he turned "the battle as far as possible into the likeness of a siege,"[5] by building around them a "palisade" of solid timber. How large a part this "palisade" plays in Mr. Freeman's story may be gathered from the fact that it is mentioned at least a score of times in his account of the great battle. This "fortress of timber," with its "wooden walls," had "a triple gate of entrance," and was composed of "firm barricades of ash and other timber, wattled in so close together that not a crevice could be seen."

It would be easier for me to deal with this "palisade" if one could form a clear idea of what it represented to Mr. Freeman's mind. Judging from the passages quoted above,

himself had quoted this wild story (iii. 729) and suggested quite a different explanation, namely, that it originated, not in the Battle of Hastings, but in some real "naval operations."

[4] Since this passage appeared in print my opponents themselves have written of the Battle of Hastings (*sic*), and Mr. Archer has admitted that "to speak of Senlac in ordinary conversation, or in ordinary writing, is a piece of pedantry" (*Academy ut supra*). On my own use of the word before I had examined Mr. Freeman's authority, see p. 353.

[5] *Norm. Conq.,* iii. 444.

and from his praising Henry of Huntingdon for his "admirable comparison of Harold's camp to a castle"; [6] I was led to believe that he imagined precisely such a timber wall as crowned in those days a castle mound. Such a defence is well shown in the Bayeux Tapestry, crowning the castle mound which William threw up at Hastings. Now, this very parallel is suggested by Mr. Freeman himself. Describing Harold's position as "not without reason called a fortress" [where?] he suggested that "its defences might be nearly equal to those of William's own camp at Hastings" (p. 447). Following up this parallel, we find Mr. Freeman writing of this latter :—

A portion of English ground was already entrenched and *palisaded*, and changed into a Norman fortress (p. 418). . . . He saw the carpenters come out with their axes ; he saw the fosse dug, and the *palisade* thrown up (p. 419). They had already built a fort and had fenced it in with a *palisade* (p. 420).

Without binding Mr. Freeman down to a defence precisely of this character—and, indeed, in this as in other matters, he may not even himself have formed a clear idea of what he meant—it gives us, I think we may fairly say, a general idea of his "palisade." It was certainly no mere row of stakes,[7] no heap of cottage window frames,[8] no fantastic array of shields tied to sticks,[9] no "*abattis* of some sort"[10] that Mr. Freeman had in view, whatever his cham-

---

[6] *Ibid.*, p. 757.

[7] Mr. Archer writes :—"*Pel* is literally 'stake,' and originally, of course, represented the upright or horizontal stakes which go to make a palisade" (*Eng. Hist. Rev.*, ix. 6).

[8] *Ibid.*, p. 10. The word which Mr. Freeman (and others) rendered "ash" is rendered "windows of farm dwellings" by Mr. Archer (see below, p. 402).

[9] Mr. Archer would have us believe that "Mr. Freeman really had in his mind . . . a real wall of real shields and stakes" (*ibid.*, p. 16), and that the English would "strap up their shields to the stakes," would combine "their shields and poles," and so forth (p. 20).

[10] This is Mr. Oman's third and (up to now) final explanation (*Academy*, 9th June, 1894).

pions may pretend. As for the defenders of the "palisade," they cannot even agree among themselves as to what it really was. Mr. Archer produces a new explanation, only to throw it over almost as soon as it is produced.[11] One seeks to know for certain what one is expected to deal with; but, so far as it is possible to learn, nobody can tell one. There is only a succession of dissolving views, and one is left to deal with a nebulous hypothesis.[12]

Mr. Freeman wrote of his "palisade" as a mere "development of the usual tactics of the shield-wall"; but this is an obvious misconception. It might, indeed, be used as a substitute for the "shield-wall," and would enable the troops behind it to adopt a looser formation; but to suppose that they were ranged "closely together in the thick array of the shield-wall," with this second wall in front of them, is surely absurd. Till the "wooden walls" were broken the "shield-wall" was needless. To retain the disadvantages of its close order, when that order had been rendered needless, would have been simply insane. Yet this insanity, in our author's eyes, was "the master-skill of Harold." Was there time, moreover, to construct such a fortress, if "the battle followed almost immediately," as we learn, "on the arrival of Harold"? Lastly, would there be material on the spot for a palisade (see ground plan) about a mile in length?[18] These awkward points may not have occurred to Mr. Freeman; but to others they will, I think, cause some uneasiness. Let us then examine Mr. Freeman's authorities for the existence of this palisade

[11] *Eng. Hist. Rev.*, ix. 232.

[12] See *Eng. Hist. Rev.*, ix. 232-3, 237-8, 240.

[18] The difficulty of hauling timber even a short distance over broken and hilly ground "in an October of those days" (*N. C.*, iii. 446) must not be forgotten.

Mr. Freeman's Authorities For It.

In his note on "The Details of the Battle of Senlac" (iii. 756), Mr. Freeman explained that he had given the authorities on which his statements rested, adding :—

Each reader can therefore judge for himself how far my narrative is borne out by my authorities.

Loyally keeping to this principle, I propose to test his statements by the authorities he gives for them himself. I therefore address myself to the passages in Henry of Huntingdon and in Wace.

(1) *Henry of Huntingdon.*

The passage relied on by the historian, is this :—

Quum ergo Haroldus totam gentem suam in una acie strictissime locasset *et quasi castellum inde construxisset* [14] impenetrabiles erant Normannis (iii. 444, note).

Mr. Freeman thus paraphrased Henry's words,—

He occupied and fortified, as thoroughly as the time and the means at his command would allow, a post of great natural strength, which he made into what is distinctly spoken of as a castle (*ibid.*).[15]

Although the writer made it his complaint against one of the editors in the Rolls series that he could not "construe his Latin," we see that the same failing led him here himself into error. *Inde* refers, and can only refer, to Harold's troops themselves. A fortress Harold wrought; but he wrought it of flesh and blood : it was behind no ramparts that the soldiers of England awaited the onset of the chivalry of France.

The metaphor, of course, is a common one. Henry of Huntingdon himself recurs to it, when describing that "acies," at the Battle of Lincoln, which Stephen "circa se . . . strictissime collocavit" (p. 271), as Harold, he wrote, "gentem suam in una acie strictissime locasset"

---

[14] The italics are Mr. Freeman's own.
[15] He even spoke of it as "the main castle" (*Arch. Journ.*, xl. 359).

(p. 203). For he shows us Stephen's "acies" assailed "sicut castellum."[16] In the same spirit an Irish bard tells us how his countrymen, on the battle-field of Dysert O'Dea (10th May, 1318), closed in their ranks, "like a strong fortress," as their enemies surged around them. It was felicitous, indeed, to describe as "quasi castellum" that immovable mass of warriors girt by their shield-wall,[17] that "fortress of shields," as Mr. Freeman termed it, at Hastings itself (iii. 492), at Stamford Bridge (iii. 372), at Maldon (i. 272), and even in earlier days (i. 151).

It was Mr. Freeman's initial error in thus materializing a metaphor (through misconstruing his Latin) that first led me to doubt the existence of the "palisade." His champion, Mr. Archer, in his first article,[18] was ominously silent as to this error: in the second, he had to confess of this passage, the first of Mr. Freeman's proofs, that he himself "should never think of using it to prove a palisade.[19] *Exit*, therefore, Henry of Huntingdon.

(2) *Wace.*

Two passages, and two alone, are in question—

(A) ll. 6991-6994, which Mr. Freeman has paraphrased thus :—

WACE.	MR. FREEMAN.
Heraut a le lieu esgarde,	He occupied the hill; he surrounded it on all its accessible sides by a palisade, with a triple gate of entrance, and defended it to the south by an artificial ditch (iii. 447).
Closre le fist de boen fosse,	
De treis parz laissa treis entrees	
Qu'il a garder a commandees.	

[16] Miss Norgate (*Angevin Kings*) follows him, speaking of their assailants striving "to assault them as if besieging a fortress." One is reminded of Mr. Freeman's remark as to Hastings, that Harold turned "the battle as far as possible into the likeness of a siege" (see above).

[17] "Men ranged so closely together in the thick array of the shield-wall" (iii. 471).

[18] *Cont. Rev.*, March, 1893.   [19] *Eng. Hist. Rev.*, ix. 12.

My criticism on this has been from the first that Wace here speaks *only* of a ditch, and that Mr. Freeman has not only introduced here the alleged palisade, from which Wace's "fosse" was quite distinct, but has also transferred to that palisade the "treis entrees" of the fosse. That Mr. Freeman did treat the "palisade" and the "fosse" as distinct and considerably apart is proved by this passage:—

The Normans had crossed the [*sic*] English fosse, and were now at the foot of the hill with the palisades and the axes right before them (iii. 476).

The "fosse" is that "artificial ditch" of which Mr. Freeman speaks in the above passage, the only one of which he does speak. Therefore, that "artificial ditch" was, in his view, down in the valley to the south, and had nothing to do with that "palisade" which he placed on the hill. There is thus no possible doubt as to Mr. Freeman's view. On his own showing, the above lines make no mention of a palisade on the hill.[20]

(B) ll. 7815-26: The passage in question runs thus:—

> Fet orent devant els *escuz*
> De fenestres è d'altres fuz,
> Devant els les orent levez,
> Come cleies joinz è serrez;
> Fait en orent devant closture,
> N'i laissierent nule jointure,
> Par onc Normant entr'els venist
> Qui desconfire les volsist.
> D'escuz e d'ais s'avironoent,
> Issi deffendie se quidoent
> Et s'il se fussent bien tenu,
> Ia ne fussent le ior vencu.

In his first edition, writing, I believe, under the influence of Taylor's version, Mr. Freeman gave these lines in a footnote to his narrative of the battle, and appears to have

[20] My detailed reply to Mr. Archer's attempt to confuse the "fosse" and the palisade will be found in *E.H.R.*, ix. 213, 214

then looked on them as describing his palisade.[21]   But in his "second edition, revised," in preparing which he went "minutely through every line, and corrected or improved whatever seemed to need correction or improvement" (p.v.), he transferred these lines to his appendix on the battle, where he wrote concerning them as follows :—

[(At Maldon) the English stood, *as at Senlac*, in the array common to them and their enemies—a strong line, or rather wedge, of in-fantry, forming a wall with their shields (i. 271).][22]

Of the array of the shield-wall we have often heard already, as at Maldon (see vol. i. p. 271), but it is at Senlac that we get the fullest descriptions of it [*sic*] all the better for coming in the mouths of enemies.   Wace gives his description, 12941 :

> " Fet orent devant els escuz
> De fenestres è d'altres fuz ;
> Devant els les orent levez.
>
> .   .   .   .
>
> Et s'il se fussent bien tenu
> Ja ne fussent li jor vencu."

So William of Malmesbury, 241.   " Pedites omnes cum bipennibus, conserta ante se scutorum testudine, impenetrabilem cuneum faciunt ; quod profecto illis eâ die saluti fuisset, nisi Normanni simulatâ fugâ more suo confertos manipulos laxassent."   So at the battle of the Standard, according to Æthelred of Rievaux (343), " scutis scuta junguntur, lateribus latera conseruntur " (iii. 763-4).

The unquestionable meaning of Mr. Freeman's words is that Wace's lines (like the other passages) describe the time-honoured shield-wall, "the fortress of shields, so often sung of alike in English and in Scandinavian minstrelsy " (iii. 372).

Appealing to this, his own verdict, in my original article,[23] I spoke of these lines as referring to the "shield-wall," and

---

[21] He paraphrased "escuz de fenestres è d'altres fuz" as "firm barri-cades of ash and other timber."

[22] I supply the passage in square brackets (the italics are my own) from the earlier volume to explain Mr. Freeman's reference.

Quarterly Review, July, 1892, p. 14

maintained that "escuz" meant shields, not "barricades." This also, it will be seen, must have been Mr. Freeman's view, when he pronounced these lines to be a description of the shield-wall. I therefore declared that the only evidence he adduced for his palisade had been demonstrably obtained by misconstruing his Latin, and (on his own showing) by mistranslating his French.

This has been my case from the first: it remains my case now. Unlike our forefathers on the hill of battle, I will not be decoyed into breaking "the line of the shield-wall." [24]

---

[24] I am loth to introduce into the text the wearisome details of controversy, especially where they are *nihil ad rem*, and have no bearing on my argument. But, lest I should be charged with ignoring any defence of Mr. Freeman, I will briefly explain in this note the attitude adopted by his champions.

In the *Contemporary Review* of March, 1893, Mr. T. A. Archer produced a reply to my original article (*Quarterly Review*, July, 1892), or rather, to that part of it which dealt with the Battle of Hastings. Declaring my attack on the palisade to be my "only definite and palpable charge against Mr. Freeman's account" (p. 353), which, it will be found, is not the case—he undertook to "show Mr. Freeman to have been entirely right in the view he took of the whole question" (p. 344). To do this, he deliberately suppressed the fatal passage (iii. 763-4) I have printed above,—to which, in my article, I had prominently appealed,—in order to represent me as alone in seeing a description of the shield-wall in Wace's lines (p. 344). He then insisted that "there are six distinct objections to translating this passage as if it referred to a shield-wall" (p. 349).

Instantly reminded by me (*Athenæum*, March 18th, April 8th, 1893), that Mr. Freeman himself had taken it as a description of the shield-wall, and challenged to account for the fact, again charged (*Quarterly Review*, July, 1893, p. 88), with "ignoring a fact in the presence of which his elaborate argument collapses like a house of cards," further challenged (*Academy*, 16th September, 1893) to reconcile Mr. Freeman's words (iii. 763-4), with his representation of the historian's position, Mr. Archer continued to shirk the point, till in the *English Historical Review* of January, 1894, he grudgingly confessed that "the discovery that a shield-wall (of some sort or other) was implied in this so-called 'crucial passage,' is due to Mr. Freeman" (p. 3), but he and Miss Norgate endeavoured to urge that it could not be as I imagined, the shield-wall that he had always spoken of (pp. 3, 16, 62). Even this feeble evasion, now seems to be dropped since I disposed of it (*ibid.*, 225-227).

MY ARGUMENT AGAINST IT.

In order to show clearly that I adhere to my original position, I need only reprint my argument as it appeared in the *Quarterly Review*.

It is clear that if he (Mr. Freeman) found it needful, in his story of the great battle, to mention this barricade about a score of times, it must have occupied a prominent place in every contemporary narrative. And yet we assert without fear of contradiction that (dismissing the 'Roman de Rou') in no chronicle or poem, among all Mr. Freeman's authorities, could he find any ground for this singular delusion; while the Bayeux Tapestry itself, which he rightly places at their head, will be searched in vain for a palisade, or for anything faintly resembling it, from beginning to end of the battle.[25]

On this passage we take our stand: it is the very essence of our case. We made our statement "without fear of contradiction"; and it is not contradicted. Moreover, we can now further strengthen it by appealing to Baudri's poem,[26] an authority of the first rank, in which, as in the others, there is no allusion to the existence of any "palisade."

It will be observed that, in this passage, we expressly excluded Wace's poem. We did so because—although, as we have seen, Mr. Freeman failed to produce from it any proof of a palisade—we preferred to leave it an open question whether Wace did or did not believe the English to have fought behind a palisade. In rebutting Mr. Freeman's evidence, that question did not arise.

There is another argument that we refrained from bringing forward because we thought it superfluous. The Normans, of course, as Mr. Freeman reminds us, magnified the odds against them: "Nothing but the special favour of God could have given his servants a victory over their enemies, which was truly miraculous" (p. 440). William of Poitiers, he adds (p. 479), sets forth their difficulties in detail:—

"Angli nimium adjuvantur superioris loci opportunitate, quem sine procursu tenent, et maxime conferti; atque ingenti quoque numerositate suâ atque validissimâ corpulentiâ; præterea pugnæ instrumentis, quæ facile per scuta vel alia tegmina viam inveniunt."

Now William who was not only a contemporary writer, but, says

---

[25] *Q. R.*, July, 1892, p. 15.
[26] See below, p. 368.

Mr. Freeman (p. 757), "understood" the site, had, obviously, every inducement to include, among the difficulties of the Normans, that special "development," which according to Mr. Freeman (p. 444, 468), "the foresight of Harold" had introduced on this occasion, and which, he assures us, involved "a frightful slaughter" of the Normans. And yet this writer is absolutely silent, both here and throughout the battle, as to the existence of a barricade of any sort or kind.[27]

Here I would briefly refer to certain misrepresentations. Mr. Archer claimed, in his original article (*Cont. Rev.*, 344) to "mainly rely" upon Wace, on the ground that I did so myself. I was obliged to describe this statement at once as "the exact converse of the truth."[28] For it will be seen, I expressly excluded Wace from the authorities on whom I relied, and specially rested my case, from the first, on the evidence of the Bayeux Tapestry. It is much to be regretted that Mr. Archer has deliberately repeated his statement,[29] though even his ally reluctantly admits that it was "not very happily worded."[30]

Mr. Archer might well seek to avoid the Bayeux Tapestry, for its evidence is dead against him, and he cannot explain it away. His first attempt was a brief allusion, accepting its authority without question, but suggesting that it might represent that part of the line where the barricade was absent.[31] Of this suggestion I at once disposed by showing that it is "not only absolutely without foundation, but is directly opposed to Mr. Freeman's theory, and, indeed, to his express statements."[32] Forced to drop this explanation, my opponent, in his next article, fell back on the desperate device of repudiating the authority of the Tapestry,[33] "the most authentic record" of the battle according to the late Professor, who was never weary of insisting on its "paramount importance." On my showing, beyond the possibility of question, that this amounted to rejecting

[27] *Q. R.*, July 1893, p. 84.
[28] *Athenæum*, March 18, 1893.
[29] *Eng. Hist. Rev.*, ix. 40.   [30] *Ibid.*, p. 58.   [31] *Cont. Rev.*, 351.
[32] *Q. R.*, July, 1893, pp. 93-4.   [33] *Eng. Hist. Rev.*, ix. 27, 28.

everything that Mr. Freeman had written on the subject,[34] Mr. Archer once more shifts his tactics, and now writes thus :—

> If any fact in Hastings is more certain than another, it is that at the beginning of the battle the main body of the English was posted *on a hill.* Now "the priceless record"—the Bayeux Tapestry—represents them *on a plain.* If the Tapestry could leave out this central feature—the hill of Senlac—from its picture of the *opening* battle, still more easily could it leave out the intricate barriers upon the hill.[35]

This *ad captandum* argument is disposed of as easily as the others. The Tapestry does not concern itself with landscape, and shows us neither a hill nor a plain. It could not, on a narrow strip, shew us " the hill of Senlac," but it could—and would—show us the alleged palisade. For not only does it strive under every difficulty to represent such objects as churches, castles and houses, but it faithfully shows us the " palisade "[36] raised by William at Hastings itself. And if it be urged that it could not depict men fighting behind such a defence, let us turn to the scene at Dinan. If we compare it with the opening scene of the great battle itself, we see precisely similar horsemen advancing to the attack, similar infantry resisting that attack, and similar spears flying between them. But at Dinan the defenders have a palisade, and on the hill of battle they have not.[37]

[34] *Eng. Hist. Rev.*, 219-225.

[35] *Ibid.*, ix. 607. The italics are Mr. Archer's own. His own trusted authority, Wace, posts the English in " un champ" (ii. 7729, 7769) !

[36] *Norman Conquest*, iii. 419, 420.

[37] No one, of course, would treat the Tapestry like a modern illustrated journal ; but if it be fairly treated, in Mr. Freeman's spirit, one's real wonder is that, under such obvious limitations, the designer should have been so successful as he has. Nowhere, perhaps, is the painstaking accuracy of the Bayeux Tapestry better seen than in its miniature representation of the fortress at Dinan. It shows us the *motte,* or artificial mound, surrounded by its ditch, and even the bank beyond the ditch, together with the wooden bridge springing (as we know it did in such castles) from that bank to the summit of the mound.

As to Mr. Archer's attempts to show that Mr. Freeman in one or two

But although the evidence of the Bayeux Tapestry, Mr. Freeman's own supreme authority, remains absolutely unshaken, it must not be supposed that I rely on that evidence alone. I attach as much importance as ever—and so will, I think, all prejudiced persons—to the other portion of my argument, that if there had been a barricade playing so

instances did not value so highly as he did what he deemed the supreme authority for the battle, I need only print Mr. Freeman's words, parallel with his own comments, to show how their character is distorted.

Mr Freeman.	Mr. Archer.
The testimony of Florence is confirmed by a witness more unexceptionable than all, by the earliest and most trustworthy witness on the Norman side, by the contemporary Tapestry . . . in every statement but one . . . . The Tapestry implies—*it can hardly be said directly to affirm*—that the consecrator was Stigand (iii. 582). The representation in the Tapestry is singular. *It does not show Stigand crowning or anointing Harold* (iii. 620).	He rejects the Tapestry's account of Harold's coronation, following Florence of Worcester's statement — that Harold was crowned by Aldred, Archbishop of York—in avowed opposition to his own reading of the Tapestry, *i.e.*, that Harold was crowned by Stigand.
It has been remarked by Mr. Planché and others, that at this point the order of time is forsaken; the burial of Eadward is placed before his deathbed and death. On this Dr. Bruce says *very truly*: "the seeming inconsistency is very easily explained," etc., etc. (iii. 587) . . I do not think that any one who makes the comparison minutely (between the Tapestry and the Life) will attach much importance to the sceptical remarks of Mr. Planché (*ib.*).	He rejects *in toto* the Tapestry's version of Edward the Confessor's death, for that "priceless record" makes *Edward buried before he died*! Mr. Freeman, and perhaps not altogether without reason, follows the saner notion of other authorities, that Edward died before he was buried (*E.H.R.*, ix. 607).

One would hardly imagine from Mr. Archer's sneers that Mr. Freeman had really vindicated the Tapestry from its "seeming inconsistency," did one not know him, as a writer, to be *capable de tout*.

important a part in the battle that Mr. Freeman found it needful to mention it at least a score of times, it is practically inconceivable that all the authorities I enumerate should have absolutely ignored its existence. Judging from Mr. Freeman's own experience, it would be simply impossible to describe the battle without mentioning the " palisade."

It is very significant that when we turn to a real feature of the English line, namely its close array, we find the above authorities as unanimous in mentioning the fact as they are in ignoring that " curious defence,"[88] those " intricate barriers," as Mr. Archer terms them, " upon the hill."[89]

The fight has raged so fiercely around this " palisade" that I have been obliged to discuss it at somewhat disproportionate length. But to sum up, we have now seen, firstly, that the alleged palisade was a new " development," and needs, as such, special proof of its existence ; secondly, that of Mr. Freeman's proofs, one at least must admittedly be abandoned, while he himself has impugned the other ;[40] thirdly, that the evidence, both positive and presumptive, is altogether opposed to the existence of a palisade. In the narrative of the battle we shall find Mr. Freeman interpolating the alleged defence solely from his own imagination, such references proving, on inquiry, to be imaginary and imaginary alone.[41]

---

[88] *Cont. Rev.*, p. 351.

[89] *Eng. Hist. Rev.*, ix. 607.

[40] I wish, as I have done throughout, to make it absolutely clear that I am here concerned only with Mr. Freeman's rendering of Wace. If we are to go outside that rendering and discuss Wace *de novo*, it is best to do so in a fresh section. This I hope to do below, when I shall discuss the question of his authority (which has not yet arisen), and shall also propound my own explanation of the now famous disputed passage.

[41] In my first article (*Q. R.*, July, 1892, pp. 15-16) I pointed out that the great weight attached to Mr. Freeman's statements had of course " secured universal acceptance" for the palisade, and that it figures "now in every history." Mr. Archer, in his latest paper, refers to these

remarks (*Eng. Hist Rev.*, ix. 602) and triumphantly charges me with self-contradiction in having myself once accepted it, like every one else. He refers to an incidental allusion by me in the *Dictionary of National Biography* so many years ago that I was unaware of its existence. I am particularly glad to be reminded of the fact that I did allude, in early days, to the "palisade" and to "Senlac," for it emphasizes the very point of my case, namely, that the mischievous superstition of Mr. Freeman's unfailing accuracy must be ruthlessly destroyed lest others should be taught, as I was, to accept his authority as supreme.

My opponent writes :—

"Mr. Round . . . in direct contradiction to the *Quarterly* reviewer, has found for it [the palisade] an authority in William of Poitiers, and *has gone far beyond Mr. Freeman himself in giving us the name of the man who first broke it down.*"

How has Mr. Archer produced the alleged "contradiction"? He has taken a passage from my notice of Robert de Beaumont, written years before I had made any independent investigation of the Battle of Hastings, and when I thought, like the rest of the world, that I might, here at any rate, safely follow Mr. Freeman, when it was only a matter of a passing allusion to the fight. The following parallel passages will prove, beyond the shadow of doubt, that I here merely followed Mr. Freeman, accepting his own authority—William of Poitiers—for the incident. Any one in my place would have done the same. But Mr. Archer asserts that, on the contrary, I went "far beyond Mr. Freeman himself in giving us the name of the man who first broke it down." Let us see if this definite statement is true :—

MR. FREEMAN.	MY ARTICLE.
The new castle was placed in the keeping of Henry, the younger son of Roger of Beaumont. A great estate in the shire also fell to Henry's elder brother, Robert, Count of Melent, who, at the head of the French auxiliaries, had been *the first to break down the English palisade* at Senlac—*Norman Conquest*, iv. [1871] 191-2. See also iii. 486, and *Will. Rufus*, i. 185, ii. 135, 402.	Of these [sons] Robert fought at Senlac . . . [and] was *the first to break down the English palisade* . . . he was rewarded with large grants in Warwickshire, and Warwick Castle was entrusted to his brother Henry.—*Dict. Nat., Biog.*, iv. 64. (Mr. Freeman's works, of course, are given among the authorities for the article.)

So much for Mr. Archer's assertion that I made an independent statement not found in Mr. Freeman's pages. It is obviously impossible to conduct a controversy with an opponent who does not restrict himself to fact.

B.H.   A A

THE SHIELD-WALL.

It is a pleasure to find myself here in complete agreement with Mr. Freeman. In his very latest study of the battle Mr. Freeman wrote as follows :—

> The English clave to the old Teutonic tactics. They fought on foot in the close array of the shield-wall.[42]

Mr. Archer says they cannot have done so.[43] There was also, according to Mr. Freeman, a barricade, in front of— and distinct from—the shield-wall, being a special development which, he tells us, "the foresight of Harold" had introduced on this occasion (pp. 444, 468). The barricade is denied by me, the shield-wall by Mr. Archer. Whichever of us is right, Mr. Freeman's accuracy is, in either case, equally impugned.

It is essential to remember that Mr. Freeman, throughout, treated the palisade and the shield-wall as *separate and distinct*. Thus he wrote so late as 1880—

> Besides the palisade the front ranks made a kind of inner defence with their shields, called the shield-wall. The Norman writers were specially struck with the close array of the English.[44]

So in his great work we read of "the shield-wall *and the* triple palisade still unbroken" (iii. 467). Later still "the shield-wall still stood *behind the* palisade" (p. 487). Even when "the English palisade was gone *the English shield-wall* was still a formidable hindrance in the way of the assailants (p. 491). The array of the shield-wall was still kept, though now without the help of the barricades" (p. 491). Here we have the very phrase of note NN, "the array of the shield-wall,"[45] and it is shown beyond question that Mr. Freeman's shield-wall, whatever Mr. Archer may

---

[42] *William the Conqueror* (1888), p. 90.
[43] " Had they done so, they must have been set so close that they could not have used their weapons with any freedom " (*Cont. Rev.*, p, 346).
[44] *Short History*, p. 79.
[45] *Norm. Conq.*, iii. 763, *ut supra.*

pretend, was quite distinct from the palisade, and was a shield-wall "pure and simple."

Let it also be clearly understood what Mr. Freeman meant by that "array of the shield-wall," of which the disputed passage in Wace was, he held, a description. He shows us the whole English army "ranged so closely together in the thick array of the shield-wall, that while they only kept their ground the success of an assailant was hopeless." [46] He describes them as, "a strong line, or rather wedge, of infantry, forming a wall with their shields," [47] and he ascribes their defeat to their "breaking the line of the shield-wall." [48]

Of this shield-wall my opponent rashly wrote :—

The Reviewer's (*sic*) theory of an extended shield-wall vanishes like smoke. If Wace is any authority . . . the question is settled once and for all. There was no extended shield-wall at Hastings. [49]

Of course, "the Reviewer's theory" here is no other than Mr. Freeman's own.

If, in spite of the above evidence, it should still be pretended by any one that the plain meaning of Mr. Freeman's words is not their meaning, I will refer them not to my own interpretation, but to that of Mr. Freeman's friend and colleague, the Rev. W. Hunt, who wrote in the historian's lifetime, "at his request" and by his "invitation," and whose proofs were revised by Mr. Freeman himself. [50] This is Mr. Hunt's version:—

Set in close array behind a palisade forming a kind of fortification, *shoulder to shoulder and shield to shield*, the army of Harold presented a steady and immovable front to the Norman attack . . . Fatal was the national formation of the English battle, when *men stood in the closest order, forming a wall with their shields*. While no mode of array could be stronger so long as the line remained unbroken it made it hard to form the line again. [51]

[46] *Ib.*, iii. p. 471.　　[47] i. 271 ; cf. *W.R.*, ii. 411.　　[48] iii. 732.
[49] *Cont. Rev.*, 348.
[50] *Norman Britain* (S. P. C. K.), p. vi.　　[51] *Ibid.*, pp. 79,80

So, again, in his life of Harold—

> All the heavy-armed force fought in close order, *shield touching shield*, so as to present a complete wall to the enemy.[52]

Here we have no tortuous imaginings, but, in plain and straightforward words, "what historians in general evidently mean" when they speak of a "shield-wall," what it meant to Mr. Freeman, what it means to Mr. Hunt, and it is admitted, to myself.[53] Such was the English shield-wall, according to Mr. Freeman, at "Senlac"; it was what Mr. Archer definitely declares it cannot possibly have been.

Lastly, as to the ground on which Mr. Archer pronounces impossible a continuous shield-wall [54]—namely, that the English could not have fought in such close order,[55] and that the axe-men being "shieldless . . . could not have formed the shield-wall"; one need only confront him with Mr. Freeman's words.

Mr. Freeman.	Mr. Archer.
Referring to the mode of fighting of an English army in that age, and to "the usual tactics of the shield-wall," Mr. Freeman wrote of "the close array of the battle-axe men" (p. 444). He had already written of "the English house carls with their . . . huge battle-axes," accustomed to fight in "the close array of the shield-wall." [56] "They still formed their shield-wall and fought with their great axes."[57]	It is enough for me that common sense, the tapestry, Wace,[58] our Italian chronicler, and his later Old French translator all show that the English axe-men could not or did not form the shield-wall (*E.H.R.*, ix. p. 14). Possibly they [the house carls] may have formed a genuine shield-wall; but while forming it they cannot have been *using* the "bipennis," or the two-handed axe (*E.H.R.*, p. 20, note).

[52] *Dict. Nat. Biography* (1890), xxx. 424.
[53] *Eng. Hist. Rev.*, ix. 2.
[54] *Cont. Rev.*, p. 348.
[55] *Ibid.*, p. 346.
[56] *Q.R.*, July, 1893, p. 90.
[57] *Old English History*, p. 335.
[58] Wace, of course, is the only one worth mentioning of the three last,

I am compelled to repeat what I said in the *Quarterly Review*.

> We almost hesitate to waste our own and our readers' time on a writer who, professing to vindicate Mr. Freeman's view as against us, devotes his energies to proving that view to be utterly absurd.[59]

Nor will Mr. Archer derive comfort from "our only English 'specialist' on mediæval warfare";[60] who holds, as I had pointed out, that "the English axemen" did fight "arranged in a compact mass."[61]

It is significant that the fact Mr. Archer so confidently rejects is precisely that on which I am at one with Mr. Freeman, Mr. Hunt, and Mr. Oman, and to which the original authorities bear witness with peculiar unanimity. Thus William of Poitiers, an authority of the first rank, describes the English as "maxime conferti," speaks of their "nimia densitas," and proceeds to dwell on the terrible effect of their weapon, the famous battle-axe. William of Malmesbury tells us that the axemen "impenetrabilem cuneum faciunt." Even Mr. Archer's authority, Wace, writes of these warriors :—

> A pie furent *serrement*.

Baudri describes the English as "consertos,"[62] and the *Brevis Relatio* as "spissum agmen." Bishop Guy writes of the "spissum nemus Angligenarum," and styles them "densissima turba"; Henry of Huntingdon, we saw, tells us that they were arranged "in una acie strictissime," and were thus "impenetrabiles Normannis."

and even his "decisive words" prove to be only a personal opinion (" *ço me semble*") that the axeman's shield must have hampered him (see *Cont. Rev.*, 348, and *N. C.*, iii. 765).

[59] *Q.R.*, July, 1893, p. 91.

[60] *Eng. Hist. Rev.*, ix. 607.

[61] Oman's *Art of War in the Middle Ages*, 24 (see *Q.R.*, July, 1893, p. 90).

[62] Compare (as Mr. Freeman does) Æthelred's description of the English array of the Battle of the Standard: "lateribus latera conseruntur."

No feature of the great battle is more absolutely beyond dispute. It was the denseness of the English ranks that most vividly struck their foes. "Shield to shield, and shoulder to shoulder," as Æthelred describes them at the Battle of the Standard, they wedged themselves together so tightly that the wounded could not move, nor even the corpses drop. And so they stood together, the living and the dead.[63]

And we must remember that this mass of men was "ranged so closely together in the thick array *of the shield-wall*, that while they only kept their ground the success of an assailant was hopeless."[64]   The Conqueror saw, Mr. Freeman reminds us, "that his only chance was to tempt the English to break their shield-wall."[65]   I need not insist on the point further: I need not even have said so much, but that some of those who read these pages may not have realised the true character of Mr. Archer's phantasies. The "scutorum testudo," as William of Malmesbury describes the famous shield-wall,[66] is depicted, with his usual pains-taking care, by the designer of the Bayeux Tapestry. We read of the "testudo" at Ashdown fight, even in the days of Alfred;[67] it was, again, with the shield-wall that "glorious Æthelstan" won the day on the hard-fought field of Brunanburh (937);[68] we hear of it at Maldon (991), where Brihtnoth, we read, "bade his men work the war-hedge,"— "that is, had made his men form the shield-wall, a sort of fortress made by holding their shields close together."[69] And we do, in Mr. Freeman's words, meet with it "down to the end," when the war-hedge of Maldon was wrought anew, by Harold, on the hill of battle, and stood once more as if a fortress—"quasi castellum."

[63] *Norm. Conq.*, iii. 491.   [64] *Ibid.*, p. 471.
[65] *Old English History*, p. 334.
[66] *Norm. Conq.*, iii. 764; cf. *Eng. Hist. Rev.*, ix. 18.
[67] "This is the *shield-wall*, the famous tactic of the English and Danes alike. We shall hear of it in all the great battles down to the end." (Freeman's *Old English History*, p. 112).
[68] *Ibid.*, p. 155.   [69] *Ibid.*, 196.

THE DISPOSITION OF THE ENGLISH.

To render clear the problem involved, I must first sketch as briefly as possible the nature of the ground the English held. The hill of battle is so fully described in Mr. Freeman's narrative that I here need only explain that it was a long narrow spur of the downs, running nearly east and west, of which the south front was defended by the English and attacked by the Normans. The one and only point that is certain is that "on the very crown of the hill," the site of the high altar in the future, was erected the standard of Harold.[70] This, then, the centre of the hill, was the centre of the English host. But the ground to which our attention is directed, as having "really played the most decisive part in the great event of the place," lay to the west of this, "where the slope is gentlest of all, where the access to the natural citadel is least difficult."[71] Mr. Freeman assumes that this ground—the "English right," as he terms it— where the "ascent is easiest in itself," was allotted to "the least trustworthy portion of the English army," to "the sudden levies of the southern shires."[72] For this assumption, I hasten to add, there is no authority whatever. He further assumes that the first English to leave their post, in pursuit of the enemy, "were, of course, some of the defenders of the English right."[73] William, he holds, at the crisis of the battle, resolved to draw them again from their post by a partial feigned retreat, that "meanwhile another division might reach the summit through the gap thus left open." Accordingly, tempted by this stratagem, "the English on the right wing rushed down and pursued," and their error proved "fatal to England."[74]

The Duke's great object was now gained; the main end of Harold's skilful tactics had been frustrated by the inconsiderate ardour of the least valuable portion of his troops. Through the rash descent of the light-armed on the right, the whole English army lost

---

[70] *N.C.*, III. p. viii. [71] *Ibid.*, 445-6
[72] *Ibid.*, 472. [73] *Ibid.*, 480. [74] *Ibid.*, pp. 488, 490.

its vantage-ground. The pursuing English had left the most easily accessible portion of the hill open to the approach of the enemy . . . The main body of the Normans made their way on to the hill, no doubt by the gentle slope at the point west of the present buildings. The great advantage of the ground was now lost; the Normans were at last on the hill.[76]

Such is Mr. Freeman's explanation of how the battle was won,[76] for in this episode he discovers the decisive turning-point of the day.[77] Now, let us consider what is involved in the theory here set forth. "Harold's skilful tactics," we find, consisted in entrusting his weakest point, the least defensible portion of his position, to "the least trustworthy portion of the English army." The natural result of these insane tactics was that his weak point was forced, and the English right turned.[78] And Mr. Freeman, having made this clear, complains of "the criticisms of monks on the conduct of a consummate general," and insists that "nowhere is Harold's military greatness so distinctly felt as when . . . we tread the battle-field of his own choice." But there is worse to come. Such tactics as these would have been mad enough, even if these raw peasants had stood behind a barricade; but if, as I hold, that barricade is a purely imaginary creation, we ask ourselves what would have happened to these unhappy creatures, protected by no "shield-wall," and armed with "such rustic weapons as forks and sharp stakes,"[79] when, first riddled by Norman arrows and then

---

[76] *Ibid.*, 490.

[76] "The battle was lost through the error of those light-armed troops who, in disobedience to the King's orders, broke their line to pursue" (*Ib.*, 505).

[77] "The day had now turned decidedly in favour of the invaders" (*Ib.*, 491). I am obliged to quote these two passages, because my opponents have not shrunk from impugning (*Cont. Rev.*, 353; *E.H.R.*, ix. 70) the accuracy of the words in the text (which are from *Q.R.*, July, 1892, p. 17).

[78] *Q.R.*, July, 1893, 101.

[79] *N.C.*, iii. 472.

attacked by Norman infantry, they were finally, broken and defenceless, charged by heavy cavalry. The first onslaught would have scattered them to the winds, and have won, in so doing, the key of the English position.[80] Remembering this, it is strange to learn that "the consummate general-ship of Harold is nowhere more conspicuously shown than in this memorable campaign," and that his was "that true skill of the leader of armies, which would have placed both Harold and William high among the captains of any age." But if the generalship of Harold was shown by entrusting to his worst troops his weakest and most important point, while posting "the flower of the English army" just where his ground was strongest, what are we to say of "the generalship of William, his ready eye, his quick thought," if he failed to detect and avail himself of this glaring blunder? For instead of concentrating his attack upon Harold's weak point, he left it to be assailed, we learn, by "what was most likely the least esteemed" portion of his host,[81] while he himself with his picked troops dashed him-self against an impregnable position like a mad bull against a wall. "We read," says Mr. Freeman, "with equal admiration of the consummate skill with which Harold chose his position and his general scheme of action, and of the wonderful readiness with which William formed and varied his plans." For myself, I should have thought that the tactics he describes—tactics which stirred him to a burst of admiration for "the two greatest of living captains"—would have disgraced the most incompetent commander that ever took the field.

But Harold, after all, was no fool. Are we then justified

[80] To have placed some of them as an advanced post on the "small detached hill" in front would have been to leave them *en l'air*, exposed to certain destruction from an attack which they could not check. For Mr. Freeman held that, even if occupied by an outpost, it was only by the "light-armed." (See *Q.R.*, July, 1893, pp. 99, 100.)

[81] On what ground are the Bretons so described? Guy, quoted by Mr. Freeman (iii. 459) writes of them here : "Gensque Britannorum quorum decus exstat in armis, Tellus ni fugiat est fuga nulla quibus."

in accusing him of this supreme folly? Mr. Freeman held that "the relative position of the different divisions in the two armies seems beyond doubt." There is, however, as I said, absolutely no evidence for Mr. Freeman's assumption that the English right was entrusted to the raw levies. Against it is the fact that in this quarter the first assault was soonest repulsed: against it also is all analogy drawn from the study of English tactics. Snorro's description of Stamfordbridge is evidence, at least, that "the fortress of shields" had a continuous line of bucklers along its whole front: Æthelred gives us the reason in his story of the Battle of the Standard; namely, that it was the front line which had to meet the shock ("periculosum dicebant si primo aggressu inermes armatis occurrerent"). It was therefore an essential principle of tactics "quatinus armati armatos impeterent, milites congrederentur militibus."[82] Therefore on Cowton Moor (1138), as (I hold) on the hill of Battle (1066), we find the "strenuissimi milites in prima fronte locati."[83]

The words "and the lighter troops behind them," which originally followed here, have been objected to by Miss Norgate, who had originally made the same statement,[84] but who now wishes to withdraw it.[85] Henry of Huntingdon, however,—like Æthelred, a contemporary authority— agrees with him in describing the dismounted knights, men with shields and *loricæ* like the "housecarls" at Hastings, as forming an "iron wall" along the English front.[86] If

[82] I have replied in *E.H.R.* (ix. 255) to Miss Norgate's characteristic quibble (*Ib.*, p. 75) that these quotations apply to the Scottish army alone— for the principle applies alike to "armati" and "armatos," to "milites" and to "militibus."

[83] Down to this point the present section is all reprinted from my original article (*Q.R.*, July, 1892), as not calling for any alteration or correction.

[84] "The general mass of the less well-armed troops of the shire in the rear." (*England under the Angevin Kings*, i. 290.)

[85] *E.H.R.*, ix. 611.

[86] When the Scotch, he writes, "amentatis missilibus et lanceis longis-

then mailed warriors formed the front line, it is difficult to
see where the " inermis plebs," as Æthelred terms it, could
be but " behind them." The fact is that the Battle of the
Standard, for which we have excellent authorities, is of no
small value for the study of the Battle of Hastings, as my
opponents seem to be uncomfortably aware. " The tactics,"
Mr. Freeman admits, " were English." We find there
again the same dense array,[87] the same tactics for defence,
though now rendered less passive by the development of
the bowman.[88] There can, I think, be little question, if we
combine the several accounts, that the Standard, with the
older chiefs around it, formed the kernel of the host;[89] that
the rude levies of the shire were massed round about them;[90]
and that the outer rim was formed by the mailed knights,

simis super aciem equitum nostrorum loricatam percutiunt, quasi muro
ferreo offendentes, impenetrabiles [compare the "impenetrabiles" ranks
of the English at Hastings, *supra*, p. 357] invenerunt . . . Equitantes
enim nulla ratione diu persistere potuerunt contra milites loricatos
pede persistentes et immobiliter coacervatos" (pp. 264-5). Miss Norgate
follows him, writing : "The wild Celts of Galloway dashed headlong upon
the English front, only to find their spears and javelins glance off from
the helmets and shields of the knights as from an iron wall."

[87] Tota namque gens Normannorum et Anglorum in una acie circum
Standard conglobata, persistebant immobiles" (Hen. Hunt.) "Australes,
quoniam pauci erant, in unum cuneum sapientissime glomerantur" (*Æth.
Riv.*)

[88] It is no less interesting than curious that the Bayeux Tapestry
enables us to see how the archers were combined with the mailed knights
at the Battle of the Standard. It shows us (on its principle of giving a
type) an English archer of whom Mr. Freeman has well observed :—"He
is a small man without armour crouching under the shield of a tall
Housecarl, like Teukros under that of Aias" (iii. 472). So Æthelred writes
that the mailed warriors "sagittarios ita sibi inseruerunt ut, *militaribus
armis protecti*, tanto acrius quanto securius vel in hostes irruerent, vel
exciperent irruentes."

[89] "Proceres qui maturioris ætatis fuerunt . . . circa signum
regium constituuntur, quibusdam altius ceteris in ipsa machina collatis"
(*Æth. Riv.*). "Circum Standard in pectore belli condensantur"(*Ric. Hex.*).

[90] "Reliqua autem multitudo undique conglomerata eos circum-
vallabat" (*Ib.*)

with the archers crouching for shelter behind their "iron wall."

Harking back to Sherstone fight (1016), we encounter precisely the same formation. "The King," Mr. Freeman writes, "placed his best troops in front, and the inferior part of his army in the rear." And he added, "we must remember these tactics when we come to the great fight of Senlac."[91] This was, unhappily, just what he failed to do. "William of Poitiers," he strangely complained, "has his head full of Agamemnon and of Xerxes, but this obvious analogy does not seem to have occurred to him." Have we also the reason why our author himself overlooked these obvious analogies in the fact that to illustrate the Battle of Hastings he quotes some five and twenty times from the Odyssey and the Iliad, from Herodotus and Xenophon, from Æschylus, Plutarch, and Dio Cassius; from Livy, Tacitus, Ammianus, and even Ælius Spartianus? In his later edition, however, he inserted in a footnote the words:— "On placing the inferior troops in the rear, see the tactics of Eadmund at Sherstone."[92] "In the *rear?*" Yes, but that is precisely my contention. The assumption that I am assailing is that they formed the *wings*.

But we are not even here at the end of Mr. Freeman's confusion. He had meanwhile, in another work, published about the same time as the first edition of his third volume, written thus:—

> As far as I can see, King Harold put these bad troops *in the back* . . . But his picked men he put *in front*, where the best troops of the enemy were likely to come.[93]

This is exactly my own view; it is that "essential principle of tactics" on which I have insisted throughout, and on which Miss Norgate has rashly endeavoured to pour contempt.[94] Mr. Freeman, moreover, further on, wrote of his "light armed" as "the troops *in the rear*,"[95] which is

[91] *N.C.*, i. 383. [92] *Ib.*, iii. 472.
[93] *Old English History*, p. 331.
[94] *E.H.R.*, ix. 75. [95] *Old English History*, p. 333.

again my contention. What seems to have happened is
that he got into his head (I can imagine how) that the
"light-armed" formed the wings, and arranged the battle
on that asssumption. Then remembering, when it was too
late, that, according to his own precedent, they ought to
have been in the rear, he hesitated to introduce a change
which would affect his whole theory of the battle, and
compel him to approach it *de novo*.[96]

But indeed, even apart from this, it seems doubtful,
examining Mr. Freeman's narrative, whether he had
formed a clear conception of how the English troops were
arranged, and whether, if so, he kept it in view, consistently, throughout. If we honestly seek to learn what his
conception was, a careful comparison of pp. 472, 473, 475,
490, and 505, with the ground-plan, will show that the
whole right wing was composed of "light-armed troops,
who broke their line to pursue." And this view seems to
be accepted and defended by Miss Norgate, who, writing as
his champion, declares that to her the conclusion embodied
in his ground-plan "seems irresistible."[97] On the other
hand, pp. 471, 480, 487, and 732 most undoubtedly convey
the impression that, as I have maintained, the heavy-armed
English were extended along the whole front,[98] and that
their defeat, in Mr. Freeman's words (p. 732) was "owing
to their breaking the line of the shield-wall." I suspect
that he was led thus to contradict himself by the obvious
concentration of his interest on "the great personal
struggle which was going on beneath the standard" (p.
487). Here, as is often the case throughout his work,
Mr. Freeman's treatment of his subject was essentially
dramatic. To bring his heroes into high relief, he thrust
into the background the rest of his scene as of compara-

---

[96] Miss Norgate, unable to deny the glaring "self-contradiction" involved in Mr. Freeman's words, dismisses it as a "matter of secondary
importance" (*E.H.R.*, ix. 74).

[97] *E.H.R.*, ix. 74.

[98] *Q.R.*, July, 1892, p. 19.

tively small account. In this spirit, for instance, he wrote :—

A new act in the awful drama of that day had now begun. The Duke himself, at the head of his own Normans, again pressed towards the standard. . . A few moments more and the mighty rivals might have met face to face, and the war-club of the Bastard might have clashed against the lifted axe of the Emperor of Britain (p. 483).

Homer, doubtless, would have made them meet; but a great dramatic opportunity was lost : the "mighty rivals" seem never to have got within striking distance. Meanwhile, however, the warring hosts are left quite in the background ; their fate is that of a stage crowd engaged in a stage battle. I do not mean, of course, that Mr. Freeman ignores them, but that he was so engrossed in the personal exploits of his heroes as to be impatient of that careful study which the battle as a whole required, and comparatively careless of consistency in his allusions to the English array.

The charge, in short, that I have brought throughout against the disposition of the English in Mr Freeman's narrative is that his view, "with all that it involves, was based on no authority, was merely the offspring of his own imagination, and was directly at variance with the only precedent that he vouched for the purpose."[99] There is absolutely not a scrap of evidence that—as shown on the "accurate" ground-plan—the English army was drawn up in three divisions, the "housecarls" forming the centre, and the "light-armed" the two wings. We do not even know that it formed an almost straight line.[100] The whole arrangement is sheer guesswork, and analogy, here our only guide, is wholly against it.

[99] *Q.R.*, July, 1893, pp. 102-3 ; cf. *Q.R.*, July 1892, p. 18 ; *E.H.R.*, ix. 254.

[100] It might, for all we know, have formed a crescent or semicircle, its wings resting strongly on the rear-slopes of the hill; or even a "wedge," as, indeed, Mr. Freeman twice described it (i. 271, iii. 471).

I cannot insist too strongly on the charge I have here made. It is no "matter of secondary importance";[101] nor is it the case that my argument as to the "palisade" is, as Mr. Archer pretended, "the only definite and palpable charge" that I bring "against Mr. Freeman's account of the great battle."[102] For, as I wrote from the very first, "rejecting Mr. Freeman's views on the grouping of the English host, we reject with them *in toto* the story he has built upon them."[103]

My own view is based upon the fact that, in the military tactics as in the military architecture of the age, the defence trusted largely to its power of passive resistance : this was the essential principle of the ponderous Norman keep ; and precisely as the walls of that keep were formed of an ashlar face of masonry backed by masses of rubble, so the fighting line of a force standing on the defensive was composed of a compact facing of heavily-armed troops backed by a rabble of half-armed peasants, or at best by what we may term the light infantry of the day. When the foe was advancing to the attack, these rear lines could discharge such weapons as they possessed—darts, arrows, stones, etc.,—from behind the shelter of their comrades,[104] while at the moment of actual shock they would form a passive backing, which would save the front ranks from being broken by the enemy's impact. As the great object of the attack was to break through the line, a formation which virtually gave the advantage now possessed by a solid over a hollow square would naturally commend itself to the defence.

---

[101] *E. H. R.*, ix. 74.   [102] *Cont. Rev.*, p. 353.

[103] *Q.R.*, July, 1892, p. 19.

[104] Since this passage appeared (as it stands) in my original article (*Q.R.*, July, 1892, p. 19), I have noted a curious confirmation in Æthelred's words where he speaks of the archers at the Battle of the Standard as "militaribus armis protecti [ut] tanto acrius quanto securius vel in hostes irruerent, vel exciperent irruentes." For, as I wrote (p. 20), "it would naturally be they who, like cavalry in modern times, would harass and follow up a retreating foe."

Now in these tactics we have the key to the true story of the battle. But, first, we must dismiss from our minds Mr. Freeman's fundamental assumption, and understand that the English "hoplites" were not massed in the centre, but were extended along the whole front, precisely as they were in battles fought both before and after. The fighting face of Harold's host was composed of this heavy soldiery, clad in helmets and mail. Arrayed in the closest order, they presented to an advancing enemy the aspect of a living rampart (quasi castellum ").

How the Normans attacked that rampart it will now be my task to show.

THE NORMAN ADVANCE.

From Telham Hill Duke William scanned that living rampart, and saw clearly that "his only chance was to tempt the English to break their shield-wall."[105] It is chiefly from Baudri's poem that we learn how he set about it.[106]

There is no question that the fight began with ance an adv of the Norman infantry. William of Poitiers and Bishop Guy are in complete accordance on the fact.[107] But as my description of the infantry has been challenged, [108] I may show that it is quite beyond dispute.[109] To my argument,

---

[105] *Old English History*, p. 334.

[106] For Baudri's poem see *Q.R.*, July, 1893, pp. 73-5. As to Baudri's authority, I need only repeat what I wrote in the *English Hist. Rev.* (ix. 217): "Mr. Archer endeavours, of course to pooh-pooh it. Now I call special attention to the fact that the test I apply to Baudri is that which Mr. Freeman applied to the Tapestry, the obvious test of internal evidence. But Mr. Archer's ways are not as those of other historians : instead of examining, as I did, Baudri's account in detail he dismisses it on the ground that the writer's ' description *of the world*' at that date could not be accurate (*Ib.*, 29). We are not dealing with his ' description of the world'; we are dealing with his lines on the battle of Hastings."

[107] *N.C.*, iii. 467, 477.

[108] *E.H.R.*, ix. 42-3, 603.

[109] Though I have already done so in *E.H.R.*, ix. 250.

as reprinted below, it has been objected that I fail "to take account of the distinction between light-armed and heavy-armed infantry."[110] It will be seen that my argument turns, not on the armour, but on the *weapons* of the foot. I have challenged my opponents to produce mention of any weapons but crossbows,[111] or bows and arrows, and need scarcely say that they cannot.

Describing the "armour and weapons of the Normans," Mr. Freeman, avowedly following the Tapestry, represented the infantry as all archers,[112] and divided them into two classes: (1) "those "without defensive harness"; (2) those who "wore the defences common to the horse and foot of both armies . . . the close-fitting coat of mail . . . and the conical helmet."[113] Now this division is exactly reproduced in the words of William of Poitiers, who divides his "pedites" into two classes, distinguished only by the fact that in one were the "firmiores et loricatos." He does not say that the latter were *not* archers, or crossbowmen, nor did Mr. Freeman venture to assign them any other weapons.[114] Bishop Guy, moreover, distinctly tells us that they were crossbowmen (*vide infra*). The advance,

---

[110] *E.H.R.*, ix. 42.

[111] Mr. Freeman rendered the "sagittis armatos et balistis" of William by "archers, slingers, and crossbowmen." "Balistæ" can hardly mean slings *and* crossbows, and I think, on consideration, it is best referred to the latter; but the question is not of much importance.

[112] So, too, in *Arch. Journ.*, xl. 359: "You may call up the march of archers and horsemen across the low ground between the hills."

[113] *N.C.*, iii. 462. I regret that I must call attention to the fact that I gave (*E.H.R.*, ix. 250) this precise reference for my statement that, according to Mr. Freeman, the infantry were all archers, explaining that in another passage (p. 467) William of Poitiers had led him to take a somewhat different view. Mr. Archer, however, has printed (*E.H.R.*, ix. 603) the other passage (p. 467) in triumph by the side of my statement. He further denies that Mr. Freeman held, even on p. 462, that the infantry were all archers. Anyone can test the value of Mr. Archer's denial for himself by referring to *N.C.*, iii. 462, where he will find that Mr. Freeman, describing the Norman host, mentions no infantry but archers.

[114] As he had merely copied from the Tapestry on p. 462, so he copied William of Poitiers on p. 467.

therefore, in modern language, consisted of skirmishers, represented by archers and perhaps some crossbowmen; supports, namely, crossbowmen who, as a somewhat superior class, would mostly have defensive armour; and, lastly, the cavalry as reserve.[115]

Now what was the intention of this advance? Mr. Freeman assumed, without hesitation, that the foot "were to strive to break down the palisades . . . and so to make ready the way for the charge of the horse" (p. 467); that "the infantry were, therefore, exposed to the first and most terrible danger" (*ib.*); "that the French infantry had to toil up the hill, and to break down the palisade" (p. 477).[116] But we find, on reference, that the above writers say nothing of any such intention, and do not even mention the existence of a palisade.[117] Moreover, the only weapons

---

[115] The distinction between archers and crossbowmen is of little or no consequence, the missile being common to both.

[116] My opponents complain that in the former passage Mr. Freeman assigns this task to "the heavier foot" only; but my point is that no palisade is here mentioned, and no attack on it by *any* infantry, heavy or light, and no weapons assigned to that infantry of any use for the purpose.

[117] This is an excellent instance of what I said as to Mr. Freeman's "imaginary" references to the now famous palisade. I have challenged my opponents to disprove my statement that none of Mr. Freeman's own authorities says anything here of a palisade. And, of course, they cannot do so.

Here is another instance in point. We read on pp. 486-7 that Robert of Beaumont was specially distinguished in the work of breaking down the "barricade" (see also *supra*, p. 353). But when we turn to William of Poitiers, the authority cited, we find no mention of a "barricade," but read only of him "irruens ac sternens magnâ cum audaciâ." As the writer had just described how the Duke "*stravit* adversam gentem," we see that Robert, in his charge, laid low, not a barricade, but "adversam gentem."

This brings me to an extraordinary case of mediæval plagiarism. The author of the Ely history has applied this description of Robert's exploits to the Conqueror himself at Ely (*Liber Eliensis*, pp. 244-5). The passages "Exardentes Normanni—deleverunt ea," "Egit enim quod—magna cum audaciâ," "Scriptor Thebaidos vel Æneidos," *et sq.*, are all "lifted" bodily from William's narrative of the Battle of Hastings and applied to the storming of the Isle of Ely!

they speak of are crossbows and bows and arrows, which
are scarcely the tools for pioneers. But William of Poitiers
puts us on the track of a very different explanation:
"Pedites itaque Normanni propius accedentes *provocant*
Anglos, missilibus in eos vulnera dirigunt atque necem."
Here Baudri comes to our aid :—

> Nam neque Normannus consertos audet adire
>   Nec valet a cuneo quemlibet excipere.
> Arcubus utantur dux imperat atque balistis ;
>   Nam prius has mortes Anglia tunc didicit.
> Tunc didicere mori quam non novere sagitta
>   Creditur a cælo mors super ingruere
> Hos velut a longe comitatur militis agmen,
>   Palantes post se miles ut excipiat.

The Normans dared not face the serried ranks of the English: the maxim that cavalry should not charge unbroken
infantry was asserting itself already. But the only means
of breaking those ranks, of throwing the English into confusion, was to gall them by archers and slingers till some
of them should sally forth, when their assailants would
turn tail and leave them to be caught in the open and
ridden down. As Bishop Guy expresses it :—

> Præmisit pedites committere bella sagittis,
>   Et balistantes inserit in medio,
> Quatinus infigant volitantia vultibus arma,
>   Vulneribusque datis ora retro faciant,
> Ordine post pedites sperat stabilire Quirites.

These tactics, says Baudri, were crowned with success; the
maddened English, as they dashed forth to strike their
tormentors to the ground, were cut off in every direction
by the horsemen waiting their chance :—

> Tunc præ tristitia gens effera præque pudore
>   Egreditur palans, insequiturque vagos.
> Normanni simulantque fugam fugiuntque fugantes,
>   Intercepit eos undique præpes equus.
> Ilico cæduntur ; sic paulatim minuuntur,
>   Nec minuebatur callidus ordo ducis.

This account is both intelligible and consistent, but differs wholly from that of Mr. Freeman. It had, however, been virtually anticipated by Mr. Oman, who in his *Art of War in the Middle Ages* (p. 25), points out, with much felicity, that

the archers, if unsupported by the knights, could easily have been driven off the field by a general charge. United, however, by the skilful tactics of William, the two divisions of the invading army won the day. The Saxon mass was subjected to exactly the same trial which befell the British squares in the battle of Waterloo : incessant charges by a gallant cavalry were alternated with a destructive fire of missiles. Nothing can be more maddening than such an ordeal to the infantry soldier, rooted to the spot by the necessities of his formation.

Let us compare the two theories. Mr. Freeman's, here again, is not even consistent. He first tells us that for the knights to charge, with "the triple palisade still unbroken, would have been sheer madness"; in fact it was "altogether useless" for them to advance until the infantry had broken down the palisade.[118] But this the infantry failed to do,[119] whereupon—the cavalry charged "the impenetrable fortress of timber" (p. 479)! One is surely reminded of the immortal Don, when "a todo el galope de Rocinante," he charged the windmill.

My own theory involves no such inconsistencies. I hold —not as a conjecture based on a hypothetical palisade, but on the excellent authority of Baudri and William of Poitiers, that the infantry were used for the definite purpose of galling the English by their missiles, and so enticing them to leave their ranks and become a prey to the horse. As soon as their line had thus been broken, the cavalry were to charge.

Up to this point, the English army, as a whole, had kept

---

[118] *N.C.*, iii. 467.

[119] "The Norman infantry had now done its best, but that best had been in vain" (*Ib.* 479).

its formation; but now the strain on its patience had become too great to be borne. Breaking its ranks, with one accord, the whole host rushed upon its foes, and drove them before it in confusion right up to the Duke's post:—

> Tandem jactura gens irritata frequenti,
>   Ordinibus spretis irruit unanimis.
> Tunc quoque plus solito fugientum terga cecidit,
>   Et miles vultum fugit ad usque ducis.

This explains what had always been to me a difficulty, namely, the panic-stricken flight of the Normans at this stage of the battle. That they should have "lost heart" (p. 480) at the firmness of the English is natural enough; but that they should have "turned and fled" (*ib.*) from a force which did not pursue them seemed improbable. The difficulty is solved by Baudri's mention of the wild onslaught by the English. Moreover, Bishop Guy's description of the rout of the assailants—which Mr. Freeman assigned to this stage of the battle—agrees well with that of Baudri :—

> Anglorum populus, numero superante, repellit
>   Hostes inque retro compulit ora dari ;
> Et fuga ficta prius fit tunc virtute coacta ;
>   Normanni fugiunt, dorsa tegunt clipei.

Again, Baudri's poem suggests a novel view by its definite statement that the Normans in their flight reached the Duke's post. Mr. Freeman imagined that the Duke himself had been fighting in the front line (pp. 479, 480), but a careful comparison of his two authorities, William of Poitiers and Bishop Guy (p. 482), will show that, on the contrary, they support Baudri's statement. Each speaks of the Duke as "meeting" (*occurrens—occurrit*) the fugitives, a difficulty which Mr. Freeman evaded by writing that "he met *or pursued* the fugitives."

From this flight the Normans were rallied by the desperate efforts of the Duke himself, who, as is usual at such moments, was believed to have fallen. I deem this episode a fixed point, and it conveniently divides the battle. All our four leading authorities—the Tapestry, William of Poitiers, Bishop Guy, and Baudri—are here in complete agreement. William describes the Duke as "nudato insuper capite"; Guy tells us that "iratus galea nudat et ipse caput"; Baudri writes "subito galeam submovet a capite"; in the Tapestry, "William (writes Dr. Bruce), when he wishes to show himself in order to contradict the rumour that he has been killed, is obliged to lift his helmet almost off his head" (p. 98). It is singular that so striking and well-established an episode is wholly ignored by Wace.

THE FOSSE DISASTER.

The serious character of the assailants' flight is duly recognised by Mr. Freeman.[120] We could have no more eloquent witness to the fact than the admission even by William of Poitiers that the Duke's Normans themselves gave way, or the description of them by Bishop Guy as "gens sua victa." The only point in question here is whether what I call "the fosse disaster" was an incident of this headlong flight or happened at a later stage of the battle. Mr. Freeman, discussing "the order of events,"[121] faced the difficulty frankly, observing that Guy had placed the feigned flight before what I have termed above the dividing incident of the day, and that this view "may be thought to be confirmed by the Tapestry," etc., etc. We have here perhaps the most difficult problem raised in the course of the battle, and one which it would be easier and safer to pass over in silence. As to Guy, I suggest, as a possible solution—it does not profess to be more—that what he was describing was not the great feigned flight but the lesser manœuvres of the same character described by Baudri above. He may, of course, have transferred to these the importance of the later episode. On the real flight, at least, he is sound. Of the

[120] *N. C.*, iii. p. 481.   [121] *N. C.*, iii. 767-8.

Tapestry I would speak with more confidence. " In the nature of things," Mr. Freeman wrote, "exact chronological order is not its strongest point" (p. 768). But in this case there was nothing to make it depart from that order, no reason why it should not place the incident of "the fosse disaster" after the central incident of the day, instead of before, if that were its right position. Moreover, it is here, we find, in the closest agreement with Wace; and though I claim, as did Mr. Freeman, the right of rejecting his testimony when wholly unsupported (and still more, when opposed to probability), yet such marked agreement as this is not to be lightly cast aside.

In any case, nothing can be more unfortunate than Mr. Freeman's treatment of what he describes as the "great slaughter of the French in the western ravine" (p. 489). This is a scene invented by Mr. Freeman alone, and illustrates the peculiar use he made, at times, of his authorities. There is no question that the Norman knights suffered, in the course of the day, at least one such disaster as the nobles of France at Courtrai (1302) or her cuirassiers at Waterloo. But five authorities, so far as one can see, place the incident in the thick of the battle, while three others assign it to the pursuit of the defeated English. It is not strange, therefore, that some writers should have held that there was but one such incident : Mr. Freeman, however, holds that there were two; and I expressly disclaim questioning his view, the matter being one of opinion. Assuming then, as he does, that the episode occurred in the course of the battle, I turn to the spirited version of Wace, as Mr. Archer defies me to "impeach Wace's authority" (p. 346). The "old Norman poet" is here very precise. He first tells us (ll. 7869-70, 8103-6) that the English had made a " fosse," which the Normans had passed unnoticed in their advance.[122] These passages Mr. Freeman accepts

[122] " Un fosse ont d'une part fait
Qui parmi la champaigne vait

. . . . .

without question (p. 476). But then Wace proceeds to
state (ll. 8107-20) that the Normans, driven back, as we
have seen, by the English, tumbled, men and horses, into
this treacherous "fosse" and perished in great numbers.
Now Wace, far from standing alone, is here in curiously
close agreement with the Tapestry of Bayeux. Two successive scenes in that "most authentic record" are styled
" Hic ceciderunt simul Angli et Franci in prœlio ; hic Odo
episcopus baculum tenens confortat pueros." Wace describes these scenes in thirty-six lines (ll. 8103-8138).
devoting eighteen lines to the first and the same number
to the second. Actual comparison alone can show how
close the agreement is. Henry of Huntingdon, we may
add, independently confirms the statement that English as
well as French perished in the fatal fosse.[128]

Now all this is quite opposed to Mr. Freeman's "conception of the battle." He had, therefore, to adapt, with no
gentle hands, his authorities to his requirements. Cin-
derella's step-mother, when her daughter's foot could not
be got into the golden shoe, armed herself, we read, with
axe and scissors, and trimmed it to the requisite shape.
With no less decision the late Professor set about his own
task. Wace's evidence he simply suppressed ; Henry of
Huntingdon's he ignored ; but that of the Bayeux Tapestry
could not be so easily disposed of. I invite particular
attention to his treatment of this, his "highest authority."
Retaining in its natural place (pp. 481-2) the second of the
two scenes we have described, he threw forward the one

> En la champaigne out un fosse :
> Normanz l'aueient adosse
> En beliuant l'orent passé
> Ne l'aueint mie esgarde."

I had followed Taylor in my rendering of this passage ; but Miss Norgate (*E. H. R.*, ix. 46) would prefer to say that the Normans did not heed,
than that they did not notice the fosse. "The passage," as she says, "is
somewhat obscure."

[128] Miss Norgate has rightly pointed out (ix. 47) that Henry places the
disaster during the great feigned flight.

preceding it to a later stage of the battle (p. 490). Nor did his vigorous adaptation stop even here. The scene thus wrenched from its place depicts a single incident : mounted Normans are tumbling headlong into a ditch at the foot of a mound, on which "light-armed" English stand assailing them with their weapons. The fight is hand to hand ; the bodies touch. And yet the Professor treats this scene as a description of two quite separate events happening at a distance from each other. These he terms (p. 489) the "stand of the English at the detached hill"; and the "great slaughter of the French in the western ravine." But on referring to his own ground-plan, we find that this "ravine" and the "detached hill" were a quarter of a mile apart, with the slopes of the main hill between them.

My criticism here is twofold. In the first place, Mr. Freeman endeavoured to conceal the liberties he had taken with his leading authority. No one would gather from his narrative of the battle that any such violence had been used ; nor would anyone who read of the "hill" episode that "the scene is vividly shown in the Tapestry" (p. 489), and, subsequently, of the "ravine" disaster, that "this scene is most vividly shown in the Tapestry" (p. 490), imagine that "the incidents of the ravine and the little hill" (p. 768) are in the Tapestry one and the same. In the second place, the large part which the writer's own imagination plays in his narrative of the fight is here clearly seen. There is nothing, for instance, in any authority to connect "the western ravine" with "the great slaughter of the French." It is placed by those who mention it in a "fosse," "fossatum," or "fovea." "If Wace is any authority," to quote Mr. Archer's words "the question is settled once and for all"; [124] the slaughter took place not in the "ravine," but in a ditch which according to him, the English had dug to the south of the hill, and which, according to Henry of Huntingdon, they

[124] *Cont. Rev.*, p. 348.

had cunningly concealed. Mr. Freeman produces no authority in support of his own fancy ; his only argument is that the slaughter

must have happened somewhere to the south or south-west of the hill. The small ravine to the south-west seems exactly what is wanted (p. 771).

The "western ravine," however, does not fulfil these requirements (see ground-plan, where it lies to the north-west of the hill); while Wace's "fosse," which—though here ignoring it—he had already accepted, lay, as required, to the south of the hill. Wace mentions another instance (ll. 1737-50) in which this stratagem was adopted,[125] but whether our ditch was dug, as he states, expressly or not, the fact of its existence does not depend on his evidence alone.

To resume : accepting provisionally Mr. Freeman's view (iii. 770) that there were two disasters to the horse, one "happening comparatively early in the battle," and the other "which William of Poitiers, Orderic and the Battle chronicler place at the very end of the battle," as occurring in the pursuit of the defeated English, we find that the former is mentioned by five writers. The Tapestry and Wace agree absolutely in making it an episode of the real flight of the Normans before the great rally ; Henry of Huntingdon assigns it to the great feigned flight, later in the battle ; William of Malmesbury seems to make it happen during the pursuit by the Normans after their feigned flight ; the anonymous writer quoted by Andresen (ii. 713) from Le Prevost may be left out of the question. Yet, in spite of all this contradiction, Mr. Freeman assigns this

---

[125] Compare the death of Robert Marmion, at Coventry, under Stephen, when he fell into one of the ditches he had dug to entrap the enemy's horse. The passage quoted by Andresen in his Wace (ii. 713) from Michel's notes to Benoit is very precise : —" Fecerant autem Angli foveam quandam caute et ingeniose, quam ipsi ex obliquo curantes maximam multitudinem Normannorum in ea præcipitaverant. Et plures etiam ex eis insequentes et tracti ab aliis in eadem perierunt."

striking episode, not as a conjecture, but as historic fact, to the pursuit of the English by the "Bretons" [126] after the feigned flight (p. 489). Let me make my position clear. We expect an historian to weigh, as an expert, the evidence before him : we look to him for guidance where that evidence is conflicting. But we have a right to protest against the statement, as historic fact, of hypotheses which cannot be established, and which are quite possibly wrong. Where the evidence is flatly contradictory, the fact that it is so should be made clear ; conflicting statements should not be evaded, nor evidence, such as that of the Tapestry, appealed to, when it proves to be opposed to, not in favour of, the writer's hypothesis. Dealing with the Conqueror's march on London, after his great victory, Mr. Parker has insisted with much force, on the principle for which I am contending.

Though, by leaving out here and there the discrepancies, the residue may be worked up into a consecutive and consistent series of events, such a process amounts to making history, not writing it. Amidst a mass of contradictory evidence, it is impossible to arrive at any sure conclusion. . . . It is, however, comparatively easy to piece together such details as will fit of the various stories, and still more easy to discover reasons for the results which such mosaic work produces. . . . [but] it cannot be reasonably regarded as real history. The method by which the results are obtained bears too close a resemblance to that by which . . . some of the legends described in the fifth chapter have come to be accepted as historical narratives. [127]

That is the danger. Such a narrative as that which Mr. Freeman has given us must "come to be accepted as historical" if allowed to pass current without a grave warning. It will doubtless be replied that in his appendices, he frankly admits that "it is often hard to reconcile the various accounts" ; but the question at issue is whether one is justified when, as here, the various accounts are not

---

[126] See below, p. 380.
[127] *Early Oxford*, pp. 191, 192. And see my preface.

only " hard " but impossible to reconcile, in constructing a definite narrative at all, instead of honestly admitting that the matter must be left in doubt.

THE GREAT FEIGNED FLIGHT.

There is no feature of the famous battle more familiar or more certain than that of the feigned retreat. It is necessary here to grasp Mr. Freeman's view, because he discovers in this manœuvre and its results the decisive turning point of the day.[128]

That there was a great feigned flight, which induced a large portion of the English to break their formation and pursue their foes, is beyond question.[129]   But Mr. Freeman, on this foundation, built up a legend, for which, we shall find, there exists no evidence whatever. He first assumed that it was "most likely" the left wing of the assailants which "turned in seeming flight"[130] (p. 488), and that it was, consequently, "the English on the right wing" who " rushed down and pursued them." Thus—

Through the rash descent of the light-armed on the right, the whole English army lost its vantage ground. The pursuing English had left the most easily accessible portion of the hill open to the approach of the enemy (p. 490).

The result, of course, was that "the main body of the Normans made their way on the hill, no doubt by the gentle slope " at this point (*ib.*).

The great advantage of the ground was now lost; the Normans were at last on the hill. Instead of having to cut their way up the slope, and through the palisades, they could now charge to the east right against the defenders of the standard (*ib.*).

[128] See above, p. 360, for Mr. Freeman's view.

[129] Angli vero, illos putantes vere fugere, cœperunt post eos currere volentes eos si possent interficere" (*Brevis Relatio*).   "Ausa sunt, ut superius, aliquot millia quas ivolante cursu, quos fugere putabant urgere (*Will. Pict.*).

[130] Though admitting, in a footnote, that the "Brevis Relatio" was opposed to this assumption.

These words are most important. They set forth Mr. Freeman's theory that Harold now found the Normans charging down upon his right flank instead of attacking him in front. It was in this sense I wrote "that his weak point was forced, and the English right turned," as the natural result of the "insane" tactics attributed to him by his champion.[181] The manœuvre assigned by Mr. Freeman to the Duke is, in fact, that by which Marlborough won the battle of Ramillies, where he got on to the hill by dislodging the French right, and then wheeled to his own right, outflanking the French centre.

When we turn from this elaborate theory to the authorities on which it is supposed to be based, we find, with some astonishment, that it is all sheer imagination. William of Poitiers, on whom the writer seemed mainly to rely for the feigned flight, states that—

Normanni sociaque turba ┆ . . terga dederunt, fugam ex industriâ simulantes—

words which distinctly imply that this feigned flight was general. Henry of Huntingdon merely writes: "Docuit Dux Willelmus *genti suæ* fugam simulare." No one, certainly, says or implies that it was restricted to the left wing. As for the theory that "the main body of the Normans" were, by this manœuvre, enabled to seize the western portion of the hill, and thus attack Harold on his flank, it is more imaginary, if possible, still.

The fact is that, as I explained in my original article,[182] Mr. Freeman had wholly misconceived the nature of William's manœuvre. The feigned flight was not a simple (as he supposed), but a combined movement. The best account of that movement is found in the Battle Chronicle :—

Tandem strenuissimus Boloniæ comes Eustachius clam, callida præmeditata arte—fugam cum exercitu duce simulante—super Anglos sparsim agiliter insequentes cum manu valida a tergo irruit, *sicque et*

[181] *Supra*, p. 360   [182] *Q.R.*, July, 1892, p. 20.

duce hostes ferociter invadente ipsis interclusis utrinque prosternuntur innumeri.

This precise statement, which Mr. Freeman omits, [188] affords the clue we seek, explaining the words of William of Poitiers, "interceptos et inclusos undique mactaverunt." The retreat of the pursuing English was cut off by the Count's squadrons, and, caught "between two fires," they were cut down and butchered. The supposition that, while this was going on, the main body of the Normans was riding on to the hill is baseless. The whole host, we have seen, were below, surrounding the English who had left the hill. Had Mr. Freeman kept in mind, as he had intended to do, the employment of this old Norman device at the relief of Arques (1053), he would have seen more clearly what really happened. But this, precisely as with his Sherstone precedent, he failed to do.

THE RELIEF OF ARQUES.

To illustrate the feigned flight by analogy, I append this passage relating to the stratagem at Arques.

A plan was speedily devised; an ambush was laid; a smaller party was sent forth to practise that stratagem of pretended flight which Norman craft was to display thirteen years later [1066] on a greater scale. The Normans turned; the French pursued; presently the liers-in-wait were upon them, and the noblest and bravest of the invading host were slaughtered or taken prisoners before the eyes of their king (iii. 133).

The manœuvre is elaborately described by Wace (ll. 3491-3514) in a passage which ought to be compared, in places, with that on the great "feinte fuie" itself (ll. 8203-8270).

---

[188] Miss Norgate has indignantly retorted (*E.H.R.*, ix. 50) that Mr. Freeman "only" omitted the words from "sicque" onwards. But it is precisely on these words that my statement is based. Mr. Freeman, moreover, did not even quote the rest *à propos* of the feigned flight, where we should look for it.

He carefully distinguishes the two parties essential to the stratagem :—[184]

> Partie pristrent des Normanz,
> Des forz e des mielz cumbatanz,
>
> .   .   .   .   .
>
> Puis pristrent une autre partie, etc., etc.

The latter detachment turned in flight and decoyed some of the leading Frenchmen past the spot where the ambush was laid. Then, facing round, they caught their rash pursuers "between two fires." I have shown above, from the "precise statement" which is found in the "Battle Chronicle," that the great manœuvre which deceived the English was a similarly combined one. Mr. Freeman, completely missing this point, makes the Norman "division," which did not take part in the flight "ride up the hill," (p. 490) where its slopes were deserted, whereas, on the contrary, they thrust themselves between the pursuers and the hill, and then charged on their rear, riding, of course, not on to, but away from the hill.

So close is the Arques parallel that in Wace we find the same words occurring in both cases :—

A cels kis alouent chazant
E quis alouent leidissant
Sunt enmi le vis tresturne,
E Franceis sunt a els mesdle (ll. 3501-4;

Engleis les aloent gabant
E de paroles laidissant

.   .   .   .   .

Torne lor sunt enmi le vis

.   .   .   .   .

E as Engleis entremesler (ll. 8241-2, 8262-4);

while William of Malmesbury describes the French king as thus "astutia insidiis exceptus," just as he describes Harold, in turn as thus "astutiâ Willelmi circumventus." Mr. Freeman quoted both passages, yet failed to note the parallel.

---

[184] So does Will. Gem., as quoted by Mr. Freeman (iii. 133) :—" de suis miserunt si quos forte hostium a regio cœtu abstraherent, qous illi in latibulis degentes incautos exciperent." See also my Addenda.

I speak, it will be seen, of "the relief of Arques." As my critic so rashly assumed that in my original article I exhausted Mr. Freeman's errors,[185] I may point out that this subject introduces us, at once, to fresh ones. Our author, for instance, held that Arques was not relieved. Let us see. We are first rightly told, on the authority of William of Poitiers, that the Duke blockaded the stronghold (*munitio*) by erecting a *castellum* at its foot (p. 128). On the next page we are told that the latter was "a wooden tower"— which is precisely what it was not—and that it "is described as a *munitio*" by William of Poitiers, whereas that term, as we have just seen, denoted, on the contrary, the rebel stronghold itself. Then we are told that the French king marched to the relief of the rebels, bringing with him "a good stock of provisions, of corn, and of wine" for the purpose, but "was far from being successful in his enterprise" (p. 131). In fact, he "went home, having done nothing towards the immediate object of his journey—the relief of the besieged" (p. 137). Mr. Freeman added in a note: "So I understand the not very clear statement of William of Poitiers that the King went away." Now, William's statement (which is quoted by him) is absolutely clear :—

Perveniens tamen quo ire intenderat, Rex exacerbatissimis animis summâ vi præsidium attentavit : Willelmum ab ærumnis uti eriperet, pariter decrementum sui, stragem suorum vindicaret.

The King, that is, in spite of the ambush, reached his destination (the blockaded stronghold) and then furiously attacked the *castellum* below, with the double object of raising the blockade and of avenging the death of his followers. Wace is, if possible, even more explicit. After describing the affair of the ambush, he proceeds thus :—

> Les somiers fist apareilier,
> La garisun prendre e chargier,
> *A la tur d' Arches fist porter,*
> Il meisme fu al mener (II. ll. 3519-3522).

[185] *Cont. Rev.*, p. 354.

Arques, therefore, was duly relieved ; the blockading party being only strong enough to defend, when attacked, its own *castellum*.

We will certainly not say of Mr. Freeman that he had not read his Wace "with common care"—to quote from his criticism on Professor Pearson—but really, when *more suo* he corrected *ex cathedrâ* the faults of others, he might at least have made sure of his facts. We will take (from the narrative of the Battle of Hastings) the case of the knighting of Harold on the eve of the Breton war :—

WACE.	MR. FREEMAN.
E Heraut out iloc geu,	Mr. Planché says that Wace
E par la Lande fu passez,	lays the scene at Avranches. He
Quant il fu al duc amenez,	probably refers to the Roman de
Qui a Aurenches donc esteit	Rou, 13723, but the knighthood
E en Bretaigne aler deueit,	is not there spoken of (p. 229).
La le fist li dus chevalier	
[ll. 13720--25].	

But it is only the feigned flight that connects the Battle of Hastings with Arques and its blockade. We read, as the battle is about to begin, of "the aged Walter Giffard, the lord of Longueville, the hero of Arques and Mortemer" (p. 457). As our author breaks the thread of his narrative (pp. 128-137) to tell us in detail about those whose names occur in it, we need not scruple in this instance to do the same. Turning back, therefore, we read :—

The chief who now commanded below the steep of Arques lived to refuse to bear the banner of Normandy below the steep of Senlac . . . and to found, like so many others among the baronage of Normandy, a short-lived earldom in the land which he helped to conquer (p. 123).

In the act of that refusal he is thus described :—

Even in the days of Arques [1053] and Mortimer [1054] he was an aged man, and now [1066] he was old indeed ; his hair was white, his arm was failing (p. 465).

B. II.   C. C.

Yet we meet the veteran again, a generation later, as "old Walter Giffard, now [1090] Earl of Buckingham, in England . . . the aged warrior of Arques and Senlac" (*W. R.*, i. 231). "Nor do we wonder," we read, "to find," among the supporters of William Rufus in 1095, "the name of Walter Giffard, him (*sic*) who appeared as an aged man forty years before" (*W. R.*, i. 472). But even Mr. Freeman admits that, "we are somewhat surprised to find," among the opponents of Henry I. in 1101, "now at the very end of his long life, the aged Walter Giffard, lord of Longueville, and Earl of Buckingham" (*W. R.*, ii. 395). Surprised? We are indeed ; for, if he was "an aged man" half a century before, what must he have been when he joined the rebels in 1101? It reminds one of a delightful passage in the quaint "Memorie of the Somervells," where the artless author, speaking of the action, in 1213, of his ancestor "being then near the nyntieth and fourth year of his age," observes :—

What could have induced him . . . to join himself with the rebellious barrons at such an age, when he could not act any in all human probabilitie, and was as unfit for counsel, is a thing to be admired, but not understood or knowne.

One need scarcely point out that Mr. Freeman has confused two successive bearers of the name. The confusion is avoided by the Duchess of Cleveland in her work on "The Battle Abbey Roll," as it had been by Planché and previous writers.

I here notice it chiefly as illustrating Mr. Freeman's ready acceptance of even glaring improbabilities.

But one of the most singular flaws in the late Professor's work was his evident tendency to confuse two or more persons bearing the same name. Three or four Leofstans of London were rolled by him into one ; Henry of Essex was identified with a Henry who had a different father and who lived in Cumberland ; while a whole string of erroneous conclusions followed, we saw, from identifying Osbern "filius Ricardi" with Osbern "cognomine Pentecost."[136] It is strange that one who was so severe on confusion of identity where places were concerned[137] should have been, in the case of persons, guilty of that confusion.

SUMMARY.

I would now briefly recapitulate the points I claim to have established. We have seen, in the first place, that Mr. Freeman's disposition of the English forces is, with all that it involves, nothing but a sheer guess—a guess to which he did not consistently adhere, and to which his own precedent, moreover, is directly opposed. Secondly, as to the "palisade" which formed, according to him, so prominent a feature of the battle, we have found that of the passages he vouched for its existence only one need even be considered; and that one, according to himself, where he last quotes and deals with it, describes, not a palisade but the time-honoured "array of the shield-wall."[138] Then, passing to the battle and taking it stage by stage, I have shown that on its opening phase he went utterly astray in search of an imaginary assault on a phantom palisade; we have seen how another such guess transported to "the western ravine" a catastrophe which, even on his own showing, must have happened somewhere else, and assigned it to a stage of the battle which is quite possibly the wrong one. We have watched him missing the point of the great feigned flight and failing to see how Norman craft caught the English in a trap. And lastly, the critical manœuvre of the day, by which the Duke's great object was gained, and "the great advantage of the ground lost" to the English, proves on inquiry—although introduced, like other assertions, as a historic fact—to be yet another unsupported guess: for the statement that by this manœuvre "the Normans were at last on the hill" and could thus "charge

[136] See above, p. 323. [137] See above, p. 334.
[138] *N. C.*, iii. 763-4.

to the east right against the defenders of the Standard there is absolutely no foundation.

We have now—confining ourselves to points as to which there can be no question—examined Mr. Freeman's account of the Battle of Hastings. It is, as I showed at the outset, the very crown and flower of his work, and it is, I venture to assert, mistaken in its essential points. Must it, then, be cast aside as simply erroneous and misleading? Hardly. In the words of his own criticism on Mr. Coote's *Romans in Britain:* "It ought to be read, if only as a curious study, to show how utterly astray an ingenious and thoroughly well-informed man can go." For there is the true conclusion. The possession of exhaustive knowledge, the devotion of unsparing pains—neither of these were wanting. Then "wanting is—what?" Men have differed, and will always differ, as to how history should be written; but on one point we are all agreed. The true historian is he, and he only, who, from the evidence before him, can divine the facts. Other qualities are welcome, but this is the essential gift. And it was because, here at least, he lacked it that, in spite of all his advantages, in spite of his genius and his zeal, our author, in his story of this battle, failed as we have seen.

Mr. Freeman held that his predecessors, Thierry and Sir Francis Palgrave, "singularly resemble each other in a certain lack of critical power." His own lack, as I conceive it, was of a somewhat different kind. For if he studied the text and weighed the value of his authorities, yet he was often liable to danger from his tendency to a *parti pris*. Setting out with his own impression, he read his texts in the light of that impression rather than with an open mind. Thus we might say of his "very lucid and original account" of the great battle, as he said of Mr. Coote's work: "The truth of the whole matter is that all this very ingenious but baseless fabric has been built upon the foundation of a single error." Had he not stumbled at the outset over that "quasi castellum," he might never have erected that "ingenious but baseless fabric." As it is, while the battle should be largely rewritten, preserving only such incidents as are taken straight from the authorities, the accompanying plan must be wholly destroyed. Till then, as Dr. Stubbs has said of the discovery that "Ingulf" was a forgery, "it remains a warning light, a wandering marsh-fire, to caution the reader not to accept too abjectly the conclusions of his authority."

What then remains, it may be asked, of Mr. Freeman's narrative? When one remembers its superb vividness, carrying us away in spite of ourselves, one is tempted to reply, in his own words on the saga of Stamfordbridge :—

We have, indeed, a glorious description which, when critically examined, proves to be hardly more worthy of belief than a battle-piece in the Iliad. . . . Such is the magnificent legend which has been commonly accepted as the history of this famous battle. . . . And it is disappointing that, for so detailed and glowing a tale, we have so little of authentic history to substitute (pp. 365-8).

For, as he has so justly observed, when dismissing as "mythical" this "famous and magnificent saga" (pp. 328-9), "a void is left which history cannot fill, and which it is forbidden to the historian to fill up from the resources of his own imagination."

Accepting the principle here enunciated by Mr. Freeman himself, I do not merely reject demonstrably erroneous statements. I protest against his giving us a narrative drawn "from the resources of his own imagination." It is no answer to say that his guesses cannot be actually proved to be wrong ; the historian cannot distinguish too sharply between statements drawn from his authorities and guesses, however ingenious, representing imagination alone. No one, I am sure, reading Mr. Freeman's brilliant narrative, could imagine how largely his story of the battle is based on mere conjecture.

What the battle really was may be thus tersely expressed—it was Waterloo without the Prussians. The Normans could avail nothing against that serried mass.

> Dash'd on every rocky square,
> Their surging charges foam'd themselves away.

As Mr. Oman has so well observed, the Norman horse might have surged for ever "around the impenetrable shield-wall."[189] It was only, as he and Mr. Hunt[140] have shown, by the skilful combination of horsemen and archers by the maddening showers of arrows between the charges of the horse, that the English, especially the lighter armed, were stung into breaking their formation and abandoning that passive defence to which they were unfortunately restricted. "While no mode of array could be stronger so long as the line remained unbroken, it made it hard to form the line again." Dazzled by the rapid movements of their foes, now advancing, now retreating, either in feint or in earnest, the English, in places, broke their line, and then the Duke, as Mr. Oman writes, "thrust his horsemen into the gaps."[142] All this is quite certain, and is what the authorities plainly describe. Let us, then, keep to what we know. Is it not enough for us to picture the English line stubbornly striving to the last to close its broken ranks, the awful scene of slaughter and confusion, as the Old Guard of Harold, tortured by Norman arrows, found the horsemen among them at last, slashing and piercing right and left. Still the battle-axe blindly smote; dog-gedly, grimly still they fought, till the axes dropped from their lifeless grasp. And so they fell.

Mr. Archer, when he first came forward to defend " Mr.

---

[180] *Social England*, i. 299. "Mr. Oman, like Mr. J. H. Round, knows nothing of the famous 'palisade,' but only of the 'shield-wall' of the English" (*Speaker*, 2 Dec., 1893).

[140] *Norman Britain*, p. 79.

[141] *Ibid.*, p. 80.

[142] *Social England*, p. 300.

Freeman's account of the great battle,"[143] observed that I claimed "here to prove the entire inadequacy of Mr. Freeman's work," that I held him "wrong, completely wrong in his whole conception of the battle."[144] And he admitted that

" such a contention, it will at once be perceived, is very different from any mere criticism of detail; it affects the centre and the very heart of Mr. Freeman's work. If he could blunder here in the most careful elaborated passage of his whole history, he could blunder anywhere; his reputation for accuracy would be gone almost beyond hope of retrieving it" (p. 336).

"Blunder," surely, is a harsh word. I would rather say that the historian is seen here at his strongest and at his weakest : at his weakest in his tendency to follow blindly individual authorities in turn, instead of grasping them as a whole, and, worse still, in adapting them, at need, to his own preconceived notions ; at his strongest, in his Homeric power of making the actors in his drama live and move before us. Not in vain has "the wand of the enchanter," as an ardent admirer once termed it, been waved around Harold and his host. We are learning from recent German researches how the narratives of early Irish warfare are " perfectly surrounded with magic "; how, for instance, at the battle of Culdreimne "a Druid wove a magic hedge, which he placed before the army as a hindrance to the enemy." But spells are now no longer wrought

> With woven paces and with waving hands ;

and the Druid's hedge must go the way of our own magician's " palisade."

But, as I foresaw, in his eagerness to prove, at least, the existence of a palisade, my critic was soon reduced to impugning Mr. Freeman's own supreme authority, and at last to throwing over Mr. Freeman himself. " Incidit in Scyllam cupiens vitare Charybdim." Sneering[145] at what

---

[143] *Cont. Rev.*, p. 353.   [144] *Ibid.*, p. 335.
[145] *E.H.R.*, ix. 607.

the historian termed his "highest," his "primary" authority, that "precious monument," the Bayeux Tapestry —merely because it will not square with his views—he rejects utterly Mr. Freeman's theory as to its date and origin,[146] and substitutes one which the Professor described as "utterly inconceivable."[147] He has further informed us that "common sense" tells him that the English axemen cannot possibly have fought "in the close array of the shield-wall," as Mr. Freeman says they did.[148] And then he finally demolishes Mr. Freeman's "conception of the battle" by dismissing "an imaginary shield-wall,"[149] and assuring us that the absurd vision of "an extended shield-wall vanishes like smoke."[150]

It is impossible not to pity Mr. Freeman's would-be champion. Scorning, at the outset, the thought that his hero could err "in the most carefully elaborated passage of his whole history,"[151] his attitude of bold defiance was a joy to Mr. Freeman's friends.[152]

> ἀμφὶ δ᾽ἄρ᾽ αὐτῷ βαῖνε λέων ὧς ἀλκὶ πεποιθώς,
> πρόσθε δέ οἱ δύρυ τ᾽ ἔσχε καὶ ἀσπίδα πάντος ἐΐσην,
> τὸν κτάμεναι μεμαὼς ὅς τις τοῦ γ᾽ ἀντίος ἔλθοι,
> σμερδαλέα ἰάχων.

But his wildly brandished weapon proved more deadly to friend than foe: he discovered, as I knew, he could only oppose me by making jettison of Mr. Freeman's views. Of this we have seen above examples striking enough; but the climax was reached in his chief contention, namely, that the lines in the *Roman de Rou*, which describe, Mr. Freeman asserted, "the array of the shield-wall,"[158] cannot,

---

[146] *E.H.R.*, ix. 219-225.   [147] *Ibid.*, 224, 257.
[148] *N.C.*, ii. 469 ; and *supra*, p. 356.
[149] *Cont. Rev.*, 352.   [150] *Ibid.*, 348.
[151] *Cont. Rev.*, 335-336.
[152] The Reviewer . . . tells us that . . . Mr. Freeman . . . wrong, completely wrong, in his whole conception of the battle. . . His attack must be held to have failed" (*Cont. Rev.*, pp. 335, 353).
[158] *N.C.*, iii. 763.

on many grounds, be " referred to a shield-wall." [154] No contradiction could be more complete. So he now finds himself forced to write :—

I do not say—I have *never* said—that I agree with every word that Mr. Freeman has written about the great battle; but I do regard his account of Hastings as the noblest battle-piece in our historical literature—perhaps in that of the world.[155]

"O most lame and impotent conclusion!" We are discussing whether that account is "right," not whether it is "noble." To the splendour of that narrative I have borne no sparing witness. I have spoken of its "superb vividness," I have praised its "epic grandeur," I have dwelt on the writer's "Homeric power of making the actors in his drama live and move before us," and have compared his tale with the "glorious description" in the saga of Stamford Bridge. But the nearer it approaches to the epic and the saga, the less likely is that stirring tale to be rigidly confined to fact.

I will not say of Mr. Archer, "his attack must be held to have failed," for that would imperfectly express its utter and absolute collapse. The whole of my original argument as to the narrative of the battle remains not merely unshaken, but, it will be seen, untouched. Mr. Archer himself has now pleaded that "the only" point he "took up directly" was that of the disputed passage in Wace;[156] and here he could only make even the semblance of a case by deliberately ignoring and suppressing Mr. Freeman's own verdict (iii. 763-4), to which, from the very first, I have persistently referred. In his latest, as in his earliest article, he adheres to this deliberate suppression, and falsely represents "Mr. Freeman's interpretation" as "a palisade or barricade" alone.[157]

Those who may object to plain speaking should rather

<hr />

[154] *Cont. Rev.*, p. 349. Cf. Mr. Archer's articles *passim*.
[155] *E.H.R.*, ix. 22
[156] *E.H.R.*, ix. 607. [157] *E.H.R.*, ix. 606. *Supra*, p. 347.

denounce the tactics that make such speaking necessary. When my adversary claims that his case is proved, if the disputed passage does not describe a shield-wall, he is perfectly aware that Mr. Freeman distinctly asserted that it did. To suppress that fact, as Mr. Archer does,[158] can only be described as dishonest.

Judging from the desperate tactics to which my opponent resorted, it would seem that my "attack" on Mr. Freeman's work cannot here be impugned by any straightforward means.   The impotent wrath aroused by its success will lead, no doubt, to other attempts equally unscrupulous and equally futile.   But truth cannot be silenced, facts cannot be obscured.   I appeal, sure of my ground, to the verdict of historical scholars, awaiting, with confidence and calm, the inevitable triumph of the truth.

CONCLUSION.

" History is philosophy teaching by examples." In one sense the period of the Conquest was, as Mr. Freeman asserted in his preface, "a period of our history which is full alike of political instruction and of living personal interest." In one sense, it is an object-lesson never more urgently needed than it is at the present hour. Only that lesson is one which Mr. Freeman could never teach, because it is the bitterest commentary on the doctrines he most adored. In the hands of a patriot, in the hands of a writer who placed England before party, the tale might have burned like a beacon-fire, warning us that what happened in the past, might happen now, to-day. The Battle of Hastings has its moral and its moral is for us. An almost anarchical excess of liberty, the want of a strong centralized system, the absorption in party strife, the belief that politics are statesmanship, and that oratory will save

[158] *E.H.R.*, ix. 606, 607.   My readers are invited to refer to this article and to that in the *Cont. Rev.* (March, 1893), and test my statement for themselves.

a people—these are the dangers of which it warns us, and to which the majority of Englishmen are subject now as then. But Mr. Freeman, like the Bourbons, never learnt, and never forgot. A democrat first, an historian afterwards, History was for him, unhappily, ever "past politics." If he worshipped Harold with a blind enthusiasm, it was chiefly because he was a *novus homo*, "who reigned purely by the will of the people." He insisted that the English, on the hill of battle, were beaten through lack of discipline, through lack of obedience to their king; but he could not see that the system in which he gloried, a system which made the people "a co-ordinate authority" with their king, was the worst of all trainings for the hour of battle; he could not see that, like Poland, England fell, in large measure, from the want of a strong rule, and from excess of liberty. To him the voice of "a sovereign people" was "the most spirit-stirring of earthly sounds;" but it availed about as much to check the Norman Conquest as the fetish of an African savage, or the yells of Asiatic hordes. We trace in his history of Sicily the same blindness to fact. Dionysius was for him, as he was for Dante, merely,—

> Dionisio fero
> Che fe' Cicilia aver dolorosi anni.

But, in truth, the same excess of liberty that left England a prey to the Normans had left Sicily, in her day, a prey to Carthage: the same internal jealousies paralysed her strength. And yet he could not forgive Dionysius, the man who gave Sicily what she lacked, the rule of a "strong man armed," because, in a democrat's eyes, Dionysius was a "tyrant." That I am strictly just in my criticism of Mr. Freeman's attitude at the Conquest, is, I think, abundantly manifest, when even so ardent a democrat as Mr. Grant Allen admits that

a people so helpless, so utterly anarchic, so incapable of united action, deserved to undergo a severe training from the hard taskmasters of Romance civilization. The nation remained, but it remained as a conquered race, to be drilled in the stern school of the conquerors.[159]

Such were the bitter fruits of Old-English freedom. And, in the teeth of this awful lesson, Mr. Freeman could still look back with longing to "a free and pure Teutonic England,"[160] could still exult in the thought that a democratic age is bringing England ever nearer to her state "before the Norman set foot upon her shores."

But the school of which he was a champion has long seen its day. A reactionary movement, as has been pointed out by scholars in America, as in Russia [161] has invaded the study of history, has assailed the supremacy of the Liberal school, and has begun to preach, as the teaching of the past, the dangers of unfettered freedom.

Politics are not statesmanship. Mr. Freeman confused the two. There rang from his successor a truer note when, as he traversed the seas that bind the links of the Empire, he penned those words that appeal to the sons of an imperial race, sunk in the strife of parties or the politics of a parish pump, to rise to the level of their high inheritance among the nations of the earth. What was the Empire, what was India—we all remember that historic phrase—to one whose ideal, it would seem, of statesmanship was that of an orator in Hyde Park? Godwine, the ambitious, the unscrupulous agitator, is always for him "the great deliverer." Whether in the Sicily of the "tyrants," or the England of Edward the Confessor, we are presented, under the guise of history with a glorification of demagogy.

No man ever deserved a higher or a more lasting place in national gratitude than the first man who, being neither King nor Priest, stands forth in English history as endowed with all the highest attributes of

---

[159] *Anglo-Saxon Britain*, p. 172.
[160] *Norman Conquest*, iii. 454.
[161] *e.g.* Vinogradoff and Dr. Andrews.

the statesman. In him, in those distant times, we can revere the great minister, the unrivalled parliamentary leader, the man who could sway councils and assemblies at his will, etc., etc. [162]

We know of whom the writer was thinking, when he praised that "irresistible tongue"; [163] he had surely before him a living model, who, if not a statesman, was, no doubt, an "unrivalled parliamentary leader." Do we not recognise the portrait?—

The mighty voice, the speaking look and gesture of that old man eloquent, could again sway assemblies of Englishmen at his will. [164]

The voice which had so often swayed assemblies of Englishmen, was heard once more in all the fulness of its eloquence. [165]

But it was not an "irresistible tongue," nor "the harangue of a practised orator," of which England stood in need. Forts and soldiers, not tongues, are England's want now as then. But to the late Regius Professor, if there was one thing more hateful than "castles," more hateful even than hereditary rule, it was a standing army. When the Franco-German war had made us look to our harness, he set himself at once, with superb blindness, to sneer at what he termed "the panic," to suggest the application of democracy to the army, and to express his characteristic aversion to the thought of "an officer and a gentleman." [166] How could such a writer teach the lesson of the Norman Conquest?

"The long, long canker of peace" had done its work— "vivebatur enim tunc pene ubique in Angliâ perditis moribus, et pro pacis affluentia deliciarum fervebat luxus." [167] The land was ripe for the invader, and a saviour of Society

[162] *Norm. Conq.*, ii. 352   [163] *Ibid.*, 327.
[164] *Ibid.*, 326.   [165] *Ibid.*, 332.
[166] "We shall get rid of the talk about 'an officer and a gentleman.'" (*Macmillan's*, xxiv. 10).
[167] *Vita Wlstani.*

was at hand. While our fathers were playing at democracy, watching the strife of rival houses, as men might
now watch the contest of rival parties, the terrible Duke
of the Normans was girding himself for war. *De nobis fabula
narratur.*

MASTER WACE.

MR. FREEMAN.	MR. ARCHER.
Of the array of the shield-wall we have often heard already as at Maldon, but it is at Senlac that we get the fullest descriptions of it, all the better for coming in the mouths of enemies. Wace gives his description, 12941 :— (*Norm. Conq.*, iii. 763).	Now, there are six distinct objections to translating this passage [of Wace] as if it referred to a shield-wall. These objections are, of course, of unequal value ; but some of them would, by themselves, suffice to overthrow such a theory (*Cont. Rev.* 349).

IN discussing Mr. Freeman's treatment of the great battle, we saw that the only passage he vouched for the existence of a palisade,[1] consisted of certain lines from Wace's *Roman de Rou*, which he ultimately declared to be, on the contrary, a description of " the array of the shield-wall."[2] The question, therefore, as to their meaning—on which my critics have throughout endeavoured to represent the controversy as turning—did not even arise so far as Mr. Freeman was concerned. Still less had I occasion to discuss the authority of Wace, Mr. Freeman's explicit verdict on the lines (iii. 763-4) having removed them, as concerns his own narrative, from the sphere of controversy. The case, however, is at once altered when Mr. Archer

---

[1] Dismissing *ut supra* the " fosse " passage, which neither mentions nor implies it, together with the passage from Henry of Huntingdon.

[2] *N.C.*, iii. 763-4. I have shown in the *E. H. R.* (ix. 225) that he meant here by the shield-wall " exactly what he meant by it elsewhere," a shield-wall and nothing else.

insists on ignoring Mr. Freeman's words, and makes an independent examination of the lines, quoting also other passages which were not vouched by Mr. Freeman, as proving "beyond the shadow of a doubt that Wace did mean to represent the English at Hastings as fighting behind a palisade."[3] So long as I make it clearly understood that this question in no way affects the controversy as to Mr. Freeman, I am quite willing to discuss the question thus raised by Mr. Archer.

It is most naturally treated under these three heads :—

(1) Did Wace believe and assert that there was a palisade?

(2) If so, what weight ought to be attached to his authority?

(3) If we reject it, can we explain how his mistake arose?

WACE'S MEANING.

I have elsewhere[4] discussed "the disputed passage," (*supra*, p. 345), and agreed with Mr. Archer that there are "four views which have been suggested" as to its meaning.[5] Two of them, I there showed, were successively, held by Mr. Freeman, and the two others, successively advanced by Mr. Archer. When I add (anticipating) that according to M. Paris, "le passage de Wace présente quelque obscurité,"[6] and that M. Meyer introduced yet another element of doubt in a special kind of shield ("de grands écus") not previously suggested, it will be obvious, quite apart from any opinion of my own, that the passage presents difficulties.

So long as I only dealt with Mr. Freeman's work, I relied on his admission that the passage described the shield-wall.[7] Now that we are leaving his work aside, I fall back on my own conclusion, namely, that the passage is

---

[3] *Cont. Rev.*, 344.
[4] *E.H.R.*, ix. 231-240
[5] *Ib.*, ix. 2.
[6] *Ib.*, 260.
[7] *N.C.*, iii. 763-4

with equal difficulty referred either to a palisade or to a shield-wall. The word "escuz," it will be seen, occurs twice in the passage. Mr. Archer held, at first, that in neither case did it mean real "shields,"[8] but he afterwards assigned that meaning to the second of the two "escuz," while still rendering the first "in a metaphorical sense."[9] It is obvious that when Mr. Freeman took the lines to describe "the array of the shield-wall," he must have done so on the ground that "escuz" meant "shields." That is my own contention. While fully recognising the obstacles to translating "the disputed passage" as if it referred throughout to a shield-wall, I maintain that "escu" means shield, as a term "which is one of the commonest in Wace" and invariably means shield.[10]

But to cut short a long story, it was decided by Mr. Gardiner to settle this issue by submitting the disputed passage to the verdict of MM. Gaston Paris and Paul Meyer. In spite of my protest, this was done without my articles and my solution of the problem[11] being laid before them at the same time. A snap verdict was thus secured before they had seen the evidence. I am sure that Mr. Gardiner must have thought this fair, and editors, we know, cannot err; but it seems to me quite possible that these distinguished French scholars were not familiar with the shield-wall, an Old English tactic, and were not aware that this information was the great feature of the battle. Had all this, as I wished, been duly set before

---

[8] *Cont. Rev.*, p. 348.   [9] *E.H.R.*, ix. 17-20.

[10] I explained, in one of my replies to Mr. Archer, that this statement applied *only* to its usage "*in Wace*" (*Academy*, 16th Sept., 1893), but, characteristically, he has not hesitated to suppress this explanation, and renew his sneers at my knowledge of "Old French," on the ground of a statement which, I had explained, was not my meaning (*E.H.R.* ix. 604). It is difficult to describe such devices as these.

Common as the word is in Wace, I have never found any other instance of its use (*i.e.*, by him) in a metaphorical sense, nor, if there is one, has Mr. Archer attempted to produce it.

[11] *Infra*, pp. 409-416.

B.H.   D D

them, their verdict would, of course, have carried much greater weight.

But having said this much, I frankly admit that their verdict is in favour of Mr. Archer's contention, and, so far as the first "escuz" is concerned, against my own.[12] They may not agree in detail with each other, or with either of Mr. Archer's views, but, on the broad issue, he has a perfect right to claim that their verdict is for him so long as he does not pretend that it also confirms "Mr. Freeman's interpretation," by ignoring the historian's own latest and explicit words.[13] It must also be remembered that this admission in no way diminishes the obscurity of the passage, which, as we have seen, is beyond dispute, and which forms an important element in my own solution of the problem.[14]

Having now shown how the matter stands with regard to "the disputed passage," I need not linger over those which Mr. Freeman ignored, and which Mr. Archer adduced to strengthen his views as to the main passage. I have dealt with these elsewhere,[15] and need here only refer to ll. 8585-90, because that passage raises a point of historical interest quite apart from personal controversy. I have maintained that it can only be accepted at the cost of "throwing over Mr. Freeman's conception of the battle,"[16] and have proved, by quoting his own words, that he placed the standard with Harold at his foot "in the very fore-

---

[12] *E.H.R.*, ix. 260   [13] *N.C.*, iii. 736-4.

[14] The word "fenestres," for instance, which Mr. Archer first rendered "ash," out of deference to Mr. Freeman and his predecessors, but subsequently "windows" (*E.H.R.*, ix. 18) is either a corruption or quite inexplicable. "If it pleases Mr. Archer," as I wrote (*ib.*, 236), "to construct a barricade, of which 'windows' are the chief ingredient, on an uninhabited Sussex down, in 1066, he is perfectly welcome to do so." I may add that the rendering adopted by the two French scholars does not in the least alter my view as to the improbability, or rather absurdity, of the suggestion.

[15] *E.H.R.*, ix. 244.

[16] *Q.R.*, July, 1893, p. 95.

front of the fight." [17]   I do not say that he was right in
doing so : he was, I think, very probably wrong, and was
influenced here, as elsewhere, by his dramatic treatment of
Harold. But as this can only be matter of opinion, I have
not challenged his view ; I only say that those who accept
it cannot consistently appeal to a passage in Wace which
places the standard in the rear of the English host.

WACE'S AUTHORITY.

Assuming then, for the sake of argument, that Wace
mentions a defence of some kind,[18] even though not consistently [19] in front of the English troops, let us see whether
his statement is corroborated, whether, it is in harmony
with the other evidence, and whether, if it is neither corroborated nor in such agreement, his authority is sufficient
nevertheless, to warrant its acceptance.

As to corroboration, Mr. Archer undertook "to produce
corroborative evidence from other sources " ; [20] but this at
once dwindled down to one line—"tending in the same
direction " [21]—from Benoît de St. Maur, who does not even
mention a palisade.[22]   There is therefore, on his own
showing, not a shred of corroborative evidence.

As to the second point, I may refer to my arguments

[17] *E.H.R.* ix. 251-3.   I was careful to add that "if it be claimed that
his text is contradictory, this would but prove further how confused his
mind really was as to the battle " (p. 252).   Mr. Archer, as I anticipated,
now prints, as a conclusive reply (*ib.*, ix. 603), words which look the other
way, ignoring, as usual, the quotations on which I explicitly relied.   He
has thereby, as I said, only proved how confused, here as elsewhere,
Mr. Freeman's conception was.

[18] Mr. Archer now prefers to leave its details doubtful (*E.H.R.*, ix. 606).

[19] As I have shown in *E.H.R..* ix. 244-5.

[20] *Cont. Rev.*, 344.

[21] *Ib.*, 346.

[22] I have shown (*Academy*, 16th Sept., 1893) by reference to Godefroi
and Michel that either Mr. Archer or they must here have been ignorant
of Old French.   The former alternative seems to be accepted.

against the palisade,[23] where I showed that none of our authorities is here in agreement with Wace.

We come, therefore, to our third point, namely, the weight to which Wace's testimony, when standing alone, is entitled. Here, as elsewhere, I adhere to my position. As I have written in the *Quarterly Review*—

Even if Wace, clearly and consistently, mentioned a palisade throughout his account of the battle, we should certainly reject the statement of a witness, writing a century after it, when we find him at variance with every authority (for that is our point), just as Mr. Freeman rejected the bridge at Varaville,[24] or the "falsehood" of the burning of the ships, or the "blunder" of making the Duke land at Hastings, or his anachronisms, or his chronology. For, "of course," in the Professor's own words, "whenever he [Wace] departs from contemporary authority, and merely sets down floating traditions nearly a hundred years after the latest events which he records, his statements need to be very carefully weighed."[25]

Let me specially lay stress upon the points on which, when Wace and the Tapestry differ, the preference is given by Mr. Freeman himself to the Tapestry as against Wace:—

Had the tapestry been a work of later date, it is hardly possible that it could have given the simple and truthful account of these matters which it does give. A work of the twelfth or thirteenth century[26] would have brought in, *as even honest Wace does in some degree*, the notions of the twelfth or thirteenth century. One

---

[23] *Supra*, pp. 348-9.
[24] The case of the battle of Varaville, in 1058, is precisely similar in this respect to that of the Battle of Hastings. Of the former Mr. Freeman writes :—" Wace alone speaks, throughout his narrative, of a bridge. All the other writers speak only of a ford " (iii. 173). Now Wace's authority was better for this, the earlier battle, because, says Mr. Freeman, he knew the ground. Yet the Professor did not hesitate to reject his " bridge." So again, in "the campaign of Hastings," Mr. Freeman rejects "the falsehood of the story of William burning his ships, of which the first traces appear in Wace" (iii. 408). So much for placing our reliance upon Wace, when he stands alone.
[25] *Q.R.*, July, 1893, p 96.
[26] Mr. Archer's limit is 1066-1210.

cannot conceive an artist of the time of Henry II., still less an artist later than the French conquest of Normandy, agreeing so remarkably with the authentic writings of the eleventh century (iii. 573).

[In the Tapestry] every antiquarian detail is accurate—the lack of armour on the horses (iii. 574). [But] Wace speaks of the horse of William Fitz-Osbern as "all covered with iron" (iii. 570).

Wace, again, is "hardly accurate" (iii. 765), we read, as to the English weapons, because he differs from the Tapestry. As to Harold's wound, "Wace places it too early in the battle" (iii. 497); Mr. Freeman follows the Tapestry. As to the landing of the Normans at Pevensey—

Venit ad Pevenesæ, says the Tapestry . . . Wace . . . altogether reverses the geography, making the army land at Hastings, and go to Pevensey afterwards" (iii. 402).

As to the "Mora," the Duke's ship, the Tapestry shows "the child with his horn"; Wace describes him "Saete et arc tendu portant." Mr. Freeman adopts the "horn" (iii. 382). Harold, says Mr. Freeman, was imprisoned at Beaurain.

This is quite plain from the Tapestry: "Dux eum ad Belrem et ibi eum tenuit." Wace says, "A Abevile l'ont mené . . . ." This I conceive to arise from a misconception of the words of William of Jumièges (iii. 224).

This illustrates, I would remind Mr. Archer, the difference between a primary authority and a mere late compiler.

To these examples I may add Wace's mention of Harold's *vizor (ventaille)*. Mr. Freeman pointed out the superior accuracy of the Tapestry in "the nose-pieces" (iii. 574), and observed that "the vizor" was a much later introduction (iii. 497).[27] Here again we see the soundness of

[27] We have, I suspect, a similar instance in Wace's *gisarmes* (ll. 7794, 7814, 8328, 8332, 8342, 8587, 8629, 8656). An excellent vindication of the Bayeux Tapestry—oddly enough overlooked by Mr. Freeman—namely, M. Delauney's "Origine de la Tapisserie de Bayeux prouvée

Mr. Freeman's view that Wace could not help introducing "the notions" of his own time into his account of the battle. Miss Norgate admits that he "transferred to his mythical battles the colouring of the actual battles of his own day," but urges that these narratives illustrate the "warfare of Wace's own . . . contemporaries."[23] Quite so. But the battle of Hastings belonged to an older and obsolete style of warfare. That is what his champions always forget. If Miss Norgate's argument has any meaning, it is that the men who fought in that battle were "Wace's own contemporaries."

But, even where Wace's authority is in actual agreement with the Tapestry, Mr. Freeman did not hesitate to reject, or rather, ignore it, as we saw in the matter of the fosse disaster.

As to Wace's sources of information, and the *prima facie* evidence for his authority, a question of considerable interest is raised. Mr. Archer discusses it from his own

---

par elle-même" (Caen, 1824)—discusses the weapons, the author observing : " La hache d'armes ressemble à celle de nos sapeurs ; celle des temps postèrieurs au xie siècle à, dans les monuments, une espèce de petite lance au-dessus de la douille du côté opposé au tranchant" (see Jubinal, *La Tapisserie de Bayeux*, p. 17). This exactly describes the true *gisarme*, a later introduction. So again, Wace makes the *chevalier* who has hurried from Hastings exclaim to Harold—

> "Un chastel i ont ia ferme
> De *breteschese* de fosse" (ll. 6717-8),

whereas *bretasches* of course were impossible at the time. One is reminded of the description, by Piramus, of the coming of the English, when "over the broad sea Britain they sought" :—

> "Leuent bresteches od kernels,
> Ke cuntrevalent bons chastels,
> De herituns [? hericuns] e de paliz
> Les cernent, si funt riulez
> Del quer des cheygnes, forze e halz,
> Ki ne criement sieges ne asalz."
>   (*Vie Seint Edmund le Rey*, ll. 228-33).

[23] *E.H.R.*, ix. 66.

standpoint.[29]   On Wace's life, age and work, facts are few and speculations many.   These have been collected and patiently sifted in Andresen's great work, with the following result :—

Wace was certainly living not merely in 1170,[30] but in 1174, for he alludes to the siege of Rouen (August, 1174) in his epilogue to the second part of the "Roman."[31]   It is admitted on all hands, though Mr. Archer does not mention it, that he did not even begin the third part till after the coronation of the younger Henry (June 14, 1170).[32]   Allowing for its great length, he cannot have come to his account of the battle *at the very earliest* till 1171, 105 years after the event.   For my part, I think that it was probably written even some years later.   But imagine in any case an Englishman, ignorant of Belgium, writing an account of Waterloo, mainly *from oral tradition*, in 1920.

Mr. Archer contends that Wace was born "probably between the years 1100 and 1110" (*ante*, p. 31).   Andresen holds that the earliest date we can venture to assign is 1110,[33] forty-four years after the battle.   Special stress is laid by Mr. Archer on Wace's oral information :—

He had seen and talked with many men who recollected things anterior to Hastings and the Hastings campaign.   Among his informants for this latter was his own father, then, we may suppose, a well-grown lad, if not an actual participator in the fight (*ante*, p. 32).

"We may suppose"—where all is supposition—exactly the contrary.   If Wace was born, as we may safely say, more than forty years after the battle, "we may suppose"

[29] *Ib.*, 31-7, 17-18, and throughout his paper.

[30] *E.H.R.*, ix. 32.

[31] "Al siege de Rouen le quidierent gaber " (l. 62).

[32] "Demn nicht etwa am Schlusse, sondern gleich zu Anfang des genannten Theiles " (l. 179) "spricht er von den drei Königen Heinrich die er gesehen und gekannt" (p. xciv.).

[33] "Nimmt man das Jahr 1110 als Geburtsjahr des Dichters an," etc. (p. xciv.).

that his father was not even born before it. All this talk
about Wace's father is based on ll. 6445-7, of which Andresen truly remarks, "Die Verse 'Mais co oi dire a mon
pere, Bien m'en souient mais Vaslet ere, Que set cenz nes,
quatre meins, furent,' u.s.w., sind viel zu unbestimmt
gehalten, so dass wir aus ihnen streng genommen nicht
einmal entnehmen können, ob der Vater im Jahre 1066
schon auf der Welt war oder nicht" (p. lxx). I venture
to take my own case. Born within forty years of Waterloo,
I can say with Wace that I remember my father telling
me, as a boy, stories of the battle. But he was born after
it. The information was second-hand. Over and over
again does Mr. Archer lay stress on the fact (*ut supra*)
that Wace gives us "the reminiscences of the old heroes
who fought at Hastings as no one else has cared to do."[34]
I must insist that Wace himself nowhere mentions having
seen or spoken to them. He does mention having seen men
who remembered the great comet (Mr. Archer italicises
the lines[35]); but this exactly confirms my point. For when
Wace *had* seen eye-witnesses he was careful, we see, to
mention the fact. Men would remember the comet, though
little children at the time. One of my own very earliest
recollections is that of a great comet, even though it did
not create the sensation of the comet in 1066. Wace had
talked with those who had been children, not with those
who had been fighting men, in 1066.

I need only invite attention to one more point. Mr.
Archer assures us that "Wace is a very sober writer,"
with "something of the shrewd scepticism" of modern
scholars.[36] What shall we say then, of his long story (ll.
7005-7100) of the night visit, by Harold and Gyrth, to the
Norman camp, to which Mr. Archer appeals as evidence

[34] *E.H.R.*, ix. 33. It need scarcely be said that these "old heroes"
would be found rather in England than in Normandy.

[35] *Ib.*, ix. 17.   "Assez vi homes qui la virent,
             Qui ainz e pois longues vesquirent."

[36] *E.H.R.*, ix. 33.

for the *lices* (l. 7010)? "Nothing," replies Mr. Freeman (iii. 449), "could be less trustworthy. . . . No power short of divination could have revealed it."[87] Mr. Archer tells us he has only space for one instance[88] of Wace's conscientiousness. That instance is his story of the negotiation between William and Baldwin of Flanders on the eve of the Conquest. Of this story Mr. Freeman writes:—

Of the intercourse between William and Baldwin in his character of sovereign of Flanders Wace has a tale which strikes me as so purely legendary that I did not venture to introduce it into the text . . . The whole story seems quite inconsistent with the real relations between William and Baldwin (iii. 718-9).

Comment is superfluous.

Having now shown that Wace's evidence is not corroborated, is not in accordance with that of contemporary witnesses, and cannot on the sound canons of criticism recognised by Mr. Freeman himself, be accepted under these circumstances, I propose to show that my case can be carried further still, and that I can even trace to its origin the confused statement in his "disputed passage" which is said to describe a palisade or defence of some sort or other.

WACE AND HIS SOURCES.[39]

In studying the authorities for the Battle of Hastings, I was led to a conclusion which, so far as I know, had never occurred to any one. It is that William of Malmesbury's "Gesta Regum" was among the sources used by Wace. Neither in Korting's elaborate treatise, "Ueber die Quellen des Roman de Rou," nor in Andresen's notes to his well-known edition of the "Roman" (ii. 708), can I find any

---

[87] Compare his scornful rejection (iii. 469-71) of Wace's tales in ll. 7875-7950.

[88] *E.H.R.*, ix. 34.

[39] Reprinted from the *English Historical Review*, October, 1893.

suggestion to this effect. Dr. Stubbs, in his edition of the "Gesta Regum," dwells on the popularity of the work both at home and abroad, but does not include Wace among the writers who availed themselves of it; and the late Mr. Freeman, though frequently compelled to notice the agreement between Wace and William, never thought, it appears, of suggesting the theory of derivation; indeed, he speaks of the two writers as independent witnesses, when dealing with one of these coincidences.[40] The more one studies Wace, the more evident it becomes that the "Roman" requires to be used with the greatest caution. Based on a *congeries* of authorities, on tradition, and occasionally of course, on the poetic invention of the *trouveur* it presents a whole in which it is almost impossible to disentangle the various sources of the narrative. Before dealing with the passage which led me to believe that the "Gesta Regum" must have been known to Wace, I will glance at some other coincidences. We have first the alleged landing of William at Hastings instead of Pevensey. On this Mr. Freeman observed :—

Venit ad Pevenesæ, says the Tapestry. Sơ William of Poitiers and William of Jumièges. William of Malmesbury says carelessly, *Placido cursu Hastingas appulerunt.* So Wace, who altogether reverses the geography, making the army land at Hastings and go to Pevensey afterwards.[41]

Here William of Malmesbury, who was probably using "Hastingas" as loosely as when he applied that term to Battle, appears to be responsible for the mistake of Wace, who may have tried to harmonise him with William of Jumièges by making the Normans proceed to Pevensey after having landed. Take again the hotly disputed burial of Harold at Waltham. On this question Mr. Freeman writes :—

William of Malmesbury, after saying that the body was given to

Gytha, adds, *acceptum itaque apud Waltham sepelivit.* . . . Wace had evidently heard two or three stories, and, with his usual discretion, he avoided committing himself, but he distinctly asserts a burial at Waltham.[42]

This, then, is another coincidence between the two writers, while, as before, Wace found himself in the presence of a conflict of authorities. On yet another difficult point, the accession of Harold, I see a marked agreement, though Mr. Freeman did not. Harold, according to William of Malmesbury, *extorta a principibus fide, arripuit diadema,* and *diademate fastigiatus, nihil de pactis inter se et Willelmum cogitabat.* Wace's version runs :—

> Heraut ki ert manant è forz
> Se fist énoindre è coroner ;
> Unkes al duc n'en volt parler,
> Homages prist è féeltez
> Des plus riches è des ainz nes.

Not only is the attitude of Wace and William towards Harold's action here virtually identical, but the mention of his exaction of homage seems special to them both.

The passages, however, on which I would specially rest my case are those in which these two writers describe the visit of Harold's spies to the Norman camp before the battle of Hastings. This legend is peculiar to William of Malmesbury and Wace, and though it may be suggested that they had heard it independently, the correspondence —it will, I think, be admitted—is too close to admit of that solution.

On the next page I print these passages side by side.

[42] lii. 782.

WILLIAM OF MALMESBURY.

Premisit tamen qui numerum
hostium et vires specularentur.

Quos intra castra deprehensos
Willelmus circum tentoria duci,
moxque, largis eduliis pastos,
domino incolumes remitti jubet.

Redeuntes percunctatur Haroldus quid rerum apportent : illi,
verbis amplissimis ductoris mag-
nificam confidentiam prosecuti,
serio addiderunt pene omnes in
exercitu illo presbyteros videri,
quod totam faciem cum utroque
labio rasam haberent ; . . .
subrisit rex fatuitatem referen-
tinum, lepido insecutus cachinno,
quia non essent presbyteri, sed
milites validi, armis invicti.

(§ 239).

WACE.

Heraut enveia dous espies
Por espier quels compagnies
E quanz barons e quanz armez
Aueit li dus od sei menez.
        Ia esteient a l'ost uenu,
Quant il furent aparceu
A Guillaume furent mene,
Forment furent espoente.
Mais quant il sout que il quereient
E que ses genz esmer ueneient,
Par tos les tres les fist mener
E tote l'ost lor fist mostrer ;
Bien les fist paistre e abeurer,
Pois les laissa quites aler,
Nes volt laidir ne destorber.
    Quant il vindrent a lor seignor,
Del duc distrent mult grant enor.
Un des Engleis, qui out veuz
Les Normans toz res e tonduz,
Quida que tuit proueire fussent
E que messes chanter peussent,
Kar tuit erent tondu e res,
Ne lor esteit guernon remes.
Cil dist a Heraut que li dus
Aueit od sei proueies plus
Que chevaliers ne altre gent ;
De co se merueillout forment
Que tuit erent res e tondu.
E Heraut li a respondu
Que co sunt cheualiers uaillanz,
Hardi e proz e combatanz.
" N'ont mie barbes ne guernons,"
Co dist Heraut, "com nos auons."

(ll. 7101-34).

The story is just one of those that William of Malmesbury
would have picked up, and Wace has simply, in metrical
paraphrase, transferred it from his pages to his own.

Yet another story, on which Mr. Freeman looked with

some just suspicion, is common to these two writers, and virtually to them alone. It is that of "the contrast between the way in which the night before the battle was spent by the Normans and the English" (iii. 760). Wace, says Mr. Freeman, "gives us the same account" as William "in more detail," while William "gives us a shorter account." I here again append the passages side by side, insisting on the fact mentioned by Mr. Freeman, that Wace expands the story "in more detail."

Itaque utrinque animosi duces disponunt acies. . . . Angli, ut accepimus, totam noctem insompnem cantibus potibusque ducentes.

. . . . .

Contra Normanni, nocte tota confessioni peccatorum vacantes, mane Dominico corpore communicarunt.

(§§ 241, 242.)

Quant la bataille dut ioster,
La noit auant, c'oi conter,
Furent Engleis forment haitie,
Mult riant e mult enueisie.
Tote noit maingierent e burent,
Onques la noit en lit ne jurent.
Mult les veissiez demener,
Treper e saillir e chanter.

. . . .

E li Normant e li Franceis
Tote noit firent oreisons
E furent en afflictions.
De lor pechiez confes se firent,
As proueires les regehirent,
E qui nen out proueires pres,
A son ueisin se fist confes.

. . . .

Quant les messes furent chantees,
Qui bien matin furent finees, . . .
(ll. 7349-56, 7362-68, 7407-8.)

This brings me to my destination, namely, § 241 of the "Gesta Regum." We may divide this section into three successive parts : (1) the description of the way in which the English spent the night—which is repeated, we have seen, by Wace ; (2) the array of the English, with which I shall deal below ; (3) the dismounting of Harold at the foot of the standard. I here subjoin the parallels for the third, calling special attention to the phrases, "d'or e de pierres (auro et lapidibus)" and "Guil. pois cele victoire Le

fist porter a l'apostoire (post victorium papae misit Willelmus)."

Rex ipse pedes juxta vexillum
stabat cum fratribus, ut, in commune periculo aequato, nemo de
fuga cogitaret.　Vexillum illud
post victoriam papae mi i Willelmus, quod erat in hominis pug
nantis figura, auro et lapidibus
arte sumptuosa intextum.

Quant Heraut out tot apreste
E co qu'il uolt out commande
Enmi les Engleis est uenuz,
Lez l'estandart est descenduz
Lewine e Guert furent od lui
Frere Heraut furent andui,
Assez out barons enuiron ;
Heraut fu lez son gonfanon.
Li gonfanon fu mult vaillanz,
D'or e de pierres reluissanz.
Guill. pois cele victoire
Le fist porter a l'apostoire,
Por mostrer e metre en memoire
Son grant conquest e sa grant
　　gloire.
　　　　　　(ll. 7853-66.)

The only part of § 241 which remains to be dealt with is
the second.　The two passages run thus :—

Pedites omnes cum bipennibus conserta ante se *scutorum*
testudine, impenetrabilem cuneum faciunt ; quod profecto illis
ea die saluti fuisset, nisi Normanni, simulata fuga more suo
confertos manipulos laxassent.
　　　　　　(§ 241.)

Geldons engleis haches portoent
E gisarmes qui bien trenchoent
Fait orent deuant els *escuz*
De fenestres e d'altres fuz,
Deuant els les orent leuez,
Comme cleies joinz e serrez ;
Fait en orent deuant closture,
N'i laissierent nule iointure,
Par onc Normant entr'els venist
Qui desconfire les volsist.
D'escuz e d'ais s'auironoent,
Issi deffendre se quidoent ;
Et s'il se fussent bien tenu,
Ia ne fussent *le ior* uencu.
　　　　　　(ll. 7813-26.)

Mr. Freeman, of course, observed the parallel, but, oddly
enough, missed the point.　He first quoted the lines from
Wace, and then immediately added, "So William of Malmes-

bury" (iii. 764), thus reversing the natural order. The word that really gave me the clue was the *escuz* of Wace. It was obvious, I held, that, here as elsewhere,[48] it must mean "shield"; and Mr. Freeman consequently saw in the passage an undoubted description of the "shield-wall" (iii. 763). Moreover, the phrase *lever escuz* is, in Wace, a familiar one, describing preparation for action, thus, for instance :

> Mult ueissiez Engleis fremir
>
> .   .   .   .   .   .
>
> Armes saisir, escuz leuer.
>
> (ll. 8030, 8033.)

On the other hand, there are, in spite of Mr. Freeman, undoubted difficulties in rendering the passage as a description of the "shield-wall," just as there are in taking *escuz* to mean "barricades" (iii. 471). The result was that, perhaps unconsciously, Mr. Freeman gave the passage, in succession, two contradictory renderings (iii. 471, 763). Now, starting from the fact that the disputed passage supported, and also opposed both renderings, I arrived at the conclusion that it must represent some confusion of Wace's own. He had, evidently, himself no clear idea of what he was describing. But the whole confusion is at once accounted for if we admit him to have here also followed William of Malmesbury. His *escuz*—otherwise impossible to explain —faithfully renders the *scuta* of William, while the latter's *testudo*, though strictly accurate, clearly led him astray. The fact is that William of Malmesbury must have been quite familiar with the "shield-wall," if indeed he had seen seen the fyrd actually forming it.[44] Wace, on the contrary, living later, and in Normandy instead of England, cannot have seen, or even understood, this famous formation, with which his cavalry fight of the twelfth century had nothing

[48] I mean, as I explained above, elsewhere in Wace.

[44] He describes, as Mr. Freeman observed, King Henry bidding the English "meet the charge of the Norman knights by standing firm in the array of the ancient shield-wall" (*W. Rufus*, ii. 411)

in common. It is natural therefore that his version should betray some confusion, though his *Fait en orent deuant closture* clearly renders William of Malmesbury's *conserta ante se scutorum testudine*. There is no question as to William's meaning, for a *tetudo* of shields is excellent Latin for the shield-wall formed by the Romans against a flight of arrows. Moreover, the construction of William's Latin (*conserta*) accounts for that use by Wace of the plu-perfect tense on which stress has been laid as proof that the passage must describe a "barricade."[45] That Wace could, occasionally, be led astray by misunderstanding his authority, is shown by his taking Harold to Abbeville, after his capture on the French coast, a statement which arose, in Mr. Freeman's opinion, "from a misconception of the words of William of Jumièges (iii. 224)." No one, I think, can read dispassionately the extracts I have printed side by side, without accepting the explanation I offer of this disputed passage in Wace, namely, that it is nothing but a metrical, elaborate, and somewhat confused paraphrase of the words of William of Malmesbury.

Passing from William of Malmesbury to the Bayeux Tapestry, we find a general recognition of the difficulty of determining Wace's knowledge of it. I can only, like others, leave the point undecided. On the one hand, his narrative, as a whole, does not follow the Tapestry; on the other, it is hard to believe that the writer of ll. 8103-8138 had not seen that famous work. His description of the scene is marvellously exact, and the Tapestry phrase, in which Odo *confortat pueros*—often a subject of discussion— is at once explained by his making the *pueri* whom Odo "comforted " to be—

> Vaslez, qui al herneis esteient
> E le herneis garder deueient.

Of these varlets in charge of the "harness" he had already spoken (ll. 7963-7). The difficulty of accounting for Wace,

[45] *Cont. Rev.*, March, 1893, p. 351.

as a canon of Bayeux, being unacquainted with the Tapestry is, of course, obvious. But in any case he cannot have used it, as we do ourselves, among his foremost authorities.

In discussing his use of William of Jumièges, we stand on much surer ground. It certainly strikes one as strange that in mentioning the obvious error by which Wace makes Harold receive his wound in the eye early in the fight (l. 8185), before the great feigned flight, Mr. Freeman does not suggest its derivation from William of Jumièges, though he proceeds to add (p. 771):—

> I need hardly stop to refute the strange mistake of William of Jumièges, followed by Orderic: "Heraldus ipse in primo militum progressu ['Congressu,' *Ord.*] vulneribus letaliter confossus occubuit."

But a worse instance of the contradictions involved by the patchwork and secondary character of Wace's narrative is found in his statement as to Harold's arrival on the field of battle. "Wace," says Mr. Freeman, "makes the English reach Senlac on Thursday night" (p. 441). So he does, even adding that Harold

> fist son estandart drecier
> Et fist son gonfanon fichier
> Iloc tot dreit ou l'abeie
> De la Bataille est establie. (ll. 6985-8.)

But Mr. Freeman must have overlooked the very significant fact that when the battle is about to begin, Wace tells a different story, and makes Harold only occupy the battlefield on the Saturday morning.

> Heraut sout que Normant vendreient
> E que par main se combatreient:
> Un champ out *par matin* porpris,
> Ou il a toz ses Engleis mis.
> *Par matin* les fist toz armer
> E a bataille conreer. (ll. 7768-72.)

I have little doubt that he here follows William of Jumi-

B.H.   E E èges : "[Heraldus] in campo belli apparuit mane," and that he was thus led to contradict himself.

Mr. Freeman had a weakness for Wace, and did not conceal it : he insisted on the poet's "honesty." But "honesty" is not knowledge ; and in dealing with the battle, it is not allowable to slur over Wace's imperfect knowledge. Mr. Freeman admits that "probably he did not know the ground, and did not take in the distance between Hastings and Battle" (p. 762). But he charitably suggests that "it is possible that when he says 'en un tertre s'estut li dus' he meant the hill of Telham, only without any notion of its distance from Hastings." But, in spite of this attempt to smooth over the discrepancy, it is impossible to reconcile Wace's narrative with that of Mr. Freeman. The latter makes the duke deliver his speech at Hastings, and then march with his knights to Telham, and there arm. But Wace imagined that they armed in their quarters at Hastings ("Issi sunt as tentes ale"), and straightway fought. The events immediately preceding the battle are far more doubtful and difficult to determine than could be imagined from Mr. Freeman's narrative, but I must confine myself to Wace's version. I have shown that his account is not consistent as to the movements of Harold, while as to the topography, "his primary blunder," as Mr. Freeman terms it, "of reversing the geographical order, by making William land at Hastings and thence go to Pevensey," together with his obvious ignorance of the character and position of the battle-field, must, of course, lower our opinion of his accuracy, and of the value of the oral tradition at his disposal.

To rely "mainly" [46] on such a writer, in preference to the original authorities he confused, or to follow him when, in Mr. Freeman's words, he actually "departs from contemporary authority, and merely sets down floating traditions nearly a hundred years after the latest events which he records"—betrays the absence of a critical faculty, or the consciousness of a hopeless cause.

[46] "It is upon Wace that we shall mainly rely." *Cont. Rev.*, p. 344.

NOTE ON THE PSEUDO-INGULF.

I OWE to my friend Mr. Hubert Hall the suggestion that the great battle described by the Pseudo-Ingulf as taking place between the English and the Danes in 870,—and all accepted as sober fact by Turner in his *History of the Anglo-Saxons*,—may be a concoction based on the facts of the battle of Hastings. This is also the theory Mr. Freeman advanced as to Snorro's story of the battle of Stamford Bridge. The coincidence is very striking. In both narratives the defending force is formed with "the dense shield-wall";[1] in both it breaks at length that formation; in both it is, consequently, overwhelmed; and in both cases the attacking force consists of horsemen and archers. But the most curious coincidence is found in the principal weapon of the defending force. In Snorro's narrative, as Mr. Freeman renders it, "a dense wood of spears bristles in front of the circle to receive the charge of the English horsemen";[2] in the Pseudo-Ingulf the defending force "contra violentiam equitum densissimam aciem lancearum prætendebant."[3] Such a defence savours of the days when the knight, fighting on foot with his lance,[4] had replaced the housecarl with his battle-axe: it was not that of Harold's host, but one which we meet with in the twelfth century.

There are marks, however, in the Pseudo-Ingulf, of study not merely of the Battle of Hastings, but of William of Malmesbury's account of it. From him, it would seem, are

[1] *Norm. Conq.*, iii. 367.   [2] *Ibid.*, p. 365.   [3] Ed. 1684, p. 21.
[4] *Vide supra*, p. 362.   Cf. the fight at Jaffa, 5 Aug., 1192.

taken the words "testudo" and "tumulus." The first
parallel passages are these :—

WILLIAM.	"INGULF."
Conserta ante se *scutorum testudine*, impenetrabilem cuneum faciunt.	In unum cuneum conglobati, . . . *testudinem clypeorum* prætendebant.

Again, after the disaster caused, in each case, by a feigned
flight, we have the rally thus described :—

WILLIAM.	"INGULF."
nec tamen ultioni suæ defuere, quin crebro consistentes . . . occupato *tumulo*, Normannos, calore succensos acriter ad superiora nitentes, in vallem dejiciunt.	in quodam campi *tumulo* cetera planitie aliquantulum altiore in orbem conferti, barbaros arietantes diutissime sustinuerunt . . . suum sanguinem vindicantes.

The Pseudo-Ingulf alludes but briefly to the Battle of
Hastings itself. Yet here again we have traces of William
of Malmesbury's words in "nec de toto exercitu, præter
paucissimos eum aliquis concomitatur" and "more gregarii militis manu ad manum congrediens," which
phrases are applied to Harold.

REGENBALD, PRIEST AND CHANCELLOR.

NO better illustration could be given of the fact that valuable historical evidence may lurk, even in print, unknown, than the charters printed, from the Cirencester Cartulary, by Sir Thomas Phillips in *Archæologia* (1836).[1] One can imagine how highly prized they would have been by Mr. Freeman, had he only known of their existence.

Regenbald, of whom Sir Thomas would seem never to have heard, was the first chancellor of England.[2] Mr. Freeman called him, I know not on what authority, "the Norman chancellor of Eadward." Whatever his nationality, it is well established that he was that king's chancellor. He occurs repeatedly in Domesday, where he is distinguished as "Canceler," "Presbyter," and "de Cirencestre." We learn also from its pages that he held land in at least three counties—Berkshire, Herefordshire, and Dorset T.R.E., and that he seems to have received further grants from King William in his return.[3]

The three charters of which I treat are found in the Cirencester Cartulary and are in Anglo-Saxon. The first is one of King Edward's in favour of "Reinbold min preost," and is a confirmation to him of soc and sac, toll and team etc., as his predecessors had enjoyed it "on Cnutes kinges

---

[1] Vol. xxvi., p. 256.

[2] Not counting Leofric, styled "regis cancellarius" by Florence in 1046.

[3] See my life of him in *Dictionary of National Biography.*

daie." The third is a notification from King William that
"ic hæbbe geunnen Regenbald minan preoste eall his lond"
as "he hit under Edþearde hædde mine meie." The chief
points to be noticed here are that the land is granted *de
novo*, not confirmed, and that the Conqueror speaks of
Regenbald as "minan preoste," implying that he has taken
him into his service.

It is the second of these charters that is of quite extraordinary importance. I here append it *in extenso* as printed
by Sir Thomas Phillips:—

"Vyllelm king gret Hereman b. & Wulstan b. & Eustace
eorl & Eadrich & Bristrich & ealle mine þegenes on Þyltone-
shyre & on Glouc'shyre fronliche & ic cuþe eop ic habbe
geunnan Reinbold mina preost þ land æt Esi & þ land æt
Latton & ealle þæra þinge þ þar to liŏ binnan port & buten
miŏ sace & miŏ socne spa full and spa forŏ spa his furmest
on hondan stodan Harald kinge on ællan þingan on dæge
& æfter to atheonne spa spa ealra lefest ys & ic nelle
nenna men geþafian þ him fram honda teo ænig þære þinga
þæs þa ic him geunne habbe bi minan freonshype."

The relevant entry in Domesday speaks for itself:—

Reinbaldus presbyter tenet Latone et Aisi. Duo taini tenuerunt
pro. II. Maneriis T.R.E. Heraldus comes junxit in unum. Geldabat
pro ix. hidis (68*b*).

If the charter were nothing more than a grant from the
Conqueror to a private individual of lands duly entered in
Domesday, it would, I believe, as such be unique. Historians have long and vainly sought for any genuine charter
of the kind; and here it has been in print for nearly sixty
years.

But the document, I hope to show, does far more for us
than this: it opens a new chapter in the history of the
Norman Conquest.

We first notice that the writ is addressed not to Norman,
but to English authorities. The only exception is Count

Eustace, who was, of course, not a Norman, and who was known in England before the Conquest as brother-in-law to Edward the Confessor. The obvious inference is that, at the time this writ was issued, Norman government had not yet been set up in the district. Urse d'Abetot, for instance, the dreaded sheriff of Worcestershire, would probably have been addressed in conjunction with Bishop Wulstan had he been then in power. But we know that he came into power soon after the Conquest, for he had time to be guilty of oppression and to be rebuked for it by Ealdred before that Primate's death in 1069. But as our writ is of this early date, it must be previous to the treason of Count Eustace in 1067. It must therefore belong to the beginning of that year, when William had only recently been crowned king.

We see then here, I think, the Conqueror, in his first days as an English king, addressing his subjects, in a part of the realm not yet under Norman sway, and doing so in their own tongue and in the forms to which they were accustomed. As King Edward in his charter to Regenbald had greeted bishops, earls, and sheriffs, so here his successor greets two bishops, "Eustace Eorl," and two Englishmen representing the power of the sheriff. And so again in his charter to London he began by greeting the Bishop and the Portreeve.[4]

The writ, it will be seen, is addressed to the authorities of Gloucestershire and Wilts. The estate lay in the latter county, but the connexion of Regenbald de "Cirencestre" with Glo'stershire may account for the inclusion of that county. Can we identify "Eadrich" and "Bristrich" with any local magnates? With some confidence I boldly suggest that the latter was no other than the "Bristricus"

---

[4] It might even be suggested that not only this charter but the Essex writ in favour of Deorman (addressed to Bishop William and Swegen the sheriff) belonged to the same early period. Compare, however, the Conqueror's Old English writ that I have discussed ("Londoners and the Chase") in the *Athenæum* of June 30, 1894.

of the Exon Domesday, that famous Brihtric, the son of
Ælfgar, who, to quote from the appendix Mr. Freeman de-
votes to him, "appears distinctly as a great landowner in
most of the western shires," one from whose vast domains
was carved out later the great Honour of Gloucester.
Until now, all we have known of him has been derived
from the Domesday entries of his estates T.R.E. and from
the legend which associates his name with that of Queen
Matilda. But this charter enables us to say that he was
living and still holding his great position in the west in
the early days of William's reign.[5]

From "Bristric" I turn to "Eadric," and ask if we may
not here recognise "Eadric the Wild" himself? This can
only be matter of conjecture, but it is certain that these
two Englishmen are here assigned the place that would be
given to a sheriff, and that "Eadric the Wild"—quidam
præpotens minister," as Florence terms him—was a magnate in the west (Herefordshire and Shropshire) at the
time of the Conquest. Mr. Freeman terms him "a man
about whom we should gladly know more." It is stated
by Orderic that he was one of those who came in and submitted to William at the outset. But Mr. Freeman held it
"far more likely that he did not submit till a much later
time," because Florence says of him in William's absence :
"se dedere Regi dedignabatur." Orderic's statement, however, is not denied, and Florence's words seem to me quite
explicable by the hypothesis that Eadric had refused the
"dangerous honour," as Mr. Freeman terms it, of following
William to Normandy in 1067 among "his English atten-
dants or hostages." Harried, in consequence, by his Norman neighbours, he retaliated by ravaging Herefordshire
in August of that year; while Count Eustace also threw
off his allegiance and made his descent on Dover.

If the identity of "Eadric" is matter of conjecture, that

[5] It is a noteworthy coincidence that "Brihtricus princeps" and
"Eadricus princeps" are among the witnesses to Harold's Waltham
charter in 1062, which Regenbald himself also attests as Chancellor.

of "Eustace eorl" is certain. But no one has known, or even suspected, that he held, at this period, high position in the west. It may be that, as I have already hinted, he was sent by William to a district, as yet only nominally subject, as being, from his previous connexion with England, less obnoxious than a Norman was likely to prove. It would be refining overmuch to suggest that William might also intend to establish him as far as possible from his base of operations at Boulogne.

In any case, we have in this charter a welcome addition to our scanty knowledge of that obscure period when William, as it were, was feeling his feet as an English king. Nor is it its least important feature that it shows us William, contrary to what Mr. Freeman held to be his fundamental rule, speaking of his predecessor as "Harald kinge."

Before taking leave of Regenbald, we may glance at one of the Domesday entries relating to his lands. Mr. Freeman, in two distinct passages, wrote as follows:—

An entry in 99 reads as if the same Regenbald had been defrauded of land by a Norman tenant of his own. "Ricardus tenet in Rode i. hidam, quam ipse tenuit de Rainboldo presbytero licentia regis, ut dicit. Reinbold vero tenuit T.R E." (*Norm. Conq.*, v. 751.)

The rights of the antecessor are handed on to the grantee of his land. . . . So in Exon 432. "Ricardus interpres habet i. hidam terræ in Roda quam ipse emit de Rainboldo sacerdote [Eadward's chancellor?] per licentiam regis, ut dicit qui tenuit eam die qua Rex E. fuit[6] et mortuus." (*Ib.*, p. 784.)

Although these two passages are found in two different appendices, the entries thus diversely adduced are, of course, one and the same. But, it will be seen, the "tenuit" of Domesday is equated by the "emit" of the Exon book. One of the two must be wrong. I should accept the Exon text because "emit licentia regis" is the right

[6] *sic.*

Domesday phrase, because it makes better sense, and because it is a sound principle of textual criticism that the Exchequer scribe was more likely to write the usual "tenuit" for the exceptional "emit" than the Exon scribe to do the converse. I should then read the passage thus:—
"emit de Rainboldo sacerdote—per licentiam regis, ut dicit, —qui tenuit eam die," etc.

If my view be adopted, we here detect noteworthy error in our great and sacrosanct record.

The charter of Henry I. to Cirencester Abbey—in which he had placed Canons Regular, and of which he claimed to be the founder—sets, as it were, the coping-stone on the story of Regenbald.[7]   In it we read :—

Dedi et concessi . . .   totam tenuram Reimbaldi presbyteri in terris et ecclesiis, et ceteris omnibus quæ subscripta sunt. . . .

De rebus autem predictis quæ fuerunt Rembaldi hec statuimus.

The details of Regenbald's possessions are given, and are of special value for collation with Domesday. They set him before us not only as a landowner in five different counties, but also as the first great pluralist. Sixteen churches, rich in tithes and glebe—one might really term them "fat livings "—had passed into the hands of Regenbald "the priest." From the king's phrase, "*dedi* et concessi," he would seem to have been not merely confirming an endowment by Regenbald, but granting lands which had escheated to himself.[8] And this conclusion is confirmed by the fact that the king, while granting them, especially reserved the life interest of the Bishop of Salisbury and of two others—one of them, alas! a bishop's nephew—who must have acquired their rights since Regenbald's death.

This charter, apart from its contents, is of great interest from its mention of the place where and the time when it

[7] See *Monast. Anglic.*, ii. 177.

[8] It is possible, I think, that the only endowment entered to the church at Cirencester in Domesday, viz., two hides at Cirencester, had been originally given by Regenbald.

was granted, together with its list of witnesses. These
were the two Archbishops, the Bishops of Salisbury, Winchester, Lincoln, Durham, Ely, Hereford, and Rochester:
Robert "de Sigillo," Robert de Ver, Miles of Gloucester,
Robert d'Oilli, Hugh Bigot, Robert de Curci, Payne "filius
Johannis et Eustacio et Willelmo fratribus ejus, et Willelmo
de Albini Britone." The charter was granted "apud Buro
nam in transfretatione mea anno incarnationis Domini
MCXXXIII. regni vero mei XXXIII."; and "Burna," as I
have elsewhere shown,[9] was Westbourne in Sussex, on the
border of Hampshire, then in the king's hands by forfeiture
and near the coast. Here therefore we see the king, when
leaving England for the last time, surrounded by his prelates and ministers, and are enabled to say positively who
were with him. I would note the predominance of the
official class represented by the Bishops of Salisbury, Lincoln, and Ely, by the late chancellor, the Bishop of Durham, and by laymen who are found specially entrusted
with administrative work. A long list of witnesses such
as this is specially characteristic of the closing period of
the reign,[19] and, of course, always possesses biographical
value.[11]

Another English writ of the Conqueror, which may be
profitably compared with that we have discussed, is found
in one of the cartularies of Bury St. Edmund's.[12] Its address, as rendered in the transcript, runs :—

William [*sic*] kyng gret Ægelmær Bischop and Raulf Eorl and
Nordman and ealle myne thegnaes on Sudfolke frendliche.

This writ is obviously previous to the deposition of Bishop
Æthelmær in April, 1070, but how far previous it is not

---

[9] Henry I. at "Burne." (*Engl. Hist. Rev.*, 1895.)

[10] As in the charters to Aubrey de Vere (*Baronia Anglica*, 158) and
William Mauduit.

[11] Here, it would seem, is further proof of the Bishops of Ely and Durham assuming their styles before consecration (*infra*, p. 484).

[12] Harl. MS., 743, fo. 8*d*,

easy to say. " Nordman " is clearly the sheriff of Suffolk, who appears in Domesday as " Normannus Vicecomes " (II. 438). His name affords presumption, though not proof, that he was of English birth ;[13] and as his Domesday holding consisted only of rights over two Ipswich burgesses (which he may have acquired during his shrievalty) he is hardly likely to have been one of the conquering race. Of the third official, Earl Ralf, we know a good deal. Mr. Freeman was much puzzled by this " somewhat mysterious person,"[14] but eventually came to the conclusion that " there were two Ralfs in Norfolk, father and son, the younger being the son of a Breton mother : the elder was staller under Edward and Earl under William." The younger was the Earl of Norfolk (or " of the East Angles "), who rebelled and was forfeited in 1075 ; the elder was that " Rawulf " who, in the words of the chronicle, " wæs Englisc and wæs geboren on Norðfolce." Putting our evidence together, I lean strongly to the view that we have here, as in the case of Regenbald, a writ addressed to English authorities before Norfolk had passed into the hands of Norman authorities. Mr. Freeman held that a passage in Domesday (II. 194), to which he had given much attention, should be read—" Hanc terram habuit A[rfastus] episcopus in tempore utrorumque [Radulforum],' and that therefore " the elder Ralph was living as late as 1070, in which year the episcopate of Erfast begins." But the context clearly shows that we should read " A[ilmarus] episcopus," and that, therefore, the elder Ralf died before Æthelmær was deposed. Moreover, Norwich, we are specially told, was entrusted by the Conqueror to William fitz Osbern before his departure from England in March, 1067. William was placed, some two years later, in charge of York castle, and we read in Mr. Freeman's work that " the man who now (autumn, 1069) commanded at Norwich, and who was already, or soon afterwards, invested

---

[13] Mr. Freeman held him to be an Englishman.
[14] *Norm. Conq.* [2nd Ed.], iii. 773. Cf. 1st Ed., iii. 752-3 ; iv. 277.

with the East-Anglian Earldom was the renegade native
of the shire, Ralf of Wader."[15] This, it will be seen, contradicts his own, and supports my reading of the Domesday passage quoted above. Everything therefore points
to the "Raulf Eorl" of our writ dying or being deposed
shortly after the Conquest.

Before taking leave of this writ we may note that, dealing as it does with Suffolk, it is addressed to Earl Ralf as
Earl, not merely of Norfolk, but of East Anglia. This is
of some importance, because Mr. Freeman wrote, speaking
of the Regents appointed in 1067 :—

There was no longer to be an Earl of the West Saxons or an Earl of
the East Angles. . . . Returning in this to earlier English practice, the Earl under William was to have the rule of a single shire
only, or if two shires were ever set under one Earl they were at least
not to be adjoining shires. The results of this change have been
of the highest moment. (iv. 70.)

Yet on page 253, as we have seen, we read of "the East
Anglian Earldom," and on page 573 that the younger
Ralph "had received the Earldom of East Anglia"—
Florence of Worcester distinctly terming him "East-An-
glorum comite." Mr. Freeman, indeed, was led by this
passage to style him "Earl of Norfolk or of the East Angles."[16] I believe this latter style to be perfectly correct,
and, as I have shown in my *Geoffrey de Mandeville* (p. 191),
to apply even to the Bigod earldom in the days of Stephen.

The curious English writ that has suggested these con-
siderations ought to be compared with a Latin one, also in
favour of St. Edmund's, on which I lighted in examining
the "Registrum Album" of the Abbey. It is one of those
exceedingly rare documents that find their correlatives in
Domesday. The words of the writ are these :—

W. rex Anglor' E. epo. B. Abbi. W. Malet salm. sciatis vos mei
fideles me concessisse servitium de Liuremere quam Werno hactenus

---

[15] *Norm. Conq.*, iv. (1st Ed.) 252-3.
[16] iii. (2nd Ed.) 773.

de me tenuit sancto Ædmundo Et filia Guernonis in vita sua de Abbate B. tenuit. [17]

The last clause is clearly an addition by the cartulary scribe. Now this charter being addressed, like the other, to Æthelmær ("Ethelmerus"), Bishop of the East Angles, is, of course, previous to April, 1070. I should, therefore, also place it previous to the capture of William Malet at York in September, 1069. But this, unlike the other date, is matter of probability rather than of proof. Mr. Freeman believed that William returned, and died "in the marshes of Ely" (1071), but this is only a guess in which I cannot concur. [18] In any case, we have evidence here of this well-known man having held a position in Suffolk (where he owned the great Honour of Eye) analogous to that of sheriff. He may have succeeded Northman in that office.

The relevant Domesday entry is as follows :—

Hujus terram rex accepit de abbate et dedit Guernoni depeiz [de Peiz]. Postea licencia regis deveniens monachus reddidit terram." (363 *b*.)

The charter records, I take it, the "licencia regis" of Domesday. [19]

[17] Add. MS., 14, 314, fo. 32*b* (pencil).

[18] See my letter on "the death of William Malet" in *Academy* of Aug. 26, 1884.

[19] Since this paper was written, there has appeared the valuable Bath Cartulary (Somerset Record Society) containing a most remarkable charter (p. 36), which should be closely compared with those to Regenbald. It is issued by William the King and William the Earl, and must undoubtedly be assigned to the former's absence from England, March-December, 1067. It shows us therefore William fitz Osbern acting as Regent and anticipating the office of the later Great Justiciar by inserting in the document his own name. This charter, like that to Regenbald, is addressed to the still English authorities of an unconquered district.

THE CONQUEROR AT EXETER.

"And y seide nay, and proved hit by Domesday."[1]

FOR a companion study to the Battle of Hastings, one could not select a better subject than the Siege of Exeter by William in 1068. It is so, because, in the tale of the Conquest, "No city of England," in Mr. Freeman's words, "comes so distinctly to the front as Exeter";[2] and because, as editor of "Historic Towns," he chose Exeter, out of all others, as the town to be reserved for himself.[3] "Its siege by William," we are told, "is one of the most important events of his reign";[4] but it was doubtless the alleged "federal" character of Exeter's attitude at this crisis that gave its story for him an interest so unique. This episode, moreover, has many advantages: it is complete in itself; it is rich in suggestion; it is taken from the period in which the Professor described himself as "most at home"; and its scene is laid within his own borders, his own West Saxon land. It presents an admirable test of Mr. Freeman's work at the point where he was admittedly strongest, and his thoroughly typical treatment of it affords a perfect illustration of the method he employed.

[1] Letter from John Shillingford, Mayor of Exeter, 1447.

[2] *Exeter* (1887), p. 34.

[3] It was also the subject of a special paper in his "Historic Towns and Districts" (1883) reprinted from *Arch. Journ.*, xxx. 297, pp. 49 et sq., and *Sat. Rev.*, xxix. 764-5.

[4] *Sat. Rev.*, xxix. 765.

The year 1067 was drawing to its close when the Conqueror, summoned back from Normandy by the tidings of pressing danger, returned to spend his Christmas at Westminster amidst "the sea of troubles which still awaited him in his half-conquered island-kingdom."[5] Threatened at once by foes within and without the realm, he perceived the vital necessity of severing their forces by instant suppression of the "rebellions" at home, *swift* suppression before the invaders were upon him, *stern* suppression before the movement spread. Let us bear in mind these twin motives, by which his policy must at this juncture have been shaped, the need for *swiftness*, with invasion in prospect, and the need for *sternness* as a warning to "rebels."

Of all the "rebellious" movements on foot, that at Exeter, as Mr. Freeman admits, was "specially hateful in William's eyes."[6] It was against Exeter, therefore, that the Conqueror directed his first blow. In the depths of winter, in the early days of the new year, "he fared to Devonshire." Such is the brief statement of the English Chronicle. We hear of William at Westminster; we next hear of him before the walls of Exeter: all that intervenes is a sheer blank. Of what happened on this long westward march not a single detail is preserved to us in the Chronicle, in Orderic or in Florence. Now it is precisely such a blank as this that, to Mr. Freeman, was irresistible. We shall see below how, a few months later, we have, in William's march from Warwick to Nottingham, a blank exactly parallel.[7] There also Mr. Freeman succumbed to the temptation. He seized, in each case, on the empty canvas, and, by a few rapid and suggestive touches, he has boldly filled it in with the outlines of historical events, not merely events for which there is no sufficient evidence,

---

[5] *Norman Conquest*, iv. 123. The metaphor of a "sea" waiting in an "island" is sufficiently original to be deserving of notice.

[6] *Ibid.*, iv. 140.

[7] See "The alleged destruction of Leicester," *infra*, p. 456.

but events which can be proved, by demonstration, to have had no foundation in fact.

The scene elaborated by Mr. Freeman to enliven the void between the departure from London and the entrance into Devonshire is THE RESISTANCE AND THE DOWNFALL OF "THE CIVIC LEAGUE."[8]   This striking incident in the Exeter campaign I propose to analyse without further delay.

It must, in the first place, be pointed out that we have no proof whatever of this "Civic League" having even existed.   To apply Mr. Freeman's words to his own narrative,—

The story is perfectly possible. We only ask for the proof. Show us the proof; . . . then we will believe. Without such a proof we will not believe.[9]

For proof of its existence Mr. Freeman relies on a solitary passage in Orderic.[10]   But Orderic, it will at once be seen, does not say that any such league was effected; he does not even say that the league which was contemplated was intended to be an exclusively Civic League. What he does say is that the men of Exeter sought for allies in the neighbouring coasts (*plagæ*)[11] and in other cities.   The Dorset townlets, such as Bridport, with its 120 houses, would scarcely represent these "cities."   Mr. Freeman assumed, however, that "the Civic League" was formed, assumed that the Dorset towns had "doubtless" joined it, and finally assumed that they were "no doubt"

---

[8] iv. 151.   "It is certain," Mr. Freeman had written, "that what William had to strive against in the West was a league of towns" (*Sat. Rev.*, xxix. 765).

[9] *Cont. Rev.*, June, 1877, p. 22.   See also Preface.

[10] "Hi nimirum socios e plagis finitimis inquiete arcessebant . . . alias quoque civitates ad conspirandum in eadem legationibus instiga-bant."—*Ord. Vit.*, 510 A (quoted in *Norman Conquest*, iv. 140).

[11] Mr. Freeman rendered it "neighbouring shires," but I am not at all sure that, taken in conjunction with the words just before about the accessibility of Exeter from Ireland and Brittany, and those just after, about "mercatores advenas," *plagæ* does not refer to the shores from which these merchants came.

B. H.   F F

besieged by William in consequence.[12]   These assumptions he boldly connected with the entries on the towns in Domesday, entries which we shall analyse below, and which are not only incorrectly rendered, but are directly opposed to the above assumptions.

What, then, is the inference to be drawn? Simply this. The "Civic League" must share the fate of the "palisade on Senlac." The sieges which took place "probably" never took place at all; the League never resisted; the League never fell; in short, there is not a scrap of evidence that there was ever such a League at all. The existence of such a League would be, unquestionably, a fact of great importance. But its very importance imperatively requires that its existence should be estabished by indisputable proof. Of such proof there is none. One can imagine how severely Mr. Freeman would have handled such guesses from others. For he wrote of a deceased Somersetshire historian who boldly connects the story of Gisa with the banishment of Godwine":—

One is inclined to ask with Henry II., "Quære a rustico illo utrum hoc somniaverit?" But these things have their use. Every instance in the growth of a legend affords practice in the art of distinguishing legend from history.

It should, however, in justice be at once added that this story did not originate wholly with Mr. Freeman himself. He refers us on the subject of the League to his predecessor, Sir Francis Palgrave. The brilliant imagination of that graceful writer was indeed led captive by the fascinating vision of "the first Federal Commonwealth," yet he did not allow himself, when dealing with the facts, to deviate from the exact truth. His statement that Exeter "*attempted to form* a defensive confederation" reproduces with scrupulous accuracy Orderic's words. And even when he

[12] The boroughs of Dorset were doubtless among the towns which had joined in the civic league. Probably they stood sieges and were taken by storm" (*N. C.*, iv. 151).

passed from fact to conjecture, there was nothing in his conjecture at variance from fact. From him we have no suggestion that the Dorset towns resisted William or "stood sieges." It was left for Mr. Freeman to carry into action Palgrave's line of thought, and, by forcing the evidence of the Domesday Survey into harmony with the story he had evolved, to show us, in his own words, "the growth of a legend." For, as he observed with perfect truth,—

What we call the growth of a story is really the result of the action of a number of human wills. The convenient metaphor must not delude us into thinking that a story really grows of itself as a tree grows. In a crowd of cases . . . the story comes of a state of mind which does not willingly sin against historical truth, but which has not yet learned that there is such a thing as historical truth.

Had Mr. Freeman done so himself? Did he ever really learn to distinguish conjecture from fact? One asks this because within the covers of a single work, his *English Towns and Districts*, that Civic League which in the *Norman Conquest* is said to have existed "no doubt," is in one place said to have existed "perhaps," and in another is set forth as an undoubted historic fact :—

Exeter stood forth for one moment . . . the chief of a con-federation of the lesser towns of the West. . . . A confederation of the western towns, with the great city of the district at their head, suddenly started into life to check the progress of the Conqueror.

Finally, in his "Exeter" (1887), the same story again appears, without a word of caution, as absolute historic fact. Exeter, we read, was

the head of a gathering of smaller commonwealths around her ; . . . the towns of Dorset were in league with Exeter. . . . We have no record of the march, but it is plain that the towns of Dorset were fearfully harried.

Through all Mr. Freeman's work we trace this same ten-dency to confuse his own conjectures with proved historic fact.

For the details of this fearful harrying we are referred to the Domesday Survey. It was "no doubt," we learn, when William marched on Exeter (1068), that

Dorchester, Bridport, Wareham, and Shaftesbury underwent that fearful harrying, the result of which is recorded in Domesday. Bridport was utterly ruined; not a house seems to have been able to pay taxes at the time of the Survey. At Dorchester, the old Roman settlement, the chief town of the shire, only a small remnant of the houses escaped destruction. These facts are signs, etc., etc.

"These facts," we find, will not bear investigation. To refute them in the case of Bridport, "there is nothing to be done but to turn to the proper place in the great Survey." Following this, his own, precept, we learn that there is nothing in Domesday of our author's "utter ruin"; and that so far from "not a house" being "able to pay taxes," Domesday tells us that four-fifths of the houses then existing could and did pay them. Here, again, the errors arose from not reading Domesday "with common care." The entry runs: "Modo sunt ibi c. domus, et xx. sunt ita destitutæ," etc. The meaning, of course, is that twenty houses were impoverished. Mr. Freeman must have hurriedly misconstrued his Latin, and read it as a hundred and twenty. No error that he detected in Mr. Froude could be worse than representing Bridport, on the authority of Domesday, as the greatest sufferer among the Dorset towns, when Domesday itself proves that it suffered least of all. And so, too, with Dorchester. On turning to Domesday, we learn with surprise that the "small remnant" of houses remaining there was eighty-eight as against one hundred and seventy-two in the days of King Edward. From an appendix of our author's to which we are referred, we glean the fact that

at Dorchester, out of a hundred and seventy-two houses no less than a hundred and twenty-eight were "penitus destructæ a tempore Hugonis vicecomitis usque nunc."

Here, again, Mr. Freeman's error can be traced beyond

the possibility of question, to a misreading of Domesday : the entry runs, "modo sunt ibi quater xx. et viii. [88] domus, et c. [sunt] penitus destructæ." Mr. Freeman must have hurriedly ignored the "quater," and then added the "twenty-eight" thus evolved to the hundred houses that were destroyed. All this Mr. Freeman did, and we have in "that great record, from which there is no appeal," the proof of the fact. Clearly, in the notable words of M. Bémont (*Revue Historique*), "il est prudent de revoir après lui les textes qu'il invoque." [13]

The strange thing is, that Sir Henry Ellis's work, though "far from being up to the present standard of historical scholarship" could have saved him, here also, from error as it gives the correct figures from Domesday.

But passing from "facts" to theories, we find Mr. Freeman holding that "no doubt," "doubtless," "probably," the destruction recorded in Domesday was wrought by the Conqueror himself in 1068. Why should this guesswork be substituted for history, when we have "always the means," as our author himself wrote, "of at once turning to the law and testimony to see whether these things are so?" A glance at Domesday effectually disposes of Mr. Freeman's theory; for the Survey is here peculiarly explicit: with anxious care, with painful iteration, it assures us that, in the case of Wareham, the devastation was wrought "a tempore Hugonis vicecomitis," and that, in the case of Shaftesbury and in the case of Dorchester, it was wrought "a tempore Hugonis vicecomitis usque nunc." These categorical statements are conclusive: they place the whole of the devastation subsequent to the accession of the Norman sheriff, Hugh FitzGrip. Mr. Eyton, in hi work on the Dorset Domesday, held that they fix it as

---

[13] Mr. Archer deemed it sufficient reply to all these "trifling blunders" to admit that "Mr. Freeman did misread 128 for 100" (*Cont. Rev.*, March, 1893, p. 337). I invite comparison of the errors I have corrected, and of all the edifice built upon them, with this disingenuous attempt to represent them as unimportant "slips" (*Ibid.*, p. 354).

having occurred between 1070 and 1084; the words, however, "usque nunc" carry it on down to 1086, and, but that I must now come to Exeter, I could show the real bearing of these allusions to Sheriff Hugh.

The breakdown, when tested, of the alleged " Civic League" strangely vindicates the sound insight of that sagacious historian who explicitly asserted that the English boroughs

never, as was the case in Scotland and in Germany, adopted a confederate bond of union, or organised themselves in leagues.[14]

Yet, in his *English Towns and Districts*, Mr. Freeman was led by his own tale of the resistance of the western lands and their capital to argue from it as from a proved historic fact :—

When Exeter stood forth for one moment . . . *the chief of a confederation of the lesser towns of the West* . . . we see that the path was opening by which Exeter might have come to be another Lubeck, the head of a Damnonian Hanse, another Bern, the mistress of the subject-lands of the western peninsula. Such a dream sounds wild in our ears.[15]

It does indeed. But it does so for the reason that it is founded on a fact which has no historic existence. Yet, for Mr. Freeman, with his fertile imagination afire with the glories of ancient Greece and of countless mediæval Commonwealths, this same "wild dream" possessed an irresistible fascination. "It is none the less true," he hastened to add, that—

when a confederation of the western towns, with the great city of the district at their head, suddenly started into life to check the progress of the Conqueror, it shows that a spirit had been kindled, etc., etc. . . . It is worth while to stop and think how near England once was to running the same course as other lands, etc., etc.[16]

set forth his doings there are short, pithy, and terrible. He took what vengeance he would for the slaughter of his men (iii. 533-4).

Dover, on the contrary, made no resistance, but surrendered before he "had thrown up a bank, or shot an arrow." It was, therefore, "plainly his policy to show himself mild and *debonnair* as it had been his policy at Romney to show himself beyond measure stark." [27]

Such being William's settled principle, what might the citizens of Exeter expect? Even before the siege began the fear that they had sinned too deeply for forgiveness made them disown the capitulation their leaders had arranged.[28] The reference is doubtless to conduct similar to that which had brought upon Romney William's merciless vengeance.[29] But how stood the case at its close?

(1) They were rebels. And for these "rebels, as they were deemed in Norman eyes" (iv. 135), confiscation was the penalty (iv. 127-8).

(2) "The movement at Exeter" was not merely a rebellion, but one which was "specially hateful in William's eyes" (iv. 140).

(3) They had been guilty of "cruel and insulting treatment" to William's earlier emissaries (iv. 138).

(4) They had offered William himself an "insult as unseemly as it was senseless" (iv. 155).

(5) They had flung to the winds their own capitulation with such audacity that William "ira repletus est" (iv. 152).

(6) They had offered a prolonged and desperate resistance, costing the lives of many of his men (iv. 156).

Verily, in William's eyes, the cup of Exeter's iniquities must have been exceeding full.

Even in cases of ordinary resistance his practice, we

[27] iii. 536-7.

[28] "Supplicia pro reatu nimis metuebant."

[29] "Militibus crudeliter et contumeliose illuserant quos ipse de Normannia miserat et tempestas ad portum illorum appulerat."

learn, was so uniform that Mr. Freeman could take it for granted, " after the fall of Exeter," that—

the heavy destruction which fell on the town of Barnstaple, in the north-western part of Devonshire, and the still heavier destruction which fell on the town of Lidford, might seem to show that these two boroughs were special scenes of resistance (iv. 163).[80]

Therefore, in the aggravated case of Exeter, we could but expect him to deal with its citizens as he had dealt with those of Alençon,[81] and as he was to deal, hereafter, with the sturdy defenders of Ely.[82] A fearful vengeance was their certain doom. There was, moreover, as I stated at the outset, a need for sternness at this juncture that might justify William, apart from vengeance, in inflicting such signal punishment as should deter all other " rebels."

Yet what do we find ? The citizens, we read, were " favourably received," and " assured of the safe possession of their lives and goods." Nay, William even " secured the gates with a strong guard of men whom he could trust in order to preserve the goods of the citizens from any breaches of discipline." [83] The dreaded Conqueror, " post tot iras terribilesque minas," had suddenly become mild as a lamb, and Mr. Freeman accepts it all quite as a matter of course.

Such conduct would, surely, have been a positive premium on revolt.

[80] So too we read of Torkesey, a little later on, that it suffered so " severely as to suggest the idea that William met with some serious resistance at this point " (iv. 217) ; while speaking of the " Fall of Chester," Mr. Freeman wrote : " We know that the resistance which William met with in this his last conquest was enough to lead him to apply the same stern remedy which he had applied north of the Humber. A fearful harrying fell on city and shire, and on the lands round about " (iv. 314-5).

[81] " The Conqueror, faithful to his fearful oath, now gave the first of that long list of instances of indifference to human suffering," etc. (ii. 285).

[82] " At Ely, as at Alençon, the Conqueror felt no scruple against inflicting punishments which to our notions might seem more frightful than death itself " (iv. 476).

[83] iv. 160.

A castle, of course, was raised; but this was inevitable, whether a town submitted peaceably or not. For instance, "it is plain," Mr. Freeman wrote, "that Lincolnshire submitted more peaceably, and was dealt with more tenderly, than most parts of the kingdom" (iv. 216); but "a castle was, of course, raised at Lincoln, as well as elsewhere," and "involved the destruction of a large number of houses" (217-8), very many more than at Exeter.

One "penalty," however, remains as the price that Exeter was called upon to pay for all her guilt. This, we read, was "the raising of its tribune to lessen the wealth which had enabled it to resist." [34] For its wealth is admitted. Now, before criticising Mr. Freeman's view, let us clearly understand what that view was. Taking, as is right, his latest work—though his view had not altered— we read of Exeter in 1050:—

The city which had been the morning-gift of Norman Emma was now, along with Winchester, part of the morning-gift of English Edith, daughter of Godwine, sister of Harold. At Exeter she was on her own ground; the royal revenues within the city were hers. [85]

In 1086, we learn—

The whole payment was eighteen pounds yearly. Of this sum six pounds—that is the earl's third penny—went to the Sheriff Baldwin. . . . The other twelve pounds had formed part of the morning-gift of the lady, and though Edith had been dead eleven years, they are entered separately as hers. [86]

So far, all is consistent and clear enough. But we find it immediately added that—

This regular yearly payment of eighteen pounds had taken the place of various uncertain payments and services. . . . Thus the citizens of Exeter, who had offered to pay to William what they had paid to former kings, found their burthens far heavier than they had been in the old time. And the lady, while she lived, reaped her full share of the increased contributions of her own city. [87]

[34] *English Towns and Districts.*
[85] *Exeter* (1887), p. 32.   [86] *Ibid.*, pp. 43-4.
[37] *Ibid.*, p. 44.

Or, as expressed in his great work,—

The money payment was now raised from an occasional half-mark of silver to eighteen pounds yearly. The rights of the old lady were not forgotten, and Eadgyth received two-thirds of the increased burthen laid upon her morning-gift.[38]

If the "twelve pounds had formed part of the morning-gift of the lady," and were accordingly received by her, as we learn,[39] in the days of King Edward, how could they possibly form part of a new "burthen" laid upon Exeter, as a punishment for its resistance, by William? And if the only payment due, under Edward, was an occasional half-mark of silver "for the use of the soldiers"[40] what were "the royal revenues" from Exeter that Edith was drawing in 1050? A moment's thought is enough to show that Mr. Freeman's statements contradict themselves, as, indeed, he must have seen, had he stopped to think. But this he sometimes failed to do.

The whole source of Mr. Freeman's confusion was his inexplicable misunderstanding of the Domesday entry on the city.[41] We must first note that both his predecessors— Palgrave, who was lacking in "critical faculty," and Ellis, who was "far from being up to the present standard of historical scholarship"—had read this entry rightly, and given, independently, its gist. It will best enable my readers to understand the point at issue if I print side by side the paraphrases of Exeter's offer given by Palgrave and by our author.

---

[38] *N.C.*, iv. 162.   [39] *Exeter*, p. 32.

[40] *Exeter*, p. 44; *Norm. Conq.*, iv. 147.

[41] This grave confusion, with all that it involves, was one of the "trifling slips," as Mr. Archer terms them (*Cont. Rev.*, p. 354), exposed in my original article (*Q.R.*, July, 1892). Such a description is either dishonest, or must imply that Mr. Archer, who boasts that he has a sterner criterion" than myself (*E.H.R.*, ix. 606), deems such errors of no consequence.

PALGRAVE.	FREEMAN.
Tribute or gafol they would proffer to their king such as was due to his predecessors. . . . They (1) would weigh out the eighteen pounds of silver; (2) the geld would be paid, if London, York, and Winchester submitted to the tax; and (3) if war arose, the king should have the quota of service imposed upon five hydes of land. . . . But the citizens refused to become the men . . . of their sovereign; they would not . . . allow the Basileus to enter within their walls.	We are ready to pay to him the tribute which we have been used to pay to former kings. . . . The city paid in money only when London, York, and Winchester paid, and the sum to be paid was a single half mark of silver. When the king summoned his *fyrd* to his standard by sea or by land, Exeter supplied the same number of men as were supplied by five hides of land. . . . But the men of Exeter would not, each citizen personally, become his men; they would not receive so dangerous a visitor within their walls.[42]

I have numbered the clauses in Palgrave's paraphrase which render the three successive clauses in the Domesday Book entry. The first refers to the *firma* of the town, payable to its lord (the king);[43] the second to the "geld" (tax), payable to the king *qua* king;[44] the third to its military service.[45] The distinction between the three clauses is admirably seen under Totnes (i. 108, *b*), and the sense of Domesday is absolutely certain to any one familiar with its formulas.[46]

[42] *N.C.*, iv. 146-7.

[43] "Hec reddit xviii. lib. per annum" (100).

[44] "Hæc civitas T.R.E. non geldabat nisi quando Londonia et Eboracum et Wintonia geldabant, et hoc erat dimidia marka Argenti ad opus militum" (100).

[45] "Quando expeditio ibat per terram aut per mare, serviebat hæc civitas quantum v. hidæ terræ" (100).

[46] The practice in the Survey of Devon was to state the render in 1086, and, if it had been different formerly, to add a note to that effect. Thus we read on 100*b*: "Reddit xlviii. lib. ad pensam. Ante Balduinum reddebat xxiii. lib." So, too, of Totnes: "Inter omnes redd' viii. lib. ad numerum. Olim reddebant iii. lib. ad pensam et arsuram" (108*b*)

The "commutation of geldability" (as Mr. Eyton termed it) was by no means peculiar to Exeter. Totnes paid, "when Exeter paid," the same sum of half a mark "pro geldo." Bridport paid the same "ad opus Huscarlium regis" (75), Dorchester and Wareham a mark each, and Shaftesbury two marks (Eyton's *Dorset Domesday* 70-72). In these Dorset instances, one mark represented an assessment of ten hides.

What Mr. Freeman did was to confuse the first clause with the second, and to suppose that both referred to the "money payment" of the town, the first under William, the second under Edward. He thus evolved the statement that under William "the money payment was raised from an occasional half-mark of silver to eighteen pounds yearly." This is roughly equivalent to saying of a house rented at fifty pounds, and paying a tax of one pound, that its "money payment" was raised from one pound to fifty.

But this confusion, with all its results, is carried further still. Edith's share of the eighteen pounds is entered in Domesday as "xii. lib[ras] ad numerum." This Mr. Freeman rightly gave as the amount in 1086;[47] but turning back a few pages, we actually read that—

In Domesday twelve houses in Exeter appear as "liberæ ad numerum in ministeriis Edid reginæ.[48]

This is, of course, the same entry, only that here our author changed pounds into houses, and *libras* into *liberæ*. What idea was conveyed to his mind by a house "libera ad numerum" I do not profess to explain. But, oddly enough, as he here turned pounds into houses, so in a passage of his *William Rufus* he turned houses into pence.[49]

The essence of the whole matter is that the "burdens" to which Exeter was subject were not raised at all, but remained precisely the same as had been paid to former

[47] iv. 162.   [48] *Ibid.*, 139.
[49] Reading "Eudo Dapifer [tenet] v. denarios," where Domesday (ii. 106) has, of course, "v. d[omus]."

kings. And this fact is the more notable, because, as Mr. Freeman had to admit, "even the tribute imposed by William" [on his own hypothesis] "was not large for so great a city," and, one may add, a rich one.[50] Indeed, it was so small as to fairly call for increase.[51] Even Lincoln, which, according to Mr. Freeman, received "favourable" treatment from William, had its "tribute largely raised"[52] in fact, more than trebled.[53] What we have to account for, therefore, is the fact that a city which had defied, insulted, and outraged William, received not only "a free pardon,"[54] but peculiar favour at his hands.

The paradox itself is beyond dispute, whatever may be said of my solution.

For a solution there is. Only it is not to miracles or legends, nor to the flatterings of courtly chaplains that we must look to learn the truth, but, in the words of a memorable essay, to "the few unerring notices in Domesday and the chronicles."[55] As yet we have not, it must be remembered, heard the story from the English side. Let us turn, therefore, to the English version, to what Mr. Freeman described as "the short but weighty account in the Worcester Chronicle, which gives hints which we should be well pleased to see drawn out at greater length."[56] These

---

[50] Mr. Freeman held that Domesday hinted it might be classed with London, York, and Winchester (*Norm. Conq.*, iv. 147 ; *Exeter*, 45), and quotes William of Malmesbury's description of its wealth and importance. Even in earlier days, he wrote, "both the commercial and the military importance of the city were of the first rank" (i. 308).

[51] The *firma* of Gloucester had been raised to £60, and that of Chester to over £70, while at Wallingford, where the king had about as many houses as at Exeter, it was £80.

[52] *Norm. Conq.*, iv. 213.

[53] "T.R.E. reddebat civitas Lincolia regi xx. libras et comiti x. libras. Modo reddit c. libras ad numerum inter regem et comitem" (D. B., i. 336*b*).

[54] *Norm. Conq.*, iv. 160.

[55] Mr. Freeman's "Pedigrees and Pedigree-makers" (*Cont. Rev.*, June, 1887, p. 33).

[56] *N.C.*, iv. 151.

B. H.   G G

hints I shall now examine, though I doubt if Mr. Freeman's friends will be well pleased with the result.

We have in the Chronicle a straightforward story, not only intelligible in itself, but also thoroughly in harmony with the known facts of the case. The king finds himself compelled to lay formal siege to Exeter (" besæt þa burh "); he is detained before its walls day after day (" xviii. dægas ") in the depth of an English winter, "and þær wearð micel his heres forfaren." The need for sternness was there indeed; but swiftness was to him, for the moment, a matter of life and death. Held at bay by those stubborn walls, learning the might of those "two generals"—January and February—in whom the Emperor Nicholas put his trust, William was in sore straits. Take Mr. Freeman's own words:

The disaffected were intriguing for foreign help; . . . there was a chance of his having to struggle for his crown against Swend of Denmark; . . . men were everywhere seeking to shake off the yoke, or to escape it in their own persons. Even where no outbreak took place local conspiracies were rife.[57]

Swend was in his rear, half England on his flank; before him reared their head the walls of dauntless Exeter.[58] In that bleak wilderness of frost and snow his men were falling around him, and, in very bitterness of spirit, the Conqueror bowed himself for need. So, at least, I boldly suggest. He fell back on his "arts of policy," and set himself to win by alluring terms the men whom he could not conquer. In the words of the chronicle, he promised them well (" ac he heom well behet ").

[57] *N.C.*, iv. pp. 103, 118. So too *ibid.*, p. 126: "There was the imminent fear of an invasion from Denmark, and the threatening aspect of the still independent west and north. William had need of all his arts of war and policy to triumph over the combination of so many enemies at once."

[58] "Cives eam tenebant furiosi, copiosæ multitudinis, infestissimi mortalibus Gallici generis."—*Ord. Vit.*

This solution, of course, differs *toto cœlo* from Mr. Freeman's narrative. We have seen that he blindly accepted
the statements of that "abandoned flatterer, William of
Poitiers (whom Orderic had here "doubtless followed" [59])—
against whom he elsewhere warned us—and combined them
with a miracle from William of Malmesbury, which he
euhemerized in the style that he himself had ridiculed in
Thierry.[60] And as he could not harmonise the courtly version with the "short but weighty account" in the Chronicle
he cut the knot by dismissing the latter, and pronouncing
his own version "the most likely." [61]

Resuming the narrative, we learn that the thegns—the
party of non-resistance from the first—must have seized
this opportunity for impressing on their "concives" the
necessity of embracing the offer, whereupon the latter, in
the words of the chronicle, "gave up the town because
the thegns had betrayed them." It is just possible that the
word "geswicon" may point to some direct treachery, but
it seems best and most naturally explained as referring to
their unpatriotic advice, which would naturally appear to
English eyes a "betrayal" of the national cause. There
can be little doubt, from the admissions of William of
Poitiers (through the mouth of Orderic), that the terms
of agreement included not only a free pardon for all past
offences, and for the city's aggravated resistance, but also
security for person and property from plunder by the
Norman soldiery. And the witness of "the great record"
implies that "the Exeter patricians," as Mr. Freeman
styled them [62]—"the civic aristocracy" [63]—gained their
original selfish aim, and secured an undertaking that they

---

[59] *N.C.*, iv. 146.

[60] It is curious to see how Thierry waters down the miracle : 'Son
cheval, glissant sur le pavé, s'abattit et le froissa dans sa chute.' Of
course this is likely enough to have been the kernel of truth in the legend,
but no man has a right to tell the tale in this shape as if it were undoubted fact."—*Norm. Conq.*, iv. 291.

[61] *Norm. Conq.*, iv. 151-2.

[62] *Ibid.*, 146.   [63] *Ibid.*, p. 147.

should not pay a penny more than their "tributum ex consuetudine pristina."

What security, it may be asked, could they obtain for the terms they seem to have exacted? Bold as it may seem, I would here venture to read between the lines, and to make the suggestion—it is nothing more—that when there issued from the gates "the clergy of the city, bearing their sacred books and other holy things" (as Mr. Freeman rendered the words of Orderic), the real object of their coming forth was to make the king swear upon their relics [64] to the observance of the terms they had obtained. It was indeed the irony of fate if William, who was ever insisting on the breach of Harold's oath, was driven, by the force of circumstances, to take such an oath himself.

But, it may be urged, should we be justified in treating thus drastically the witness of Orderic, or rather, of William of Poitiers? At Alençon, I reply, in Mr. Freeman's words:—

> William of Poitiers is silent altogether, both as to the vengeance and as to the insult. Neither subject was perhaps altogether agreeable to a professed panegyrist (*Norm. Conq.*, ii. 285).

Stronger, however, is the case of Le Mans, and more directly to the point. "William," we read, "followed the same policy against Exeter (1068) which he had followed against Le Mans" (1063); [65] and so, in 1073, we find him "calling on the men of Le Mans, as he had called on the men of Exeter," to submit peacefully, and escape his wrath. [66] Unlike "the Exeter patricians," indeed, "the magistrates of Le Mans" did receive the king peacefully within their walls; they did not incur the guilt of offering armed resistance. But the essential point at Le Mans is that—

the Norman version simply tells how they brought the keys of

---

[64] Cf. the familiar phrase, "Tactis sacris evangeliis," with Orderic's words here, "sacros libros."

[65] *Norm. Conq.*, iv. 151.

[66] *Ibid.*, 559.

the city, how they threw themselves on William's mercy, and were graciously received by him. The local writer speaks in another tone. The interview between the king and the magistrates of Le Mans is described by a word often used to express conferences—in a word, *parliaments*—whether between prince and prince, or between princes and the estates of their dominions. They submitted themselves to William's authority as their sovereign, but they received his oath to observe the ancient customs and *justices* of the city. Le Mans was no longer to be a sovereign commonwealth, but it was to remain a privileged municipality.[67]

The words "acceptis ab eo sacramentis, tam de impunitate perfidiæ quam de conservandis antiquis ejusdem civitatis consuetudinibus"[68] would apply exactly to the case of Exeter, and William may well have done there what he actually did, we here read, at Le Mans. There would have been at Exeter even greater need for an oath, in that its "perfidia" had been so much the worse.

But now comes the curious parallel. Though quoting and scrutinising so closely the meagre accounts of the Exeter campaign, Mr. Freeman seems to have oddly overlooked the significant words of Florence, although, of course, familiar with his narrative. Florence, we find, employs a phrase corresponding with that in the *Vetera Analecta*.

FLORENCE.	"VET. AN."
Cives autem *dextris acceptis* regi se dedebant.	*Acceptis ab eo sacramentis . . .* sese et sua omnia dederunt.

Mr. Freeman argues from the case of Le Mans that *dedere* in these times did not imply the fulness of a Roman *deditio*.[69] But we are not merely dependent upon this. The words, "dextris acceptis," I contend, imply a promise and a pledge for its performance, and cannot therefore be reconciled with an unconditional surrender.

Now if it were not for the fortunate preservation of the

[67] *Norm. Conq.*, iv. 560.   [68] *Ibid.*
[69] iv. 560.

Vetera Analecta in the case of Le Mans, Mr. Freeman would there also, as at Exeter, have been hoodwinked by "the Norman version."[70]   I am anxious not to employ a phrase which might be deemed offensive or unjust, so I restrict myself to that which he himself applied to his predecessor, Palgrave, when, speaking of the story of Eadric and his brother, he wrote that Sir Francis Palgrave "swallowed the whole tale.[71]   Whether my solution be accepted or not, it is, I repeat, conjectural.   I have, at least, shown that there is a mystery to be solved, that Mr. Freeman's version fails to solve it, and that, so far from Domesday recording the punishment inflicted upon Exeter, it actually heightens the mystery of the case by proving that Exeter obtained exceptionally favourable treatment.

It is not merely a question of how Exeter fell.   The issue illustrates the policy and affects the character of William.   The lame manner in which Mr. Freeman accounts for his sudden conversion from fury to lamblike gentleness is no less unsatisfactory than his treatment of the "weighty account" in the Chronicle when he found that this, his valued authority, rendered the problem difficult.   Even at Le Mans more was needed than merely to print both stories.   The fact that we find in "the Norman version" the truth conveniently glossed over ought to be insisted on and duly applied.   Time after time in Mr. Freeman's work we find him paraphrasing patches of chronicles, under the impression that he was writing history.   The statements of witnesses are laid before us, neatly pieced together, but they are not subjected to more than a perfunctory cross-examination.   Even if the accurate reproduction of testimony were all that we sought from the historian, we should not, so far as Domesday is concerned, obtain it in this instance.   But the case of

[70] "Edicta regalia suis opportune intimavit, et urbanis imperiose mandavit, ut prudenter sibi consulerent" (*Ord Vit.*, ii. 255).

[71] *Norm. Conq.*, i. 662.

Exeter is one where something more is needed, where even accuracy is not sufficient without the possession of that higher gift, the power of seizing upon the truth when the evidence is misleading and contradictory. The paraphrasing of evidence is the work of a reporter; from the historian we have a right to expect the skilled summing-up of the judge.

THE ALLEGED DESTRUCTION OF LEICESTER (1068).

THIS question was raised and discussed by Mr. Freeman in his "History of the Norman Conquest" (iv. 196-7). We there read as follows :—

Is it possible that in the case of Leicester, at least, no power was left either to follow or to resist? While we have no evidence either way on which we can rely with confidence, one of those secondary and local records, which sometimes contain fragments of authentic tradition, suggests, in a perfectly casual way, that a doom fell upon Leicester, which might, doubtless, with some exaggeration, be spoken of as utter destruction. And this incidental hint may perhaps draw some indirect confirmation from the highest evidence of all [Domesday] . . . and it may be that Leicester earned its overthrow by a defence worthy of a borough which was to give its name to the greatest of England's later worthies.

The "record referred to is quoted in a footnote, and is a history of the foundation of Leicester Abbey, one of a class of narratives notoriously inaccurate and corrupt :—

Robertus Comes Mellenti, veniens in Angliam cum Willelmo Duce Normanniæ, adeptus consulatum Leycestriæ, ex dono dicti Ducis et Conquestoris Angliæ, *destructa prius civitate Leicestriæ* cum castello et ecclesia infra castellum tempore prædicti Conquestoris, reædificavit ipsam æcclesiam Sancta Mariæ infra castellum.

Now, it strikes one in the first place as somewhat unlikely that William, on his arrival at Leicester, should find a castle to destroy. But, further, how could Robert have obtained the "consulatus" of Leicester from the Conqueror, when he is well known to have first obtained it (under very peculiar circumstances) from Henry the First? If this known event has been so glaringly antedated, may not the alleged "destruction" be so likewise? These it may be said are only doubts. But, as it happens, we can not only discredit the suggested "destruction" in the days of the Conqueror: we can actually fix its date as the reign of Henry the First.

We learn from Orderic that the town of Leicester ("urbs Legrecestria") was divided into four quarters, of which Ivo de Grantmesnil possessed two, one in his own right, and one (which was the King's share) as the King's reeve and representative. We also learn that he was among the "seditiosi proceres," who rebelled against Henry in 1101, and that of these, "aliqui contra fideles vicinos guerram arripuerunt et gremium almæ telluris rapacitatibus et incendiis, cruentisque cædibus maculaverunt." Ivo is again mentioned by Orderic in 1102, not only among the "proditores" of the previous year, who were now called to account, but also as a special ringleader in that internecine conflict to which he had already referred. He tells us that Henry

Ivonem quoque, quia guerram in Anglia cœperat et vicinorum rura suorum incendia combusserat (quod in illa regione crimen est inusitatum nec sine grave ultione fit expiatum), rigidus censor accusatum nec purgatum ingentis pecuniæ redditione oneravit, et plurimo angore tribulatum mæstificavit.

In short, as Dr. Stubbs reminds us, Ivo "has the evil reputation of being the first to introduce the horrors of private warfare into England." Bearing in mind the divided authority from which Leicester suffered, and the statement that Ivo, ruling half the town, plundered and made fierce war upon his neighbours, we arrive at the conclusion that the "destruction," which, in the *Monasticon* narrative, precedes the accession of the Count of Meulan to the *comitatus* of Leicester, may be assigned, without a shadow of doubt, to the struggle of 1101.

On Ivo's disgrace, as is well known, the wily Count stepped at once into his shoes, "et auxilio regis suâque calliditate totam sibi civitatem mancipavit, et inde consul in Anglia factus." There is no reason to doubt the statement that St. Mary "de Castro" was rebuilt and refounded by Count Robert after his obtaining this position at Leicester.

It is singular that just as the *Monasticon* seems to have misled Mr. Freeman at Leicester, so it is responsible for Thierry's "story of the fighting monks of Oxford," at about the same time, a story of which Mr. Freeman wrote that "the whole story is a dream," and "would not have been allowable even in an historical novel" (iv. 779-780).

ELY AND HER DESPOILERS

(1072-75)

THE elaborate record of this trial is only found, I believe, in the Trinity College (Cambridge) MS., O. 2,
1 (fos. 210*b*-213*b*) from which it has been printed by Mr.
Hamilton in his *Inquisitio Comitatus Cantabrigiensis* (pp.
192-195). This " placitum," therefore, would seem to have
remained unknown till the publication of that work (1876.)

The date of this important document can be fixed within
a few years. It mentions Earl Waltheof among those
before whom the plea was held, so that it cannot be later
than 1075 ; and as it also mentions " Rodulfus comes," it is
evidently previous to the revolt of the earls in that year.
On the other hand, it is later than the death of William
Malet, for it mentions his son Robert as in possession, and
later, therefore, than the restoration of Waltheof at the
beginning of 1070. Moreover, it is subsequent to the death
of Stigand ("post obitum illius "). Now Stigand was not
even deposed till the spring of 1070 ; and we know from
Domesday and other sources that he lived some time afterwards. We may safely say, therefore, that this " placitum "
did not take place till after the suppression of the Ely
revolt in the autumn of 1071. Practically, therefore, our
document belongs to the years 1072-1075. Now, as Abbot
Thurstan did not die till 1076—the date given in the
" Liber Eliensis," and accepted by Mr. Freeman—it follows
that this great act of restitution in favour of the Abbey
took place under Abbot Thurstan himself, a fact unmen-

tioned by the chroniclers, and unsuspected by Mr. Freeman, who held that he found no favour in William's eyes.

The great length of this document—so important for its bearing on Domesday—precludes its discussion in detail. But its opening clause must be given and some of its features pointed out.

Ad illud placitum quo pontifices Gosfridus et Remigius, consul vero Waltheuus, necnon vicecom[ites] Picotus atque Ilbertus jussu Willelmi Dei dispositione Anglor[um] regis, cum omni vicecomitatu sicut rex preceperat, convenerunt, testimonio hominum rei veritatem cognoscentium determinaverunt terras que injuste fuerant ablate ab ecclesia sancte Dei genitricis Marie de insulâ ely . . . quatinus de dominio fuerant, tempore videlicet regis Ædwardi, ad dominium sine alicujus contradictione redirent quicunque eas possideret.

The mention of Count Eustace among those withholding lands proves that at the date of this document he was already restored to his possessions. Another individual whose name occurs several times in this document is Lisois (De Monasteriis"), the hero of the passage of the Aire. Collating its evidence with that of Domesday, we find that Lisois had been succeeded, at the date of the great record, by the well-known Eudo Dapifer in a fief, ranging over at least five counties—Cambridgeshire, Bedfordshire, Norfolk, Suffolk, and Essex—in all of which Domesday records his name as the predecessor of Eudo. This is of the more interest because Mr. Freeman wrote :—

The only notice of this Lisois which I can find in Domesday is in ii. 49*b*, where he appears in possession, but seemingly illegal possession, of a small holding in Essex.

So again we have in our document this passage relating to Stigand :—

He sunt proprie ville monasterii insule Ely quos Stigandus archipresul tenebat, unde per annum victum fratribus reddidit tantum quantum pertinet ad hoc. Has vero tenet rex noster W. post obitum illius, Methelwald et Crokestune et Snegelwelle et Dictun.

Now Stigand, according to the *Liber Eliensis* "quasdam illius optimas possessiones sicut Liber Terrarum insinuat, ad maximum loci dispendium retinuit." Our document identifies these "possessiones" with Methwold and Croxton in Norfolk, Snailwell and Ditton in Cambridgeshire, and thus disposes of Mr. Freeman's very unfortunate suggestion—advanced, of course, to justify Stigand—that the *Liber Eliensis* here referred to a tiny Hampshire estate, which the Abbey had held under Stigand T.R.E.[1]

In my paper on Domesday I have pointed out the importance of this document in its bearing on socmen and their services, while we saw in investigating knight-service that its language affords, in this matter, a valuable gloss on that of Domesday. Close examination of its details shows that the aggressions on the Abbey's property which it records, were, in spite of the verdict on this occasion, persisted in, if not increased. Those, for instance, of Hardwin may be recognised in the duplicate entries in Domesday Book, representing the conflicting claims.[2] On persons as on lands we have some fresh information. Ilbert the Sheriff was, I believe, identical with that "Ilbert de Hertford," who is alluded to in Domesday (i. 200), and would thus be a pre-Domesday Sheriff of Herts.[3] The entry, "tenet Rotbertus homo Bainardi in Reoden de soca," when compared with the holding of "Rienduna" by Ralf "Baignardi" in Domesday (ii. 414), suggests that we have in Bainard the father (hitherto unknown) of this Domesday tenant-in-chief. Bainard would thus be a Christian name, as was also Mainard, which occurs in this same document.

[1] D.B., i. 40*b*.   [2] See p. 23 *supra*.

[3] Domesday (i. 200*b*) styles him, "Ilbertus de Hertford," and connects him with "Risedene," a Hertfordshire Manor. On the other hand, the I.C.C. makes him "Ilbertus de Hereforda" (p. 56), and "Ilbertus vicecomes" is actually found in Herefordshire (D.B., i. 179*b*) But what could he be doing in Cambridgeshire?

THE LORDS OF ARDRES

IN the *History of the Norman Conquest* (2nd Ed.) we read of Eustace of Boulogne :—

An incidental notice of one of his followers throws some light on the class of men who flocked to William's banners, and on the rewards which they received. One Geoffrey, an officer of the Abbey of Saint Bertin at Saint Omer, who had the charge of its possessions in the County of Guines, sent his sons, Arnold and Geoffrey, to the war . . . and in the end they received a grant of lands both in Essex and in the border shires of Mercia and East-Anglia, under the superiority of their patron Count Eustace (iii. 314).

In an Appendix on "Arnold of Ardres," which Mr. Freeman devoted to this subject (iii. 725-26), he gave the "Historia Comitum Ardensium" (of Lambert of Ardres) for his authority, and he verified, by Domesday, the Manors which Lambert assigns to "these adventurers," holding that a Bedfordshire estate was omitted, while "Stebintonia," which he identified with Stibbington, Hunts, was wrongly included, as it was "held of Count Eustace by Lunen."

The first point to be noticed here is that "these adventurers" were the sons (as Lambert explains) not of any "Geoffrey," a mere Abbey officer, but of a local magnate, Arnold, Lord of Ardres. The next is that Lambert was quite correct in his list of Manors.

In the fourth series of his historical essays Mr. Freeman included a paper on "The Lords of Ardres," for which he availed himself of Dr. Heller's edition of Lambert in the *Monumenta* (vol. xxiv.). In this edition the passage runs :—

Feodum Stevintoniam et pertinencias eius, Dokeswordiam, Tropintoniam, Leilefordiam, Toleshondiam, et Hoilandiam (cap. 113, p. 615).

Dr. Heller, on this, notes :—

Secundum "Domesday Book" recepit Ernulfus de Arda Dochesworde, Trupintone (com. Cantabrig.) et Stiventone (comit. Bedford) a comite Eustacio . . . e contra Toheshunt [*sic*] Hoiland, Leleford recepit ab eodem comite Adelolfus de Merc (prope Calais).

This note enabled Mr. Freeman to identify "Adelolfus" (which he had failed to do in the *Norman Conquest*), though he must have overlooked the identification of "Stevintonia" (namely Stevington, Beds.), for we find him still writing :—

But of the English possessions reckoned up by our author two only . . . can be identified in Domesday as held by Arnold . . . The local writer seems to have mixed up the possessions of Arnold with those of a less famous adventurer from the same reign, Adelolf—our Athelwulf—of Merck (pp. 184-5)

And he again insisted that "Arnold had other lands in Bedfordshire."

We will now turn to an entry in the *Testa de Nevill* from the "milites tenentes de honore Bononie" :—

Comes de Gines tenet xii. milites, scilicet—in Bedefordescire, in *Stiveton* et Parva Wahull 111 milites, in Cantabr' in *Dukesword*, et *Trumpeton* 111 milites . . . in Essex, *Tholehunt* et Galdhangr' 111 milites, in *Hoyland'* et *Lalesford* ibidem 111 milites.

Here we have all the Manors mentioned by Lambert (with their appurtenances) assigned to the Count of Guines, the heir of Arnold of Ardres ; and we can thus believe the *Testa* entry (p. 272) of Tolleshunt and Holland, "quas idem comes et antecessores sui tenuerunt de conquestu Angliæ." But the *Testa* does more than this ; it informs us that Holland and Lawford were held of the Count by "Henry de Merk." Now, "Adelolf" de Merk is found in Domesday holding many Manors direct from Eustace of Boulogne, and these Manors are divided in the *Testa* between his descendants Simon and Henry de Merk.[1] It is, therefore, possible that he held the three Essex Manors in 1086, not directly from Count Eustace, but, like his descendant, from their under-tenant (Arnold). This raises, of course, an important question as to Domesday.[2]

It is interesting to observe that the village of Marck in the Pas de Calais has, through Adelolf and his heirs, transferred its name to the Essex parish of Mark's Tey, though not to that of Marks Hall (so named in Domesday).

While on the subject of the Lords of Ardres, it may be convenient to give the reference to a letter of mine to the *Academy* (28th May, 1892), explaining that Lambert's "Albericus Aper," who puzzled Dr. Heller and Mr. Freeman, was our own Aubrey de Vere, first Earl of Oxford, and that Lambert's statement (accepted by Mr. Freeman) as to the parentage of Emma, wife of Count Manasses, had been disproved by Stapleton.

[1] An interesting charter belonging to the close of Stephen's reign shows us Queen Matilda compensating Henry "de Merch" for his land at Donyland (one of these Manors)—which she was giving to St. John's, Colchester—"de redditibus transmarinis ad suam voluntatem." Another and earlier charter from her father and mother (printed by Mr. E. J. L. Scott in the *Athenæum* of 2nd December, 1893) has Fulco de merc and M. de merc among the witnesses.

[2] The non-appearance of Arnold's brother, "Geoffrey," in Domesday which has been deemed a difficulty, is accounted for by Lambert's statement that he made over his English possessions to Arnold.

EARLY IRISH TRADE WITH CHESTER AND ROUEN [1]

THE eighth report of the Royal Commission on Histori- cal Manuscripts speaks of the records of the city of Chester as "beginning with Henry the Second's writ of license to the citizens of Chester to trade in Durham [*sic*] as they were wont to do in the time of Henry the First" (p. xv.). The records themselves are similarly described in the actual report on them (pp. 355-403) as "beginning with a curious writ, addressed by Henry the Second to his bailiffs of the city of Durham" [*sic*]. This, which is among those items spoken of as "especially interesting and im- portant," figures thus at the head of the calendar:—

(1) Henry II. License to the burgesses of Chester to buy and sell at Durham [*sic*] as they were wont to do in the time of Henry I. —" Henricus Dei gratia Rex Anglie et Dux Normannie et Aquitanie et Comes Andegavie balluis [*sic*] de Dunelina [*sic*] salutem:— Precipio quod Burgenses Cestrie possint emere et vendere ad detail- lum [*or* doraillum] apud Dunelinam [*sic*] habendo et faciendo eas- dem consuetudines quas faciebant tempore Regis Henrici avi mei et easdem ibi habeant rectitudines et libertates et liberas consuetudines quas tempore illo habere solebant, teste, Willelmo filio Ald' dapifero Apud Wintoniam.

Durham is not only a most improbable place for such a writ to refer to, but is also an impossible rendering of the

---

[1] The error as to the Chester writ was explained by me in a letter to the *Academy* (No. 734).

B.H.   H H

Latin name. The interest and importance of this " curious writ" has, in short, been obscured and lost through the ignorance of Mr. J. C. Jeaffreson, to whom the report was entrusted. The charters which follow the writ, and which are printed on the same page, refer to this writ as relating to Ireland; and the town, of course, to which it refers is not Durham but Dublin (*Duuelina*).

We have, therefore, in this writ an almost, if not quite, unique reference by Henry the Second to Dublin in the days of his grandfather, and a confirmation of the "liber-tates, etc., which the men of Chester had then enjoyed there, just as if his grandfather had been in his own position. Secondly, we have here record evidence, not merely of a recognised connection, but of what might be termed treaty relations between the traders of Chester and the Ostmen of Dublin, long previous to the Conquest of Ireland, thus confirming Mr. Green's observation, "the port of Chester depended on the trade with Ireland, which had sprung up since the settlement of the Northmen along the Irish Coasts.[2] And this has, of course, a bearing on the question of "a Danish settlement" at Chester. Thirdly, we learn from this document that at the date of its issue Dublin was governed by bailiffs of the King (*ballivi sui*).

What, then, was its date? The clue, unfortunately, is slight; but it may not improbably belong to the close of 1175 or early part of 1176. This brings us to the interesting question, why was such a writ issued? Remembering that during his stay at Dublin (November, 1171—January, 1172) Henry II. had granted that city to his men of Bristol, we may hold it in accordance with the spirit of the time, and, indeed, a matter of virtual certainty, that Bristol would have striven on the strength of this grant to exclude "its rival port" (*Conquest of England*, p. 443) from the benefits of the Dublin trade. Chester would, therefore, appeal to the King on the strength of its antecedent rights,

[2] *Conquest of England*, p. 440.

and would thus have obtained from him this writ, recognising and confirming their validity.

The Domesday customs of the city (i. 262*b*) contain a curious allusion to its Irish trade:—

> Si habentibus martrinas pelles juberet prepositus regis ut nulli venderet donec sibi prius ostensas compararet, qui hoc non observabat xl. solidis emendabat . . . Hæc civitas tunc reddebat de firma xlv. lib et iii. timbres pellium martrinium.

There is nothing to show where these marten skins came from, or why they are mentioned under Chester alone. But on turning to the customs of Rouen, as recorded in the charters of Duke Henry (1150-1) and King John (1199), we find they were imported from Ireland.

> Quæcunque navis de Hibernia venerit, ex quo caput de Gernes [Guernsey] transierit, Rothomagum veniat, unde ego habeam de unaquâque nave unum tymbrium de martris aut decem libras Rothomagi, si ejusdem navis mercatores jurare poterint se ideo non mercatos fuisse illas martras ut auferrent consuetudinem ducis Normanniæ, et vicecomes Rothomagi de unaquaque habeat viginti solidos Rothomagi et Camerarius Tancarvillæ unam accipitrem aut sexdecim solidos Rothomagi.

Giraldus Cambrensis, it may be remembered, alludes to the abundance of martens in Ireland,[8] and describes how they were captured. We thus have evidence in Domesday of the Irish trade with Chester, even in the days of Edward the Confessor.

[8] " Martrinarum copia abundant hic silvestria " (*Top. Hib.*, i. 24).

WALTER TIREL AND HIS WIFE

IN his detailed examination of all the evidence bearing on the death of William Rufus, the late Mr. Freeman carefully collected the few facts that are known relative to Walter Tirel. They are, however, so few that he could add nothing to what Lappenberg had set forth (ii. 207) in 1834. He was, however, less confident than his predecessor as to the identity of Walter Tirel with the Essex tenant of that name in Domesday. I hope now to establish the facts beyond dispute, to restore the identity of Walter Tirel, and also to show for the first time who his wife really was.

The three passages we have first to consider are these,— taking them in the same order as Mr. Freeman :—

Adelidam filiam Ricardi de sublimi prosapia Gifardorum conjugem habuit, quæ Hugonem de Pice, strenuissimum militem, marito suo peperit (*Ord. Vit.*).

Laingaham tenet Walterus Tirelde R. quod tenuit Phin daous pro ii. hidis et dimidia et pro uno manerio (*Domesday*, ii. 41).

Adeliz uxor Walteri Tirelli reddit compotum de x. marcis argenti de eisdem placitis de La Wingeham (*Rot. Pip.*, 31 Hen. I.).

Dealing first with the Domesday entry, which comes, as Mr. Freeman observed, "among the estates of Richard of Clare," I would point out that though Ellis (who misled Mr. Freemam) thought that "Tirelde" was the name, the right reading is "tenet Walterus Tirel de R[icardo]," two words (as is not unusual) being written as one. Turning next to the words of Orderic, we find that Lappenberg renders them " Adelaide, Tochter des Richard Giffard," and Mr. Freeman

as "a wife Adelaide by name, of the great line of Giffard."
But there is no trace of a Richard Giffard, nor can " Adelida" herself be identified among the Giffards. The explanation of the mystery, I hold, is that she was the
daughter, not of a Giffard, but of Richard *de Clare*, by his
wife Rohese, daughter of Walter Giffard the elder. It is
noteworthy that Orderic employs a precisely similar expression in the case of another Adeliza, the daughter of Robert
de Grentmesnil. He terms her "soror Hugonis de Grente-
maisnil de clara stirpe Geroianorum," though she was only
descended from the famous Geroy through her mother.
Richard's daughter was sufficiently described as " Adelida
filia Ricardi," just as her brothers were known as "Gilbertus filius Ricardi," "Rogerus filius Ricardi," etc. The
position of that mighty family was such that this description was enough, and they were even known collectively
as the " Ricardi," or " Richardenses" (*Mon. Ang.*, iv. 609),
This is well illustrated by the passage in the Ely writer,
describing Adeliza's brother Richard, Abbot of Ely, as

parentum undique grege vallatus, quorum familiam ex Ricardis
et Gifardis constare tota Anglia et novit et sensit. Ricardi enim et
Gifardi, duæ scilicet ex propinquo venientes familiæ, virtutis fama et
generis copia illustres effecerat.

The above forms are curious, but not without parallel.
Thus the descendants of Urse d'Abetot are spoken of as
"Ursini" in Heming's Cartulary. Æthelred of Rievaulx
speaks of "Poncii" and "Morini" as present at the battle
of the Standard ; Gerald, in a well-known passage (v. 335),
speaks of the "Giraldidæ" and "Stephanidæ," and Orderic,
we have seen, of the "Geroiani."

The doubly influential character of this descent is well
illustrated in this passage (*quantum valeat*) from the chronicle of St. John's Abbey, Colchester.

Parcebatur tamen Eudoni, propter genus uxoris ipsius Rohaisæ :
erat enim hæc de genere nobilissimo Normannorum, filia scilicet
Ricardi, qui fuit filius Gilberti Comitis, duxitque Rohaisam uxorem,

quæ erat soror Willelmi Giffardi, Episcopi Wintoniæ. Itaque, cum fratres et propinqui junioris Rohaisæ quoslibet motus machinaturi putarentur, si contra maritum ipsius aliquid durius decerneretur, sic factum est ut interventu predicti Episcopi," etc., etc.

This passage is, I believe, the sole evidence for the real parentage of Bishop William. It was clearly unknown to Canon Venables, who wrote the Bishop's life for the *Dictionary of National Biography*.

Like most of these "foundation" histories, this document is in part untrustworthy. But it is Dugdale who has misread it, and not the document itself that is responsible for the grave error (*Baronage*, i. 110) that Eudo's wife was "Rohese, daughter of Walter Giffard, Earl of Buckingham." Here again, as in the Tirel case, the daughter of a Clare, by a Giffard, is converted into a Giffard. The error arose from referring the "qui" to Eudo instead of to his father-in-law, Richard. The "Historia" is perfectly consistent throughout in its identification of the younger Rohese, of whom it states that "commorata est marito annis triginta duobus, cui ante habiles annos nupta est" (iv. 609).

In asserting under "Clare" (*Baronage*, i. 208) that Eudo married the widow (not the daughter) of Richard, Dugdale relied on another and more inaccurate document (*Mon. Ang.*, v. 269) which actually does speak of

Rohesia una sororum Walteri [Giffard secundi]—duas plures enim habuit—conjuncta in matrimonio Ricardo filio Gilberti, qui in re militari, tempore Conquestoris, omnes sui temporis magnates præcessit—

as marrying Eudo Dapifer after her husband's death. But we must decide in favour of the Colchester narrative: Eudo's wife was her daughter and namesake.

We see then that Walter Tirel was son-in-law to Richard de Clare, who had enfeoffed him in "Laingaham" before 1086. Now this "Laingaham" was Langham in Essex, just north of Colchester, which gives us an important clue, Walter's widow "Adeliz" was in possession in 1130 (*Rot.*

Pip., Hen. I.) because, as we have seen, it was probably given her by her father " in maritagio." But her son Hugh held it under Stephen, and Anstis saw among the muniments of the Duchy of Lancaster a mortgage of it by Hugh to Gervase "Justiciar of London." I have not yet identified this "mortgage," but the confirmation of it to Gervase de Cornhill by Earl Gilbert de Clare, as chief lord of the fee, is extant,[1] and its first witness is Earl Gilbert of Pembroke, so that it cannot be later than 1148, or earlier than 1138 (or 1139). Moreover in yet another quarter (Lansdown MS. 203, 15 dors.) we find a copy of a charter by this latter Earl Gilbert, belonging to the same occasion, which runs as follows:—

Com. Gilb. de Penbroc omnibus hominibus Francis et Anglis sal. Sciatis me concessisse illam convencionem et vendicionem quam Hugo Tirell fecit Gervasio de Chorhella de manerio suo de Laingham parte mea. Nam Comes de Clara ex parte sua illud idem concessit, de cuius feodo predictum manerium movet.

Both charters contain the curious "movet" formula, in England so rare that I think I have not met with any other instance. It is, of course, equivalent to the regular French phrase: "sous sa mouvance." This mortgage or sale was probably effected as a preliminary to the crusade of 1147, in which Hugh Tirel is known to have taken part. Now the above Gervase, as I have shown in my *Geoffrey de Mandeville* was no other than Gervase de Cornhill, and after his death we find Langham duly in the possession of his son, Henry de Cornhill.[2] The chain of evidence is thus complete, and the identity of the Tirels and of their Manor placed beyond question.

[1] Duchy of Lancaster: Grants in boxes, A. 157. It is there described as "conventionem et venditionem quam Hugo Tirell' fecit Gervasio de cornhella de manerio suo de lauhingeham," which implies an actual sale rather than a mortgage. The seal of Earl Gilbert, with the three chevrons on his shield, is, I claim, an earlier instance, by far, of coat-armour on a seal than any hitherto known (see my paper in *Arch Journ.*, II. 46).

[2] Duchy of Lancaster: Royal Charters, No. 42.

But returning to the parentage of Walter's wife, we find
that it raises a curious question by the family circle to
which it introduces us. For we now learn that Gilbert and
Roger, sons of Richard de Clare, who were present at
Brockenhurst when the King was killed, were brothers-in-
law of Walter Tirel, while Richard, another brother-in-law,
was promptly selected to be Abbot of Ely by Henry I., who
further gave the see of Winchester, as his first act, to
William Giffard, another member of the same powerful
family circle.[8]   Moreover, the members of the house of
Clare were in constant attendance at Henry's court, and
"Eudo Dapifer," whose wife was a Clare, was one of his
favourites.   I do not say that all this points to some
secret conspiracy, to which Henry was privy, but it shows
at least that he was on excellent terms with Walter Tirel's
relatives.

I have explained in my article on the Clares in the *Dictionary of National Biography* that there has been much
confusion as to the family history. As the errors are very
pesistent, it may perhaps be of some service, especially for
identifying names, if I append a pedigree for the period of
the Tirel connexion, which will distinguish the descendants of Count Gilbert, "illustrious alike in his forefathers
and his descendants."

Two charters will illustrate the attendance of the family
at court in the early days of Henry I. An interesting
charter belonging to Christmas, 1101, is attested by "Gislebertus filius Ricardi et Robertus filius Baldwini et Ricardus
frater ejus," while the attestations to one of 3rd September,
1101, comprise "G[islebertus] filius R[icardi] R[ogerus] (or
R[obertus]) frater suus W[alterus] frater suus. . . .
R[obertus] (or R[icardus]) filius B[aldwini].[4]

Among the most persistent of errors are those which

---

[8] A metrical epitaph, preserved by Rudborne, claims for him a descent
from Charlemagne, which implies that he, like Walter's wife, was "de
sublimi prosapia Gifardorum " (see p. 468 *supra*).

[4] See also *Geoffrey de Mandeville*, p. 329.

identify Richard "filius Baldwini" with Richard de Red-vers (who was of a different family and died long before him), and which make this compound Richard an Earl of Devon.

Planché endeavoured to slay the former of these errors, —which, originating in the *Monasticon*, is embalmed in Dugdale's Baronage,—as Taylor had previously done in his "Wace," and the Duchess of Cleveland has rightly ob-served in her *Battle Abbey Roll* (1889) that "there is not the slightest authority for assuming "the identity. But the necessity for again correcting the error is shown by its reappearance in Mr. Freeman's *Exeter* (1887) and by the life of Baldwin de Redvers, in the *Dictionary of National Biography*, by Mr. Hunt, which begins by stating that he was "the eldest son of Richard, Earl of Devon, the son of Baldwin de Moeles," whereas his father was not an Earl, and was not the son of Baldwin de Moeles.

I may also take this opportunity of pointing out that (as is shown in my *Geoffrey de Mandeville*) Richard fitz Gil-bert (d. 1136) was not an earl, the earldom of Herts having been ante-dated like that of Devon.

Dugdale again has omitted, because he failed to identify, another daughter of the house of Clare, who made a most interesting match. This was "Adelidis de Tunbridge," wife of William de Percy, a niece and namesake, I con-fidently suggest, of Walter Tirel's wife. She seems to have brought into the Percy family the names of Richard and Walter. The charters which establish, I think, her identity are those of Sallay Abbey, in which Maud (widow of William, Earl of Warwick) and her sister Agnes (ances-tress of the later Percies) speak of their mother as "Ade-lidis de Tunbridge" (*Mon. Ang.*, v. 512-3). She can only, therefore, in my opinion, have been a daughter of Gilbert "de Tunbridge"; and with this conclusion the dates har-monize well. Yet another daughter was Margaret, wife of William de Montfichet, who brought into that family the names of Gilbert and Richard.

We have yet to deal with one more member of this historic house, Baldwin fitz Gilbert, or Baldwin de Clare, ancestor, through his daughter and heir, of the family of Wake. I had always suspected that Baldwin fitz Gilbert, the recognised grandfather of Baldwin Wac (1166), could be no other than Baldwin, son of Gilbert de Clare, a well-known man. But Dugdale, under "Wake" (i. 539) positively asserts that the former was "brother to Walter de Gant, father of Gilbert de Gant, the first Earl of Lincoln of that family." This proves, however, on enquiry, to be based on an almost incredible blunder. Dugdale actually relied on a charter,[5] which includes Baldwin among the Clares, and which he himself under " Clare " rightly so interprets (*Baronage*, i. 207*b*). There is, therefore, no ground for deriving Baldwin from De Gant, or for rejecting his identity with that Baldwin *de Clare*, who addressed the troops on behalf of Stephen at the battle of Lincoln.[6]

Having made several additions to the Pedigree of De Clare, I have also to make one deduction in Robert fitz Richard's alleged younger son "Simon, to whom he gave the Lordship of Daventry in Northamptonshire" (*Baronage*, i. 218). This erroneous statement is taken from a monastic genealogy (blundering as usual) in the Daventry Cartulary.[7] The documents of that house show at once that Simon was the son of Robert fitz "Vitalis" (a benefactor to the house in 1109), not of Robert fitz Richard, and was not therefore, a Clare. Nor was he lord of Daventry.

But Dugdale's most unpardonable blunder is his identification of Maud "de St. Liz," wife of William de Albini Brito. He makes her sixty years old in 1186 (p. 113), and

---

[5] Old *Monasticon*, i. 245*b* ; and *vide infra*, p. 522. A curious sketch of the above scene in a MS. of Henry of Huntingdon (Arundel MS. 148) depicts Baldwin with two of the Clare chevrons on his shield, and a marginal note, almost illegible, duly describes him as grandfather of Baldwin Wac. This sketch is overlooked in the Brit. Mus. catalogue of drawings.

[6] See also *Rot. Pip.*, 31 Hen. I., and my *Geoffrey de Mandeville*.

[7] *Mon. Aug.*, v. 178.

yet widow of Robert fitz Richard, who died in 1134 (p. 218), finally stating that "she died in *anno* 1140" (*Ib*)! Here, as in the case of Eudo Dapifer, William's wife was the daughter, not the widow. In both cases the lady was a Clare. The fact is certain from his own authority, the cartularies of St. Neot's.[8] We have a grant that "Rob[ertus] filius Ric[ardi]" at fo. 79*b*, grants from "Matildis de Sancto Licio (*al.* 'Senliz') filia Roberti filii Ricardi" on the same fo., and on the preceding one (fo. 79) this conclusive one as to her husband :—

Ego Willelmus de Albineio Brito et Matild' uxor mea dedimus et concessimus ecclesiam de Cratefeld deo et ecclesie Sci. Neoti et monachis Beccensibus pro anima Roberti filii Ricardi et antecessorum meorum.

Then follows their son's confirmation, as "Willelmus de Albeneio filius Matillidis de Seint Liz." Next, "Willelmus de Albeneio filius Matild' de Senliz," gives land, "quam terram Domina Matild' Senliz mater mea eis prius concesserat,"—her said grant of land in Cratfield duly following as from "Matild de Senliz filia Roberti filii Ricardi." Further, we have Walter fitz Robert (fitz Richard) confirming this grant by his sister Matildis. Finally, we learn that Cratfield belonged to her in "maritagio." Now (as "Cratafelda") it belonged in Domesday to Ralf Baignard. His honour, on his forfeiture, was given to Robert fitz Richard, who was thus able to give Cratfield "in maritagio" to his daughter. Here then is independent proof of what her parentage really was, and further independent proof, if needed, is found in this entry (1185) :—

Matillis de Sainliz que fuit filia Roberti filii Ricardi, et mater Willelmi de Albeneio est de donatione Domini Regis et est lx. annorum (*Rot. de Dominabus*, p. 1).

We thus learn that, as with Avicia "de Rumilly," daughter of William Meschin, it was possible for a woman

---

[8] Cott. MS. Faustina A. iv. See also Addenda.

to bear, strange though it may seem, the maiden name of her mother. Clearly, Maud was the widow of William de Albini, who sent in his *carta* (under Leicestershire) in 1166, and died, as I reckon, from the Pipe Rolls, in Nov., 1167. She was not, as alleged, the widow of the William who fought at the Battle of Tinchebray in 1106.

Lastly, we come to the parentage of Walter Tirel himself. Mr. Freeman wrote that this was "undoubted," that "Walter was one of a family of ten, seemingly the youngest of eight sons" of Fulc, Dean of Evreux, and that "he became, by whatever means, lord of Poix in Ponthieu and of Acheres by the Seine" (*W. Rufus,* II. 322, 673).[9] But the mystery of his rise is not lessened by the fact that, as Mr. Freeman put it, most accounts "connect him with France rather than with Normandy." Closer investigation suggests that Orderic in no way identifies the Walter Tirel of 1100 with the son of Dean Fulc, and shows indeed that his French editors had specially declared the two to be distinct. In short, Walter had nothing to do with Dean Fulc or with Normandy, but was, as categorically stated, a Frenchman, the third of his name who occurs as Lord of Poix. Père Anselme identifies him with the second (who occurs in 1069), but he is probably identical with the third, who occurs in an agreement with the Count of Amiens, 1087, and who, with his wife "Adelice," founded the Priory of St. Denis de Poix,[10] and built the Abbey of St. Pierre de Sélincourt. It was he who was father of Hugh the Crusader.[11]

---

[9] Mr. Freeman rendered Walter Map's "Achaza" by "Achères." But as the Tirels always styled themselves "Sires de Poix Vicomtes d'*Equesnes*" it is probable that the latter was meant.

[10] His gift was confirmed by Geoffrey, Bishop of Amiens, who died in 1116.

[11] The essential reference occurs in the charter of 1069 granted by Ralf, Count of Amiens, which mentions "Symon filius meus et Gualterus Gualteri Tirelli natus" (Archives depart. de le Somme : Cartulaire de N.D. d'Amiens, No. 1, fo. 91). These were the first and second known bearers of the name. The latter occurs in a St. Riquier charter of 1058. Poix was some fifteen miles from Amiens, and its lordship was of con-

Here may be mentioned another name by which Walter seems to have been known. I take it from the twelfth century chronicle of Abbot Simon in the "Chartularium Sithiense,"[12] which appears to have eluded Mr. Freeman's researches when he made his collection of all the versions of the death of William Rufus :—

Willelmus prioris Willelmi regis Angliæ filius, eodem anno a Waltero *de Bekam*, ex improviso, interficitur. Qui, cum rege in saltu venatum iens, dum sagitta cervum appeteret, eadem divinitus retorta, rex occiditur. Cujus interitus sancte recordationis viro Hugoni, abbati Cluniacensi est præostensus, etc., etc.

The testimony of a St. Omer writer on the deed of the Lord of Poix is, even if traditionary, worth noting; but I do not profess to explain the "Bekam."[13]

If we now turn to the French writers, we find that the special work on the family is that of Mr. Cuvillier-Morel-d'Acy, "Archiviste-Généalogiste."[14] It savours, however, of Peerage rather than of History, and relies for its expansion of Père Anselme's somewhat jejune narrative[15] on private MS. collections instead of original authorities. This work was followed by an elaborate monograph on "Poix et ses Seigneurs" by M. l'Abbé Delgove,[16] who accepts the former writer's genealogy without question, though dealing more critically with the charters of foun-

---

siderable importance. A charter of 1030 to Rouen Cathedral is said to contain the name "Galtero Tyrello, domino de Piceio."

[12] *Cartulaire de l'Abbaye de St. Bertin* (*Documents Inédits*), pp. 267-8.

[13] I find entered in the Cartulary of Hesdin (Bibliothèque Nationale, Paris) on fo. 29, a notification "quia Walterus Tireel et filius eius Hugo hospitem unum eum omni mansione . . . apud villam Verton concesserunt," and that they have granted freedom from toll "apud Belram . . . coram militibus suis." Could "Bekam" possibly be a misprint for "Belram" [Beaurain]?

[14] *Histoire Genealogique et Héraldique de la Maison des Tyrel, Sires, puis Princes de Poix*, etc., etc. (2nd Ed.) 1869.

[15] Vol. vii., pp. 820 et seq.

[16] *Memoires de la Société d'Antiquaires de Picardies* (1876), xxv. 287 et sq.

dation for the Priory of St. Denis de Poix. He admits that these charters are not authentic in their present form, but accepts their contents as genuine. Now the endowment of St. Denis, according to them, included two marcs out of the tithes "de Lavingaham en Angleterre." Here, though these writers knew it not, we have again our Essex Langham, the "Lawingeham" of the Pipe Roll. Is this the reason why Walter required the consent of his wife "Adeline" and son Hugh to the grant?

Neither of these writers knew of the English evidence, nor did they solve the mystery of Walter Tirel's wife, whom they, like Lappenberg, imagined to be the daughter of a Richard Giffard. This tends to diminish our trust in the pedigree they give. They took a Walter Tirel to England at the Conquest, but only because Wace mentions the "Pohiers," or men of Poix, and because the name of Tirel is found in the Battle Roll. In their view, Hugh Tirel, Lord of Poix, the crusader of 1147, was grandson of the famous Walter. Now Orderic, whose evidence on the point they ignore, says, as we have seen, he was the son; and as the chronicler was contemporary both with father and son, we cannot think him mistaken. Moreover, the Pipe Roll of 1130 cannot be harmonised with their pedigree. Adeliz, wife (? widow) of Walter Tirel, then answered for Langham, and could not be "Adeline dame de Ribecourt," who was dead, according to both writers, before 1128 (or 1127), and who could not, in any case, have aught to do with Langham.

But there is other evidence, unknown to these French writers, which proves that the version they give must be utterly wrong. Among the archives at Evreux there is a charter of Hugh Tirel to the Abbey of Bec, granting "decem marcas argenti in manerio quod dicitur Lavigaham" to its daughter-house of Conflans, where, he says, his mother had taken the religious "habit," and retired to die. The Priors of Conflans, and [St. Denis of] Poix are among the witnesses; and we read of the charter's date :—

Hoc concessum est apud piceium castrum anno M.cxxxviii. ab incarnatione dominica viii. idus martii.

Even if we make this date to be 1139, we here find Hugh in posssesion of Poix and Langham at that date, whereas the French writers tell us that he only succeeded in 1145, and that his father died in that year[17] The above charter, moreover, points to his mother having survived his father, and died at Conflans as a widow. Until, therefore, evidence is produced in support of the French version, we must reject it *in toto*.

I close this study with an extract from that interesting charter by which Richard I. empowered Henry de Cornhill to enclose and impark his woods at Langham, the same day (6th Dec., 1189) on which he empowered his neighbours the burgesses of Colchester to hunt the fox, the hare and the " cat " within their borders. The words are :—

Sciatis nos dedisse et concessisse Henrico de Cornhell' licentiam includendi boscum suum in Lahingeham et faciendi sibi ibidem parcum, et ut liceat illi habere omnes bestias quos poterit ibi includere.[18]

Thus did the wealthy Londoner become a country squire seven centuries ago. Nor is it irrelevant to observe that the " Langham Lodge coverts " are familiar to this day to those who hunt with the Essex and Suffolk.

[17] M. l'Abbé Delgove produces (p. 369) a precisely similar case, in which a deed of 1315 proves John Tirel to have been already in possession of Poix, although, according to the family history, he did not die till 1315. This throws doubts, he admits, on M. Cuvillier-Morel-d'Acy's chronology.

[18] Duchy of Lancaster, Royal Charter, No. 42. *Supra*, p. 471

WALDRIC, WARRIOR AND CHANCELLOR

THE importance of fixing the sequence of chancellors, for chronological purposes and especially the dating of charters, is very great. Waldric, who preceded Ranulf as chancellor to Henry I., was, as a warrior and then a bishop, a man of mark. It has hitherto been supposed, as by Mr. Archer (who wrote his life for the *Dictionary of National Biography*), that his latest appearance as chancellor was early in 1106, before the king's departure for Normandy. His feat in taking Duke Robert prisoner at Tinchebrai (28th Sept., 1106) is well known, but was believed to be the only evidence of his presence in Normandy with the King. There is, however, in *Gallia Christiana* (vol. xi.) a valuable charter recording a "causa seu placitum," decided before King Henry at Rouen, 7th Nov., 1106, among those present being "Waldricus qui tunc temporis erat regis cancellarius." We can trace, therefore, his tenure of the office up to that date.

There is some doubt and difficulty as to another charter. Foss believed that Waldric was the "Walterus Cancellarius" who is found in a charter to Tewkesbury of "1106."[1] This charter is printed in the *Monasticon* (ii. 66) from an Inspeximus *temp*. Henry IV. There is, however, a better Inspeximus on the Charter Roll of 28 Edward I.[2] (No. 16), in which the name is clearly Waldric. But the difficuly is that the same Inspeximus contains another version of this charter (No. 2), with a fuller list of witnesses.[3]   I have

---

[1] *Judges of England*, i. 140.
[2] *30th Report of Deputy-Keeper*, p. 203.   [3] *Ibid.*, p. 204

examined the roll for myself, and there is no doubt as to the date, for the clause runs :—

Facta est hec carta Anno. . . . ab incarnacione domini M° centesimo vii° apud Wintoniam.

The other version, in the body of the charter, contains the words, " Anno Dominicæ Incarnationis millesimo centesimo sexto apud Wintoniam." I have always looked with some suspicion on these Tewkesbury charters,[4] and that suspicion is not lessened by the double version of this, or by the name of the last witness in that of 1107, namely, " Roger de Pistres." The only known bearer of that name was dead before Domesday, though this witness may just possibly be identical with Roger de Gloucester (son, I hold, of Durand de Pistres[5]) who was killed in 1106.

On the whole, it is safer to deem that Waldric's last appearance as chancellor, at present known, is in the Rouen charter of November, 1106. Ranulf, his successor, first appears, as Foss pointed out,[6] in a charter to St. Andrew's Priory, Northampton.[7] Its date is determined by the appearance among the witnesses of Maurice, Bishop of London (d. 26th Sept., 1107) and of Ranulf himself as Chancellor, combined with the statement appended to the charter that it was granted in the King's 8th year (" octavo imperii sui anno "). One must not attach too great importance to these clauses, which did not, as a rule, form part of the original charter, but in this case the names of the witnesses point to Easter—Sept., 1107 ; and it is just possible to assign to the 8th year the close of the Westminster gathering, at the beginning of August, when this charter to St. Andrew's may well have been granted.

Miss Norgate holds that Bishop Roger " probably resumed " the chancellorship in 1106, on Waldric's elevation to the Bishopric of Laon,[8] but I do not know of any evidence to that effect.

---

[4] See *Geoffrey de Mandeville*, 421, 431-2.   [5] See p. 313.
[6] *Judges of England*, i. 79.   [7] *Monasticon*, v. 191.
[8] *England under the Angevin Kings*, i. 22.

A CHARTER OF HENRY I. (1123)

A GOOD illustration of the value of charters for chronological and biographical purposes is afforded by one
which Henry I. granted to the church of Exeter. It is
printed in the *Monasticon* under Plimpton, to the foundation of which priory it is asserted to have been preliminary.
That foundation is assigned to 1121. The charter, however, is also found among those confirmed by Henry VIII.
(Confirmation Roll, 1 Hen. VIII., p. 5, No. 13), with a list
of witnesses arranged in correct order ; whereas the *Monasticon* version is taken from the pleadings under Ric. II.
(Coram Rege, Hil. 2 Ric. II., Rot. 20, Devon), and records
the witnesses in grievous disorder. The explanation of
such disorder is that the clerk in the latter case was not
familiar with the system on which the attestations to these
charters were arranged. the names of the leading witnesses
being placed in a line above the others. This will be made
evident from the two lists of witnesses :—

Right Order.	*Wrong Order.*
King Henry	
Queen Adeliza	Queen Adeliza
William, archbishop of Canter-bury	William, archbishop of Canter-bury
Thurstan, archbishop of York	Robert, earl of Gloucester
Richard, bishop of London	Thurstan, archbishop of York
William, bishop of Winchester	William, earl of Surrey
Roger, bishop of Salisbury	Roger, bishop of Salisbury
Alexander, bishop of Lincoln	Roger, earl of Warwick
Evrard, bishop of Norwich	Alexander, bishop of Lincoln

Hervey, bishop of Ely
Ralf, bishop of Chichester
Ranulf, bishop of Durham
Robert, bishop of Coventry
"Theold," bishop of Worcester
Bernard, bishop of St. David's
Richard, bishop of Hereford
Godfrey, bishop of Bath
Geoffrey the chancellor
Geoffrey, abbot of St. Peter's, Winchester
Osbert, abbot of Tavistock
Thurstan, abbot of Sherborne
Vincent, abbot of Abingdon
Seffrid, abbot of Glastonbury
Robert, earl of Gloucester
William, earl of Surrey
David, earl of Huntingdon
Ranulf, earl of Chester
Roger, earl of Warwick
Robert, earl of Leicester
Hugh Bigot, *dapifer*
William de Pirou, *dapifer*
William d'Aubeny
Nigel d'Aubeny
Richard fitz Baldwin
Baldwin de Redvers
Johel de Berdestaple
Guy de Totness
Robert de "Badentona"
William fitz Odo
Goislin de Pomereda
Rainald de Valle Torta
William fitz Richard
Herbert de Alneto
Humfrey de Bohun
Walter fitz Thurstan

Robert, earl of Leicester
Evrard, bishop of Norwich
Hugh Bigot, *dapifer*
Hervey, bishop of Ely
William de Pirou, *dapifer*
Ralf, bishop of Chichester
William d'Aubeny
Ranulf, bishop of Durham
Nigel d'Aubeny
Robert, bishop of Coventry

Richard fitz Baldwin
"Theold," bishop of Worcester
Baldwin de Redvers
Bernard, bishop of St. David's
Johel de Berdestaple
Richard, bishop of Hereford
Guy de Totness
Godfrey, bishop of Bath
Robert de Cadentona (*sic*)
Geoffrey the chancellor
William fitz Odo
Geoffrey, abbot of St. Peter's, Winchester
Goislin de Pomereda
Osbert, abbot of Tavistock
Rainald de Valle Torta
Thurstan, abbot of Sherborne
William fitz Richard
Vincent, abbot of Abingdon
Herbert de Alneto
Seffrid, abbot of Glastonbury
Humfrey de Bohun
William, abbot of Cerne
Walter fitz Thurstan[1]

[1] It will be observed that this list omits the bishops of London and Winchester and the earls of Huntingdon and Chester, but adds the abbot of Cerne.

It is obvious that this charter was granted before the
death of the Bishop of Worcester (20th Oct., 1123), and before
the King's departure from England (June, 1123). But it
must be subsequent to the death of the previous chancellor,
Ranulf (Christmas, 1122), and to the appointment or consecration (February, 1123) of Archbishop William. The
narrow limit thus ascertained points to the Easter court of
1123 at Winchester, the great gathering of bishops and
earls implying some such occasion. Easter fell that year
on 15th April.

Now two sees had fallen vacant at the beginning of the
year, those of Lincoln and of Bath. Lincoln was given to
Alexander, whether at Easter (Winchester), as stated by
Henry of Huntingdon, or in Lent, as asserted by the continuator of Florence; but he was not consecrated till 22nd
July. Bath was bestowed on Godfrey, whose consecration
did not take place till 26th August, though Henry of Huntingdon assigns his appointment, like that of Alexander, to
Easter (Winchester). Both these bishops, it will be seen,
attest the above charter, which proves that it cannot be
earlier than Easter (15th April), while the evidence below
practically limits it to the Easter court at Winchester.

The first point to be observed is that these two bishops
attest as such (not as "elect") long before their consecration. As it is generally held that bishops never did so, this
point is of importance (always assuming the accuracy of
the evidence) for its bearing on other charters.[2] Secondly,
four of the witnesses—the two archbishops, the Bishop of
St. David's, and the Abbot of Glastonbury—are said by the
continuator to have left for Rome after Alexander's appointment. From this charter it is clear that they did not leave
till after Easter. The third point is that Earl Roger of

[4] An excellent instance of this practice is found, ten years later, in the
case of Bishop Nigel, who attested three charters in 1133, before the
king's departure, as Bishop of Ely, though he was not consecrated till
some months later. They are those found in *Monasticon*, vi. 1174, 1274,
and that which granted the chamberlainship to Aubrey de Vere.

Warwick had, at the date of this charter, succeeded his father, Henry.

Turning to Geoffrey the chancellor, we find in this charter perhaps his earliest appearance. Foss, in his useful work, is here a year out. He wrongly assigned the death of the preceding chancellor, Ranulf, to Christmas, 1123, instead of Christmas, 1122, and he assumed that our charter must be subsequent to Bishop Godfrey's consecration (26th August, 1123), and, in fact, that it belonged to 1124 (to which year he wrongly assigned the death of Bishop Theowulf). It is important for chronological purposes to date the change of chancellor correctly. I have already determined (p. 481) the date of Ranulf's accession to the post.

The correction of this date of Ranulf's death affects that of the foundation of Laund Priory, Leicestershire, which is assigned by Nichols and by the Editors of the *Monasticon* to "about 1125." As the foundation charter is addressed to William, Archbishop of Canterbury, and Alexander, Bishop of Lincoln, it must be subsequent to Alexander's promotion in the spring of 1123 (if not to his consecration on June 22nd). This is admitted by Foss, who accepts the charter without question. There is nothing in the document to excite suspicion, nor do I impugn it without reluctance. But the awkward fact remains that it is witnessed by Ranulf the chancellor, who died, as we have seen, at the beginning of 1123, and actually in the lifetime of Bishop Robert, Alexander's predecessor at Lincoln. There can be no question as to Ranulf's death, for the sequence of events is inexorable. Henry of Huntingdon tells us that (1) the king spent Christmas (1122) at Dunstable; that (2) he went thence to Berkhampstead, where Ranulf was accidentally killed; that (3) he then visited Woodstock, where Bishop Robert met with an equally sudden death; that (4) at the Purification (2nd Feb., 1123) he gave the See of Canterbury to William of Corbeuil; that (5) he gave (at Winchester) the see of Lincoln to Alexander at Easter. It is singular that the members of the foundation had two strings to their bow, another charter of Henry I. being adduced for Inspeximus. Its witnesses imply a later date, and their names do not involve any chronological difficulty.

We have in this Exeter charter one of the earliest attestations (according to my theory) of Robert as earl of Gloucester. It should be noted that he takes at once precedence of all other earls, just as he had taken, before his elevation, precedence of all laymen under the rank of earl.

Of the barons most are familiar. Richard fitz Baldwin was the son and successor of the famous Baldwin of Exeter, and was, like him, sheriff of Devon (see p. 301). Baldwin de Redvers was the son of Richard de Redvers, and became subsequently first earl of Devon (the confusion of these two families, from the similarity of name, seems to be incorrigible).[3] The lords of the great honours of Barnstaple and Totnes[4] are followed by Robert of Bampton, who had succeeded to the Domesday fief of Walter de Douai, and who, as I have shown (*English Historical Review*, v. 746), was afterwards a rebel against Stephen. Goislin de Pomerey was the heir of Ralf de Pomerey, the Domesday

---

[3] It has found its way, under "Baldwin," into the *Dictionary of National Biography*.

[4] The *Guido de Totteneys* of this charter seems to be identical with the *Wido de Nunant* of the charter granted by Henry II. to this priory. This conjecture is confirmed by the entry in the Pipe Role of 31 Hen. I. : "Wido de Nunant reddit comp. de x. marcis pro concessione ferie de Totneis" (p. 154). There is a story quoted by Dugdale, under Totnes priory, from the records of the abbey of Angers, that Juhel "of Totnes," the Domesday baron, was expelled by William Rufus, and his lands given to Roger de Nunant. I certainly find Roger de Nonant attesting in 1091 the foundation charter of Salisbury Cathedral in conjunction with William fitz Baldwin (see pp. 330, 472) ; and Manors belonging to Juhel in 1086 are found afterwards belonging to Valletort, Nonant's successor, as part of his honour of Totnes. But it would seem that Juhel retained part of his honour of Barnstaple, while the Nonants held the rest as the honour of Totnes. Indeed, he must have held both *capita* so late as 1113, when, say the monks of Laon, "venimus ad castrum, quod dicitur Bannistaplum, ubi manebat quidam princeps nomine Joellus de Totenes," etc. (*Hermannus*, ii. 17), adding that they afterwards visited Totnes "præfati principis castrum" (*ibid.* 18).

baron; and Reginald (Rainaldus) de Vautort was a great
under-tenant of the honour of Mortain. William fitz
Richard I identify with that great Cornish magnate, whose
daughter and heiress carried his fief to Reginald, afterwards earl of Cornwall. Herbert de Alneto also was a
Cornish baron, father of that Richard who, in 1130, paid
£100 for his succession (*Rot. Pip.*, 31 Hen. I., p. 158).
Specially interesting, however, is the name of William fitz
Odo, in whom I detect not the William fitz *Otho*, of Essex
and Middlesex (with whom he is confused in the Index to
the 1130 Pipe Roll), but the son of "Odo filius Gamelin";
a Devonshire tenant-in-chief (D.B., i. 116 *b*). I see him in
that "—filius Odonis," who is entered on the damaged
Devonshire roll (*Rot. Pip.*, 31 Hen. I., p. 157) in connexion
with 34 shillings, which proves that he held a considerable estate. The fief of "Odo filius Gamelin" was assessed
at $21\frac{3}{16}$ hides, representing in Devon large estates.[5]

[5] Reprinted, with additions from *Eng. Hist. Review.*

THE ORIGIN OF THE NEVILLES

I T is difficult to believe that so interesting a genealogical
question as the origin of this famous house should have
remained as yet undetermined. I have shewn above (p.
166) that we can identify in Domesday Gilbert and Ralph
de Neville, the earliest bearers of the name in England,
as knightly tenants of the Abbot of Peterborough ; but the
existing house, as is well known, descends from them only
through a female. It is at its origin in the male line that
I here glance. The innumerable quarters in which, unfortunately, information of this kind has been published
makes it impossible for me to say whether I have been
forestalled. So far, however, as I can find at present, two
different versions are in the field.

First, there is Dugdale's view that Robert fitz Maldred,
their founder, was " son of Dolfin, son of Earl Gospatric,
son of Maldred fitz Crinan by Algitha daughter of Uchtred, Earl of Northumberland, who was son-in-law to King
Æthelred." This was, apparently, Mr. Shirley's view, for,
in his *Noble and Gentle Men of England* he derives the
Nevilles from " Gospatric, the Saxon Earl of Northumberland," though he makes Robert fitz Maldred his *great-*
grandson, as Rowland had done in his work on the House
of Nevill (1830), by placing Maldred between Dolfin and
Robert fitz Maldred. Even that sceptical genealogist, Mr.
Foster, admitted in his peerage their descent from this
Earl Gospatric. The immediate ancestry, however, of their
founder, Robert fitz Maldred, can be proved, and is as
follows :—

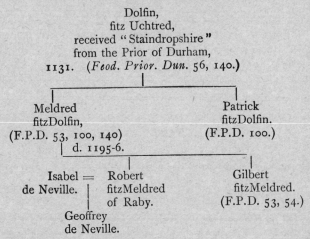

Drummond's *Noble British Familes* (1842) set out a new origin for the family without any hesitation, and this was adopted by the Duchess of Cleveland, whose elaborate work on the Battle Abbey Roll has much excellent genealogy. Their patriarch Dolfin was now made the son of that Uchtred, who was a grandson and namesake of Dugdale's Earl Uchtred, *temp.* King Æthelred. A chart pedigree is required to show the descent of the earls :—

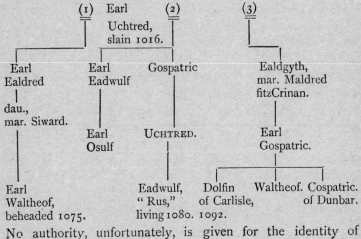

No authority, unfortunately, is given for the identity of

this Uchtred with Uchtred, father of Dolfin, and the assumption of that identity involves the conclusion that
Eadwulf "Rus," who took the lead in the murder of Bishop
Walcher (1080), was brother to Dolfin who received Staindrop in 1131, and uncle to a man who died in 1195 or 1196!
We cannot therefore accept this descent as it stands, or
carry the pedigree at present beyond Dolfin fitz Uchtred
(1131).   But as this Dolfin, when doing homage to the
Prior of Durham for Staindrop, reserved his homage to the
kings of England and of Scotland, as well as the Bishop of
Durham, he was, no doubt, a man of consequence, and was
probably of High Northumbrian birth.   It may be worth
throwing out, as a hint, the suggestion that his father
Uchtred might have been identical with Uchtred, son of
Ligulf, that great Northumbrian thegn who was slain at
Durham in 1080. But this is only a guess. One cannot,
in fact, be too careful, as I have shown in my two papers
on "Odard of Carlisle" and "Odard the Sheriff,"[1] in identifying two individuals of the same Christian names, when,
in these northern districts, the names in question were
so widely borne.   The Whitby cartulary, for instance,
proves that Thomas de Hastings was (maternal) grandson
of Alan, son of Thorphin "de Alverstain," son of Uchtred
(son of Cospatric), which Uchtred gave the Church of Crosby
Ravensworth to the abbey in the time, it would seem, of
William Ruffus.   But who Cospatric, his father, was has
not been clearly ascertained.   The skilled genealogists of
the north may be able to decide these points, and to tell us
the true-descent of "Dolfin, the son of Uchtred."

[1] *Genealogist*, N. S., v. 25-8; viii. 200.

THE ALLEGED INVASION OF
ENGLAND IN 1147

WHEN Mr. Richard Howlett, in the preface to his edition of the *Gesta Stephani* for the Rolls series, announced that we were indebted to its "careful author" for the knowledge of an invasion of England by Henry FitzEmpress in 1147, "unrecorded by any other chronicler," and endeavoured at considerable length to establish this proposition,[1] it was received, from all that I can learn, with general incredulity. As however, in the volume which he has since edited, he reiterates his belief in this alleged invasion,[2] it becomes necessary to examine in detail the evidence for a discovery so authoritatively announced in the pages of the Rolls series.

The accepted view of Henry's movements has hitherto been that, by his father's permission, in the autumn of 1142 he accompanied the Earl of Gloucester to England; that he remained there about four years; that, by his father's wish, at the end of 1146 or beginning of 1147 he returned from England; that he then spent two years and four months over sea; that in the spring of 1149 he again came to England, and was knighted at Carlisle by the king of Scots on 22nd May. As to the above long visit, commencing in 1142, Gervase of Canterbury is our chief authority, but the other chroniclers (omitting for the present the *Gesta Stephani*) harmonise well with his account.

[1] *Chronicles*, Stephen, Henry II., Richard I., vol. iii. pp. xvi.-x.x, 130.
[2] *Ib.*, vol. iv. pp. xxi-xxii.

Gervase and Robert of Torigni alike mention but one arrival of Henry (1142) and one departure (1146 or 1147), thus distinctly implying there was then only one visit— namely, that visit which Gervase tells us lasted four years. The only slight discrepancy between Gervase and Robert is found in the date of Henry's departure. Robert places that event under 1147, and mentions that Henry visited Bec 29th May in that year. There is also, Mr. Howlett has pointed out, charter evidence implying that Henry was back in Normandy in March or April. Now Gervase says distinctly that he was away from England two years and four months. The chroniclers, Gervase included, say that he returned to England in the middle of May, 1149. Counting back the two years and four months, this would bring us to January, 1147, as the date of his departure from England. But there is a charter of his to Salisbury Cathedral, tested, as Mr. Howlett observes, at Devizes, 13th April, 1149. If this evidence be trustworthy, it would take us back to December, 1146, instead of January, 1147. It is easy to see how Gervase may have included in 1146, and Robert in 1147, an event which appears to have taken place about the end of the one or the beginning of the year.

Much has been made of the alleged circumstance that Gervase assigned the Earl of Gloucester's death to 1146, whereas he is known to have died in 1147. But reference to his text will show that he does nothing of the kind. Writing of Henry's departure at the close of 1146, he tells us that the earl was destined never to see him again, for he died in November [*i.e.* November, 1147]. He is here obviously anticipating.

Such being the evidence on which is based the accepted view of Henry's movements, let us now turn to the *Gesta Stephani*. Though Mr. Howlett's knowledge of the period is great and quite exceptional, I cannot but think that he has been led astray by his admiration for this fascinating chronicle. Miss Norgate sensibly observes that "there must be something wrong in the story" as actually preserved in the *Gesta*,[3] but Mr. Howlett, unwilling to admit the possibility of error in his chronicle, boldly asserts that the "romantic account"[4] of Henry's adventures which it contains does not refer to his visit in 1149, but to a hitherto unknown invasion in 1147. He appears to imagine that the only objection in accepting this story is found in the fact that Henry was but just fourteen at the time.[5] But this is not so. Putting aside this objection, as also the silence of other chroniclers, there remains the chronological difficulty. How is the alleged visit to be fitted in? Its inventor, who suggests "about April, 1147," for its date, must first take Henry back to Normandy (why or when he does not even suggest) and then bring him back to England as an invader, neither his alleged going or coming being recorded by any chronicler. Then he assigns to his second return to Normandy (after the alleged invasion) the only passages in Gervase and Robert which speak of his returning at all. Surely nothing could be more improbable than that Henry should rush back to England just after he had left it, and had returned to his victorious father, and this at a time when his cause seemed as hopeless there as it was prosperous over the sea.

The evidence of the *Gesta Stephani* would have, indeed, to be beyond question if we are to accept, on its sole authority, so improbable a story. But what does that evidence amount to? The *Gesta*, unlike other chronicles, not being arranged chronologically under years, the only definite note of time here afforded in its text is found in the passage, "Consuluit [Henricus] et avunculum (*sic*) Glaorniæ comitem, sed ipse suis sacculis avide incumbens, rebus tantum sibi necessariis occurrere maluit."[6]

[3] *England under the Angevin Kings*, i. 377.
[4] *Ibid.*
[5] "The invasion of England by Henry in 1147, when he was but a boy of fourteen, a piece of history which has hitherto been rejected solely on the ground of improbability."—Preface (*ut supra*), p. xxi.
[6] *Gesta* (ed. Howlett), p. 131.

As Earl Robert is known to have died in the autumn of
1147, the word *avunculus* does, undoubtedly, fix these
events as prior to that date.   But is not *avunculus* a slip
of the writer for *cognatus*?   Is not the reference to Earl
William rather than to his father, Earl Robert?[7]   Such a
slip is no mere conjecture ; the statement that Earl Robert
was too avaricious to assist his beloved nephew in his hour
of need is not only absolutely contrary to all that we know
of his character, but is virtually discredited by the *Gesta*
itself when its author tells us, further on—

Comes deinde Glaorniæ ut erat regis adversariorum strenuissimus
et ad magna quevis struenda paratissimus, iterum atque iterum
exercitum comparare, jugi hortaminis et admonitionis stimulo
complices suos incitavit ; illos minis, istos promissis sibi et præmiis
conjugare ; quatinus omnes in unam concordiam, in unum animum
conspirati, exercitum e diverso ad idem velle repararent, et collectis
undecumque agminibus, vive et constanter in regem insurgerent.[8]

How can such language as this be reconciled with the
statement as to Earl Robert's apathy at the very time
when Henry's efforts offered him a unique opportunity of
pursuing his war against the king?   Mr. Howlett does not
attempt to meet, or even notice, this objection.   Moreover,
when the *Gesta* proceeds to describe Earl William of
Gloucester as devoted to his own pleasures rather than to
war,[9] we see that the conduct so incredible in his father
would in him be what we might expect.

I will not follow Mr. Howlett in his lengthy argument

---

[7] There is a precisely similar slip, by John of Salisbury, in the *Historia
Pontificalis* (Pertz, xx. 532), where the "Duke" of Normandy is referred
to in 1148 as "qui modo rex est" (*i.e.* Henry).   Mr. Howlett himself has
pointed out (*Academy*, 12th Nov., 1887) that the author "slipped in the
words 'qui modo rex est,' and thus transferred to Henry a narrative
which assuredly relates to his father."   The slip in question, as he
observed, had sadly misled Miss Norgate.

[8] *Gesta* (Ed. Howlett), p. 134.

[9] "Successit in comitatum suum Willelmus filius suus, senior quidem
ætate, sed vir mollis, et thalamorum magis quam militiæ appetitor"
(*Gesta*, Ed. Howlett, p. 134).

relative to the knighting of Eustace and Henry, because he himself admits that it is based only on conjecture.[10] It is sufficient to observe that if the "romantic" narrative in the *Gesta* refers to the events of 1149,[11] then the knighting of Eustace, which is a pendant to that narrative, belongs, as the other chroniclers assert, to 1149. The statement, I may add, that Henry applied for help to his mother, by no means involves, as Mr. Howlett assumes, her presence in England at the time.

I would suggest, then, that the whole hypothesis of this invasion in 1147 is based on nothing more than a confusion in the *Gesta*. Mr. Howlett, indeed, claims that "medieval history would simply disappear if the evidence of chroniclers were to be treated in this way,"[12] and detects "among some modern writers a tendency to incautious rejection," etc.[13] But he himself goes out of his way to denounce, in this connexion, as a "blundering interpolation" a passage in John of Hexham, which he assigns to notes being "carelessly misplaced" and "ignorantly miscopied."[14] The *Gesta*, to my knowledge, is by no means immaculate; its unbroken narrative and vagueness as to dates render its chronology a matter of difficulty; and the circumstance that the passage in dispute occurs towards its close renders

[10] Mr. Howlett incidentally claims that knighthood was a necessary preliminary to comital rank, and appeals to the fact that the younger Henry was even carefully knighted before his coronation (*Gesta*, p. xxii.). But what has he to say to the knighting of Earl Richard of Clare by Henry VI., and more especially to the knighting of Malcolm, already Earl of Huntingdon and king of Scots, by Henry II., in 1159? (*Robert of Torigni*, p. 203).

[11] Mr. Howlett asserts (*Gesta*, p. 130, note) that "when Henry made his better known visit in 1149 his acts were quite different" from those recorded in the *Gesta*. But if, as he himself admits, in 1149 Henry visited Devizes on his way to Carlisle, what more natural than that he should pass by Cricklade and Bourton (the two places mentioned in the *Gesta*), which lay directly on his road?

[12] Preface to *Gesta*, p. xx.

[13] Preface to Robert of Torigni, p. xxii.

[14] Preface to *Gesta* (*ut supra*), p. xvi.

it impossible to test it as we could wish by comparison with later portions. The weakness of Mr. Howlett's case is shown by his desperate appeal to "the exact precedent" set by Fulk Nerra, and no talk about the contrast presented by "physical science" and that "fragmentary tale of human inconsistencies which we term history" can justify the inclusion of this alleged invasion as a fact beyond dispute in so formal and authoritative a quarter as the preface to a Rolls volume.

THE ALLEGED DEBATE ON DANE-GELD (1163)

THE great importance attached by historians to the financial dispute at the council of Woodstock in 1163 renders it desirable that the point at issue should be clearly stated and understood. As I venture to believe that the accepted view on the matter in dispute is erroneous, I here submit the reasons which have led me to that conclusion. "Two most important points," writes Dr. Stubbs, "stand out" on this occasion: (1) "this is the first case of any express opposition being made to the king's financial dealings since the Conquest"; (2) "the first fruit of the first constitutional opposition is the abolition of the most ancient property-tax [danegeld] imposed as a bribe for the Danes."[1] It is with the second of these points that I propose especially to deal.

The passage which forms our best evidence is found in Grim's *Life of St. Thomas*, and its relative portion is as follows:—

---

[1] *Early Plantagenets*, pp. 69, 70. So, too, Miss Norgate : "It seems, therefore, that for the first time in English history since the Norman Conquest the right of the nation's representatives to oppose the financial demands of the crown was asserted in the Council of Woodstock, and asserted with such success that the king was obliged not merely to abandon his project, but to obliterate the last trace of the tradition on which it was founded" (*Angevin Kings*, ii. 16).

B. H.   K K

Movetur quæstio de consuetudine quadam quae in Anglia teneba-
tur. Dabantur de hida bini solidi ministris regis qui vicecomitum
loco comitatus servabant, quos voluit rex conscribere fisco et reditibus propriis associare. Cui archiepiscopus in faciem restitit, dicens,
non debere eos exigi pro reditibus, "nec pro reditu," inquit, "dabi-
mus eos, domine rex, salvo beneplacito vestro : sed si digne nobis
servierint vicecomites, et servientes vel ministri provinciarum, et
homines notros manutenuerint, nequaquam eis deerimus in auxilium." Rex autem aegre ferens archiepiscopi responsionem, "Per
oculos Dei," ait, "dabuntur pro reditu, et in scriptura regis scriben-
tur."

On this passage Dr. Stubbs thus comments :—

A tax so described can hardly have been anything else than the
danegeld, which was an impost of two shillings on the hide, and was
collected by the sheriffs, being possibly compounded for at a certain
rate and paid by them into the exchequer. As the danegeld from
this very year 1163 ceases to appear as a distinct item of account in
the Pipe Rolls, it is impossible to avoid connecting the two ideas,
even if we may not identify them. Whether the king's object in
making this proposition was to collect the danegeld in full amount,
putting an end to the nominal assessment which had so long been in
use, and so depriving the sheriffs of such profits as they made from
it, or whether he had some other end in view, it is impossible now
to determine; and consequently it is difficult to understand the
position taken by the archbishop.[2]

The attempt to identify the payment in dispute with the
danegeld does indeed lead to the greatest possible difficulties, and Miss Norgate, who follows closely in Dr. Stubbs'
footsteps, is no more successful in answering them ;[3] for, in
the first place, the words of Grim do not apply to the danegeld if taken in their natural sense ; and in the second
the proceeds of the danegeld were already royal revenue,

[2] *Cont. Hist.* i. 462 ; so, too, *Early Plantagenets*, pp. 68-70 ; and
Select Charters, p. 29, where it is described as " Henry's proposal to
appropriate the sheriffs' share of danegeld,"

[3] *Angevin Kings*, ii. 15, 16

and were duly paid in, as such, at the exchequer. To meet
this latter and obvious difficulty Dr. Stubbs suggests that—

as the sums paid into the exchequer under that name (danegeld)
were very small compared with the extent of land that paid the tax,
it is probable that the sheriffs paid a fixed composition and retained
the surplus as wages for their services (etc.).[4]

So, too, Miss Norgate urges that the danegeld "still occasionally made its appearance in the treasury rolls, but in
such small amount that it is evident the sheriffs, if they
collected it in full, paid only a fixed composition to the
crown, and kept the greater part as a remuneration for
their own services."[5] Now this suggestion raises the
whole question as to the revenue from danegeld. We are
told that "the danegeld was a very unpopular tax, probably because it was the plea on which the sheriffs made
their greatest profit . . . having become in the long
lapse of years a mere composition paid by the sheriff to
the exchequer, while the balance of the whole sums exacted
on that account went to swell his own income."[6]
As against this view I venture to hold that the danegeld
was in no way compounded for, but that every penny
raised by its agency was due to the royal treasury, leaving
no profit whatever to the sheriff. The test is easily applied:
let us take the case of Dorset. The Domesday assessment
of this county, according to the late Mr. Eyton, who had
investigated it with his usual painstaking labour, and
collated it with the geld-rolls of two years before, was
about 2,300 hides.[7] This assessment would produce, at
two shilllings on the hide, about £230. Now the actual

---

[4] *Early Plantagenets*, p. 69.

[5] But the Auctor Anonymus makes it clear that the king was not
asking for the balance of the sums raised, but for the entirety: "duo
illi solidi . . . si in unum conferuntur immensum efficere possunt
cumulum."

[6] Stubbs, *Const. Hist.*, i 381, 582.

[7] *Dorset Domesday*, p. 144.

amount accounted for on the Pipe Roll of 1130 is £228 5s.;
on that of 1156 it is £228 5s.; and on that of 1162, the last
levy, it is £247 5s.[8]   There is certainly no margin of profit
for the sheriff here.   In other counties we find that the
proceeds of the danegeld in 1130, 1156, and 1162, whilst
slightly fluctuating, roughly correspond, as, indeed, they
were bound to do, the Domesday assessment remaining
unchanged.[9]   I can therefore find no ground for the alleged
discrepancy between the amounts accounted for by the
sheriffs and those which the assessment ought to have
produced.

This being so, the solitary explanation suggested for
Henry's action falls to the ground, and it becomes clear
that the payment in dispute could not have been the danegeld, as the proposed change could not increase the amount
it produced already.   As a matter of fact, the last occasion
on which danegeld *eo nomine* was levied was in 1162, but
to connect that circumstance with the Woodstock dispute
of 1163 is an instance of the *post hoc propter hoc* argument,
more especially as the danegeld was not in dispute, still
less its abolition.   On the contrary, the primate desired to
keep things as they were.   What, then, was this mysterious payment but the *auxilium vicecomitis*, or "sheriff's
aid"?   Garnier distinctly states that this is what it was,[10]

---

[8] Thus accounted for (*Rot. Pip.*, 8 Hen. II.) :—

	£	s.	d.
Paid in	141	10	0
Paid out previously . . .	63	0	0
Allowed for remissions . . .	20	1	2
Balance due	22	13	10
	£247	5	0

N.B.   The roll sums up the remissions as £21 [*sic*] 1s. 2d., but the
total of the items is £20 1s. 2d.

[9] Oxfordshire, for instance, where the amounts were £239 9s. 3d.,
£249 6s. 5d., £242 0s. 10d.; or Wiltshire, where they run £388 13s.,
£389 13s., £388 11s. 11d.

[10] *L'Aide al Vescunte*, as quoted by Miss Norgate, who observes there-

and Grim's words no less unmistakably point to the same conclusion. To institutional students of the twelfth and thirteenth centuries the *auxilium vicecomitis* is familiar enough. It was, writes Dr. Stubbs, a "payment made to the sheriff for his services,"[11] and was, it may be added, a customary charge, varying in amount,[12] paid over locally to the sheriffs. It may fairly be said to have stood to the danegeld in the relation of rates to taxes.

On this hypothesis the difficulties of the case vanish at once, and Henry's object is made plain. To add this regular annual levy to his own revenues would be all clear gain, and would relieve him *pro tanto* from the necessity of spasmodic and irregular taxation. As for the sheriffs and the districts beneath their sway, they were possibly to be left to their own devices to find a substitute for the lost " aid," like a modern county council bereft of its wheel tax ; for the thought suggests itself that Henry was attempting to reverse the process that we have lately witnessed, by relieving the taxes at the expense of the rates, instead of the rates at the expense of the taxes. Whether, therefore, the attitude of the primate can be described as " opposition to the king's will in the matter of taxation" is perhaps just open to question. He took his stand on the sure ground of existing " custom," recognised at that time as binding on all.[18] One is tempted to discern

on, " This payment, although described as customary rather than legal, and called the 'sheriffs' aid,' seems really to have been nothing else than the danegeld. . . . His (Garnier's) story points directly to the danegeld."

[11] *Const. Hist.*, i. 382.

[12] In this detail alone Grim appears to have confused it with the uniform two shilling rate of the danegeld. The record in the *Testa de Nevill* (pp. 85, 86) of the " auxilium vicecomitis," due from the Vills in the Wapentake of Framelund (Leic.), illustrates well the payment.

[18] Thus the statement that he " declared at Woodstock that the lands of his church should not pay a penny to the danegeld " (*Const. Hist.*, is 578) misrepresents his position by making him repudiate his undoubted obligation.

a grim irony in Henry's action when he promptly proceeded to turn the tables on his old friend by appealing to the *avitae consuetudines* as obviously binding on so rigid a constitutional purist as the primate.[14]

[14] This and the preceding and succeeding papers are reprinted from the *Eng. Hist. Review*.

A GLIMPSE OF THE YOUNG KING'S COURT (1·170)

THE charter given below is cited by Madox as evidence that in the days of Henry II. the exchequer was still "sometimes holden in other places" than Westminster. Contrary to his usual practice, he does not print the charter; so, wishing to ascertain what light it might throw on the private transaction it records, I referred to its original enrolment.[1] Finding that its evidence would prove of some historical value, I decided to edit it for the use of students.[2]

Willelmus comes de Essex' omnibus hominibus ⁊ amicis suis, Francis ⁊ Anglis, clericis ⁊ laicis, tam futuris quam presentibus, salutem. Sciatis me dedisse ⁊ concessisse ⁊ hac carta mea confirmasse Rogero filio Ricardi ⁊ suis heredibus villam de Aynho cum omnibus pertinen [ciis] in escambio pro Cunctonia hereditarie tenendam de me ⁊ heredibus meis sibi ⁊ heredibus suis per servicium unius militis ⁊ dimidii, libere et quiete ⁊ honorifice sicut unquam antecessores mei liberius ⁊ honorificencius eam tenuerunt ⁊ habuerunt; scilicet in bosco ⁊ in plano, in pratis et pascuis, in viis ⁊ semitis, in aquis, ⁊ molendinis, ⁊ in omnibus predicte ville adjacentibus. Et insuper dedi ⁊ concessi predicto Rogero filio Ricardi terram de Wlauynton' quam pater meus comes Gal[fridus] dedit Willelmo de Moretonio, per servicium michi faciendum quod

---

[1] Madox gives a misleading reference. The charter occurs among the Clavering enrolments of m. 17 (not 19) of the L.T.R. Memoranda of the Exchequer, containing the Michaelmas *communia* of 5 Ed. II.

[2] Mr. Hubert Hall, of the Public Record Office, kindly undertook to transcribe the charter for me.

predictus Willelmus patri meo facere debuit, hereditarie tenendum [*sic*] de me ꝿ heredibus meis, illi ꝿ heredibus suis.   Quare volo ꝿ firmiter precipio quod ista donacio rata ꝿ inconcussa permaneat. Et notum sit omnibus quod istud eschambium factum fuit apud Wynconiam [*sic*] ad Scaccarium coram domino Rege Henrico filio regis Henrici Secundi ꝿ Baronibus suis.   Tesꝿte [*sic*] Reg' comite, Bac'[8] de Luc[i], Willelmo de Sancto Johanne, Galfrido Archidiacono Cantuar', Ricardo Archidiacono Pick[tavensi], Hunfrido de Buh[un] constant[e],[4]   Manser' Biset dap[ifero], Gilberto Malet dap[ifero], Hugone de Gundvil[la], Alano de Nevill[a], Thoma Basset, Willelmo filio Audel[ini], Johanne Mereschal, Roberto de Bussone, Johanne const[abulario] Cestr[iae], Ranulpho de Glanvile, Gaufrido de Say, Gerard de Kanvill[a], Oseberto filio Ricardi, David de Jarpenvilla, Ricardo filio Hugonis, Johanne Burd, Willelmo filio Gill[eberti], Roberto de Sancto Claro, Johanne de Roch, Hasculfo Capellano, Henrico clerico, Roberto clerico, qui hanc cartam scripsit, ꝿ multis aliis.

The purpose of the charter is soon disposed of; it records a grant by the Earl of Essex to Roger fitz Richard (who had married the earl's aunt " Alice of Essex "[5]) of Aynho, Northants, in exchange for Compton, co. Warwick.   Both Manors were in the Mandeville fief, and the former was to be held, as the latter had been (in 1166[6]), "per servicium unius militis et dimidii."

The interest of the document is to be sought in its witnesses, and its place of testing, and above all in the date which, I hope to show, they suggest.   The mention of the two inseparable archdeacons proves that this date cannot be later than 1174, and consequently, as the young king was present, must have been previous to his revolt in 1173, and therefore to his departure from England about the close of 1172.   On the other hand, the date must be subsequent to June, 1170, when the young king was

---

[8] Read *Ric[ardo]*.   [4] Read *constab[ulo]*.

[5] See my paper on " Who was Alice of Essex ? " in the *Essex Arch. Transactions.*

[6] " Rogerus filius Ricardi i. militem et tres partes unius militis. Probably the quarter fee was a separate holding.

crowned, and therefore probably to the meeting at Fréteval (22nd July, 1170), at which the Archdeacon of Canterbury was present.

Thus we obtain a limit of date. Within this limit we may exclude the young king's stay in England after the departure of the two archdeacons (Dec., 1170), as also his subsequent presence in England in 1171-2 while his father was in Ireland, for William fitz Aldelin was in Ireland with him. Indeed, we are told by Giraldus (v. 286) that when the king left Ireland (April, 1172) William was left behind in charge of Wexford.[7] As the young king then accompanied his father over sea, the only period remaining (except July-December, 1170) to which we could assign the document is August-November, 1172, when he visited England, with his consort Margaret, for his second coronation. This ceremony took place at Winchester, but we cannot tell whether William fitz Aldelin had yet returned from Ireland, or whether any other of our witnesses were present on that occasion.[8]

But if we turn to the other possible period, the latter half of 1170, we find an occasion when six of the witnesses to the above charter can actually be shown to have been present, under circumstances of peculiar interest, with the young king at Winchester.

The evidence of charters is so deficient at this period of the reign that from August, 1170, to June, 1171, Mr. Eyton could only adduce two charters "quite problematically" and one more "safely," as he claims, but erroneously, as his own pages show.[9] If, then, our charter belongs to this

[7] Humphrey de Buhun also and Hugh de Gundeville were left behind at Waterford.

[8] Foss (*Judges of England*, i. 235) states positively that Hugh de Gundeville did not leave Ireland till 1173, at the time of the rebellion. This, if true, would dispose at once of an 1172 date for our charter; but, unfortunately, he does not give his authority, and I have not succeeded in finding it.

[6] *Court, etc., of Henry II.*, pp. 147, 154. The Archdeacon of Canterbury attests the Chinon charter, which Mr. Eyton "safely" assigns to

period, its evidence is proportionately valuable.   Now all
that we know of the movements of the young king at the
time is that he was at Westminster on 5th October, and
that he kept his Christmas at Winchester.   Mr. Eyton's
book must here be used with great caution.   He has been
misled by R. de Diceto (i. 342)[10] into the statement that
Henry was at Woodstock when Becket sought to visit him
in December; and adds—by a confusion, it would seem,
with his October movements—"The young king is at
Windsor" (4th Dec.[11]).   Henry was neither at Woodstock
nor Windsor at this time, but at Winchester.   Becket's
biographers are unanimous in stating that he sent his
envoy before him to the young king at Winchester.

Landing on 1st December, and entering Canterbury next
day, the primate (says William fitz Stephen), "post octo
dierum moram in sede,"[12] sent Richard, prior of Dover
(who was destined to be his own successor), to the young
king to ask permission to visit him "tanquam regem et
dominum suum."   Richard "veniens Wintoniam, regem
invenit, ubi optimates regni . . . coegerat."[13]

The purpose of this special assembly was connected with
the scheme for an irregular election to the vacant sees, at
the court of the elder king, by deputations whom his son
was to send over.[14]   Prior Richard was confronted by

the middle of October, 1170, adding that he had "apparently been with
the king ever since the peace of Fréteval" (22nd July).   But he is known
to have been with the young king at Westminster on 5th October, as
indeed Mr. Eyton elsewhere observes (p. 151).

[10] Becket, he says, visited London on his way, "ad videndam faciem
novi regis, qui tunc temporis morabatur apud Wdestoc" (*sic*).

[11] "Court of King Henry the Younger" (Eyton, pp. 151-2).

[12] *Materials*, p. 121.   William of Canterbury places Richard's despatch
"post aliquot dies reditus sui" (*ib.* i. 106).

[13] *Ib.*, i. 106; so Garnier (p. 166, Ed. Hippeau)—
> "Le juefne Rei aveit à Wincestre trové.
> Là èrent del païs li barun assemblé."

[14] *Ib.*, i. 106; so Garnier—
> "Pur c' èrent assemblé cele genz à cel jur,
> Et li prince et li cunte et des baruns plusur."

the young king's guardians (three of whom attest our charter).[15]   He himself, on receiving the application, sent (as I read it) to consult Geoffrey Ridel, who was believed to know his father's wishes, and who, with the Archdeacon of Poitiers, was at Southampton, waiting to cross.[16]   Turning, for their movements, to William Fitz Stephen, we learn that, while on their way to cross from a Kentish port, the two archdeacons, on entering the county, learnt that the primate had arrived at Canterbury, and, turning their horses' heads, made for a more westerly port.[17]   Southampton clearly was the port they made for, and on their way thither they must have visited the young king at Winchester.   This is admitted in the case of Geoffrey, who went there, says Becket, to lay before him the complaint of the excommunicated bishops.

I believe that our charter belongs to this occasion, when the two attesting archdeacons were at Winchester.   *Reg'* no doubt is Earl Reginald of Cornwall, who was certainly present at the same time[18] and who is probably referred to in "li cunte" of Garnier.   This will establish the presence of six of our witnesses.   Of the others, Richard de Luci takes precedence as justiciar; Alan de Nevill, Thomas Basset, and the great Glanville were, like the two archdeacons and the three guardians of the king, members

[15] "Veniens itaque legatus ad curiam, convenit tutores regis . . . Willelmum de Sancto Johanne, Willelmum filium Aldelinae, Hugonem de Gundulfivilla, Randulfum filium Stephani" (i. 108-9).

[16] "Qui de portu Suthamtune transfretaturi erant" (i. 111).   Geoffrey sent back a scornful reply (see also Garnier) expressing his wonder that the young king could think of meeting a man who meant to disinherit him.   This statement agrees with Becket's own complaint (vii. 406) that his *archidiabolus* Geoffrey was instructed to make this charge.

[17] III. 120.   "Duo archidiaconi . . . jam in Cantiam venerant, ad regem illac transfretaturi.   Audito autem quod archiepiscopus appulsus Cantuariae esset, lora statim diverterunt, ad occidentales maris portus tendentes."   This convicts Mr. Eyton of error in asserting that on 1st December the two archdeacons were at Dover, waiting to cross (p. 149).

[18] *Ib.*, i. 111

of the judicial body; Humfrey de Bohun, Gilbert Malet, and Manasser Bisset were present as officers of the household; John, constable of Chester, was (then or afterwards) son-in-law to the grantee's wife, and Geoffrey de Say was the son of the earl's aunt; Osbert Fitz Richard and David de Jarpenville (probably John de Rochelle also) were among the earl's feudal tenants and are found attesting another of his charters; and Hasculf was the enterprising chaplain who had plotted to carry off the late earl's corpse and present it to the nuns of Chicksand.   The only person whose presence need puzzle us is the Earl of Essex himself; for William fitz Stephen [19] asserts that he was despatched from Henry's court after the arrival there of the excommunicated prelates and the Archdeacon of Poitou.   Either, then, he had previously paid a flying visit to Winchester, or he must have been absent when this transaction was recorded.

[19] *Memorials*, iii. 127.

THE FIRST KNOWN FINE (1175)

IN his masterly introduction to *Select Pleas of the Crown*, Professor Maitland, with his usual skill, discusses the evolution of the *Curia Regis* and the relation of the central to the itinerant courts. An appendix to this introduction is devoted to " early fines " ; and the conclusion arrived at, as to the date when regular fines began, is that " the evidence seems to point to the year 1178 or thereabouts, just, that is, to the time when King Henry was remodelling the Curia Regis ; thenceforward we have traces of a fairly continuous series of fines " (p. xxvii.). More definitely still, in his latest work, he traces the existence of fines " from the year 1179."

The earlier document I here print from the valuable cartulary of Evesham (*Vesp* B. xxiv., fo. 71, etc.) is, I contend, a true fine, and is fortunately dated with exactitude (20th July) :—

Hæc est finalis concordia facta in curia domini Regis apud Evesham ad proximum festum sancte Margarete post mortem comitis Reginaldi [2] Cornub' coram Willelmo filio Audelini et Willelmo filio Radulfi et Willelmo Basset et aliis justiciariis domini regis qui ibi tunc aderant, inter Rogerum filium Willelmi et Robertum Trunket de terra de Ragl' unde placitum fuit inter eos in curia domini Regis. Scilicet quod predictus Wibertus Trunket clamavit quietam predicto Rogero terram illam de Ragl' et (*sic*) feud[um] et hereditatem suam et totum jus suum quod in predicta terra

---

[1] Vol. i. (Selden Society).

[2] "Reg." MS. The earl died 1st July, 1175. This fine further confirms the accuracy of the *Gesta Henrici* (see Eyton, p. 192).

habebat, et ipse trunchet reddidit in curia domini Regis terram illam de Ragl' in manu (*sic*) abbatis de Evesham, et ipse abbas ibi statim in curia Regis reddidit eam predicto Rogero. Pro hac autem concessione dedit predictus Rogerus predicto trunchet xx. marcas argenti, et predictus abbas dedit truchet unum anulum argenteum cum cural.

The transcript of this fine is immediately followed by a royal charter confirming it, and establishing Roger in possession :—

H. dei gratia . . . Sciatis me concessisse et presenti carta confirmasse finem que factus fuit in curia mea inter, etc., etc. . . . et Wibertus eam reddidit solutam et quietam in manu abbatis de evesham de cujus feodo terra illa est. . . . Et ideo volo et firmiter precipio. . . . Test. Willelmo Audelin', Willelmo filio Radulfi, Willelmo Basset, Berteram de Verdun, Gaufrido Salvagio. Apud Evesham.

Mr. Eyton, to whom this fine was unknown, does not, in his *Court and Itinerary of Henry II.*, include Evesham among the places visited by the king in 1175, but makes him visit Feckenham about October (p. 196). But as we learn from the above fine that Henry was at Evesham on July 20, Mr. Eyton's conclusions must be reconsidered. Henry, according to him, was at Woodstock July 8 and at Nottingham August 1. Now this latter date is derived from a Nottingham charter (p. 193), among the witnesses to which are William fitz Audelin "Dapifer," William Basset, and William fitz Ralf, the very three justices before whom our fine had been levied at Evesham on July 20th. I hold, therefore, that Henry proceeded (possibly through Lichfield, as Mr. Eyton asserts) from Woodstock to Nottingham *via* Evesham ; and, further, that he visited Feckenham (to the north of Evesham) on this occasion, and not, as Mr. Eyton imagined, in October. We find accordingly that of the Feckenham charters quoted by that writer (p. 196), one is witnessed by all three of our officers, William fitz Audelin "Dapifer," William fitz Ralf, and

William Basset; one by William fitz Audelin and William fitz Ralf; and the third by William fitz Ralf and William Basset.

Now, working from the Pipe Rolls, Mr. Eyton discovered that—

while the king was in Staffordshire there were pleas held in that country which are expressed to have been held by William fitz Ralph, Bertram de Verdon, and William Basset *in curia Regis* (p. 193).

He also noted that—

the Pipe-Roll of 1175, after duly recounting the results of the ordinary assizes, held by William de Lanvall and Thomas Basset (who appear to have visited York while the king was there), contains the following (in regard to a different kind of judicature than that at which the two justiciars presided), and which probably took place in a court of which the king in person was president :

"Placita et conventiones per Willelmum filius Radulfi, Bertram de Verdon, et Willelmum Basset, in curia Regis." These *Placita* were apparently nothing more than fines with the crown (p. 194).

So, too, he found that at Northampton—

the three justiciars who had attended him in his special *curia* in Staffordshire and at York, negotiated a fine by Robert de Nevill, "pro rehabenda saisina de Uppetona quæ fuit Radulfi de Waltervilla" (p. 194).

My own evidence proves that the same three justiciars had been with him, earlier in the summer, in his special *curia* at Evesham, where an actual fine was levied.

Thus we have proof that in the summer of 1175 the king was accompanied on his progress by a special group of justices, with whose assistance he held pleas, just as, a generation later, John, in his ninth year, "was journeying about the country with three judges in his train—Simon Pateshull, Potterne, and Pont Audemer."[8] While he was doing this, as Eyton has shown, two great eyres were going on throughout the country, one of them conducted by

[8] Maitland's *Select Pleas of the Crown*, I. xv.

William de Lanvall[ei] and Thomas Basset, the other by
Ranulf de Glanville and Hugh de Cressi. It is noteworthy
that all these four are found, with William fitz Audelin,
among the witnesses to a royal charter assigned by Mr.
Eyton—rightly no doubt—to the king's stay at York (*circ.*
10th Aug., 1175), as they also are among the witnesses to
the Nottingham charter mentioned above (p. 510), assigned
by Eyton to August 1st. The latter, therefore, brings together the king's own party of three or four justices with
the four justices in eyre.

The great importance of this royal *iter* consists in its
bearing on the evolution of the *curia regis*. The years
1175 and 1176 from a critical epoch in this institutional
development. Dr. Stubbs, writing on this subject, reminds
us that "the first *placita curiæ regis* mentioned by Madox
are in 1175" (i. 600), and speaks of the "two circuits of
the justices in 1175, and the six circuits of the judges in
1176 " (*ib.*). So far, indeed, all is clear. The two judicial
eyres of 1175 are known to us from the Pipe-Rolls ; the six
of 1176 are found in the chronicles also, for they were
settled by the Assize of Northampton in January of that
year (i. 484-5). The really difficult subject is the king's
own *iter*, for which, we have seen, there is clear evidence,
but of which Dr. Stubbs, working from Madox, seems to
have been unaware.   His words are :—

All the eighteen justices of 1176 were officers of the Exchequer ;
some of them are found in 1175 holding "placita curiæ regis" in
bodies of three or four judges, and not in the same combinations in
which they took their judicial journeys. We can scarcely help the
conclusion that the new jurisprudence was being administered by
committees of the general body of justices, who were equally
qualified to sit in the Curia and Exchequer, and to undertake the
fiscal and judicial work of the eyre.

[*Note.* For instance, in 1176, William Fitz Ralf, Bertram de
Verdun, and William Basset hear pleas in Curia Regis touching
Bucks. and Beds. ; yet, on the eyre, these two counties are visited
by three other judges, etc.].

These statements are based on Madox's extracts from the Pipe-Rolls,[4] which afford, however, more definite evidence than Dr. Stubbs discovered. In the Pipe-Roll of 1175 and its immediate successor we find "Placita *in Curia Regis*" held by a single group of judges—William fitz Ralf, Bertram de Verdon, and William Basset (Thomas Basset is a substitute in one case and William fitz Audelin, we have seen, in another)—quite distinct from the "placita" of the justices in eyre, which were not described as "in curia regis." The view, therefore, that I now advance is that these pleas "in curia regis" were held by a separate group of judges in the train of the king himself, whose *iter* began at Reading, June, 1175.[5] It was there, I believe, that were held the "placita" for Bucks, and Beds., duly recorded in the Pipe-Roll of 1175. That this royal *iter* was continued through the Exchequer year 1175-6 seems to be well established, and the chronological difficulty of distinguishing between the two years renders the discovery of a fixed point, such as that afforded by the Evesham fine, of special value. Its evidence also establishes the presence of the king in person,[6] whose charter of confirmation should be carefully noted on account of its reciting the fine.

Having now traced the royal *iter*, of which the pleas are distinguished on the Pipe-Rolls as held "in curia regis," I turn to the circuits of the judges. I have fortunately lighted, in the course of my researches, on two more fines earlier than any known to Prof. Maitland. And, better still, one of these is the original document itself. The date of the first is July 1 and of the second June 29, 1176. The justices named in each case are those who are known to have gone the circuits, in which Leicester and Oxford

---

[4] *History of the Exchequer* (Ed. 1711), pp. 64, 65.

[5] Eyton's *Itinerary*, p. 191.

[6] Prof. Maitland has explained that this presence was formal (*Select Pleas of the Crown*, I. xiv.).

were respectively comprised.[7]   The importance of these
documents demands that they should be printed *in extenso*.

I.

Hec est finalis concordia facta apud Legr[ecestr]am proxima die
Jovis post proximum festum apostolorum petri et pauli postquam
Hugucio legatus Rome pervenit in Angliam,[8] coram Hugonem de
Gundevile et Willelmo filio Radulfi et Willelmo Basset, Justiciariis
domini Regis, et ceteris Baronibus qui ibi tunc aderant Inter Galfridum Ridel et Bertramum de Verdun de terrra de Madeleye, unde
placitum fuit inter eos in curia Domini Regis, Videlicet quod Galfridus Ridel dedit Bertrammo [*sic*] de Verdun feodum 1 militis in
Leycest'syre, scilicet servitium viii. car. terre quas Robert Devel
tenet in Swineford et in Walecote et servitium ii. car terre quas Walterus de Folevile tenet in parva Essebi et servitium 1 car. terre quam
peverel tenet in Flekeneye, et servitium i. car. terre quam Hardeui-
[nus] tenet in eadem Flekeneye.   Et has xii. car. terre dedit ei et
concessit in feodo et hereditate per servicium unius militis.   Et in
Staffordesyre dedit predictus Galfridus prenominato Bretamo [*sic*]
xii. bov. terre quas habebat in Crokestene de feodo de Madelye et
servitium de Foxwiss et de Hanekote per v. sol. inde annuatim red-
dendos Galfrido pro omnibus que ad illum pertinent.   Has vero
terras in Leycest'syre et in Staffordsyre dedit Galfridus Ridel et concessit Bertramo et heredibus suis tenendas de illo et de heredibus suis
in feodo et hereditate libere et quiete per prenominatum servitium
pro omnibus que ad illum pertinent, et pro ista donatione et concessione Bertrammus [*sic*] de Werdun [*sic*] totam calumpniam quam
habuit versus Galfridum in Madeleye quietum clamavit de illo et de
heredibus suis Galfrido Ridel et heredibus suis.[9]

II.

Hec est finalis concordia que facta fuit apud Ox[eneforde] in curia
Regis coram Ricardo Giffard et Rogero filio Reinfr[idi] et Johanne
de Caerdif Justitiis Regis . . . proximum festum apostolorum
petri et pauli postquam dominus Rex cepit ligantiam baronum Scotie

[7] Except that Robert fitz Bernard's place is taken by John of Cardiff.
[8] 27th October, 1175.
[9] Sloane Charter xxxi. 4, No. 34.   See also Addenda.

apud [Ebo]racum [10] inter Canonicos Oseneie et Ingream et tres filias eius scilicet Gundream et Isabella et Margaretam de terre de Oxenef[orde] unde placitum fuerat inter eos in curia Regis scilicet quod Ingrea et tres filie sue prenominate clamaverunt predictis canonicis quietam terram illam in Oxenenef[orde] de se et de heredibus suis pro xx. sol. quos canonici illi dederunt et omne jus quod in eadem terra habebant quietum illis clamaverunt. [11]

It will be observed that the Oxford fine is described as made "in curia regis," while the Leicester one is not. It would seem, then, that in spite of the distinction drawn at first on the rolls, the phrase "curia regis" was already creeping in as describing a court at which the king was not present.

I have also discovered, in MS., a "fine" of some ten or twelve years earlier, most valuable for comparison with those which I have here discussed. We have there a similar charter of confirmation, in which the king describes the transaction as "finem illum quem Abbas Willelmus de Hulmo fecit coram me," [12] and the document confirmed, moreover, describes itself as a "finis" between the Abbot of Holme and William and Henry de Neville, brothers. [18] But the form is very different from that of the true fine, which is fully developed in our example of 1175. The Holme "fine" may be safely assigned to March 1163-March, 1166, [14] and as it was "made" at Westminster, it not improbably belongs to the series of proceedings there *circ.* 8th March, 1163. It may fairly be presumed that if, at the date of this fine, the fully developed form existed it would have been duly employed at Westminster on this occasion. We may therefore safely assert, at least, that it came into use between the dates of these two transactions.

[10] August, 1175.   [11] Cotton Charter, xi. 73 (original).
[12] Galba, E., II., fo. 31*b*.   [18] *Ibid.*, 62*b*.
[14] The witnesses to the fine and the charter confirming it included Richard Archdeacon of Poitiers and Robert Earl of Leicester. The former gives us the limit March, 1163, and the king was not in England in the lifetime of the latter after March, 1166.

As bearing on the evolution of the fine, the charter of Henry II., confirming a "finis et concordia," and assigned by me to 1163-1170,[15] ought to be compared with the Holme charter, as indicating, perhaps, some advance, though the close resemblance between the clauses, in these royal charters, confirming the fine points to an almost common stage of development.

HOLME.	LEWES.
Quare volo et firmiter precipio quod finis ille sicut coram me factus est stabilis sit, et firmiter et inconcusse ex utraque parte teneatur.	Et ideo volo et firmiter precipio ut finis iste et concordia stabilis sit et firma maneat et inconcusse inter eos teneatur, sicut facta fuit coram me et utrobique concessa.

The part played by William fitz Audelin in the affairs, at this time, of Ireland, gives also some importance to this proof of his presence at Evesham on the 20th of July, 1175. It brings us, indeed, in contact with the great "Laudabiliter" controversy. Miss Norgate holds that William fitz Audelin was sent to Ireland in charge (with the Prior of Wallingford) of that contested document in 1175.[6] Prof. Tout, in his biography of William, writes on the contrary, oddly enough, that he was "sent in 1174 or 1175" (*sic*) on this mission, but "soon left Ireland, for he appears as a witness of the treaty of Falaise in October 1174 (*sic*), and in 1175 and 1176 he was constantly in attendance at court in discharge of his duties as steward or seneschal."[17] This confusion, however, is slight when compared with the statements as to William's tenure of

[15] See my *Ancient Charters*, pp. 67-8.

[16] "It is acknowledged on all hands that there is no sign of any attempt on Henry's part to publish the letter in Ireland . . . before 1175. In that year Gerald states that the latter was read . . . at Waterford." *Eng. Hist. Rev.*, viii. 44. Cf. p. 31. See also *Angevin Kings*, ii. 182.

[17] *Dictionary of National Biography.* I differ wholly from both writers, and take the view, based on record evidence, that, contrary to the accepted belief, William visited Ireland some two years earlier.

the government of Ireland. It is agreed that he was sent
to succeed Earl Richard (who died 5th April, 1176); but
while Miss Norgate holds that "early in the next year
Henry found it necessary to recall him,"[18] Prof. Tout
places his recall in 1179, consequent on complaints against
him to the king in January of that year. Without undertaking to decide the question, I may suggest that William
had returned to England by May, 1177,—for he is proved
by charters to have attended the Oxford council of that
date,—when Henry replaced him, as governor, by Hugh de
Lacy, but entrusted him, as Hoveden states, with Wexford.
We have only to assume that Gerald, by mistake, assigns
to 1172 his Wexford appointment, which really belonged
to 1177 (Prof. Tout thinks this probable), and then the
solution I suggest satisfies all the requirements.

William Fitz-Audelin, I may add, has been peculiarly
the sport of genealogists. Having been selected by them
as ancestor to the great Irish house of Burke (" De Burgo ")
he was further transformed, by a flight of fancy even
wilder than usual, into a lineal descendant of Charlemagne.
Who he really was seems to have remained unknown, for
his life in the *Dictionary of National Biography* treats with
suspicion, though duly mentioning, his alleged descent from
Charlemagne. Moreover, his very name would seem to
have been left in doubt. It would, of couse, be difficult
to distinguish " Aldelinus " from " Aldelmus " in MS., and
I confess to having looked on the latter—which is the
form adopted by Prof. Tout in the *Dictionary of National
Biography*, as by Miss Norgate and others—as probable
enough from its likeness to the English " Aldhelm." But
the " fitz Audeline " of the Anglo-Norman poem on the
Conquest of Ireland seems decisive. " Willelmus filius
Audelini, domini regis dapifer " was the style he used in
his own charters.[19]

[18] *England under the Angevin Kings*, ii. 183.
[19] The name of " Audelin " is extant as a surname. I have met with
it in London.

Having always kept a look-out for him in Yorkshire, I recognised William at once in a charter which is among those abstracted in the Report on the Portland MSS.[20] This is a confirmation by Roger de Mowbray of a grant to Fountains by "Aldelin de Aldefeld and Ralph his son and his other sons." Among the witnesses are "Ralph son of Aldelin, William his brother," and at the close, "Amelin son of Aldel." Now, if we turn to the *cartæ* of 1166, we find, under Yorkshire, that Ralph "filius Aldelin" held half a knight's fee of Roger de Mowbray, and William filius Aldelin one fee of Henry de Lacy. Here we recognise the two brothers mentioned in the charters above.[21] The small fief of William "filius Aldelin" himself is entered under Hampshire, where it is described as "terra quam dominus Rex dedit Willelmo filio Aldelin, Marscallo suo, cum Juliana filia Roberti Dorsnelli."

It is through this Juliana that we obtain the coping-stone of proof. Her charter granting Little Maplestead, Essex, to the Hospitallers, has for its first witness "Radulfo filio Adelini," who, as we have seen above, was her husband's brother.[22] And he is also the first witness to William's confirmation of her gift.[23]

The parentage and the true name of William fitz Audelin are thus, at length, clearly established.

[20] 13th Report Hist. MSS., App. ii., p. 4. We are indebted, I believe, to Mr. Maxwell Lyte for these interesting abstracts.

[21] The name seems to be preserved in Thorpe-Audlin (*vulgo* Audling), a township in the W. Riding of Yorkshire, some 4½ miles from Pontefract.

[22] It seems to be printed only in a footnote to Morant's *Essex* (i. 282). "Radulfo filio Willelmi domini mei" is a witness, which certainly suggests that William had been married before.

[23] See *Monasticon*. Prof. Tout seems to have been unaware of these charters of William, one of which is dated. Indeed he only says that William "is said to have married" Juliana, giving the *carta* (1166) as his authority.

THE MONTMORENCY IMPOSTURE.

MANY a jest has been levelled at the Irish family of Morres for seeking and obtaining permission from the crown, some eighty years ago, to assume the glorious name of "De Montmorency" in lieu of their own, as having been originally that of their family.[1] They have since borne, as is well-known, not merely the name, but even the arms and the proud device of that illustrious house. Moreover, the introduction of the name Bouchard, borne by the present Lord Mountmorres, proves the determination of the family to persist in their lofty pretensions.

I am not aware whether these pretensions have ever been regularly exposed: they seem to have been thought too fantastic for serious criticism. At the same time, it must be remembered that they have been formally and officially recognised by Sir W. Betham as Deputy Ulster, by the English crown (on the strength of his statement) and by the Chevalier De la Rue, "garde-général des archives du Royaume," on the French side, in 1818. On the other hand, it must not be forgotten that MM. de Montmorency at the time, in spite of the repeated and strenuous appeals of the Morres family, declined to admit their claim to be members of the house of Montmorency.

To the indignant protest of Col. Hervey Morres (styling himself "de Montmorency-Morres") against this action of the French house, we owe the most complete exposition of

[1] See, for instance, the *Complete Peerage* of G. E. C. *sub* "Frankfort de Montmorency."

the case on behalf of his family.[2]   On it, therefore, my
criticisms will be based.   Nor will these criticisms be
destructive only : they will show that the pedigrees upheld
by Col. Morres and his opponents were both alike erroneous,
and will establish the real facts, which, it will be found,
completely vindicate the accuracy of Giraldus Cambrensis.

The controversy hinged on a well-known personage.
" Herveius de Monte Mauricii," as Giraldus terms him.
The French house, taking their stand on the historians of
their family, insisted that he was the only Montmorency
who had gone to Ireland in his time, and that as he had,
admittedly, left no legitimate issue, the Morres claim was
untenable.   The Irish house contended that, on the contrary, others of the family had come over also, and that
they were lineally descended from one of Hervey's brothers,
but the whole story undoubtedly sprang from the mention
of this Hervey—the sole connecting link—and from the
curious form in which Giraldus chose to latinise his name.

Now Duchesne, the historian of the house of Montmorency, whose version Desormeaux and Père Anselme
did but follow in the main, wrote thus of Hervey :—

Il espousa Elizabeth de Meullent veuve de Gislebert de Claire,
Comte de Pembroc en Angleterre et mère de Richard de Claire,
surnommé Strongbow, Comte de Pembroke, dompteur de l'Hibernie,
duquel à raison de cette alliance un Autheur du temps le qualifie
parastre ou beaupère (p. 92).[3]

But this " Autheur " is Giraldus Cambrensis, on whom
Duchesne based his account, and who, we find, does not
speak of Hervey as stepfather, but as paternal uncle of
Strongbow :—

Herveius de Monte Mauricii, vir quoque fugitivus a facie fortunæ,

   [2] *Les Montmorency de France et les Montmorency d'Irlande, ou
Précis historique des démarches faites à l'occasion de la reprise du nom
de ses ancêtres par la branche de Montmorency-marisco-morres.*   Paris,
1828.

   [3] *Histoire de la maison de Montmorency.*   Paris, 1624.

inermis et inops, ex parte Richardi comitis cujus *patruus* erat, explorator potius quam expugnator advenit (i. 3).

Duchesne's version, therefore, is out of court, although it was repeated by Père Anselme, and even adopted in the *Genealogist* by so skilled and able a genealogist as Mr. G. W. Watson.[4]

Col. Hervey Morres went so far as to accuse Duchesne and Desormeaux "d'adulation, d'immoralité, et de mauvaise foi" in giving this account of his great namesake ; and he proceeded to substitute a version of his own, severing the hapless man and converting him into two ! To make this clear, I must print the essential part of the pedigree as given by him.

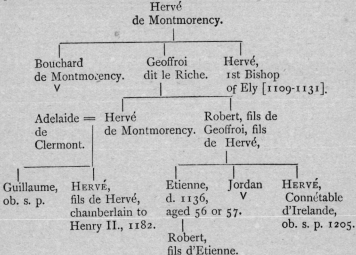

The explanation is extremely simple : the whole pedigree is concocted with a view to making the Irish Hervey uncle to—— Robert Fitz Stephen. This was done to satisfy the supposed requirements of Giraldus, whose words Col. Morres thus triumphantly quoted :—

Robertus Stephanides . . . Inter cæteros *Herveius de*

[4] Vol. x. p. 6.

Montemaurisco ROBERTI PATRUUS, *nepoti suo se* comitem præbuit (p. 77).

Unfortunately for him, he had gone, not to Giraldus, but to "Stonyhurst de rebus Hibernicis i. 69-70, *d'après Giraldus Cambrensis.*" Stonyhurst had carelessly made Giraldus speak of Hervey as uncle, not to Earl Richard, but to Robert Fitz Stephen, and the pedigree was accordingly constructed to fit this error. When the error is corrected, the pedigree collapses; and the very passage which is quoted to confirm it at once unmasks the concoction.

And now having made it clear that both sides were in error, I shall set forth the true explanation of the words of Giraldus. The clue is given us by those Deeping charters which, oddly enough, Col. Morres duly quoted and appealed to. The first is found in the *Monasticon*, ii. 601 :—

Adeliz, uxor Gilberti filii Ricardi et Gillebertus, et Baldewinus, et Rohaisia pueri Gilberti episcopo Lincolniensi . . . salutem . . . Hiis testibus, Gilberto filio Gilberti, Galterio, *Hervæo*, Baldwino fratribus ejus et Rohaisia sorore eorum, etc., etc.

The next is the confirmation of this grant by Robert Bishop of Lincoln, (ob. 1123) as "donum Adelidæ *de Montemoraci*" (p. 602). The third is a charter of "Adeliz, mater comitis Gilberti" (p. 603), who is also styled in the Thorney Register "Adelitia de Claromonte." Col. Morres also relied much on a grant to Castleacre by "Adalicia de Claromonte," to which the first witness is "Her. de Montemorentino,"[6] but the relationship of the witness to the grantor is not stated. Hervey de Montmorency is also mentioned in the Bilegh Abbey confirmation charter of Ric. I., but it gives us no information.

We have now, however, sufficient evidence to recover the true genealogy, which is interesting enough.

[6] Blomefield's *Norfolk*, ix. 5

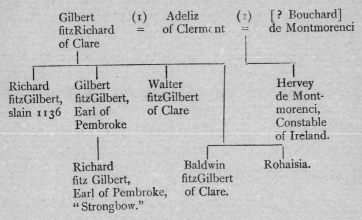

This shows us how Hervey was "paternal uncle" to Strongbow,[6] and why he witnessed his mother's charter (*ut supra*) with his brothers and sister, but did not join in their grant. We see, also, how Duchesne's error arose from his making the widow not of Gilbert, but of his son and namesake the first Earl of Pembroke, marry a Montmorenci. The error is not surprising in the case of such a family as the Clares, whose alliances and ramifications are made specially puzzling by the repetition of their Christian names.

On the other hand, the "dimidiation" of Hervey in the pedigree put forward by the Morres family was merely the fruit of the resolve to make him at all costs uncle to Robert Fitz Stephen, as the words of Giraldus were supposed to require, in their misquoted form.

Poor Hervey has, indeed, been the sport of genealogists and historians. Mr. Dimock, in his Rolls edition of Giraldus, renders his name as "Mont-Maurice," Miss Norgate as "Mountmorris,"[7] Mrs. Green as Mount Moriss.[8]

[6] Since this article was written, Mr. Hunt's life of Hervey has appeared in the *Dict. Nat. Biog.* He has arrived at precisely the same conclusions as myself.

[7] *England under the Angevin Kings*, ii. 101, 112.

[8] *Henry the Second*, p. 159.

Mr. Hunt, who has written his life in the *Dictionary of National Biography* as Mount-Maurice, and even Mr. Orpen, in his admirable edition of the Anglo-Norman poem on the Conquest, as " Montmaurice " (p. 335). This last is the strangest case, because the forms found in the poem are " Mumoreci " and " Momorci," while, as Mr. Orpen duly points out, it is " Munmoreci " in the Register of St. Thomas's, and " Mundmorici " in the Cartulary of St. Mary's (p. 266). Hervey was constable to his nephew Earl Richard's troops in Ireland, and described himself as " Marescallus Domini Regis de Hibernia, et senescallus de tota terra Ricardi Comitis."

Having now shown that the alleged descent can be absolutely disproved so far as concerns the only Montmorenci whose name occurs in connexion with Ireland, I proceed to glance at his supposed relatives, none of whom, it is important to remember, even bore the name of Montmorency.

The chart pedigree printed above (p. 512) will show how Robert Fitz Stephen was converted into a Montmorenci, though the parentage of his father Stephen, constable of Cardigan, is wholly unknown. It need scarcely be said that no proof is, or can be, given for this filiation ; but the following passage on Stephen is an excellent illustration of the sort of evidence which is vouched for this wholly imaginary pedigree :—

Ce seigneur, très-jeune encore, en 1087, confirma conjointement avec son père et son aïeul Hervé, fils de Bouchard, la donation faite par Turillus le Gros à l'abbaye de St. Florent de Saumur de certaines bénéfices.

Sig. Hervei filii Burchardi, Sig. Roberti filii ejus, Sig. Stephani militis ejus.

All that is needed, we are told, is to read grandson (" petit fils ") instead of *filius* for Robert, and great-grandson for *miles*,—on the ground that *miles* sometimes meant " un jeune homme " ! Such is a type of the " proofs " on which this pedigree rests. But its absurdities and inconsistencies go even further than this. The dates work out as follows :—

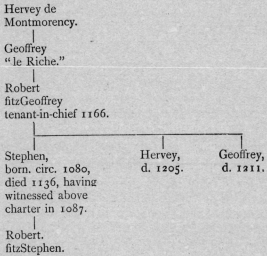

Hervey de
Montmorency.

Geoffrey
"le Riche."

Robert
fitzGeoffrey
tenant-in-chief 1166.

Stephen,
born. circ. 1080,
died 1136, having
witnessed above
charter in 1087.

Hervey,
d. 1205.

Geoffrey,
d. 1211.

Robert.
fitzStephen.

Thus Stephen, who was born about 1080, and was a witness in 1087, would be *son* to a man who flourished in 1166, and *brother* to men who died in 1205 and 1211.[9]

But what are we to say when we learn further that this Stephen, who died in "1136," is the Stephanus de Marisco" who appears in the *Liber Niger* as a tenant of the Bishop of Ely in 1166! The probable, and indeed only, explanation is that Col. Morres did not even know when the returns in the *Liber Niger* were compiled. Their real date again destroys this cock-and-bull pedigree, or genealogical nightmare, which for sheer topsy-turveydom, has, I venture to assert, never been surpassed.

I strongly suspect that the whole story arose from the occurrence in Ireland, in the thirteenth century, of the Latinised name "De Marisco" or "De Mariscis," which represents of course, neither Montmorenci nor Morres, but

---

[9] "Etienne de Mariscis (*sic*) . . . fut tué en 1136 par les Gallois lorsqu'il gouvernait ce pays" (p. 74). "Il n'était agé lors de sa mort que de cinquante six ou cinquante sept ans" (p. 75).

simply Marsh. Genealogists, no doubt, were attracted by the form "De Monte Maurisco" into tracing a connexion; but, so far as can be understood, Col. Morres discarded this resemblance, and represented his alleged ancestors as "seigneurs de Mariscis ou des marches" in England, connecting them with the fen district in Cambridgeshire. It would be easy to show that the early pedigree positively teems with absurdities similar to those I have already exposed, but it would be sheer waste of time to devote any more attention to proofs, which Col. Morres proudly boasted were "vérifiés avec la plus scrupuleuse attention par l'autorité competente et sanctionnés désormais par l'autorisation du prince qui gouverne aujourd'hui l'empire britannique" (p. 25).

I do not hesitate to say that a more impudent claim was never successfully foisted on the authorities and the public. The chief sinner in the matter was, of course, Sir. W. Betham, who certified (29th June, 1815) that this audacious concoction was "established on evidence of the most unquestionable authority, chiefly from the ancient public records" (p. 203). The Crown naturally could only accept the statement of its own officer of arms, and accordingly described the alleged descent as being duly proved and recorded.[10] As for the French expert, the Chevalier de la Rue, of whose investigation and favourable verdict (17th April, 1818) so much has been made, it will scarcely be believed that he actually, with the sole exception of the *Monasticon*, did not attempt to verify the "proofs" set before him! It will be seen from his own words that his decision was subject to their genuineness :—

Toutes les citations puisées par monsieur de Morrès dans les monuments, registres, et terriers publics d'Angleterre étant, *comme je n'en doute pas*, aussi exactes que celles du Monasticon (p. 37).

The value of his loudly-trumpeted verdict may be estimated from this admission.

[10] *London Gazette*, Sept. 9th, 1815 ; *Dublin Gazette*, Aug. 12, 1815.

It is only right that MM. de Montmorency and all those in France who are interested in historical genealogy should understand that no one among ourselves, whose opinion is worth having, would dream of defending this gross usurpation. We may hope and believe that in the present day no officer of arms would behave like Sir W. Betham, and certify, as "established on evidence of the most unquestionable authority" a descent which is not merely "not proven," but can be absolutely disproved. It cannot be stated too emphatically, or known too widely, that the house of Morres has no more right, by hereditary descent, to the name and arms of "De Montmorency" than any of the numerous families of Morris, or indeed, for the matter of that, the family of Smith.[11]

[11] For an even more illustrious foreign descent, see my paper, "Our English Hapsburgs : a great delusion" (*Genealogist*, N. S., x. 193).

THE OXFORD DEBATE ON FOREIGN SERVICE (1197)

GREAT importance is rightly assigned to the first instances of "a constitutional opposition to a royal demand for money,"[1] of which the two alleged earliest cases are "the opposition of St. Thomas to the king's manipulation of the danegeld [1163], and the refusal by St. Hugh of Lincoln to furnish money for Richard's war in France [1197]."[2] These two precedents are always classed together : Dr. Stubbs writes of St. Hugh's action :—

The only formal resistance to the king in the national council proceeds from St. Hugh of Lincoln and Bishop Herbert of Salisbury, who refuse to consent to grant him an aid in knights and money for his foreign warfare . . . an act which stands out prominently by the side of St. Thomas's protest against Henry's proposal to appropriate the sheriff's share of danegeld.[3]

And Mr. Freeman repeats the parallel :—

Thomas . . . withstands, and withstands successfully, the levying of a danegeld. . . . As Thomas of London had withstood the demands of the father, Hugh of Avalon withstood the demands of the son. In a great council . . . [he] spoke up for the laws and rights of Englishmen . . . no men or money were they bound to contribute for undertakings beyond the sea.[4]

---

[1] Stubbs, *Const. Hist.* (1874), i. 510.   [2] *Ibid.*, p. 577.
[3] *Select Charters* (1870), pp. 28-9. So too, preface to Rog. Hoveden (1871) : "It may be placed on a par with St. Thomas's opposition to Henry II. in 1163" (IV. pp. xci.-xcii.). So also *Early Plantagenets* (1876), p. 126, and *Const. Hist.*, i. 510.
[4] *Norm. Conq.*, v. 675, 695.

Having already discussed the earlier instance,[5] and advanced the view that the Woodstock debate [1163] did not relate to danegeld at all, but to an attempt of the king to seize for himself the *auxilium vicecomitis* (a local levy) I now approach the later instance.

"This occasion," we read, "is a memorable one":[6] it is that of an "event of great importance,"[7] of "a landmark in constitutional history."[8] No apology, therefore, is needed for endeavouring to throw some further light on an event of such cardinal importance. But, to clear the ground, let us first define what we mean by "opposition to a royal demand for money." However autocratic the king may have been—and on this point there is not only a difference of opinion but a difference in fact corresponding with his strength at any given period—there were limits set by law or custom (or, should we rather say, limits, both written and unwritten?) beyond which he could not pass. "Domesday," for instance, was a written limit: if the king claimed from a Manor assessed at ten hides the danegeld due from twenty, the tenant need only appeal to "Domesday" (*poneret se super rotulum Winton'*). Or, again, if from a feudal tenant owing the forty days' service the king were to claim eighty days, he would be transgressing unwritten custom as binding as a written record. But outside these limits there lay a debatable ground where that elastic term *auxilium* proved conveniently expansive. It was here that the crown could increase its demands, and here that a conflict would arise as to where the limit should be placed, a conflict to be determined not by law, but by a trial of strength between the crown and its opponents. We have, then, to decide to which of these spheres the action of St. Hugh should be assigned, whether to that of the lawyer appealing to the letter of the bond, or to that of the popular leader opposing the demands of the king, though they did not contravene the law. If one may use the terms, for

---

[5] See above, p. 497.   [6] *Early Plantagenets*, p. 126.   [7] *Const. Hist.*, i. 509
[8] *Ibid.*, p. 510, and pref. to Rog. Hoveden, iv. pp. xci.-xcii.

convenience sake, it was a question of law or a question of
politics; and only if it was the latter had it a true constitutional importance.

The two chief accounts of the Oxford debate are found
in Roger Hoveden and the *Magna Vita St. Hugonis*. As
they are both printed in *Select Charters*, I need not repeat them here. There is, however, an independent version in the *Vita* of Giraldus Cambrensis, which it may be
desirable to add :—

In Anglicanam coepit [rex] ecclesiam duris exactionibus debacchari.
Unde collecto in unum regni clero, habitoque contra insolitum et
tam urgens incommodum districtiore consilio, verbum ad importunas
pariter et importabiles impositiones contradictionis et cleri totius pro
ecclesiastica libertate responsionis, in ore Lincolnensis tanquam
personae prae ceteris approbatae religionis authenticae magis communi omnium desiderio est assignatum (vii. 103-4).

Gerald's editor impugns the correctness of these statements, on the grounds that the assembly was not clerical
merely and that the bishop did not speak on behalf of the
whole church. But the passage seems to me to refer to a
meeting of the clergy in which it was decided that St.
Hugh should be their spokesman at the council. Of the
other objection I shall treat below.

According to Hoveden, Richard asked for either (1) three
hundred knights who would serve him, at their own costs,
for a year, or (2) a sum sufficient to enable him to hire
three hundred knights for a year at the rate of three
shillings a day. The *Magna Vita*, however, implies that
the former alternative alone was laid before the council.
The grounds on which St. Hugh protested are thus given
by our two authorites :—

Respondit pro se, quod ipse in hoc voluntati regis nequaquam
adquiesceret, tum quia processu temporis in ecclesiae suae detri-
mentum redundaret, tum quia successores sui dicerent, "Patres
nostri comederunt uvam acerbam, et dentes filiorum obstupescunt"
(Hoveden).

Scio equidem ad militare sevitium domino regi, sed in hac terra
solummodo exhibendum, Lincolniensem ecclesiam teneri; extra

metas vero Angliae nil tale ab ea deberi. Unde mihi consultius arbitror ad natale solum repedare . . . quam hic pontificatum gerere et ecclesiam mihi commissam, antiquas immunitates perdendo, insolitis angariis subjugare (*Magna Vita*).

Two points stand out clearly—one that St. Hugh took his stand on the prescriptive rights of his church, rights infringed by the king's demand ; the other, that he spoke for himself alone, not for the church, still less for the barons, and least of all for the nation. Our authorities, however, are so vague that they leave in doubt the precise point "taken" by the saintly prelate. Mr. Freeman, we have seen, confidently assumes that he "spoke up for the laws and rights of Englishmen"; Miss Norgate holds that he took up the position of Thomas and Anselm as a champion of constitutional liberty," [9] whatever that may mean ; even Dr. Stubbs claims that he "acted on behalf of the nation to which he had joined himself." [10]

I venture to think that the clue to the enigma is to be found in quite another quarter. In the chronicle of Jocelin de Brakelond we find a most instructive passage, which refers, it cannot be doubted, to the same episode. The story is told somewhat differently, but the point raised is the same. King Richard, we are told, demanded that knights should be sent him from England, in the proportion of one from every ten due by the church "baronies." The *servitium debitum* of St. Edmund's being forty, the abbot was called upon to send four. [11] That the principle of joint equipment, which had been adopted under Henry II. in 1157, [12] and again I think by Longchamp in 1191, [13]

---

[9] *England under the Angevin Kings*, ii. 350.

[10] *Early Plantagenets*, p. 126.

[11] " Precepit rex Ricardus omnibus episcopis et abbatibus Angliae ut de suis baroniis novem milites facerent decimum, et sine dilacione venirent ad eum in Normanniam, cum equis et armis in auxilium contra Regem Franciae. Unde et abbatem oportuit respondere de iiii. militibus mittendis " (ed. Camden Soc., p. 63).

[12] " Præparavit maximam expeditionem ita ut duo milites de tota Anglia tertium pararent ad opprimendum Gualenses." Robert de Torigni.

[13] "Tertium cum omnibus armis totius Angliae militem die nominato mandavit venire Wintoniam." Ric. Devizes (Rolls Series), p. 409.

was resorted to on this occasion is the more probable
because a few years later (1205) we find King John similarly demanding "quod novem milites per totam Angliam
invenirent decimum militem, bene paratum equis et armis,
ad defensionem regni nostri." I admit, however, that it is
not mentioned in the other versions of our episode, and
Jocelin speaks only of the demand upon the church fiefs.
But the point is that when the abbot consulted his tenants
as to sending the four knights required, they protested that
they were liable to pay scutage, but not to serve out of
England.[14] Now this is a *locus classicus* on the institution
of scutage. Its bearing I shall examine below, after finish-
ing the story. The abbot, we read, finding himself in a
strait, crossed the sea in search of the king, who told him
that a fine would not avail ; he wanted men, not money.[15]

Surely we have here the key to the position taken by St.
Hugh. When he claimed that his fief was not bound "ad
servitium militare . . . extra metas Angliae" he cannot have referred to the payment of scutage, for that had
been paid by his predecessors and himself without infringing
the liberties of their church.[16] He must, therefore, have
referred not to "money," but to *personal* service outside the
realm. But was this exemption peculiar to the church of
Lincoln? If we find the same privilege existing at St.
Edmund's and at Salisbury, may we not infer that the
church contingents were only bound to serve in person for

[14] "Cumque summoneri fecisset omnes milites suos, et eos inde con-
venisset, responderunt feudos suos, quos de Sancto Ædmundo tenuerunt,
hoc non debere, nec se nec patres eorum unquam Angliam exisse, set
scutagium aliquando ad praeceptum regis dedisse" (*Ibid.*).

[15] Abbas vero in arcto posito, hinc videns libertatem suorum militum
periclitari, illinc timens ne amitteret saisinam baronie sue pro defectu
servicii regis, sicut contigerat Episcopo Lundonensi [? Lincolnensi] et
multis baronibus Angliæ, statim transfretavit, et . . . in primis
nullum potuit facere finem cum rege per denarios. Dicenti ergo se non
indigere auro nec argento, sed quatuor milites instanter exigenti," etc. (*ib.*)

[16] "In quibus conservandis sive exhibendis hactenus fere per tredecim
annos a rectis praedecessorum meorum vestigiis non recessi" (*Magna
Vita*).

"defence, not defiance,"[17] and that we have here the
perfect explanation of the fact that scutage, as commutation for service, is an institution, when it first appears,
peculiar to church fiefs? The medieval dread of creating
a precedent preyed on the abbot as on the saint. From the
council of Lillebonne to the Bedford *auxilium* (1224) it was
always the same cry :—

> Creiment k'il seit en feu tornez
> Et en costume seit tenu
> Et par costume seit rendu.

It was in this spirit that Hugh of Avalon, I take it, made
his stand : other prelates might waive the point, in consideration of the king's necessities, but he, at least, would
never allow a standing exemption to be broken through
and thus impaired for all time.

His attitude, we are told, proved fatal to the scheme
compelling the king and his ministers to abandon it in
impotent wrath. But perhaps his biographer exaggerates
the defeat, for the Bishop of Salisbury, we know, had to
purchase the king's pardon for his action by a heavy fine,
while the Abbot of St. Edmund's had to compromise the
matter by the payment of a large sum.[18] It seems pro-

---

[17] "Ad publicam rem tuendam" (*Abingdon Cart.*), ii. 3).

[18] "Quatuor milites stipendiarios optulit abbas. Quos cum rex recepis-
set, apud castellum de Hou misit. Abbas autem in instanti eis xxxvi.
marcas dedit ad expensas xl. dierum. In crastino autem venerunt quidam
familiares regis, consuelentes abbati ut sibi caute provideret, dicentes
werram posse durare per annum integrum vel amplius, et expensas militum excrescere et multiplicari in perpetuum dampnum ei et ecclesiae
suae. Et ideo consulebant ut, antequam recederet de curia, finem faceret
cum rege, unde posset quietus esse de militibus predictis post xl. dies.
Abbas autem, sano usus consilio, centum libras regi dedit pro tali quiet-
antia" (*Jocelin*, p. 63). It is noteworthy that thirty-six marcs would
represent just three shillings a day (for forty days) for each knight, the
very sum named by Hoveden. In 1205 the pay named in John's writ
was two shillings a day (home service), but both these sums are largely
in excess of the eight pence a day paid, as we have seen, under Henry II.,
the discrepancy being incomprehensible, unless the higher wage implied
a larger following.

bable that similar compromises would be arranged in other cases where the request was not complied with.

If, then, I am right in the solution I offer, St. Hugh must have taken the narrowest ground, and have acted on behalf of ecclesiastical privilege, and only incidentally even for that, his protest being limited to his own church.[19] And, further, it follows that, like St. Thomas, he was acting strictly on the defensive. To say that his action affords "the first clear case of the refusal of a money grant demanded directly by the crown, and a most valuable precedent, for later times,"[20] is, I submit with all respect, to set it in a quite erroneous light. In 1197, as in 1163, the crown was trying to infringe on well-established rights, and St. Hugh like St. Thomas, resisted that infringement, so far as his own rights were concerned, just as he would have resisted an attempt of the crown to deprive his see of a Manor, of feudal services, or of goods. The crown might take its pound of flesh, but more than that it should not have; never, through any action of his, should his church be deprived of its prescriptive rights.[21]

Here this article originally closed; but I am tempted to refer to one touching on the same subject which appeared a year later in the pages of the same review.[22] Alluding to "the question of foreign service" as a prominent grievance under John,[23] I wrote:—

Ralf of Coggeshall, and Walter of Coventry, assert that the northern barons denied their liability to foreign service in respect of lands held in England. John retorted that the principle had been admitted in the days of his father and his brother, and there-

---

[19] Dr. Stubbs held [1870] that he acted "not on ecclesiastical but on constitutional grounds" (*Select Charters*, p. 28), though he subsequently [1871] doubted whether "the grounds of the opposition" were "ecclesiastical or constitutional" (Pref. to Hoveden, iv. p. xci.), and even admitted that "the opposition of St. Hugh was based not on his right as a member of the national council, but on the immunities of the church" (*Const. Hist.*, i. 578).

[21] Hoveden, iv. xcii.   [21] "Antiquas immunitates perdendo."

[22] "An Unknown Charter of Liberties." *English Historical Review*, viii. 288 et sq.   [23] See Dr. Stubbs' Pref. to W. Coventry, p. lxiv.

fore claimed it *tanquam debitum*. This justifies the fears expressed sixteen years before by St. Hugh of Lincoln, and explains what I termed, in examining his action, the mediæval dread of creating a precedent.[24]

The final loss of Normandy had, of course, altered the case, but even while it still formed part of an English King's possessions, there must always have been scope for argument as to feudal obligations. To quote once more from the same article :—

The question must have been complicated by the growth of the king's dominions. Did the feudatories owe service to the king, as their lord, in whatever war he was engaged? Or were they only bound to follow him as King of England? Or were they, as holding *a conquestu*, only bound to serve in the dominions of the Conqueror who enfeoffed them, *i.e.* in England and Normandy.[25]

On the death of the Conqueror, the question would arise for the King of the English and the Duke of the Normans were no longer one and the same. It comes to the front accordingly in a gathering of the barons at Winchester, which Mr. Freeman assigns to Easter, 1090.[26] Orderic, here his authority, places it under 1089, and although his chronology is not to be always blindly followed, there is no ground for supposing here that the date is wrong. When he is following out a story or carried on by allusion, Orderic, like other chroniclers, anticipates or wanders in his dates; but this gathering has no connexion with what precedes or follows; there is, therefore, nothing to account for his placing it under 1089, if it really belonged to 1090.

But the point to which I would call attention is the nature and intention of this gathering. Orderic writes :—

Confirmatus itaque in regno, turmas optimatum ascivit, et Guentoniæ congregatis, quæ intrinsecus ruminabat sic ore deprompsit.

Mr. Freeman attaches to the speech that follows no small importance. Holding that the king " was now ready to take the decisive step of crossing the sea himself or sending others to cross it," he pointed out that—

[24] *E.H.R.*, viii. 293.   [25] *Ibid.*   [26] *Will. Rufus*, i. 222.

even William Rufus, in all his pride and self-confidence, knew that it did not depend wholly on himself to send either native or adopted Englishmen on such an errand. He had learned enough of English constitutional law not to think of venturing on a foreign war without the constitutional sanction of his kingdom. In a Gemot [*sic*] at Winchester, seemingly the Easter Gemot of the third year of his reign, he laid his schemes before the assembled Witan [*sic*], and obtained their consent to a war with the Duke of the Normans.[27]

Of course, in reading Mr. Freeman's works we must reconcile ourselves to "Gemot" and "Witan," being thrust upon us at every turn, however radically false a conception these words may convey. At the close of his dealing with this episode, he refers us, as a parallel, to the "full Gemot" of 1047, in which "the popular character of the assembly still," we learn, "impresses itself on the language of history." Now Orderic describes those who were summoned to our Winchester gathering as "turmas optimatum"; he makes William begin his speech "nostri egregii barones"; and he places in his mouth language essentially feudal and Norman :—

Nunc igitur commoneo vos omnes, qui patris mei homines fuistis, et feudos vestros in Normannia et Anglia de illo tenuistis[28] . . . coenobia quæ patres nostri construxerunt in Neustria . . . Decet ergo ut, sicut nomen ejus [*i.e.* Willelmi] et diadema gero, sic ad defensionem patriæ inhæream ejus [*i.e.* Normanniæ] studio.

Mr. Freeman expressed astonishment and delight at William's "constitutional language," and declared that though, in its actual wording, the speech, of course was Orderic's,

the constitutional doctrines which he has worked into his speech cannot fail to set forth the ordinary constitutional usage of the time. Even in the darkest hour in which England had any settled government at all, etc., etc.[29]

[27] *Will. Rufus*, i. 222.

[28] Mr. Freeman quotes this passage, and duly renders it in his text (i. 232).   [29] i. 22

And then follows the usual lament for "the days of King Eadward," when it was not a "cabinet," but a crowd, that dealt with the delicate question of peace or war.

Now even the late Professor's most ardent followers cannot represent my criticism here as "trifling," or un-important. Mr. Freeman, I hold, had misconceived the matter altogether. The whole thing is sheer delusion. William's appeal, as set before us, was not the fruit of studies in English "constitutional law": it was the appeal of a feudal lord to "barons" holding by feudal tenure. Should there be any one who feels the slightest doubt upon the question, let him turn to Mr. Freeman's own account of the great "Assembly of Lillebonne." He could not himself avoid a passing glance at the parallel, when he wrote that "William. the Red had as good reasons to give for an invasion of Normandy as his father had once had to give for an invasion of England." [80] Contrasting that Assembly (1066) with an English Gemót, he wrote that "in William's Assembly we hear of none but barons." [81] Precisely. But that remark is equally true of his son's Assembly at Winchester. [82] And when we learn, a few years later, the composition of his Assembly, we find it admittedly restricted to tenants-in-chief. [83] Of the two Assemblies, that of Lille-bonne revealed a more active opposition, showed more "parliamentary boldness," than that of Winchester. [84] The latter merely applauded, we read, the King's appeal. Like his father, he appealed to his barons to follow him on foreign service; like him also, he pleaded his wrongs and the justice of his righteous cause.

Of the two, the father seems, as I have said, to have met with more opposition than the son. One might therefore produce an argument *ad absurdum*, and contend that, on Mr. Freeman's showing, an English King was not less, but more, absolute than a Norman Duke. In any case we have

[80] i. 222. [81] *Norm. Conq.*, iii. 290.
[82] "Turmas optimatum "—"barones." Cf. *supra*, pp. 247 262.
[83] *Will. Rufus*, ii. 56-7. [84] *Norm. Conq.*, iii. 294-296, 298.

now seen that the ideas about "constitutional usage," and so forth, imported here by Mr. Freeman, were nothing but a figment of his brain. The Assembly of Winchester no more resulted from "English constitutional law" than did the Assembly of Lillebonne, convened for a similar purpose. William Rufus had to deal with barons who could not be anxious to invade Normandy merely to make him Duke of the Normans. If they had any preference in the matter, it would be rather for Robert than for William, for a weak rather than a strong ruler; but, apart from preference, the barons would be loth to engage in internecine warfare merely for the personal advantage of one brother or the other. This was seen in the peaceful close of the invasion by Duke Robert, as with that of Duke Henry half a century later. The question, in short, that arose in 1066, when a Duke of the Normans asked his barons to make him King of the English, arose once more in the days of his son, when a King of the English asked his barons to make him Duke of the Normans.

It was here no question of "the laws and rights of Englishmen":[85] it was to no folkmoot that William Rufus spoke. When we read of the King in his court, composed of his tenants-in-chief,[86] as surrounded by "no small part of the nation,"[87] when we hear of the mass of "the Assembly . . . crying Yea, yea";[88] when we learn that "a great numerical proportion, most likely a numerical majority, were natives,"[89] we are fairly prepared for the astounding statement that—

The wide fields which had seen the great review and the great homage in the days of the elder William, could alone hold the crowd which came together to share in the great court of doom which was holden by the younger.[40]

For we see that in all these fantasies of a brain viewing plain facts through a mist of moots and "witan," we have what can only be termed history in masquerade.

[85] *Supra*, p. 528.   [86] At Salisbury, 13th Jan., 1096.
[87] *Will. Rufus*, ii. 57.   [88] *Ibid.*, 59.   [89] *Ibid.*, 57.   [40] *Ibid.*, 56.

RICHARD THE FIRST'S CHANGE OF SEAL (1198)

> With the superficial student and the empiric politician, it is too common to relegate the investigation of such changes to the domain of archæology. I shall not attempt to rebut the imputation ; only, if such things are archæology, then archæology is history.—STUBBS, Preface to *R. Hoveden*, IV., lxxx.

HISTORICAL research is about to pass, if indeed it is not already passing, into a new sphere—the sphere of Archæology. The central idea of that great advance which the present generation has witnessed in the domain of history has been the rebuilding of the historical fabric on the relatively sure foundation of original and contemporary authorities, studied in the purest texts. Chronicles, however, are not inexhaustible : for many periods they are all too few. The reaper has almost done his work ; the turn of the gleaner has come. The smaller *quellen* of history have now to be diligently examined and made to yield those fragments of information which will supplement, often where most needed, our existing stock of knowledge.

But this is not our only gain as we leave the broad highways trodden by so many before us. Those precious fragments which are to form our spoils will enable us to do more than supplement the statements of our standard chroniclers : they will afford the means of checking, of testing, by independent evidence, these statements, of submitting our witnesses to a cross-examination which may shake their testimony and their credit in a most unexpected manner.

As an instance of the results to be attained by archæological research, I have selected Richard the First's celebrated change of seal. Interesting as being the occasion on which the three lions first appear as the Royal arms of England—arms unchanged to the present day—it possesses exceptional historical importance from the circumstances by which it was accompanied, and which led, admittedly, to its adoption.

Historians have agreed, without the least hesitation, to refer this event to the year 1194, and to place it subsequent to the truce of Tillières or about the beginning of August. "That Richard I.," writes a veteran student,[1] "adopted a new seal upon his return from the Holy Land is a matter of notoriety." Speed, in fact, had shown the way. We are told by him that "the king caused [1194] a new broad seale to be made, requiring that all charters granted under his former seale should be confirmed under this, whereby he drew a great masse of money to his treasurie."[2] The Bishop of Oxford, with his wonted accuracy, faithfully reproduces the statement of Hoveden (the original and sole authority we shall find for the story), telling us that "Amongst other oppressive acts he [Richard] took the seal from his unscrupulous but faithful chancellor, and, having ordered a new one to be made, proclaimed the nullity of all charters which had been sealed with the old one."[3] Mr. Freeman similarly places the episode just before "the licenses for the tournaments" (20th August, 1194), and consistently refers to Dr. Stubbs's history.[4]

[1] Canon Raine, *Historiæ Dunelmensis Scriptores Tres* (Surtees Soc.), p. 379.

[2] Speed's History (1611).

[3] *Const. Hist.*, i. 506.

[4] *Norman Conquest*, v. 693. Compare *The Office of the Historical Professor*, pp. 16, 17 :—"In a long and careful study of the Bishop of Chester's writings . . . I have never found a flaw in the statement of

Miss Norgate, in her valuable work, our latest authority on the period, assigns the event to the same date, and tells us that "Rog. Hoveden's very confused account of the seals is made clear by Bishop Stubbs."[5]   Mr. Maitland, in his noble edition of "Bracton's Note-book," gives a case (ii. 69) in which a charter sealed "secundo sigillo Regis Ricardi" was actually produced in court (1219), and explains that "Richard had a new seal made in 1194," referring to Hoveden for his authority.[6]

It should be observed that all these writers rely merely on Hoveden, none of them throwing any light on the process of confirmation, or telling us how it was effected, and whether any traces of it remain.   An independent writer, M. Boivin-Champeaux, in his monograph on William Longchamp, discusses the episode at some length, and asserts that the repudiated documents were "assujettis, pour leur revalidation, à une nouvelle et coûteuse scellure." Like the others, however, he relies on the authority of Hoveden, and consequently repeats the same date.

In the course of examining some ancient charters, I recognised one of them as nothing less than an actual instance of a confirmation consequent on this change of seal. But its incomprehensible feature was that the charter was confirmed on the 22nd August, 1198, having originally been granted, "sub primo sigillo," so recently as the 7th January preceding.   How could this be possible if the great seal had been changed so early as August, 1194, and if the first seal, as stated by Dr. Stubbs, was "broken" on that occasion?   Careful and prolonged research among the charters of the period (both in the original and in transcripts) has enabled me to answer the question, and to prove that (as, of course, the above charter implies) the

his evidence.   If I have now and then lighted on something that looked like oversight, I have always found in the end that the oversight was mine and not his."

[5] *England under the Angevin Kings*, ii. 343.

[6] I have been able to identify this very charter.

change of seal did not take place in 1194, but 1198, and between January and May of that year.

Original charters under the second seal, confirming grants under the first, are distinctly rare. I have found, as yet, but one in the Public Record Office, and only two at the British Museum. But of originals and transcripts together I have noted twenty-eight. The dates of the original grants range from 5th September, 1189, to 7th January, 1198 (1197-8), and of the confirmations from 27th May, 1198, to 5th April, 1199.[7]

In a single instance there is fortunately preserved not only the text of the confirmation charter, but also that of the original grant.[8] From this we learn that the charter of confirmation did not necessarily give the wording, but only the gist ("tenor") of the original grant. We are thus brought to the instructive formula invariably used in these charters :—

Is erat tenor carte nostre in primo sigillo nostro. Quod quia aliquando perditum fuit, et, dum capti essemus in alem[anniâ], in aliena potestate constitutum, mutatum est. Huius autem innovationis testes sunt Hii, etc.. etc.

We may here turn to the passage in Hoveden [Ed. Stubbs, iii. 267] on which historians have relied, and see how far the reasons for the change given in the charters themselves correspond with those alleged by the chronicler.

Fecit sibi novum sigillum fieri, et mandavit, per singulas terras suas, quod nihil ratum foret quod fuerat per vetus sigillum suum ; tum quia cancellarius ille operatus fuerat inde minus discrete quam esset necesse, tum quia sigillum illud perditum erat, quando Rogerus Malus Catulus, vicecancellarius suus, submersus erat in mari ante insulam de Cipro, et præcepit rex quod omnes qui cartas habebant venirent ad novum sigillum ad cartas suas renovandas.

[7] This is the only confirmation I have found later than 3rd March. If the date can be relied on, it is of special interest as being the day before the king died.

[8] Charters to W. Briwere, 22nd June, 1190, and 11th March, 1199 (1198-9), transcribed in the Great Coucher (Duchy of Lancaster).

In both cases we find there are two reasons given; but while one of these is the same in both, namely the temporary loss of the seal when Roger Malchael was drowned, the other is wholly and essentially different. The whole aspect of the transaction is thus altered. To illustrate this I shall now place side by side the independent glosses of the Bishop of Oxford and of M. Boivin-Champeaux :—

Richard's first seal was lost when the vice-chancellor was drowned between Rhodes and Cyprus in 1190; but it was re-covered with his dead body. The seal that was now broken must have been the one which the chancellor had used during the king's absence. Richard, how-ever, when he was at Messina, had allowed his seal to be set to various grants for which he took money, but which he never in-tended to confirm. Therefore probably he found it convenient now to have a new seal in lieu of both the former ones, although he threw the blame of the trans-actions annulled upon the chan-cellor. The importance of the seal is already very great. (*Const. Hist.*, i. 506, note.)

Sur deux exemplaires usuels du grand sceau, le premier, que portait le vice-chancelier Mau-chien, avait été perdu lors de l'ouragan qui, en vue de Chypre avait assailli la flotte Anglo-Normande, le second était resté en Angleterre; mais il avait subi, par suite de la revolution du 10 octobre, de nombreuses vicissi-tudes. Richard se prévalut de ces circonstances jointes au désaveu de la trève de Tillières pour publier un édit aux termes duquels tous les actes publics passés sous son règne, qui avaient été légalisés avec les anciens sceaux étaient frappés de nullité et assujettis, pour leur revalidation à une nouvelle et coûteuse scellure. Cette ordon-nance aurait pu, à la rigueur, se colorer, si elle n'avait concerné que les actes ...ccomplis pendant l'expédition et la captivité du roi; mais le comble de l'impu-dence et de l'iniquité était de l'appliquer même a ceux qui avaient précéde son départ ou suivi son retour (p. 223).

Thus both writers assume that there were two seals, one

which remained in England with the chancellor, and one which accompanied the king to the east. They further (though Dr. Stubbs is somewhat obscure) hold that the two excuses given refer respectively to the two seals, thus discrediting both. But when we turn to the charters themselves, we find but one seal mentioned, and to that one seal alone both the excuses refer. The king explains that on two occasions it was, so to speak, "out on the loose"—(1) when his vice-chancellor was drowned; (2) when he himself was captured in Germany. This was, of course, the seal which accompanied him to the east.[9] The king makes no allusion to any other or to the chancellor. Such charters and grants as are known to us all proceed from the king himself, either before he left Messina or after he had reached Germany on his return. No charter or grant of Longchamp, as representing him, is known. In short, the whole of our record evidence points one way: the charters which the king proclaimed must be confirmed, and which we find brought to him for that purpose were those which he had himself granted, and no other. Lastly, even had we nothing before us but the passage in Hoveden which all have followed, I contend that it may, and indeed ought to be, read as referring to a single seal. But it is, as Miss Norgate justly observes, "very confused," from its allusion to the chancellor's use of the seal. That allusion, however, would most naturally refer to the truce of Tillières, and not to the use of a separate seal in England. Therefore even if we accepted, which I do not, Hoveden's statement, it would not warrant the inference that has been drawn.

Again, when Miss Norgate writes of the "withdrawal of the seal from William," and when Dr. Stubbs tells us that

---

[9] Dr. Stubbs, indeed, writes, as we have seen, that "the seal that was now broken must have been the one which the chancellor had used during the king's absence." But Longchamp had been ejected from the chancellorship in October, 1191, whereas Richard limits the period of abuse to the duration of his captivity, which did not begin till 20th December, 1192.

the king "took the seal from" him, these statements may have two meanings. But M. Boivin-Champeaux is more precise: "L'emploi de ces procédés emportait le mépris et la violation non seulement de tous les actes étrangers au chancelier, mais encore de tous ceux où il avait mis la main. Il ne pouvait décemment conserver les sceaux. Le roi les lui enleva." This is a distinct assertion that Longchamp was deprived of his office. Yet all our evidence points to the conclusion that he remained chancellor to the day of his death.

Dismissing Hoveden for the time, and returning to the testimony of the charters, we have seen that they point to the event we are discussing having taken place in 1198, between the 7th of January, at which date the first seal was still in use, and the 27th of May, when charters were already being brought for confirmation under the second seal. Passing now from the charters to the seals still in existence, we learn from Mr. Wyon's magnificent work [10] (which has appeared since I completed my own investigation) that the first seal was still in use on the 1st of April, 1198,[11] while an impression of the second is found as early as the 22nd of May, 1198.[12] Thus our limit of time for the change is narrowed to 1st April—22nd May, 1198.[13] The evidence of the charters and of the seals being thus in perfect harmony, let us see whether this limit of date corresponds with a time of financial difficulty. For so desperate a device as that of the king's repudiation of his charters would only have been resorted to at a time of extreme pressure. What do we find? We find that the

---

[10] *The Great Seals of England* (Stock), p. 149.

[11] Its impression is attached to a charter tested at Tours, now at Lambeth Palace. If the date of this charter is correctly given, it is an important contribution to the Itinerary of Richard.

[12] *Ibid.*, p. 19.

[13] It is singular that Mr. Wyon, while giving these *data*, should himself assign the change to "*circ.* 1197," and still more singular that he should elsewhere (p. 20) accept the usual passage from Hoveden iii. 267).

B. H.   N N

time of this change of seal corresponds with the great
financial crisis of Richard's reign. The Church had at
length lost patience, and had actually in the Council at
Oxford (December, 1197) raised a protest. The "want of
money," in Miss Norgate's words, was "a difficulty which
. . . must have seemed well-nigh insurmountable." Pre-
parations were being made for a huge levy at five shillings
on every ploughland. It was at this moment that the
desperate king repudiated all the charters he had granted
throughout his reign, and proclaimed that they must be
"brought to him for confirmation; in other words . . .
paid for a second time."[14]

Let us now look at the other chroniclers. R. Coggeshall
is independent and precise :—

Accessit autem ad totius mali cumulum, juxta vitæ ejus terminum,
prioris sigilli sui renovatio, quo exiit edictum per totum ejus regnum
ut omnes cartæ, confirmationes, ac privilegiatæ libertates quæ prioris
sigilli impressione roboraverat, irrita forent nec alicujus libertatis
vigorem obtinerent, nisi posteriori sigillo roborarentur. In quibus
renovandis et iterum comparandis innumerabilis pecunia congesta
est (p. 93).

This is in complete accordance with the now ascertained
fact that Richard changed his seal, and regranted the old
charters, within the last year of his life. Similarly independent and precise evidence is afforded by the Annals of
Waverley :—

MCXCVIII. Anno x. regis Ricardi præcepit idem rex omnes cartas
in regno suo emptas reformari, et novo sigilli sui impressione
roborari, vel omnes cassari, cujuscunque dignitatis aut ordinis
essent, qui vellent sua protectione defensari, vel universa bona sua
confiscari.[15]

Further, we read in the Annals of Worcester[16] and in

[14] Miss Norgate (1194), ii. 343.
[15] *Annales Monastici*, ii. 251.
[16] *Ibid.*, iv. 389 (Vespasian E, iv.)

the *Historia Major* of M. Paris (ii. 450-451)[17] that in 1198, "circaque festum sancti Michaelis, mutatæ sunt carte quas prius fecerat rex Ricardus, novo sigillo suo." Now this Michaelmas fell just in the heart of the period within which the process of confirmation is proved to have been going on.

We see, then, that the evidence (1) of the seals, (2) of the charters, (3) of the circumstances of the time, (4) of other chroniclers, all concur in pointing to the spring of 1198. And now we will lastly appeal to Hoveden against himself. After telling us of the king's proclamation on the refusal ot the religious to contribute to the carucage in the spring of 1198, he adds:—

> Præterea præcepit idem rex ut omnes, tam clerici quam laici, qui cartas sive confirmationes habebant de sigillo suo veteri deferrent eas ad sigillum suum novum renovandas, et nisi fecerint, nihil quod actum fuerat per sigillum suum vetus ratum haberetur (iv. 66).

This passage, which ought to be compared with Coggeshall, is merely ignored by Dr. Stubbs. Miss Norgate, however, boldly explains it as "a renewal of the decree requiring all charters granted under the king's old seal to be brought up for confirmation under the new one" (ii. 356). But the passage stands by itself, as describing a new measure.[18]

The only conclusion to be drawn from this cumulative evidence is that the earlier passage in Hoveden (1194)

[17] Faust A. 8. fo. 136. It is a striking instance of the confusion and blundering to be met with even in our best chronicles that M. Paris (*Chron. Maj.*, ii. 356) has an independent allusion to the king's change of seal (as a "factum Ricardi regis enorme") in which he gives us a circumstantial account of the event and of the prior of St. Alban's going over to France to secure the confirmation, "cum effusione multæ pecuniæ et laboris," but assigns it to the year 1189. Hoveden's error pales before such a blunder as this, which has been accepted without question by the learned editor, Dr. Luard.

[18] Hoveden, by placing it wrongly (p. 66) *after* Hubert's resignation (p. 48), to which it was some two months previous, has misled Miss Norgate into the belief that it was the work of his successor, Geoffrey.

which has been so universally accepted, must be rejected altogether. Against the facts I have adduced it cannot stand.

Incredible though it may seem that a court official, a chronicler so able and well informed, indeed, in the words of his editor, "our primary authority for the period,"[19] should have misstated so grossly an event, as it were, under his own eyes, we must remember that "Hoveden's personality is to a certain degree vindicated by a sort of carelessness about exact dates."[20] Yet even so, "few are the points," our supreme authority assures us, "in which a very close examination and collation with contemporary authors can detect chronological error in Hoveden."[21] Nor, of the eight anachronisms laboriously established by Dr. Stubbs, does any one approach in magnitude the error I have here exposed. The importance of every anachronism in its bearing on the authorship of the chronicle is by him clearly explained.

How far does the rejection of this statement on the change of seal affect the statement which precedes it as to the Truce of Tillières? Hoveden places the latter and the former in the relation of cause and effect:—

Deinde veniens in Normanniam moleste tulit quicquid factum fuerat de supradictis treugis, et imputans cancellario suo hoc per eum fuisse factum, abstulit ab eo sigillum suum, et fecit, etc. (iii. 267).

This is rendered by Dr. Stubbs in the margin: "He annuls the truce and all the acts of the chancellor passed under the old seal." The passage has also been so read by M. Boivin-Champeaux (p. 221); but if that is the meaning, which I think is by no means certain, Hoveden contradicts himself. For he speaks five months later of the truce ("Treuga quæ inter eos statuta fuerat duratura usque ad festum omnium sanctorum") as not having stopped

---

[19] Stubbs's *Hoveden*, IV. xxxii.
[20] *Ibid.*, p. xxv.
[21] *Ibid.*, p. xxxi.

private raids on either side.[22]   R. de Diceto, mentioning,
the truce (ii. 120), says nothing of it being annulled, nor
does R. Newburgh in his careful account.   On the contrary,
he implies that it held good, though the terms were thought
dishonourable to Richard (ii. 420).   I should, therefore,
read Hoveden as stating simply that Richard was much
annoyed at ("moleste tulit") its terms, and was wroth with
the chancellor for accepting them.

In addition to correcting the received date for Richard
the First's change of seal, the evidence I have collected
enables us, for the first time, to learn how and to what
extent the confirmation of the charters was effected.   We
find that it was no sweeping process, carried out on a
single occasion, but that it was gradually and slowly proceeding during the last eleven months of the king's life.
Here, then, is the explanation of another fact (also hitherto
overlooked), namely that only a minority of the charters
were ever confirmed under the second seal.[23]   For the
king's death abruptly stopped the operation of that oppressive decree which was being so reluctantly obeyed.

It should be superfluous for me to add that, in thus
correcting previous statements, I have not impeached the
accuracy of our greatest living historian, who could only
form his judgment from the evidence before him.   The
result of my researches has been to show that the evidence
itself breaks down when submitted to the test of fact.

---

[22] iii. 276.   This distinctly implies that the truce had been nominally
in full force.   Note that it is here spoken of as "*till* All Saints,"
while in the document itself (iii. 259) it is made for a year *from* All
Saints.   Miss Norgate (ii. 367) speaks of it as "till All Saints" (1194),
but I think it was made from July 1194 to All Saints 1195.

[23] I have not found a single charter of municipal liberties, though the
reign was so rich in them, among these confirmations.   Nor since this
article first appeared, in 1888 (*Archæol. Rev.*, vol. i.), have I found more
than four additional cases of re-sealed charters, raising the total to 28.
Of these a detailed list is given on the next page.

Granted	*at*	*Confirmed*
16 April, 1194 [1] . . .	Winchester . .	27 May, 1198 . . .
2 December, 1189. .	Canterbury . .	15 June, 1198 . . .
10 October, 1189 . .	Westminster . .	1 July, 1198 . . .
28 November, 1189. ・	Canterbury . .	1 July, 1198 . . .
1 July, 1190. . . .	Dangu . . .	3 July, 1198 . . .
5 Sept, 1189 } . . .	Westminster } . .	30 July, 1198 . . .
17 Sept, 1189 } . . .	Geddington } . .	
25 April, 1194 . . .		22 August, 1198 . .
12 December, 1194. .	Chinon . . .	22 August, 1198 . .
7 January, 1198. . .	Vaudreuil . .	22 August, 1198 . .
8 December, 1189. .	Dover	10 September [1198] .
6 December, 1189. .	Dover	15 September [1198] .
14 March, 1190. . .	Nonancourt . .	18 September, 1198 .
23 March, 1190. . .	Rouen. . . .	19 September, 1198 .
29 November, 1189 .	Canterbury . .	9 October, 1198 . .
6 October, 1189 .	Westminster . .	20 October, 1198 . .
7 December, 1189 .	Dover	24 October, 1198 . .
23 March, 1190 . .	Rouen . . .	5 November, 1198 .
7 December, 1189 .	Dover. . . .	10 November, 1198 .
17 September, 1189 .	Geddington . .	12 November [1198] .
28 November, [2] 1189 .	Canterbnry . .	13 November, 1198 .
27 July, 1197 . . .	Isle d'Andely .	14 November, 1198 .
10 November, 1189 .	Westminster .	30 November, 1198 .
5 August, 1190 . .	Marseilles . .	7 December, 1198 .
September, 1197. .	Rouen . . .	17 December, 1198 .
1189. .	[No place] . .	24 January, 1199 . .
15 April, 1190 . . .	Evreux . .	3 March, 1199 . .
22 June, 1190. . . .	Chinon . . .	11 March, 1199 . .
25 April, 1194 . . .	Portsmouth . .	5 April, 1199. . .

[1] " Scilicet die secunda coronationis nostræ."
[2] " December " in Cart. Ant., which date is accepted in Gibson's " Monastery of Tynmouth."

at	Grantee	Authority
Lions	Robert fitz Roger	Cart. Ant. EE. 6
Château Gaillard	Hugh Bardulf	Ditto EE. 10
Ditto, ditto	Ely	Ditto JJ. 43
Ditto, ditto	Ely	Ditto NN. 26
Ditto, ditto	William Longchamp	Ditto JJ. 46
Lire	Rievaulx Abbey	Rievaulx Cartulary (Surtees Soc.), p. 308
	Thomas Basset	Hist. MSS., 9th Report, ii. 404
Roche d'Orival	Alan Basset	Cott. Cart. xvi. 1 (Rymer i. 67)
Ditto, ditto	Alan Basset	Anc. Deeds, Ser. A. No. 5924.
Château Gaillard	Shaftesbury Abbey	Harl. MS. 61, fo. 26
Ditto, ditto	Peterborough Abbey	Cart. Ant. EE. 21
Ditto, ditto	Waltham Abbey	Ditto RR. 7 & 8
Ditto, ditto	Roger de Sancto Manveo	Ditto BB. 6
Ditto, ditto	Fontevrault	Ditto F. 1
Lions	St. Leonard's, Stratford	Add. MS. 6,166, fo. 341
Château Gaillard	Stratford Langthorne Abbey	Cart. Ant. E. 1
Ditto, ditto	St. Jacques de Boishallebout	Add. Cart. (Brit. Mus.) No. 3
Ditto, ditto	Boxley Abbey	Cart. Ant. Q. 8
Ditto, ditto	St. Alban's Abbey	Ancient Deeds, A. 1050
Ditto, ditto	Tynmouth Priory	Cart. Ant. BB. 18
Ditto, ditto	Llanthony Abbey	Ditto B. 26
Lions	The Templars	Deville's Transcripts
Ditto	Church of Durham	Surtees Soc., vol. IX. p. lvi.
"Sanctum Ebruskum"	Domus Dei (Southampton)	Cart. Ant. D. 30
Cahagnes	Spalding Priory	Add. MS. 5844, fo. 228
Château du Loir	Gilbert fitz Roger	Hist. MSS. 10th Report 325
Chinon	W. Briwerre	Great Coucher II. 1, 67 IV. (1, 2)
[No place]	Noel " serviens "	Cart. Ant. D. 30

COMMUNAL HOUSE DEMOLITION

THERE was a strange custom peculiar to the ancient community of the Cinque Ports, which has not, so far as I know, been found elsewhere in England. If a member of any one of these towns was elected to serve as Mayor or " Jurat " (the governing bodies consisting of a Mayor and twelve " Jurats "), and refused to accept the office, his house was publicly demolished by the community. An extract from the Custumal of Sandwich, headed " Pena maioris electi recusantis officium suum," will make the custom clear :—

Si maior sic electus officium suum recipere noluit, primo et secundo et tercio monitus, tota communitas ibit ad capitale messua- gium suum, si habuerit proprium, et illud cum armis omnimodo quo poterit prosternat usque ad terram. . . . Similiter quicunque juratus fuerit electus, et jurare noluerit, simile judicium." [1]

Although the custom of house demolition is apparently, as I have said, peculiar in England to the Cinque Ports, it was of widespread occurrence abroad. Thither, therefore, we must turn our steps in order to investigate its history.

It is in Flanders and in Northern France, and in Picardy, most of all, that we find this singular custom prevailing, and discover its inseparable connexion with the institution of the *Commune*. It would seem that the penalty of house demolition was originally decreed for offences against the *commune* in its corporate capacity. Thierry, basing his

[1] Boys' *Sandwich*, p. 431.

conclusions mainly on the charters of the *commune* of Amiens and the daughter-charter of Abbeville writes :—

Celui qui se soustrait à la justice de la Commune est puni de banissement, et sa maison est abattue. Celui qui tient des propos injurieux contre la Commune encourt la même peine. Voilà pour les dispositions communes aux chartes d'Amiens et d'Abbeville, c'est-à-dire pour celles qui authentiquement sont plus anciennes que l'acte royal de 1190. Si l'on ne s'y arrête pas et qu'on relève dans cet acte d'autres dispositions, probablement primitives aussi, on trouvera les peines du crime politique, *l'abatis de maison* et le banissement, appliquées à celui qui viole sciemment les constitutions de la Commune et à celui qui, blessé dans une querelle, refuse la composition en justice et refuse pareillement de donner sécurité à son adversaire.

Une peine moindre, car elle se réduit à ce que la maison du délinquant soit abattue s'il n'aime mieux en payer la valeur, est appliquée à celui qui addresse des injures au Maire dans l'exercice de ses fonctions, et à celui qui frappe un de ses Jurés devant les magistrats, en pleine audience. Ainsi l'abatis de maison, vengeance de la Commune lésée ou offensée, était à la fois un châtiment par lui-même et le signe qui rendait plus terrible aux imaginations la sentence de banissement conditionnel ou absolu. Il avait lieu dans la plupart . . . des communes du nord de la France avec un appareil sombre et imposant; en présence des citoyens, convoqués à son de cloche, le Maire frappait un coup de marteau contre la demeure du condamné, et des ouvriers, requis pour service public, procédaient à la démolition qu'ils poursuivaient jusqu'à ce qu'il ne restât plus pierre sur pierre.[2]

The public character of the ceremony, which was no less marked at Sandwich (*vide supra*), is well illustrated in the

[2] *Monographie de la Constitution communale d'Amiens* (*Essai sur l'Histoire* . . . *du Tiers-Etat*, pp. 347-8). The charter of Abbeville prescribed this penalty ("domus ejus et omnia ad ejus mancionem pertinentia prosternantur") for homicide, which lies outside the class of "political offences." Giry, in his *Etablissements de Rouen* (1883), speaks of the "abattis de maison" as "caractéristique du droit municipal du Nord" (i. 431), but I do not find that he anywhere mentions it as the penalty appointed for refusing office.

Ordonnances of Philip of Alsace (*circ.* 1178) on the powers of his *baillis* in Flanders :—

Domus diruenda Judicio Scabinorum, post quindenam a scabinis indultam, quandocunque comes præceperit, aut ballivus ejus, diruetur a communia villæ, campana pulsata per Scabinos ; et qui ad diruendam illam non venerit, in forisfacto erit, etc., etc.

This ringing of the communal bell—parallel to the moot-bell of England—is an important feature in the matter. Without insisting upon a stray allusion, one may ask whether an entry in the Colchester records in the 16th century, threatening that if an offending burgess does not make amends, the town will "ring him out of his freedom," may not be explained by this practice.

There are plenty of other early instances of this house demolition in recognised *Communes*. At Bruges we read (*circ.* 1190) : "Si scabini voluerint domum eius prosternere, poterunt," etc., etc. So, too, at Roye, the charter (*circ.* 1183) provides : "Domus forisfactoris diruetur si Major voluerit, et si Major redempcionem accipiet de domibus diruendis," etc., etc. . . . "Si quis extraneus . . . forisfactum fecerit . . . Major et homines ville ad diruendam domum ejus exeant ; quæ si sit adeo fortis ut vi Burgensium dirui non possit, ad eam diruendam vim et auxilium conferemus."[3] So essential was the power of distraint, as we might term it, given to the community over its members, by the possession of a house, that it was sometimes made compulsory on a new member to become possessed of a house within a year of his joining. This was the case at Laon, one of the oldest of the *Communes*, the charter of Louis VI. (1128) providing that "Quicunque autem in Pace ista recipiatur, infra anni spatium aut domum sibi edificet, aut vineas emet . . . per que justiciari possit, si quid forte in eum querele evenerit." Where, in the absence of such provision, the culprit had no house to be demolished, it would seem that, in some cases, he had to procure one, for the express purpose of being demolished, before he could be restored to his membership. Thus, at Abbeville, the charter of *Commune* provides that "si domum non habuerit, antequam villam intret, domum centum solidorum, quam communia prosternat, inveniet."

Thierry pointed out how the "commune" of north-eastern France found its way, through its adoption in Normandy, to the opposite corner of the country "sur les terres de la domination Anglaise."[4] The form "jurats" adopted by the Cinque Ports for the members of their governing body suggests, indeed, some connexion with Gascony, to which region, as Thierry observed, it more especially belongs.[5] I was much struck, when visiting Bayonne, with its interesting municipal history. Thierry alludes to its peculiar character;[6] and, as the town had commercial relations with the Cinque Ports, and illustrates, moreover, the tendency of a commercial port to adopt, from other regions, a constitution peculiar to itself, I shall here give from its local customs the provisions as to house demolition.

Appended to John's charter granting a *communa* to Bayonne (19th April, 1215) we find a code of communal

[4] So also p. 263, where he calls attention to "l'établissement de la constitution communale de Rouen et de Falaise dans quatre des provinces annexées au XIIᵉ siècle à la domination anglo-normande"; and to "cette adoption de la commune jurée selon le type donné par les grandes villes de la Normandie, événement auquel contribua sans doute la politique des rois d'Angleterre."

[5] "A Bordeaux . . . le principal titre de magistrature était celui de Jurats, titre qu'on retrouve dans une foule de villes, depuis la Gironde jusqu'au milieu de la chaîne des Pyrénées" (p. 247).

[6] "Au milieu de cette unité d'organisation administrative et judiciaire la ville de Bayonne se détache, et contraste avec toutes les autres. On la voit, au commencement du XIIIᵉ siècle, abandonner le régime municipal indigène et chercher de loin une constitution étrangère, celle des communes normandes, transportée et perfectionée dans les villes du Poitou et de la Saintonge; c'est une double cause, la suzeraineté des rois d'Angleterre étendue de la Normandie aux Pyrénées, et le commerce d'une ville maritime, qui amène ainsi aux extrémités de la zone municipale du Midi la commune jurée dans sa forme native, avec toutes ses règles et ses pratiques" (p. 249).

ordinances based partly on those in the Rouen and Falaise charters and partly on the customs of La Rochelle. In this code the penalty of destroying the offender's house was decreed for a magistrate who accepted bribes,[7] for a citizen who shirked his military service,[8] for a perjured man,[9] for a thief.[10]

It again appears as the penalty for receiving bribes in the local Custumal assigned to 1273 :—"La soe maison sera darrocade, et que jameis ed ni son her no hage juridiccion en le communi."[8] In the foundation-charter granted to Sanabria by Alphonso IX. of Leon, in 1220, we find this penalty similarly assigned to perjury ("que la su casa sea derribada por esta razon"); but when the charter was altered by Alphonso X. (1st Sept., 1258), the penalty was commuted for a pecuniary fine of sixty "sueldos," on the ground that the destruction of the house was an injury to the city and to himself.[11] This is important as affording an instance of the actual introduction of commutation.

Now, my contention is, that as the practice of communal house demolition wandered down into Gascony, and thence actually crossed the Pyrenees into Spain, so—in the opposite direction—it crossed the channel and established itself in the Cinque Ports. As these movements become better understood, we are learning to treat them scientifically, and to trace them through their growth to their origin. In the case of the *commune,* the principle of filiation enables us to accomplish this with remarkable success.

But, it may be asked, is there any instance, on the other side of the channel, of house demolition being the penalty prescribed for refusal to accept office as Mayor or Jurat?

[7] "La soe maizon, so es del maire o d'aquet quiu loguer aura pres, sera darrocade seins contredit."

[8] "E en merce de la comunie, de sa maizon darrocar."

[9] "Sera en merce dou maire e dous pars de sa maizon darrocar."

[10] "La maison ons ed estaue sera abatude per les justizies de la comunie."

[11] "Ca esto tornarie en dano de Nos e de la nuestra Puebla." (*Boletin de la real Academia de la Historia,* Oct., 1888.)

It is, I reply, at Amiens the very penalty prescribed for
that offence! The Custumal of Amiens contained these two
clauses :—

> Et convient que chis qui pris est faiche le serment de le mairie ;
> et se il ne veult faire, on abatera se maison, et demourra en le
> merchy du roy au jugement de esquevins.
>
> Derekief se li maires qui eslus seroit refusoit le mairie et vausist
> souffrir le damage, jà pour che ne demouerroit qu'il ne fesist l'office ;
> et se aucuns refusoit l'esquevinage, on abateroit sa maison et l'amen-
> deroit au jugement de esquevins, et pour chou ne demoureroit mie
> que il ne fesist l'office de l'esquevinage.[12]

Thierry, who was ignorant of the Cinque Ports custom—
as the historians of the Cinque Ports appear to have been
ignorant of that at Amiens—describes this provision as
"loi remarquable en ce qu'elle faisait revivre et sanction-
nait par des garanties toutes nouvelles ce principe de la
législation romaine, que les offices municipaux sont une
charge obligatoire."[13] But this brings us face to face with
the difficult and disputed question of the persistence of
Roman institutions. Personally, I have always thought it
rash to accept similarity as proof of continuity. Here, for
instance, the occurrence of this practice at Sandwich might
lead to the inference that the institutions of Sandwich were
of direct Roman origin. Yet, if this practice was imported
from France, we see how erroneous that inference would
be. A *reductio ad absurdum* of this rash argument, as I
have elsewhere pointed out, would be found in the suggestion that every modern borough rejoicing in the possession
of aldermen had derived its institutions continuously from
Anglo-Saxon times. In the particular instance of this practice, we should note that it occurs (*a*) in that portion of
France where the municipal development was least Roman

[12] Ancienne Coutume d'Amiens " (*Recueil des Monum. inéd. de
l'Histoire du Tiers-Etat*, I. pp. 159, 160).

[13] He refers us to the Theodosian Code. Lib. XII., tit. 1, "de de-
curionibus," and D., Lib. 1, tit. 4, " de muneribus et honoribus."

in character; (*b*) in a peculiar and original form—the "garanties toutes nouvelles" of Thierry.

Again, we find the infliction of fines for non-acceptance of municipal office a familiar custom in England even to the present day. These fines were undoubtedly commutations for an original expulsion from the community; and at Colchester, for example, we have a case of a man being deprived of "his freedom" for declining the office of alderman, and of his having to make "submission" and pay a fine before it was restored. The fact is, that in every community, whether urban or rural, where office was a necessary but burdensome duty—like modern jury-service or mediæval "suit"—a penalty had to be imposed upon those who declined to discharge it. The peculiarity of the Sandwich and Amiens cases consists not in the imposition of a penalty, but in the character of the penalty imposed.

Pass we now from the consideration of this penalty to the wider and important conclusions suggested by its local occurrence.

I have always been puzzled by the peculiar phenomena presented by the "Cinque Ports" organisation. To other writers it would seem to present no such difficulty; but to me it is unique in England, and inexplicable on English lines. In that able monograph of Professor Burrows,[13] which is the latest contribution on the subject, the writer, I venture to think, leaves the problem as obscure as ever. I shall now, therefore, advance the suggestion, which has long been taking form in my mind, that the "Cinque Ports" corporation was of foreign origin, and was an offshoot of the communal movement in Northern France.

From Picardy, which faced the Cinque Ports, they derived, I believe, their confederation. To quote Thierry:

La région du nord, qui est le berceau, et pour ainsi dire la terre classique des communes jurées, comprend la Picardie, l'Artois, etc.

---

[13] *Cinque Ports* (Historic Towns Series), by Montagu Burrows.

. . . Parmi ces provinces, la Picardie est celle qui renferme le plus grand nombre de communes proprement dites, où cette forme de régime atteint le plus haut degré d'indépendance et ou dans ses applications, elle offre le plus de variété. Les communes de Picardie avaient en général toute justice, haute, moyenne et basse. Non-seulement dans cette province les chartes municipales des villes se trouvaient appliquées à de simples villages, dont quelques-uns n'existent plus, mais encore *il y avait des confédérations de plusieurs villages ou hameaux réunis en municipalités sous une charte et une magistrature collectives.*" [14]

Let me briefly summarise the arguments on which I base my hypothesis :—

(1) There is no parallel to the Cinque Ports confederation in England,[15] but there is in Picardy.

(2) The very name "Cinque Ports" betrays a foreign origin,[16] as does the fact that the oath taken by the King's Warden to the Corporation was termed, not an oath, but a "serement" (as in France).

(3) The English Merchant-Guild [17] and the English "Alderman" [18] were unknown to the Cinque Ports constitutions ; but they all possessed the typical constitution of the *Communes* of Northern France, namely a Mayor, with a Council of twelve, these twelve councillors having the French name of *Jurats*.[19]

(4) In the Cinque Ports, as in the French *Communes*, we

[14] *Essai sur l'Histoire du Tiers-Etat*, p. 240. (The italics are my own).

[15] The Danish " Five Boroughs " stand apart, as a temporary confederation, the character of which we do not know.

[16] Professor Burrows makes light of this name, asserting that "it is hard to say when the French form came into common use " (p. 56). But "the five Cinque Ports," which he admits to be the correct style, is a pleonasm which proves the " Cinque " to be older than the Five."

[17] " London and the Cinque Ports stand isolated from their fellows in the common absence of the institution " (Burrows, p. 43).

[18] " The same may be said of the office of 'Alderman' . . . The term seems to be only accidentally, if not erroneously used " (*Ib.*, p. 44).

[19] The mayor and his twelve *pairs*, *jurats* (or *jurés*) or *échevins*, were an essential feature of the *Commune*, and spread with the communal movement.

find side by side with this elective administration, a royal officer, with us a Warden, with them the *Sénéchal* (or *Prévôt* or *Bailli*) *du Roi.*

(5) the very same penalty of house demolition for refusal to accept office as Mayor or Jurat was exacted in the Cinque Ports (and nowhere else in England) as at Amiens.

I do not contend that the French "Commune" was adopted intact by the Cinque Ports, for of course it was not so. In the matter of names alone, they are not styled a "commune," nor are the members of their community termed "jurés" (*jurati*), but "barons" (*barones*). The study, however, of the "Commune" in France itself reveals the adaptation to environment it underwent on transplantation. And, the salient feature of the Cinque Ports organisation, the fact that they formed a single community, possessing a single assembly, and receiving a joint charter, is paralleled most remarkably in the joint "communes" of Picardy, containing from four to eight separate "Vills."[20]

It would be very satisfactory if the French "Communes" could throw light on the obscure title of "Barons" appertaining to the men of the Cinque Ports, and to them, I maintain (against Prof. Burrows), alone among English burgesses. I have elsewhere shown that there is evidence of the use of this term at an earlier period than is supposed, viz., in the early years of Stephen;[21] but on its origin the

[20] *Recueil des Ordonnances des Rois de France*, xi. 231, 237, 245, 277, 291, 308, 315. The text must now be modified in the light of my further criticism, in the next paper, of the early date alleged for the confederation of the Ports.

[21] This was written in reliance on the statement by Mr. Howlett (*Chronicles of the reigns of Stephen, Henry II. and Richard I.*, vol. iii. p. xl.) that an interesting writ he quoted from "the cartulary of St Benet-at-Hulme" was "safely attributable to the year 1137." It is a writ of Robert, Earl of Leicester, acting as justiciary, and "gives," says Mr. Howlett, "a clear idea of the Earl's position at the opening of the reign." As he has made himself master of the period, and has specially studied its manuscript sources, I accepted his assurance without question.

"Commune" throws no light. One can only quote the parallel afforded by the "Commune" of Niort, and this is taken from a late document (1579). Its officers are said to hold of the King "à droit de baronie, à foi et homage-lige, au devoir d'un gant ou cinq sols tournois, pour tous devoirs, payables à chaque mutation de seigneur."[22] This "devoir" is parallel, it will be seen, to the "canopy-service" (or "Honours at Court") of the Cinque Ports, rendered as it was, in practice, "à chaque mutation de seigneur." It is noteworthy that a French royal charter of 1196 contains the clause: "prefati quatuor ville exercitum et equitationem nobis debent *sicut alie communie nostre*";[23] but one can scarcely connect this with the naval service of the Cinque Ports. Yet it was part, undoubtedly, of the communal principle that the "commune" should hold directly of the King, and not of any mediate

But as it subsequently struck me that such a writ was more likely to be issued by the Earl when justiciary under Henry II., I referred to the cartulary and found that the writ contained the words "avi regis," proving it, of course, to belong to the reign, not of Stephen, but of Henry II. :—

"R. Com(es) leg(recestriæ) Baronibus regis de Hastingg' salutem. Precipio quod abbas et monachi de Hulmo teneant bene et in pace et juste terras suas in Gernemut . . . sicut eas melius tenuerunt tempore Regis H. *avi regis* . . . T. R. Basset per breve regis de ultra mare" (Galba E. 2, fo. 33*b*).

We can only, therefore, say of its date that it is previous to the Earl's death in 1168. In any case, however, it is of much interest as connecting Yarmouth with Hastings alone, not, as alleged, with the Cinque Ports as a whole. This is in perfect accordance with the fact that John's charter to Hastings in 1205 duly mentions its rights at Yarmouth, of which there is no mention in his charters to the other ports.

I have noted in this same cartulary, and on the same page, an interesting confirmation by Henry II. to the Abbey of the land, "quam lefwinus et Robertus presbyteri et Bonefacius et ceteri barones mei de Hastingges eidem ecclesie dederunt in Gernemut' apud Den . . . Test' Thom' cancellario. Apud Westmonasterium." The name of Thomas fixes the date as not later than 1158. In the charters of 1205, the people of Hastings are styled "barons," but those of the other ports only "homines."

[22] This represents the "esporle" of South-Western France (cf. p. 310, n. 278).   [23] *Recueil (ut supra)*, xi. 277.

lord, and this principle would explain the style " barones regis" applied to the men of the Cinque Ports.

To sum up, there are features about the Cinque Ports organisation which can only be accounted for, it seems to me, by the hypothesis here advanced. If this novel solution be accepted,[24] a question at once arises as to the date at which this communal confederacy was established. From what we know of the origin of the "Commune," we can scarcely believe in its adoption here till a generation, at least, after the Conquest. "Only the least informed and most sceptical," writes Prof. Burrows, "have placed the act of incorporation later than the date of the Conqueror,"[25] but a wider knowledge of municipal institutions would lead to the opposite conclusion. It is possible that the reign of Henry I. may have witnessed the superimposing of a communal confederacy on the existing institutions of the several ports ; it is impossible, at any rate, to trace it in Domesday, and difficult, indeed, to reconcile with its existence the evidence afforded by the Great Survey. It is conceivable that the position already attained, in the Conqueror's days, by Dover, may have served as a model for the other Ports, when they learnt the power of the principle that lay at the root of the *Commune*—" L'union fait la force."[26]

[24] I can find no trace of it in Prof. Burrows' careful *résumé* of the factors in the Cinque Ports organisation.

[25] *Cinque Ports*, p. 56.

[26] Professor Burrows is very severe on those who question the alleged charter of Edward the Confessor to the Ports and "the sweeping franchises" that it conferred (pp. 55-6, 59). But the sole evidence for its alleged existence is the charter of 1278, which does not even, I think, necessarily imply it. For the allusion to the liberties the Ports possessed in the days of Edward and his successors might well be taken from such a charter as that of Henry II. to Lincoln, in which he grants to the citizens all the liberties "quas habuerunt tempore Edwardi et Willelmi et Henrici regum Anglorum." This does not imply that those kings had granted charters.

[The result of my further investigation has been to develop much further the position here *Arch. Rev.*, Dec., 1889 adopted, and to modify accordingly the closing paragraph in the text].

THE CINQUE PORT CHARTERS

I HAVE allowed the preceding paper to stand as it was written, in spite of the rejoinder by Professor Burrows, entitled, "The Antiquity of the Cinque Port Charters."[1]

So far as regards my French analogies, Professor Burrows adopts the argument that I have not proved a parallel sufficiently close and complete. But this does not meet my contention : (1) that in the Cinque Ports organisation we find peculiar words and things; (2) that these peculiarities are not found elsewhere in England; (3) that they are found in France. Admitting, however, that "the earliest title is Norman French," the Professor urges that Edward the Confessor was a "half-Norman king," and that "nothing is more likely than that he should grant his charter to the Confederation under a Norman name."[2]

This brings us at once to Edward's alleged charter ; and, indeed, my critic recurs at the outset to his belief in "the Ports having been chartered as a Confederation by Edward the Confessor" (p. 439). At the close of the article he reminds us again that he "accepted the charter of Edward the Confessor as a faithful landmark, and showed how the history of our early kings and their institutions appeared to coincide with the statement." But he adds that "if proof can be brought against the issue of such a charter," he will be "the first to recognise it."

It is curious that my critic cannot perceive what must be

---

[1] *Archæological Review*, iv. 439-444.

[2] *Ibid.*, p. 441.

obvious to all those who are familiar with "the history of our early kings and their institutions," namely that the *onus probandi* rests, not, as he alleges, on those who question, but on those who maintain the startling proposition that Edward the Confessor issued such a charter of incorporation. Nothing short of proof positive could induce us to accept so unheard-of an anticipation of later times. That proof Professor Burrows claims to find in the great charter of Edward I. to the Ports. He contends that, according to this document, Edward "saw" the Confessor's charter,[3] and blames me for omitting its statement to that effect (p. 443). Unfortunately he quotes the words, as indeed he had done in his book, from an English translation only, and that a misleading one. The actual words (as given by Jeake), confirm to the Ports their liberties as held—

temporibus Regum Angliæ Edwardi, Willelmi primi et secundi, Henrici regis proavi nostri, et temporibus Regis Richardi et Regis Johannis avi nostri et Domini Henrici Regis patris nostri per cartas eorundem, sicut cartæ illæ quas iidem Barones nostri inde habent, et quas inspeximus, rationabiliter testantur.

In this peculiar wording we notice two points: (1) that it divides the kings into two groups, and that Henry II. is placed in the first group, not, as we should expect, with his sons ; (2) that Edward does not say that he has "inspected" charters of all the kings named, but only "cartæ *illæ* quas iidem Barones nostri inde habent."[4] I claim, therefore, to read the words as not implying that Edward had actually seen any charter older than that of Richard, whose name heads what I have termed the second group of kings. It is noteworthy that Richard's is the earliest charter of which the contents are known to ourselves.

But let us see how the matter stands with reference to previous charters. Professor Burrows holds that the form

---

[3] *Cinque Ports*, p. 64.

[4] Had he seen them all, the wording would have run, " per cartas eorundem, quas iidem," etc.

of Edward the First's charter "certainly supposes that the former charters were granted" also to the Ports collectively.[5] Indeed, he "need not point out," we read, "that the charters referred to are charters to the Confederation, not to separate Ports" (p 444). Where do we find them? "That the charter of Henry," we are told (p. 439), "which we know about from those of his sons, has no more survived than those of his predecessors, has always seemed to me an argument of some weight." But no charter of Henry II. to the Confederation is spoken of by his sons. We have in the *Rotuli Chartarum* what Professor Burrows terms "the series of six charters, dated June 6, and 7, 1205." Each port on this occasion received a separate charter, and in each case reference is made to that port's charter from Henry II. Of a collective charter we hear nothing. Nor are John's charters even identical in form: to quote once more Professor Burrows :—

It should also be noted that the franchises of Sandwich are to be such as the town enjoyed in the reigns of "William and Henry"; of Dover, as in that of "Edward"; of Hythe, as in those of "Edward, William I., William II., and Henry."[6]

And in none of them is any charter mentioned earlier than that of Henry II.

These charters of John are most important, but have not, so far as I know, received scientific treatment. The charter to Hastings is in many ways distinct from the others. It alone speaks of the "Honours at Court," the rights at Yarmouth, and the ship-service due, and alone mentions that this service was rendered "pro hiis libertatibus." The charter to Rye and Winchelsea is modelled on that of Hastings, and neither of them goes back beyond the charter of Henry II. The charters to Dover and to Hythe, it will be found, are closely parallel, and in both cases the privileges are to be enjoyed as in the times of Edward, William I., William II., and Henry [I.]. Sand-

---

[5] *Cinque Ports*, p. 63.   [6] *Cinque Ports*, p. 71.

wich has her liberties confirmed as in the days of Henry I., King William, "and our predecessors"; Romney as in the days of Henry I.

If it be urged that the rights of Yarmouth, though only specified in the Hastings charter, were included under general liberties in the charters to the other ports, I appeal, in reply, to that writ of Henry II.[7] which treats the Barons of Hastings alone as possessing authority at Yarmouth. The charter and the writ confirm one another.

We see, then, that when we interpret the great charter of Edward I. to the ports (1278) in the light of evidence, not of supposition, we find that Henry II. and John did grant separate charters to the different ports as to other towns (not a collective charter to them all), and that these therefore must have been the charters referred to in the general confirmation of 1278. In other words, it was Edward I., not Edward the Confessor, who granted the first "Charter to the Confederation," as a whole. Utterly subversive though it be of Professor Burrows' view, this is the only conclusion in harmony with the known facts.

Thus the sole result of examining my critic's evidence is to make me carry my scepticism further still. I now hold that even so late as the days of John, the Ports had individual relations to the crown, although their relations *inter se* were becoming of a closer character, as was illustrated by the fact that their several charters were all obtained at the same time. Hastings alone, as yet, had rights at Yarmouth recognised : hers were the only portsmen styled "barons" by the crown.

It is always, in these matters, necessary to bear in mind that the local organisation was apt to be ahead of the crown, and that communal institutions and municipal developments might be winked at for a time to avoid formal recognition. In this way I believe the rights and privileges belonging in strictness to Hastings alone were gradually extended in practice to the other ports. There is,

[7] *Supra*, p. 561.

for instance, a St. Bertin charter granted by the so-called "Barons of Dover," although the formal legend on their seal styles them only "burgesses." The portsmen may all in practice have been loosely styled "barons," even though Hastings alone had a special right to that distinction. Professor Burrows speaks of "its acknowledged claim to be the Premier Port of the Confederation" as "a circumstance of the greatest significance in our inquiry,"[8] and here I entirely agree with him. But I cannot think his explanation of that pre-eminence in any way satisfactory. He lays great stress on "the identification lately established beyond any reasonable doubt between the town in the Bourne valley and the 'New Burgh' of Domesday Book." I have searched long and in vain for this identification, but, whether it be accepted or not, it throws no light on the old town, the King's town, of Hastings.[9]

The importance of Hastings before the Conquest is shown not only by the action of its ships in 1049, but also by its possessing a mint. Yet the only mention of this town in Domesday is the incidental entry that the Abbot of Fécamp had " in Hastings " apurtenant to his Manor of Brede, "iiii. burgenses et xiiii. bordarios."[10] One is fairly

[8] *The Cinque Ports*, p. 26.

[9] The Professor's argument that "the lordship of St. Denis over the Saxon Hastings had ceased—probably when the Northmen took possession of the Seine valley and blocked out the French ; that of Fécamp was the renewal of the old idea on an adjoining territory" (*Cinque Ports*, p. 27), is as baseless as that which follows it as to Winchelsea and Rye. For the "charter of Offa, king of the Mercians" (p. 25), granting Hastings to St. Denis, has been conclusively shown by Mr. Stevenson to be a forgery.

[10] One cannot, of course, speak positively without seeing that "identification" on which Professor Burrows relies. But, unless there is evidence to the contrary, it seems difficult to resist the conclusion that this estate of the Abbey " in Hastings " was identical with that which it actually possessed in the Bourne Valley. For this by no means included the whole "town in the Bourne Valley," but only that portion of it at the foot of the West Hill, which is bordered by Courthouse Street, Bourne Street, John Street, and High Street, together with St. Clement's Church and its block of buildings (*Sussex Arch. Coll.*, xiv. 67). And this conclusion

driven to the bold hypothesis that Hastings, which ought to have figured at the head of the county survey (as did Dover in Kent), was one of the important towns wholly omitted in Domesday.[11] The fact that its ship-service, when first mentioned, was as large as that of Dover is a further proof of its importance.

The geographical position of Hastings also severs its case, as widely as do its privileges, from those of the Kentish ports. It is therefore difficult to resist the impression that the distinction in John's charter had a real origin and meaning. The "Barons" of Hastings were, I believe, the men of the *King's* town (not, as alleged, the Abbot's) and so far from the Abbot's men being admitted to share their distinction, we find the latter, at Rye and Winchelsea, styled in John's charter "homines," not even "homines nostri."

The accepted view as to Rye and Winchelsea is thus set forth by Professor Burrows :—

The Confessor had evidently intended to make the little group of Sussex towns, the "New Burgh," Winchelsea, and Rye, a strong link of communication between England and Normandy; but Godwin and Harold had contrived to prevent the two latter from becoming the property of the Abbey of Fécamp, to which Edward granted them in the early part of his reign; and this formed one of the Norman grievances. William promised to restore them to the Abbey, and when he had conquered England he kept his word. . . . .

is strengthened by the fact that in Domesday its rents are 63*s.* "in Hastings," and 158*s.* in the "novus burgus," while at the Dissolution they were only 35*s.* 4*d.* in Hastings. In that case we must after all look for the "novus burgus" of Domesday at Winchelsea or Rye.

Nor is the history of Hastings harbour at all as clear as could be wished. "The ancient Harbour once occupied," no doubt, "Priory Valley" (*Cinque Ports*, p. 9); but I can find no trace of a haven "formed by the Bourne between the East and West Hills," which replaced it on its sitting-up. On the contrary, the old map of Hastings in 1746 (*Sussex Arch. Coll.*, vol. xii.) shows us the "haven" (with ships) in the Priory Valley to the west of the Castle Hill. Was not this a later harbour (1637), and the real original one out to the south?

[11] Chichester, Lewes, and Pevensey are all duly entered, under the names of their respective lords.

Of the grant of Winchelsea and Rye to the same Abbey as part of the lands of Steyning we have distinct evidence in the charter of resumption issued by Henry III. in 1247 (p. 27; cf. *supra.* p. 319).

Although this view has always been held by local historians and antiquaries, it seems to me obvious that there must be error somewhere. Rye and Winchelsea belonged geographically to the Abbey's lordship of Brede in the extreme west of the county; its lordship of Steyning was in East Sussex. On examining for myself the charter of resumption and comparing it with the Abbey's claims as to Brede at the *quo warranto* inquiry, I discovered the solution of the mystery. Rye and Winchelsea were not, as alleged, appurtenant to Steyning, but belonged to the Manor of Brede. The Abbey, however, claimed on behalf of its Manor of Brede (including Rye and Winchelsea) all the franchises granted to Steyning, contending that they were meant to extend to all its lands in Sussex. This claim was urged and recognised in the case of the charter of resumption (1246), the source of the whole misapprehension.

But to return to the "Barons," Professor Burrows, discussing the title, writes thus :—[12]

It is admitted that the title was at first only held by the Portsmen in common with the citizens of several other places, as that of a responsible man in a privileged community, of a " baro " or " vir " of some dignity; but, of course, not in the least in the sense of a " baron " such as the word came to mean in the twelfth and thirteenth centuries.

I do not know which were these "several other places"; but I think the word "baron" can be shown to have here had a definite connotation. The exemption from "wardship and marriage," for instance, granted by Edward I. (1278), implies that these "barons" were subject to the burdens of tenants-in-chief, while their extraordinary appeal, after the battle of St. Mahé (1293), to " the judg-

[12] *The Cinque Ports*, pp. 77-79.

ment of their peers, earls, and barons "[13] has not, so far as I know, received the attention it deserves. By such a phrase the Cinque Port "barons" virtually claimed the privilege of peers of the realm.

But one must not wander too far along these tempting paths. When tradition is replaced, as it may be in part, by evidence, we shall have, not improbably, to unlearn much that now passes current as genuine Cinque Ports history. On the other hand, there may be in store for us glimpses of much that is interesting and new.[14]

Apart, however, from problems as yet difficult and obscure, we shall be standing on sure ground in asserting that the charter of Edward I. is the first that was granted to the Ports collectively, and that the rights and liberties it confirmed were those which had been granted to the separate ports by Henry II. and John, and which it then made uniform and applicable to the whole confederation. As at London,[15] we have always to remember that com-

---

[13] *The Cinque Ports*, p. 123. Compare the banishment of the Despencers (1321) by the "piers de la terre, countes et barouns."

[14] The courts of the Cinque Ports, for instance, greatly need investigation. One can only throw out as a mere conjecture the suggestion that if the Court of Guestling derived its name, as Professor Burrows admits is probable, from Guestling (the *caput* of a Hundred), midway between Hastings and Winchelsea, it may have been originally a *Sussex* Court for the Hastings group, while the Court of Broadhill—afterwards "Broderield" and "Brotherhood" (*The Cinque Ports*, p. 178)—may have been the Kentish one. The admitted corruption in the traditional derivation of both names, together with the court's change of *locale*, shows how much obscurity surrounds their true origin. Few, I think, would accept Professor Burrows' view that, because the Brodhull, when we first have record of it, was held "near the village of Dymchurch" (p. 46), it was named from "the 'broad hill' of Dymchurch, which may well have been some portion of the wall which extended for three miles along the beach" (p. 47). As the Guestling was not a court of "Guests," so "the broad hill," from which the meeting derived its name, must have been originally somewhere else than down "on Dymchurch beach" (p. 75), between Romney Marsh and the sea.

[15] See my paper on the origin of "The Mayoralty of London," in *Archæological Journal* (1894).

munal institutions might develop locally before their existence is proved by the crown's formal recognition. Delay in that recognition is not proof of their non-existence. What complicates so greatly the study of the Cinque Ports polity is the difficulty of disentangling its three component elements: the old English institutions common to other towns; the special relation to the crown in connexion with their ship-service; and the foreign or communal factor on which I have myself insisted. No impartial student, I believe, will deny that I have fairly established the existence of this third element. Its relative importance and its sphere of action must remain, of course, as yet matter of conjecture.

ADDENDA

----

pp. 7, 125. In case I should not have made sufficiently clear my views as to the filiation of the Domesday MSS., it may be well to explain that what I deny on p. 8 is that the *Inq. Com. Cant.* and the *Inq. El.* can both have been copied from a third document intermediate between them and the original returns. But, as I state on pp. 7, 146, it cannot be *proved* that the *Inq. Com. Cant.* was itself transcribed direct from the original returns, as it might, possibly, be only a copy of an earlier transcript of these returns.

p. 21. A remarkable instance of the occasional untrustworthiness of the figures given in these texts is afforded by the Manors of Stretham and Wilburton, co. Camb., which were farmed together. The correct figures for their ploughteams were these :—

	Dominium.	Homines.	Total.
Stretham . . .	4^1 .	5 .	9
Wilburton . .	3^2 .	4 .	7^3
	7	9	

The footnotes show the errors.

Thus the A text, which is the best known, gives two figures out of three wrongly for Wilburton, and Mr. Pell,

[1] A, B, and C give this figure as 3 (p. 170). Their own title requires 4.

[2] A, B, and C give this figure as 3 (p. 170), but elsewhere (wrongly) as 4 (p. 117).

[3] A gives this figure as 6 (p. 117), but B and C, rightly, as 7

by accepting as genuine these two erroneous figures, was led to quite erroneous conclusions.

pp. 72-3. The parallel for this system of counting by threes and sixes is found in the wergild of Scandinavia, with its *rétt* of 3 marks, or 6, or 12, the 6 or the 12 *aurar*, the 12 ells or the 12 feet of *vadmal*.

For the *formulæ* on p. 72 an instructive parallel is found in the Frostathing's Law :—

If a *haulld* wounds a man, he is liable to pay 6 *baugar* (rings) to the king, and 12 *aurar* are in each ring . . . a *lendrmann* 12, a jarl 24, a king 48, 12 *aurar* being in each ring.

Thus we find in Scandinavia the counterpart of the system of counting found in the "Danish" districts of England, just as we find in Angeln and Ditmarsh the counterpart of the "hide," with its four "yards," found in southern England (*Archæologia*, xxxvii. 380).

p. 122. For the election of *juratores* we may compare the Abingdon Abbey case, under Henry II. : "ex utroque parte seniores viri eligerentur qui secundum quod eis verum videretur . . . jurarent ; . . . segregati qui jurarent diversis opinionibus causam suam confundebant." For juries of eight or sixteen we may compare Jocelin de Brakelonde's narrative of a suit for an advowson in 1191 :— "delatum est juramentum per consensum utriusque partis sexdecim legalibus de hundredo."

p. 151. Compare here Mr. Freeman's text (iii. 413-4) :—

There can be little doubt that William's ravages were not only done systematically, but were done with a fixed and politic purpose. . . . It is impossible to doubt that the systematic harrying of the whole country round Hastings was done with the deliberate purpose of provoking the English king. . . . The work was done with a completeness which shows that it was something more than the mere passing damage wrought by an enemy in need of food.

Domesday is appealed to, as in the Appendix, for this view.

p. 257. Though I have spoken in the text of *William* de Montfichet, following, like Dugdale, the *Liber Niger*, I have since found that the tenant of the fief, in 1166, was his son Gilbert, the *carta* being wrongly assigned in the *Liber Niger* itself to William. There are similar and instructive errors to be found in it.

p. 312. The succession of Schelin, the Domesday under-tenant by his son Robert, in 1095 identifies the former with Schelin, the Dorset tenant-in-chief, from whom Shilling Ockford took its name, and who was succeeded in Dorset also by his son Robert (*Montacute Cartulary*).

pp. 381-3. To guard (as I have to do at every turn) against misrepresentation, I may explain that the Battle Chronicle is the primary authority I follow for the feigned flight. Its words, "fugam cum exercitu duce simulante," distinctly assert that the Duke himself, with the main body of his army, "turned in seeming flight." It must, surely, be because this evidence is quite opposed to Mr. Freeman's view that he ignored it in his text (pp. 488-490). The essential point to grasp, according to my own view, is that a detachment, told off for the purpose, thrust itself between the pursuing English and the hill to cut off their retreat, and that the main body of the Normans then faced about. The English, one may add, are hardly likely to have ventured down into the plain unless the feigned flight was so general as to make them think they could safely do so.

p. 407. "Mainly from oral tradition." This refers, of course, to Mr. Archer's contention.

p. 469. On the great influence, by their connection, of the Clares see also the *Becket Memorials* (iii. 43), where Fitz Stephen writes (1163):—

Illi autem comiti de Clara fere omnes nobiles Angliæ propinquitate adhærebant, qui et pulcherrimam totius regni sororem habebat, quam rex aliquando concupierat.

We are reminded here of the curious story in the *Monasticon* (iv. 608) that, some forty years before, Roheis de Clare, the wife of Eudo Dapifer, was, on his death (1120), destined by her brethren for the second wife of Henry I., a story which illustrates, at least, the position attributed to the family.

pp. 472-3. The Montfichet match is not shown in the chart pedigree, nor is the important marriage of Adeliza, another daughter of Gilbert (fitz Richard) de Clare, to Aubrey de Vere, the Chamberlain, which is well ascertained (*Geoffrey de Mandeville,* pp. 390-392). By him she had *inter alios* a daughter, with the Clare name of " Rohese," who married Geoffrey de Mandeville, first Earl of Essex (*Ibid.*). The existence of this Adeliza may be held to be against my affiliation of " Adelidis de Tunbridge," which avowedly is only a conjecture.

p. 475. A chart pedigree is here given to illustrate the connection of Robert fitz Richard (de Clare), through his wife, with the Earls of Northampton and the Scottish kings:—

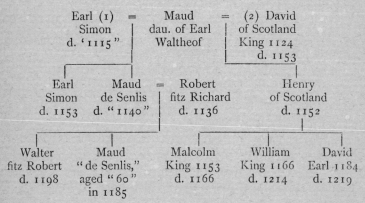

Robert fitz Richard and his children (see p. 474) are included in this pedigree, in order to show that their ages present no chronological difficulty, and that the length of time they survived him is clearly due to his marrying rather late in life.

p. 513. I have identified a third fine, since this book was

in type, as belonging to the great circuits of 1176. It proves that they began early in the year.

As a corollary to my conclusions on pp. 511-513, I should like to allude to the well-known changes in 1178-80. Great importance is attached to the passage in the *Gesta Regis Henrici*, which describes how the king selected five justices "de privata familia sua" in the place of the eighteen previously appointed, who, as I read the passage, were to accompany his court. I cannot think that this reform, if it took place, enured, for the central body that we really meet with from 1179 onwards is, it seems to me, distinctly different. It consists of the Bishops of Winchester, Ely, and Norwich, whom, says R. de Diceto, in a passage to which the Bishop of Oxford rightly draws attention, Henry, in 1179, appointed "archijustitiarios regni," with Glanvill, who soon became a chief justiciar with them. These four continue to hold a position severed from that of the other justices, of whom some act with them at one time and some at another. The earliest appearance at present known to me of this well-defined central group is at Oxford, Feb. 11, 1180. We there find the three bishops, associated with five justices, headed by Ranulf Glanvill, recorded on a fine. Now, we happen to know that the king was at Oxford about this very time, for he decided there on the issue of his new coinage.[4] His presence would account for this gathering of the four leading justiciars, so that we need not hesitate to connect the two phenomena. We have then here record evidence of the true *personnel* at the time of the central judicial body, together with the fact of its presence with the king, the fact which had not till now been proved, on his progress through the land.

[4] So Eyton (p. 230), not giving his authority; nor have I found it.

INDEX

—·—